THEOLOGICAL PROPÆDEUTIC

A GENERAL INTRODUCTION TO THE

STUDY OF THEOLOGY

EXEGETICAL, HISTORICAL, SYSTEMATIC, AND PRACTICAL

INCLUDING

ENCYCLOPÆDIA, METHODOLOGY, AND BIBLIOGRAPHY

A MANUAL FOR STUDENTS

BY

PHILIP SCHAFF, D.D., LL.D.
PROFESSOR OF CHURCH HISTORY IN THE UNION THEOLOGICAL SEMINARY
NEW YORK

Wipf & Stock
PUBLISHERS
Eugene, Oregon

Wipf and Stock Publishers
199 W 8th Ave, Suite 3
Eugene, OR 97401

Theological Propaedeutic
A General Introduction to the Study of Theology
By Schaff, Philip
ISBN 13: 978-1-55635-272-0
ISBN 10: 1-55635-272-7
Publication date 2/9/2007
Previously published by Charles Scribner's Sons, 1893

PREFACE.

This book is intended to be a guide for theological students in the first year of their course of preparation for the ministry of the gospel. It gives an outline of the various departments of theology, defines their nature and aim, their boundary lines and organic connection, their respective functions and value; it sketches their history, and indicates the best methods of prosecuting their study. It answers the purposes of a map for orientation. Formal Encyclopædia, Methodology and Bibliography are here combined.

The new title PROPÆDEUTIC, which I have chosen after a good deal of reflection, is more comprehensive and more appropriate than the usual title ENCYCLOPÆDIA, which does not necessarily include Methodology and Bibliography, and is almost exclusively understood among us in the sense of an alphabetical dictionary of the *matter* of knowledge.*

I beg the indulgence of the English reader for introducing a uniform terminology in the singular form for the several departments, as *Isagogic, Canonic, Patristic, Apologetic, Dogmatic, Ethic, Symbolic, Polemic, Statistic, Homiletic, Catechetic, Liturgic, Poimenic, Evangelistic.* Some of these terms are new and sound strange, but they are coined after analogy from the Greek, like most of our scientific designations. The singular form is shorter than the plural and more in accordance with Greek and German usage. The English usage is inconsistent almost beyond remedy; for while we have *Logic* (from λογική, sc. τέχνη, or ἐπιστήμη), *Rhetoric, Music, Arithmetic* (which are not likely

---

* When I was appointed, in 1869, "Professor of Encyclopædia and Symbolic," in the Union Theological Seminary, a doctor of divinity and editor of a leading religious periodical asked me, "Pray, tell me the name of your professorship." When I told him, he said with an expression of surprise: "As to Symbolic, I never heard of it in all my life; and as to Encyclopædia, if you are a professor of that, they need no other professor!"

ever to be changed into *Logics, Rhetorics, Musics, Arithmetics)*, we have, on the other hand, *Mathematics, Metaphysics, Ethics, Statistics*, etc. (which are as unlikely to be changed into the singular form). I am no authority in such matters, but I had to choose a uniform system.

This is the first original work on *Propædeutic* in America. It aims to answer the same purpose for English-speaking students as the well-known *Encyclopädie und Methodologie* of the late Dr. Hagenbach of Basel (whom I knew very well) has served and still serves for German students (who prize it as a useful *Studentenbuch*). Although we have now a good translation of it by my Methodist friends, Dr. Crooks and Bishop Hurst, with valuable bibliographical supplements, yet it must be remembered that Hagenbach wrote from the German standpoint for German and Swiss students, and is constantly undergoing improvements at the hands of new editors. The twelfth edition by Professor Reischle, which appeared in 1889, is enlarged to 600 pages.

I have taught Propædeutic for many years, first at Mercersburg and later in New York, and have allowed the students to circulate imperfect copies of my lectures. These will now be superseded by the printed book.

Propædeutic is as yet a new study in this country, but it should be taught in every theological institution. No course is more necessary and useful for beginners. It is hoped that this manual will meet a growing demand of teachers and students.

PHILIP SCHAFF.

Union Theological Seminary,
NEW YORK, Sept. 18, 1893.

CONTENTS.

INTRODUCTION.

CHAPTER	PAGE
1. Education.	3
2. Theological Propædeutic.	6
3. Encyclopædia.	6
4. Formal and Material Encyclopædia.	8
5. General and Special Encyclopædia.	8
6. Theological Encyclopædia.	9
7. Methodology and Bibliography.	10
8. Division and Arrangement.	10
9. History and Literature.	11
10. A Select List of Works Introductory to the Study of Theology.	12

BOOK I.

RELIGION AND THEOLOGY.

FIRST SECTION: RELIGION.

11. General Definition of Religion.	17

PART I.—OBJECTIVE RELIGION.

12. Science of Religion.	19
13. History of Religion.	19
14. Philosophy of Religion.	20
15. Value of the Science of Religion.	20
16. The Religious World.—Statistics.	21
17. Classification of Religions.	29
18. Natural and Revealed Religions.	29
19. Dualism, Polytheism, Pantheism, Monotheism.	31
20. Civilized, Semi-civilized, and Barbarian Religions.	32
21. Sensual, Ascetic, and Ethical Religions.	33
22. Division according to Psychological Faculties.	33
23. Turanian, Semitic, and Aryan Religions.	34
24. Division according to the Ruling Ideas and Aims.	35
25. Tribal, National, and Universal Religions.	35
26. Designations of Ethnic Religions.	36

vi   CONTENTS.

CHAPTER	PAGE
27. The Origin of Idolatry	37
28. The Bible View of the Heathen World	38
29. Fetichism	41
30. Confucianism	41
31. Brahmanism	43
32. Buddhism .*	45
33. Zoroastrianism	49
34. The Religion of Ancient Egypt	50
35. Classical Paganism	52
36. The Scandinavian and Teutonic Mythology	53
37. The Jewish Religion	55
38. Mohammedanism	57
39. Christianity	59

PART II.—SUBJECTIVE RELIGION.

40. The Religious Constitution of Man	63
41. Religion and the Mental Faculties.—The Psychology of Religion	64
42. The Intellectual Theory.—Piety and Knowledge	65
43. Piety and Orthodoxy	67
44. The Moral Theory.—Piety and Morality	69
45. The Emotional Theory.—Piety and Feeling	71
46. The Life Theory	73
47. Individual, Denominational, and Catholic Piety	75

SECOND SECTION: THEOLOGY.

48. Definitions of Theology	77
49. Natural and Revealed Theology	79
50. Theology and Religion	80
51. Theology and Philosophy	82
52. Theology and the Gospel Ministry	85
53. Hints for the Study of Theology	87
54. The Student's Library	91
55. Division of Theology	92

BOOK II.

EXEGETICAL THEOLOGY.

EXEGETIC.—BIBLICAL LEARNING.

56. General Conception of Exegetical Theology	93
57. Departments of Exegetical Theology	94
58. The Bible	94
59. General Hints for the Study of the Bible	96
Select Tributes to the Bible	97

CONTENTS. vii

FIRST SECTION: BIBLICAL PHILOLOGY (PHILOLOGIA SACRA).

CHAPTER | PAGE
60. Importance of the Study of the Original Languages 101
61. Classification of Languages................................... 103
62. The Semitic Languages....................................... 104
63. The Hebrew... 106
64. History of Hebrew Learning................................. 109
65. The other Semitic Languages................................ 114
66. The Aramaic Languages 115
67. The Biblical Aramaic and the Rabbinical Hebrew 116
68. The Syriac and the Samaritan................................ 117
69. The Assyrian.. 118
70. The Arabic.. 121
71. The Study of the Classics................................... 123
72. Christianity and the Greek Language......................... 123
73. The Dialects of the Greek Language......................... 125
74. The Hellenistic Dialect...................................... 126
75. The Septuagint 127
76. The Apostolic Greek... 127
77. Peculiarities of the New Testament Writers 130
78. History of the Study of Hellenistic Greek 135
79. The Sub-Apostolic Greek..................................... 137
80. The Ecclesiastical Greek..................................... 138

SECOND SECTION: BIBLICAL ARCHÆOLOGY (INCLUDING GEOGRAPHY, NATURAL HISTORY, AND SACRED ARCHÆOLOGY).

81. Idea of Biblical Archæology.................................. 140
82. Parts of Archæology 141
83. Sources of Archæology...................................... 142
84. Biblical Geography 143
85. Natural History of the Bible................................. 144
86. Archæology Proper.. 145
87. History of Archæology...................................... 146
88. Literature of Archæology.................................... 148

THIRD SECTION: BIBLICAL ISAGOGIC (HISTORICO-CRITICAL INTRODUCTION TO THE BIBLE).

89. Nature of Isagogic... 149
90. Object and Value of Isagogic................................. 150
91. Method and Arrangement of Isagogic 150
92. Parts of Isagogic 151
93. History of Isagogic 151
94. Biblical Criticism.. 153
95. Textual Criticism.—Its Aim.................................. 154
96. Necessity of Textual Criticism............................... 154
97. Classes of Textual Variations................................. 155

CHAPTER	PAGE
98. Number and Value of Various Readings	156
99. Textual Criticism of the Old Testament	158
100. Sources of the Old Testament Text	159
101. The Hebrew Original and the Greek Septuagint	160
102. Sources of the Text of the New Testament	163
103. The Received Text and the True Text	166
104. Canonic, or the Theory of the Canon	168
105. The Canon of the Old Testament	169
106. Origin of the Jewish Canon	170
107. The Canon of the New Testament in the Ancient Church	172
108. The Final Settlement of the Canon	175
109. Protestantism and the Canon	175
110. Special Isagogic	177
111. Historical or Higher Criticism	177
112. Authorship	179
113. Known and Unknown Authorship	180
114. Present State of Higher Criticism	181
115. The Final Result	184

FOURTH SECTION: BIBLICAL HERMENEUTIC AND EXEGESIS.

116. Nature of Hermeneutic	186
117. Aim of Interpretation	187
118. Qualifications of an Interpreter	188
119. Translation, Paraphrase, Commentary	189
120. The English Version and Revision	190
121. Philological and Historical Exegesis	194
122. Theological Exegesis	195
123. Practical and Homiletical Exegesis	196
124. Exhaustive Commentaries	196
125. Popular Commentaries	197
126. Exegesis of the Old and New Testaments	197
127. History of Exegesis	199
128. Jewish Exegesis	200
129. Jewish Exegesis before Christ	201
130. Jewish Exegesis after Christ	203
131. Epochs of Christian Exegesis	204
132. Patristic Exegesis. A.D. 100–600	204
133. Mediæval Exegesis. A.D. 600–1500	207
134. The Period of the Renaissance	209
135. Exegesis of the Reformers	212
136. Protestant Exegesis of the Seventeenth to the Middle of the Eighteenth Century	215
137. Roman Catholic Exegesis of the Sixteenth down to the Eighteenth Century	222
138. Rationalistic Exegesis	223
139. Swedenborgian Exegesis	226
140. Exegesis of the Nineteenth Century	227
141. Biblical History and Biblical Theology	232
142. Hints for Exegetical Study	232

BOOK III.

HISTORICAL THEOLOGY.

CHAPTER	PAGE
143. General Conception of Historical Theology	234
144. Biblical and Ecclesiastical History	235
145. Agents of History	236
146. Historical Development	239
147. Central Position of Christ in History	241
148. Auxiliary Sciences: Ecclesiastical Philology, Geography, Chronology, Diplomatic, Secular History	241
149. Branches of Church History	244
150. History of Missions	244
151. History of Persecutions	245
152. History of Religious Liberty	246
153. History of Organization	246
154. History of Councils	247
155. History of Worship	248
156. History of Christian Life	248
157. History of Doctrines and Dogmas	249
158. Sources of Church History	251
159. The Written Sources	251
160. The Unwritten Sources	253
161. Duty of the Historian	254
162. The Mastery of the Sources	255
163. Artistic Composition	256
164. The Christian Spirit	257
165. Uses of Church History	258
166. Periods and Epochs	259
167. Periods of Biblical History	260
168. Periods of Christian Church History	260
169. History of Israel	264
170. History of Biblical Times	267
171. The Life of Christ	268
172. Literature on the Life of Christ	270
173. The Apostolic Age	272
174. Patrology and Patristic	273
175. Patristic Literature	276
176. Christian Archæology	280
177. The Reformation	280
178. American Church History.—Roman Catholic America	285
179. Church History of the United States	289
180. Ecclesiastical Monography	294
181. Literature of General Church History	296
182. Historians before the Reformation	297
183. Historians of the Sixteenth and Seventeenth Centuries	298

CONTENTS.

CHAPTER	PAGE
184. Historians of the Eighteenth Century	300
185. Historians of the Nineteenth Century	301
186. Manuals, Text-books, and Tables of General Church History	304
187. Hints for the Study of Church History	305

BOOK IV.

SYSTEMATIC THEOLOGY.

188. General Conception 307
189. Departments of Systematic Theology 307

FIRST SECTION: APOLOGETIC.

190. Idea and Aim of Apologetic 309
191. Necessity of Apologetic 310
192. Limits of Apologetic 311
193. Value and Use of Apologetic 312
194. Epochs of Apologetic 313
195. Literature of Apologetic 314

SECOND SECTION: BIBLICAL THEOLOGY.

196. Nature and Object of Biblical Theology 316
197. Connection of Biblical Theology with other Branches 317
198. Importance of Biblical Theology 318
199. Division and Method 319
200. The Old and New Testaments 320
201. Theology of the Old Testament 321
202. Theology of the New Testament: The Teaching of Jesus 325
203. The Teaching of the Apostles 327
204. History of Biblical Theology 328
205. Literature of Biblical Theology 330

THIRD SECTION: DOGMATIC THEOLOGY.

206. Definition and Contents of Dogmatic Theology 333
207. The Sources of Dogmatic Theology 334
208. Biblical Dogmatic 335
209. Confessional or Churchly Dogmatic 336
210. Dogmatic Theology of the Greek Catholic Church 337
211. Dogmatic Theology of the Roman Catholic Church 338
212. Dogmatic Theology of the Lutheran Church 339
213. Dogmatic Theology of the Reformed and Calvinistic Churches .. 342
214. Dogmatic Theology of the Anglican Church 344
215. Arminian and Methodist Theology 346

CHAPTER	PAGE
216. Socinian and Unitarian Theology	348
217. Rationalistic Theology	350
218. Evangelical Union Theology	352
219. The Theology of Ritschl	355
220. Speculative and Critical Dogmatic	360
221. Christocentric Theology	362
222. History of Dogmatic Theology.—The Patristic Period	364
223. The Scholastic Period	368
224. The Theology of the Reformation	371
225. American Theology	374
226. Calvinistic Theology in America	375
227. New England Theology	377
228. Channing and Bushnell	386
229. Presbyterian Theology	388
230. German Theology in America	402

FOURTH SECTION: SYMBOLIC, POLEMIC, AND IRENIC.

231. Symbols of Faith, or Creeds and Confessions	406
232. Classification of Creeds	408
233. Symbolic	410
234. Historical Symbolic	411
235. Polemical Symbolic	411
236. Irenic	412
237. Method and Arrangement	416
238. History of Symbolic	417
239. Symbolical Literature	419

FIFTH SECTION: ETHIC.

240. Christian Ethic	421
241. Ethic and Dogmatic	422
242. Philosophical and Christian Ethic	423
243. Pagan and Christian Morality	424
244. Ascetic and Evangelical Morality	426
245. History of Christian Ethic	428
246. Mediæval Morals	434
247. History of Protestant Ethic	436
248. Literature on Ethic	440
249. Casuistic	441
250. Sociology	442

SIXTH SECTION: GEOGRAPHY AND STATISTIC.

251. Ecclesiastical Geography and Statistic	444
252. Material for Statistic	445
253. Comparative Statistic.—Lessons of Statistic	446

BOOK V.

PRACTICAL THEOLOGY.

CHAPTER	PAGE
254. General Conception of Practical Theology	448
255. Branches of Practical Theology	449
256. History and Literature of Practical Theology	451
257. Theory of the Christian Ministry	454
258. Different Conceptions of the Ministry	454
259. Ecclesiology	455
260. Church Law	457
261. Collections and Manuals of Church Law	461
262. Church Polity	463
263. Literature on Church Polity	467
264. Church and State	467
265. Toleration and Liberty	469
266. Homiletic or Keryctic	472
267. Different Kinds of Preaching	474
268. Homiletic Hints	475
269. History of the Pulpit to the Time of the Reformation	477
270. The Protestant Pulpit on the Continent	483
271. The English Pulpit	488
272. The American Pulpit	496
273. Homiletical Literature	499
274. Catechetic	500
275. Typical Catechisms	502
276. Catechetical Literature	504
277. The American Sunday-School	505
278. Poimenic or Pastoral Theology	507
279. Liturgic	508
280. Liturgical Literature	508
281. Worship and Art	509
282. Hymnology	510
283. History of Hymnody	511
284. Hymnological Literature	515
285. Evangelistic	517
286. Epochs of Missions	518
287. Missionary Literature	522
Topical Index	525
Index of Authors	532
Bibliography	537

THEOLOGICAL PROPÆDEUTIC.

INTRODUCTION.

CHAPTER I.

EDUCATION.

1. *Nature and Object of Education.*

Education* is the harmonious development of all the faculties of man, or the training of head and heart, to the highest attainable degree of perfection and usefulness. This is the ultimate aim, though the ideal is never fully realized in this world.

The pursuit of knowledge is based on the inborn love of truth; it is an intense enjoyment and carries in it its own exceeding great reward. The possession of knowledge is still better; else God omniscient could not be perfect in bliss, and man's future state would not be an advance upon the present. Hence Lessing's preference for the search of truth to the possession of truth must be qualified.

2. *Kinds of Education.*

There are three kinds: moral, intellectual, and religious. These should be preceded and accompanied by physical education, *i.e.*, the healthy development of the body, as the organ of the mind, according to the maxim, "*Sana mens in corpore sano.*"

(a) Intellectual culture embraces all the knowledge, human and divine, which may be acquired by the cognitive faculty. It embraces in its widest sense æsthetic education as well, that is. the cultivation of the imaginative faculty, the sense of the beautiful, and the taste for art.

(b) Moral training is the cultivation of the will and the affections, and builds up character, which is even more important than knowledge.

---

* From *educere, educare,* to lead forth, to draw out, to bring up, to educate.

(c) Religious education develops the spiritual or God-ward nature of man, and trains him for holiness, which is the highest order of goodness, and connects his temporal with his eternal welfare. Piety is the soul of morality. Man feels and fulfils his duty to his fellow-men in proportion as he realizes his relation and duty to God.

3. *Value of Education.*

(a) The material value: Education stores the mind with useful information and sound principles.

(b) Formal value: Education strengthens and sharpens the various faculties to an easy and vigorous exercise, and practical efficiency.

Knowledge, next to virtue, is the greatest power, and far more desirable than material wealth. But it may be a power for evil as well as for good, according to its spirit and tendency. Hence the prime importance of connecting moral and religious culture with intellectual. No true culture without virtue, no virtue without piety, no love to men without love to God.

Beware of the pride of knowledge. Superficial knowledge puffs up (I. Cor. 8:1); thorough knowledge makes humble. Genuine scholarship is modest, and knows how little we do know and how much more might be known, and will be known hereafter. Sir Isaac Newton says: "I am but a little child, picking up pebbles on the shore of the vast ocean of truth." There is an humble and Christian as well as a proud and unchristian agnosticism. The former arises from a knowledge of the boundaries of the human capacity and a sense of the infinite depth, height, and breadth of the truth, which we can here know only in part and see in a mirror darkly, but which we may hope to see hereafter face to face (I. Cor. 13: 9); the latter starts in indifferentism or skepticism and ends in pessimism and nihilism. The one says: There *is* a God, and we know him as far as he has revealed himself in nature, in reason, and in history (including the Church and the Bible), but no further; the other says: There *may* be a God, but we do not know it; there is probably none, and we need not care for him.

4. *Means and Schools of Education.*

It is carried on and promoted through countless natural and social influences; the whole world of nature, the rising and setting sun, the flowers of the field, the mountains and valleys, father and mother, friends and neighbors, books and newspapers, are educators. In the school, education is reduced to a system and methodical process under the superintendence of competent teachers, who devote their whole strength to this noble work, and who are the true philanthropists and benefactors of the race.

There are school-trained, self-taught, and God-inspired men; but the difference is relative. Most educated men belong to the first class; a few to the second (Shakespeare, Bœhme, Franklin, Lincoln); still fewer to the third class (Prophets and Apostles who were θεοδίδακτοι and θεόπνευστοι). Christ differs from all, being self-taught and God-taught, without any special inspiration, but by a permanent indwelling of the Father in him (Col. 2 : 9). He taught the world as one who owed nothing to it, who came directly from God as "the Light of the world" (John 8 : 12).

5. *Degrees of Education.*

It is a process which grows with our growth.

(*a*) Domestic Education or home-training is carried on under the supervision of the parents. The mother is the first and most impressive teacher of the child.

The fifth commandment—child's prayer—child's catechism—the spelling-book—Mother Goose—Grimm's Household Tales—Work and Play—The Infant Sunday School—The Kindergarten.

(*b*) Elementary or Common Education. Either in close connection with the parish (Parochial School); or under the supervision of the government (State School, Public School); or under private tuition.

The Common School—the Sunday School—Catechetical Instruction.

(*c*) Liberal or Classical Education begins in the Academy (in the American sense), or Preparatory Grammar School, and is carried forward in the College (Gymnasium, Lyceum).

Classical education embraces Latin and Greek, Geography and History, Mathematics, Natural Science, Mental and Moral Philosophy, Literature, and Poetry. All necessary for a professional scholar and an accomplished gentleman.

(*d*) Professional Education in the University (*Universitas Literarum*), where all knowledge, human and divine, is taught in the highest branches, or in special professional colleges and seminaries. The mediæval Universities distinguished four learned professions or faculties: Theology, law, medicine, philosophy. This division now requires enlargement corresponding to the growth of science, with a suitable multiplication of academic degrees in history, philology, natural sciences, mathematics, fine arts, and useful arts, etc.

(e) Theology is the chief among the professional studies, and prepares for the practical duties of the Christian ministry. It should be cultivated both as the knowledge of divine things for its own intrinsic value, and as a means for building up the Church. It is the queen of sciences (*regina scientiarum*), by far the noblest and sublimest branch of knowledge. "*A Deo docetur, Deum docet, et ad Deum ducit.*"

CHAPTER II.

THEOLOGICAL PROPÆDEUTIC.

Theological Propædeutic * is a general introduction to the scientific study of the Christian religion in its origin, progress, and present condition.

It embraces Encyclopædia (in the formal or systematic sense), Methodology, and Bibliography.

The first is the principal part, the other two are auxiliary.

Encyclopædia teaches what to study; Methodology, how to study; Bibliography, what books to study. The first is concerned with the matter, the second with the method, the third with the means or helps.

CHAPTER III.

ENCYCLOPÆDIA.

Encyclopædia (literally, instruction in a circle, or a circle of instruction) † is a general survey of the sciences and arts, or a summary of general knowledge.

* From προπαιδεία, preparatory or elementary teaching of a boy (παῖς); προπαιδεύω, to teach beforehand. Both words are used by Plato and Aristotle. Προπαίδευσις, προπαίδευμα, ἐγκύκλιον προπαίδευμα, occur in later writers. I have coined this term for theological use after the analogy of *logic, rhetoric, arithmetic,* etc. Other terms proposed, instead of the misleading term *Encyclopædia,* are: *Isagogic, Hodegetic, Theologic.*

† From ἐν κύκλῳ, or ἐγκύκλιος παιδεία, ἐγκυκλοπαιδεία, also ἐγκύκλιος ἀγωγή, instruction in general knowledge. Classical writers use: ἡ ἐγκύκλιος

It embraced originally the cycle of liberal arts and sciences (*artes liberales*, or *ingenuæ*), that is, the school learning which constituted a liberal education,* and which a free-born Greek or Roman youth had to acquire before he was fit for public life. These arts and sciences were gradually increased to seven; namely, grammar, dialectic (logic), rhetoric; music, arithmetic, geometry, and astronomy. In the middle ages, the first three were called *Trivium*, the other four, *Quadrivium*. Seven, three, and four were all regarded as sacred numbers.†

In modern times the cycle of sciences and arts is greatly enlarged, especially by the immense progress of the knowledge of nature, philology, ethnology, and history in all its ramifications.

Encyclopædic knowledge is a general knowledge of all that is worth knowing; but it is, of course, limited and fragmentary, even with the most comprehensive scholars. A universal genius is the greatest rarity. There is a difference between encyclopædic and polyhistoric knowledge. The former is systematic and comprehensive, the latter is disconnected and incoherent. The one digests, the other devours, books. Examples of a philosophic, well-ordered and unified universality of knowledge: Aristotle, Leibnitz, Alexander von Humboldt, Hegel, Goethe. Example of a chaotic universality of knowledge: Robert Burton, the anatomist of melancholy (well described by Taine, in his *History of English Literature*, I. 209).

παιδεία, τὰ ἐγκύκλια μαθήματα, or τὰ ἐγκύκλια, and somewhat later the compound word ἐγκυκλοπαιδεία, *orbis doctrinæ*. Quintilian (*Inst.* I. 10, 1): "*Orbis ille doctrinæ quem Græci ἐγκύκλιον παιδείαν vocant.*" To this Turnebus adds the remark: "*Quæ ostendit, inter omnes artes esse conjunctionem quandam et communionem.*" The compound ἐγκυκλοπαιδεία (a barbarism) was first used perhaps by Galenus (d. c. 201). An '*encyclical* letter," or *encyclical*, is a letter intended for a certain number of persons or congregations, and addressed to all at once or in turn; at present it is confined to letters of the Pope to all the bishops of the Roman church.

* ἐλευθέρα or ἐλευθερία παιδεία, the liberal education of a boy or youth (παῖς).
† The division is derived from St. Augustin (*De Ordine* II. 12 sqq.) and Cassiodorus (*De Artibus ac Disciplinis Liberalium Artium*; *Opera*, ed. Migne II. 1150–1218). Augustin connects *poëtica* with *musica*. (See Schaff, *Hist. of the Chr. Church*, IV. 611 sqq.) The division is expressed in the verse:

"*Grammatica loquitur, Dialectica verba docet, Rhetorica verba colorat;
Musica canit, Arithmetica numerat, Geometria ponderat, Astronomia colit astra.*"

CHAPTER IV.

FORMAL AND MATERIAL ENCYCLOPÆDIA.

Encyclopædia is either formal or material (real), according as it is treated with reference chiefly either to the form, or to the matter of knowledge. To avoid confusion, the former might be called "Encyclopædia" proper, the latter "Cyclopædia." But the terms are used indiscriminately.

1. Formal Encyclopædia is a general outline of human knowledge in all its branches, showing the organic unity and universality of knowledge, and proceeding from a common central principle which is constitutive and regulative. All branches of knowledge have their origin and unity in God. Science is the investigation and knowledge of truth; and truth is one in origin, essence, and aim, but involves infinite variety.

The different sciences must, therefore, agree and form a living unit or an organic whole. They are related to each other as the branches of a tree, or as the members of the human body. None can be thoroughly understood and perfected without the rest. As they all proceed from God, they must ultimately return to him, that he may be "all in all." Science and philosophy superficially tasted may lead away from God, but thoroughly exhausted, they lead back to him. (Bacon.)

2. Material Cyclopædia is a summary of human knowledge as to its matter or contents. It may be arranged either in the systematic order of subjects according to their logical connection, or lexicographically in alphabetical order for convenient reference. A good alphabetical Cyclopædia is a necessity for every educated man. (*Encyclopædia Britannica;* Chambers, Johnson, Appleton, Pierre Larousse, Brockhaus, Meyer, Ersch and Gruber.)

CHAPTER V.

GENERAL AND SPECIAL ENCYCLOPÆDIA.

Encyclopædia may be further divided into general and special, according to its extent.

1. General Encyclopædia embraces all sciences and arts, or all branches of human knowledge. It is a condensed reference library.

2. Special Encyclopædia embraces one or more departments of human knowledge. Thus we have Encyclopædias of theology, law, medicine, philosophy, philology, physical sciences, biography, history, poetry, music, architecture, sculpture, painting, the mechanical arts, general and particular literature, etc.

CHAPTER VI.

THEOLOGICAL ENCYCLOPÆDIA.

In Theological Encyclopædia we must likewise distinguish between formal and material.

1. The formal Theological Encyclopædia is a general introduction to the study of theology and its various departments. It is an outline of the science of theology, giving an idea of its general character and aim, and showing the number, unity, variety, order, and connection of its different branches. It is, so to speak, a theological map, and furnishes a standpoint (δός μοι ποῦ στῶ) from which the student may survey the whole field for preparatory orientation.

It is impossible to avoid entering to some extent into the concrete contents of the science itself and to anticipate much positive information, but the main object must be always to bring out the organism of theology and to present a clear view of the nature, aim, and limits of the parts which constitute the whole. We must take our stand in the vestibule, rather than in the interior of the temple, and, looking from without, we shall be better able to sketch the architectural design and structure of the whole building.

Formal Encyclopædia stands related to theology in general, as Biblical Introduction is related to exegetical theology. It embraces in one connected whole all the introductory information which precedes the several departments of theology, as Biblical Introduction comprehends the introductory chapters to the several books of the Old and New Testaments and weaves them into a literary history of the Bible.

2. The material Theological Cyclopædia gives the matter of information in all departments of theological science. It may either follow the systematic or the alphabetical method. The latter is the more convenient for use.

Works of this kind a student ought to have for constant

reference. A general theological Encyclopædia and a Bible Dictionary are—next to the Bible itself, with Grammar, Lexicon, and Concordance—the most indispensable and useful books of a working library and a pastor's study. (General Theological Encyclopædias: Herzog, Schaff-Herzog, Wetzer & Welte, McClintock & Strong, Jackson. Bible Dictionaries: Winer, Schenkel, Riehm, Kitto, Fairbairn, Smith, Schaff. See the Bibliography at the end of this volume.)

CHAPTER VII.

METHODOLOGY AND BIBLIOGRAPHY.

Methodology gives directions how to study to the best advantage. Bibliography indicates the best helps to study.

It is a good part of study to know how to do it and where to go for information.* Method in the use of time gains and economizes time and strength. A judicious distribution of hours and objects of study facilitates it. Books are to a student what tools are to a mechanic, what furniture is to a housekeeper, what arms are to a soldier. Every student ought to acquire a library of standard works for constant use, and this can be done only gradually and under proper direction.

It is the object of this book to combine Encyclopædia, Methodology, and Bibliography. Methodology accompanies Encyclopædia by giving hints and suggestions as to the best way of pursuing the study of the several branches. Bibliography constitutes a separate department, and is put at the end of the volume for more convenient reference.

CHAPTER VIII.

DIVISION AND ARRANGEMENT.

The method and arrangement must correspond to the division of theological study, or the several parts which compose the organic whole of theology. But before the parts can be examined, we must have a general idea of the whole.

* *"Scire ubi aliquid possis invenire, magna pars eruditionis est."*

We purpose to divide the work into five parts, or books, as follows:

BOOK I. RELIGION AND THEOLOGY IN GENERAL.

Nature, character, value, and aim of religion and theology; their relation to philosophy, to the Church, and to the ministry.

BOOK II. EXEGETICAL (BIBLICAL) THEOLOGY.

Christianity in its origin and authentic records. This includes also the Scriptures of the Old Testament as a preparation for Christianity.

BOOK III. HISTORICAL (ECCLESIASTICAL) THEOLOGY.

Christianity in its past history down to the present time.

BOOK IV. SYSTEMATIC (PHILOSOPHICAL) THEOLOGY.

Christianity in its present state: apologetic, dogmatic, ethic, etc.

BOOK V. PRACTICAL THEOLOGY.

Christianity in its aim and action for the future.

CHAPTER IX.

HISTORY AND LITERATURE.

Manuals for the use of theological students and ministers are almost as old as theology itself, and were known under different names, such as *Studium theologicum; Ratio* or *Methodus studii theologici; Doctrina Christiana; Enchiridion; Introductio in theologiam universam; Isagoge historico-theologica,* etc. They were at first confined to Biblical and patristic studies, and gradually enlarged in topics with the growth of history and theological science. They embrace miscellaneous information and directions, without system or order, and without any idea of the extent and organic unity of the theological sciences. Many of the older works, however, have still a historical and practical value, and deserve to be studied as mirrors of the theological education of their age and for the influence they have exerted.

The term "Encyclopædia" in the sense here used was first applied to theology towards the end of the eighteenth century

by S. Mursinna, Professor of Reformed Theology at Halle (d. 1795).*
A systematic and scientific treatment began with Schleiermacher, who is the founder of the modern theological Encyclopædia. Since his time it has been specially cultivated in Germany by Hagenbach, Pelt, Räbiger, and others; since 1884 also in England by Drummond and Cave. America has not yet produced an original work on the subject, but has made Hagenbach accessible to American students.

CHAPTER X.

A SELECT LIST OF WORKS INTRODUCTORY TO THE STUDY OF THEOLOGY.†

The most important are marked by a *.

I. PATRISTIC and SCHOLASTIC Works. They are mostly confined to Biblical studies and the duties of the clergy.

*CHRYSOSTOM (d. 407): *De Sacerdotio* (Περὶ ἱερωσύνης). Best English translation, with notes, by Stephens, in Schaff's "Nicene and Post-Nicene Library," First Series, vol. IX. (New York, 1889).

AMBROSE (d. 397): *De Officiis Ministrorum.*

*AUGUSTIN (d. 430): *De Doctrina Christiana.* Translated by Shaw, in Schaff's "Nic. and P.-Nic. Libr.," First Series, vol. II. (1887).

CASSIODORUS (d. 562): *De Institutione Divinarum Literarum* (for the training of monks).

GREGORY I. (d. 604): *Regula Pastoralis.*

ISIDOR OF SEVILLE (d. 636): *Originum S. Etymologiarum libri XX.* (embracing all the knowledge of his age).

RABANUS MAURUS (middle of the ninth cent.): *De Institutione Clericorum.*

HUGO OF ST. VICTOR (d. 1141): *Didascalion.*

VINCENTIUS DE BEAUVAIS (Bellovacensis, d. 1264): *Speculum Doctrinale.*

II. WORKS FROM THE REFORMATION TO SCHLEIERMACHER, 1519–1811.

*ERASMUS (d. 1536): *Ratio seu Methodus * * * * ad veram theologiam* (1519, 1522, etc.).

MELANCHTHON (d. 1560): *Brevis Ratio discendæ Theologiæ.* Only a few pages recommending the study of the New Testament before the Old, and

---

* In his *Primæ Lineæ Encyclopædiæ*, Halle, 1784; second ed., 1794. The term had been used before in reference to legal and medical sciences.

† For a fuller list of literature see Pelt, *Encyklopädie*, 47 sqq.; Hagenbach, *Encyklopädie*, Appendix to § 33 (92–114 of the 12th ed.); Räbiger, *Theologik*, 2–91 (a critical digest); Cave, *Introd. to Theol.*, 32–37.

in the New Testament the Epistle to the Romans first, and the Gospel of John last, so that the doctrines of faith and of justification might be the beginning and end of theology.

BULLINGER (d. 1575): *Ratio studii theologici*. Very practical, and going into the details of the daily life of the student.

Similar works by THAMER, CHYTRÆUS, WELLER, HYPERIUS, JOHN GERHARD, ALSTED, CALIXTUS, BUDDE, PFAFF, J. G. WALCH, SEMLER (the father of rationalistic criticism), MURSINNA.

*HERDER'S *Briefe über das Studium der Theologie* (2d ed., 1785, in 4 vols.) marks an epoch as an inspiring work of genius with universal sympathies, and is full of useful suggestions (especially on Hebrew poetry), but neither systematic nor complete.

Works which more nearly approach the modern idea are the Encyclopædias of NÖSSELT (1786), PLANCK (1794), TITTMANN (1798), KLEUKER (1800), NIEMEYER (1803).

Roman Catholic works by ANT. POSSEVINUS (*Bibliotheca selecta de Ratione Studiorum*, 1607); *L. ELLIES DU PIN (*Methode pour étudier la théologie*, 1716, translated into several languages); OBERTHÜR (*Encyclopædia et Methodologia*, 1786, German edition, 1828); J. SEB. DREY (*Kurze Einleitung in das Studium der Theologie*, 1819).

III. WORKS FROM SCHLEIERMACHER TO THE PRESENT TIME, 1811–1890.

*FRIEDRICH SCHLEIERMACHER (Prof. of Theology in Berlin, 1768–1834): *Kurze Darstellung des theologischen Studiums zum Behuf einleitender Vorlesungen*. Berlin, 1811, 2d ed., 1830. (English translation by William Farrer: *Brief Outline of the Study of Theology, with Lücke's Reminiscences of Schleiermacher*. Edinburgh, T. & T. Clark, 1850.)

This is a mere sketch, but the sketch of a master architect. It struck the key-note for his successors. Schleiermacher defines theology as a positive and practical science for the service and government of the Church, and divides it into three parts—*philosophical, historical*, and *practical*. In the first he includes apologetic and polemic, in the second exegesis, church history, and systematic theology. He limits the first, overloads the second, and obliterates the distinction between exegetical, historical, and systematic theology. The whole scheme is wrong; but, nevertheless, the book is full of stimulating suggestions. Schleiermacher was the Origen of German Protestantism, neither orthodox nor heretical, but independent, original, emancipating, and stimulating in different directions. Those systems are gone, but the inspiration remains.

KARL ROSENKRANZ (Hegelian philosopher, d. 1879): *Encyclopädie der theologischen Wissenschaften* (*Encyclopædia of Theological Sciences*), Halle, 1831; 2d ed., 1845, much altered. This book enters more into the concrete contents, while Schleiermacher dwells exclusively on the form. Rosenkranz gives an epitome of historical, philosophical, and practical theology, like Hegel who, in his *Philosophical Encyclopædia*, gives his whole system of philosophy in a nutshell. It is, in fact, a material encyclopædia in systematic form, and condensed into a compend.

F. A. STAUDENMEIER (Rom. Cath.): *Encyclopädie der theologischen Wissenschaften*. Mainz, 1836, 2d ed., 1840. He divides theology into speculative, practical, and historical, and dwells mainly on the first. Very prolix.

Jo. CLARISSE: *Encyl. theol. Epitome.* Lugd. Batav., 1832, ed. II., 1835. Very full in the bibliographical department, including English books which are unknown to the majority of German divines.

G. C. AD. HARLESS (Orthodox Lutheran, d. 1879): *Theologische Encyklopädie und Methodologie vom Standpunkte der protestantischen Kirche (Theological Encyclopædia and Methodology from the Standpoint of the Protestant Church),* Nürnberg, 1837. With copious literature and valuable sketches of the history of the theological sciences.

ANT. F. L. PELT (Prof. in Kiel, d. 1861): *Theol. Encyklopädie als System, etc. (Theological Encyclopædia as a System),* Hamb. and Gotha, 1843. Valuable for much historical and literary information, Christian spirit, and sound judgment. Three parts: I. Historical Theology (including Biblical Exegesis and Church History). II. Systematic Theology. III. Practical Theology.

*K. R. HAGENBACH (Swiss Reformed, Prof. of Church History, School of Neander, d. 1874): *Encyklopædie und Methodologie der theologischen Wissenschaften (Encyclopædia and Methodology of Theol. Sciences),* Leipzig, 1833; 9th ed., 1874 (the author's last, with a very modest preface); 10th ed., revised by *E. Kautzsch* (then Prof. at Tübingen, now at Halle); 11th ed., by the same, 1884 (544 pp.); 12th ed., again revised and enlarged by Prof. *Max Reischle,* 1889 (600 pp.). Follows independently in the track of Schleiermacher, but is more full, popular, and practical, and includes extensive lists of books (mostly German). A most useful handbook for German and Swiss students (" *ein rechtes Studentenbuch* "), written in excellent Christian spirit, and kept alive by constant improvements. Divided into General and Special Encyclopædia, and the latter subdivided into Exegetical, Historical, Systematic, and Practical Theology.—A Hungarian translation by *J. Revesz,* Pest, 1857. An English translation and transformation by *Crooks* and *Hurst;* and an abridgment by *Weidner* (see below).

H. G. KIENLEN: *Encyclopédie des sciences de la theologie chrétienne,* Strasbourg, 1842; enlarged by the author in the Germ. ed., Darmstadt, 1845. On the basis of Schleiermacher.

HOFSTEDE DE GROOT and L. G. PAREAU: *Encyclopædia Theologi Christiani,* Groningen, 3d ed., 1857. Represents the Groningen school, which stands between the orthodoxy of Utrecht and the rationalism of Leiden.

JOHN M'CLINTOCK (d. 1872): *Lectures on Theological Encyclopædia and Methodology,* ed. by *John T. Short,* Cincinnati and New York, 1873. A posthumous publication and imperfect outline of lectures freely delivered, but never elaborated for publication by the author.

JOHN BAPT. WIRTHMÜLLER (R. Cath. Prof. at Würzburg): *Encyclopädie der kathol. Theologie. Eine propädeutische Einleitung in ihr Studium.* Landshut, 1874 (pp. 975). Divided into three parts: I. *Realencyclopädie der Theologie;* II. *Idealencyclopädie der Theologie;* III. *Systematische Encyclopädie der Theologie.*

I. T. DOEDES (Prof. of Theol. in Utrecht): *Encyclopedie der Christlclijke Theologie,* Utrecht, 1876; 2d ed., 1883 (272 pp). Divided into Exegetical, Historical, Dogmatic, and Practical Theology. Important for Dutch literature.

J. P. LANGE (d. 1884): *Grundriss der theologischen Encyklopädie mit*

INTRODUCTION. 15

Einschluss der Methodologie, Heidelberg, 1877 (pp. 232). Original and suggestive. Divided into General and Special Encyclopædia, and the latter again into Historical and Didactic Theology. Intended as a supplement to Hagenbach, with constant reference to his lists of literature.

RICHARD ROTHE (Prof. in Heidelberg, d. 1867): *Theologische Encyclopädie. Aus seinem Nachlasse herausgegeben von Hermann Ruppelius,* Wittenberg, 1880 (pp. 158). Posthumous lectures of one of the greatest speculative divines of the 19th century, full of valuable thoughts, but not elaborated for publication. He divides theology, somewhat like Schleiermacher, into Speculative, Historical (including Exegetical), and Practical.

J. K. VON HOFMANN (Prof. at Erlangen, d. 1877): *Encyklopädie der Theologie nach Vorlesungen und Manuscripten,* Nördlingen, 1879. A posthumous work, ed. by BESTMANN. A compendium of the author's own theology, in three divisions, systematic, historical (including Biblical), and practical.

*J. F. RÄBIGER (Prof. in Breslau): *Theologik oder Encyklopädie der Theologie,* Leipzig, 1880 (pp. 554). With an Appendix: *Zur Theologischen Encyklopädie. Kritische Betrachtungen* (on Hofmann and Rothe), Breslau, 1882. A material as well as formal encyclopædia, representing theology itself in a nutshell (like Rosenkranz's work); combines the Schleiermacherian and Hegelian modes of thought. Substitutes the term Theologic for Encyclopædia. Divided, like Hagenbach's, into General and Special Encyclopædia, and the Special into Exegetical, Historical, Systematic, and Practical. Literature is omitted, except in the Introduction. English translation by Rev. John Macpherson, Edinburgh (T. & T. Clark), 1884–85, 2 vols., with notes and additions to literature.

*GEO. R. CROOKS (Prof. in Drew Seminary, Madison, N. J.) and Bishop JOHN F. HURST (both Methodists): *Theological Encyclopædia and Methodology. On the basis of Hagenbach.* New York, 1884 (pp. 596). A useful adaptation of Hagenbach's book to the Anglo-American student, with additions of English and American literature. The translators do not state the edition of Hagenbach on which their work is based, nor distinguish between the original and the additions.

REVERE FRANKLIN WEIDNER (Prof. in the Swedish Lutheran Seminary at Rock Island, Ill.): *Theological Encyclopædia and Methodology. Based on Hagenbach and Krauth* (his unpublished lectures in the Luth. Seminary of Philadelphia). Rock Island, Augustana Book Concern, 1885–90, in four parts. The title sufficiently indicates the character of this compilation.

JAMES DRUMMOND, LL.D. (Unitarian, Prof. of Theol. in Manchester New College, London): *Introduction to the Study of Theology.* London (Macmillan & Co.), 1884 (pp. 262). Deals with the scientific form, not with the matter, of theology, and sets forth "the nature, method, and mutual relations of the various branches of theological study, so that the student may see more clearly the bearing of his labors, and view the several departments of his work, not as incoherent fragments, but as constituent members, each with an appropriate place, in a collective organism which embraces them all." The first clear definition, in English, of formal Encyclopædia. Drummond distinguishes six departments I. Philosophy; II. Comparative Religion; III. Biblical Theology; IV. Ecclesiastical History; V. Systematic Theology; VI. Practical Theology.

*ALFRED CAVE (Independent, Principal, and Professor of Theology, of Hackney College, London): *An Introduction to Theology: its Principles, its Branches, its Results, and its Literature*, Edinburgh (T. & T. Clark), 1886 (pp. 576). The best original work on the subject in the English language; with select lists of books, Continental, English, and American. Sixfold division of Theology: I. Natural Theology; II. Ethnic Theology; III. Biblical Theology; IV. Ecclesiastical Theology; V. Comparative Theology; VI. Pastoral Theology.

E. MARTIN: *Introduction à l'étude de la théologie protestante*. Genève, 1883. An attempt at an independent reconstruction.

A. GRETILLAT (Prof. of Theol. in the Independent Faculty of Neuchâtel, and colleague of F. Godet, the commentator): *Exposé de Théologie systématique. Tome I. Propédeutique*. Neuchâtel, 1885 (pp. 356).

*OTTO ZÖCKLER (Prof. of Church History in Greifswald, representing a mild and irenic type of evangelical Lutheran orthodoxy): *Handbuch der theologischen Wissenschaften in encyclopädischer Darstellung*. Nördlingen, 1883, 3d. ed., 1890, 4 vols. A useful work of a number of specialists under the editorial care of Zöckler. Combines formal and material Encyclopædia, and consists of a series of manuals on all the departments of theological science by eighteen writers—CREMER, GRAU, HARNACK (THEODOSIUS), HÖLSCHER, KÜBEL, LINDNER, LUTHARDT, VON ORELLI, SCHÄFER, VON SCHEELE, FR. W. SCHULTZ, VIKTOR SCHULTZE, L. SCHULZE, STRACK, VOLCK, VON ZEZSCHWITZ, PLATH, P. ZELLER. Zöckler prepared the introductory part (*Grundlegung*), the general church history, and, in part, dogmatic. He follows the fourfold division of Hagenbach, with departures in subdivisions.

*HEINRICH KIHN (Professor in Würzburg): *Encyklopädie und Methodologie der Theologie*. Freiburg i.-B. (Herder), 1892 (pp. 573). The best work from a Roman Catholic, with full lists of literature.

JOS. HENRY THAYER (Professor of N. T. Criticism or Interpretation in Harvard University): *Books and their Use*. Boston, 1893. With a select bibliography for students of the New Testament.

MARVIN R. VINCENT (Professor of Sacred Literature in Union Theological Seminary, New York): *Student's Handbook of Topics and Literature in New Testament Introduction*. New York, 1893. A preparation for the use of larger works on New Testament Introduction. The topics of the critical study of the New Testament, and the literature of each; a sketch of New Testament Criticism from the end of the fourth century to the present time; a statement of the critical questions raised by each book, and a select catalogue of commentaries and illustrative works.

*GEORG HEINRICI (Professor in Leipzig, formerly in Marburg): *Theologische Encyklopädie*. Freiburg-i.-B., 1893 (pp. 372). The best since Hagenbach. One of a series of short theological text books from the school of Ritschl, published by Mohr (Siebeck) at Freiburg i. B. Heinrici divides theology into two divisions: I. Historical: (1) Exegesis; (2) Church History. II. Normative: (1) Systematic Theology (Dogmatic and Ethic); (2) Practical Theology.

BOOK I.

RELIGION AND THEOLOGY.

FIRST SECTION: RELIGION.

CHAPTER XI.

GENERAL DEFINITION OF RELIGION.

Theology is the science of religion.* It has religion for its contents and object. Christian theology is the science of the Christian religion, as revealed in the Bible, developed in history, and believed and practiced in the Church.

Religion is the relation of man to God. It is confined to rational creatures. It is fully realized in Christianity, as the universal religion of union and communion of man with God in Christ.

The term *religion* (being Latin) does not occur in the original Bible, but it has been naturalized in all the Romanic and Germanic languages, and also occurs in the English Bible.†

---
* Strictly speaking, *theology* (from θεός and λόγος) is the knowledge of God and divine things (λόγος περὶ θεοῦ καὶ τῶν θείων). It is "*a Deo, de Deo, in Deum.*" But it necessarily includes also the knowledge of God's relation to man. Religion combines both factors.

† Acts 26 : 5 (for θρησκεία); Gal. 1 : 13, 14 ("Jews' religion," for 'Ιουδαισμός); James 1 : 26, 27 (for θρησκεία). The adjective *religious* occurs Acts 13 : 43; James 1 : 26. The Revised Version retains the word except in Acts 13 : 43, where it substitutes "devout proselytes" for "religious proselytes" (σεβομένων προσηλύτων). The word might have been properly used in the address of Paul to the Athenians, Acts 17 : 22, for δεισιδαιμονεστέρους, "very religious," "over-religious" (*religiosiores, sehr gottesfürchtig*)—that is, more religious than others, in building an altar even to "an unknown God," who is the true God in Christ, whom they unknowingly or unconsciously worshipped. The A. V. is certainly wrong in translating "too superstitious." Paul did not begin with insulting the Athenians, but with gaining their good will (*captatio benevolentiæ*). The R. V. substitutes "somewhat superstitious," with the margin "religious." The Amer. Rev. better, "very religious."

It expresses both the subjective side, or religion in the heart of man (like our corresponding terms piety, godliness, holiness, etc.), and the objective aspect, namely, religion in its outward manifestation as an institution, or organization, or form of worship. It is the most general designation of the relation of man to God. The Bible terms are more concrete and specific.*

The meaning of religion does not depend on its etymology, which is uncertain. The most popular and significant, though perhaps not the correct, derivation is that of Lactantius from *religare*, to re-bind, re-unite—viz., man to God.†

This derivation gives the precise idea of religion as actualized in Christianity. It implies:

1. An original union of God and man—state of innocence.
2. A separation in consequence of the fall—state of sin and death.
3. A reconciliation by the atonement of Christ, the God Man and Mediator, and a consequent reunion of God and man—state of redemption.

Other derivations from *relegere* (to reflect, to meditate) ‡; *reëligere* (to re-elect, viz., God whom we lost); *relinquere* (to forsake, viz., the world, a monkish derivation), are less significant, or liable to philological objections.

We treat of religion first objectively, then subjectively.

* Such as "fear of God," "love of God," "godliness" (εὐσέβεια and εὐσεβής, several times), "faith," "righteousness," "holiness," "worship," "service." These terms represent various aspects and states of religion or piety.

† Lactantius, called "the Christian Cicero" on account of his elegant Latinity, *Inst. Div.*, IV. 28: "*Hoc vinculo pietatis obstricti Deo religati sumus; unde ipsa religio nomen accepit, non, ut Cicero interpretatus est, a relegendo.*" The objection that this derivation would require *religatio* does not hold; for we have *rebellio* from *rebellare*, *optio* from *optare*, *postulio* from *postulare*, etc. Most theologians accept the etymology of Lactantius. The word might be derived from an obsolete verb, *ligere* (comp. the Sanscrit *lok*, the Latin *lucere, lux*, the Swiss-German *lugen*, the English *look*), like *diligere, intelligere, negligere* (*dilexi, intellexi, neglexi*, not *dilegi*, etc.), and would convey the fundamental idea of looking back with *respect, reverence*, which underlies all religion. "The fear of God is the beginning of wisdom."

‡ This is Cicero's derivation, *De Natura Deorum*, II. 28, where he draws a line of distinction between *superstitio* (*nomen vitii*) and *religio* (*nomen laudis*), and says: "*Qui omnia quæ ad cultum deorum pertinerent, diligenter retractarent et tamquam relegerent, ii dicti sunt religiosi ex relegendo, tamquam ex intelligendo intelligentes.*" Grammatically not impossible; comp. *legio* from *legere, regio* from *regere, contagio, oblivio*, and other nouns in *io* from the verbs of the third conjugation. Nitzsch (in the "*Studien und Kritiken*," Vol. I., No. 3, and again in his "*System der Christl. Lehre*," 6th ed., § 6, p. 8) defends this derivation, but in the sense of *respectus, observantia*. So also A. Peip, *Religionsphilosophie* (1879), p. 83.

PART I.

OBJECTIVE RELIGION.

CHAPTER XII.

THE SCIENCE OF RELIGION.

Recent discoveries and the study of comparative philology have brought all the religions of the world within the reach of our knowledge. The architectural and sculptural monuments and hieroglyphic inscriptions of Egypt, the ruins and cuneiform literature of Assyria and Babylonia, the study of Sanscrit and the sacred books of India and Persia, the opening of the immense empire of China and the writings of Confucius, the contact with Japan, the explorations of the interior of Africa and acquaintance with its savage tribes—have enormously enlarged the field of observation.

It is the aim of the Science of Religion to work up the results of these discoveries and researches into a connected whole. This may be done historically, or philosophically. Hence we have two branches of the Science of Religion, both of recent growth and great importance—History of Religion, and Philosphy of Religion. They supplement each other: one gives the facts, the other a rational explanation of the facts.

CHAPTER XIII.

HISTORY OF RELIGION.

The History of Religion is an account of the origin, development, and characteristic features of all religions, from those of the lowest savage tribes to those of the most cultivated nations. The historian deals with facts as an accurate observer and impartial judge. He may be purely objective, or comparative in his treatment. Comparative History of Religion corresponds to Comparative Geography, Comparative Philology, Comparative Anatomy, all of which are of recent origin. It also resembles Symbolic or Comparative Dogmatic, with this difference: the science of Comparative Religion has to do with all religions, including Christianity as one of them; Symbolic is confined to the Christian religion, and discusses only the doctrinal controversies within the Church.

CHAPTER XIV.

PHILOSOPHY OF RELIGION.

The Philosophy of Religion rests upon the History of Religion, and reduces its facts and phenomena to general principles. It goes to the root of the matter, explains the religious nature of man and the essential character of religion, shows the relationship, the virtues and defects of the various religions, traces the laws of development from the lower to the higher forms, and ends with a vindication of Christianity, as the most rational and universal religion.

The Philosophy of Religion forms the connecting link between Philosophy and Theology, and approaches the domain of Apologetic and Dogmatic.

Schleiermacher was the first to make the psychological nature of religion the subject of a keen scientific analysis; while Hegel first attempted a philosophical classification of religions on the basis of historical development or evolution. To English travellers and writers we owe most of our information about the religions of Asia and Africa.

CHAPTER XV.

VALUE OF THE SCIENCE OF RELIGION.

The study of the Science of Religion, both in its historical and philosophical aspects, is of great value to the theologian, and especially also to the missionary in heathen lands. It enlarges and liberalizes the vision and furnishes the best proof for the following important facts:

1. That religion forms the deepest current of the world's his-

tory. It shapes public and private morals and controls more or less the course of government, science, art and civilization. In ancient times, and in the middle ages, religious and secular history were inseparably interwoven; in modern times they are more distinct in proportion as the separation of Church and State and the principle of religious freedom advance; nevertheless they everywhere act and react upon each other.

2. That Christianity is immeasurably superior to all other religions and is all the time progressing, with the certainty of ultimate supremacy. Comparison and contrast teach full knowledge. We cannot fully understand the English language without knowing the Saxon, Norman, Celtic and other elements of which it is composed; nor can we fully understand and appreciate Christianity till we compare it with the heathen, Jewish and Mohammedan religions.

3. That the best elements in the other religions are combined and perfected in the Christian, but remain an unfulfilled prophecy without it. Christianity meets and satisfies the noblest tendencies and deepest wants of the human mind and heart. It is true in the broadest sense that Christ came " not to destroy, but to fulfil."

In the history of religion, heathenism may be compared to the starry night, Judaism to the full moon and early dawn, Christianity to the bright sun.

CHAPTER XVI.

THE RELIGIOUS WORLD.—STATISTICS.

The religious world is divided into Christian, Jewish, Mohammedan, and heathen. The entire population of the globe numbers now (in 1891), in round figures, 1,467,600,000. The Christian religion embraces about 450,000,000; that is, more than one-fourth of it. Among heathen religions, Confucianism, Buddhism, and Brahmanism count the largest following. Then comes Mohammedanism, and last, though not least, the Hebrew religion, the most tenacious of all.

It should be kept in mind that numerical estimates usually refer only to nominal membership, without regard to internal condition. Only in the United States a distinction is made between communicant members and nominal members or hearers.

The Christian religion prevails all over Europe and America, and is the only religion of these two continents (with the exception of the Jews scattered over both, the followers of Islam in Constantinople and the Balkan States, and the remnant of heathen Indians in America). It has also a large following in the other three continents, without distinction of race and language. It is divided into three great sections: the Greek Church in the East; the Roman Church in the South of both hemispheres and all other parts of the world; and the Protestant Churches, chiefly among the Northern and Western nations.

The total number of Christians in the year 1891 probably exceeds 450 millions, and may be thus divided: Roman Catholics, about 220 millions; Protestants, 140 millions; Orientals or Greeks (including the Eastern Schismatics), 90 millions.

The comparative statistics of this century are in favor of Protestantism. According to the statement of Dr. Zöckler, the Protestants have, from 1786 to 1886, increased 230 per cent., the Greek Church 207 per cent., the Roman Catholic Church 192 per cent. It should be remembered, however, that Protestantism is divided into a large number of denominations and sects; while the Roman Catholic Church is one compact and centralized organization. The progress of the Greek Church is due chiefly to the growth and conquests of the Russian Empire; the progress of Protestantism, to the superior intelligence, energy, enterprise, and westward spread of the Protestant nations, especially the English and American.

The Jews are scattered among all Christian and Mohammedan nations, and prosper most in Germany, England and the United States.

Mohammedanism, or Islam, controls the Turkish Empire, and is widely spread in Persia, India, Egypt, and among the negroes in the interior of Africa, but has no hold on Europe (except in Constantinople), and no followers in America and Australia.

Brahmanism is the dominant religion of India, but is honeycombed by Christian ideas and influences. Buddhism extends over Thibet, the Burmese Empire, China, Japan, Siam, Ceylon, etc. Confucianism is the state religion of China. None of these three Asiatic religions has any foothold in Africa, Europe, or America. Christianity is the only religion which by its omnipresence on earth betrays its universal adaptation to men.

STATISTICAL TABLES.

The following statistical tables represent the latest estimates, varying from 1880 to 1890.*

THE WORLD'S POPULATION IN 1890.

From Petermann's *Mittheilungen, Ergänzungsheft No.* 101. *Die Bevölkerung der Erde,* ed. by Wagner & Supan. Gotha, 1891.

Europe	357,379,000
Asia	825,954,000
Africa	163,953,000
Australia	3,230,000
America	121,713,000
Oceanic Islands	7,420,000
Polar Regions	80,400
Total	1,479,729,400

GENERAL RELIGIOUS STATISTICS, 1885.

Christians, total number, about	†430,284,500
Jews	7,000,000
Mohammedans	230,000,000
Heathen	794,000,000
Total	1,461,284,500

STATISTICS OF THE CHRISTIAN RELIGION ACCORDING TO ITS THREE CHIEF DIVISIONS, 1885.

	R. Catholics.	Protestants.	Orientals.	Christians in all.
Europe	154,479,500	78,875,000	71,405,000	304,759,500
America	49,780,000	45,200,000	10,000	94,097,000
Asia	8,829,000	2,866,000	9,402,000	21,097,000
Africa	2,148,000	1,092,000	3,200,000	6,440,000
Australia	702,000	2,296,000	....	2,998,000
Total	215,938,500	130,329,000	84,017,000	429,391,500

---

* I have used the last issues of the best statistical authorities, viz., *The Statesman's Year Book* for 1893, edited by J. Scott Keltie (London, Macmillan & Co.); *Whitaker's Almanack* for 1893 (London); *Boehm und Wagner's Die Bevölkerung der Erde* (Gotha); Wagner's *Geographisches Jahrbuch* (Gotha, 1888 and 1889); *Statistisches Jahrbuch des Deutscher Reichs* (Berlin, 1887); Zöckler's statistical tables in his *Handbuch der Theol. Wissenschaften*, 3d ed., 1889, Bd. II. 820 sqq. The statistics of the United States are drawn from the official *Census Bulletin* of Washington (1890 and 1891) as published at Washington, 1893, and from a summary of the *New-York Independent*.

† This was a low estimate; the latest estimates count about 450,000,000 Christians.

STATISTICS OF DIFFERENT COUNTRIES.

RUSSIA, 1888.

Orthodox Greek Catholics, without army and navy	69,808,497
United Church and Armenians	55,000
Roman Catholics	8,300,000
Protestants	2,950,000
Jews	3,000,000
Mohammedans	2,600,000
Pagans	26,000

FRANCE, CENSUS OF 1881.

Roman Catholics .... 29,201,703 — $78\frac{5}{10}$ of total population.
Protestants .... 692,800 — $1\frac{8}{10}$ "
 (as compared with 584,757 in 1872)
Jews 53,436
Non-declarants of religious belief. 7,684,906
Various creeds 33,042

SWITZERLAND, 1888.

Protestants	1,724,257
Roman Catholics	1,190,008
Jews	8,386

GERMAN EMPIRE, 1880 AND 1885.

	1880.	Per cent. of Pop.	1885.	Per cent. of Pop.
Protestants	28,331,152	$62\frac{6}{10}$	29,369,847	$62\frac{7}{10}$
Roman Catholics	16,232,651	$35\frac{9}{10}$	16,785,734	$35\frac{8}{10}$
Other Christians	78,031	$\frac{2}{10}$	125,673	$\frac{2}{100}$
Jews	561,612	$1\frac{2}{10}$	563,172	$1\frac{2}{10}$
Others and unclassified	30,615	$\frac{1}{100}$	11,278	$\frac{2}{100}$

Total population in 1885, 46,855,704; in 1890, 49,424,135.

Adherents of the Greek Church are included in "Roman Catholics"; but the Old Catholics are reckoned among "Other Christians." Certain changes were introduced in 1885 in the grouping of "Other Christians" and "Others," which explain the differences between the returns for these groups for 1880 and 1885.

ENGLAND AND WALES, 1887.*

Established Church (Episcopal)	13,500,000
Dissenters of all descriptions	12,500,000
Roman Catholics (in 1887)	1,354,000
Jews (estimated in 1883)	70,000

* *Whitaker's Almanack* for 1892, p. 249, makes the extraordinary statement that the number of religious denominations in England is 254. The *Statesman's Manual*, p. 50, speaks of 180. This is about as misleading as Voltaire's frivolous remark that England had fifty religions and only one kind of soup. In the table of Religious Statistics in *Whitaker's Almanack*, p. 387, we find the following societies counted as separate "denominations": Christian Soldiers, Blue Ribbon Gospel Army, British Israelites, Church of Islam, Crusade Mission Army, Hosanna Army, Nazarenes, Open Brethren, Polish Jews, Psalms of David Society, Woman's Mission, Worshippers of God, etc., etc.

STATISTICAL TABLES. 25

SCOTLAND, 1889.

Presbyterians: 1. Established Church (1889) ... 587,954
              2. Free Church (1890).......... 1,165,000
              3. United Presbyterian Church . 184,354
Roman Catholic Church 326,000
Episcopal Church .... 80,000.

IRELAND, 1881.

Roman Catholics........	3,960,891	Independents	6,210
Episcopalians...........	620,000	Baptists	4,879
Presbyterians...........	470,734	Quakers	3,645
Methodists.............	48,839	Jews	472

ESTIMATED NUMBERS OF RELIGIOUS DENOMINATIONS AMONGST ENGLISH-SPEAKING COMMUNITIES THROUGHOUT THE WORLD, 1890.

[From *Whitaker's Almanack* for 1892, p. 387.]

Episcopalians................................ 23,000,000
Methodists of all denominations.............. 16,960,000
Roman Catholics............................. 15,200,000
Presbyterians of all descriptions 11,100,000
Baptists of all descriptions 8,600,000
Congregationalists 5,500,000
Free Thought, various 3,500,000
Unitarians, under several names.............. 1,250,000
Minor religious sects 4,000,000
German, or Dutch, Lutheran, etc. 1,750,000
Of no particular religion .... 13,500,000 .

English-speaking population 104,360,000

RELIGIOUS STATISTICS OF THE UNITED STATES.

[From an elaborate article in *The Independent*, New-York, July 31, 1890.]

GENERAL SUMMARY BY FAMILIES.

	1889			1890		
	Chs.	Min.	Com.	Chs.	Min.	Com.
Adventists..........	1,575	840	100,712	1,773.	765	58,742
Baptists	46,624	32,017	4,078,589	48,371	32,343	4,292,291
Christian Union.....	1,500	500	120,000	1,500	500	120,000
Congregationalists ..	4,569	4,408	475,608	4,689	4,640	491,985
Friends.............	763	1,017	106,930	763	1,017	106,930
German Evangel. Ch.	675	560	125,000	850	665	160,000
Lutherans	6,971	4,151	988,008	7,911	4,612	1,086,048
Mennonites	420	605	100,000	563	665	102,671
Methodists..........	50,680	29,770	4,723,881	54,711	31,765	4,980,240
Moravians	98	111	11,219	101	114	11,358
New Jerusalem	100	113	6,000	100	113	6,000
Presbyterians	13,349	9,786	1,180,113	13,619	9,974	1,229,012
Episcopalians	5,159	4,012	459,642	5,227	4,100	480,176
Reformed...	2,058	1,378	277,542	2,081	1,379	282,856
Roman Catholics....	7,424	7,996	*7,855,294	7,523	8,332	*8,277,039
Salvation Army.....	...	...	...	360	1,024	8,771
Unitarians..........	381	491	20,000	407	510	20,000
Universalists	721	691	38,780	732	685	42,952.
Grand Total	142,767	98,436	20,667,318	151,261	103,303	21,757,171

* Catholic population (nominal). This applies also to Lutherans.

THEOLOGICAL PROPÆDEUTIC.

STANDING ACCORDING TO NUMBERS.

BY FAMILIES.

		Chs.		Min.		Com.
1	Methodists	54,711	..	31,765	..	4,980,240
2	Roman Catholics*	7,523	..	8,332	..	4,676,292
3	Baptists	48,371	..	32,343	..	4,292,291
4	Presbyterians	13,619	..	9,974	..	1,229,012
5	Lutherans	7,911	..	4,612	..	1,086,048
6	Congregationalists	4,689	..	4,640	..	491,985
7	Episcopalians	5,227	..	4,100	..	480,176

BY DENOMINATIONS.

		Chs.		Min.		Com.
1	Roman Catholics	7,523	..	8,332	..	4,676,292
2	Regular Baptists†	33,588	..	21,175	..	3,070,047
3	Methodist Episcopal	22,103	..	13,279	..	2,236,463
4	Methodist Episcopal South	11,767	..	4,862	..	1,161,666
5	Presbyterian (Northern)	6,727	..	5,936	..	753,749
6	Disciples of Christ	7,250	..	3,600	..	750,000
7	Congregationalists	4,689	..	4,640	..	491,985
8	Protestant Episcopal	5,118	..	3,980	..	470,076
9	African M. E. Zion	3,500	..	3,000	..	412,513
10	African M. E.	3,800	..	3,000	..	400,000
11	Lutheran Synodical Conference	1,811	..	1,291	..	365,620
12	" General Council	1,557	..	899	..	264,235
13	United Brethren	4,265	..	1,455	..	199,709
14	Reformed (German)	1,535	..	813	..	194,044
15	Colored Methodist Episcopal	2,100	..	1,800	..	170,000
16	Presbyterian (Southern)	2,321	..	1,145	..	161,742
17	" Cumberland	2,689	..	1,595	..	160,185
18	German Evangelical	850	..	665	..	160,000
19	Lutheran General Synod	1,423	..	951	..	151,365
20	Methodist Protestant	2,003	..	1,441	..	147,604
21	Evangelical Association	1,958	..	1,187	..	145,703

ACCORDING TO POLITY.

We do not claim that the following classification is perfect. It is difficult to know where to place the Lutherans. They claim to be Congregational in polity; but they give to Synod a function which pure Congregationalism does not permit. Therefore we classify them as Presbyterian.

Episcopal.	Chs.		Min.		Com.
Methodists	50,924	..	29,318	..	4,780,406
Roman Catholics	7,523	..	8,332	..	4,676,292
Episcopalians	5,227	..	4,100	..	480,176
Moravians	101	..	114	..	11,358
Total Episcopal	63,775	..	41,864	..	9,948,232
In 1889	61,507	..	39,958	..	9,433,196

* "We estimate the number of Catholic communicants on the basis of 8,277,039 Catholic population, using the ratio which Lutheran statistics has established between souls and communicants in the Synodical Conference, viz., 1.77."—Ed. of *The Independent*.

† Really three denominations.

STATISTICAL TABLES.

Congregational.	Chs.	Min.	Com.
Baptists	48,371	32,343	4,292,291
Christian Union	1,500	500	120,000
Congregationalists	4,689	4,640	491,985
Friends	763	1,017	106,930
Adventists	830	546	31,000
Methodists	85	130	9,000
Miscellaneous	1,239	1,308	68,952
Total Congregational	57,477	40,484	5,120,158
In 1889	56,478	39,719	4,928,619

Presbyterian.	Chs.	Min.	Com.
Presbyterians	13,619	9,974	1,229,012
Lutherans	7,911	4,612	1,086,048
Reformed	2,081	1,379	282,856
Methodists	3,702	2,317	191,104
German Evangelical	850	665	160,000
Mennonites	563	665	102,671
Church of God	525	491	33,000
Adventists	943	218	27,742
Total Presbyterian	30,194	20,321	3,112,433
In 1889	25,722	19,065	2,888,228

AS TO MEMBERS.

Episcopal polity	9,948,232
Congregational polity	5,120,158
Presbyterian polity	3,112,533

AS TO MINISTERS.

Episcopal polity	41,864
Congregational polity	39,484
Presbyterian polity	20,321

AS TO CHURCHES.

Episcopal polity	63,875
Congregational polity	57,477
Presbyterian polity	30,094

CATHOLIC STATISTICS OF THE UNITED STATES.

[From the third *Census Bulletin*, No. 101, issued at Washington, D. C., July 23, 1891.]

This represents all the bodies calling themselves "Catholic." The Roman Catholic Church has congregations in every State and Territory of the Union, including Alaska and the District of Columbia. It is divided into 13 provinces, which embrace 13 archdioceses, 66 dioceses, 5 vicariates apostolic, and 1 prefecture apostolic. The other "Catholic" bodies are confined to one or more States. The statistics were gathered under the care of Henry K. Carroll, LL.D. (one of the editors of *The Independent*).

Churches.	Number of organizations.	Church edifices.	Seating capacity.	Value of church property.	Communicants or members.
Roman Catholic	10,221	8,765⅝	3,366,633	$118,381,516	*6,250,045
Greek Catholic (Uniates)	14	13	5,228	63,300	10,850
Russian Orthodox	12	23	3,150	220,000	13,504
Greek Orthodox	1	1	75	5,000	100
Armenian	6	....	....	....	335
Old Catholic	4	3	700	13,320	665
Reformed Catholic	8	....	....	....	1,000

* This figure differs from the one given in *The Independent* in the preceding table, which gives the total number of Roman Catholics 8,277,039, and the number of communicants 4,676,292.

ADDITIONAL RELIGIOUS STATISTICS OF THE UNITED STATES IN 1892.

The Religious Statistics of the Eleventh Census are in course of preparation under the care of Henry K. Carroll, LL. D., and will show the number of congregations, ministers, church edifices, and communicants of each denomination, with the seating capacity and value of all houses of worship.

The number of denominations is stated to be over 140, besides many independent congregations.

We give the official figures for some of the minor denominations not mentioned in the preceding pages:

Denominations.	Number of organizations.	Church edifices.	Seating capacity.	Value of church property.	Communicants or members.
United Presbyterian Church	866	$831\frac{1}{2}$	264,298	$5,408,084	94,402
Church of the New Jerusalem	154	$87\frac{3}{4}$	20,810	1,386,455	7,095
Catholic Apostolic Church	10	3	750	66,050	1,394
Salvation Army	329	27	12,055	37,350	8,662
Advent Christian Church	580	$294\frac{1}{12}$	80,286	465,605	25,816
Evangelical Adventists	30	$22\frac{7}{8}$	5,855	61,400	1,147
Life and Advent Union	28	$7\frac{11}{12}$	2,250	16,790	1,018
Seventh-day Baptists	106	$78\frac{1}{2}$	21,467	264,010	9,123
Seventh-day Baptists (German)	6	$3\frac{3}{8}$	1,960	14,550	194
General Six Principle Baptists	18	$13\frac{1}{2}$	3,600	19,600	937
Christian Church, South	143	135	46,005	137,000	13,004
Schwenkfeldians	4	6	1,925	12,200	306
Theosophical Society	40	1	200	600	695
Brethren in Christ	63	34	13,605	57,750	2,080
Cumberland Presbyterian Church	2,791	$2,008\frac{7}{30}$	662,807	3,515,511	164,940
Church of Jesus Christ of Latter-day Saints (Mormons)	425	$265\frac{3}{5}$	92,102	825,506	144,352
Reformed Episcopal Church	83	84	23,925	1,615,101	8,455
Moravian Church	94	114	31,615	681,250	11,781
German Evangelical Synod of North America	870	$785\frac{1}{12}$	245,781	4,614,490	187,432
German Evangelical Protestant Church of North America	52	52	35,175	1,187,450	36,156
Plymouth Brethren, I	109	....	......	....	2,279
" " II	87	1	......	1,265	2,364
" " III	....	1	......	200	1,081
" " IV	....	....	......	....	446
Seventh Day Adventist	995	$418\frac{1}{3}$	94,627	644,675	28,891
Church of God (Seventh Day)	29	1	200	1,400	647
Christian Connection	1,281	$962\frac{5}{6}$	301,692	1,637,202	90,718
Cumberland Presbyterian Church, (Colored)	238	$192\frac{5}{6}$	53,914	202,961	13,439
Reorganized Church of Christ of Latter-day Saints	431	$122\frac{1}{2}$	30,790	226,285	21,773
Dunkards (Old Order)	720	$854\frac{29}{180}$	353,586	1,121,541	61,101
" (Conservative)	57	$31\frac{5}{6}$	6,250	24,970	2,088
" (Progressive)	128	$95\frac{17}{20}$	32,740	145,770	8,089
Jewish, Orthodox	316	122	46,837	2,802,050	57,597
Jewish Reformed	217	179	92,397	6,952,225	72,899
Welsh Calvinistic Methodist	187	$189\frac{1}{2}$	44,445	625,875	12,722
Spiritualists	334	30	20,450	573,650	45,030
Free Methodist	....	1102	......	805,085	22,113
Social Brethren	20	$11\frac{1}{12}$	8,700	8,700	913
Christian Scientists	7	7	......	40,666	7,889
Christian Reformed	99	106	33,755	428,500	12,470
Shakers	15	16	5,650	36,800	1,728
United Zion's Children	25	25	3,100	8,300	525
Independent Churches of Christ in Christian Union	294	$183\frac{1}{2}$	68,000	234,450	18,214
Friends (Hicksite)	201	213	72,568	1,661,850	21,992
" (Wilburite)	52	52	13,169	67,000	4,329
" (Primitive)	9	5	1,050	16,700	232

CHAPTER XVII.

CLASSIFICATION OF RELIGIONS.

The most popular classification of the religious world is: Christianity, Judaism, Mohammedanism, and Heathenism.*

But Heathenism implies an indefinite number of distinct religions which demand more specific classifications. These vary according to the principle of distinction and the standpoint from which the religions are viewed.

The religions may be classified according to their origin, or the controlling idea of God, or their relation to culture and literature, or their moral character and aim, or the predominant psychological faculty, or the prevailing race and nationality, or the extent of influence and destination.

In every one of these aspects, Christianity stands first, without a rival, and derives from comparison and contrast a new evidence for its divine origin and character. The sacred books of the non-Christian religions—the King of Confucius, the Vedas of the Brahmans, the Tripitaka of the Buddhists, the Koran of the Mohammedans, and the Talmud of the Jews—contain many germs of truth and lessons of wisdom, but bear no comparison with the Bible, which outshines them all as the sun outshines the moon. It is the only book of religion adapted to all races, nationalities, classes, and conditions of men, and is constantly making conquests in all countries and languages of the globe.

CHAPTER XVIII.

NATURAL AND REVEALED RELIGIONS.

In regard to origin, the religions are divided into two classes: natural and revealed. This is the most important distinction, and determines all other differences.

1. Natural religions: all forms of heathenism and idolatry.

They grow wild in the soil of human nature and produce wild fruits. Man, though fallen, weak and corrupt, still remains a

---

* James Freeman Clarke counts *Ten Great Religions*. See his two popular works under this title. Boston, 1871 and 1883. Several editions.

religious being and gropes in the dark for the true religion, under the guidance of God, who "suffered all the Gentiles to walk in their own ways, and yet left not himself without witness" (Acts 14: 16, 17), who "made of one every nation of men . . . that they should seek God, if haply they might feel after him and find him." (Acts 18: 26, 27.) The heathen religions are the prodigal children who waste their inheritance, but remember their father's house and will penitently return to it in their own appointed time. They are essentially false, but with glimpses of truth. No error can live without some element of truth, of which it is the caricature and the perversion. Of all forms of paganism, Buddhism makes the nearest approach to the truth; and yet in its final issue (Nirvâna) it is farthest from the truth.

2. Revealed religions: Christianity and Judaism.

They proceed from God, and teach the truth and the way of salvation. They are recorded in the Holy Scriptures and exemplified in the history of Israel and the history of the Christian Church. They rest on the testimony of divinely called and inspired prophets and apostles and on the supreme authority of Jesus Christ.

Judaism, or the religion of the Old Covenant (from Abraham to John the Baptist), is the preparatory revelation, the truth in its genesis, Christianity in shadowy anticipation.* It becomes false by becoming anti-Messianic or anti-Christian. Christianity, or the religion of the New Covenant, is the full and final revelation of the will of God concerning our faith and duty and the way of life. Judaism is relatively true, Christianity is absolutely true. The Old Covenant has the truth in the form of promise and type; the New Covenant has the truth in the form of fulfilment and substance. "The New Testament is concealed in the Old; the Old Testament is revealed in the New" (St. Augustin.) "The law was given by Moses; grace and truth came by Jesus Christ." (John 1: 17.)

No higher religion than the Christian can be expected, but its apprehension and application are gradual and progressive, like the revelation itself; for God deals with men as a wise educator who adapts himself to the differences of age, capacity and condition.

Mohammedanism is a mixture of heathen, Jewish and Chris-

* *Das werdende Christentum,* or *das Christentum im Werden.*

tian doctrines and practices. It has greater force and tenacity than Paganism because it involves more truth, especially the sublime truth of one omnipotent, omnipresent and all-merciful God, the Maker and Ruler of all things.

CHAPTER XIX.

DUALISM, POLYTHEISM, PANTHEISM, MONOTHEISM.

The idea of the Godhead, or a supreme, superhuman and supernatural power upon which all creatures depend, underlies and controls all religions. It is in one form or other as universal as the human race. Hegel says: "The idea of God constitutes the general basis of a people." It shapes its fundamental laws and institutions, and is the bond of society.

Making this idea the principle of distinction, we have dualistic, polytheistic, pantheistic and monotheistic religions.

1. Dualism: Zoroastrianism, Manichæism (old and new) and nearly all the schools of Gnosticism. Two coëternal principles, God and Matter, or Good and Evil in antagonism. Evil is eternalized (*ab ante*), and redemption is made impossible Annihilation of matter is substituted for redemption.

2. Polytheism: a plurality of gods (hence idols), without fixed limits. The Athenians were not sure whether they had exhausted the number, and built an altar to "an unknown god." Here belong the various forms of idolatry. The most cultivated are the mythologies of Greece and Rome. The gods are fictitious men and women exaggerated and intensified both in their virtues and vices. The plurality of gods destroys the absoluteness, therefore, the very essence, of God.

3. Pantheism or Atheism: Brahmanism and Buddhism. Brahmanism connects an ideal pantheism with gross idolatry. Buddhism begins apparently in Atheism and ends in nihilism. Its *summum bonum* is Nirvâna, that is absorption, annihilation, the absolute nothing. Yet Nirvâna means also the highest stage of spiritual liberty and bliss. Atheism may be only a negative expression for pantheism or a denial of the personality of the Godhead, and not of the Godhead itself. Strictly speaking, Atheism, as a negation of the supernatural, is incompatible with the idea of religion, for it denies the existence of one of its two factors. Burnouf's conclusion as to the meaning

of Nirvâna is: "For Buddhist theists, it is the absorption of the individual life in God; for atheists, the absorption of this individual life in the nothing; but for both it is deliverance from all evil, it is supreme affranchisement." Buddhism is pessimistic, Christianity is optimistic; so far they are antipodes.

4. Monotheism: Judaism, Mohammedanism, Christianity.

But there is considerable difference in their conception of the Divine unity. The monotheism of the Old Testament admits distinctions in the Divine being and moves towards the triunity of the New Testament; the post-biblical or Talmudic, and especially the Mohammedan monotheism is abstract, monotonous, unitarian and antitrinitarian; while the Christian idea of the Divine unity implies fulness of life, an internal intercommunion of Father, Son and Spirit, and an external self-revelation of the Godhead under these three aspects in His works of creation, redemption and sanctification. Hence the doctrine of the Trinity is the most comprehensive of Christian dogmas, but most offensive to Jews and Moslems, who regard it as a species of idolatry.

CHAPTER XX.

CIVILIZED, SEMI-CIVILIZED, AND BARBARIAN RELIGIONS.

Looking at the grade of culture, or want of culture, we may divide the religions into civilized, semi-civilized and barbarian.

1. Religions of civilized and semi-civilized nations still living: Christianity, Judaism, Mohammedanism, Confucianism, Brahmanism, Buddhism. These religions have a more or less elaborate ritual, and are recorded in sacred books. They have also a vast body of literature in poetry and prose. The Christian literature is by far the most extensive and important.

2. Religions of civilized and semi-civilized nations which have passed away and live only in history: Zoroastrism, the Egyptian, Babylonian, Phœnician, ancient Greek, Roman, and Teutonic (Scandinavian) religions. The most important of these are the religions of ancient Greece and Rome on account of their classical literature and close contact with early Christianity and higher education.

3. Religions of savage and barbarian tribes are found among the aborigines in Africa, America and Australasia. The lowest form is Fetichism.

CHAPTER XXI.

SENSUAL, ASCETIC, AND ETHICAL RELIGIONS.

In regard to moral character, we may distinguish three classes.*

1. Sensual and immoral religions are controlled by passion for self-indulgence and the gratification of the natural instincts and appetites. Some forms of heathenism ascribe all human vices to the gods, and sanction even lewdness as a part of worship. Mohammedanism also has a sensual element; for, while it commands total abstinence from intoxicating drinks and is so far ethical, it legalizes polygamy on earth and carries it into paradise.

2. Ascetic religions are characterized by penal self-mortifications based upon a dualistic view of the antagonism between matter and spirit, and aim at a destruction of nature rather than its transformation. The Buddhist and Parsee religions belong to this class and several schools of Gnosticism and Manichæism, which influenced the mediæval sects of the Paulicians, Bogomiles and Albigenses.

3. Ethical religions start from the idea of the holiness and love of God and aim at the salvation of the whole man, body, soul and spirit. Regeneration and sanctification are the leading ideas. Here again Christianity and Judaism stand first. The moral code of the gospel is the purest that can be conceived, and is practically embodied in the perfect life of Christ. Confucianism is also an ethical religion, but of a lower order, with its face turned to earth rather than to heaven, and enjoining simply a secular morality, without poetry and spirituality.

CHAPTER XXII.

DIVISION ACCORDING TO PSYCHOLOGICAL FACULTIES.

If we look to the mental faculty which dominates religion, we get a psychological division, which was developed by Hegel

---

* This division is an improvement on Schleiermacher's distinction between æsthetic and teleological religions. *Der Christliche Glaube,* § 9 (voL i, 53 sq.).

and his followers. They distinguish, in a rising scale, religions of feeling or desire; religions of imagination (the Indian and the Greek); a religion of the understanding (the Roman); and the religion of reason (the Christian). But Christianity acts upon all the intellectual, moral and emotional faculties of man.

CHAPTER XXIII.

TURANIAN, SEMITIC, AND ARYAN RELIGIONS.

Max Müller, one of the foremost writers on this subject, applies his principles of comparative philology to the science of comparative religion, and suggests a classification corresponding to the three great divisions of languages—the Turanian, Aryan, and Semitic. He assumes a primitive religion in each before their separation into various ramifications.

1. The Turanian branch: the old religion of China and of the cognate Turanian tribes, such as the Mandthus, the Mongolians, the Tartars, the Finns or Lapps. But of their religion we know very little, and that is not enough to justify us in speaking of a Turanian religion.

2. The Semitic (or Shemitic) family:

(a) The polytheistic religions of the Babylonians, Phœnicians, Carthaginians, Moabites, Philistines, and Arabs before Mohammed.

(b) The monotheistic creeds of Judaism, Mohammedanism, and Christianity.

3. The Aryan family embraces the Hindoo, Persian, Græco-Roman, and the old Teutonic religions. But these are too different to be classed under one head.

The Semitic family has produced the highest forms of religion—the monotheistic, because it was chosen to be the bearer of the worship of the only true and living God. "Japheth dwells in the tents of Shem." (Gen. 9: 27.) This old prophecy of Noah is literally fulfilled in Europe and America. The West lives on the religious ideas of the East.

But Christianity, while it is Semitic in origin, lives in all languages and in all nationalities, and has found a more congenial home among the Latin, Celtic and Germanic races than in the land of its birth.

CHAPTER XXIV.

DIVISION ACCORDING TO THE RULING IDEAS AND AIMS.

Confucianism is built upon reverence for parents and superiors, and is the most conservative religion in its influence upon society and the state. Buddhism represents the idea of self-mortification and final extinction of passion and desire (Nirvâna).

Ancient Zoroastrism and Manichæism are ruled by a deep sense of an irreconcilable antagonism between light and darkness, good and evil. Ancient Egypt had a religion of mystery, with a strong belief in immortality and resurrection. The religion of Greece is a religion of beauty and art. The Roman religion was one of policy and conquest. Judaism aims at holiness or conformity to God's law.

Christianity is essentially gospel, or the religion of salvation. But it embraces at the same time the virtues of all other religions, without their vices and errors, and supplements their defects. It has a higher morality than Confucianism and Judaism, and is progressive as well as conservative; it inspires more heroic self-denial than Buddhism, and secures eternal happiness instead of extinction; it feels and solves, by redemption, the antagonism of good and evil, which Zoroastrism could not solve; it gives, on the ground of Christ's resurrection, a certain hope of immortality and bliss, which Egypt could not give; it produces the highest and purest works of art, excelling the masterpieces of Greece and Rome; it aims at the redemption, sanctification and perfection of the whole human race.

CHAPTER XXV.

TRIBAL, NATIONAL, AND UNIVERSAL RELIGIONS.

As regards extent and destination, we may distinguish three classes of religion.

1. Tribal religions. Here belong the lowest forms of worship by savage tribes who are not yet organized into national life, have no literature or architecture or music.

2. National or ethnic religions, which are confined to one nation or cognate nations: Confucianism in China, Brahman-

ism in India, Zoroastrism in Persia, the Assyrian and Babylonian, the Egyptian, Greek, Roman, Celtic, Teutonic and Slavonic religions. Judaism is likewise limited to one nation, but cherished the Messianic hope of converting all the Gentiles.

3. Missionary religions which aimed at universal dominion, but failed: Buddhism and Mohammedanism. The former spread over Thibet, Ceylon, China, Japan and other countries; the latter converted Arabs, Turks, Persians, Egyptians, Hindus, and Negroes, and was for several centuries a dangerous rival of Christianity, aiming at universal dominion. But both have been arrested in their progress and have no hold on the Western nations in Europe, America and Australasia, and consequently no prospects for the future.

4. The universal religion: Christianity. It is as wide as humanity. It started with the claim of universality, and is realizing it more and more by its missionary operations in all countries and among all the races and nations of the earth.

CHAPTER XXVI.

DESIGNATIONS OF ETHNIC RELIGIONS.

The ethnic religions are designated by the terms idolatry, paganism, and heathenism.

"Idolatry" means image-worship, or worship of false gods.* The most common designation in the Scriptures and patristic writings. An "idolater" is a worshiper of false gods (1 Cor. 5:10; Rev. 22:8).

The term "Paganism," or Peasant Religion,† dates from the end of the fourth century, when Christianity was already triumphantly established in the cities of the Roman empire, and idolatry lingered only in remote country places.

"Heathenism" ‡ is of similar import: a "heathen" is one living on the heaths or moors, and not in a walled town, an ignorant backwoodsman. In the English Scriptures the "heathen," or "Gentiles," § mean all nations except the Jews,

* εἰδωλολατρεία from εἴδωλον, *idolum*, an image of the Divinity as an object of worship. Comp. εἶδος, that which is seen, form, figure. Gal. 5:20; 1 Cor. 10:14.

† From *pagus*, village; *paganus*, villager, peasant, rustic.

‡ From *heath*, as the German *Heidentum* from *Heide*.

§ τὰ ἔθνη, ἐθνικοί, *haggojim*, *gentes*, *gentiles*, in the O. T., and Matt. 4:15; 6:32; Rom. 3:29; 9:24; Gal. 2:8.

who were "the people" of God, the chosen people of the covenant.*

We now exempt from the heathen all who worship one God, or all Monotheists, i.e., Jews and Mohammedans, as well as Christians. The Mohammedans hate and abhor idolatry as much as the Jews.

CHAPTER XXVII.

THE ORIGIN OF IDOLATRY.

The different theories on the origin of the heathen theo-mythologies may be divided into two classes: those which maintain, and those which deny, the reality of the false gods.

I. The gods are real beings:

1. Demons, fallen angels under the lead of the Devil, the father of idolatry. So the Church fathers, on the ground of Gen. 6:2; Ps. 96:5, 1 Cor. 10:20.

2. Kings, heroes, sages, navigators, discoverers; in one word, great men, who were idealized and idolized after their death. So Euhemerus, an Epicurean philosopher of the Alexandrian age. Epicurus himself held that the gods were higher beings, but idle and unconcerned about the world, which he thought was governed by chance.

3. Scripture characters perverted: Saturn derived from Adam, Vulcan from Tubal-cain, Apollo from Jubal, Venus from Naamah (Gen. 4: 22), Hercules from Samson.—G. J. Voss, a Dutch divine (d. 1649).

4. A theogonic process which has its ultimate ground in ante-historic, transcendental relations, or real divine powers which successively took possession of the human consciousness. This view is pantheistic, and involves God himself in a gradual process of development.—Schelling, in his "Introduction to the Philosophy of Mythology," assumes an objective and subjective evolution of the idea of God from a primitive monotheism through polytheism to absolute monotheism.

II. The gods are unreal and imaginary:

1. The invention of priests and lawgivers for selfish ends. A very low view.

* ὁ λαός (for the Hebrew *am*), often with the addition τοῦ θεοῦ, the peculiar people of God whom he has chosen for himself, Matt. 2:6; Luke 1:68; Heb. 11:25, and very often in the Septuagint.

2. The innocent creations of poets, especially Homer and Hesiod. But the poets made only the theogony (as Herodotus says), not the gods themselves. They gave poetic shape and form to the popular belief which preceded them and which they shared.

3. Personifications of the powers of nature.—The view of Empedocles, Aristotle, and the Stoics.

4. Deifications of men; impersonations of human passions, virtues and vices reflected from the mind of man.

5. A poetic cosmogony, astronomy, chronology and philosophy of nature, invented by philospohers. Dionysos = wine; Phoibos = light, etc.—G. Hermann (1817).

6. The production of human hope and fear, especially of fear. —Hume.

7. The broken fragments of a primitive and underlying monotheism, which arose after the division of nations.—Creuzer regards polytheism as a disorganized and scattered monotheism.

8. A development of man's religious and moral consciousness in its departure from the worship of the true God, and a successive deterioration to the grossest creature-worship and corresponding unnatural immorality.

This is the true view, suggested by Paul (Rom. 1:19–32). He gives a fearful picture of the heathen world, which is abundantly confirmed by the testimony of contemporary writers, as Seneca, Tacitus, and Juvenal. But he assumes, at the same time, an original knowledge of God from the outward and inward manifestation of God, which leaves the heathen without excuse, if they do not live up to the light of nature. His view does not exclude, on the one hand, the agency of evil spirits, nor, on the other, the elements of truth and beauty which remained under the rubbish of perversion. For fallen human nature is a strange compound of good and evil; it is the battle-ground between God and his great adversary. Religion reflects this double nature of man in its most intense form.

CHAPTER XXVIII.

THE BIBLE VIEW OF THE HEATHEN WORLD.

In the Old Testament idolatry is represented as a worship of demons or evil spirits (Gen. 6:2; Ps. 96:5; comp. 1 Cor. 10:

20), and as the greatest sin, because it robs God of the honor and glory which is due to him alone, as the only true and living God. It was a political as well as a religious offence; it was a violation of the sacred covenant of Jehovah with his people, and therefore rebellion and high treason against his majesty. The first and second commandments are directed against idolatry in every form. The idolater was devoted to destruction and stoned to death (Ex. 22 : 20; Deut. 13 : 2-10; 17 : 2-5). The Canaanites were exterminated in punishment of their abominable idolatry (Ex. 34 : 15, 16 ; Deut. 12 : 29-31).

In the Christian Church, after the union of Church and State in the fourth century, heresy came to be regarded in the same light as idolatry among the Jews, both as a religious and civil crime, and was made punishable by death. Theodosius I. introduced the penal legislation against idolatry and heresy into the Roman code, from which it passed into all the countries of Catholic Europe. Under these laws Hus was burned at Constance in 1415, Servetus at Geneva in 1553, and Giordano Bruno at Rome in 1600.

But the denunciation of heathen idolatry is not a condemnation of all the heathen. The Old Testament recognizes worshipers of the true God outside of the Mosaic dispensation. Melchisedek and Job are the chief types of these holy outsiders. The book of Jonah is a rebuke to Jewish bigotry, and teaches the great lesson that the working of the Spirit of God was not confined to Israel. The Wise Men from the East, Matt. 2 : 1, represent the nobler heathen who, in the darkness of error, are longing for the light of truth.

Our Saviour rebuked the bigotry of the Jews in the parable of the good Samaritan, who, though a heretic and schismatic in their eyes, put to shame the priest and the Levite by the exercise of the chief of virtues (Luke 10 : 33). He told them that the only grateful leper of the ten whom he healed was a Samaritan (Luke 17 : 16). He expressed astonishment at the faith of the heathen centurion at Capernaum and said: "Verily I say unto you, I have not found so great faith, no, not in Israel" (Matt. 8 : 10). The Syro-Phœnician woman whose daughter he healed, is another instance of that "great faith," which smouldered beneath the ashes of a false worship (Matt. 15 : 28). Christ warned the unbelieving Jews that the men of Nineveh, of Tyre and of Sidon shall rise up in the day of judgment against them (Matt. 11 : 21-24; 12 : 41, 42). He pointed to his "other sheep" outside of the Jewish fold, who shall hear his voice (John 10 : 16).

John teaches, in the prologue to the fourth Gospel, that the Divine Logos before his incarnation shone "in the darkness," and that he "lighteth every man that cometh into the world" (John 1 : 5, 9, 10).

According to the teaching of Paul, God has never left himself "without witness" (Acts 14 : 16, 17). He revealed himself even to the heathen; externally, in the works of nature, where the reflecting mind may discern "his eternal power and divinity, so that they are without excuse" (Rom. 1 : 19–21); and internally, in their reason and conscience, so that the Gentiles, having not the written law of Moses, "are a law unto themselves; in that they show the work of the law written in their hearts, their conscience bearing witness therewith, and their thoughts one with another accusing or else excusing them" (Rom. 2 : 14, 15). Hence the same apostle, when proclaiming to the Athenians the "unknown God," to whom they had built an altar in testimony of their unsatisfied religious wants, hesitates not to quote, with approbation, a passage from the heathen poet (Aratus), on the indwelling of God in man, and to adduce it as proof of the possibility of seeking and finding God (Acts 17 : 27, 28).

Peter discovered in Cornelius the marks of prevenient grace, and acknowledged that there are in every nation such as "fear God and work righteousness" and are "acceptable to him" (Acts 10 : 35). He does not mean by this that man can at all fulfill the divine law and be saved without Christ (which would contradict his own teaching, Acts 4 : 12); but he does mean that there are everywhere Gentiles with honest and earnest longings after salvation, who, like Cornelius, will readily receive the gospel, as soon as it is brought within their reach, and will find in it satisfaction and peace.

It was just among such God-fearing heathen, like Cornelius and Lydia, that Christianity made most progress in the Apostolic age.

CHAPTER XXIX.

FETICHISM.

Fetichism* is the lowest form of idolatrous superstition. It is found among the savage tribes in all countries, especially among the Negroes, Zulus and Hottentots in Africa. It consists in the worship of any material, dead or animate, object of nature (as a stone, a tree, a stream, or a serpent), supposed to be bewitched and inhabited by good or evil spirits. It is connected with cruel practices, such as burning widows, the slaughter of servants in honor of their chief, to keep him company in the other world. It has little force of resistance, and is easily swept away by the approach of Mohammedanism or Christianity.

Remnants of Fetichism survive even in Christian lands (especially among the Negroes in the Southern States), in the popular superstitions of witchcraft, sorcery, enchantments, fortune-telling, necromancy, the wearing of amulets and charms as a protection against harm, and the worship of dead relics and belief in their wonder-working power.

CHAPTER XXX.

CONFUCIANISM.

Confucianism is the state religion of the immense empire of China. It has its name from Kong-fu-tse, "the prince of wisdom," who lived five hundred years before the Christian era, a king without a kingdom, who yet rules in the hearts of millions of men. He was, however, not "a maker," but "a transmitter" of an older religion. Some parts of the sacred books which he collected and improved are dated back eighteen hundred years before his time.

These sacred books, called the "King," contain the ancient history of China from B.C. 2357–627, poems, rites and ceremonies, laws and maxims of conduct, and the table-talk of Confucius and his disciples. They are the text-books in all institutions of learning, and the substratum of the vast Chinese litera-

---

* *Fetich*, or *fetish*, is derived from the Portuguese *feitiço*, sorcery, charm; as this is derived from the Latin *facticius*, artificial, factitious.

ture. A knowledge of them is necessary for any promotion in the competitive examinations. China is governed by an aristocracy of scholars.

The Confucian system is based upon filial piety or reverence for parents and superiors. It is a worship of ancestors. It holds the living in bondage to the dead. Every house has its ancestral tablets, before which the members of the family bow down with tapers and burning incense, the head acting as priest. There are more dead gods in China than living men. The Chinese worship also heaven and earth, as the father and mother of all things. This is an approach to the worship of a supreme deity, but the deity (Tî and Shang Tî) is confounded with the material heaven (Thien). Christian missionaries find it difficult to translate the words "God" and "sin" into the Chinese language, because the ideas are wanting.

Confucianism illustrates the beauty and power of the fifth commandment, but also the weakness of a morality that is not based on religion or the love of God. It teaches the golden rule, but only in its negative form, and furnishes no unselfish motive for its exercise. It produces a colorless, prosy, monosyllabic, utilitarian, and materialistic morality. It is intensely conservative and stationary. It excludes progress as a kind of treason.

For more than two thousand years China kept aloof from the rest of the world, and looked down upon all foreigners as outside barbarians; but is now open to Christian missions and Western civilization. It is humiliating that Christian England, in breaking down the walls of China, forced the curse of the opium traffic upon a heathen land; but the Christian religion is innocent of national and political crimes, and God overrules even the wrath of men for the progress of his kingdom. The bad treatment of the Chinese on the Pacific coast, and the causeless war of France against China in 1885, have stirred up resentment and retarded the progress of the gospel. On the other hand, many Chinamen are educated and converted in Europe and America for future work in their native land. Christianity will assume a peculiar type in that intellectual, frugal, industrious, and utilitarian race. It will be intellectual and ethical rather than emotional and spiritual. The respect for parents is a good foundation, although in other respects also a hindrance.

Besides Confucianism, there are two other heathen religions

in China, Buddhism and Taoism. The latter was founded by Laotse, a contemporary of Confucius, and has a pantheistic character, teaching that the Tao (way) is one and all from which all things have proceeded and to which they will return. Taoism combines the worship of ancestors with the worship of a multitude of idols.

CHAPTER XXXI.

BRAHMANISM.

Brahmanism (Brahminism) or Hinduism is the ruling religion of East India. It has its name from "Brahm" or "Brahma" (neuter), which means worship, prayer, hymn, and also the impersonal deity, the ineffable, absolute essence.* It arose a thousand or fifteen hundred years before Christ. Its sacred books are chiefly the Vedas, which issued like a breath from the deity, the Laws of Manu, and the two great epics, Mahabharata and Ramayana (the former numbering about two hundred and twenty thousand lines, the latter about fifty thousand). These books contain hymns, prayers, incantations, the laws, customs, and morals of the Hindus. Veda means knowledge.† There are four Vedas, the Rigveda (which contains the oldest Aryan hymns, addressed to Brahm and the lesser gods), the Samaveda (the book of penitential chants), the Yarulveda (the book of sacrificial rites), and the Atharvaveda (the book of spells and incantations). To the Vedas are attached the Aranyakas, and especially the Upanishads,—prose-writings which contain comments on the Vedic hymns, ritualistic precepts, and mystical speculations on the problems of the universe. The Vedic books are the foundation of the literature of India. They are a strange compound of beautiful poetry, wise maxims and precepts with gorgeous fancies, absurdities, and impossibilities. They are written in Sanskrit.

Brahmanism is both pantheistic and polytheistic. Brahm is the absolute essence, the universal, self-existent soul, and unfolds

---

* "Brahma" in the masculine gender means a worshiper, a priest, or composer of hymns; in the later Hindu literature also the personified Brahm, or the ineffable essence conceived as God. A "Brahman" or "Brahmin" is a member of the sacerdotal caste.

† From the same Sanskrit root are derived the Greek *oida*, the Latin *videre*, the German *wissen*, the English *wit*.

itself in infinite self-manifestations. It is the light in the sun, the brilliancy in the fire, the sound in the air, the fragrance in the flowers, the life and light in all life and light. Nothing really exists except Brahm. All things are Maya or illusion. Men are emanations of Brahm, sparks from the central fire, separated for a season, and absorbed at last. "Our life," says a Brahman proverb, "is as a drop that trembles on the lotus-leaf, fleeting and quickly gone."

But if God is all, then every thing is a part of God. Pantheism is thus consistent with Polytheism. The gods are portions of Brahm, like men, only higher in degree. There are said to be three hundred and thirty millions of gods in the Hindu pantheon, chiefly personifications of the forces of nature. The Hindus worship sacred cows, monkeys, serpents, stones, trees and rivers. The Ganges is the holiest of rivers, which washes away all sins and is lined with thousands of temples and priests to aid the ablutions of penitent bathers.

The Hindu Trimurtti, or the three-faced god, often represented in sculpture and painting, is a triple impersonation of the deity, and expresses the creation, preservation, and destruction of the universe. This triad consists of Brahma (a personification of Brahm), the Creator; Vishnu, the Preserver; and Siva, the Destroyer. Their functions are interchangeable, so that each may take the place of the other, and be "first, second, third among the blessed three."

The gods undergo for the benefit of mankind many avatars or incarnations. The chief are the ten avatars of Vishnu, who appeared successively as fish, tortoise, boar, and man, and will at last appear for the tenth time to destroy all vice and wickedness.

Brahmanism teaches the emanation of the world from Brahm, the transmigration of the soul, a priestly hierarchy, and a severe asceticism, as a means of self-redemption. The Brahmans are the hereditary priests and mediators between god and men, and are worshiped as demi-gods. Their occupation consists in studying and teaching the Vedas, offering five daily sacrifices, acting as physicians, giving alms, and sitting in judgment. Theoretically, the life of the Brahmans is divided into four stages, those of student, householder, anchorite, and ascetic. Final perfection is attained by abstraction of the mind from external objects, intense meditation, total extinction of sensual instincts, complete knowledge of the divine essence, and absorption into the universal soul.

Hinduism has its saints, the Yogi or Fakirs. They are vagabond hermits, and carry austerity and self-torture to the highest degrees of eccentricity: going about naked, or wearing filthy rags, with hair uncombed, nails uncut, the body and face besmeared with ashes, begging on the road-side, sleeping on cow-dung, delighting in filth and obscenity with great show of sanctity, hoping to be absorbed at last in Brahm.

Hindu society is based upon a rigorous system of hereditary caste, sanctioned by religion. There are four distinct castes: the Brahmans, the Warriors, the Merchants and Farmers, and the Sudras or Servants. The first class emanated from the mouth of Brahma, the second from his arms, the third from his side, the fourth from his feet. This system prevents the lower classes from rising, and is the greatest obstacle to the progress of Christianity.

Hinduism is honeycombed by Western ideas and doomed to collapse. A remarkable phenomenon produced by this contact is the society of Brahmo-Somaj, a theistic form of Brahmanism in its movement towards a Unitarian Christianity. Its chief advocate, Keshub Chunder Sen, a Brahman, weary of his ancestral faith, said that Jesus is the power which will conquer and hold the bright and precious diadem of India. Other Brahmans have embraced the evangelical type of Christianity, and their number is increasing.

CHAPTER XXXII.

BUDDHISM.

Buddhism arose in India, but was expelled from its native land and spread rapidly over a large part of Asia. It has more followers than any heathen religion, with the exception, perhaps, of Confucianism.* That a religion, apparently atheistic

---

* Max Müller, Rhys Davids, and Sir Edwin Arnold estimate the number of Buddhists as high as 450,000,000, or even 475,000,000, which would equal or exceed the number of Christians. But this is probably a great exaggeration, and seems to include many millions of Confucianists. Professor Monier Williams reduces the number of Buddhists to 100,000,000, and Dr. A. P. Harper (an American missionary in China, who wrote to me on the subject) to 90,000,000.

and nihilistic in its issue, should command such a long and widespread influence is a mystery, but it is confined to one continent. It may be called "the light of Asia," but it certainly is not and never can be "the Light of the world."

It is divided into two great schools: Southern Buddhism in Ceylon, Burmah, and Siam, and Northern Buddhism in Thibet, Mongolia, China, and Japan.

The sacred books of Buddhism are the legendary life of Buddha, and collections of didactic poems, rites and ceremonies, and maxims of wisdom. They form the basis of the two great schools just mentioned. The books of the Southern Buddhists are written in the Pali language, and are more reliable and complete. The Dhammapada, or "Path of Life," is believed to contain the utterances of Buddha himself (in four hundred and twenty-four verses). The books of the Northern Buddhists are written in Sanskrit, and abound in absurd and miraculous legends. The date of this literature is uncertain. For centuries the Buddhist religion was transmitted by oral tradition before it was reduced to writing.

The name of this religion is derived from "Buddha," that is, the Sage, the Enlightened (not a personal name, but an official title, like "Christ"). It was founded by Gautama, the Buddha, also called Sakya-Muni, that is, the Hermit or Sage of Sakya. He lived about five hundred years before Christ (between B.C. 556 and 477, or, according to another conjecture, between B.C. 622 and 543).

Gautama was a moral reformer and philanthropist. The story of his life bears a striking resemblance to that of Jesus, as recorded in the apocryphal Gospels, and is interwoven with the wildest legends and incredible marvels. He left a royal throne, and devoted himself in poverty and self-denial to the service of his fellow-men. He went about doing good, preaching a new doctrine, rebuking sin, reconciling strife, and exerting a humanizing influence upon his followers. According to the tradition of the Northern Buddhists, he descended of his own accord from heaven into his mother's womb, and was without an earthly father. Angels assisted at his birth, after which he immediately walked three steps and in a voice of thunder proclaimed his own greatness. When a babe of five months, he was left under a tree, where he worked himself into a trance; five wise men who were journeying through the air were miraculously stopped and came down to worship him. He is believed by his followers to have been sinless and perfect, and is worshiped as a god.*

Like Socrates and Christ, Gautama wrote nothing, but, unlike them, he lived in a mythological mist, which makes it impossible to ascertain the real facts. The oldest Buddhist writings were not composed till four hundred years after his death.

Buddhism sprang from Brahmanism. It is Brahmanism spiritualized, humanized, and popularized.

It was a revolt of philosophy against sacerdotalism, of democracy against the oppression of caste. It emphasizes intelligence and moral interests. It uses preaching as a means of conversion, and is tolerant. It is, in its spirit, similarly related to Brahmanism as Christianity is to Judaism, and as Protestantism is to Romanism, but, in its outward form and ceremonial, it resembles Romanism far more than Protestantism.

Buddhism retains the Hindu pantheon and cosmogony, with some modifications; it assumes an infinite number of worlds, an endless series of æons, with perpetually recurring periods of destruction and renovation; it teaches the wanderings of souls through six orders of beings, so that death is but a birth into a new mode of existence, organic or inorganic. Its objects of worship are the images and relics of Buddha and the other holy men of the legends.

Its chief aim is the removal of pain and the escape from the terrible curse of metempsychosis, which lies like an incubus on the Hindu and Buddhist mind. The present life is a probation. Those who do not attain the end of probation by a sort of moral suicide, must pass the fearful round of transmigration and may have to spend æons of pain in infernal regions. This accounts for the apparent folly of the Buddhist self-mortification unto final absorption. The alternative is: either Nirvâna, or endless migration and repetition of earthly misery.

The precise meaning of Nirvâna is a matter of dispute. It is usually understood to mean annihilation. But Max Müller

* Sir Edwin Arnold (in the Preface to his *The Light of Asia*) calls Gautama "the highest, gentlest, holiest, and most beneficent personality, with one exception, in the History of Thought," who "united the truest princely qualities with the intellect of a sage and the passionate devotion of a martyr. * * * Forests of flowers are daily laid upon his stainless shrines, and countless millions of lips daily repeat the formula, 'I take refuge in Buddha!'"

thinks that Nirvâna is something like the Elysian Fields or the Mohammedan Paradise.* He also denies the alleged atheism of Buddhism.

The principal Buddhist doctrines are these: 1. Suffering exists, and existence is suffering. 2. It is caused by passion or desire. 3. Desire may be ended by Nirvâna, which means annihilation, or rather absolute and unceasing apathy. 4. Nirvâna is attained by mortification of the passions and affections.

The five moral precepts of Buddha which apply to all men resemble the second table of Moses. They are all negative: Do not kill; Do not steal; Do not commit adultery; Do not lie; Do not become intoxicated. The last is substituted for the evil desire.

One of the most remarkable features in Buddhism is its resemblance to Romanism. It has its hermits, monks and abbots, vows of celibacy, voluntary poverty and obedience, nunneries for women, worship of saints and relics, bells, tonsure, rosary, censer, incense, holy water, purgatory, masses for the dead, confession and absolution, pilgrimages, psalmody, chanting of prayers in an unknown tongue, almsgiving, penances, excessive asceticism, and even a sort of pope in the Dalai Lama in Thibet, who is worshiped as an incarnation of the Deity. The first Roman missionaries who visited Buddhist countries were much struck with this resemblance, and either derived Buddhism from Christian sources, or from the devil, "the monkey of God," who counterfeited the true religion. But both hypotheses are set aside by the pre-Christian origin of those institutions and ceremonies. The true explanation is that Buddhism and Romanism have the same root in human nature.

Buddhism, when it became properly known towards the middle of the nineteenth century, had the charm of a new revela-

---

* His argument is that Buddha, after having already seen Nirvâna, still abides on earth, and appears to his disciples after his death. Sir Edwin Arnold puts into the mouth of his imaginary Buddhist votary this description of Nirvâna:

"If any teach NIRVÂNA is to cease,
Say unto such they lie.

If any teach NIRVÂNA is to live,
Say unto such they err; not knowing this,
Nor what light shines beyond their broken lamps,
Nor lifeless, timeless bliss."

tion. Its transient popularity is due in part to its affinity with Western pessimism, as represented in philosophy by Schopenhauer and Von Hartmann.

In some respects Buddhism makes of all religions the nearest approach to Christianity, both in the life of its founder as compared with Jesus, and in its moral code as compared with the Sermon on the Mount. But the resemblance is more apparent than real, more outward than inward. Both start from a profound sense of sin and guilt, but Buddhism, by teaching an impossible self-redemption through mortifications of the flesh, casts a gloom over the whole life; while Christianity, by revealing a personal God of saving love and overruling wisdom, gives peace and joy. Buddhism is pessimistic in its start, and ends in the inexplicable silence of Nirvâna; Christianity is optimistic, and ends in resurrection and life eternal.

CHAPTER XXXIII.

ZOROASTRIANISM.

Zoroastrianism, or Fire-worship, is the ancient Persian religion, and traced to Zoroaster (Zarathustra), a priest in the temple of the Sun, who lived about B.C. 1300. It was the religion of Cyrus, Darius Hystaspis, and Xerxes, and of the Wise Men from the East who came to worship the new-born Messiah at Bethlehem. It is laid down in the Zend-Avesta, a book of worship, a collection of hymns and prayers to Ormazd and to a multitude of subordinate divinities.

It is a system of dualism with a monad behind and, possibly, a reconciliation in prospect. Ormazd is the good principle (the sun, the light), and Ahriman, the evil principle (darkness, winter), who corresponds to the Devil of the Scriptures; yet both were created by Zerâna-Akerana. They are in constant antagonism, and have hosts of good and bad angels under their banners. There is incessant war going on in heaven as well as on earth. At last Ormazd sends his prophet (a kind of Messiah) to convert mankind; then follows a general resurrection, and a separation of the just from the sinners.

The sum of the moral code, or the supreme command, is: Think purely, speak purely, act purely.

The followers of this religion worship with the face turned

towards the sun or the fire upon the altar; hence they are called fire-worshipers.

The old Parsism had considerable influence upon early Christianity, through Gnosticism and Manichæism, but with the exception of a small remnant in India and Persia, it has been swept away by Christianity and Mohammedanism. It is a defunct religion.

CHAPTER XXXIV.

THE RELIGION OF ANCIENT EGYPT.

The religion of the ancient Egyptians may be read to-day in innumerable hieroglyphic inscriptions and pictures on temple-ruins, tombs, pyramids, obelisks, and other architectural monuments which are profusely scattered over the valley of the Nile.

It was a religion of mystery, well symbolized in the hieroglyphics, the mysterious sphinx, and the veil of the temple of Sais. It reflects a half-conscious dream-life.

The Egyptians in the time of Herodotus were "of all men the most excessively attentive to the gods." Wilkinson calls them "the most pious nation of all antiquity." It was more easy to find a god than a man along the banks of the Nile. Every month and every day was governed by a god. The Egyptians were the greatest builders, and their architectural masterpieces were temples, whose ruins (at Luxor, Karnak, Dendera, Edfu, Aboo-Simbel, etc.) still excite the admiration of travellers by their colossal proportions. They had a very strong belief in the immortality and transmigration of the soul, in its final reunion with the body, and in a judgment after death. Hence the care with which they embalmed the body. The pyramids are royal monuments and sepulchres for the preservation of the royal mummies. The "Book of the Dead," which was often deposited with a mummy, is a funeral liturgy with prayers and directions to the departing soul on its lonely journey to Hades, where it is to be judged by Osiris and his forty-two assessors. The lotus-flower opening with the early sun, and the fabulous Phenix rising from its ashes, are characteristic of the land of the Pharoahs. "To die is to begin to live."

The religion of the Egyptians is zoölatry, or worship of the divinity in animals. Paul no doubt refers to them when he speaks of the worship of "birds, and four-footed beasts, and creeping things" (Rom. 1: 23). They worshiped and embalmed more than half of the animals of their country, especially the bull (Apis), the ibis, the crocodile, the cat, the beetle (Scarabæus). Their gods often wear the heads of animals. Ammon-Ra, the god of the sun, is represented as a hawk-headed man, his forehead encircled with the solar disk. Osiris is represented as a mummied figure, with a crocodile's head, wearing on either side an ostrich feather and holding in his hands a shepherd's crook and a flail. The Sphinxes, also, who keep sleepless watch over the vast necropolis, are a monstrous union of man and beast, and have always the body of a lion and either the head of a man (never of a woman) or of a ram. The former are called Andro-Sphinxes, the latter Krio-Sphinxes.

The gods are divided into three orders. Manetho calls them dynasties. The first is known only to priests; the third, the circle of Osiris and Isis, is for the people. The gods share all the wants, vices and fortunes of mortals. Osiris marries his sister Isis, to whom he was wedded before their birth from Seb and Nut (earth and heaven); he came down from heaven as an incarnate god and reigned over Egypt, was murdered and cut to pieces by Typhon, his enemy (the devil), and thrown into the Nile; but was made alive again by his wife Isis, who put the fragments together; now he lives forever enthroned in the judgment hall of the invisible world. Their son, Horus, assuming the shape of a lion with a human head, avenged the death of Osiris, and slew Typhon. This may be regarded as a confused foreboding of the incarnation, death, resurrection and exaltation of Christ. But it was a hidden mystery reserved for the initiated.

Osiris, Isis, and Horus are the Egyptian triad, and represent the fructifying and fruitful life of nature.

The river Nile is also an object of worship. What Herodotus said nearly five hundred years before the Christian era is as true to-day,—" Egypt is the gift of the Nile." Descending from a mysterious source far away in the land of the sun, and spreading fertility east and west, in its long course over the sandy plain, it was and is to the Egyptians literally a river of life,

> "Whose waves have cast
> More riches round them, as the current rolled
> Through many climes its solitary flood,
> Than if they surged with gold."

CHAPTER XXXV.

CLASSICAL PAGANISM.

Greek and Roman Mythology is connected with the highest intellectual and æsthetic culture attained and attainable without the aid of Christianity. It still lingers among us in the names of stars (Jupiter, Venus, Mars), of days (Sunday, Saturday), and of months (January, March, June, August, etc.), as well as in the epics of Homer and Vergil, the orations of Demosthenes and Cicero, the philosophies of Plato and Aristotle. Greece and Rome took a prominent part in the providential preparation of the world for the reception of Christianity: Greece in the department of language, philosophy, literature and art; Rome by her conquests, polity and laws. They died out in the fourth and fifth centuries, but their works of genius continue as inspiring aids to Christian culture and learning.

The Greek and Roman religions agree in the worship of deified *men* and *women*, who bear the characteristic virtues and vices of the two nationalities in an exaggerated form. They are essentially man-worship, and so far much higher than the animal-worship of Egypt. In Greece and Rome man felt himself to be a man, as distinct from and above the animal. Their conception of humanity determines the character of their religion and their literature.

1. The Greek religion is æsthetic, a religion of art and beauty, Zeus (Zio, Jov, Sanskrit Dyu), Pallas-Athene (his motherless daughter), and Apollo (his son) form the highest divine triad. Hermes, Dionysos, Poseidon, Plutos, Demeter, Aphrodite, etc., are subordinate divinities. The earth, the sea, and the sky are inhabited by invisible beings; every department of nature is ruled by a god or goddess. The Athenians, in their superstitious anxiety to worship all possible divinities, erected an altar to an "unknown god," and made room for Paul to preach to them the only true God and his Son Jesus Christ (Acts 17: 22 sqq.).

The Greek myths of Pandora, Tantalus, Titan, Prometheus are very significant, and contain reminiscences of a golden age of innocence and dreamy foreshadowings of a future redemption. Prometheus was chained to the rock for his rebellion against

Zeus, and after long penal sufferings, was delivered by Hercules, the demi-god, the divine man. The Furies (Erinys, Eumenides) or goddesses of revenge, as described by Æschylos, represent the personified evil conscience and the curses pronounced upon the guilty criminal; they are daughters of the night, born in the moment when the first crime was committed on earth; they carry a dagger and unceasingly pursue and torture the guilty sinner; serpents are twined in their hair, and blood drops from their eyes. The poems of Homer, Pindar, Æschylos, and Sophocles, the philosophy of Plato and Aristotle, the moral treatises of Cicero, Seneca, Marcus Aurelius, Epictetos, and Plutarch, contain many beautiful religious ideas and moral maxims which come very near to the teaching of Christ and the Apostles, and prove the God-ward and Christ-ward tendency of the human mind and heart when they follow their purest and highest aspirations.

2. The Roman Mythology is political and utilitarian, a religion of the state and military conquest. Jupiter (*Jovis pater*), Juno (his sister and wife), and Minerva (his daughter) correspond to the Greek triad; Mercury, Mars, Janus, Diana, Venus, etc., to the minor divinities. The domestic gods are Lares, Penates, etc. Each town, each family, each man had a special god. Varro counted thirty thousand gods.

The Roman religion was less poetic, but more moral and practical than the Greek. Vesta, the immaculate Virgin, protected the private and public hearth, and served as a heathen prototype of the Virgin Mary. The gods were guardians of justice, property, conjugal fidelity. Cicero saw great wisdom in the close union of the Roman religion with the civil government, as it united the magistrates and priests in saving the state. The ruler of the state was the ruler of religion (*pontifex maximus*); the priests were officers of the state; the gods were national, and accompanied the legions on their conquering marches.

CHAPTER XXXVI.

THE SCANDINAVIAN AND TEUTONIC MYTHOLOGY.

The religions of the Celtic, Teutonic or Germanic, and Slavonic barbarians who emigrated in successive waves from

Asia, and settled in central, northern and western Europe, disappeared with their conversion to Christianity during the Middle Ages; but they left traces in many popular superstitions, and in the names of our week-days,—Tuesday, Wednesday, Thursday, Friday. Cæsar gives us the best account of the Celtic Gauls of his day, and Tacitus, of the Germans. The Norsemen, now so domestic and peaceful, were once the terror of Europe. Bold and fearless navigators and pirates, they invaded England, France, Southern Italy, Sicily, and threatened Constantinople. They founded Normandy, conquered the Anglo-Saxons, and out of both sprang the English race.

The Germanic and Scandinavian mythology and hero-worship is contained in the Eddas and Sagas of Iceland. This island was discovered by the sea-kings of Norway in the ninth century, and in its isolation preserved Teutonic views and customs for centuries.

The elder Edda (which means Great-Grandmother), consists of thirty-seven songs and ballads of ancient times, first collected and published by Saemund, a Christian priest and bard of Iceland, who was born in 1076 and died in 1133. The younger Edda is written in prose, and is ascribed to Snorri Sturluson, of Iceland, in the first half of the thirteenth century (1179–1241). The Eddas furnished the material for the German Nibelungen Lied, as the pre-Homeric ballad literature of Greece, concerning the siege of Troy and the adventures of Ulysses, furnished the material for the Iliad and Odyssey.

The chief Teutonic divinities are ODIN, or WODAN, the Allfather, the creator of gods and men (though himself one of the three sons of BOR), with the Earth, his wife; his eldest son THOR (Thonar, Donner, Thunder); ZIO, or TUI (the Indian Dyu, the Greek Zeus, the Roman Jupiter); FREYR and FREYA (Frowa, Frau, Mistress); LOKI, the evil god, the calumniator of the gods, the contriver of all frauds and mischief; BALDER, or BALDUR, the second son of Odin, the fairest, wisest and best among the gods, who is beloved by all. The gods are always fighting or feasting. They dwell in Valhalla, with the heroes who fell in battle, eating the flesh of boars and drinking mead out of curved horns. There is a constant conflict of the gods with the dark powers. The conflict ends with the downfall of all the gods, and a universal conflagration; but after this a new sun shall shine on a new earth, and Balder, the god of peace, shall rule with the descendants of the gods. An unconscious prophecy of Christianity.

The Teutonic mythology has several points of resemblance with Zoroastrianism: Odin corresponds to Ormazd, Loki to Ahriman, Baldur to Sraosho. They teach a constant warfare between the gods and their good and evil angels, a final conflagration, and a subsequent new creation of peace and joy.

CHAPTER XXXVII.

THE JEWISH RELIGION.

Judaism, as recorded in the Scriptures of the Old Covenant, and represented by the Patriarchs, Moses, and the Prophets down to John the Baptist, was the true religion before Christ, but not perfect, or final. It is the cradle of Christianity; for "salvation comes from the Jews" (John 4:22; Luke 24:47; Rom. 9:4, 5). It was like an oasis in the wilderness, surrounded by various forms of idolatry, but isolated and free from foreign admixture. It is, in its prominent features, monotheistic, legalistic, prophetical, and typical, and finds its fulfilment in Christianity.

1. Monotheism. Jehovah (Jahveh) is the only true and living God, the almighty Maker and Ruler of all things. He claims supreme devotion from his creatures. The unity of the Godhead, in opposition to all forms of idolatry, is the fundamental article of the Jewish faith. It is put at the head of the Decalogue: "I am Jehovah, thy God, thou shalt have no other gods before me" (Ex. 20:2, 3), and in the form of a dogma: "Hear, O Israel: Jehovah our God is one Jehovah" (Deut. 6:4).* This dogmatic declaration of the Divine unity, which excludes all polytheism, is made the basis for the highest moral precept—supreme love to God—in opposition to all practical idolatry (Deut. 6:5): "And thou shalt love Jehovah, thy God, with all thine heart, and with all thy soul, and with all thy

---

* The Hebrew may also be rendered: "Jehovah our God, Jehovah is one," if we connect "one" as predicate with the second "Jehovah." (So Oehler, *Theol. des A. Test.*, I. 159.) The Revised E. V. puts two other renderings on the margin: "The Lord is our God, the Lord is one," or "The Lord is our God, the Lord alone." For *Jehovah* the critical writers, following the etymology, now use *Jahveh* or *Yahveh*. (Driver spells *Jahweh*.)

might." Hence, our Lord quotes this passage as "the first of all commandments" (Mark 12 : 29).*

2. Judaism is the religion of law, and hence of repentance. The law reveals the holy will of God; leads by contrast to the knowledge of sin (Rom. 3 : 20); excites a longing after redemption, and thus serves as a tutor to bring men to Christ (Gal. 3 : 24). The seventh chapter of the Romans illustrates the discipline of the law, as a school for Christian freedom, by the experience of Paul. Judaism alone of all ancient religions has a proper conception of the holiness of God and the sinfulness of man. It reveals the infinite distance between God and man and the awful guilt of apostasy; and therefore prepares the way for the reconciliation (Rom. 5 : 11; 2 Cor. 5 : 18, 19). The moral disease must be fully known and felt, and be brought to a crisis, before it can be healed. To do this, is the mission of the moral and ceremonial law with its duties and sacrifices.

3. Judaism is prophetical and typical. It is a religion of Divine promise, and therefore of hope. The promise of redemption antedates the law, which came in between the promise and the fulfilment as an interimistic dispensation. It prevails in the patriarchal period. It goes back to the very beginning of history, the protevangelium, as it is called, which was given to our first parents, as an anchor of hope, after their expulsion from paradise. "The woman's seed," *i.e.*, Christ, which is the ultimate meaning, "shall bruise" the serpent's "head," *i.e.*, destroy the power of the devil (Gen. 3 : 15). The promise was essentially Messianic, pointing to a divine-human redeemer and reconciler of God and man, who was to proceed from Abraham and the house of David, and bless all the nations of the earth. The Messianic prophecies of the Old Testament, running like a golden thread through many centuries, apply to their own time, but have an ulterior meaning for the future, and culminate in the person of Jesus of Nazareth. He alone is the Christ.

The Mosaic religion is also a religion of types and shadows pointing forward to the substance and reality. Its leaders, institutions, sacrifices and ceremonies prefigure the Christ and his gospel. The Epistle to the Hebrews sets forth the typical

---

* Comp. also Deut. 4 : 35, 39; 2 Sam. 7 : 22; 22 : 32; 1 Kgs. 8 : 60; 1 Chr. 17 : 20; Ps. 56 : 10; Is. 43 : 10; 44 : 6, 8; 45 : 22. Confirmed in the N. T., Mk. 12 : 29; Luke 10 : 27; John 17 : 3; 1 Cor. 8 : 4; Gal. 3 : 20; 1 Thess. 1 : 9; 1 Tim. 2 : 5.

significance of the Old Testament in regard to the eternal priesthood and eternal sacrifice of Christ.

4. Judaism is a religion of the future. Both the law and the promise, and all the types, point beyond themselves: the law by awakening a sense of the need of redemption; the promise by directing the desire of redemption to a personal Redeemer, who will surely come in the fullness of time.

John the Baptist preaching repentance, pointing his own pupils to Jesus as the Messiah, and willing to decrease that Christ might increase, is the best as well as the last representative of the Old Testament religion. Genuine Judaism lived for Christianity and died with the birth of Christianity. The Old Testament is the inheritance of the Christian Church, and is understood only in the light of the gospel.

Unbelieving Judaism, after crucifying the Saviour, has become antichristian, vainly hoping for the Messiah, who will come again indeed, but to judge those who reject his great salvation. Yet, after "the fullness of the Gentiles" has come in, "all Israel shall be saved" (Rom. 11:26), and the Jewish race is preserved by Providence for that glorious end.

CHAPTER XXXVIII.

MOHAMMEDANISM.

Mohammedanism (from its founder*), or Islâm (from its chief virtue, submission to God), is an eclectic religion. It combines Jewish, Christian and heathen elements, which are held together and animated by an intensely fanatical monotheism in the form of antitrinitarian Unitarianism.

The Koran is the Bible of the Mohammedans, and contains their creed, their code of laws and their liturgy. It claims to be inspired by the archangel Gabriel (who performed the function of the Holy Spirit in the Scriptures). It consists of 114 Suras (revelations or chapters), and 6,225 verses; each Sura begins with the formula (of Jewish origin): "In the name of Allah, the God of mercy, the Merciful." It resembles in form the

* Mohammed or Mohammad (also Muhammad) means the *Praised*, the *Glorified*. The more usual spelling "Mahomet" and "Mahometanism" is incorrect.

Psalter, but is far inferior to it in spirit. It is a strange mixture of sublime poetry, religious fervor, and wise maxims, with bombast, absurdities and sensuality, and abounds in vain repetitions and contradictions.

1. Mohammedanism may be called a bastard Judaism, standing in the same relation to the religion of the Old Testament as Ishmael, the wild son of the desert, stood to Isaac, the legitimate son of promise. It is Judaism deformed by heathenism, or rather heathenism raised up to a Jewish monotheism. It is a worship of the one omnipotent, omnipresent God, but without Messianic hopes and aspirations, and therefore hostile to Christianity. Circumcision is retained. Friday is substituted for the Sabbath, but not as rigorously observed. The cultus is puritanic. All pictures and works of sculpture (except unmeaning arabesque figures) are strictly forbidden, as in the second commandment. Idolatry is regarded as the greatest sin.

2. Islâm also borrowed some features from heretical and corrupt forms of Christianity, and recognizes Jesus as the greatest prophet next to Mohammed, but not as the Son of God.

3. The motto of Islâm is: "There is no god but God (Allah),* and Mohammed is his prophet." This is the fundamental dogma of the Jewish religion (Deut. 6:4), with the spurious addition of "Mohammed is his prophet." The truth is thus turned into a heresy, and monotheism is made antichristian by its antagonism to the Trinity, and the divinity of Christ. Allah is the god of iron fate. Absolute resignation (Islâm) to his will is the capital virtue, which is carried to the excess of fatalism and apathy.

4. Morals. Prayer, fasting and alms-giving are enjoined, pork and wine forbidden. Polygamy is allowed, with the normal restriction to four lawful wives, but with liberty to the caliphs of filling their harems to the extent of their wealth and desire.† This heathen sensualism destroys home-life and pollutes even the Mohammedan picture of paradise. The sword

---

* Allah is contracted from the article *al*, and *ilah*, and signifies in Arabic the true God, the only God.

† Mohammed himself had eleven wives and several concubines. He was surpassed by Brigham Young (d. 1877), the second founder of Mormonism (American Mohammedanism), who had nineteen lawful wives (besides so-called spiritual wives) and left fifty-four children. One of his wives rebelled and exposed him in a book entitled "Number Nineteen."

is the legitimate means for the propagation of Islâm, and the conquered Christians are held in abject servitude. Apostasy is punished by death.*

5. Relation to Islâm of Christianity. This has two aspects. The Mohammedan religion, viewed in its relation to Eastern Christianity which is reduced to a state of slavery, was a curse and a divine judgment; viewed in its relation to heathenism which is converted by conquest, it is a blessing and marks a great progress. Its mission was to break down idolatry in Asia and Africa, and to raise savages to the worship of one God, and to some degree of civilization. Like the law of Moses, it may prove a schoolmaster, to lead its followers ultimately to a purer form of Christianity than has hitherto prevailed in the East. But this will not be done till its political power in Turkey is broken, which has been kept alive of late only by the jealousy of Christian governments. By the sword Islâm has conquered Constantinople, by the sword (of Russia or other nations) it will be driven out; by the moral power of the gospel it will be converted.

CHAPTER XXXIX.

CHRISTIANITY.

Christianity is the perfect religion of God for the whole human race. It is the end of all religions, and will itself have no end. It is the final revelation of God to men. All further religious progress will be a growth of humanity in (but not beyond) Christianity, or a more complete apprehension and application of the spirit and example of Christ. The kingdom of God on earth is intended to embrace all nations and to last forever.

The characteristic features which distinguish the Christian religion from all other religions, and which constitute its perfection, are the following:

1. Christianity is the religion of the incarnation. "The Word became flesh." It is the nearest possible approach of God to man and the highest uplifting of man to God, exhibited in the char-

* After the Crimean war in 1855, the death penalty for apostasy was nominally abolished, and the International Treaty of Berlin (July, 1878) guaranteed religious liberty in Turkey. But the promises of Turkey to Christian Europe mean nothing. Christian sects are tolerated and allowed to proselyte among themselves, but not among Mohammedans, who are as fanatical as ever. This is the amount of Turkish toleration.

acter of its founder. For Christ is the God-Man, who unites in his person forever the fullness of the Godhead and the fulness of manhood, without sin, and who communicates this harmony to his followers. The avatars of the Indian, and the theanthropogenies of the Greek and Roman mythologies, are carnal anticipations and foreshadowings of the one historical incarnation of God in Christ.

The incarnation of the Eternal Logos is emphasized by the Orthodox Greek Church, and made the cardinal doctrine of theology.

2. Christianity is the religion of salvation or redemption from sin and death. It is just such a religion as sinners need. It is the atonement (in the old sense of at-one-ment) or reconciliation ($καταλλαγή$) of man with God through Christ, the Mediator. It fully realizes the idea of all religion, *i.e.*, a re-union or reconciliation of man with God. It is not merely a striving after, or a preparation for, deliverance from sin, but it is complete salvation accomplished once for all. Christ is the all-sufficient Saviour of mankind, and there is no defect whatever in his work. Jesus "came not to call the righteous, but sinners" (Matt. 9 : 13). Self-righteous Pharisees and proud Stoics cannot appreciate the gospel which addresses itself to those who feel their need of salvation. Hence there is no use of arguing with a proud and self-contented infidel.

The saving character of Christianity is emphasized by the Evangelical Churches. Luther laid chief stress upon gratuitous justification by faith, Calvin on eternal election.

3. Christianity, in its subjective character, is the religion of regeneration and sanctification. It not only removes the guilt, but breaks also the power of sin. It not only reforms and improves the old character, but it creates a new moral character, by imparting the life of Christ through the agency of the Holy Spirit. The process of regeneration is carried on through sanctification to perfection and glorification. The perfect Christian is at the same time a perfect man. Christianity blends piety and morality. It is the harmony of all virtues and graces. It is supreme love to God and love to our fellow-men, and thus fulfils the whole law of God, in imitation of the perfect example of Christ.

4. Christianity is the most rational of all religions, and is consistent with the highest culture. Its doctrines and facts are in-

deed above, but not against reason, and the more reason is elevated and purified, the nearer it approaches revelation. The Christian religion commands the homage of the greatest intellects, as well as of the humblest child. We may mention the names of the Apostle Paul, Origen, Athanasius, Chrysostom, Augustin, Jerome, Charlemagne, Anselm, Thomas Aquinas, Dante, Luther, Calvin, Bacon, Milton, Newton, Kepler, Bossuet, Pascal, Fenelon, Leibnitz, Schelling, Schleiermacher, Lotze, among the great men and profound thinkers who bowed their knees before Christ as their Lord and Saviour. Other religions cannot bear the touch of criticism, nor survive an advanced stage of intellectual culture.

5. Christianity is the religion of humanity. It is catholic or universal, *i.e.*, adapted to the whole human race, while all other religions in capacity and extent are ethnic, *i.e.*, limited to one or more nations.

This is abundantly proved by history. Christianity has made converts by purely spiritual means, among Jews, Greeks, Romans, the Celtic, Germanic, and Slavonic nationalities, Hindus, Chinese, Negroes, Indians, and all other races, civilized and barbarian, bond and free. Judaism has made some proselytes; Mohammedanism has made subjects and slaves by the sword; Buddhism has spread widely by preaching, but only in Asia; and all have reached their zenith of strength and influence. Christianity retains its peaceful conquests, and is steadily advancing. It may be weakened for a time in one country or among some nations, but it always advances in other directions and gains more than it loses. It makes day by day converts from all religions, while apostasies from Christianity to any other religion are exceptional and abnormal occurrences, and nearly always traceable to compulsion or selfish motives. When educated men forsake Christianity, they generally renounce all religion and become infidels.

6. Christianity is universal not only as to extent, but also internally, in that it is suited to all classes, states and conditions of man. It brings the same blessings to all, it requires the same duties from all. It is compatible with every form of government, with every kind of society, with every grade of culture, with the largest progress and development, physical, intellectual, and moral. It can never be replaced or superseded.

7. Christianity is pleromatic. It is the fullness and harmony of all the truths which are scattered through the different religions, without their corresponding errors and defects. It is the central truth which comprehends all other truths.

8. Christianity is the religion of Christ, who personally embodies its whole meaning and power. He is the incarnate Son of God, the Saviour of the world; the perfect Man without sin, the Way, the Truth, and the Life, the same yesterday, to-day, and forever. In him the central ideas of our religion are fully united and actualized. Christianity is only the manifestation of the divine-human life of its Founder and ever present, ever-living Head. Beyond him it is impossible to go in virtue and piety.*

* See the collection of impartial testimonies to the perfection of Christ's character by Rousseau, Napoleon, Goethe, Carlyle, Strauss, Renan, Keim, Lecky and others, in my book on *The Person of Christ* (N.Y. 12th ed. 1882).

PART II.

SUBJECTIVE RELIGION.

CHAPTER XL.

THE RELIGIOUS CONSTITUTION OF MAN.

Man is constitutionally a supernatural as well as a natural being in the sense that he is descended from, and destined for, a world lying beyond the limits of time and space. Being made in the image of God, he is capable of knowing God, communing with him, and enjoying him in endless felicity. He is the prophet, priest, and king of nature, and is at the same time above nature. Religion is the bond which unites man to God and represents his higher, spiritual and eternal relations. Only men and angels are capable of religion. Animals have no conception of God and no moral sense.

Religion is the deepest, strongest and most universal interest of man. It accompanies him from the cradle to the grave; it belongs to him on the heights of knowledge and happiness, and in the depths of ignorance and misery. No one can be indifferent to it. Irreligion is only a bad religion; a man who will not worship God, will worship an idol, or himself, or the evil spirit. Even demons believe that there is a God, and shudder. Religion is either man's crown and glory, or his degradation and shame. It emancipates or enslaves; it blesses or curses, according as it is true or false, pure or corrupt, the original of God or the caricature of his great antagonist. It has the power to raise man above the angels, or to sink him beneath the demons. The best and the worst things are done in the name of religion. From its inspirations proceed the purest motives, the noblest impulses, the highest thoughts, the brightest hopes, the holiest joys, but also the darkest crimes, the bloodiest persecutions, the fiercest wars.

"What should it profit a man if he gain the whole world, and forfeit his life? Or what should a man give in exchange for his life?" (Matt. 16 : 26.) Unless a man fulfils his highest mission and becomes united to God, his life is worse than a failure, and it would be better for him never to have been born. Happiness and misery are always in proportion to the capacities. As man can rise infinitely above the animal, so he can also sink infinitely below the animal; he may become the companion of God and holy angels in heaven, or of the devil and evil spirits in the regions of despair.

Religion being inseparable from the rational and moral constitution of man, is found in some form or other in every nation and tribe. Plutarch, a heathen philosopher of the Platonic school, asserts the universal prevalence of religion as far as the knowledge of his age extended. "There has never been," he says, "a state of Atheists. You may travel over the world and you may find cities without walls, without king, without mint, without theatre or gymnasium; but you will never find a city without God, without prayer, without oracle, without sacrifice. Sooner may a city stand without foundations, than a state without belief in the gods. This is the bond of all society and the pillar of all legislation."*

The same religious impulse of man in its normal tendency will lead him to choose Christianity before all other religions. The soul, according to Tertullian, is naturally or constitutionally a Christian. Though corrupted by sin and perverted by bad training, the soul still longs for the only true God, and if left to its own higher and nobler instincts, will embrace Christianity as soon as it is presented, because it is the perfect religion and alone can give rest and peace. "*Tu nos fecisti ad Te,*" says the great Augustin, "*et inquietum est cor nostrum, donec requiescat in Te.*"

CHAPTER XLI.

RELIGION AND THE MENTAL FACULTIES.—THE PSYCHOLOGY OF RELIGION.

We may divide the faculties or powers of the human soul into three.

1. Cognition, or the theoretical faculty, the intellect, the

*Adv. Colotem (an Epicurean), ch. xxxi. (*Moralia*, VI. 255, ed. Tauchnitz).

reason. This is receptive, and appropriates, by the internalizing process of learning or mental digestion, the objective world by which we are surrounded.

2. Volition, or the practical faculty, the will. This is productive and works spontaneously from within, forming thoughts into resolutions and resolutions into actions, and thus exerting an influence upon the world.

3. Feeling, or the emotional faculty, the sensibility. This is not so much an activity of the mind as a state or sensation, either of pleasure or pain, which accompanies the actions of the intellect and the will. A man does not feel, except he knows or wills something which excites emotion.

These three faculties constitute the trinity in man who is made in the image of God. They reflect the Divine Trinity. They are one in essence, but different in function and operation. They are not to be considered as separate parts or organs, which act independently, like the brain, the heart, the eye, the ear, in the body. They are the capacities, manifestations and states of the one undivided personality, the Ego, which is wholly present and active in all. It is the rational soul itself which is predominantly in a state of knowledge, or will, or feeling.

On this psychological basis we may form three or four different theories of religion, according as we identify it with one of the three faculties, or assign it a distinct sphere:

I. The intellectual or rational theory.
II. The practical or moral theory.
III. The emotional theory.
IV. The theory of life, including all the faculties of man in their relation to God.

CHAPTER XLII.

THE INTELLECTUAL THEORY.—PIETY AND KNOWLEDGE.

The intellectual or rational theory holds that religion is essentially knowledge of divine things.*

* "*Modus Deum cognoscendi*," usually, however, with the addition "*et colendi*." Max Müller defines religion as "the perception of the infinite"; Alfred Cave (*Introd. to Theol.*, p. 49) more fully as "the perception or knowledge of the supernatural, together with the effects of that perception upon the complex nature of man." The various schools of ancient and modern Gnosticism, from Valentinus down to Hegel, put knowledge (γνωσις) above faith (πιστις), and resolve religion at last into philosophy. Abelard, the Ration-

This is true, but one-sided. No religion without knowledge, but knowledge is only one element of religion.

There can be no Christian piety without some knowledge of God, of Christ, and the way of salvation. Christ is a prophet as well as a king, the truth as well as the way and the life; he is "the light of the world," and in him are "hid all the treasures of wisdom and knowledge" (Col. 2 : 3). Knowledge is a gift of grace, and highly prized by John (17 : 3), Paul and Peter. Christianity is the mother of the highest culture.

But knowledge alone is not religion, and religion is more than knowledge. Else theological scholars would be the best Christians; men and adults would be more religious than women and children; even the demons, who are by no means deficient in knowledge (James 2 : 19), would have some claim to piety.

Experience teaches a different lesson. Religion usually passes from the heart to the head, and not from the head to the heart.* We must first love divine things before we can properly know them. Faith precedes understanding.† Childlike simplicity is the beginning and the soul of piety (Matt. 18 : 3). Christ praises his heavenly Father that he hid the mysteries of his kingdom from the worldly-wise and prudent, and revealed them unto babes (Matt. 11 : 25).‡ He selected his apostles, not from the learned rabbis of Jerusalem, nor the philosophers of Athens, nor the statesmen of Rome, but from the illiterate fishermen of Galilee. Only one apostle was a scholar, and he exchanged his

---

alist among the mediæval schoolmen, advocated the principle that knowledge precedes faith (*Intellectus præcedit fidem*). The champions of orthodoxy emphasize the correctness of belief (RECHT*gläubigkeit*) rather than belief itself (*Recht*GLÄUBIGKEIT), and thus likewise put the essence of religion in knowledge.

* Pascal says : "*Les vérités divines entrent du cœur dans l'esprit, et non pas de l'esprit dans le cœur, pour humilier cette superbe puissance du raisonnement qui prétend devoir être juge des choses que la volonté choisit, et pour guérir cette volonté infirme, qui s'est corrompue par ses sales attachements.* * * * *Les saints disent en parlant des choses divines qu'il faut les aimer pour les connaître, et qu'on n'entre dans la vérité que par la charité.*"

† "*Fides præcedit intellectum*" is St. Augustin's and Anselm's theological principle. Schleiermacher has chosen as the motto of his work *Der Christliche Glaube*, the sentence of Anselm : "*Neque enim quæro intelligere ut credam, sed credo ut intelligam. Nam qui non crediderit, non experietur, et qui expertus non fuerit, non intelliget*" (*Proslog. I. de fide trin.* 2).

‡ The finest lines which Schiller ever wrote are:

"*Was kein Verstand der Verständigen sieht,
Das glaubet in Einfalt ein kindlich Gemüth.*"

And next to it is his distich :

"*Religion des Kreuzes, nur du verknüpfest in Einem
Kranze, der Demuth und Kraft doppelte Palme zugleich.*"

rabbinical learning for the simplicity of Christ. A man who understands all mysteries and is able to speak with the tongues of angels, yet lacks love, is in the eyes of Paul but as "sounding brass or a clanging cymbal" (1 Cor. 13 : 1). Paul represents the religion of the cross as a stumbling-block to the self-righteous Jew and as foolishness to the wise Greek, and lays it down as a rule that God "chose the foolish things of the world that he might put to shame them that are wise," and that he "chose the weak things of the world that he might put to shame the things that are strong" (1 Cor. 1 : 19–31). The world is to be converted "by the foolishness of the preaching" (1 Cor. 1 : 21), *i.e.*, not by foolish preaching, but by the preaching of the apparent folly of God which turns out to be the greatest wisdom. While Paul duly appreciates sound knowledge, he condemns, on the other hand, that knowledge "which puffeth up" (1 Cor. 8 : 1), "the knowledge falsely so called" (1 Tim. 6 : 20), which profiteth nothing, but creates strife, dissension and distraction. He warns Timothy and Titus earnestly against that very tendency which was afterwards more fully developed in the Gnostic systems, and which reappears from time to time in the various phases of a one-sided intellectualism and rationalism, whether gnostic or agnostic.

CHAPTER XLIII.

PIETY AND ORTHODOXY.

A modification of the intellectual theory identifies religion with correctness or soundness of belief in divine things, or with orthodoxy in opposition to heterodoxy or heresy.*

---

* The terms, orthodoxy (ὀρθοδοξία, ὀρθοτομία) and heterodoxy, or heresy (ἑτεροδοξία, αἵρεσις), presuppose a publicly recognized standard of faith or creed (κανὼν τῆς ἀληθείας or τῆς πίστεως, regula veritatis or fidei). They are of patristic origin, and were much used during the Arian controversy. Athanasius was called by Epiphanius "the father of orthodoxy" for his valiant, persistent, and successful defense of the divinity of Christ and the holy Trinity. The nearest Scripture expressions are διδασκαλία ὑγιαίνουσα, sound teaching, λόγος ὑγιαίνων, sound word (1 Tim. 1 : 10 ; 6:3), and the verbs ὀρθοτομέω τὸν λόγον τῆς ἀληθείας, to cut straight, to expound soundly, to handle aright the Word of truth (2 Tim. 2 : 15), and ἑτεροδιδασκαλέω, to teach otherwise, to teach a different doctrine (1 Tim. 6 : 3). The term αἵρεσις, which is translated *heresy* in the English Authorized Version, means faction, division, party, sect (1 Cor. 11 : 19 ; Gal. 5 : 20 ; 2 Pet. 2 : 1). Christianity itself is called a sect (Acts 24 : 14). Every departure from an established creed at first appears heretical, but may turn out to be a new truth, or a progress in the knowledge of the old truth.

But orthodoxy cannot be the standard of piety because it is purely a matter of the head. Orthodoxy consists in theoretical assent to a denominational or sectarian creed; hence there are as many orthodoxies as creeds and sects: a Greek orthodoxy, a Roman Catholic orthodoxy, an Anglican orthodoxy, a Lutheran orthodoxy, a Calvinistic orthodoxy, etc. These doxies are in part antagonistic and exclusive. They may all be connected with practical piety, or they may not. One may be thoroughly acquainted with the creed of his Church and convinced of its truth, and yet be entirely destitute of spirituality, or even of decent morality. The Church of Ephesus is commended for its zeal for pure doctrine, but blamed for having left her first love (Rev. 2: 1–6). The Greek Church calls herself the orthodox Church above all others, but is the most stagnant. Pietism in Germany and Methodism in England were protests of practical piety against dead orthodoxy and formalism.

A one-sided orthodoxism, whether Greek, Roman, or Protestant, is generally intolerant, bigoted, uncharitable, and capable of the greatest injustice and cruelty, as the history of persecutions proves. Tolerance is one of the last lessons which the selfish human heart learns. The most intolerant kind of intolerance is the intolerance of infidelity, as the reign of terror in the first French Revolution has shown.

On the other hand, there have been in all ages pious heretics and schismatics. There is an unchurchly and separatistic as well as a churchly piety. Some of the most pious men have been burnt as heretics. Uncharitableness and intolerance is the worst heresy. Gottfried Arnold, a pietist who was persecuted by the orthodox Lutherans, wrote a learned Church History as a history of pious heretics and schismatics.

Nevertheless, orthodoxy is an important element in a normal state of religion. As a rule, there is a harmony between one's views and practices, although there are happy and unhappy inconsistencies, and many men are better or worse than their creed. The apostles lay great stress on soundness of knowledge (1 Tim. 1: 10; 6: 3; 2 Tim. 1: 23; 4: 3; Tit. 1: 9; 2: 1), and warn against errors. It is the duty of the Church to maintain the purity of doctrine, and to make it an essential condition of admission to the ministry that the candidate be sound in the faith and teach no error. The best kind of orthodoxy is Scripturalness, or conformity to the teaching of God's Word; but in view of the conflicting interpretations of the Bible, subordinate standards of orthodoxy called Creeds or Confessions of Faith, are necessary; only they should be confined to the essential and fundamental articles, and not embarrass the consciences of honest men or encourage mental reservations. Unfortunately, the Protestant Confessions of the sixteenth and seventeenth centuries contain too much metaphysical and polemical theology, which should be left to the school. There is a great difference between a system of theology and a creed of the Church.

CHAPTER XLIV.

THE PRACTICAL THEORY.—PIETY AND MORALITY.

According to this theory, religion resides in the will and is essentially action, that is, moral action in obedience to the will of God as expressed in our conscience and in his revealed law, and in imitation of the example of Christ as the pattern.*

All this is true as far as it goes, but becomes false by excluding other truths and by identifying piety with morality. There is no sound piety without morality, and no perfect morality without piety. Yet there are morbid forms of piety which consist in entire withdrawal from the world, in meditation and prayer (Anchoretism, Quietism, Mysticism); other forms run into antinomianism; even the darkest crimes have been committed in the name of religion.

On the other hand, there are forms of morality which are indifferent or hostile to religion. Even publicans and harlots are more easily converted than self-righteous Pharisees and proud Stoics.

These facts, however abnormal, prove that there is a difference between the two.

The Bible lays great stress on obedience and holiness, and knows no happiness without holiness. We must not only hear

---

* Various forms of this theory: The religion of Confucius; Greek and Roman Stoicism; Jewish and Christian legalism; Pelagianism; Deism; Unitarianism. Kant's moralism makes religion to consist simply in this, that we regard our moral duties as *Divine* commandments; morality is the essence, religion the accident, the outside form. Unitarianism comes nearer the truth by making much account of the example of Christ, though only under a humanitarian view and overlooking his Divine character and his priestly and kingly office.

the Word and say "Lord, Lord," but do the will of God in order to enter his kingdom (Matt. 7: 21, 24; John 13: 17; James 1: 22, 25, 27). We must aim to be perfect even as our Father in heaven is perfect (Matt. 5: 48). Faith without works is dead (James 2: 24). But works without faith are dead also and of no value before God (Rom. chs. 3 and 4). Faith precedes good works, as the tree is before the fruit, the root before the tree.

Piety is primarily not moral action, no work of our own, but a receptive attitude of the soul to God, a child-like disposition and readiness to be acted upon by him. We must first believe in God before we can obey his commandments; we must suffer ourselves to be loved by him before we can love him in turn and love our fellow-men. We are not to earn our salvation by our own efforts, but to accept salvation already and completely wrought out for us once for all, and then to show our gratitude for it by consecrating ourselves to the service of Christ. The gospel religion is not a system of ordinances, commandments and duties, but of divine promises, fulfilments and blessings. It begins on the Mount of Beatitudes; it is the story of the boundless love of God to sinners in the sacrifice of his Son. This love of God works miracles. It alone produces love and gratitude in man, which is the heart and soul of all true morality. It is the motive which determines the moral character of an action, and the highest motive under which man can act is love to God. But love to God is a religious affection.

Consequently religion is distinct from morality, and at the same time the source of true morality. Religion quickens the moral sense, enlightens it with the knowledge of God, kindles it with the love of God and man, directs all our energies to his glory and the welfare of the race.

To cut morality loose from faith in God and to make it independent of religious opinions, is to dry up its fountain, and to strangle its noblest aspirations. Morality without religion is either an idle abstraction, or a lifeless legality, a selfish virtue, which is indeed far better for society than immorality, and has its uses for this world, but no value before God.*

---

* Benjamin Franklin presents, perhaps, the most respectable specimen of a great man who aimed at moral perfection without the aid of (revealed) religion. He conceived, as he tells us in his *Autobiography*, "the bold and arduous project of arriving at perfection," and gathered for this purpose from his reading a catalogue of thirteen virtues of which temperance was the first, humility the last, with the direction under this head, "Imitate

CHAPTER XLV.

THE EMOTIONAL THEORY.—PIETY AND FEELING.

Piety is essentially emotional. It is feeling, more particularly a feeling of absolute dependence on God, as the almighty and omnipresent Maker, Preserver, and Ruler of all things.*
Feeling plays an important part in prayer and praise and all other acts of worship. It enters into all the exercises and experiences of private and public devotion, of repentance and holy

---

Jesus and Socrates." As if they were quite independent of each other, he practiced these virtues one by one, devoting thirteen days to the course and repeating the course four times in a year. What an atomistic, mechanical conception! Christian morality, on the contrary, begins with humility, with a sense of sin and guilt and entire dependence on God for grace and strength. It is characteristic that he at first omitted humility altogether, but added it at the suggestion of a Quaker. He found it the severest task to conquer his *pride*. "Disguise it" (he wrote in 1784), "struggle with it, beat it down, stifle it, mortify it as much as one pleases, it is still alive, and will every now and then peep out and show itself; you will see it, perhaps, often in this history; for, even if I could conceive that I had completely overcome it, I should probably be proud of my humility." Franklin found, however, in the practice of his virtues that he was "much fuller of faults" than he had imagined. Deist as he was, he yet had a respect for the religion of the Bible, and was fond of hearing the great revival preacher Whitefield. He wrote to his daughter in 1764: "Go constantly to church, whoever preaches. The act of devotion in the Common Prayer Book is your principal business there, and, if properly attended to, will do more towards amending the heart than sermons generally can do. For they were composed by men of much greater piety and wisdom than our common composers of sermons can pretend to be; and therefore I wish you would never miss the prayer days; yet I do not mean you should despise sermons even of the preachers you dislike, for the discourse is often much better than the man, as sweet and clear waters come through very dirty earth." *Autobiography*, edition of John Bigelow, Philad. (1868), p 213.

* The emotional theory is held by various schools of mysticism, and has been brought into a scientific shape by Schleiermacher, first in his *Discourses on Religion* (1799), which were directed against the superficial rationalism and moralism of the last century; then in his work on Dogmatic (*Der Christliche Glaube*, 1821, third ed., 1835, § 4). He defines religion as the feeling of absolute dependence on God (*das schlechthinige Abhängigkeitsgefühl*), but asserts at the same time that it influences the intellect and the will. By feeling he understands the immediate consciousness (*das unmittelbare Bewusstsein*). In his posthumous *Dialectic*, he defines feeling to be the unity of our being in the alternation between intelligence and will (*die Einheit unseres Wesens im Wechsel zwischen Wissen und Wollen*). To feel *absolutely* dependent is to feel dependent on God, the absolute being, or to be *religious*. Religion is *Gottesbewusstsein*, as distinct from *Weltbewusstsein* and *Selbstbewusstsein*. Schleiermacher's theory has an affinity with Calvinism, which rests on the doctrine of the absolute sovereignty of God and the absolute dependence of man. It was advocated by Twesten, De Wette, Elwert, Alexander Schweizer, and Hagenbach, but opposed by Hegel (who condescended to a cynic witticism about the dog and his master), Marheineke and Rosenkranz, who maintained the supremacy of thinking. Räbiger and Pfleiderer seek to mediate between Schleiermacher and Hegel.

grief, of joy and peace, of faith and love. Religion must be felt as a personal concern of our own. Without feeling it is unreal and imaginary. Religion begins with a state of feeling, *i.e.*, the felt need of redemption, and ends with a state of feeling, *i.e.*, perfect blessedness in holy union with God. The Bible represents the heart (καρδία), which is the seat and centre of emotions, as the fountain head from which are the issues of life and from which proceed all good and evil thoughts and actions (comp. Prov. 4 : 23; Matt. 15 : 19).

Religious feeling is a consciousness of absolute dependence on God, but at the same time a feeling of confidence, trust and freedom in God. Christians are children as well as servants of God, and enjoy all the family privileges. In the Old Covenant the sense of dependence and the fear of God prevailed; in the New Covenant the sense of freedom and the love of God prevail. To serve God in a child-like spirit, with a cheerful mind, is true freedom.

Moreover, the state and degree of religion cannot be measured by the state and degree of feeling. The argument which Schleiermacher uses against the intellectual and moral theory, viz., that it would make piety depend upon the degree of knowledge or morality, holds with the same force against his own theory. Neither the depth, nor the liveliness of feeling are sure tests of piety. Emotional and excitable people are not always or necessarily more religious than those of a cooler and calmer disposition. The reverse is often the case. A man may have much more piety than he is conscious of; yea, the possession of Christian graces is often in inverse proportion to the degree of consciousness. The greatest saints sometimes pass through a gloom of despondency to the very brink of despair and foretaste of damnation, while, in fact, they are as near and dear to God as in the opposite state of feeling; they have only lost the sense, not the possession, of God's favor, who "behind a frowning providence hides a smiling face."

The theory of disinterested love which should be willing to renounce the bliss of heaven and suffer for others the torments of hell, rests on a false exegesis of Rom. 9 : 3 (comp. Ex. 32 : 32) and a mistaken conception of the relation of love to happiness, of virtue to reward (which God has joined together), but it has nevertheless been connected with most spiritual and lovely forms of piety. (Mad. Guyon, Fénelon.)

The emotional theory is apt to run out into extreme subjectivism, sentimentalism, and doctrinal indifferentism. Nothing is more deceptive and changeable than those fleeting children of the moment which we call feelings. Religion must have a more solid foundation in clear views, strong convictions, and fixed determinations which cannot be moved by transient impressions.

CHAPTER XLVI.

THE LIFE THEORY.

We have seen that religion, although involving knowledge, action, and feeling, is not commensurate with any of them, but broader and more comprehensive than a single faculty of the soul separately considered. The force which lies behind the faculties as their common ground and centre, we call *life*. It is the human personality as a unit, of which thinking, acting, and feeling are but various manifestations.

Religion in general is the life of the human soul brought into actual contact with the divine life as its fountain. Christian piety in particular may be defined to be a vital union of man with God in and through Christ, the God-Man and Saviour; or the life of Christ planted in the soul of man through the power of the Holy Spirit and gradually pervading and sanctifying all the faculties. Christianity alone can bring about such a union in a real and permanent way, but all forms of religion are at least an effort and striving after it.

The incarnation, or the Divine Logos in abiding union with human nature, is the central fact of objective Christianity. So we may say that the measure of the union and harmony of our whole being with God in Christ, is also the measure of religion; the closer this union, the purer and stronger is also the piety. As far as our intelligence moves in the sphere of divine truth, it is a religious intelligence; as far as our will obeys the divine will, it is sanctified will; and as far as our feeling realizes both our dependence on God and our filial freedom in God, or his absolute sovereignty as well as his loving fatherhood over us, it is religious feeling.

This view is scriptural. The first definition of piety in the Old Testament is given in the words that Enoch "walked with God," which means, that he lived in the constant sense of his presence and conformed his thoughts and actions to his will (Gen. 5:22). The same is said of Noah (6:9), and Abraham (17:1). Righteousness and holiness consist in observing the law of God, which is the expression of his will, and commands us to love him with all our heart, and our neighbor as ourselves (Deut. 6:5; Lev. 19:18).

The New Testament presents the same view in a more perfect form. Supreme love to God and men is declared by Christ to be the very essence, the sum and substance of piety, the fulfilment of the whole law (Matt. 22:37-40; Rom. 13:9). Christianity appeared as a fact, as the manifestation of the Divine life in human form. Christ is the prophet, priest, and king of humanity, the Way, the Truth, and the Life. So Christian piety begins in the individual with a divine fact, with the regeneration of the whole inner man, and ends with the resurrection of the body to life everlasting. It purifies, transforms and sanctifies all the faculties of the soul, it lifts the intellect into the sphere of truth, it brings the will into harmony with the will of God, and gives peace and joy to the heart. The Christian is a follower of Christ; he is united to him as the member is to the head, as the branch is to the vine (John 15:1-5). He is "a new creature" in Christ, and "all things are become new" (2 Cor. 5:17; Gal. 6:15). Believers are constantly represented in the New Testament as being "in Christ," that is, as having their life in Christ, from whom they receive all spiritual strength and nourishment. "I live no longer myself," says Paul, "but Christ liveth in me" (Gal. 2:20). "When Christ, who is our life, shall appear, then ye shall also appear with him in glory" (Col. 3:4). The *vital* union of the believer with Christ is one of the most precious doctrines of the Bible.

What our Saviour says of the kingdom of heaven, that it is like unto leaven which a woman took and hid in three measures of meal, till the whole was leavened (Matt. 13:33), applies to the effect of the kingdom upon individual life as well as upon humanity at large. It is an all-pervading and all-transforming power working invisibly from within upon every department of life. A perfect Christian is a perfect man, and the perfect kingdom of heaven is perfect humanity.

All life consists in a double activity, a receptive and spontaneous action, corresponding to the in-breathing and out-breathing of the vital air in our bodily existence. Both are necessary to sustain life. When the process of respiration is stopped, the circulation of blood through the lungs is retarded, carbonic acid accumulates in the blood, and asphyxia and death are the inevitable consequence. Thus also the religious life has the twofold form of faith and of love; and if one ceases, the spiritual life itself must die out. By faith we assimilate to ourselves the divine life; it is the organ for the supernatural, the spiritual hand and mouth, by which we receive Christ himself and all the benefits of his work. Faith is not merely an assent of the intellect or a state of feeling, but also a motion of the will, and unites our whole person with the life of Christ. Only in this living form can faith be said to justify and to save men. As a mere theoretic belief, opinion or even conviction, it may be possessed by demons who tremble (James 2 : 10). But this divine life which we must first receive by faith, cannot remain shut up within us; it will manifest and exert itself and pass over into others. This is love, the necessary fruit of faith, or faith itself turned outward, as it were, made practical in relation to God and to man. Hence the apostle speaks of "faith working by love" (πίστις δι' ἀγάπης ἐνεργουμένη, Gal. 5: 6), as the sum and substance of true Christian piety. Prayer, of course, is likewise a necessary exercise of piety; it represents the emotional element, as faith represents the theoretical or intellectual, and love the practical or moral element. Prayer is an ascension of the soul to God, and is followed by his blessing in return.

CHAPTER XLVII.

INDIVIDUAL, DENOMINATIONAL, AND CATHOLIC PIETY.

Religion has various degrees and forms as regards its extent or circumference.

1. Individual or personal piety. Religion is a matter between God and the individual conscience. Each man must settle it for himself. No man can be pious or moral for another any more than he can eat and drink and sleep for another. Every Christian must repent, believe and show his faith by a holy life. Every one must work out with trembling and fear his own salvation.

2. Social piety. Man is a social being, and religion is eminently

social. Temporary retirement and seclusion is necessary and helpful for the development of character. Every serious man wants from time to time to be alone with God. Moses, Elijah, John the Baptist, and our Saviour, spent days and nights and weeks in solitude, but they came out with new vigor and fresh power to do the will of God and to benefit their fellow-men. The anchorets fled from the world and the Church, but they carried the evil heart and the temptations of flesh and blood into the desert, and experienced the truth of the sentence: "Woe to him who stands alone, for if he falls he has no one to raise him up." The object of Christian piety is not to go out of society, but to improve it, and to transform the world into the kingdom of God.

3. Congregational or churchly piety. This is the first form of an expansion of personal religion into social religion. It identifies itself with a particular congregation, and takes an active interest in its devotions and activities.

4. Denominational piety goes further and extends to a whole denomination or confession. Every one should be loyal to his denomination and promote its welfare. But denominational loyalty often degenerates into bigotry and sectarianism, which puts a part above the whole, and is only an extended selfishness.

5. Catholic piety is in sympathy with the whole Church of Christ in all lands and nations. It springs from a hearty belief in "the holy Catholic Church and the communion of saints." It is the best cure of selfish individualism and sectarian bigotry. It must not be confounded with latitudinarianism and indifferentism, which is a negative and hollow pseudo-catholicity. True catholicity is positive and inclusive. It rests on a broad and comprehensive view of Christianity in all its types, phases, and manifestations, and kisses the image of the Saviour in every one of his followers. It breathes the spirit of Christ's sacerdotal prayer for the perfect unity of all believers. Its motto is: "I am a Christian, and no stranger to any thing that is Christian." It thanks God for every progress of Christ's kingdom, for the conversion of every soul, for the building of every church and benevolent institution, no matter by what denomination or party. "I rejoice," says Paul, "yea, and I will rejoice" if "Christ is proclaimed, whether in pretense or in truth" (Phil. 1: 18).

SECOND SECTION: THEOLOGY.

CHAPTER XLVIII.

DEFINITIONS OF THEOLOGY.

THEOLOGY (from θεός and λόγος) or DIVINITY (*Gottesgelehrtheit*) means, literally, a discourse concerning God, or the knowledge of God.

It was so used by the Greeks with reference to their theogonies, or theories concerning the origin and genealogy of the gods. Those who were well informed on the nature and history of the gods and taught that knowledge, were called "theologians." Sometimes the term was restricted to those who described the cosmogony as a theogony, in distinction from the "physiologians," who explained the genesis of the world as a development of the elements of nature. There were also "semi-theologians" or "mixed theologians," who took a middle ground and combined the theological with the physiological theory. Aristotle gives to the highest branch of philosophy the name *theology*.*

Each religion of some degree of culture has its own theology: heathen mythology is based on myths; rabbinical theology, on the Old Testament and the Talmud; Mohammedan theology, on the Koran and its commentators.

Christian theology is the science of the religion of the Bible and the Church. It is, however, variously defined according to extent.

1. Theology in the narrowest sense: The doctrine of the

---

* Aristotle divides philosophy into theoretical, practical, and poetical; and theoretical philosophy again, he classes under the heads of Physic, Mathematic, and Theology (*Metaph.*, xi. 7: τρία γένη τῶν θεωρητικῶν ἐστί, φυσική, μαθηματική, θεολογική). The last he identifies with metaphysic or "the first philosophy" (πρώτη φιλοσοφία), which culminates in the doctrine of God. He places it above all other sciences. Practical philosophy he divided into Ethic, Economic, and Politic. Philo calls Moses ὁ θεολόγος.

Deity of Christ, the Logos (ὁ λόγος is θεός, John 1 : 1), or also the doctrine of the Trinity.

In this sense, John the Evangelist was called "the theologian" or "the Divine" par excellence, on account of the clearness and emphasis with which he sets forth the Deity of Christ, especially in the Prologue to his Gospel. The English version affixes the title to the heading of the Apocalypse, but without manuscript authority. Gregory of Nazianzus also was honored with this title for his theological orations in vindication of Christ's Divinity against the Arian heresy. This use of the word is restricted to the fathers of the Nicene age and has passed away.

2. In a wider sense: The Doctrine of God (his existence, attributes, unity and trinity), in distinction from Christology, Pneumatology, Anthropology, Soteriology, Eschatology, and other parts of Dogmatic theology.

This is in strict conformity to the etymology, and is still in use.

3. Didactic Theology or Dogmatic; that is, a systematic exposition and vindication of all the articles of the Christian faith. This is regarded as the principal branch of Systematic Theology, and formerly included also Christian Ethic, or an exposition of Christian duty.

So Augustin, the mediæval schoolmen, the Reformers and older Protestant divines. In this sense Calvin was called "the theologian" by Melanchthon (at the Colloquy at Worms in 1541). It is still the prevailing use among English and American divines, who entitle their dogmatic works "Theology" or "Systematic Theology" (Hill, Dick, Hodge, Strong), or "Dogmatic Theology" (Shedd); while on the Continent it has given way to the more definite terms "Dogmatic" (*Glaubenslehre*) and "Ethic" (*Sittenlehre*).

4. In the widest sense: The whole science of the Christian religion, as revealed in the Bible, developed in history, and carried forward in the life of the Church through the functions of the gospel ministry.

This definition embraces all departments of sacred learning, exegetical, historical, systematic, and practical. This is now the usual understanding of the term, when we speak of the "study of Theology," "Theological Seminaries," "Theological Libraries," "Theological Encyclopædias," etc. German divines use it always either in this last and widest, or in the second restricted, sense; while the first is antiquated, and the third is better expressed by Dogmatic or Dogmatic Theology.

CHAPTER XLIX.

NATURAL AND REVEALED THEOLOGY.

The distinction between Natural and Revealed Religion and Theology refers to the source from which they are derived. Strictly speaking, it applies only to religion; for theology is neither natural nor revealed, but the science of one or the other.

Natural Theology deals with those truths which may be inferred from the creation, the rational and moral constitution of man, and the general course of history, and which are found with different degrees of clearness in all the religions of civilized nations. These truths are the being, power, wisdom and goodness of God, his providence, the freedom and moral responsibility of man, the immortality of the soul, the future reward of the good and the punishment of the wicked. Paul expressly concedes to the heathen a certain knowledge of God as the Creator, and a moral sense of right and wrong.*

But the truths of Natural Religion are only imperfectly known outside of Christendom, and associated with errors in all heathen religions. They become fully known in the light of the Christian revelation. There is a great difference between reason in its natural state and reason as enlightened by the Scriptures and by Christian education. A well-trained Christian child knows more about the truths of natural religion than a heathen priest or an infidel philosopher.

Revealed Theology embraces the supernatural truths of the Christian religion which can be known only from the Bible and the Church, such as the Trinity, the Divinity of Christ and the Holy Spirit, the atonement, the Church and the Sacraments, regeneration and sanctification, the general resurrection and life everlasting.

Augustin made a distinction between *lumen naturæ* and *lumen gratiæ*, and this distinction runs through the whole scholastic theology. Raymond de Sabunde, a Spaniard and professor of

---

* Rom. 1:19-21; 2:14, 15; Acts 14:15-17; 17:24-29. Comp. Ps. 19: 1-4; Ps. 104.

philosophy and theology at Toulouse, first carried out this distinction in his *Theologia Naturalis* or *Liber Creaturarum* in 1436. He is the father of Natural Theology. He maintains that the book of nature and the book of the Bible are both revealed by God, and harmonize. Every creature is a certain letter written by the finger of God, and out of these letters the universe is composed. But it is not sufficient; and hence the second book was given to men to enable them how to read the first.

English Theists of the seventeenth century, especially the Cambridge Platonists (Cudworth, More, Whichcote, Wilkins, Stillingfleet, Baxter, Boyle, Samuel Clarke, etc.) cultivated Natural Theology in the interest of Revealed Theology against the rising skepticism.

But the Deists (Lord Herbert, Collins, Toland, Woolston, Tindal, etc.) turned the weapons forged in defense of Christianity, against it. They exaggerated the truths of Natural Religion at the expense of Revealed Religion, and declared the latter superfluous or denied it altogether.

The anti-Deistic writers (Butler, Lardner, Paley) resumed the defense of the Revealed Religion of the Bible and showed its superiority over, and agreement with, Natural Religion. They also proved that the same objections which the Deists raised against Revealed Religion, may be raised against Natural Religion; while on closer examination both will be found to be in harmony with the constitution and course of nature.

The scientific study of nature necessitates in its ultimate consequences the belief in a supernatural personality of supreme intelligence and goodness, as the only sufficient cause of the stupendous result of this universe.

Dogmatic Theology must embrace all the doctrines of Natural and Revealed Religion in systematic order.

CHAPTER L.

THEOLOGY AND RELIGION.

Religion and Theology are related to each other as life and knowledge, or as practice and theory. Theology is the scientific consciousness of religion. Herein lies their unity and their difference.

1. Religion is universal; theology is limited to scholars. Every human being has a capacity for religion, and ought to be religious in order to attain the true aim of life. But only ministers and teachers of the Church are called to theological scholarship. The theologians are the brains, the eyes, and ears in the body of the Church. Beating hearts, working hands and ready feet are just as necessary.

But a popular knowledge of theology expands with Christian civilization. There is growing up a theological lay-public, larger in the Protestant than in the Greek or Latin churches, and largest in Great Britain and in North America, where popular theological books are most numerous and have by far the widest circulation. The laity are no longer under the control of the clergy; they read and think for themselves, and are becoming more and more interested in theological questions as far as they touch practical Christian life.

2. Religion precedes theology. It furnishes all the material to work upon. So nature is before natural science, man before anthropology and psychology, the earth before geography, history before historiography. *Pistis* is the mother of *Gnosis*. "*Fides præcedit intellectum.*"

3. Religion produces theology. The science of theology is not born from the barren womb of skepticism or indifferentism, but from faith in God and love of truth. "*Credo ut intelligam*" (Anselm). The Christian divine is as sure of his faith as he is of his reason, yea, of his very existence.

Des Cartes, in opposition to the dogmatic assumptions of scholasticism, starts with the purely negative principle: "*De omnibus dubitandum est.*" But this applies only to historical criticism, which can take nothing for granted on mere authority, and must proceed without prejudice and prepossession. Theology rests on the best authority, on divine revelation. Philosophy has its origin in love of the truth and in an honest desire to know it. Heresy and infidelity no doubt stimulate the investigation of truth and are, negatively, of great benefit to it, but the propelling force of theology and philosophy is intrinsic and inherent. In the full assurance of faith and its harmony with reason, theology may boldly venture on speculation and the closest critical examination. Even Des Cartes must admit a positive starting-point for philosophy, viz., the certainty of self-conscious existence: "*Cogito, ergo sum.*" It is God's exclusive privilege to create the world *ex nihilo;* but as for man, the maxim holds good: *"Ex nihilo nihil fit."*

4. Theology reacts favorably or unfavorably on the state of religion. The fruit contains new seed. The power of ideas is irresistible. Ideas rule the intellectual and spiritual world.* They pass from the university to the pulpit, from the pulpit to the congregation, from the congregation to the family. The theology of the Reformation shook the Church and the world, and opened new avenues of thought and action. On the other hand, a bad theology has the opposite effect. Rationalism and infidelity have wrought fearful devastation in the Churches on the Continent of Europe, though only temporarily.

Religion and theology are therefore inseparably connected, they decay or flourish together.

CHAPTER LI.

THEOLOGY AND PHILOSOPHY.

Theology is related to Philosophy as revelation is to reason, as the order of grace is to the order of nature.

Philosophy is the fundamental science, the science of the general laws of all existence, the science of sciences. It penetrates from the surface to the depth beneath, from the outward phenomena to the underlying laws, from the particulars to the general. Every branch of knowledge has its philosophy or may be treated philosophically, as well as empirically and historically.

1. Theology is limited to the sphere of religion or the relation of man to God; its connection with other departments of knowledge is indirect. Philosophy has a much more extensive range of subjects, and embraces God, man, and nature; it is as wide as the spiritual and material universe.

2. On the other hand, theology is more comprehensive in the sphere of religion, and covers all the details of exegesis, Church history and the practical work of the ministry. Philosophy is confined to the speculative or metaphysical part of religion, to dogmatic and moral theology. There is, however, room also for a philosophy of church history, which would deal with the laws

---

* The German proverb, *Geld regiert die Welt,* applies only to the material world. The "almighty dollar," however useful as a means to an end, can not produce a single idea.

of development and the leading characteristics of the several epochs and types of Christianity. Such a work is greatly needed and worthy of a life's study.

3. Theology starts from revelation and the consciousness of God (*Gottesbewusstsein*); philosophy starts from reason and self-consciousness (*Selbstbewusstsein*). The theologian begins with faith and has for his motto: "CREDO, *ergo sum; Fides præcedit intellectum.*" The philosopher begins with thought and says: "COGITO, *ergo sum; Intellectus præcedit fidem.*" The former is guided by the revealed word of God, the latter by the laws of thought. Theological truth is measured by agreement with the Scriptures, philosophical truth, by logical consistency and conclusiveness. Sound theology must be biblical, sound philosophy must be rational. The theologian tries to comprehend and explain the divinely revealed order of grace and the way to salvation; the philosopher reconstructs the universe *a priori*, out of his own mind.

4. Theology is in possession of the truth; philosophy is in quest of truth.* Theology has an infallible guide in the sure word of prophecy concerning the supernatural world and the order of salvation. Theology is the science of revelation, philosophy is the science of reason. Theology knows that there *is* a God, and that man *is* immortal for weal or woe. Philosophy teaches that on principles of sound reasoning there *may* be a God and there ought to be a God, that man *may* be and probably is immortal; but it cannot give certainty. Theology knows the poison of sin and its antidote in salvation by Christ; philosophy must admit the terrible fact of moral disorder and misery in the world, but it cannot explain and remedy it. Philosophy may, however, show the possibility and the necessity of a divine revelation and aid in comprehending it.

5. Philosophy is purely speculative, and takes for granted the knowledge of facts and details. Theology is to a large extent positive and empirical, dealing with given facts, and minute investigations, as in Exegesis and Church History; but it is also speculative in Dogmatic and Ethic, where it deals with doctrines and principles, and endeavors not only to prove them from the Bible and the confessions of faith, but also to vindicate them before the tribunal of reason.

Systematic theology and philosophy go over the same ground

* Picus a Mirandola: "*Philosophia quærit, religio possidet veritatem.*"

and have the same end in view. To Christian Dogmatic corresponds Philosophy of Religion; to Christian Ethic corresponds Moral Philosophy or Philosophical Ethic. The doctrinal part of Church History, since the Christian era, runs parallel with the History of Philosophy. They cannot be indifferent to each other, but are either friendly or hostile. Higher philosophy must notice the doctrines of revelation, *e.g.*, the trinity, incarnation and atonement; while theology on its part must pay attention to the tenets of natural religion, as the existence and attributes of God, the freedom of the will, the immortality of the soul.

6. There is no fundamental (principial) or necessary antagonism between philosophy and theology, as little as there is between reason and revelation, knowledge and faith, nature and grace. They proceed from the same God of truth, and will ultimately meet in perfect harmony. They pursue independent parallel lines of investigation, and may agree or disagree. If they disagree, the fault lies not in philosophy or theology as such, but in the imperfection of the philosopher or theologian. There have always been Christian philosophers as well as philosophical (speculative) theologians. The same is true of the relation of natural sciences to religion. The Bible teaches religion, but does not profess to teach geography, geology, astronomy, biology, chronology, or any other science; and hence does not contradict them or forbid their freest and fullest development. Science and religion represent different interests, and must be pursued independently.

Examples of Christian philosophers and scientists, and speculative theologians: Justin Martyr, Clement of Alexandria, Origen, Athanasius, Gregory of Nyssa, John of Damascus, Augustin, Anselm, Thomas Aquinas, Calvin, Jonathan Edwards, Jacob Boehme, Bacon, Newton, Kepler, Leibnitz, Schelling, Jacobi, Schleiermacher, Ulrici, Lotze, Coleridge, Sir William Hamilton, Rothe, Dorner. "*Philosophia obiter libata abducit a Deo, penitus hausta reducit ad eundem.*" (Bacon).

7. The normal relation of theology and philosophy in the present order of things is similar to that between Church and State in America, *i.e.*, a peaceful and friendly independence. A state of subserviency of the one to the other retards or obstructs the normal progress of both. Every age has its own ruling system of philosophy, which reflects the spirit of the age in its

highest scientific self-consciousness; but theology should rise above the ever-changing currents of human speculation and derive its inspiration from the eternal Word of God. *"Amicus Plato, amicus Aristoteles, sed magis amica veritas."* " Thy word is truth " (John 17 : 17).

8. Use of the study of philosophy to the theologian:

(a) Material use. It enables him to measure the extent of the speculative capacity of the human mind in grasping the truth, and to compare the various and varying systems of philosophy with the system of revelation.

(b) Formal use. It is the best discipline of the mind and indispensable for a successful cultivation of systematic theology. Philosophy can remove the obstacles to faith, refute the objections, and prove that the doctrines of revelation, although above reason, are not contrary to reason. A false philosophy may make proud unbelievers, true philosophy makes humble and reverent believers. The end of philosophy is, to show the need of revelation.*

CHAPTER LII.

THEOLOGY AND THE GOSPEL MINISTRY.

1. Theology is necessary for the well-being of the Church and for an efficient ministry of the gospel.

(a) The minister is first of all a preacher of the Word of God (*Verbi divini minister*), and an educator of the people in the way of Life. He should be thoroughly furnished for the efficient and faithful discharge of this sublime duty. He must be familiar with the Holy Scriptures, and be able clearly and forcibly to expound and apply them to the wants of the congregation in the present age. Paul requires bishops and presbyters to be "apt to teach." But no man can teach who has not been taught himself, and knows much more than his pupils.

(b) The minister must lead the devotions, administer the sacraments, and conduct the whole public worship. This requires fervor, dignity, and solemnity, and much careful prepara-

---

* *" Studire nur und raste nie,*
  Du bringst's nicht weit mit deinen Schlüssen.
 Das ist das Ende der Philosophie :
   Zu wissen, dass wir glauben müssen.' (Em. Geibel.)

tion. He is a priest, not in a literal, but spiritual sense.* All Christian believers are priests, having a direct access to the throne of grace, and are directed to offer spiritual sacrifices of prayer and praise; but the minister takes the lead.

(c) As a pastor or shepherd ($ποιμήν$), the minister has to lead the flock of Christ, to feed the sheep and lambs, to be the spiritual counselor and comforter of immortal souls in their moral relations, trials and temptations, and to conduct them from the cradle to the threshold of eternity; all of which requires knowledge of the human heart, wisdom, discretion, experience and a high order of moral character.

2. Theology is especially important for the Protestant minister, and in the present age.

The Greek or Roman priest has less need of a thorough education. He is seldom required to preach; he is chiefly a functionary; he depends upon the objective teaching of the Church and the prescribed liturgical forms; his principal duty is to read mass; his throne is the altar and the confessional.

The Protestant minister must expound and enforce the Scriptures in every regular service; his throne is the pulpit. He stands or falls with his personal character and merit. He cannot shelter himself behind the dignity of his office. He will lose his authority over the thinking classes unless he keeps pace with the progress of knowledge and practices what he preaches.

The editor is a powerful rival of the preacher; the daily press is a daily pulpit, with the largest audience. Our age is distinguished for high scientific culture, the diffusion of knowledge, the spirit of inquiry, the pride of reason.

Yet, after all, the minister must depend on spiritual and moral rather than intellectual power; and in this chief department he need fear no rivalry. The ministry will be indispensable as long as men are religious and have immortal souls to save. It administers counsel, comfort, and blessing at every important stage of life from the cradle to the grave, in seasons of prosperity and adversity, and can less be spared for the well-

* The English word "priest" and the German "Priester" are contracted from "presbyter;" but in the New Testament $πρεσβύτερος$ is equivalent to $ἐπίσκοπος$, and means ruler and teacher, not $ἱερεύς$ or *sacerdos*. The literal sacerdotal idea, with the corresponding ideas of altar and sacrifice, was introduced into the Christian ministry by Cyprian in the third century.

being of society and the happiness of the home than any other profession or occupation.

3. The Church has always demanded a suitable preparation for the ministry and provided the means for it.

Examples from the Bible: Moses learned in all the wisdom of Egypt; the training of the Prophets; the school of John the Baptist; the personal instruction of Christ; the pentecostal outfit; Paul's hellenistic and rabbinical training. From the history of the Church: the catechetical schools and theological seminaries of Alexandria, Antioch, etc.; convents; cathedral schools; universities; theological colleges, and seminaries.

4. Theological learning is not sufficient to qualify a man for the gospel ministry. The most learned divine may be a very poor preacher and pastor; while, on the other hand, moral and spiritual qualities may to a considerable extent make up for serious defects of education. Familiarity with the Bible, knowledge of human nature, sound common sense, and fervent piety are more important for a successful ministry than any amount of scholastic learning. Moreover, God is not bound to any rules. He can call prophets from the plough or the sheepfold or the net as well as from colleges and universities.

5. A minister must first of all be called by the Holy Spirit and prompted by love to God and to immortal souls. He must be a man of living faith and fervent zeal. He must keep in view the salvation of the world as the great practical end of the ministerial office. It is the harmonious development of intellectual and spiritual training that constitutes the true theologian or divine. He must be taught of God as well as of men, and therefore able to teach others the way of life by word and example.

CHAPTER LIII.

HINTS FOR THE PROFITABLE STUDY OF THEOLOGY.

1. Study Devoutly and Prayerfully.

In the old trio of qualifications which constitute the theologian, *oratio* is put first, and is followed by *meditatio* and *temptatio*. To Luther is ascribed the saying: "*Bene orasse est bene studuisse.*" He practiced it, like all great and good preachers before and after him. Reverence is essential to all piety. Theology is a sacred science. "*Sancta sancte tractanda.*" On its portal stands the inscription: "*Procul abeste profani.*" It is the science of God, and God is an object of adoration and praise, rather than of curious speculation. By thinking we seek God; by prayer we find him. Study makes a scholar; prayer makes a saint. Goodness is better than greatness; godliness better than scholarship. We admire learning, we respect and love virtue. Aim to combine both.

Refresh yourselves from the fountain of life before you open your books. Put the spiritual before the intellectual, the devotional before the critical. The secret communion with God is the best consecration of your studies and makes them fruitful for the welfare of your fellow-men and the building up of the Redeemer's kingdom.

2. *Study Enthusiastically.*

Nothing great and good can be done without enthusiasm. It inspires the mind, it stirs the heart, it stimulates the will, it gives itself wholly to the pursuit of the object of its choice. One of the finest gifts of youth is that unquenchable ardor of the soul, that burning thirst for knowledge, that energy and courage, which shrinks from no difficulty. A double-minded and half-hearted man never accomplishes much in this world. He is "unstable in all his ways."

Throw, then, your whole mind into your studies; be *totus in illis.* Be all ear while you hear; be all eye while you read; be all thought while you think. In this way you will accomplish more in a day than a slow and indifferent student can in a week.

3. *Study Judiciously.*

Genuine enthusiasm is not inconsistent with moderation and judgment. Μηδὲν ἄγαν. "*Ne quid nimis.*" Moderation in all things. The best thing may be undone by being overdone. Many a scholar, in this stimulating climate of ours, studies himself away to an untimely grave by a neglect of needed rest and healthy exercise.

4. "*Sana Mens in Corpore Sano.*"

"Cleanliness is next to godliness." Keep your body clean,

healthy, and vigorous, that it may be an efficient organ of the immortal soul.

Give a portion of each day to innocent recreation in the open air, either alone with your God, or in the company of congenial friends, which of itself is one of the best recreations.

The ascetic contempt and neglect of the body springs from the radical error that matter is essentially evil, and that the body is the prison of the soul. This error crept into the ancient Church through Gnosticism; and, though theoretically repudiated as a heresy, it perpetuated itself practically in monasticism. There were hermits in Egypt who thought that godliness thrives best in filth, and who never washed their face nor combed their hair, except on holy Easter.

Christianity begins with the washing of regeneration and ends with the resurrection of the body. In the life of our Saviour you look in vain for any trace of ascetic austerity and self-mortification. Every thing in him was healthy, serene, hopeful. He associated freely with men and women, and loved little children. He rejoiced with the rejoicing. He attended the wedding feast and turned water into wine. He admired the birds of the air and the flowers of the field, and, in his incomparable parables, drew sublime lessons from the book of Nature.

5. *Study Systematically.*

"Time is money," says the proverb. Rather, it is more than money; for money may be replaced, but time cannot; once lost, it is lost forever. Agassiz declined a tempting offer to deliver a course of lectures at a thousand dollars a lecture, because "he could not afford time to make money." A noble sentiment, well worth remembering in this age of the degrading worship of Mammon. Economize your precious time so as to turn it to the best account. This can only be done by order and system.

Be regular in your habits, punctual in your appointments. Sleep no longer than is necessary for health. Make a wise distribution of the day between study and recreation and between the different kinds of study. Get up early in the morning* and

---

* The German proverb says: "*Morgenstunde hat Gold im Munde.*" The English proverb is still better:

"Early to bed and early to rise
Makes a man healthy, wealthy and wise."

keep wide awake during the day. The last is the most important.

Do not put off till to-morrow what you can do to-day. "Strike the iron while it is hot." Answer a letter at once; if you wait a week, you have to read it over again and lose that much time. Give your first hour to prayer and devotional reading. Then take up your regular studies, dividing and adjusting the time according to your lectures and the particular stage of your course. Postpone the lighter studies and miscellaneous reading to the afternoon or evening. We must acquaint ourselves with the march of events and the state of public opinion on the great questions of the day if we would exert a wholesome influence on the living generation. Yet true scholarship is not born of ephemeral productions, which pass away with the fleeting moment; it comes from the thorough mastery of works of profound thought and earnest research, which outlive the author and his age.

6. *Study Faithfully.*

Enter upon your studies in the fulness of faith; faith in the existence and the supreme value of truth. The knowledge of truth, the whole truth, and nothing but the truth, is the object of study.

Skepticism may stimulate inquiry, explode prejudices, dispel superstition, and provoke abler and stronger defences of the truth. But the mission of doubt is negative. It can destroy, but it cannot build up. Faith is the fruitful mother of knowledge, the pioneer of inventions, discoveries, and all great enterprises. Faith can remove mountains of difficulties, and is sure to succeed at last. Go forth, then, in the panoply of faith, and boldly meet the mocking Goliath of unbelief. A little stone from the brook can slay him, if you hit his brain.

7. *On Reading.*

Study the best books of the best authors, and the Bible most of all. "*Non multa, sed multum.*"

Digest as you read, and impress the contents indelibly on your mind. Use the pen and note down or mark on the margin what is most important and worth remembering. "*Legere sine calamo est dormire."* Lord Bacon says: "Reading makes a full man, conference a ready man, writing an exact man."

So exercise your memory as to become in a measure independent of books. Make your memory a library, which you can use anywhere and at any time. It is of inestimable value to have in your brain a treasury of Bible passages, hymns, and a perennial flower garden of classical poetry.

CHAPTER LIV.

THE STUDENT'S LIBRARY.

A library is the student's working tool and armory. Books are his best friends, always on hand to give instruction, entertainment, and encouragement. A book contains the author's best thoughts in his best words. Some books are better than their authors; but some authors are greater and better than their books. Some exercise most influence through what they do or write; others by what they are, or by their personal magnetism. Milton says: "A good book is the precious life-blood of a master-spirit embalmed and treasured up on purpose to a life beyond life."

Books that live cannot be manufactured to order; they grow spontaneously like trees. But most books fall still-born from the press.

Great care should be taken by the student in selecting his library. It can only be done gradually as he progresses.

The following are some hints.

1. The value of the library depends on its quality rather than its quantity. A selection is better than a collection. A few classics outweigh hundreds of indifferent works. Books, like friends, should be few and well chosen.

2. Get the best books of the best authors in the best editions.

3. Old editions of good books when superseded by the author's corrections and improvements, become bad, being the enemies of the better. This applies especially to exegetical and historical works in an age of rapid progress in discovery and research like ours.

4. The dearest books are the cheapest when they are the most useful. (The same is true of bindings.)

5. Those books are the best which instruct and stimulate most and last longest.

6. Miscellaneous and ephemeral books only burden the shelves; bad books are a nuisance.

7. A theological library should contain:

(*a*) The Bible in the original Hebrew and Greek as well as in English (Authorized and Revised Vers.), with grammars, dictionaries, concordances, and other exegetical helps.

(*b*) Standard works on Church history, Doctrine history, Dogmatic, Ethic, homiletic and pastoral Theology.

(*c*) A Bible Dictionary and a general theological and religious Encyclopædia for convenient reference.

(*d*) Ancient and modern classics, especially poets, for the cultivation of taste and style and the feeding of the flame of enthusiasm for the ideal, the beautiful, and the pure.

CHAPTER LV.

DIVISION OF THEOLOGY.

We divide Theology into four divisions: EXEGETICAL, HISTORICAL, SYSTEMATIC, and PRACTICAL. The first has to do with the normative beginning and infallible record of Christianity; the second with its past history; the third with its present status; and the fourth with its future prospects.

EXEGETIC explains the inspired documents of the Christian religion, which constitute its immovable foundation.

CHURCH HISTORY traces the origin and growth of Christianity from the founding of the Church to the present generation.

SYSTEMATIC Theology systematizes and defends its doctrines and duties, as now held and understood on the basis of the Scriptures and the history of Christianity.

PRACTICAL Theology sets forth its task and progressive work, and connects the professor's chair with the pastor's pulpit.

BOOK II.

EXEGETICAL THEOLOGY.

EXEGETIC.—BIBLICAL LEARNING.

CHAPTER LVI.

GENERAL CONCEPTION OF EXEGETICAL THEOLOGY.

EXEGETICAL Theology or EXEGETIC embraces all that belongs to the learned explanation of the Sacred Scriptures of the Old and New Testaments, or the whole extent of Biblical Literature. It is the science and practice of Biblical interpretation.

It is the first branch of theological study, both in the order of time and in importance, and furnishes the foundation for all other branches. Hence it may be called FUNDAMENTAL Theology. No knowledge is more useful and indispensable to a minister of the gospel than that of the Word of God which is contained in the Bible, and which is the only infallible rule of Christian faith and duty.

Exegesis (ἐξήγησις, from ἐξηγέομαι, to lead out, to explain) signified, at Athens, the interpretation of the religious rites and ceremonies, the signs of heaven, the meaning of oracles, etc. *Exegetes* (ἐξηγηταί) were the sacred interpreters, originally the Eutrepides, afterwards three men appointed by the oracle of Delphi for that office. The theological signification may be derived from John 1:18, where Christ, the Logos, is called the Interpreter or Revealer of God (ἐκεῖνος ἐξηγήσατο, used emphatically, without an object, as *regnat = rex est; docet = doctor est*). The exegetical divine must expound and unfold the hidden meaning of the *written* Word, which reflects the *personal* Word (the Logos, which in Greek signifies both reason and speech, *ratio* and *oratio*).

Etymologically, *Exegetic* and *Hermeneutic* (ἑρμενευ-ική διδαχή, from ἑρμηνεύω, to explain) have the same meaning; but the former is used in a wider sense and embraces both the theory and the practice of interpretation (*Auslegungswissenschaft* and *Auslegungskunst*); while the latter is confined to the principles of interpretation.

CHAPTER LVII.

DEPARTMENTS OF EXEGETIC.

Exegetical theology includes, besides exegesis proper, a number of sciences which are either preparatory or supplementary, and which sum up the scattered results of exegesis in a systematic form. The following scheme exhibits the various branches:
1. Biblical Philology.
    (*a*) Hebrew (and Aramaic).
    (*b*) Greek (Classical and Hellenistic).
2. Biblical Geography.
3. Biblical Natural History.
4. Biblical Archæology or Antiquities.
5. Biblical Introduction or Isagogic.
6. Biblical Criticism.
    (*a*) Textual Criticism.
    (*b*) Literary Criticism.
7. Biblical Canonic.
8. Biblical Hermeneutic.
9. Biblical History (with Contemporary History of the Old and New Testaments, *Zeitgeschichte*).
10. Biblical Theology.

The last two branches are a systematic summary of the results of exegesis and connect it with Church History and Systematic Theology, where they more properly belong.

CHAPTER LVIII.

THE BIBLE.

The Scriptures of the Old and New Covenants are the subjects of exegesis and the material on which it is employed. They are the sacred books of the Christians, the inspired record of divine revelation and the supreme rule of faith and practice.

In one aspect the Bible is like any other book or literary production, and must be interpreted according to the laws of human thought and human speech. In another aspect it is different from all other books, and must be handled with peculiar care and reverence. It has a double origin and double character melted into one. Like the person and work of our Lord and Saviour, who is himself the central theme and guiding light of the Bible, it is theanthropic or divine-human. It has a truly human body, but the animating spirit is the eternal truth of God. As the Divine Logos became flesh and assumed our human nature—body, soul, and spirit, so the Word of God became flesh in the letter of the Scriptures.

The mechanical theory of a literal inspiration ignores or minimizes the human element: it confounds inspiration with dictation and reduces the sacred writers to passive organs or clerks of the Holy Spirit, contrary to the dealings of God with men as free and responsible agents; while the rationalistic theory ignores or minimizes the divine element and obliterates the specific distinction between biblical inspiration and extra-biblical illumination.

And as to the relationship of the two elements, we must avoid a confusion on the one hand, and a mechanical separation on the other. The Bible is both divine and human all through, but without mixture and without separation.* We cannot say that the thoughts only are divine; while the words are altogether human. Both thoughts and words, contents and form, are divine, and human as well. They constitute one life, which kindles life in the heart of the believing reader. The Spirit of God dwelt in the Prophets and Apostles and directed them in the process of meditation and composition, but in a free way, and through the medium of the ordinary mental faculties. Every biblical writer has not only his own style, but also his own conception of divine truth, his own mode of reasoning, and used his memory and judgment and all available means of information as much as any ordinary writer (compare the preface to Luke 1: 1–4); and yet it is equally true that the Prophets "spake from God, being moved by the Holy Spirit" (2 Peter 1: 21). The more we study James, Peter, Paul, and John, and the four Evangelists, the more we find the pervading variety of human individualities and the pervading unity of divine truth in all of them, and in their thoughts as well as their style.

The *fact* of inspiration, that is, the action of the divine mind upon the Prophets and Apostles, is as clear and undeniable as the action of the human soul upon the human body; but the *mode*

* Hence we may say of the Bible with Origen: πάντα θεῖα καὶ ἀνθρώπινα πάντα.

of inspiration is as mysterious as the mode of the soul's operation upon the body. The Christian creeds and confessions assert or assume the fact, but do not define the mode, of inspiration, and leave this an open question for theological science.*

The doctrine of inspiration, as we have intimated, runs parallel with Christology, and the false theories correspond to the Christological errors which must be carefully avoided: (1) Ebionism, which denies the divine nature of Christ; (2) Gnosticism and Docetism, which deny his human nature; (3) Apollinarianism, which admits only a partial incarnation and denies that Christ had a human spirit (the divine Logos taking the place of reason); (4) Nestorianism, which admits both natures, but separates them abstractly; (5) Eutychianism and Monophysitism, which confound and mix the two natures or absorb the human in the divine; (6) the Kenosis theory, which suspends the divine nature of Christ during the state of humiliation.

CHAPTER LIX.

GENERAL HINTS FOR THE STUDY OF THE BIBLE.

1. Study the Bible as a book divine as well as human; as the Word of God; as the book of life; as the rule of faith.
2. Study it reverently and devoutly as well as critically and scientifically. A purely critical study is a profanation, and deprives us of the spiritual benefit of the Bible.
3. Study it more frequently, earnestly, thoroughly than any other work.
4. Read it often in the original, face to face.
5. Use the best helps: grammar, dictionary, concordance, and commentaries.
6. Read the Bible in the light and faith of Christ, who is the Alpha and Omega, the essence and center of it. Without him it is a sealed book; with him it is the power and wisdom of God unto salvation, the very gate of heaven.
7. Commit the most important passages of the Psalms, the Gospels, and Epistles to memory, as a living concordance ready for constant use.

---

* The only exception is the Helvetic Consensus Formula (1675), which teaches the literal inspiration of the Scriptures and the integrity of the Masoretic text of the Old Testament, including vowels and consonants; but it had only local and ephemeral authority in Switzerland.

SELECT TRIBUTES TO THE BIBLE.

JEROME: "*Qui nescit Scripturas, nescit Dei virtutem, ejusque sapientiam. Ignoratio Scripturarum ignoratio Christi est.*"

AUGUSTIN: "*Habet Scriptura haustus primos, habet secundos, habet tertios, habet infinitos.*"

WESTMINSTER CONFESSION OF FAITH (Ch. I., Sect. IV.): "The authority of the Holy Scripture, for which it ought to be believed and obeyed, dependeth not upon the testimony of any man or church, but wholly upon God (who is truth itself), the author thereof; and therefore it is to be received, because it is the Word of God."—(Yet for the authorship and canonicity of the several books of the Bible we need the testimony of tradition and the judgment of the Church, as witnesses.)

IZAAK WALTON:
"Every hour
I read you, kills a sin,
Or lets a virtue in
To fight against it."

WALTER SCOTT, on his death-bed, called for the reading of *the* book, and, being asked by Lockhart, his son-in-law, what book he meant, replied: "There is but one book." He meant the Bible, of which he wrote (in *The Monastery*) the well-known lines:

"Within that awful volume lies
The mystery of mysteries!
Happiest they of human race,
To whom the Lord has granted grace
To read, to fear, to hope, to pray,
To lift the latch, and force the way;
And better had they ne'er been born,
Who read to doubt, or read to scorn."

GOETHE made the remark: "I am convinced that the Bible grows in beauty the more we understand it, that is, the more we see that every word to which we give a general meaning and a particular application to ourselves, has had a specific and direct reference to definite conditions of time and place." *

HEINRICH EWALD (d. 1875), the great Hebraist and biblical scholar, the highest of the higher critics, holding a Greek Testament in his hand, said to Dean Stanley (who relates this in the Preface to the third volume of his *Lectures on the Jewish Church*, 1878), then a student from Oxford: "In this little book is contained all the wisdom of the world."

FREDERICK W. ROBERTSON.

Sermon on *Inspiration* (*Sermons*, New York ed., pp. 828, 829).
"It is this universal applicability of Holy Scripture which has made

---

* "*Ich bin überzeugt, dass die Bibel immer schöner wird, je mehr man sie versteht, d. h. je mehr man einsieht und anschaut, dass jedes Wort, das wir allgemein auffassen und im besondern auf uns anwenden, nach gewissen Umständen, nach Zeit- und Ortsverhältnissen einen eigenen, besondern, unmittelbar individuellen Bezug gehabt hat.*" (*Gespräche mit Eckermann.*)

the influence of the Bible universal: this book has held spellbound the hearts of nations, in a way in which no single book has ever held men before. Remember, too, in order to enhance the marvelousness of this, that the nation from which it emanated was a despised people. For the last eighteen hundred years the Jews have been proverbially a by-word and a reproach. But that contempt for Israel is nothing new to the world, for before even the Roman despised them, the Assyrian and Egyptian regarded them with scorn. Yet the words which came from Israel's prophets have been the life-blood of the world's devotions. And the teachers, the psalmists, the prophets, and the law-givers of this despised nation spoke out truths that have struck the key-note of the heart of man; and this, not because they were of Jewish, but just because they were of universal application.

"This collection of books has been to the world what no other book has ever been to a nation. States have been founded on its principles. Kings rule by a compact based on it. Men hold the Bible in their hands when they prepare to give solemn evidence affecting life, death or property; the sick man is almost afraid to die unless the book be within reach of his hands; the battle-ship goes into action with one on board whose office is to expound it; its prayers, its psalms are the language which we use when we speak to God; eighteen centuries have found no holier, no diviner language. If ever there has been a prayer or a hymn enshrined in the heart of a nation, you are sure to find its basis in the Bible. There is no new religious idea given to the world, but it is merely the development of something given in the Bible. The very translation of it has fixed language and settled the idioms of speech. Germany and England speak as they speak because the Bible was translated. It has made the most illiterate peasant more familiar with the history, customs, and geography of ancient Palestine than with the localities of his own country. Men who know nothing of the Grampians, of Snowdon, or of Skiddaw, are at home in Zion, the Lake of Gennesareth, or among the rills of Carmel. People who know little about London, know by heart the places in Jerusalem where those blessed feet trod which were nailed to the cross. Men who know nothing of the architecture of a Christian cathedral, can yet tell you all about the pattern of the holy temple. Even this shows us the influence of the Bible. The orator holds a thousand men for half an hour breathless —a thousand men as one, listening to his single word. But this word of God has held a thousand nations for thrice a thousand years spellbound; held them by an abiding power, even the universality of its truth; and we feel it to be no more a collection of books, but *the* book."

HENRY B. SMITH.

From his sermon on the *Inspiration of the Holy Scriptures*, delivered before the Synod of New York and New Jersey, in the First Presbyterian Church at Newark, N. J., Oct. 7, 1855.

"Central in this marvelous volume, its very center of unity, is the Godman, our Saviour, our Prophet, Priest and King, the ever-living Head of a divine kingdom, which is never to pass away. Miracles attest his divine commission, and that of his Prophets and Apostles also; while Prophecy speaks of him in her most exalted strains, proclaiming his advent through thousands of years, and announcing the perpetuity and final victory of his kingdom in those daring promises, which only Omniscience could truly utter, which Omnipotence alone could carry into execution in a manner so indubitable and unexampled.

"And all this is presented in such a wondrous style and method, that human literature has nothing of stateliness or of simplicity, of poetic inspiration or prosaic fidelity, of that self-forgetfulness in the writers which is one of the surest tests of genius, of largeness of grasp and accuracy of delineation, of fervid eloquence, touching appeal and concentrated aim, to be compared even in fugitive analogy with these utterances of the seers of Judæa and the Apostles of Jesus.

"History and experience, too, add their testimony; for this Book of books has had a divine efficacy; its words are spirit and life; penitence still confesses its abasement in the language of David; faith lingers upon the rapt visions of Isaiah; with John we meditate upon the very words of Jesus; with Paul we receive the assurance of redemption in looking unto Christ; with the oldest of the prophets we still anticipate the day when the seed of the woman shall crush all the powers of sin. The human heart knows no depth of spiritual sorrow, no height of spiritual joy, no elevation of faith, no wonder of divine or human love, for which it may not here find fitting speech. And to all the perplexing and final problems of human destiny, this same volume offers a definite, a truly rational, and an authoritative solution. Beyond its revelation no scheme of human wisdom has ever reached. The most arrogant system of pantheistic infidelity only resolves the Christian faith into barren and abstract ideas.

"Such is this Book; and if it be such—if such a work has been written by fallible and sinful men—then we claim that there is an antecedent probability that it is also from God, and not from man alone; that it is given by the inspiration of the Almighty."

PHILIP SCHAFF.

From his Preface to Lange's *Commentary on Matthew* (New York, 1864). Abridged.

"Viewed merely as a literary production, the Bible is a marvelous book, and without a rival. All the libraries of the world could not furnish material enough for so a rich a treasure of the choicest gems of genius, wisdom, and experience. It embraces works of about forty authors, representing the extremes of society, from the throne of the king to the boat of the fisherman; it was written during a period of sixteen centuries, on the banks of the Nile, in the desert of Arabia, in the land of promise, in Asia Minor, in classical Greece, and in imperial Rome; it begins with the creation, it ends with the new heavens and the new earth, and describes all the intervening stages in the revelation of God and in the spiritual development of man. It uses all forms of literary composition; it rises to the highest heights and descends to the lowest depths of humanity; it is acquainted with every joy and every woe; it contains the spiritual biography of every human heart; it is suited to every class of society; it is as universal as the race, and as boundless as eternity. This matchless combination of human excellencies points to its divine character and origin; as the absolute perfection of Christ's humanity is an evidence of His divinity.

"But the Bible is first and last a book of religion. It is a book of life for all ages and nations. It presents the religion of God, both in its preparatory growth under the law and promise, and in its completion under the gospel. It speaks to us as immortal beings on the highest themes, and with irresistible authority. It can instruct, edify, warn, terrify, appease, cheer, and encourage, as no other book. It seizes man in the hidden depths of his intellectual and moral constitution, and goes to the quick of the soul, to that mysterious point where it is connected with the unseen world and with the great Father of spirits. It purifies, ennobles, sanctifies man, and brings him into living union with God. It has light for the blind, strength for the weak, food for the hungry, drink for the thirsty; it has, in precept or example, a counsel for every relation in life, a comfort for every sorrow, a balm for every wound. Like the diamond, it casts its luster in every direction; like a torch, the more it is shaken, the more it shines; like a healing herb, the harder it is pressed, the sweeter is its fragrance. Of all the books in the world, the Bible is the only one of which we never tire, but which we admire and love more and more in proportion as we use it.

"What an unspeakable blessing, that this inexhaustible treasure of divine truth and comfort is now accessible, without material alteration, to almost every nation on earth in its own tongue, and, in Protestant countries at least, even to the humblest man and woman that can read or hear!"

HEINRICH HEINE.

Heinrich Heine, a mocking unbeliever but brilliant poetic genius, makes in the preface to the second edition of his book on *Deutsche Religion und Philosophie*, 1852, the following striking confession of his conversion from atheism to deism:

"I owe my illumination wholly to the reading of one book,—yes, one book, and it is an old plain book, modest and natural as nature itself, as common and unpretentious as the sun which warms us, as the bread which nourishes us;—a book which looks at us as familiarly and benignantly as an old grandmother who reads in it daily, with the dear trembling lips and spectacles on her nose. And this book is simply and properly called *the* book, the Bible, also the Holy Scripture. He who lost his God can find him again in this book, and he who never knew him will feel in it the breath of the divine word."

Heine repeats this confession in his *Bekenntnisse*, 1854.

FIRST SECTION: BIBLICAL PHILOLOGY.
(*Philologia Sacra.*)

CHAPTER LX.

IMPORTANCE OF THE STUDY OF THE ORIGINAL LANGUAGES.

Every branch of theology rests on a secular science; as theological Seminaries rest on Colleges, and Colleges on Academies, and Academies on elementary Schools. The necessary preparation for Exegesis is Biblical philology; that is, the knowledge of the original languages of the Bible,—the Hebrew of the Old, and the Greek of the New Testament.

Language is the key to unlock the reason, and the medium of communication of mind to mind. *Ratio* and *oratio*, the two significations of the Greek *logos*, are intimately connected. The thought is the inward word, or the speech of the mind; the word is the outward thought, its necessary form and expression. "To speak in his heart," means, in Hebrew, to think. We cannot conceive an idea, without clothing it in words, whether we utter them or not. To say, "I know it, but I cannot express it," amounts to a confession that the thought is not yet born, or is involved in obscurity.

By means of translations it is possible to get an intimate knowledge of the Bible sufficient for practical purposes. It would indeed be disastrous for the great mass of mankind, if they had to study Greek and Hebrew before they could understand the sacred volume which teaches them the way of life and salvation.

But without the knowledge of the original we would have no translation at all. And there is a difference between a popular or practical, and a critical or theological understanding and interpretation. For the latter some acquaintance with the original is indispensable. It is a general characteristic of scientific operation to go to the source, to the prime fountain and principle.

Moreover, we have no faultless translations of the Bible. God has made no provision for inspired and infallible translators any more than for infallible commentators, preachers and printers. The best translations admit of constant improvement as the language changes and as the knowledge of the original advances.

Even if we had a perfect translation, it could never be an equivalent for the original. The best translation is only a copy and an imitation. It is an inestimable privilege to study the Bible face to face as it came from the hands of its inspired authors, and to drink the water of life as it gushes fresh from the primitive rock. Zwingli said that he learned the Greek language that he might draw the doctrine of Christ from the fountain ("*ut ex fontibus doctrinam Christi haurire possem*"). Without this knowledge he could not have become a Reformer.

The study or neglect of the original languages of the Scripture is inseparably connected with the prosperity or decay of religion and pure doctrine. The period of the fathers, when the Greek was still a living tongue, was very fruitful in exegetical learning, and the most useful of the fathers were those who studied the Bible most carefully (Origen, Chrysostom, Jerome, Augustin*). In the Middle Ages the knowledge of Greek and Hebrew almost disappeared from the Latin Church; the study of the Bible was sadly neglected, and all sorts of unscriptural traditions were accumulated, and obscured the Christian faith. The Revival of Letters in the 15th and 16th centuries by Agricola, Reuchlin, Erasmus, Melanchthon, and others, was a very important preparation for the Revival of primitive Christianity. The Reformers were good Greek and Hebrew scholars, and rank among the best translators and commentators of all ages.

It must, of course, not be supposed that a knowledge of Greek and Hebrew, however profound, is of itself sufficient to make a theologian. A poor philologist may be a profound divine, while a master in the languages may be a rationalist or unbeliever. All depends at last on the proper spirit. Without faith it is impossible to understand the spiritual depths of the Bible.

* Augustin, however, often missed the sense from his defective knowledge of Greek and his ignorance of Hebrew.

CHAPTER LXI.

CLASSIFICATION OF LANGUAGES.

The languages of the world are divided into three stocks or families.

I. The SEMITIC stock embraces the languages spoken by the descendants of Sem or Shem, one of the sons of Noah (Gen. 10: 21–31); that is, by the nations of Western Asia, in Palestine, Phœnicia, Syria, Mesopotamia, Babylonia, and Arabia. It may also be called the WESTERN ASIATIC or SYRO-ARABIC stock.* It includes the Hebrew, Aramaic (Eastern and Western), Phœnician, Arabic, and Assyrian languages, besides a few subordinate dialects (the Samaritan, Hymaritic, and Ethiopic). The Arabic and New Syriac are still in active use, especially the Arabic, but the Biblical Hebrew, the Old Syriac and other Semitic languages are quite or almost dead.

II. The INDO-GERMANIC or ARYAN or JAPHETIC or INDO-EUROPEAN stock embraces the Sanscrit (the sacred language of the Hindus), the Persian, the classical languages of Greece and Rome, the Romanic, Celtic, Germanic, and Slavonic tongues, with their ramifications.†

---

* The term *Semitic* (as the French, German, and some English writers spell it), or *Shemitic* (after the more accurate transliteration of the Hebrew), has come into use since Eichhorn (1794) and Schlözer (1781), and, though not strictly correct, is preferable to the older designation, *Oriental*, which dates from Jerome, but is too comprehensive according to modern ideas of the Orient, which includes Central and Eastern Asia and Egypt as well as Western Asia. The Semitic family of nations, with corresponding languages and dialects, are: the Hebrews, Phœnicians, Aramæans, Assyro-Babylonians, Arabs, and Abyssinians. According to the ethnological table in Gen. 10 : 22, the sons of Shem were Elam, Asshur, Arpachshad, Lud, and Aram. From Arpachshad are descended the Hebrews and the Arabs. But Elam belongs to the Persian stock; while the Canaanites and Phœnicians, whose language is cognate to the Hebrew, are traced back to Cush (Ethiopia), and several Arabic tribes to Ham (10 : 5, 6).

† The term *Indo-Germanic* denotes the two geographical extremes of these languages and nationalities, but would exclude the Celts who emigrated further West than the Germans. The term *Aryan* (from the Sanscrit *árya*, excellent; akin to the name of the country, *Iran*) would only embrace the Indians and Persians (Iranians). *Indo-European* is a more comprehensive term. The agreement of the languages of this stock has been shown chiefly by Franz Bopp (1791–1867), the founder of the science of Comparative Philology, in his *Vergleichende Grammatik* (Berlin, 1833–52, 6 vols., third ed. 1868–71, 3 vols., translated into French and English). The comparative vocabulary is given in Fick's *Vergleichendes Wörterbuch der indogermanischen Sprachen*, 3d ed. Göttingen, 1874–76, 3 vols.

The Romanic family, derived from the old Latin, embraces the Italian, French, Spanish, Portuguese, and Romansh (in the Grisons, Switzerland). The Celtic family embraces the old British, Irish, Welsh, and Gaelic. The Germanic or Teutonic family: Gothic, Anglo-Saxon, German, Dutch, Danish, Swedish. The Slavonic family: Russ, Polish, Bohemian, Lithuanian.

III. The TURANIAN stock includes the Chinese and cognate languages, which consist of disconnected unchangeable words, without prefixes, suffixes, and inflections denoting relations and modifications of meaning. These languages have no connection with biblical studies, and come in contact with Christianity only on missionary ground.

CHAPTER LXII.

THE SEMITIC LANGUAGES.

Porta Linguarum Orientalium incohavit J. H. PETERMANN *continuavit* HERM. L. STRACK. Berlin, London, Paris, New York (Westermann & Co.). A series of manuals of all Semitic languages, with bibliography, chrestomathy and glossary, prepared by different scholars.—WILLIAM WRIGHT, *Lectures on the Comparative Grammar of the Semitic Languages.* Cambridge, 1890. RENAN, *Histoire Générale des Langues Sémitique.* Paris, 1855, 2d ed., 1858, 2 vols. The second part, the *Système comparé*, has not yet appeared.

There must have been a primitive Semitic race and a primitive Semitic language; but they are lost in the darkness of prehistoric times. We may infer from Gen. 11:2 that the Semites settled in the Tigris-Euphrates Valley, towards which the descendants of Noah were moving ("from the East"). They spread over Western Asia to the Mediterranean coast, and sent colonies to the Delta of Egypt, to North Africa (Carthage), and the south of France (Marseilles). They may be broadly divided into *Northern* Semites: the Aramæans, Canaanites, Phœnicians, Hebrews, Babylonians, Assyrians; and *Southern* Semites: the Arabs and Abyssinians. The Jews and the Arabs still remain, with remnants of a few other branches.

The Semitic languages and dialects resemble one another much more closely than the branches of the Aryan family, which occupy a larger territory and embrace a greater variety of nationalities. They are as closely connected as the old Norse, Gothic, High and Low German, and old English; or as the Latin languages (Roman, Italian, Spanish, Portuguese, Provençal, and French). They have a peculiar phonetic system, a simple syntax, and a limited vocabulary. They are not adapted for philosophy and science, but are very rich in emotional, proverbial, poetic and religious expressions. The Hebrew vocabulary has furnished to the languages of Christian Europe a number of religious terms for which there were no Aryan equivalents.

A striking superficial peculiarity of most Semitic books is, that they are written and read from right to left. But the Assyrian runs from left to right.

The Semitic alphabet has a variety of gutturals—the Arabic no less than six—which are breathed up from the throat and drawn as it were from the depth of the heart, but cannot be reproduced by Occidentals. Herder says of the Hebrew: "It is full of the breath of the soul, it does not *sound*, like the Greek, but it *breathes*, it *lives*."* The Arabic spoken by a native Arab in the East is much more musical than when pronounced by a Western scholar.

The consonants constitute the solid body of the words, animated by vowels, and determine the signification. The stem-words are tri-literal (consisting of three consonants), and dissyllabic. They are enriched in a phonetic manner by the multiplication of sounds, or by doubling the radical consonants, or by attaching new consonants to the root. There are only two genders (no neuter), and only two tenses of the verb,—the *perfect* and the *imperfect*; the perfect for expressing the completed, the imperfect for expressing the incomplete or hypothetical act, whether past, present, or future. The verbs predominate over the nouns. The oblique cases are not marked by case endings (although traces may be found in certain archaic forms), but by prepositions, and the genitive by the *status constructus*, that is, by closely combining the noun in the genitive with the governing noun, so as to make a compound of the two. There is a scarcity of particles and compounds. The structure of sentences is lapidary, detached, isolated, picturesque; no elaborate periods, no involutions, inversions, and transpositions for rhetorical effect. The sentences do not grow, like trees, by logical or

* " *Die Hebräische Sprache tönt nicht, aber sie haucht, sie lebt.*"

organic process, but are piled up like the stones of a building or follow each other like the waves of the sea. In the Hebrew the sentences are usually connected by "and" (*vav* and *vav consecutive*), which by a simple change of vocalization, accentuation, or position may denote simple consecution or purpose or result.

Parallelism—synthetic, or antithetic, or progressive—is characteristic of Semitic poetry, and also of sententious and elevated prose. It resembles the flapping of the two wings of a bird, or the alternate rising and falling of a fountain, or the advancing and receding flow of the tide. It constitutes a peculiar charm of the poetry of the Old Testament, and admits of easy translation into other languages.

The simplicity, boldness, and sublimity of the Semitic languages admirably adapt them to be vehicles of the early revelations of God to the human race. This is especially true of Hebrew.

CHAPTER LXIII.

THE HEBREW.

The Hebrew* is by far the most important of the Semitic languages for the theologian and minister, for all the canonical books of the Old Testament are composed in that language, with the exception of a few Aramaic passages (namely, Daniel 2 : 4–7 : 28; Ezra 4 : 8–6 : 18; 7 : 12–26; Jer. 10 : 11). The Aramaic, however, is closely related to the Hebrew both in its vocabulary and grammatical structure.

The Hebrew language is the medium of the Old Testament revelation. It is simple, natural, childlike, and yet forcible, majestic, and eminently fitted for worship. It is rich in synonyms. It is said to have 2,000 roots to 10,000 words; while the English has fewer roots, but over 200,000 words (the *Century Dictionary* gives about 215,000 words).

The Hebrew surpasses all Semitic languages in prophetic oratory. It has the most important literature. It was probably used by the Canaanites and Phœnicians before the immigration

* Derived from *Eber* or *Heber*, the ancestor of Abraham (Gen. 14 : 13). In the Old Testament it is called "the language of Canaan," or "the Jews' language"; in the New Testament, "the language of the Hebrews," or "Hebrew" ('Εβραΐς διάλεκτος, γλῶσσα τῶν Ἑβραίων, Ἑβραϊστί), is Aramaic. John 5 : 2; 19 : 13; Acts 21 : 40; 22 : 2; 26 : 14; Rev. 9 : 11; 16 : 16.

of Abraham, who originally spoke Aramaic (comp. Gen. 31 : 47). The remains of the Phœnician and the cognate Punic languages in inscriptions, tablets, coins, and sepulchral monuments, agree closely with the Hebrew.

Jewish rabbis, Christian fathers, and some of the older Protestant divines indulged the fancy that the Hebrew was the primitive language, that it was spoken by God and by angels, as well as by Adam in Paradise, and that it prevailed universally till the Flood and the dispersion of Babel. They called it *lingua Dei, lingua angelorum, lingua prophetarum*. The Buxtorfs, father and son, both distinguished for Hebrew and Talmudic scholarship, believed in the literal inspiration of the Old Testament, including the Masoretic vowel-points and accents, and advised all Christians to learn Hebrew that they might praise God in that language. This is a species of pious and learned Bibliolatry.

The Hebrew was transplanted by the patriarchs to Egypt and brought back again by the Israelites to Canaan. It was their mother-tongue during the time of their national independence, and with some modification down to the destruction of Jerusalem, and is their sacred language to this day. The Law and the Prophets are still read and the Psalter chanted from the original in the Jewish synagogues, and prayers are usually printed in Hebrew and another language in parallel columns.

The Hebrew, owing to the greater stability of the Eastern nations, and the Semitic languages as compared with the Aryan, the firm character of the Mosaic institutions, its confinement to sacred literature, and the isolation of the Jews from foreign nations, remained substantially the same during the flourishing period of its literature. Yet we may distinguish three periods in its growth and decay: the Mosaic; the Davidic and Solomonic; the Babylonian and post-exilic. The earliest pre-Mosaic, Mosaic, and post-Mosaic records are marked by grand simplicity and certain archaic forms of speech: here belong the stories of the creation and the fall, and the poetic and prophetic sections of Genesis—the song of Lamech (Gen. 4 : 23); the blessing of Noah (9 : 25–27); the blessing of Jacob (49 : 2–28); the Song of Moses (Ex. 15); the Ten Words (Ex. 20); the Farewell Song and Blessing of Moses (Deut. 32 and 33); the Prayer of Moses (Ps. 90); the Song of Deborah (Judges 5 : 2–31). With David and Solomon begins the golden age of Hebrew literature, which continued down to the exile. To it belong the older Psalms and Proverbs, the prophecies of Isaiah, Micah, Nahum, Habakkuk, Jonah, Amos, Hosea, and probably also the Book of Job, although this is often assigned to an earlier date. During the Babylonian exile the Hebrew language was assimilated to the kindred Aramaic or Chaldee, as may be seen, in various degrees, in the books of Ezra, Nehemiah, Chronicles, Esther, Jeremiah, Ezekiel, Daniel, Haggai, Zechariah, Malachi, and the later Psalms.

Gradually the Aramaic superseded the Hebrew as the living language of the people. It was the mother-tongue of Christ and the Apostles.*

The Jews of the Dispersion used the Greek with a Hebrew coloring and accent, and hence were called *Hellenists*, or Grecian Jews, as distinct from the *Hebrews* in Palestine.

The Hebrew of the Old Testament, after having accomplished its great purpose, died as a spoken tongue and became stereotyped and unalterably fixed for the benefit of future generations. It was thus protected against the changes which every living language in the process of its growth and decay must undergo. The same is the case with the Hellenistic, or Jewish Christian dialect of the New Testament. This fixed character of the Bible language is a positive advantage: it enables the reader to drink from the pure fountain of the original, and facilitates the work of the translator and commentator. The Bible can be easily reproduced in any language without losing its force and beauty by the process.

A knowledge of Hebrew is necessary, or at all events most helpful, to the minister for the understanding of the Old Testament, and also of the New; for the Gospels and Epistles constantly quote from the Law and the Prophets, and point to their fulfilment in Christ. Besides, the Hellenistic Greek is strongly Hebraistic, and many words and phrases derive their full meaning only from the vernacular Aramaic of Christ and the Apostles. The two Testaments are so closely connected in spirit

---

* When the New Testament speaks of Hebrew as then used in Palestine, the Aramaic is meant, as is evident from such words as Bethesda, Gabbatha, Golgotha, Rabbi, Messias, Mammonas, Bar Jonah, Talitha Kumi, Epphatha, Abba, Kephas, Akeldama. Josephus often uses *Hebrew* in the sense of *Aramaic*. Christ is reported by Mark to have spoken Aramaic on three occasions, when he raised the daughter of Jairus (4:41), when he opened the ears of the deaf man (7:34), and when he exclaimed on the cross, "Eloi, Eloi, lamma sabachthani" (15:35). "*Eloi*" is the Syriac form for the Hebrew *Eli* (Ps. 22:1; Matt. 27:46).

and form, that one cannot be understood without the other. "The New Testament is concealed in the Old, the Old Testament is revealed in the New." The mere knowledge of the language is, of course, not sufficient; otherwise Jewish rabbis and Hebrew grammarians would be the best interpreters of the Old Testament. It is only in the light of Christianity that we can fully comprehend the Hebrew Scriptures.

Besides the Old Testament we have a few remains of the ancient Hebrew, viz.: (1) The inscription of the Moabite stone from the ninth century before Christ (about 850), discovered at Dibon, in Moab, in 1868, by Klein, and containing in thirty-four lines an account of King Mesha of Moab, about 900 B.C., and his conflicts with Israel (comp. 2 Kings 3:4 sqq.). (2) The Siloam inscription, of the seventh century B.C., found in 1881 in a tunnel, about fifteen feet from the pool of Siloam; it narrates the completion of the tunnel. (3) Twenty cut stones (seals), containing mostly names only, partly from the period before the exile. (4) Coins of the Maccabæan prince, John Hyrcanus (B.C. 135), and his successors. The inscriptions on tombstones in the Hebrew cemeteries of ancient Rome, discovered and deciphered by Garrucci and Schürer, are mostly Greek, some Latin, but none Hebrew.

In some parts of Persia the Jews are said to use Hebrew still as their mother-tongue. It is also spoken by the Jews in Jerusalem, and the first newspaper published there was in Hebrew. Since the efforts of Moses Mendelssohn and his friend David Friedländer in the eighteenth century to raise the Hebrew from the dead, it has to a limited extent again become a spoken language in Europe, and Hebrew periodicals and works original and translated, in different departments of literature, are appearing from German, Russian, and American presses. Among recent Hebrew translations we may mention portions of Schiller, Goethe's *Faust*, Homer's *Odyssey*, Longfellow's *Excelsior*, Eugene Sue's *Mysteries of Paris*. Bunyan's *Pilgrim's Progress* was translated by S. Hoga. The New Testament has been repeatedly translated into Hebrew, by Elias Hutter (1600), Joachim Neumann, Greenfield, and others, and last by Prof. Franz Delitzsch (1876, 5th ed., revised, 1883, published by the British and Foreign Bible Society).

CHAPTER LXIV.

HISTORY OF HEBREW LEARNING.

1. The ancient Christians knew the Old Testament mostly from translations, especially the Septuagint, the Itala, and the Vulgate. The Greek and Latin fathers, with the exception of ORIGEN, EPIPHANIUS (probably a Jew by birth), EPHRAEM, and JEROME, were ignorant of Hebrew, and for this reason made

many mistakes in their exegesis. Even Augustin knew, besides his native Latin, only a little Greek, and a few Hebrew words, and relied on the defective *Itala* for his knowledge of the Bible.

Jerome learned Hebrew from Jewish rabbis in Syria, and was thus enabled to revise the *Itala* and to translate the Old Testament from the original. He taught St. Paula and other pious Roman ladies to chant the Psalter in the original. By his Vulgate Version he did an inestimable service to the mediæval Church. He had to fight his way against the ignorance and prejudice of his over-conservative assailants, and, in one of his spicy letters, he calls them "two-legged donkeys" (*bipedos asellos*), to whom " a lyre is played in vain."

In the Syrian Church, owing to the affinity of language, a knowledge of Hebrew was more common; the Peshitta or Syriac translation of the Scriptures is a noble monument of Hebrew learning. The writings of Ephraem Syrus show likewise some acquaintance with the original text of the Old Testament.

The Jews kept up a learned knowledge of their language in the schools at Tiberias. The Talmudists and Masorets (who contributed to the Masora or the body of critical traditions relating to the text of the Hebrew Scriptures) handed down the manuscripts from which our text is derived. The Masoretic text, so called, will always be the basis of translations and commentaries, but admits of considerable improvement from the Septuagint and other sources, especially the Septuagint which was derived from Hebrew manuscripts much older than those we now possess. Moreover, the quotations in the New Testament are mostly taken from the Septuagint.

2. In the Middle Ages, the Hebrew was exclusively cultivated by learned Jews (especially in Spain during the Moorish rule), such as Ibn Ezra (d. 1170), David Kimchi (1200), Moses Maimonides (d. 1204). Even the greatest scholastic divines, as Anselm, Thomas Aquinas, Bonaventura, were ignorant of Hebrew. Christians had to learn it from the Jews after the revival of letters. Nicolaus Lyra, a Franciscan monk who taught theology in Paris (d. 1340), knew Hebrew and applied it to exegesis in his brief commentaries on the Bible, which were much used by Erasmus and Luther.*

Elias Levita, a German Jew (Elihu ben Asher Hallevi, d. 1549), taught the language in Italy during the first half of the sixteenth

* See ch. cxxxiv., p. 210.

century, and put grammatical rules into Hebrew rhymes. Wessel, Agricola, and others who are named among the forerunners of the Reformation, learned the language to a limited extent.

3. The Reformation kindled an enthusiasm for the Bible and a spirit of free inquiry. Since that time the Hebrew was made a part of regular theological study, at least in the Protestant Churches. But the Reformation could not have taken place without the preceding Renaissance or the revival of ancient learning.

REUCHLIN, the great-uncle of Melanchthon, broke the path. He is the father of modern Hebrew learning among Christians. He acquired the language from John Wessel, from Matthew Adrianus (a converted Spanish Jew), and several Jewish scholars at Vienna and Rome, and taught it in Germany till his death, 1522. He coined most of the technical terms which have since been in use in Hebrew grammar (as *status absolutus, status constructus, affixum, verba imperfecta, quiescentia*, etc.), and introduced the pronunciation which prevails in Germany. His grammar, *Rudimenta Hebraica*, 1505, based upon David Kimchi, was the first Hebrew grammar written by a Christian, unless we except Pellican's *De Modo legendi et intelligendi Hebræum*, which appeared one or two years earlier (at Strassburg, 1504).* Reuchlin had to suffer much persecution from the ignorant monks, who were afraid of such studies; hence he calls himself *Hebraicarum litterarum protomartyr*. He died, however, in the Roman Catholic Church. He and Erasmus stood on the dividing line between the Renaissance and the Reformation, and between mediæval Catholicism and modern Protestantism.

Luther, Melanchthon, Zwingli, Œcolampadius, Calvin, and other reformers cultivated and highly recommended the study of Hebrew. Without such knowledge Luther could not have produced such a masterly translation of the Bible, nor could Calvin have written his unrivaled commentaries.

Even the Roman Church could not entirely neglect it. The Jesuits, Bellarmin, Huntley, and others took it up, though mostly in a polemical interest to show the necessity of church authority and to disprove the Protestant doctrine of the perspicuity of the Scriptures. Huntley showed that the very first

---

* This book was recently discovered and republished by Nestle, Tübingen, 1877. Pellican was called to Zurich as teacher of Hebrew by Zwingli in 1525. He died in 1556.

verse of Genesis admitted grammatically of eight interpretations, beside the orthodox one, and that Elohim may mean "gods," or "angels," or "magistrates," etc.

4. The dogmatic scholasticism which set in after the Reformation led again to a neglect of biblical philology and exegesis; but could not entirely stop progress. The mechanical inspiration theory of Lutheran and Reformed divines hindered the understanding of the spirit, but promoted the study of the letter, of the Bible.

The greatest Hebrew and Talmudic scholars of the seventeenth century were the two BUXTORFS of Basel, father and son, especially the father (d. 1629, author of a Hebrew grammar and lexicon). Next to them SALOMO GLASSIUS (d. 1656), professor in Jena and author of the *Philologia sacra* (1625, 1705, 1776), which was once regarded as the key for the solution of all exegetical difficulties. JOHN LIGHTFOOT (a member of the Westminster Assembly of Divines, d. 1675) prepared from his extensive reading the illustrative *Horæ Hebraicæ et Talmudicæ* (1,648) which are still used and quoted by scholars. A valuable continuation and supplement of this work was furnished in 1733 by CHRISTIAN SCHÖTTGEN (d. at Dresden, 1751) in his *Horæ Hebr. et Talm. in universum N. Test.*

5. A new epoch for Hebrew learning was opened in the nineteenth century by two great scholars, GESENIUS and EWALD, who vastly advanced the critical knowledge of the language and literature of the Old Testament, but differed widely in their spirit and method. Wilhelm Gesenius (1786–1842, Professor in Halle), a rationalist, but a very able, clear-headed, industrious, and useful Hebraist, still continues to guide beginners in the empirical study of the language by his grammar (1813), which, with the successive improvements of Rödiger and Kautzsch, has reached the twenty-fifth edition (1889), and has been several times translated into English (by Mos. Stuart, Th. J. Conant, Benj. Davis, E. C. Mitchell); while his Hebrew Lexicon (German ed. 1815, 11th ed. by Mühlau and Volck, 1890; Latin ed. 1833; English translations by Tregelles and Robinson) and his great *Thesaurus* (completed by Rödiger, 1829–58, 3 vols.) are indispensable. HEINRICH EWALD (1803–75, Professor in Göttingen, then in Tübingen, and again in Göttingen) was a genius and scholar of the first order, but eccentric, excessively independent and sublimely conceited, yet very religious (he

HISTORY OF HEBREW LEARNING. 113

looked and spoke like a prophet of Jahveh, and in his way he was a prophet). He first grasped and expounded the philosophy of the Hebrew syntax (*Lehrbuch*, 8th ed. 1870; the portion on Syntax translated by James Kennedy, 1879).

The more recent scholars have the great additional advantage of the Assyrian discoveries.

Next to these masters, must be mentioned the services of HUPFELD (1841), FÜRST (1857), DELITZSCH (father and son), DIETRICH (1846), J. OLSHAUSEN (1861), BÖTTCHER and MÜHLAU (1866-68), BICKELL (1870, well translated by Samuel Ives Curtiss, 1877), NÄGELSBACH (1856, 4th ed. 1880), SEFFER (7th ed., 1883), STADE (1879), KÖNIG (1881), STRACK (1883).

SIEGFRIED and STADE published a new Hebrew Lexicon, 1892.

The modern Hebrew learning in France, England, and Scotland is mostly dependent upon that of Germany. S. P. TREGELLES published *Heads of Hebrew Grammar* (1852), *The Englishman's Hebrew and Chaldee Concordance to the Old Testament* (1843), and a translation of Gesenius's *Lexicon* (1859). B. A. DAVIES is the author of a *Hebrew and Chaldee Lexicon* (3d ed. revised by E. C. MITCHELL, 1880). ROBERT YOUNG published an *Analytical Concordance* of the whole Bible, with the Hebrew and Greek words (1879). Professor A. B. DAVIDSON of Edinburgh has written a useful *Introductory Hebrew Grammar* (8th ed. 1891), and Canon DRIVER of Oxford a valuable *Treatise on the Use of the Tenses in Hebrew* (3d ed. 1892.)

6. The fathers of Hebrew learning in America are MOSES STUART of Andover (d. 1852), JOSEPH ADDISON ALEXANDER of Princeton (d. 1860), and EDWARD ROBINSON of the Union Theological Seminary in New York (d. 1864). They introduced the fruits of critical German scholarship, as then represented by Gesenius, but happily retained the traditional English and American reverence for the Word of God. Stuart published, besides several commentaries, a *Hebrew Grammar*, based on Gesenius. Alexander wrote commentaries on Isaiah and the Psalms (based upon Hengstenberg). Robinson prepared a *Hebrew Lexicon* (20th ed. 1881) on the basis of Gesenius, which has heretofore been the best, but is now undergoing a complete reconstruction, according to the latest Semitic discoveries and researches, by Professors BROWN and BRIGGS of the Union Theological Seminary, New York, and Canon DRIVER, Professor of Hebrew in the University of Oxford, published by

the Clarendon Press, and by Houghton, Mifflin & Co., New York, 1892 sq.

Hebrew grammars have been written by BUSH, CONANT, NORDHEIMER, GREEN, HARPER, and BISSELL. Those of Nordheimer (of Union Th. Sem., New York, 1842, 2 vols.) and Green (of Princeton, 4th ed. 1883) are of superior merit.

A new generation of Hebrew scholars, trained in German universities, is growing up and producing a revival of Semitic studies to an extent unknown before. An Oriental Society was founded at Boston in 1842, and edits a journal which corresponds to the journals of the German and French Oriental Societies. Several Theological Seminaries (Union, Princeton, Andover, Yale) provide for instruction in all the Semitic languages. An *Institute of Hebrew* was organized December 31, 1880, under the inspiration of Dr. WILLIAM R. HARPER, President of the new University of Chicago, an enthusiastic Hebraist and indefatigable worker. The *Institute* consists of thirty-seven professors of Hebrew of various denominations, and carries on a Correspondence School, and four Summer Schools, which are held for several weeks, during the summer vacation, simultaneously in Eastern and Western cities. Students, ministers, and even ladies attend. In addition to the Hebrew, the other Semitic languages are also taught in these summer schools.

Ultimately all the leading colleges will have to provide for the optional study of Hebrew and other Semitic languages. In this way the Theological Seminaries will be relieved of the preparatory grammatical drill and be able to devote their strength to the higher work of exegesis.

CHAPTER LXV.

THE OTHER SEMITIC LANGUAGES.

The study of other Semitic languages besides Hebrew is unnecessary for the great majority of theological students and pastors, who may employ their time more profitably, but it is indispensable for those who would make the Old Testament language and literature the subject of special critical and comparative research.

The Aramaic is essential for Rabbinical and Talmudic scholarship, and the Syriac gives access to a considerable body of ancient Christian literature.

The Assyrian is important not only for its close affinity with the Hebrew, but also for the parallel sections of its literature. The recovery of this language has opened a new field for comparative Semitic philology and history.

The Arabic facilitates a thorough understanding of Hebrew, and the geographical exploration of Bible lands. It has an independent literary and historical value for the student of the Koran and the history of Islâm. It is indispensable to missionaries in Mohammedan countries.

CHAPTER LXVI.

THE ARAMAIC LANGUAGES.

The Aramaic (Aramæan) group differs, especially in its earlier form, very slightly from the Hebrew. Jacob and Laban understood each other, the one speaking Hebrew, the other Aramaic (comp. Gen. 31 : 47). Gideon, or Purah, or both, understood the conversation of "the Midianites and the Amalekites, and all the children of the East" (Judges 7 : 9–15). At a later period only the educated Jews were familiar with Aramaic (2 Kings 18 : 26); but still later, after the Babylonian exile, the Aramaic supplanted the Hebrew even in Palestine, and continued to be the language of the Hebrews during the Persian, Greek, and Roman periods. It was the native language of Christ and his Apostles (who spoke the Galilean dialect; comp. Matt. 26 : 73; Mark 14 : 70).

The Aramaic is probably as old as the Hebrew, if not older, but is known to us mainly from the time of the Babylonian exile. It prevailed in Mesopotamia, Palestine, and Syria. It is still spoken in part, though corruptly, in the neighborhood of Mosul and Lake Oroomiah; but upon the whole it has been supplanted by the Arabic with the spread of Mohammedanism. It is more rough and flat in its consonants, poorer in vowels, and far less cultivated than the Hebrew. Among its peculiarities are the preponderance of consonants, the *emphatic state* of nouns (equivalent to the article in Hebrew and Arabic), the termination *in* for the plural of the masculine (as *Sanhedrin*), etc.

The principal languages of the Aramaic group are the ARAMAIC proper, or CHALDEE, and the SYRIAC. They differ mainly in pronunciation and spelling.

CHAPTER LXVII.

THE BIBLICAL ARAMAIC AND THE RABBINICAL HEBREW.

The Aramaic, or Chaldee so called, was the language of Syria; it got the upper hand of the Hebrew in ordinary use in Palestine since the fourth or fifth century before Christ.* It occurs in the later portions of the Old Testament,† in a few remains of the current speech in Palestine in the New Testament, where it is called "Hebrew"; ‡ then in the Targums (*i.e.*, translations and paraphrases of the Old Testament), the Masora, the Talmud, and the Jewish scholars of the Middle Ages (Ibn Ezra, Maimonides, Kimchi, Rashi, etc.).

The Rabbinical and Talmudic Hebrew is also called the "New Hebrew," in distinction from the Hebrew of the Old Testament, which the Rabbins endeavored artificially to imitate. It is related to the pure Hebrew as the monastic and ecclesiastical Latin is to the classical Latin of Cicero. Buxtorf, in his Chaldee-Talmudic Dictionary, notices throughout the Rabbinical vocabulary. The language of the Talmud is essentially Aramaic mixed with Hebrew; the Mishna nearly resembles the Hebrew; the style of the Gemara of Jerusalem is Aramaic, while the Gemara of Babylon more nearly approaches the Hebrew.

* The term *Chaldee* is derived from Dan. 2:4 (Septuagint), and was introduced by Jerome as a designation of the Aramaic language, but this is inappropriate, since the old Chaldæans, *i.e.*, the Babylonians, never spoke Aramaic. Yet the term is used in the Dictionaries of Buxtorf, Fürst and Gesenius, including the ninth edition: the tenth corrects it.

† Dan. 2:4–7:28; Ezra 4:8–6:18; 7:12–26; Jer. 10:11. The oldest Aramaic word in the Bible, *Jegar-sahadutha*, *i.e.*, the heap of witness, is found Gen. 31:47. The dialect used in the Old Testament is called the Biblical Aramaic.

‡ Luke 23:38; John 19:13, 17, 20.

CHAPTER LXVIII.

THE SYRIAC AND THE SAMARITAN.

The Syriac is the Christian and ecclesiastical Aramaic. It has an alphabet of its own (one common in MSS., and one for printed books). The Syriac literature extends from the second to the thirteenth century after Christ. It commences with one of the oldest and best translations of the Bible (the Peshitta, probably from the second century), and was carried forward by Ephraim the Syrian, and by the Nestorians in their theological schools at Edessa and Nisibis. It embraces translations, legends, poems, liturgies, and folk-lore. The British Museum acquired in 1845 from Coptic convents in Egypt a large number of Syriac MSS., mostly patristic, which were published by Cureton, Payne Smith, and others. This collection has been increased by later discoveries in the East. Among the most important documents are fragments of an old, perhaps the oldest, translation of the Gospels (called the Curetonian Syriac), the Syriac Ignatius, the Festal Letters of Athanasius, the Syriac Clement of Rome, and the Apology of Aristides (discovered by J. Rendel Harris on Mt. Sinai in 1889).

The Syriac is mixed with Greek, Arabic, Persian, and Latin words (mostly nouns), owing to its contact with the literature of the Greek Church, and to the wanderings of the Nestorians.

It still exists in altered and decayed forms, and is spoken by Jews and Nestorian Christians in Syria, Mesopotamia, and Koordistan. It is the sacred language of the Nestorians, Jacobites, and Maronites. But among the people since the tenth century, it has been more and more supplanted by the Arabic.

The modern Syriac has a literature of its own, partly native, partly the product of Protestant and Roman Catholic missionaries.*

To the same branch belongs the Samaritan language. It is a mixture of the Aramaic and vulgar Hebrew, and corresponds to the mixed character of the Samaritan people. In many cases it embraces the forms of both, e.g., the Hebrew article and the Aramaic emphatic state. It has twenty-two letters in the or-

* See a full list of Syriac literature, old and new, in the Appendix to Nestle's *Syriac Grammar* (1889), pp. 1–66.

der of the Hebrew alphabet; the form resembles the ancient Hebrew and Phœnician (not the later Hebrew square character). The gutturals are weak and quiescent: hence the difference in pronunciation. (Comp. John 4 : 9.) The Samaritan Literature is confined to the Samaritan *Pentateuch* (which has some critical value), the Samaritan *Targum* (of Nathaniel the high priest, B.C. 20), Samaritan *Chronicles*, *Liturgies*, and *Hymns*, mostly in MS. in the British Museum.

CHAPTER LXIX.

THE ASSYRIAN.

The Assyrian or Assyro-Babylonian language belongs to the same branch of Semitic languages as the Hebrew, and resembles it much more closely than the Arabic. It was spoken and written, with a slight dialectical difference, in Babylonia and Assyria.[*] It continued in use through the Persian and Greek periods, but was buried and forgotten for centuries till the middle of the nineteenth century, when it was dug up from the dust with the ruins of Nineveh and Babylon. Its study is a necessity for the specialist in Semitic philology, history, and religion.

The system of Assyrian writing was originally, like the Chinese and Egyptian, hieroglyphic and pictorial. The pictorial form gradually faded away, and the pictures became conventional notations. A few bold strokes sufficed to depict the object intended, and in the end the form of the letter bore very little or no resemblance to the thing from which it was derived.

Assyrian is read from left to right; its characters are composed of wedges; hence the name *cuneiform* (from *cuneus*, wedge); also *arrow-headed*. There are horizontal, perpendicular, and sloping wedges, and also double wedges. The characters contain from one to twenty wedges each, and represent

[*] Assyria is made prominent in the name because the attention of explorers and decipherers was first directed to the palaces and inscriptions of the great Assyrian kings, but the Babylonian empire and civilization was older than the Assyrian (comp. Gen. 10 : 10, 11), and survived it. Nineveh, the capital of ancient Assyria, was destroyed B.C. 607 (so Schrader); Babylon was captured and its empire overthrown by Cyrus, B.C. 538. The Babylonians were priests and built temples; the Assyrians were soldiers and built palaces.

either syllables or words. There are ideograms, *i.e.*, signs of objects or ideas, and phonograms, *i.e.*, signs for sounds. The cuneiform writing is complicated and difficult, but may be made easier by transliteration into Hebrew or Latin. The easiest method for beginners is to study the language by the use of transliterated texts.

The decipherment of the wedge-writing was made possible by the help of trilingual inscriptions (made under the Persian kings), just as the decipherment of the Egyptian hieroglyphics was made by the help of the trilingual Rosetta stone discovered in 1799. It is due to the genius and progressive efforts of Grotefend (who first deciphered a short Persian cuneiform inscription as early as 1802), Bernouf, Lassen, Rawlinson, Talbot, Hincks, Oppert, Lenormant, Benfey, Spiegel, Schrader, Haupt, Delitzsch, Hilprecht, and others. Oppert wrote the first connected Assyrian Grammar (1860), and was followed by Sayce (1872), and Friedrich Delitzsch (1889). The grammar is simple and easily acquired by one acquainted with Hebrew. A large majority of the roots are the same as in Hebrew. The verb has two forms for the imperfect: the first for expressing a continuous action, whether past, present, or future (as in Hebrew), the second for ordinary narration of past action (like the English preterit).

The Assyrian literature reaches back into the third and fourth millennium before Christ; the oldest writing of which we know was in the time of Sargon I., about B.C. 3800. The Babylonians knew the art of writing long before Abraham left Ur in Chaldæa, and some have conjectured that the Hebrew alphabet was derived from the archaic form of the Babylonian signs for words and syllables. The history which this literature unfolds is a startling revelation to the second half of the nineteenth century, as the recovery of ancient Egypt through the decipherment of the hieroglyphics was to the first half of the same century. They were brought to light by excavations in the Euphrates valley made by Botta (1842–45), Layard (1845–51), Rassam (1852–54), George Smith (1873–76), E. de Sarzec (1875–80), the American Wolfe expedition led by Ward (1884), Peters, Hilprecht (1890), and other scholars of different nations.

The cuneiform literature is inscribed on bricks, prisms, slabs of marble or alabaster, statues, obelisks, colossal bulls, on walls of temples and palaces, and on clay tables of every shape. The royal library at Nineveh had at least 30,000 clay tablets with texts of all sizes, some in such minute characters as to require a magnifying glass. The inscriptions already discovered exceed in compass the Hebrew Bible, and continue to increase in number from year to year. They record primitive traditions of the creation and the flood, lists and legends of the gods, prayers, psalms, grammars, and dictionaries, chronicles of the Assyrian and Babylonian Kings, astrological tablets, calendars, oracular deliverances, letters, proclamations, petitions, inventories, receipts, deeds of purchase and sale, bequests, wills; and thus furnish us a faithful picture of the history, geography, religion, politics, wars, culture, domestic, social, and public life of the Babylonians and Assyrians and the neighboring nations of Western Asia. These ancient treasures have been transferred to the British Museum, the Louvre of Paris, and other museums of Europe, and are thus made accessible to scholars. There is a large and growing literature on Assyriology, to which scholars of different nations have contributed.* To the biblical student the most important portions of the cuneiform literature are those which run parallel with the sacred narrative. The stories of the creation, the deluge, and the tower of Babel are vitiated by polytheism, and show by contrast the superiority of the accounts of Genesis. The gods themselves emerge from the primitive chaos, while the Bible raises the one true and living God above the world which he called into existence by his free, omnipotent will. The Babylonian flood-story agrees with Genesis in representing the deluge as a visitation of divine justice, the building of a ship, the embarkment of the family of Pir-napishtim (the Babylonian Noah), and all kinds of animals, the perishing of the race except this family, the grounding of the ship on a mountain, the sending forth of a dove (a swallow and a raven), the disembarkment, and the sacrifice of thanksgiving. But this poem also is disfigured by polytheism, and a quarrel among the gods, Bel, Ea, Ishtar, and Anu. The Nimrod of Genesis 10 : 8 sqq. has been identified with the Babylonian Gilgames, the chief hero of the great epic, in which the Babylonian flood-story forms a canto. The Babylonio-Assyrian chronology serves in part as a

* A complete list of works on modern Assyriology is given by Friedrich Delitzsch (son of the late Franz D.), in the Appendix to his *Assyrian Grammar* (Berlin, 1889, English translation by A. R. S. Kennedy, pp. 55–78).

guide through the perplexity of the more meagre Hebrew dates. The history of the Assyrian monarchy from B.C. 900 to the destruction of Nineveh is best known from these monuments, and illustrates the corresponding accounts of the Books of Kings.*

CHAPTER LXX.

THE ARABIC.

The ARABIC or Ishmaelite language appears in history about four hundred years after Christ. Of its early phases we know little or nothing. Its oldest literature consisted of ballads handed down by oral tradition. It assumed a vast importance in the seventh century through Islâm and spread with the Mohammedan conquest far beyond its original limits. In this respect the promise of God to Ishmael to make him a great nation (Gen. 16: 10; 17: 20; 21: 13, 18) has been strikingly fulfilled. The Arabic is said to be spoken by from one hundred to one hundred and twenty millions of people in the Turkish empire, in Egypt, Palestine and Syria, in Algiers, in the interior of Africa, in India and Central Asia. It is spoken not only by Mohammedans, but also by Christians under their government, as the Greeks, Maronites, Jacobites and Armenians.

The Arabic retained longest the original fullness of the Semitic forms of speech, but has at length undergone considerable corruption. It is the most opulent and cultivated of the Semitic languages, and has the richest literature. It reflects the wildness of wandering herdsmen and robbers, and, in its cultivated state, the habits of a luxurious and licentious people. It reached its flourishing period in the fourteenth and fifteenth centuries. It has a greater variety of forms than the Hebrew, and is much more difficult to learn. It numbers about 6,000 roots and 60,000 words, among them scores of terms for *camel*, *lion*, *sword*. De Sacy, one of the greatest Arabic scholars, con-

---

* See *The Cuneiform Inscriptions of Western Asia*, by Major-General Sir H. C. RAWLINSON, assisted by EDWIN NORRIS, etc. London, 1861-84, 5 vols.; SCHRADER'S *Keilinschriften und das Alte Testament*, Giessen, 1883 (English translation by Owen Whitehouse, London, 1885-88). For an excellent summary, see the articles of Prof. FRANCIS BROWN (of Union Theological Seminary) on *Assyriology and the Bible*, in the Schaff-Herzog *Enc.*, and in Jackson's *Concise Dictionary of Religious Knowledge* (1889), pp. 51-61.

fessed that he could not read a single page of Arabic poetry without a dictionary. The Arabs say that even the angel Gabriel does not know all the roots. In ordinary writing and printing, the vowel-points are omitted.

The Arabic is the sacred language of the Korân, the Mohammedan Bible, which is the ultimate standard of linguistic purity as well as of faith and practice. It claims to be inspired by Gabriel and too sacred to be translated, but has been frequently translated by Christians (into English by Sale, Rodwell, Palmer). It consists of 114 Suras (chapters) and 6,225 verses, and is composed in imperfect metre and rhyme. The other Arabic literature embraces nearly all departments of knowledge.

The Arabic in ordinary use is called the modern or vulgar Arabic.

A knowledge of Arabic is indispensable for a missionary in Bible lands, and among the Mohammedans in Africa and India.

The American missionary press in Beirût is creating a Christian Arabic literature, including translations of our best hymns, of Bunyan's *Pilgrim's Progress*, Edwards's *History of Redemption*, and especially a new Arabic version of the Bible by Eli Smith and Dr. Van Dyck, completed and printed in the Bible House at New York (1868)—a noble monument of American learning and missionary zeal. The Jesuits in Beirût, who are very active, have been stimulated by it to another Arabic version (1877), which aims at greater elegance at the expense of popularity.

The HIMYARITIC language (from Himyar, an ancient king of Yemen) is a Southern Arabic dialect as distinct from the Northern Arabic in which the Korân is written. It is known to us from numerous Himyaritic inscriptions of ancient but uncertain date (probably from the third to the seventh century).

It is the basis of the ÆTHIOPIC (called GEEZ) in Abyssinia, which after the conversion of the Æthiopians became an ecclesiastical and literary language, but has long since died out among the people. There remain numerous Æthiopic MSS., a translation of the Bible, apostolic canons and constitutions, liturgical forms, apocryphal books, notably the Book of Enoch (edited and translated by Dillmann, 1851).*

* See list of literature in the *Æthiopische Grammatik* of F. Prætorius (1886), pp. 21–28.

CHAPTER LXXI.

THE STUDY OF THE CLASSICS.

The language of the New Testament brings us into contact with the classical literature of Greece and Rome. The study of Latin and Greek is indispensable for every well-educated theologian, and will be to the end of time, because the New Testament is composed in Greek, and nearly the whole ancient and mediæval, with a great deal of the modern, literature of the Christian Church, is deposited in those two languages.

Providence has inseparably connected the fortunes of Christianity with ancient classical civilization. Plato and Aristotle, Homer and Virgil, Demosthenes and Cicero have become servants of the Church and will always be studied by Christian philosophers, poets and orators. The literature of Greece and the polity of Rome prepared the way for the Gospel. The Greek language and the Roman empire were the human forms for the divine contents of our religion.

All thorough knowledge must be genetic, and grow up from the roots. The ancient classics represent the human mind at its highest point of culture, which it could attain without supernatural aid. They reveal human nature in its strength and beauty, but also in its helplessness and inability to attain the highest end. Human nature is still the same in all its capacities, but it has been enlightened, purified, and ennobled under the influence of Christianity. Our modern ideas of God, virtue and immortality are vastly superior to those entertained by the most enlightened heathen sages on the same subjects. To study human nature in its pre-Christian condition (the *humanities* so called), we must go to the classics, and then we shall be better prepared to appreciate Christianity.

CHAPTER LXXII.

CHRISTIANITY AND THE GREEK LANGUAGE.

The Greek language, the noblest ever spoken, was at the time of Christ the universal medium of international intercourse in the Roman empire; as the Latin was in the Middle Ages, the

French in the eighteenth century, and as the English in more recent times. It was the language of government, law, diplomacy, literature and trade.

Since the conquest of Alexander the Great, a pupil of Aristotle,—the philosophical world-conqueror—the Greek language spread in the East as far as the valley of the Euphrates. It accompanied the Roman legions to the banks of the Rhine and the pillars of Hercules. It was used extensively by the Jews of the Dispersion, especially in Alexandria and Rome; it was spoken even in Palestine, on the western sea-coast, in Samaria and in Galilee ("Galilee of the Gentiles"). Greek Jews flocked by thousands from all countries to the annual festivals in Jerusalem, and aided in spreading their adopted language. The Jewish Apocrypha, and the works of Philo and Josephus were composed in Greek. Josephus, who was born and educated for the priesthood in Jerusalem, wrote, as he says, his *History of the Jewish War* first in Hebrew, "for the barbarians in the interior," afterwards in Greek, "for those under the Roman dominion." The Septuagint translation of the Old Testament was used in the synagogue long before Christ, and is usually quoted from in the New Testament. This fact makes the knowledge of the Septuagint as important as the knowledge of the Hebrew Scriptures. Hellenism was a bridge from Judaism to Christianity, and a providential preparation for the latter.

It is almost certain that our Saviour, though usually speaking the vernacular Hebrew (Aramaic), occasionally used the Greek, as when addressing a mixed multitude, or conversing with the Syro-Phœnician woman ($\gamma\upsilon\nu\grave{\eta}$ Ἑλληνίς, Mark 7: 26), with the heathen centurion (Matt. 8: 5), with the Greeks who called on him (John 12: 20), and before Herod and Pontius Pilate. Peter's sermon on the Day of Pentecost was probably in Greek, which could be understood by nearly all his hearers.

The Apostles and Evangelists, growing up in a bilingual community, must have been more or less familiar with Greek from early youth, for they wrote it, not indeed with classical purity and elegance, yet with a naturalness and ease which are seldom acquired in adult age. Paul received his first training in the Greek city of Tarsus, and was acquainted with Greek poets such as Aratus (Acts 17: 28), Epimenides (Tit. 1: 12) and Menander (1 Cor. 15: 33).

The Greek was therefore the most natural organ of Christian

literature, even in the Western Church (as we see from the Greek writings of Clement of Rome, Hermas, Irenæus, Hippolytus), and continued to be almost exclusively used until Tertullian and Cyprian in North Africa raised the Latin to the dignity of a Christian and ecclesiastical language.

The language of Homer and Herodotus, of Plato and Aristotle, accomplished its highest mission when it proclaimed the truths of the gospel of the Saviour of mankind. As the language of the New Testament, it will always have the first claim upon the attention of the theologian, even above the study of all the Semitic languages combined.

CHAPTER LXXIII.

THE DIALECTS OF THE GREEK LANGUAGE.

The Greek language has come down to us in a number of dialects and sub-dialects. The literature is chiefly deposited in four:

1. The ÆOLIC dialect, known from inscriptions and grammarians, and from remains of Alcæus, Sappho (the greatest Greek poetess, c. B.C. 650), and her friend Erinna.

2. The DORIC is rough but vigorous, immortalized by the odes of Pindar and the idyls of Theocritus.

3. The IONIC, soft and elastic. In this dialect Homer sang the Iliad, and Herodotus told his history.

4. The ATTIC dialect differs little from the Ionic, unites energy and dignity with grace and melody, and is represented by the largest literature: the tragedies of Æschylus, Sophocles, Euripides, the comedies of Aristophanes, the histories of Thucydides and Xenophon, the philosophical dialogues of Plato, and the orations of Demosthenes.

The Attic dialect, owing to its literary wealth and the military conquests of Alexander the Great, came to be the popular language not only in Greece proper, but also in the conquered provinces of Syria and Egypt. By its diffusion it lost much of its original stamp, and absorbed a number of foreign words and inflections from the Orient. But what it lost in purity, it gained in extent and popularity. It was emancipated from the trammels of nationality and intellectual aristocracy, and became cosmopolitan. It grew less artistic, but more useful.

5. In this modified form, the Attic Greek received the name of the MACEDONIAN or ALEXANDRIAN, and also the COMMON or HELLENIC language.* It was used by Aristotle, who connects the classic Attic with the Hellenic, by Polybius, Plutarch, Diodorus Siculus, Dio Cassius, Dionysius of Halicarnassus, Aelian, Herodian, Arrian, and Lucian.

CHAPTER LXXIV.

THE HELLENISTIC DIALECT.

The Hellenic dialect assumed a strongly *Hebraizing* character among the Grecian Jews, who were called *Hellenists* in distinction from the Aramaic-speaking *Hebrews*.†

In this modified form it is called the HELLENISTIC dialect.

The city of Alexandria, founded by Alexander the Great (B.C. 332), became the center of the Hellenistic dialect. There different nationalities mingled, and adopted the Greek as their medium of commercial, social, and literary intercourse. Immense libraries were collected under the rule of the Ptolemies, and every important work of Egyptian and Oriental learning was translated into Greek.

The literature of the Hellenistic dialect is all of Jewish origin, and intimately connected with religion. It embraces the Septuagint and the Jewish Apocrypha, which are incorporated in the Septuagint, and passed from it into the Latin Vulgate. Philo (B.C. 20 to c. A.D. 40), and especially Josephus (A.D. 38 to 103), the two most eminent Jewish scholars of the first century, aimed at Attic purity of style, which should commend their theological and historical writings to scholars of classical taste; but after all, they could not conceal the Hebrew spirit and coloring. The Hellenistic writings express Jewish ideas in Greek words, and carried the religion of the East to the nations of the West.

* ἡ κοινὴ διάλεκτος or Ἑλληνικὴ διάλεκτος.

† Acts 6:1. Ἕλλην, *Hellen* (John 12:20), is a native Greek, a gentile (sometimes used in the sense of a civilized man as distinct from a barbarian, Rom. 1:14, or as a representative heathen, as distinct from the Jew, ver. 16). Ἑλληνιστής, *Hellenist* (from ἑλληνίζω, to act or imitate the Greek in language or custom, to speak Greek) is a Greek-speaking Jew, Acts 6:1; 9:21; 11:20; 13:43; 17:4. Comp. ῥωμαΐζειν, to romanize, πλατωνίζειν, to follow Plato. *Hellenism* denotes a type of life and mode of speech, but not national origin. The designation *Hellenistic* for the dialect was first introduced by Scaliger.

CHAPTER LXXV.

THE SEPTUAGINT.

The Greek version of the Old Testament Scriptures, called the *Septuagint*, from the supposed number of translators (seventy or seventy-two), was gradually made by Jewish scholars in Alexandria during the reign of Ptolemy II., B.C. 285–247, and survived the ravages of the Moslem conquerors. It laid the foundation for the Hellenistic idiom. It made the Greek the vehicle of Hebrew thought. It became the accepted Bible of the Jews of the Dispersion, spread the influence of their religion among the Gentiles, and prepared the way for the introduction of Christianity. Thus an "altar was erected to Jehovah" not only "in the midst of the land of Egypt," as the prophet foretold (Isa. 19 : 19, 20, 25), but all over the Roman Empire.

The Septuagint is the basis of the Apostolic or Christian Greek. It is a remarkable fact, not yet sufficiently explained, that the great majority of direct citations from the Old Testament in the New, which amount to about 280, are taken from the Septuagint, or at all events, agree better with it than with the Hebrew original.

Jesus himself quotes from the Septuagint, according to the Evangelists. The Apostles did it in their discourses, and in their epistles. Even Paul, who was educated at Jerusalem and well versed in rabbinical lore, usually agrees with the Septuagint, except when he freely quotes from memory, or adapts the text to his argument. It has been plausibly suggested that they used an Aramaic version or periphrase current at that time among the people in Palestine; but the proof is wanting.

CHAPTER LXXVI.

THE APOSTOLIC GREEK.

PHILIP SCHAFF: *A Companion to the Greek Testament and the English Version.* New York, 1883; 4th ed., revised, 1892 (with facsimiles of ancient MSS. and standard editions of the Greek Testament).

The twenty-seven books of the New Covenant were written by Christians of Jewish birth and training, under Roman dominion, in the Greek language, which was then generally spread and understood in the civilized world, but had never before been applied to such high themes.

The language of the New Testament is therefore a peculiar, we may say, cosmopolitan, idiom, best adapted for the universal mission of the gospel. It is trichotomic: it has a Greek body, a Hebrew soul, and a Christian spirit. It is the noble language of classical civilization and the venerable language of revealed religion. It combines the best elements of the ancient world, regenerated and controlled by the spirit of a new religion, and made subservient to the highest ends. It is, moreover, so plain and simple in its diction that, both in the original and in translations, it comes home to the capacity of the common people. The New Testament is not a book for scholars only or chiefly, but for all classes and conditions of men.

The inscription on the cross was threefold (John 19: 20), in Hebrew—the language of religion, in Greek—the language of civilization, and in Latin—the language of law and power. This foretokens the universal mission of Christianity.

1. The GREEK of the New Testament is the Hellenistic dialect, as already described.

2. The HEBREW and ARAMAIC element in this dialect is the connecting link between the Mosaic and the Christian dispensations. It pervades all the writings of the New Testament more or less, but chiefly the Gospels of Matthew and Mark, the first two chapters of Luke (except the prologue 1: 1–4, which is pure Greek), and the Apocalypse. It appears in the following characteristics:

(*a*) A large number of Hebrew or Aramaic words, for which the classical Greek had no equivalents.

Examples: *Abba* (father); *Alleluia* (praise ye Jahveh); *Amen* (truly); *Boanerges* (son of thunder); *Gehenna* (the valley of Hinnom, hell); *Golgotha* (skull, the place of Christ's crucifixion, so called from its conical shape); *epphatha* (be opened); *judaize, Judaism, Jewish* (from Judah); *mammon* (riches); *manna* (the miraculous food of the Israelites in the desert); *pascha* (passover); *rabbi* and *rabbuni* (teacher, doctor); *sabbath* (rest); *Satan* (adversary); besides a number of proper names, as *Jesus, Cephas, Jacob, John, Saul, Mary, Martha.*

(*b*) Greek words with Hebrew (or Christian) meanings.

Examples: *Christ* (Messiah); *angel; apostle; evangelist; bap-*

tism; devil (slanderer, for Satan); *flesh* (in the sense of frail, mortal, corrupt nature, carnal desire); *seed* (for offspring); *synagogue.*

(c) Hebraistic phrases and modes of construction.

Examples: *from the face* (presence) *of; to taste death; by two and two, i.e.* pair-wise; *to be pleased in; to reckon unto; not all* (for no one); *to accept the face* or *person* of any one (for to be partial); *son of* (in the sense of belonging to).

(d) The simplicity of style and construction of sentences by way of succession and parallelism rather than logical sequence. The Sermon on the Mount and the parables have that correspondence of thoughts and words which forms a peculiar charm of Hebrew poetry.

3. The ROMAN element is subordinate. It consists of thirty-one Latinisms, mostly terms of war, politics and business. They found their way into the Greek after the Roman conquest, but did not change its character, like the Hebrew. They occur chiefly in Mark's Gospel, which was written in Rome for the Romans, but also in Matthew and Luke.

Examples: *centurion* (captain of a hundred soldiers); *legion; prætorium* (the governor's residence, the camp of the prætorian cohort); *custody; colony; census; mile; tavern; robber; denarius* (a Roman silver coin, equivalent to an Attic drachma, and worth about 16 cents, inaccurately translated *penny* in the Authorized Version). Besides a considerable number of Latin proper names (as *Agrippa, Cornelius, Clemens, Marc, Paul, Prisca* and *Priscilla*), and of places (as *Cæsarea, Appii Forum, Tres Tabernæ*).

4. The whole language of the Apostles and Evangelists is baptized with the spirit and fire of CHRISTIANITY. It thus received a character altogether peculiar and distinct not only from the classical, but also from the earlier Hellenistic, Greek. The genius of a new religion must either produce a new language, or inspire an old one with a new meaning. The Greek was sufficiently flexible to adapt itself to the inspiring and transforming influence of the gospel. Classical and Hellenistic words in common use were clothed with a deeper spiritual significance: they were transplanted from a lower to a higher sphere, from the order of nature to the order of grace, from mythology to revelation, from the realm of sense to the realm of faith.

This applies to the very words which express the fundamental ideas of Christianity, as *gospel, faith, love, hope, mercy, peace, light, life, repentance* (change of mind, μετάνοια), *conversion, regeneration, redemption, justification, sanctification, grace, humility, apostle, evangelist, baptism, Lord's Supper, Lord's Day, kingdom of heaven.*

Take, for instance, the word *gospel* (εὐαγγέλιον): to a Gentile Greek it would convey the idea of reward for good news (as in Homer), or any kind of good news; to a Jew, the prophecy of a future Messiah; to a Christian, the glad tidings of salvation by Christ. The word *church* (the equivalent for assembly, congregation, ἐκκλησία) passed through a secular, Jewish and Christian state, denoting first a political or any kind of assembly, then a synagogue, and lastly the Christian commonwealth and communion of saints. *Faith* (πίστις) means trust or confidence in a person or belief in a report; but in a higher sense, the saving faith in Christ. *Love* (ἀγάπη, which, however, is a purely Biblical and ecclesiastical word) rises in the New Testament from the idea of natural affection and friendship (φιλία) to the idea of the highest spiritual gift, described by Paul. The Greek terms for *humble* and *humility* (ταπεινός, ταπαινότης, ταπείνωσις) designated to the proud heathen, meanness and baseness of mind, but in the New Testament, a fundamental Christian virtue. The apostolic salutation, "Mercy and peace be unto you," is a transformation of the idea of physical health and temporal happiness, as conveyed in the Greek χαίρειν and the Hebrew *shalom l'cha*, into the idea of spiritual and eternal welfare, so that χάρις and εἰρήνη signify the blessings, objective and subjective, of the Christian salvation.

5. The peculiarity of the New Testament Greek, differing as it does from the preceding Hellenistic Greek of the Septuagint and Philo, and from the subsequent patristic Greek of Ignatius, Justin Martyr, Irenæus, and later writers, furnishes a strong argument for the genuineness of the Gospels and Epistles, as productions of the second half of the first century.

CHAPTER LXXVII.

PECULIARITIES OF THE NEW TESTAMENT WRITERS.

Every man has his own style, and "the style is the man." No two human beings, yea, no two leaves are precisely alike.

There is unity and endless variety in nature and in history, and therein is displayed the beauty of the universe, and "the manifold wisdom of God."

The apostolic writers make no exception. They have their idiosyncracies of temper, mode of thought and speech. The Holy Spirit, far from destroying these peculiarities, purifies, sanctifies, strengthens and uses them for the instruction and edification of the Church. The diversity of style in the New Testament has been felt and incidentally pointed out by the Fathers and Reformers; it was obscured by the mechanical inspiration theory which prevailed in the seventeenth century; it was emphasized by the rationalists at the expense of the essential harmony; it is now better understood and appreciated as an essential element in the divine-human character and applicability of Scripture to the tastes and wants of all classes of men.

We must not look in the Greek Testament for classical purity of diction and polished elegance of rhetoric. The Apostles and Evangelists carried the heavenly treasure in earthen vessels that the power and grace of God might become more manifest. Calvin justly remarks, with special reference to Paul, that by a singular providence of God the highest mysteries have been committed to us "*sub contemptibili verborum humilitate*," that our faith may not rest on the power of human eloquence, but solely on the efficacy of the divine Spirit. Yet the New Testament has a beauty of its own, which can be appreciated by the illiterate and the scholar alike, and which grows upon the mind and heart and will never fade away.

MATTHEW'S style is simple, calm, dignified, majestic. He has a fondness for grouping and topical arrangement. He gives prominence to the words of our Saviour and strings them together as so many precious pearls, one weighty sentence following another till the effect is overwhelming. He points out the fulfilment of prophecy with his phrase $ἵνα\ πληρωθῇ\ τὸ\ ῥηθέν$, which occurs twelve times in his Gospel. While he takes his quotations freely from the Septuagint, he adapts them to the Hebrew when it makes the fulfilment more distinct. He is less Hebraistic than Mark, and uses such a genuine classical paronomasia as: "Those wretches he will wretchedly destroy" (21 : 41). His vocabulary contains about 130 words not found elsewhere in the New Testament. He alone uses the term "the kingdom of *heaven*" (32 times); he calls God "the heavenly Father," and Jerusalem "the holy city," and "the city of the Great King."

MARK writes the poorest Greek of all the Evangelists, but has a peculiar freshness and vivacity, with a number of picturesque details, which prove his originality and independence, his intimacy with Peter and sympathy with his impulsive and impetuous temperament. He rushes from place to place, from event to event. He records chiefly the miracles which excite astonishment, and must have made a strong impression upon the Roman reader so fond of displays of conquering power. He introduces a number of Latin terms. He quotes some words and phrases in the original Aramaic, and characterizes the acting persons. His favorite adverb is "forthwith" or "straightway" ($\dot{\epsilon}\nu\theta\dot{\epsilon}\omega\varsigma$, $\epsilon\dot{\upsilon}\theta\dot{\upsilon}\varsigma$), which occurs more frequently in his Gospel than in all the other Gospels combined, and is characteristic of the rapidity of his movement, like the American "Go ahead!" With this is connected his preference for the historical present. He loves affectionate diminutives, as little child, damsel, little daughter, little dog, etc.*

LUKE, the author of the third Gospel and the Acts, is the most literary among the Evangelists. He was an educated physician and acquainted with contemporary history. He refers to the emperors Augustus, Tiberius, Claudius, to the census of Quirinius, to the Herodian family, and to the procurators Felix and Festus. He has the richest vocabulary among the Evangelists, and the largest number of words not occurring elsewhere in the New Testament (about 300 in the Gospel and 470 in the Acts). His medical knowledge appears in the accounts of miracles of healing; his familiarity with nautical terms in the last two chapters of Acts. His account of the voyage and shipwreck of Paul, whom he accompanied from Cæsarea to Rome, has been minutely investigated by an experienced Scotch seaman (Commodore James Smith, of Jordanhill), and establishes the remarkable fact that Luke, though not a professional seaman, was a close and accurate observer of the winds and storms, and the management and movements of a ship. He furnishes more information of ancient navigation in those two

---

* $\pi\alpha\iota\delta\acute{\iota}ον$, $κορ\acute{α}σιον$, $θυγ\acute{α}τριον$, $κυν\acute{α}ριον$, $\dot{\iota}χθ\acute{υ}διον$, $\dot{ω}τ\acute{α}ριον$.

chapters than any single document of antiquity.* He uses pure Greek where he writes independently, as in the historiographic preface to his Gospel (1 : 1–4), which compares favorably in style with the prefaces of Herodotus and Thucydides, and surpasses them in combined modesty and dignity. In the second part of the Acts (the "we sections" so called, beginning ch. 16 : 10, and resumed 20 : 3, and continued to the close), he reports as an eye-witness and companion of Paul. But his style is Hebraistic in those sections where he depended on older sources. This is especially the case in the first two chapters of his Gospel, in those charming songs of Zachariah, Mary, and Simeon, which are the last of the Hebrew psalms and the first of Christian hymns. The greater part of the Gospel and the first part of the Acts occupy a middle position between classical Greek and Hebrew Greek. There is a close resemblance between his style and that of Paul, as appears specially in the account of the institution of the Lord's Supper. Both are fond of such words as "grace," "mercy," "righteousness," "knowledge," "the power of the Lord."† Luke alone relates the pentecostal miracle, and uses the word "Spirit" or "Holy Spirit" again and again. He has a preference for words of joy and gladness, in accordance with the cheerful and hopeful tone of his books. His Gospel is the gospel of humanity and poetry; the Acts is the gospel of the Holy Spirit and a record of a peaceful spiritual campaign from Jerusalem to Rome, marching from victory to victory, and turning even persecution and martyrdom into an occasion of joy and praise.

PAUL has the most characteristic style of all the apostolic writers. It reflects the originality and intensity of his mind, and the violence of his transition from Judaism to Christianity, by which the fanatical persecutor became an enthusiastic friend. His style is full of force and fire, but rough and incorrect. He wrestles with the language, and tries to subdue and to mould it for his purpose. His ideas overflow the ordinary channels of speech, and the pressure of his thoughts boldly de-

* Compare his verbs for sailing: πλέω, to sail; ἀποπλέω, to sail from; βραδυπλέω, to sail slowly; ἐκπλέω, to sail away; διαπλέω, to sail through; καταπλέω, to arrive; ὑποπλέω, to sail under the lee; παραπλέω, to sail by; ἀνάγομαι, to put to sea; ἐπικέλλω, to run the ship ashore, etc.

† Holtzmann enumerates about two hundred expressions or phrases which Luke and Paul have in common, and are more or less foreign to the other writers of the New Testament.

fies the rules of grammar. He abounds in rapid leaps, sudden transitions, grammatical irregularities, antitheses, paradoxes, anacolutha, ellipses, oxymora and paronomasias. We may well say of his words, with Jerome and Calvin, that they are peals of thunder and flashes of lightning.* He "has the style of genius, but not the genius of style." Although he was trained in rabbinical schools, he departs from the simplicity of the Hebrew, and uses long and involved periods, which might be broken up into half-a-dozen English sentences, as Eph. 1: 1–14. He is dialectic and argumentative, reasoning now from Scripture, now from experience. He frequently uses logical particles.† He disclaims classical elegance and calls himself "rude in speech," though not "in knowledge." Nevertheless he rises at times to the pinnacle of lofty eloquence and poetic beauty. The triumphant pæan of faith (in the closing verses of the eighth chapter of Romans), and the seraphic ode on love (in the thirteenth chapter of First Corinthians), have no parallel in literature ancient or modern, and are alone sufficient to prove that his genius was under the power of divine inspiration.

The Epistle to the Hebrews is more pure and correct in style than the Epistles of Paul, and this difference is one of the chief arguments against its Pauline authorship. It has 168 words not occurring elsewhere in the New Testament.

JOHN differs in his style from Paul as a placid lake does from a rushing torrent, as a gentle breeze from the storm, as an anthem of peace from a trumpet of war. His style is clear, calm, serene, simple and childlike. Yet in the uncompromising discourses of the Lord against the Pharisees, and in the Apocalypse, we hear the Son of Thunder. The Apocalypse is the most Hebraistic of all New Testament books, and was probably written before the destruction of Jerusalem, about twenty years before the fourth Gospel. But the Gospel, though purer in diction, is conceived in a Hebrew spirit, which dominates the Greek form. This fact diminishes the difficulty of ascribing the two books to the same author, considering the difference of matter and the prophetic basis of the Apocalypse. John uses few particles; his favorite one is "therefore" ($o\tilde{v}\nu$), which signifies temporal

---

* Jerome: "*Non verba, sed tonitrua.*" Erasmus: "*Tonat, fulgurat, meras flammas loquitur Paulus,*" and: "*Quid unquam Cicero dixit eloquentius?*" Calvin: "*Fulmina sunt, non verba.*"

† $o\tilde{v}\nu$, ἄρα, ἄρα οὖν, γάρ, εἰ γάρ, εἰ δέ, οὐκέτι, τί οὖν, οὐ μόνον δέ, ἀλλά.

sequence and providential connection. He advances not by a dialectical process of argumentation, like Paul, but by a succession of assertions which have the force of self-evident truths. He is a mystic, not a scholastic; a seer, not a reasoner. His sentences are short and weighty. His vocabulary is limited, but includes words of the profoundest import, as "life," "light," "truth," "love," which occur again and again, and are contrasted with "death," "darkness," "falsehood," "hatred." He is "*verbis facillimus, sensu difficillimus.*" He alone calls Christ the "Logos" (the Interpreter or Revealer of the Godhead), "the Only Begotten Son," "the Light of the world," "the Bread of life," "the Good Shepherd," "the Vine"—designations which have ever since guided the Church in her devotions. He calls the Holy Spirit "the Paraclete" or Advocate, who pleads the cause of believers here on earth, while Christ, who is also a "Paraclete," intercedes for them before God's throne in heaven. He gives us the inside view of the life of Christ, and introduces us into the holy of holies.

CHAPTER LXXVIII.

HISTORY OF THE STUDY OF HELLENISTIC GREEK.

The study of Hellenistic, as distinct from classical, Greek is modern. The Greek fathers were more concerned about the doctrinal contents than the form and language of the Scripture. The Latin fathers and the mediæval schoolmen were either entirely ignorant of Greek or had only an elementary knowledge of it, and depended on the Latin Vulgate, which the Council of Trent afterwards put on a par with the original.

The Revival of Letters raised the classical Greek from oblivion, and prepared the way for the Reformers, who had a good general knowledge of Greek, but cared little for the differences of dialects. Beza and Henry Stephens first observed the differences between the classical and Hellenistic idioms, and saw in the Hebraisms an element of beauty.

The mechanical theory of inspiration which soon followed the Reformation, confounded inspiration with dictation, and led to the notion that the Greek of the New Testament must be perfect to the extent of grammatical accuracy and classical purity. Hence arose the controversy between the Purists and the Hebraists. It was carried on chiefly by Dutch and German scholars till the end of the seventeenth century, when the Hebraists gained the ascendency.

GEORG PASOR (Professor of Greek at Franeker, d. 1637) prepared a little lexicon of the New Testament, which was often republished, and left also in manuscript a grammar of the New Testament, which was published at Groningen, 1655.

A Swiss divine, CASPAR WYSS (Professor in the Theological College of Zürich, d. 1659), made the first attempt to collect and classify the peculiarities of the New Testament idiom, in his *Dialectologia sacra*, Tigur., 1650.

SALOMON GLASIUS, a Lutheran divine at Jena (d. 1656), wrote a *Philologia sacra*, in which he paid much attention to the Hebraisms of the New Testament. Then followed a long interval, till PH. H. HAAB, a Swabian pastor (d. 1833), appeared with a Hebrew-Greek Grammar of the New Testament (1815), which is very imperfect and marks no real advance.

The founder of the New Testament Grammar on the basis of the modern classical philology is GEORG BENEDICT WINER (Professor at Leipzig, d. 1858). His *Grammatik des Neutestamentlichen Sprachidioms* (1st ed., Leipzig, 1822; 7th ed. by Lünemann, 1867; two excellent translations by Moulton, and by Thayer) marks an epoch in Biblical philology. He traced the Hellenistic peculiarities to fixed principles and reduced them to a system. He gave a new impulse to a sound grammatical exegesis. The rich fruits of his labors can be seen in the commentaries of De Wette, Meyer, Weiss, Alford, Trench, Ellicott, Lightfoot. His work is still an authority on the subject, but behind the latest results of textual criticism. Besides Winer, we must mention ALEX. BUTTMANN'S *Greek Grammar of the New Testament* (1859, English translation by JOS. H. THAYER, 1873); S. A. GREEN'S *Handbook* (London, 1885); and EDWIN HATCH'S *Essays in Biblical Greek* (Oxford, 1889).

The best dictionaries of the Greek Testament are those of W. GRIMM (in Latin, 3d ed., 1887); CREMER (*Biblisch-theologisches Wörterbuch*, etc., 5th ed., 1887, English translation from the 2d ed., 1880); E. ROBINSON (English, originally based on Wahl's *Clavis*, 1836, 1850, 1879); JOS. H. THAYER (1886, based on the 2d ed. of Grimm, 1879, with valuable additions and supplements and with constant reference to the latest recensions of the text by Tischendorf, Westcott and Hort, and the Revised English Version of 1881).

Concordances of the Greek Testament by BRUDER (4th ed., 1887), and HUDSON, revised by EZRA ABBOT (1885).*

CHAPTER LXXIX.

THE SUB-APOSTOLIC GREEK.

The Apostolic Fathers so called, who are supposed to have been personal disciples of the Apostles, and wrote between the end of the first and the middle of the second century (Clement of Rome, Polycarp, Ignatius, Barnabas, Hermas, and the anonymous author of the *Didache*), belong already to a new generation of Christians and differ in style as well as in depth, vigor and originality from the Apostles. Their Greek has no more the informing Hebrew spirit and coloring of men born and bred in the synagogue It breathes the atmosphere of a native Christian community after the distinction between Jewish and Gentile converts had disappeared.

The *Didache* or *Teaching of the Twelve Apostles*, discovered and first published by Bryennios (1883), comes, of all the sub-apostolic writings, nearest to the New Testament in its style and vocabulary, and this is a strong argument for its great antiquity (probably before the close of the first century), and its Jewish-Christian origin (probably in Palestine or Syria). Its style is simple, natural, sententious, like that of the Sermon on the Mount, and shows traces of Hebrew parallelism, antithetic and synthetic. Its vocabulary embraces 552 words, of which 504 are found in the New Testament. Among these are a number of Hebraisms, such as "not all" (οὐ πᾶς, *lo col*) for no one (οὐδείς); "to accept the person" (πρόσωπον λαμβάνειν) for to favor, to show partiality; the designation "Preparation day" (παρασκευή) for Friday.†

---

* For a full list of helps to the study of the Greek Testament, see Schaff's *Companion*, pp. 1–4.

† See Schaff: *The Teaching of the Twelve Apostles*, pp. 95–113 (New York, 3d ed., 1889).

CHAPTER LXXX.

THE ECCLESIASTICAL GREEK.

The ecclesiastical or patristic and Byzantine Greek is important for the student of ancient Church History. It is the language used by Christian authors during the Roman and Byzantine periods till the fall of Constantinople (1453). It is the common Greek dialect of the time and country of the writers, but modified by the influence of the Septuagint and the New Testament. It includes a number of technical theological terms, which grew out of the theological controversies in the Nicene and Post-Nicene ages, and refer mostly to the doctrine of the trinity, the incarnation, and the person of Christ.

Examples: οὐσία, the divine essence or substance; ὑπόστασις or πρόσωπον, the divine person (Father, Son, and Spirit); ἐνανθρώπησις and ἐνσάρκωσις (*incarnatio*), the incarnation; ὁμοούσιος, equal in essence, ὁμοιούσιος, similar in essence, and ἑτεροούσιος, of a different essence (the first was the Athanasian or orthodox, the second the Semi-Arian, the third the Arian word for expressing the relation of Christ to God the Father); λόγος ἄσαρκος, the Logos before the incarnation; ἰδιότης denotes the property of each person of the Trinity, ἀγεννησία that of the Father, γεννησία that of the Son, ἐκπόρευσις that of the Holy Spirit; περιχώρησις (*inexistentia, inhabitatio*) is the term for the intercommunion of the three persons of the immanent Trinity; κοινωνία ἰδιωμάτων (*communicatio idiomatum*), the communion of attributes of the person and of the two natures of Christ; θεάνθρωπος, the God-Man; θεοτόκος, bearing God (*Deipara*), or Mother of God, applied to the Virgin Mary.

The best Greek writers among the fathers are Origen, Eusebius, Athanasius, Basil, Gregory of Nazianzus, Gregory of Nyssa, Chrysostom, Cyril of Alexandria, John of Damascus, and Photius. The later Greek commentators and theologians were mostly imitators and compilers.

The same dialect was also used by a large number of secular writers, and by the Byzantine historians, who give a vast amount of information on the manners, customs, and commerce of the Eastern Empire from the foundation of Constantinople to the conquest of the Turks (1453).

After the removal of the seat of empire to Constantinople or New Rome, the Greeks were called *Romans,* sometimes *Eastern Romans,* to distinguish them from the Western or genuine Romans; while the national term *Hellenes* was generally used by Christian writers in the same sense as pagans or idolaters.

During the reign of Constantine the Great and a short time after, the Latin was the language of the court of legislation and administration. In the reign of Justinian, the Latin disappeared from the East, but left its impress upon the Greek in many words and phrases. The Teutonic invasions, being merely transient, had no effect upon the Greek. But the Slavonians (Scythians), who since the eighth century had settled in the depopulated provinces of continental and peninsular Greece, commingled with Greek blood, adopted the Greek language and religion, and gave to it a considerable number of nouns, names of places, and the diminutive ending *-itza.*

The principal helps for the study of patristic Greek are: J. CASP. SUICER (Schweizer, Professor in the Carolinum at Zürich, d. 1684, of whom it was said that "he understood more Greek than all the Greeks taken together"): *Thesaurus ecclesiasticus e Patribus Græcis,* Amsterd., 1682, 2 vols. fol.; two enlarged edd., 1728 and 1746, with supplements. CAROLUS DU FRÈSNE (Sieur DU CANGE, an eminent French scholar and expert in mediæval philology and history, 1610–1688): *Glossarium ad Scriptores mediæ et infimæ Græcitatis,* Lugd., 1688, 2 vols. fol. He wrote also a *Glossarium mediæ et infimæ Latinitatis* (1678), best ed. by Henschel, Paris, 1840–50, in 7 vols. 4to; revised by L. Favre, 1884–87, 10 vols.

For the Byzantine Greek, E. A. SOPHOCLES: *Greek Lexicon of the Roman and Byzantine Period* (from B.C. 146 to A.D. 1100), Boston, 1870; revised ed. by Dr. JOS. H. THAYER, New York, 1887.

SECOND SECTION: BIBLICAL ARCHÆOLOGY.

CHAPTER LXXXI.

IDEA OF BIBLICAL ARCHÆOLOGY.

Biblical Archæology* or Biblical Antiquities is a systematic description of the external and internal condition of the countries and nations in which the Holy Scriptures originated and to which they refer. It must give a clear and full view of the state of civilization, the public and private life, the manners and customs of the Israelites from the beginning to the close of the apostolic age.

The art of the archæologist † consists in so grouping together the various aspects of ancient Jewish life and society with its base and surroundings as to present a complete and faithful picture, and to transfer the student to the time and situation of the authors and actors of the Bible.

Biblical Archæology is essentially Hebrew Archæology, since the Bible was mainly written by Hebrews and in Palestine. But inasmuch as the Jews themselves came in contact with other nations—the Egyptians, Phœnicians, Assyrians, Chaldæans, Medes, Persians, Greeks and Romans—these must all be noticed incidentally as far as is necessary for the illustration of the Bible.

Archæology is indispensable for the material understanding of the Bible, as grammar is indispensable for its verbal understanding. At the same time it gathers its information from the Bible itself and brings it into systematic order. It is both a preparation for exegesis and the result of exegesis. In this way archæology and exegesis mutually illustrate and supplement each other. The same applies to Biblical Isagogic.

---

* 'Αρχαιολογία, from ἀρχαῖος, *old*, and λόγος. It corresponds to the Latin *Antiquitates* (*Alterthumswissenschaft*, or *Alterthümer*).
† 'Αρχαιολόγος, *antiquarius*.

To Biblical Archæology in Exegetical Theology corresponds Christian or Ecclesiastical Archæology in Historical Theology. Sometimes they are comprehended under the common name of "Sacred Archæology," as distinct from Secular Archæology.

CHAPTER LXXXII.

PARTS OF ARCHÆOLOGY.

The boundaries of Biblical Archæology are not clearly and uniformly defined. Josephus embraces under it the whole Jewish history down to the beginning of the rebellion against the Romans; while Ewald, more appropriately, but too narrowly, confines it to the laws and customs of the Hebrew theocracy and treats it as a mere appendix to Jewish history.

I. In its widest sense, Archæology comprehends the following divisions:
1. Biblical Geography.
2. Natural History of the Bible.
3. Domestic and Social Life of the Jews.
4. Civil and Political Institutions.
5. Ecclesiastical or Religious Institutions, rites and ceremonies.
6. History of the Jews till the destruction of Jerusalem (A.D. 70) or down to the second destruction under Hadrian (135). Schürer excludes the older history; he begins with the Maccabæan period, and concludes with the age of Hadrian.
7. History of Biblical Times in the Old and New Testaments (*Biblische Zeitgeschichte*), *i.e.*, the contemporary history of the Jews and Gentile nations with which they came in contact. But this section cannot be clearly distinguished from the sixth, and coincides with it in part. Schneckenburger and Hausrath embrace under the History of New Testament Times (*Neutestamentliche Zeitgeschichte*) both the Jewish and heathen history in the time of Christ; Schürer confines it to the Jewish history. The History of Old Testament Times embraces the contemporary history of the Egyptians, Babylonians, Assyrians, Persians, Greeks, and Romans.

Some of these departments are so large as to require separate treatment. The sixth and seventh divisions belong to history rather than to archæology, but the departments are intertwined

II. Archæology, in the narrower and proper sense, should be confined to the domestic, social, civil and religious life, laws and institutions of the Jews. It describes the *results* of Jewish history, not its growth—history *at rest*, not history in motion. The latter belongs to Historical Theology.

CHAPTER LXXXII I.

SOURCES OF ARCHÆOLOGY.

1. The CANONICAL SCRIPTURES of the Old and New Testaments are the chief and most authentic source.

2. The JEWISH APOCRYPHA, especially the Books of the Maccabees, are the connecting link between the Old and New Testaments. They explain the religious and political condition, and many customs and usages of the Jews at the time of Christ.

3. The writings of PHILO of Alexandria (d. about A.D. 40), and of JOSEPHUS (a Jewish priest, b. A.D. 37, at Jerusalem, d. at Rome after 103). The *Antiquities of the Jews*, by Josephus,* is invaluable and indispensable for the contemporaneous history of the Jews down to A.D. 66. It was written about 94, with the apologetic aim to inspire the Greeks and Romans with more respect for his countrymen. His *History of the Jewish War* is the only authentic source for that important event, the destruction of Jerusalem, which closes the history of the Jewish theocracy.

4. The TALMUD (תלמוּד, *Doctrine, Corpus Doctrinæ*) gives information on the Jewish theology and jurisprudence at the time of Christ. It consists of two parts, the *Mishna* (*i.e., Repetition, the Second Law*) and the *Gemara* (*i.e., Supplement, Conclusion,* viz., of rabbinical wisdom). The Mishna is a digest of rabbinical traditions before and after Christ concerning the Mosaic law, and was reduced to writing in its present form by a wealthy and influential rabbi, Jehudah the Holy, Patriarch of Tiberias at the close of the second or early part of the third century. As it is very concisely written, it required a commentary, and this led to the Gemara. Of this there are two, the Palestinian Gemara, compiled about A.D. 390, and the Babylonian Gemara, which is much larger and was completed

* Ἰουδαϊκὴ Ἀρχαιολογία, in twenty Books. Numerous editions and translations. See Schürer, Vol. I., pp. 56 sqq.

about A.D. 500 under the supervision of the patriarch of Babylon. The Mishna is of more importance for Biblical Archæology than the Gemara.

5. The GREEK and ROMAN authors are of little account. When they speak of the despised Jews, they mostly borrow from Josephus and mix errors with facts. So Tacitus and Justinus. On the geography of Palestine, Strabo furnishes some information; on natural history, Pliny.

6. Reports of EASTERN TRAVELERS from Jerome (who lived many years in Bethlehem) to our own age, especially their descriptions of natural scenery and the manners and customs of the people, which have undergone little change from the age of the patriarchs and prophets.

7. MONUMENTAL sources, written and unwritten. These are becoming more and more important as discoveries and researches in Bible lands progress. The monumental evidences for Old Testament history from the tombs and excavated cities, and hieroglyphic and cuneiform inscriptions, outweigh critical conjectures and skeptical objections.

(*a*) For the Jews: ruins of eleven old synagogues (all in Galilee), walls, bridges, aqueducts, tombs, coins, inscriptions, and the triumphal arch of Titus in Rome, adorned with a delineation in relief of the spoils of the temple at Jerusalem.

(*b*) For the surrounding nations, and indirectly for the Jews: Phœnician remains (inscriptions); Egyptian monuments and hieroglyphic inscriptions; Assyrian, Babylonian and Persian monuments, and cuneiform inscriptions.

CHAPTER LXXXIV.

BIBLICAL GEOGRAPHY.

Biblical Geography is a description of Bible Lands, namely:
1. Egypt, the cradle of Israel.
2. The Sinaitic Peninsula, the school of Israel.
3. Palestine, the final home of Israel, the native land of Christ and the Apostles, and of the Christian Church.

The Bible Lands are the best commentary on the Bible, as the Bible is the best guide-book in Bible Lands. The Land and the Book mutually illustrate and confirm each other. Palestine has appropriately been called (by Renan) "the fifth

Gospel," lacerated and torn, but still legible. It furnishes the illustrations to the other four Gospels. It is nature's framework to the life of Christ. Palestine was sufficiently secluded to keep the Jews from contaminating contact with idolatrous nations, and yet sufficiently central between Asia, Africa and Europe and on the Mediterranean to illuminate the whole world with the gospel.

Topography is a part of geography, and deals with special localities. It is of uncommon interest in Jerusalem, involving the disputed question as to the site of the holy sepulchre.

In a wider sense, Biblical Geography touches also upon Arabia, Mesopotamia, Phœnicia, Assyria, Babylonia, Persia, Asia Minor, Greece, and Italy as far as Rome. The Bible brings us into contact with the whole ancient world.

Every student should visit Bible Lands, if he can, and finish his theological education there. They will make a deeper impression and be of more practical use to him for sermonizing and the religious instruction of youth than many commentaries. Palestine is a ruin, but an eloquent ruin, surrounded by sacred memories. Travel in the East takes away much of the poetry, but deepens and enlivens the sense of the reality.

CHAPTER LXXXV.

NATURAL HISTORY OF THE BIBLE.

(Physica Sacra.)

The Natural History of the Bible gives an account of the climate, the natural productions, minerals, plants, and animals of Palestine.

The Bible is full of allusions to nature, and turns its familiar scenes and products into symbols of ideas and vehicles of moral instruction.

The Parables of Christ rest on the correspondence between nature and man, between the material and the spiritual universe, between creation and redemption, and derive lessons of wisdom from the common objects and events of life.

The Bible most frequently mentions the rose, lily, vine, olive, fig—among plants; the dove, eagle, vulture—among birds; the horse, ox, sheep, lamb, goat, ass, camel, dog—among animals.

Rare names: The "unicorn" (Isa. 34:7; Job 39:9; Ps. 29:6) is an unfortunate translation of the Authorized Version for "wild ox" (Revised Version). The "behemoth" in Job (40:15-24) is probably the hippopotamus or river-horse of Africa. The "leviathan" (Job 41:1 sqq.; Ps. 74:14; Isa. 27:1) is the crocodile or some other sea-monster.

CHAPTER LXXXVI.

ARCHÆOLOGY PROPER.

Archæology in the strict sense, as defined in chapter lxxxii, includes:

1. DOMESTIC and SOCIAL Antiquities: an account of the tents and houses of the Hebrews, their dress and personal ornaments, their food and meals, their family relations and usages, wedding ceremonies, burial of the dead, slavery, social intercourse, nomadic life, agriculture, trade and commerce, weights and measures.

2. CIVIL and POLITICAL Antiquities: the patriarchal, the republican, and the monarchical forms of government, the administration of justice, Hebrew penalties, war and military affairs.

3. RELIGIOUS or SACRED Antiquities (*Sacra*). This is the most important part, as religion lay at the foundation of Jewish society and the Jewish state, which was a theocracy. Here belongs a description of sacred *places* (the tabernacle, the temple, the synagogue); sacred *seasons* (sabbaths, new moons, annual festivals); sacred *persons* (priests, Levites, prophets, scribes); sacred *things* (altar, furniture of the temple, priestly garments); sacred *acts*, *rites* and *ceremonies* (sacrifices, oblations, purifications, circumcision, the passover, etc.).

The Tabernacle, the Temple, the Synagogue, and the Mosaic worship in its typical import, are described in numerous monographs.

Hebrew psalmody may be treated here in connection with public worship, but belongs also to Biblical Introduction.

The religion of idolatrous nations with whom the Jews came in contact must not be forgotten, especially the service of Baal and Moloch.

4. The SCIENCE and ART of the Hebrews were closely con-

nected with their religion, but may also be separately discussed. Domestic and mechanical arts, the art of writing, music and musical instruments, and poetry.

5. Jewish THEOLOGY includes an account of the sects of the Pharisees, Sadducees, and Essenes, which originated in and after the Maccabæan period, and of the two rival schools of Hillel and Shammai, who lived shortly before Christ, and furnish some parallels to his teaching. But the influence of these rabbis was confined to Judaism, while the teaching of Christ has regenerated and benefited the world. He is the founder, not of a school or party, but of a spiritual kingdom for all mankind.

CHAPTER LXXXVII.

HISTORY OF ARCHÆOLOGY.

In the history of Biblical Archæology, we may distinguish four periods, with special reference to the geography of Palestine:

1. The period of devout pilgrimage, monastic tradition and superstition, from the pilgrimage of St. Helena (the mother of Constantine the Great) and the discovery of the supposed holy places, down to the seventeenth century.

EUSEBIUS (d. 340) is the father of Biblical geography (as well as church history) by his work on the names of places mentioned in the Scriptures. Jerome translated it into Latin.*

From the Middle Ages we have a large number of Itineraries of Christian pilgrims, monks and crusaders.

2. In the seventeenth century several Dutch divines, especially BOCHART (d. 1667) and RELAND (d. 1718), laid the foundation for a systematic and critical treatment of Archæology. Bochart's *Hierozoicon* (1663, Rosenmüller's ed., 1793, 3 vols.) is still the best work on Biblical zoology. Reland produced a standard work on Palestine down to the era of the Crusades.†
VITRINGA wrote the best book on the Synagogue (1696). A vast collection of older monographs on Biblical Archæology is

---

* Περὶ τῶν τοπικῶν ὀνομάτων τῶν ἐν τῇ θείᾳ γραφῇ, or *Onomasticon Urbium et Locorum Scripturæ Sacræ*, first printed by the Jesuit Bonfrère (Paris, 1631); best edition by De Lagarde, *Onomastica Sacra*, I., 207–304 (Göttingen, 1870 and 1887).

† *Antiquitates Sacræ Veterum Hebræorum* (Trajecti-ad-Rhenum, 1708, etc.); *Palæstina ex monumentis veteribus illustrata* (Traj., 1714, etc.).

contained in Ugolino's *Thesaurus Antiquitatum Sacrarum* (Venice, 1744–69, 34 vols. fol.).

3. The period of independent critical research and scientific travel began with the geography of CARL RITTER of Berlin, the founder of scientific geography (d. 1859),* and his friend, Edward Robinson of New York, the pioneer of Palestine exploration.† Dr. Robinson (d. 1863) was accompanied in his first journey by Dr. ELI SMITH, an American missionary in Syria, who was quite familiar with classical and vulgar Arabic. He minutely examined the Scripture localities, trusting only his own eyes and the Bible, and disregarding to an excess of independence the monastic traditions. But he could examine only the surface of Palestine.

4. A new period began with the excavations of subterranean Jerusalem and other interesting localities by the labors of the "Palestine Exploration Fund," established in England, 1865, the American Palestine Exploration Society founded in New York in 1871, and a similar German Society founded in 1878. The results of the English Society are published in Quarterly Statements, in an illustrated volume, *The Recovery of Jerusalem* (1872), and in the Map of Palestine with text (1880). The American Exploration Society has investigated the lands east of the Jordan, but stopped operations in 1878, leaving the whole field to the English. The German Society issues a periodical. The discovery of the Moabite Stone by Klein in 1868 was independent of the English society.

Many discoveries are yet to be made in Jerusalem and the lands east of the Jordan, as well as in the Sinaitic Peninsula. New and fresh arguments and illustrations of the Bible will yet be dug out from the sacred soil trod by our Saviour and covered with the rubbish of ages.

The Egyptological and Babylonio-Assyrian discoveries and researches are still in progress, and throw side-lights on Biblical archæology and history.

* The Palestine part is in *Die Erdkunde*, Vols. XIV.–XVII., revised edition, 1848–55. English translation by Gage, New York, 1866, 4 vols.

† *Biblical Researches in Palestine and Adjacent Regions*, in 1838 and 1852; 3d ed., Boston, 1867, 3 vols. Also in German. His *Physical Geography of Palestine*, 1865, is a posthumous work, and only a portion of a complete physical, historical, and topographical history of the Holy Land, which he had projected.

CHAPTER LXXXVIII.

LITERATURE OF ARCHÆOLOGY.

See the accurate lists of archæological works in the first part of Schürer's *Geschichte des jüdischen Volkes im Zeitalter Jesu Christi* (1890), pp. 4 sqq.

1. General works on Archæology: Jahn (1817–25); Rosenmüller (1818–20); De Wette (1814, 4th ed. by Räbiger, 1864); * Ewald (1844, 3d ed., 1866, translated); Saalschütz (1855); *Keil (1857, 2d ed., 1875); Fish (1876); Filion (1883); Bissel (1888) ; * Schürer (2d ed., 1890, 2 vols., Eng. transl.; by far the best for later Jewish history).

2. Bible Dictionaries of Winer, Kitto, revised by Alexander, Smith, Schenkel, Riehm, Zeller, Schaff (also the Biblical articles in the general theological encyclopedias of Herzog, and Mc Clintock and Strong). These works contain archæological information in convenient alphabetical arrangement.

3. The literature on Bible Lands and the geography of Palestine: * Reland; * Ritter (new ed., 1850–55); * Robinson (1867); * K. v. Raumer (1835 and '60); * Tobler (1845–77); Van de Velde (1854); * Stanley (1856 and '61); De Vogüé (1865–77, 2 vols.); * W. M. Thomson (new ed., 1880, in 3 vols.); * Tristram (1865, '76 and '81); Bovet (1864); Furrer (1865); Schaff (1878 and '89); Orelli (1878); Conder (1878); Merrill (1881); Guérin (1882, sqq., with magnificent illustrations); Pierotti (1882); * Stapfer (1885); Hull (1886); Dawson (1888).*

4. Topography of the Holy Land: Tristram (1876). Topography of Jerusalem and the Temple: George Williams (1849, 2 vols.) and Tobler (1854, 2 vols.).

5. Handbooks for Travelers in Bible Lands: Murray and Bädeker.

6. Maps of Palestine in all good Bible Dictionaries. *Map of Western Palestine* by Conder and Kitchener, in 26 sheets, each sheet accompanied by a memoir showing the scientific results of the survey undertaken by the Palestine Exploration Fund, London, 1880.

---

* A careful list of books on Palestine to 1850 in Ritter's *Erdkunde*, Vol. XV., pp. 33 sqq.; another down to 1856, in Appendix I. to Vol. II. of Robinson's *Biblical Researches*, pp. 533–555, and a third to 1866 in Dr. Tobler's *Bibliotheca Geographica Palestinæ* (Leipzig, 1867), pp. 265; Supplement, 1875. Tobler, a practical traveler of Switzerland who visited Palestine four times, enumerates more than one thousand (1086) writers on Palestine from A.D. 333 to 1866, of which he examined no less than eight hundred and ninety-four.

THIRD SECTION: BIBLICAL ISAGOGIC.
(*Historico-Critical Introduction to the Bible.*)

CHAPTER LXXXIX.
NATURE OF ISAGOGIC.

Biblical Isagogic is a historico-critical Introduction to the Scriptures of the Old and New Testaments. It is a literary history of the Bible from its origin to the present time. It embraces a summary of preliminary information which is necessary or useful for the understanding of the Scriptures in whole or in part. Its limits are not clearly defined, but it includes all the questions which are generally discussed in an introduction to the several books, concerning the authorship, the authenticity and integrity of the text, the time and place of composition, the aim of the writer, the class of readers, and the principal commentators.

NAMES: Εἰσαγαγωγὴ εἰς τὰς θείας γραφάς, *Isagoge*, or *Introductio in Scripturam sacram;* first used, the Greek by Adrianus in the fifth, and the Latin by Cassiodorus in the sixth century, but first properly naturalized in the Reformed Church, since 1643, by Andrew Rivetus, who wrote *Isagoge sive Introductio generalis ad Scripturam s. V. et N. T.;* and in the Lutheran Church, since 1767, by J. G. Carpzov (*Introductio ad libros canonicos Bibliorum*). The Germans, since Michaelis and Eichhorn, call it *Isagogik*, or *Einleitung*, or *Historisch-Kritische Einleitung in die heil. Schrift*. The English name chosen by the translators of German works and by Horne and Davidson is *Introduction*. The term *Isagogic* (in conformity with *Apologetic, Logic, Rhetoric*) is more scientific, but not current, although the adjective *isagogical* is used in the sense of *introductory*. Some have proposed the name *Canonic*, but this is only a part of the introduction, viz , the history and doctrine of the Canon.

DEFINITION: Formerly *Isagogic* was a name for an arbitrary collection of all sorts of antiquarian and critical information about the Bible, without any regulating principle or definable limits. Owing to the difficulty of fixing the boundaries, De Wette denies to Isagogic the character of a theological science properly so called. Hupfeld, in an essay on the method of the so-called Introduction to the Bible (1844), has first clearly defined it as a historical science. Reuss, Bleek, Weiss, Holtzmann, and others have followed this method. Yet, after all, it is no part of historical theology, but belongs to exegesis and must be treated throughout as contributory and preliminary to it.

CHAPTER XC.

OBJECT AND VALUE OF ISAGOGIC.

The object of Isagogic is to give a clear and comprehensive view of the character of the Bible as a body of literature and of the historical situation out of which it has grown, and from which alone it can be scientifically understood and interpreted.

The information must be derived from all contemporary literature and history connected with the Bible, but chiefly from the Bible itself; and so far the Introduction presupposes exegesis, while at the same time it prepares the student for exegesis.

I+s value consists in bringing together, under convenient heads and in systematic order, a complete view of the position and influence of the Bible in the history of literature and civilization, and in facilitating the understanding of its several parts.

The origin and history of the Bible should be investigated like that of all other books, without any preconceived theory on inspiration and the canon; yet the result of the investigation, if conducted in the right spirit, will sustain the claims of the Bible. It will be found to be the most remarkable phenomenon in literature, the Book of books, the Book of God as written by holy men under the inspiration of the Holy Spirit for the good of all mankind. It can never die or grow old. It bears translation into all languages without losing its vitality and beauty. It is as universal as the race. It is a perpetual and omnipresent literary miracle with ever-expanding influence and power.

According to the division of the Bible into the Old and New Testaments, Biblical Introduction is divided into Introduction to the Old Testament and Introduction to the New. Each may be treated separately.

CHAPTER XCI.

METHOD AND ARRANGEMENT OF ISAGOGIC.

I. The older and usual, but mechanical method, is to divide Isagogic into *General* and *Special*. The first treats of the names, order, division, collection, language, text, translation and interpretation of the Bible as a whole; the second of the origin, authenticity, integrity, etc., of the several books of the Bible. This method was introduced by Rivet. Eichhorn, Berthold, Hug and De Wette begin with the general part; Schott, Credner, Reuss, and Bleek reverse the order.

II. The historical method grows out of the modern conception of Introduction as a literary history of the Bible. It brings out more clearly the gradual development of the records of revelation, and their fortunes in the Christian Church.

CHAPTER XCII.

PARTS OF ISAGOGIC.

Isagogic in the widest sense of the term includes the following divisions:

I. The ORIGIN of the several books of the Bible. This is Isagogic in the strict sense of the term and embraces the contents of "Special" Introduction, so called. It presents the growth of Biblical literature as a living organism in connection with the history of the Jewish theocracy and the primitive Christian Church.

II. History of the CANON (CANONIC). The collection of these books into a body of sacred literature, distinct from all other books, and constituting the rule of faith and life for those who accept them as divinely inspired.

III. History of the TEXT: 1, the *written* text; 2, the *printed* text.

IV. History of TRANSLATIONS ancient and modern.

V. HERMENEUTIC, or the Science of Interpretation.

VI. History of INTERPRETATION.

These topics are large and important enough to be treated separately. The History of Interpretation may be made a part of Hermeneutic.

CHAPTER XCIII.

HISTORY AND LITERATURE OF ISAGOGIC.

Biblical Introduction as a science is a child of modern critical research, but the material was prepared for centuries. It has been cultivated largely by rationalists, who treat the Bible like any other book, in a purely literary and antiquarian interest, but also by orthodox and evangelical scholars who employ the art of criticism for the vindication of the Bible.

1. Imperfect preparations: AUGUSTIN: *De Doctrina Christiana;* CASSIODORUS: *De Institut. divinarum Scripturarum;* SANTES PAGNINUS of Lucca (d. 1541): *Isagoge ad S. literas* (1538); ANDR. RIVETUS: *Isagoge ad Script. V. et N. T.* (1643); J. H. HOTTINGER: *Clavis Scripturæ* (1649); J. H. HEIDEGGER: *Enchiridion Biblicum* (1681 and often); and other works on special topics.

2. The first critical work on Isagogic is the *Histoire Critique du Vieux Testament* by RICHARD SIMON, a liberal Roman Catholic (priest of the Oratory, d. 1712). It appeared at Paris, 1678, was seized and nearly destroyed, but reprinted at Amsterdam, 1680 and 1685 (English translation, 1682). It was followed by a *Critical History of the Text of the New Testament* (Rotterdam, 1689), and *of the Versions of the New Testament* (Rotterdam, 1690; English translation, London, 1692). He first divided the Old Testament Introduction from that to the New. He was not trammeled by the rigid inspiration theory of the Protestant scholastics, which was unfavorable to a free investigation of the text; but yet he had a propensity to novel opinions which endangered also the theory of his own church. Hence his books were suppressed in France at the recommendation of Bishop Bossuet.

CALMET, a very learned and industrious French Benedictine (1672–1757), wrote a commentary on the Bible, and a very popular *Historical and Critical Dictionary of the Bible* (Paris, 1730, 4 vols.), which was translated into Latin, German, and English. Best English ed. by CHARLES TAYLOR, 9th ed., London, 1847, 5 vols.

3. Since that time Isagogic has been cultivated in whole or in part chiefly by Lowth, Semler, Herder, Griesbach, Eichhorn, Berthold, De Wette, Credner, Hengstenberg, Hävernick, Keil, Guericke, Bleek, Reuss, Baur, Hilgenfeld, Wellhausen, Grau, Strack, Weiss, Holtzmann, Zahn—among Germans; Scholten, Rovers, Kuenen—in Holland; Horne, Ayre, Tregelles, Sam. Davidson, Salmon, Westcott, Hort, Dods, Sanday, Driver—among English writers; also by Roman Catholic scholars, as Jahn, Hug, Scholz, Reusch, Langen (the last two joined

the Old Catholic movement in 1870), Von Aberle, Schanz, Kaulen.

4. The latest and best general books on Old Testament Introduction: BLEEK (1860, 4th ed., revised by Wellhausen, 1878, 5th ed., 1886; English translation by G. H. Venables from the 2d ed., 1869, 2 vols.); REUSS (1881, 2d ed., 1890); KEIL (3d ed., 1873); REUSCH (Old Cath., 4th ed., 1870); STRACK (1883); KUENEN (Dutch, 2d ed., 1885); MARTIN (French, 1887); KILPATRICK (London, 1891); DRIVER (Edinburgh and New York, 1891); CORNILL (1891); CH. H. H. WRIGHT (1892).

On the New Testament: BLEEK (1860, 4th ed. by Mangold, 1886); REUSS (1842, 6th ed., 1887; English translation by Houghton, Boston, 1884, 2 vols.); VON HOFMANN (ed. by Volck, 1881); L. Schulze (1883 and 1885); HOLTZMANN (1885, 3d ed., 1892); WEISS (1886, 2d ed., 1889; English translation, Edinb. 2 vols.); SALMON (London, 1885, 4th ed., 1890); GODET (in course of preparation, 1893, 3 vols., French and English).

CHAPTER XCIV.

BIBLICAL CRITICISM.

Criticism is a method of investigation for the purpose of ascertaining the truth. It inquires into the nature and credibility of the sources of information, and determines the value of traditional opinions. It may be destructive or constructive or both. It is a sifting process which separates truth from error, and fact from fiction. It is necessary for all true progress in exegesis and history, or any other department of science.

Biblical criticism, in the technical sense, is divided into TEXTUAL or VERBAL, and LITERARY or HISTORICAL criticism. They are also distinguished as LOWER and HIGHER criticism; but this must not be understood in an invidious sense; for the one is just as important and as difficult as the other, and requires the same amount of minute and painstaking labor. Textual criticism comes first in order, and lays the basis for literary criticism. The former deals with the text or the form of the Scripture; the latter, with its contents, its literary character and historical surroundings.

Both are comparatively recent departments of Biblical study, and have been cultivated chiefly by Protestant scholars in

Germany, Holland and England. Protestantism favors original investigation. Romanism is hampered by traditionalism, whenever the Church has made a positive deliverance, as on the extent of the canon, and the authority of the Vulgate. But a number of Roman Catholic scholars, as Simon, Jahn, Hug, Scholz, Vercellone, Martin, have taken a prominent part in these studies.

CHAPTER XCV.

TEXTUAL CRITICISM—ITS AIM.

The object and aim of textual criticism is to ascertain and restore, as far as possible, the original text of the Scripture, from all accessible documentary sources. It has nothing to do with sectarian notions or private opinions as to what the Biblical authors might or ought to have written, but simply with what they actually did write. It does not enter into the domain of interpretation, but furnishes a solid foundation for the exegete. It requires patient attention to minute details, microscopic accuracy and judicial impartiality.

The number of textual critics is very small. These devout and reverent scholars took the deepest interest in the letter as well as the contents of the Bible, and devoted years of study to the restoration of the purity of the text.

CHAPTER XCVI.

NECESSITY OF TEXTUAL CRITICISM.

The need for this study arises from the loss of the Hebrew and Greek autographs, and the vast number of readings. These are inevitable in the multiplication of any book by printing, and still more so by transcribing; for manuscripts are not so easily corrected as printed books, which have the benefit of repeated proof-readings.

God has watched with special providence over the essential integrity of the Bible, but he has not chosen to exempt it, by a perpetual miracle or series of miracles, from the common fate of human compositions, and to endow the copyists, translators and printers of the Bible with infallibility. He wastes no miracles. The command, "In the sweat of thy face shalt thou eat bread," applies to intellectual and spiritual as well as physical labor.

For all practical purposes the English or any version of the Bible, on which most readers have to depend, is just as good as the original autographs, which are irrecoverably lost. The Apostles used great freedom in their quotations from the Old Testament, and thereby taught us an important lesson. "The letter killeth, the spirit giveth life" (2 Cor. 3: 6).

CHAPTER XCVII.

CLASSES OF TEXTUAL VARIATIONS.

Errors of transcription may be intentional, or accidental. The former are exceedingly rare in Biblical manuscripts; for transcribers and translators had too much respect for the Bible to venture upon wilful changes and mutilations. Marcion's mutilated Gospel of Luke is an isolated case and was generally condemned.

But accidental and unintentional errors are exceedingly numerous. They crept in very early. The further we go back, the greater was the freedom and carelessness of transcribers. Irenæus, who wrote about A.D. 170, mentions the remarkable difference of reading in the Apocalyptic number, 666 or 616 (Rev. 13: 18), which he found in old copies. Origen complained of the corruption of the text about the middle of the third century. Jerome reports that in his day there were as many distinct forms of the text as codices of the Latin Testament (*tot pœne exemplaria quot codices*), and that the text of the Gospels which were most frequently copied was in great confusion (*apud nos mixta sunt omnia*). It was only after the fifth century that the text assumed a settled and stereotyped form.

Textual variations arose partly from inadvertence, partly from mistakes of the eye in reading or the ear in hearing, partly from corrections of the copyist. They are either omissions, or insertions, or substitutions.

Omissions are rare; for purchasers wanted complete copies. They occur mostly in cases of *homœoteleuton*, or similarity of ending, *i.e.*, where a line or sentence closes with the same word as the preceding one (*e.g.*, 1 John 2: 23).

Insertions or additions were made chiefly from parallel passages (in the Gospels), or from Old Testament quotations, or from lectionaries and liturgies, or from love of paraphrase, or from marginal notes of transcribers, or from oral tradition. The most important cases of this kind are the doxology in the Lord's Prayer (Matt. 6:13), the notice about the pool of Bethesda (John 5:3, 4), the section of the woman taken in adultery (John 7:53–8:11), the concluding verses of Mark (16:9–20), and the passage of the three witnesses in heaven (1 John 5:7, 8). The last is not found in any old Greek manuscript or version or patristic quotation, and is entirely omitted in the Revised Version; while the other passages are retained, with a marginal note. The Septuagint has large additions in Esther and Daniel.

Substitutions are due to resemblances of words in spelling or pronunciation, or to the aim of harmonizing. Examples: 1 John 1:18 (θεός or υἱός); Luke 2:14 (εὐδοκία or εὐδοκίας); Rom. 5:1 (ἔχομεν or ἔχωμεν); Acts 20:28 (θεοῦ or κυρίου); 1 Tim. 3:16 (θεός or ὅς); Rev. 17:8 (καίπερ ἔστιν or καὶ παρέσται).

CHAPTER XCVIII.

THE NUMBER AND VALUE OF VARIOUS READINGS.

We can only make an approximate estimate of the number of variations.

In the Masoretic text of the Hebrew Bible a careful examiner has numbered 1314 different readings of value. Of these only 147 affect the sense or have any theological importance. But when we compare the Hebrew original with the Greek translation, the differences are much more frequent and important, and imply many omissions and additions.

The manuscripts of the Greek Testament are far more numerous than those of the Hebrew Bible and the Septuagint, or any other ancient book, and present a correspondingly large number of variations. Mill in his time (1707) counted 30,000 readings; Scrivener in our age (1874) estimated their number to be "at least fourfold that quantity."* Others run the sum up to 150,000. These include differences in the order of

* *Introduction to the Criticism of the New Testament* (Cambridge, 2d ed., 1874); repeated without change in the third edition (1883), p. 3.

words, in spelling and other trifles, which are ignored in the printed editions. But even this large number is much less in proportion than the 30,000 readings in the few copies of Terence.

The number of variations differs in the different books. Less care was bestowed upon doubtful books (the *Antilegomena*) than those which were generally received by the Church (the *Homologumena*). Dr. B. Weiss found in the five remaining uncial manuscripts of the Apocalypse, which contains about 400 verses, nearly 1,650 departures from the received text (210 in A, 110 in C, over 515 in ℵ, the rest in P, and B Apocalypse).*
The Apocalypse was the last among the apostolic writings which received canonical sanction, at least in the Eastern Church (it is omitted in the Laodicean canon of 363); hence the large number of variations in the oldest manuscripts. The settlement of the canon after the fourth century led to a systematic emendation and unification of the text.

The vast majority of variations in the Greek Testament, at least nineteen out of twenty, are analogous to trifling typographical errors, and of no consequence whatever; of the remaining twentieth part not more than about 400 affect the meaning; of these less than 100 involve any doctrinal or ethical question; and not one of them invalidates any revealed doctrine or moral duty, but only diminishes the number of proof-texts for an article of faith which is sufficiently sustained by other undoubted passages.

The abundance of variations, far from unsettling the general integrity of the text, furnishes us the material for restoring it with approximate certainty to a far greater degree than is the case with any classical author of antiquity. There is no need of resorting to uncertain conjectures and emendations. The true reading is sure to be preserved in the great mass of variations.†

---

* See his minute and careful analysis, *Die Johannes-Apocalypse*, in Gebhardt and Harnack's *Texte und Untersuchungen zur Geschichte der altchristl. Literatur*, Bd. VII., No. 1, 1891 (225 pp.). Weiss gives, in conclusion, an emended text of the Apocalypse, based chiefly upon the Codex Alexandrinus (A), and more nearly agreed with that of Westcott and Hort than that of Tischendorf, who in his eighth edition follows too much the Sinaitic Codex (ℵ).

† See the remarkable judgment of Richard Bentley, one of the greatest classical scholars and critics, and the concurrent testimonies of Tischendorf, Tregelles, Hort, and Ezra Abbot, quoted in Schaff's *Companion to the Greek Testament*, pp. 176 sqq.

Nevertheless the variations in the Bible text are sufficiently important to call for a vast amount of patient learning and research. In the Word of God nothing is indifferent. Reverence for the Bible and a desire to enjoy its primitive purity and integrity should be the strongest motive for the critic. This was the case with the great and good John Albright Bengel. When he first learned, as a student, of the variety of readings in the Greek Testament, he was somewhat disturbed; but this very fact led him to a careful investigation, which strongly confirmed him in his faith and secured him a place among the first textual critics and exegetes. "If the Holy Scriptures," he says, "which have been so often copied, were absolutely without variations, this would be so great a miracle that faith in them would be no longer faith. I am astonished, on the contrary, that from all these transcriptions there has not resulted a greater number of various readings." *

CHAPTER XCIX.

TEXTUAL CRITICISM OF THE OLD TESTAMENT.

The textual criticism of the Old Testament is as yet in its infancy. If it aims simply at the restoration of the Masoretic text, the task is much easier than the criticism of the Greek Testament. But if it aims at a restoration of the ante-Masoretic or primitive text, it is more difficult.

The restoration of the Masoretic text is confined to an examination of the Hebrew MSS. dating from the Masoretic period, which extends from the sixth to the twelfth centuries.

The Jewish rabbis, called Masorets or Traditionalists (from *masora* or *massora*, tradition, *masar*, to hand down), especially those of the school of Tiberias, searched the letter of the Scriptures most diligently, thinking that in them they had eternal life; while they were blind to the Christ of whom they bear witness (John 5: 39). Yet their bibliolatry or letter-worship served a good purpose in securing uniformity. They watched with scrupulous fidelity and unwearied patience over the purity of the text, registering every letter and the frequency of its occurrence, marking the variations (*keri*, the word *read*,

---

* See an interesting account of this chapter in his life, the biography of Burk (Stuttgart, 1831), p. 200.

and *kethib*, the word *written*), and supplying the vowel points, punctuation and accents. They introduced also the versicular division of the Old Testament; while the division into chapters is of Christian origin (from the thirteenth century). The versicular division of the poetical books existed much earlier, perhaps from the beginning, in accordance with the rhythmical structure and the parallelism of members (the lines being called στίχοι, *versus*). The versicular division of the New Testament dates from the middle of the sixteenth century (1551).

The written *Masora* embodies the results of the rabbinical labors on the text of the Hebrew Scriptures. It was originally preserved in distinct books, but was afterwards transferred to the margin of the Bible MSS., mostly with large curtailments (hence the *Masora parva*, an abridgment, as distinct from the *Masora magna*). Its most valuable part is the collection of the marginal Keris, or the readings which the Masorets themselves approved as correct, and derived either from other MSS. or from conjectures. The number of Keris, according to Elias Levita, who spent twenty years in the study of the Masora, is 848, but the Bomberg Bible contains 1171, the Plantin Bible 793.

There is only one recension of the Hebrew text, the Masoretic; and hence there is no difference in the text of the Jewish and Christian, Roman Catholic and Protestant editions of the Hebrew Bible.

Best edition of the Masoretic text by G. BAER (with preface by Delitzsch), Lipsiæ, 1869 sqq.

The most complete collection of the Masoretic material was made by GINSBURG, a converted Jewish scholar and member of the British Old Testament Revision Company.*

CHAPTER C.

SOURCES OF THE OLD TESTAMENT TEXT.

1. The chief source of the Hebrew text of the Old Testament are the manuscripts. They represent, with few variations, the Masoretic text, the older ones in its simpler form, the later ones with the full Masoretic vocalization and accentuation. The oldest known codex, containing the Prophets

* *The Massorah, Compiled from Manuscripts, Alphabetically and Lexically Arranged.* London, 1880–86, 4 vols.

with the Babylonian punctuation, is from the year 916; the oldest complete codex is from 1009 (both in the Imperial Library of St. Petersburg). The former has been republished in facsimile (1876). The Spanish MSS. are generally the most accurate, the Italian come next, the German last. There are rich collections in the libraries at Oxford, Paris, Parma, and St. Petersburg.

The number of Hebrew MSS. cannot be accurately ascertained. Kennicot (Oxford, 1776) mentions 630, of which he thoroughly collated 258, the remainder in part; De Rossi (Parma, 1784–88) collated 751. Strack (*Prolegomena Critica in V. T.*, Lips. 1873) gives a full account of lost and extant codices known at this time.*

2. The other sources for the Hebrew text are the old translations made before the Masora, and the Samaritan Pentateuch (known in Europe since 1620). Of the translations the most important are the Greek Septuagint, the Chaldee Targums, the Syriac Peshitta, and the Latin Vulgate.

Valuable attempts to improve the Masoretic text by means of the versions have been made by Wellhausen (*Text der Bücher Samuels*, 1871), Cornill (*Das Buch des Propheten Ezechiel*, 1886), and by Driver (*The Hebrew Text of the Books of Samuel*, Oxford, 1890, following in the line of Wellhausen). Much more remains to be done.

CHAPTER CI.

THE HEBREW ORIGINAL AND THE GREEK SEPTUAGINT.

There is a remarkable difference between the Hebrew Scripture and the Greek Version of Alexandria, made two hundred years before Christ, called the Septuagint (from the Jewish fable of the seventy or seventy-two inspired translators). This causes the chief difficulty of reconstructive textual criticism, which has scarcely begun. It opens up a vast field of future labor.

The Septuagint is twelve centuries older than the oldest extant Hebrew manuscript; it was in common use among the Hellenistic Jews; it is usually quoted by Christ and the Apos-

---

* Harkevy (St. Petersburg, 1884) has described about 50 newly discovered manuscripts and fragments, but they are not genuine.

tles in the New Testament, even where it differs from the Hebrew. These facts give it an authority almost equal, if not superior, to the Hebrew text as we now have it from the hands of Jewish rabbis, who certainly cannot claim an infallible authority.

The Jews before Christ believed that the Septuagint was as literally inspired as the Hebrew text, even with all the additions, but they abandoned this view when the Christians made use of the Septuagint against them. Philo of Alexandria says (in his *Life of Moses*): "We look upon the persons who made this Version, not merely as translators, but as persons chosen and set apart by divine appointment, to whom it was given to comprehend and express the sense and meaning of Moses in the fullest and clearest manner."

The early Christian fathers, who were nearly all ignorant of Hebrew—Justin Martyr, Irenæus, Augustin and others—adopted this pious superstition, which cannot stand the test of the slightest examination. The Septuagint still holds its authority in the orthodox Greek Church; but in the Latin Church it gave way to the Vulgate, which the Council of Trent placed on a par with the original, thus substituting one superstition for another.

The Septuagint was made by different persons at different times, without an attempt to revise and harmonize their work. Hence it is very unequal in the different books. In the Pentateuch (according to the testimony of Jerome, who compared it with the Hebrew manuscripts of the fourth and fifth centuries) it best agrees with the Hebrew text, and is most valuable. Ezekiel, also, is well translated, but Isaiah, Job, the Psalms, and most of the prophetical books are imperfectly rendered. The Septuagint is often too literal and obscure, as in Ezekiel and Koheleth, or too loose, periphrastic and prosy.*

With all the imperfections of the translation, the comparative study of the Septuagint and Hebrew is instructive and stimulating.

More serious than the grammatical faults of translation are the differences of matter, which have a bearing upon the original text. The Septuagint disagrees with the Hebrew (accord-

---

* Looking at these defects, Luther expressed a low estimate of the Septuagint, and Zwingli correctly said that Isaiah found an unworthy translator. Modern scholars entertain a higher opinion.

ing to Bleek) in more than 1000 places where the Masoretic text presumably preserves the original reading; but in many other places it has preserved an older and better reading, and decides between the variations of the existing manuscripts. The Revised English Version mentions some on the margin.

The greatest differences exist in the texts of Jeremiah, Job, Proverbs, Daniel and Esther. In Job, whole verses of poetry are omitted which the translator probably could not understand; while the Prologue and Epilogue of that book are enlarged. The Greek Esther contains numerous additions, which Jerome in his Vulgate has placed at the end of the book. Daniel is poorly translated and has several apocryphal additions, namely, the prayer of Azarjah and the song of the three children in the furnace (after 3 : 23, in the Vulgate 4 : 24–90), the story of Susanna (ch. 13 in the Vulgate), and the story of Bel and the Dragon (ch. 14).

In the antediluvian and patriarchal chronology the differences are irreconcilable. The Vulgate follows the shorter Hebrew chronology (which was adopted by Ussher and incorporated in the English Bible), while the majority of Protestant scholars (Vossius, Jackson, Hales, etc.) give the preference to the chronology of the Septuagint, which extends the length of the period from the Creation to the Flood, about 1000 years.

EDITIONS: The text of the Septuagint was very often copied, and underwent so many corruptions that it is almost hopelessly confused. It is contained in the Vatican, Sinaitic, and Alexandrian uncials (with many breaks), and in a large number of cursive MSS., representing three or four types or recensions, Palestinian, Egyptian, Syrian and Constantinopolitan. There are four primary printed editions, the sources of smaller editions, namely, the Complutensian (1514–17, copied in the Antwerp Polyglot), the Aldine (1518), the Roman (the Sixtina, 1587, after the Vatican MS., followed by many editions), and the Oxford (by Grabe, 1707–20). All very imperfect. The edition of HOLMES and PARSONS (Oxford, 1798–1827, 5 vols. fol.) has a large apparatus, but is behind the age. The Alexandrian Codex (A) was published in a splendid facsimile edition at London (1881–83) in three volumes. The Vatican Codex (B) was published in quasi-facsimile by VERCELLONE and COZZA (Rom. 1869–72, Vols. I.–IV.), and has since been reproduced by photography (Rom. 1891).

Manual editions by LEANDER VAN ESS (1824), and * TISCHENDORF (Leipz. 1850, 7th ed., 1887, with valuable additions by Prof. Nestle, of Tübingen, 2 vols.).

The want of a truly critical edition, which is an essential prerequisite for textual criticism, has long been felt, and is not yet satisfied, but preparations on a large scale have been made by LAGARDE of Göttingen, who edited the recension of the presbyter Lucian of Antioch (d. 311), but was interrupted by his death (Dec. 22, 1891) from finishing his task.*

The most recent and convenient edition is by Professor SWETE of Cambridge, which is based upon the Vatican Codex, with readings from the Sinaitic and Alexandrian Codices.†

CHAPTER CII.

SOURCES OF THE TEXT OF THE NEW TESTAMENT.

SCRIVENER (died 1891): *A Plain Introduction to the Criticism of the New Testament*, 3d ed., Cambridge, 1883 (pp. 712). GREGORY: *Prolegomena* to Tischendorf's eighth critical edition, Leipzig, 1884; second part, 1890 (third part not yet published). For a fuller list of works and manuscripts, see SCHAFF: *Companion to the Greek Testament*, New York, 4th ed., 1892 (pp. 82-85, 102, 133, 134).

The text of the New Testament is derived from three sources: Greek manuscripts, translations, and patristic quotations.

A. GREEK MANUSCRIPTS. These are divided into uncials, written in capital letters, and cursives, written in running hand.

I. The UNCIAL MSS. are older—from the tenth up to the fourth century—and hence more valuable. They are designated, for brevity's sake, by the capital letters of the Latin alphabet with the addition of Greek and Hebrew letters. The corrections are marked by one, two, or three stars, according as they date from the first, second, or third hand. Constantine the Great ordered the preparation of fifty MSS. of the Bible for the churches of Constantinople. The number of uncials found

---

* *Librorum Veteris Testamenti Canonicorum. Pars prior. Græce.* Göttingen, 1883, p. 541. The historical books, with the text only, without the critical apparatus. The second volume has not appeared.

† *The Old Testament in Greek, according to the Septuagint.* Cambridge (University Press), 1887, 1891, 2 vols. It is to be followed by a larger edition. HATCH and REDPATH, *Concordance to the Septuagint,* Oxford, 1892 sq.

so far amounts to about 110, but most of them are fragmentary; only one is complete (the Codex Sinaiticus).

The oldest and most important uncials are the following:

1. CODEX SINAITICUS (ℵ, Aleph), discovered by Tischendorf in the convent of St. Catharine on Mt. Sinai in the desert, 1859, now in the Imperial Library of St. Petersburg, published in quasi-facsimile style, 1862. From the age of Constantine the Great, about 330. Written on fine parchment, four columns to a page. The chief basis of Tischendorf's eighth edition.

2. CODEX ALEXANDRINUS (A), of the fifth century, presented by Cyril Lucar of Constantinople to King Charles I. (1628), preserved in the British Museum, and published in photographic facsimile, 1879. The first uncial used by critics. In the Gospels it approaches the textus receptus. It has several gaps (the first 24 chapters of Matthew, 2 chapters of John and 8 chapters of 2 Corinthians are lost), but adds, after the Apocalypse, the Epistle of Clement of Rome to the Corinthians (defective), and a fragment of a homily.

3. CODEX VATICANUS (B), from the age of Constantine, as old as the Sinaitic, and more carefully written, on very thin vellum in clear and neat uncial letters, in three columns, preserved in the Vatican Library, for a long time almost inaccessible, but at last published in photographic facsimile, 1889. It breaks off at Heb. 9:14 in the middle of the verse (with the word $\kappa\alpha\theta\alpha/\rho\iota\epsilon\tilde{\iota}$). The last chapters of Hebrews, the Pastoral Epistles, Philemon, and the Apocalypse are lost. It is upon the whole the most valuable MS. and the chief basis of the text of Lachmann, Tregelles (as far as they knew it), and Westcott and Hort.

4. CODEX EPHRAIM (C), a codex rescriptus (used for the works of Ephraim, d. 373, which are written over it), dating from the fifth century, hardly legible and very defective, preserved in the National Library of Paris, and edited by Tischendorf, 1845.

5. CODEX BEZÆ or CANTABRIGIENSIS (D), once in the possession of Beza (who procured it from a convent in Lyons), and presented by him to the University of Cambridge. It dates from the sixth century, contains only the Gospels and Acts, with a Latin version, and is full of errors, eccentricities and bold interpolations. It presents the Western text.

6. CODEX CLAROMONTANUS (D^2), for the Pauline Epistles,

with a Latin Version, a supplement to Cod. D, and of the same age. Preserved in Paris, and edited by Tischendorf, 1852.

II. The CURSIVE MSS. superseded the more costly uncials, except for splendid copies. They are written on cotton paper, which dates from the ninth century, or on linen paper, which was first introduced in the twelfth century. They date from the ninth to the middle of the fifteenth century, when the invention of the art of printing furnished a much easier and cheaper mode of multiplying books. A few were written early in the sixteenth century. They are designated by Arabic figures. Their number has much increased by recent discoveries, and amounted in 1890 to 3553, if we include 1201 Lectionaries which contain only the Scripture lessons. They present a more harmonious text, which assumed a stereotyped form after the fifth century.

These MSS. alone present a critical apparatus which is without a parallel in the history of ancient books. The Greek Testament was more frequently copied than all the Greek and Roman classics put together, some of which have come down to us only in two or three manuscripts of very late date.

B. ANCIENT TRANSLATIONS are indirect or mediate sources, except in cases of omissions and interpolations, where they are equal in authority to Greek MSS. The oldest and most important are:

1. The OLD LATIN VERSION, called *Itala* which we know only in fragments from the early Latin fathers—Tertullian, Cyprian, Ambrose, Jerome, Augustin, etc. It dates from the middle or second half of the second century, and presents many errors and variations.

2. The LATIN VULGATE, prepared by Jerome, the greatest biblical scholar of his age (d. 419), begun 388 and finished 405. It met with much opposition, even from Augustin, but by its superior merits gradually superseded the *Itala*, ruled throughout the Middle Ages, was first printed at Mayence, 1455, and sanctioned by the Council of Trent, 1546, which put it on a par with the original. All vernacular versions of the Roman Church must conform to the Vulgate. But its text has undergone many corruptions and revisions; and the pope's infallibility does not extend to biblical criticism.

3. The SYRIAC VERSION, called the *Peshitta, i.e.* the Simple, dates in its present shape from the third or fourth century. It

is called "the Queen of Ancient Versions," for its faithfulness and idiomatic character. It was first used by Beza, Walton, Mill and Wetstein. The CURETONIAN Syriac is older than the Peshitta and therefore even more valuable, but is a mere fragment of the Gospels, discovered in 1842, and published by Cureton, 1858. There are also later Syriac versions of less critical value, the PHILOXENIAN or HARCLEAN Syriac, dating from 508, and the JERUSALEM Syriac from the fifth century.

4. Three EGYPTIAN or COPTIC translations, in three dialects, the Thebaic or Sahidic, the Memphitic or Bahiric, and the Bashmuric. They are as yet in a fragmentary condition, and poorly edited.

Of less critical value are the Æthiopic, the Gothic, and the Armenian versions.

All modern versions, being made from printed copies, are of no account for ascertaining the original text.

C. PATRISTIC QUOTATIONS from the New Testament in commentaries and other writings of the ancient Christian authors. Among these the Greek fathers are more important than the Latin, since they refer to the original. The quotations of Irenæus, Hippolytus, Clement of Alexandria, Origen, Tertullian, and other ante-Nicene fathers, are older than our oldest MSS., but their text was liable to the same corruptions, and has in many places been conformed to the text in common use. The value of patristic citations is mainly corroborative, where it is supported by other ancient witnesses.

CHAPTER CIII.

THE RECEIVED TEXT AND THE TRUE TEXT.

I. The traditional or commonly received text (*textus receptus*) of the New Testament is the text which ruled supreme from the sixteenth till the close of the eighteenth century, and from which all the Protestant versions have been made. It is primarily derived from the first printed editions of the Greek text by Erasmus (1516; 4th ed., 1527; 5th ed., 1535), who never used more than eight MSS., with some improvements from the Complutensian Polyglot (printed 1514, but not published till 1520). It was further improved in the editions of Robert and

Henry Stephens (1548, 1549, 1550),* Theodore Beza (1565, 1582, 1589, 1598), and the enterprising Dutch publisher Elzevir (1624, 1633). In England the text of the third edition of Stephens of 1550, called *editio regia*, was often reproduced, and is regarded as containing the textus receptus; but on the Continent the Elzevir edition of 1633 was made the basis of all later editions.†

With all respect for these meritorious scholars and publishers who broke the ice and did the best with the means at hand, the textus receptus does not deserve that superstitious veneration in which it was held for nearly three hundred years. It was hastily derived from a few and comparatively late MSS., before the discovery of the oldest and most important uncials, without the use of the patristic quotations and ancient versions, without even a good text of the Vulgate, and with no knowledge of the principles of criticism, which was a later and gradual growth. It is essentially the Byzantine or Constantinopolitan text, which may be traced to the fifth century, and passed into all Constantinopolitan copies.

II. The true text is that which is nearest the original. We have now sufficient material approximately to restore a text as it obtained in the ante-Nicene age up to the middle of the second century. This must be derived mainly from the oldest uncial MSS., the Latin and Syriac versions, and the quotations of the ante-Nicene fathers. Yet antiquity alone, like numbers, is no absolute test; it must be supported by internal probability. Later sources must also be consulted, but are assigned a subordinate degree of authority.

Bentley, the celebrated classical critic, first suggested this correct principle (1716). Bengel followed it in the Apocalypse (1734). Lachmann first boldly carried it out (1842), but with a limited range of authorities and without regard to internal evidence, or even to the correctness of the text, aiming simply at the oldest as founded on external evidence. By the com-

---

* The first edition of Stephens which contains the versicular division was printed (at Geneva) in 1551, in 2 small vols.; the Greek text in the middle, and two Latin versions in smaller type—one to the left, the other to the right. See a facsimile in Schaff, *Companion*, etc., pp. 538, 539.

† The Elzevirs first introduced the term "textus receptus" by boldly declaring, in the preface to their neat and correct edition (the second, Leyden, 1633): "*Textum ergo habes nunc* AB OMNIBUS RECEPTUM *in quo nihil immutatum aut corruptum damus.*" The second Elzevir edition differs but slightly from the first, and both agree substantially with the third edition of Stephens. Including minute variations, they differ in 287 places. Where Elzevir departs from Stephens, he generally agrees with Beza.

bined labors of Lachmann, Tischendorf, Tregelles, and especially of Westcott and Hort (who spent twenty-seven years on their edition), we have now attained a text which in all essential points may be supposed to agree with the apostolic original. It is shorter, but also older, purer and stronger than the traditional text.*

The Revised English Version of 1881 includes the chief results of these labors. It had the benefit of the best textual critics who were members of the Revision Committee—Westcott, Hort, Lightfoot, Scrivener, and Ezra Abbot.

CHAPTER CIV.

CANONIC, OR THE THEORY OF THE CANON.

Canonic is a history of the Canon of the Old and New Testaments. The Bible is a collective whole, separate and distinct from all other collections of books. Viewed as a unit, it is called the *Canon*, because it forms the rule or standard for the belief and moral conduct of those who accept it.†

The Old Testament or the Jewish Scriptures are accepted by Jews and Christians alike, though understood very differently. The New Testament or the writings of the Evangelists and Apostles are accepted by Christians only, but by Christians of all denominations and sects. Canonicity implies inspiration, but there are degrees of canonicity as well as of inspiration, according to the difference of contents. The Jews assigned the highest place to the Pentateuch as the foundation of the theocracy; the Christians, to the Gospels as containing the authentic record of the teaching and history of Christ. Hence the Gospels were the most frequently copied and read.

The Bible itself contains no list of canonical books, which could not be made out till after they were all written and ac-

* For the best editions of the Greek Testament, see the revised list in the *Companion*, 4th ed., p. 1, and for a brief history of Textual Criticism, pp. 225–298.

† Κανών, in classical Greek, means a straight rod or line, then anything that serves to regulate or determine other things, like the Latin *regula*, *norma*. Paul uses it for leading thought, regulative principle (Gal. 6:16). In Ecclesiastical Greek the word was applied to the rule of faith (κανὼν τῆς πίστεως, κανὼν τῆς ἀληθείας, *symbolum fidei*); then to the collection of inspired writings (first by the Council of Laodicea, 363); also to disciplinary decrees of Councils; and last to the catalogue of martyrs and saints (hence *canonize*, to enroll in the catalogue of saints).

cepted. Their number was gradually determined by the judgment of the Churches. This judgment is subject to investigation. The criteria of canonicity are external and internal. The external are the testimonies of tradition and Church authority; the internal are the purity and power by which the several books authenticate themselves as inspired productions.

The Roman Church emphasizes the first, the Protestant Church the second class, of criteria. Calvin and the Reformed Confessions base the authority of the Scriptures altogether on their intrinsic excellency and the testimony of the Holy Spirit, which speaks through them to the Christian reader. No ecclesiastical decision by pope or council, synod or confession of faith, can make the Scriptures what they are not in themselves. Their authority depends on their divine inspiration, and not on their human authorship, and extends alike to the anonymous writings, as the Book of Job, Deutero-Isaiah, the orphan-Psalms, and the Epistle to the Hebrews. The Bible must stand or fall by its own intrinsic merits; but it is able to stand.

LITERATURE. The relevant sections in the Critical Introductions to the Old and New Testaments, mentioned in Chapter XCIII., page 153: REUSS: *Histoire du canon des saintes écritures dans l'église chrétienne*, Paris, 2d ed., 1864 (Eng. translation by David Hunter, Edinb. 1884). S. DAVIDSON: *The Canon of the Bible*, London, 1876, 3d ed., 1880. BRIGGS *Biblical Study*, New York, 1883, Chapter V., pp.105-138.

On the Old Testament Canon: STRACK in Herzog[2], VII. 412-451. G. WILDEBOER: *Die Entstehung des A. Tlichen Kanons*, Gotha, 1891 (translated from the Dutch). FRANTS BUHL (a Dane, successor of Delitzsch in Leipzig): *Kanon und Text des A. T.*, Leipzig, 1891 (English translation by Macpherson, Edinburgh, 1892). H. E. RYLE: *The Canon of the O. T.*, Lond. 1892.

On the New Testament Canon: CHARTERIS: *Canonicity* (based on Kirchhofer's *Quellensammlung*), Edinburgh, 1880; and *The New Testament Scriptures*, London, 1882. WESTCOTT: *History of the Canon of the N. T. in the First Four Centuries*, 6th ed., 1889. THEOD. ZAHN: *Geschichte des N. Testamentl. Kanons*, 1888 sqq., 2 vols. AD. HARNACK: *Das Neue Testament um das Jahr 200*, Freiburg, 1889.

CHAPTER CV.

THE CANON OF THE OLD TESTAMENT.

The Canon of the Old Testament rests on the testimony of the Jewish Synagogue. But this is not sufficient for Christians. We accept the Old Testament on the authority of Christ and the Apostles, who endorsed Moses and the Prophets as the organs of divine revelation. We believe first in Christ, as our Lord and Saviour; next the New Testament, as the authentic record of his teaching and example; and last the Old Testament, as bearing witness of him.

The Roman Catholic Church accepts the Canon of the Septuagint and the Vulgate, which include the so-called Apocrypha. She puts the Apocrypha on a par with the other books. The Greek Church assigns them a subordinate position. The Protestant Churches accept only the Hebrew Scriptures as canonical, but they recognize the historical importance of the Apocrypha, which fill the gap between the Old and the New Testaments, and represent the history and religious life of the Jews during that period.

Luther's Bible contains the Apocrypha, as "books which are not equal to the canonical Scriptures, yet useful and good to read." The Reformed Churches drew a sharper distinction between apocryphal and canonical books, but retained the former in the Swiss, French, Dutch and English versions. The British and Foreign Bible Society and the American Bible Society have excluded them from their editions since 1826.

CHAPTER CVI.

ORIGIN OF THE JEWISH CANON.

Jewish tradition traces the canon of the Old Testament to Ezra, the second Moses and restorer of the theocracy, in the middle of the fifth century before Christ, and to the "Great Synagogue," which he founded and which continued as a permanent ecclesiastical council till about two hundred years before the Christian era. This tradition was accepted by the Greek and Latin fathers and nearly all orthodox divines down to the present time. There is every probability that Ezra brought the Pentateuch or the Thorah into its present shape, but there is no evidence that the canon was completed before the Maccabæan age and the Alexandrian version.*

* The Fourth Book of Ezra (c. 14), at the close of the first Christian century, first reports that the Old Testament was burnt up at the destruction of Jerusalem under Nebuchadnezzar, but that Ezra, by divine inspiration, re-wrote not only the 24 canonical books, but 70 apocryphal books besides. The Greek and Latin fathers believed this wild legend.

ORIGIN OF THE JEWISH CANON. 171

There were at the time of Christ two canons differing in extent, the shorter Hebrew and the larger Hellenistic.

1. The HEBREW or PALESTINIAN (Babylonian) Canon embraces the thirty-nine (or, according to the Talmudic reckoning, twenty-four) books of the Hebrew Bible, but none of the Apocrypha.* It was recognized by the Jews generally since the beginning of the second century. It divides the books into three classes, according to the supposed historical order of their composition, namely the Law (*Thorah*), the Prophets (*Nebhiim*), and the remaining Writings (*Kethubim, Hagiographa*). The first division includes the five books of Moses. The second is subdivided into older Prophets (Joshua, Judges, Samuel, Kings), and later Prophets (Isaiah, Jeremiah, Ezekiel, and the Twelve Minor Prophets counted as one book). The third division embraces all the other books of the Hebrew Bible (Chronicles, Psalms, Job, Proverbs, Ruth, Canticles, Ecclesiastes, Lamentations, Esther, Daniel and Ezra-Nehemiah, the last two counted as one). This division was already known about B.C. 200, as we learn from the preface to the Proverbs of Jesus, the son of Sirach. It reflects the three stages in the formation of the canon.†

The authorship of the several books was fixed by the Talmud, which ascribes the Pentateuch and Job to Moses (except eight verses, Deut. 34 : 5–12, written by Joshua), the Psalter to David, Judges, Samuel and Ruth to Samuel, etc. But the Talmud is no authority for Christians.

2. The ALEXANDRIAN or HELLENISTIC Canon is represented by the Septuagint. It obliterates the distinction between the Prophets and the Hagiographa, and mixes among them several books which the Jews of Palestine either rejected or allowed only as profane literature. These are the Apocrypha, so-called, or obscure writings of unknown or uncertain origin. Their number is indefinite and varies in different copies of the Sep-

---

* Josephus, in his book against Apion, I. 8 (written c. 100), counts only 22 books, according to the number of letters in the Hebrew alphabet, by combining several books into one, but he considered all the books of our Hebrew Bible as canonical, and counted them like Origen, but arranged them differently. The Talmud counts 24 books, likewise by combining several into one. Josephus was followed by the Greek and Latin fathers, the Talmud by the Jewish scholars and the Hebrew manuscripts. The printed editions of the Hebrew Bible divide it into 39 books.

† This division is indicated in Luke 24 : 44 : "Which are written in the law of Moses, and the Prophets, and the Psalms, concerning me." The Psalms are the chief book of the third division.

tuagint. They are partly philosophical or proverbial (the Proverbs of Sirach, the Wisdom of Solomon), partly poetical (the Psalms of Solomon), partly historical and legendary (the Three Books of the Maccabees, Tobit and Judith), partly prophetical (the Book of Henoch, the Assumption of Moses, the Fourth Book of Ezra, the Book of Baruch, the Epistle of Jeremiah, the Apocalypse of Baruch), or popular additions to canonical books (to Esther and Daniel, and the Prayer of Manasseh). The apocryphal books passed from the Greek Septuagint into the Latin Vulgate. Hence the difference between the Roman Catholic and the Protestant Bibles, above referred to.

CHAPTER CVII.

THE CANON OF THE NEW TESTAMENT IN THE ANCIENT CHURCH.

The Canon of the New Testament embraces twenty-seven books, and is the same in the Greek, Roman, and all Protestant Churches.

It is the result of a gradual growth, like the canon of the Old Testament. The ancient Church was unanimous in the reception of the Gospels, Acts and the chief Epistles, but was divided in its judgment of the canonicity of seven books which are now in the canon, and of a few books now excluded from the canon. The first class of books are James, 2 Peter, 2 and 3 John, Jude, Hebrews and the Apocalypse. The second embraces the Epistle of Clement of Rome, the Epistle of Polycarp to the Philippians, the Epistle of Barnabas, the Shepherd of Hermas, perhaps also the "Teaching of the Twelve Apostles," and a few other books which were widely used in public service, some of them appended in uncial MSS. of the New Testament,* but were afterwards numbered among the Apocrypha. They sustain the same relation to the canonical books of the New Testament as the Jewish Apocrypha to the Hebrew canon.

The general ecclesiastical use in public worship, based upon a belief in the apostolic origin and divine inspiration of the books, decided the question of canonicity.

I. From the Apostolic age (30–100) we know that the Epistles

---

* The Sinaitic Bible Codex includes the Epistle of Barnabas and a portion of the Shepherd of Hermas; the Alexandrian Bible Codex contains the first Epistle of Clement of Rome, and the fragment of a second (which is not genuine, but a homily of later date).

of Paul were read in the churches to which they were addressed (1 Thess. 5 : 27; Col. 4 : 15). The same was presumably the case with the other Epistles. The prohibition to add to, or to take away from, "the words of the book of this prophecy" (Apoc. 22 : 18, 19), refers evidently only to the Book of Revelation, and has nothing to do with the canon. The first intimation of a collection of Paul's Epistles is found in 2 Peter 3 : 16 (ἐν πάσαις ἐπιστολαῖς), which are said to be misinterpreted like "the other scriptures."

The writings of the Apostolic (or rather post-Apostolic) Fathers, which date from the close of the first or from the beginning of the second century, breathe the atmosphere of the oral teaching of the Apostles and contain few quotations from their writings, which were then not yet generally circulated and collected. The author of the *Didache* was familiar with Matthew, which he calls "the Gospel of Christ." Barnabas quotes a passage from this Gospel (Matt. 22 : 14), with the solemn formula of Scripture quotation, "It is written." The Epistle of Clement of Rome shows acquaintance with Matthew, Paul and Hebrews, but has no direct quotation. The Epistles of Ignatius, and the Epistle of Polycarp are interwoven with reminiscences of John and Paul. Papias gives us valuable hints concerning the Gospels of Matthew and Mark. But in none of these writers do we find the least trace of a fixed canon.

II. In the second century, Justin Martyr, about 150, is the earliest witness for the use of the canonical Gospels in public worship on Sunday. His pupil, Tatian, about 170, wrote the first harmony of the four Gospels, which has been recently recovered in an Armenian and in an Arabic version. The heretical canon of Marcion, which embraced a mutilated Gospel of Luke and ten Epistles of Paul, presupposes a larger catholic canon about the middle of the second century; for heresy usually follows truth as its caricature.

Most of the books of the New Testament were in general use in the latter half of the second century, and are quoted as apostolic and inspired scriptures by Irenæus, Theophilus of Antioch, Clement of Alexandria, and Tertullian of Carthage.

The mutilated Muratorian fragment, of Roman origin between 160 and 220, contains a canon, which enumerates Mark, Luke (as the *third* Gospel, which explains the omission of Matthew), John, Acts, *thirteen* Epistles of Paul, *two* Epistles of John, one of Jude, the *Apocalypses* of John and Peter. It thus omits James, Hebrews, 3 John, 1 and 2 Peter, but adds an Apocalypse of Peter, with the note: "Some of our body will not have it read in the Church."*

III. In the third century we have accumulated evidence of the ecclesiastical use of nearly all the books of the New Testament in the writings of Hippolytus, Origen, Cyprian, Novatian, and in the ancient versions. The Syriac Peshitta omits only Jude, 2 Peter, 2 and 3 John, and Revelation. The old Latin Version omits probably Hebrews, James, and 2 Peter. The Sinaitic Bible includes all the twenty-seven books.

IV. Fourth Century. Eusebius, the historian (d. 340), gives us a full account of the state of the canon in the age of Constantine, and the Council of Nicæa. He distinguishes four classes of sacred books which were then in use among Christians.

1. *Homologumena, i.e.* such as were universally acknowledged: 22 out of the 27 books of the New Testament, viz., 4 Gospels, Acts, 14 Pauline Epistles (including Hebrews), 1 Peter, 1 John and Revelation. But in another passage he counts Hebrews and Revelation with the second class. The difficulty with Hebrews was its anonymity and the difference of opinion concerning its authorship; the difficulty with the Apocalypse was the mysteriousness of its contents.

2. *Antilegomena*, or controverted books, yet "familiar to most people of the Church": the Epistle of James, the Epistle of Jude, 2 Peter, 2 and 3 John (Hebrews and Apocalypse).

3. *Spurious* books (νόθα), such as the Acts of Paul, the Revelation of Peter, the Shepherd of Hermas, the Epistle of Barnabas, the so-called "Doctrines of the Apostles" (the *Didache*, rediscovered in 1873, and first published in 1883), and the Gospel according to the Hebrews (which was probably based upon the Hebrew Matthew).

4. *Heretical* books, such as the apocryphal Gospels of Peter, of Thomas, of Matthias, the Acts of Andrew, of John, and of the other Apostles.

The first Œcumenical Council of Nicæa, 325, made no deliver-

*According to one of the last papers of Bishop Lightfoot, published in his work on *S. Clement of Rome*, II. 405–413 (London, 1890), the much discussed fragment of Muratori (who discovered it in the Ambrosian Library at Milan, 1740) was originally written in Greek verse, probably by Hippolytus of Rome (who died about 236).

ance on the canon, nor did any other of the seven Œcumenical Councils do so.

CHAPTER CVIII.

THE FINAL SETTLEMENT OF THE CANON.

The canon was finally settled by a few Provincial Councils held towards the close of the fourth century, one in the East at Laodicea in Phrygia, 363 (which omits the Apocalypse), and two in North Africa, at Hippo, 393, and at Carthage, 397, both under the commanding influence of Augustin. The African canon includes the Apocrypha of the Old Testament, and so far supports the Roman Bible. Augustin was the first theologian of his age, but poorly qualified to judge on critical questions, and depended on the imperfect Latin version for his knowledge of the Bible. His elder contemporary, Jerome, was a better biblical scholar, and favored the Hebrew versus the Hellenistic canon; yet he translated the apocryphal books of the Old Testament, and his version was the common Bible of the Latin Church throughout the Middle Ages.

The Council of Trent, in 1546, formally endorsed the traditional Latin canon, without making a distinction between the canonical and apocryphal books, and pronounced an anathema on those who dissent from the decision. But the Council of Trent is no authority for Protestants, and could not alter the facts of history. It was a purely papal council, like the Vatican Council of 1870. Among the fathers of that council, mostly Italians, there was none who had any special distinction as a biblical or historical scholar. The authority of the Church outweighed all arguments of scholarship.

CHAPTER CIX.

PROTESTANTISM AND THE CANON.

The Reformers claimed the freedom of the ante-Nicene Church and revived the doubts on the Apocrypha of the Old Testament and several Antilegomena of the New. Luther especially, following a subjective instinct rather than critical principles, uttered bold and unwise opinions on Esther, the

Epistle of James, the Hebrews and the Apocalypse. He made the truth of Christ the true criterion of canonicity. From a novel and profound view of inspiration, he said in the Preface to the first edition of his version of the New Testament (1522): "That which does not teach Christ is not apostolic, though Peter and Paul should teach it; again, that which teaches Christ is apostolic, though Judas, Annas, Pilate and Herod should teach it." But the Lutheran Church retained the traditional canon, with a slight change in the order of the books.

Zwingli did not recognize the Apocalypse as apostolic.

Calvin never commented on the Apocalypse; he denied the Pauline authorship of Hebrews, and doubted the genuineness of 2 Peter, though he found in it nothing unworthy of an apostle. But he recommended no changes in the canon.

The example of the three greatest among the Reformers proves conclusively that the profoundest reverence for the Word of God in the Bible may coexist with very liberal opinions on some parts of the canon.

For all practical purposes the settlement of the canon is final; for the Roman Church with the Apocrypha, for the evangelical Churches without the Apocrypha. Our Bibles will never be enlarged or diminished.

The Church was guided by a sound religious instinct in the selection and limitation of the sacred books. Some of these books are, indeed, less important than others, yet they fill a gap and serve a useful purpose. Esther, the Song of Songs, Ecclesiastes, and the Apocalypse are sealed books to many Christians, but fountains of edification and comfort to others. The Bible provides for all tastes and wants. The Book of Esther canonizes patriotism, which may well claim a place among Christian virtues. The Song of Songs may not contain all the spiritual mysteries which many pious people read into it, but it elevates bridal love, which reflects the love of God to his creatures, and of Christ to his Church. All pure love is holy and divine, a flame kindled by the God of love.

The question of canonicity should not be confounded with the question of human authorship. The latter cannot be decided by Church authority, and must be left open to the free investigation of Christian scholarship.

CHAPTER CX.

SPECIAL ISAGOGIC.

Special Introduction has to do with the several books of the Canon in detail and constitutes the main body of Isagogic. It may be treated separately in one or more volumes.*

It deals with all the preliminary questions concerning the origin and historical environments of the several books, namely the authorship, the time and place of composition, the circle of readers, the aim of the writer, an analysis of the contents, and the history of interpretation, with a select list of the chief commentators. It thus combines in one whole the introductory information which usually precedes the commentaries.

The matter is derived partly from contemporary, extra-biblical sources, partly and mostly from the books themselves. Thus the Epistle to the Romans in connection with the Acts of the Apostles supplies all the necessary facts as to the authorship, place, time and aim of composition.

CHAPTER CXI.

HISTORICAL OR HIGHER CRITICISM.

Special Introduction is the field for the exercise of historical or higher criticism, which deals with the Bible as literature; while lower criticism deals with the text. Criticism follows the inductive method, like every true science. It ascertains, collects and classifies the facts and phenomena, and then draws such general conclusions as the facts justify. It has no apologetic or polemic or dogmatic purpose, but aims simply to establish the truth concerning the origin, history and structure of the biblical writings. It may result in the overthrow or in the confirmation or modification of traditional theories. "It proves all things and holds fast that which is good" (1 Thess. 5: 21).

The Fathers, Schoolmen and Reformers devoted their atten-

---

* Most writers on Isagogic—De Wette, Bleek, Reuss, Weiss, Holtzmann—combine in one work the general subjects of textual criticism and canonic with a special introduction; but Credner, Davidson, Salmon (*Introduction to the New Testament*) and Driver (*Introduction to the Old Testament*) confine themselves to special introduction.

tion to the doctrinal contents of the Bible in the full conviction of its divine inspiration, but cared very little about its human origin and literary form.

Biblical criticism is the product of the modern historical spirit of independent investigation, which receives nothing on mere trust and goes to the primary sources and bottom-facts. Rationalism has, since the end of the eighteenth century—the century of revolution—emancipated theology from the bondage of traditionalism and dogmatism, and cultivated every branch of biblical learning with patient industry and success, especially philology, archæology and isagogic. It starts from the principle that the Bible must be studied and explained from a purely literary and historical standpoint, like any other ancient book, without a dogmatic bias or prepossession. But there are negative and antidogmatic as well as positive and dogmatic prejudices. Strauss and Renan wrote their *Lives of Jesus* with the philosophical preconception of the impossibility of a miracle. Such a prepossession is just as uncritical and unhistorical as the opposite. If a miracle can be proven by satisfactory evidence, it has the same claim upon our belief as a natural event. We cannot absolutely emancipate ourselves from educational influences and personal experiences; but we certainly should aim first and last at the truth, the whole truth, and nothing but the truth.

There are two classes of critics, positive or conservative, and negative or radical; and between these two extremes, there are moderate, discriminating critics, who favor every genuine progress, but without breaking with the faith of the past. Neander, Bleek, Bernhard Weiss, Ezra Abbot, and Bishop Lightfoot have done as good and more enduring critical work than Baur, Strauss, Renan and the anonymous author of *Supernatural Religion*. There is a criticism of doubt which destroys, and a criticism of faith which builds up. The mission of negative criticism is to break down old prejudices, to rouse opposition and investigation, and to clear the way for a new structure. The mission of positive criticism is to reconstruct and to adjust the theory of the Bible to ascertained facts.

CHAPTER CXII.

AUTHORSHIP OF THE BIBLE.

Among the numerous topics of Special Introduction to the Bible, the question of authorship or genuineness, which refers to the origin and time of composition, occupies a prominent place.

The inspiration and canonicity of a book do not depend upon its human authorship, but upon its intrinsic value and the judgment of the Christian world. Nevertheless, the person of the author and the time of composition have an important bearing upon the degree of reliability and trustworthiness of a book. A false prophecy, or false doctrine, or historical error cannot be inspired. The nearer the source of events, the greater is the possibility and probability of accuracy; while the liability of misunderstanding, omission and addition increases in proportion to the distance of the writer from the scene of action. If Moses and his contemporaries composed the Pentateuch which bears his name, we have a much better guarantee for the historical character of the events therein narrated than if the Pentateuch was written by unknown persons several centuries later. If the Synoptic Gospels were written before the destruction of Jerusalem, and the fourth Gospel before the close of the first century, we have a solid foundation for the life of Christ by two primitive disciples and two associates of apostles; but if the fourth Gospel was the product of some Christian genius of the second century who dealt as freely with the historic Jesus of Nazareth, as Plato with Socrates, we would lose at least a considerable part of the most valuable information, which we could expect only from the bosom friend of Jesus. "Distance lends enchantment to the view," but often at the expense of reality.

Hence the great importance which the question of authorship has assumed in biblical criticism. The tendency of the rationalistic critics has heretofore been to bring the composition down to later dates and thus to weaken the historical credibility. There is an exception in the case of the Apocalypse, which for internal reasons has been by most critics put back from the traditional date under Domitian (95) to the time between the death of Nero and the destruction of Jerusalem (68–70).

The authorship of a book must be ascertained by external testimony and internal evidence. The former has the possession of the ground and should always be treated with respect, but cannot be regarded as final. The internal evidence of the book itself may outweigh the testimony of tradition. One of the surest signs of date is the allusion to facts and conditions. If a work on American history mentions the name of Lincoln or Grant, it is conclusive evidence that it cannot date from the colonial period. Moses cannot have written an account of his own death and burial, though it is included in Deuteronomy, which the Talmud ascribes to Moses. The evidence of style is also important, but less conclusive, since the same author may vary his style at different periods of life, or according to the difference of subjects. It is not impossible that the same Apostle John composed the prophetic Apocalypse in his vigorous manhood, and the historic Gospel in extreme old age. Illustrations may be found in the genuine writings of Dante, Shakespeare, Milton, Carlyle, and Goethe.

CHAPTER CXIII.

KNOWN AND UNKNOWN AUTHORSHIP.

As regards authorship, the biblical books are divided into three classes. Some are anonymous, as Job, a number of the Psalms (the Orphan-Psalms so called), Judges, Kings, Chronicles, Ruth, Esther. Others have traditional headings in the manuscripts and printed copies, as the Pentateuch, the four Gospels, the Acts. In a third class, the authors themselves indicate their names, as the Prophets, and the writers of the Epistles (except Hebrews and the three Epistles of John).

In the case of anonymous books we may never be able to advance beyond the region of conjecture and probability, and it is well to be modest and cautious. The Epistle to the Hebrews is variously ascribed to Paul, to Barnabas, to Luke, to Clement, to Apollos; but all we can ascertain from internal evidence with some degree of certainty, is that it was written from Italy by a friend of Timothy, by a disciple or companion of Paul, about the time of his Roman captivity (Heb. 13 : 23, 24). Origen wisely says: "God only knows who wrote the Epistle to the Hebrews."

In the second class, where we have to deal simply with traditional opinions of the Jewish synagogue or of the early Christian Church, as expressed in the titles, the way is open for defense, or reasonable doubt; and the question must be decided for or against tradition by internal evidence. Neither the synagogue, nor any Christian Church has ever claimed infallibility in matters of history.

In the third class, where the writer gives his name in the book itself, the alternative is truth or literary fiction, and nothing but the strongest evidence should induce us to doubt the veracity of the author.

CHAPTER CXIV.

PRESENT STATE OF HIGHER CRITICISM.

There is scarcely a book in the Bible which has not been submitted to the dissecting-knife of the most searching criticism, such as would disprove the genuineness of almost any ancient book.

I. THE NEW TESTAMENT CRITICISM. The rationalistic criticism of the apostolic literature reached its culmination in the "Tübingen School," founded by Dr. F. Christian Baur (1792–1860), Professor of Church History in the University of Tübingen, and a master-critic of the highest scholarship and power of combination. He reconstructed, in a series of critical investigations, the whole history of primitive Christianity by representing the literature of the New Testament as the battlefield of Petrine, Pauline, and mediating, irenic tendencies, which resulted, as by a dialectical process of thesis, antithesis, and synthesis, in the formation of the Catholic Church of the second century. He applied the Hegelian theory of development or evolution to literature. He went at first so far as to deny the apostolic origin of all the New Testament writings, except five—the four great Epistles of Paul (Galatians, First and Second Corinthians, and Romans) and the Apocalypse of John.

This was, however, a most important concession; for these writings confirm the historical basis of Christianity and allude to the chief events in the life of its founder, as his birth, his miracles, his crucifixion and resurrection. And it is a very significant fact that Dr. Baur made the honorable confession that the conversion of Paul from an enemy to an apostle is beyond the reach of any psychological or dialectical analysis, and cannot be explained except by a miracle of divine grace.*

In the progress of development, the Tübingen School has greatly narrowed the sphere of scepticism and conceded the genuineness of all but three or four of the thirteen Epistles of Paul.† The three Pastoral Epistles are still in dispute, because they cannot be easily located in the known life of Paul and seem to indicate a post-Pauline state of church polity and heresy; but these difficulties are not insurmountable if we accept the hypothesis of a second Roman captivity. The second Epistle to Timothy wears the unmistakable physiognomy of the aged Apostle of the Gentiles shortly before the heroic close of a heroic life. The Epistle to the Ephesians is in some respects his profoundest work and could hardly have been conceived by any other genius.

The Synoptical and the Johannean problems are approaching a satisfactory solution after every possible hypothesis has been tried. Matthew is now conceded to have been written before A.D. 70, when Jerusalem and the temple were still standing. There is no good reason why the same should not be true of Luke, who wrote independently of Matthew and had the best opportunity of composing his Gospel from earlier records and oral tradition at Cæsarea and Rome in the company of Paul. It is generally conceded that the Acts of the Apostles were written by the same author; and his companionship with Paul and credibility are conclusively proven by the "we-sections" so-called, especially the remarkably accurate account of the voyage and shipwreck, which has been verified in every particular. As regards the Gospel of Mark, the older view that it is a mere abridgment of Matthew (first suggested by St. Augustin, renewed by De Wette, Baur and Keim), has been completely reversed, and the well-nigh unanimous consensus of the latest critics recognizes its originality and independence. It reflects the fresh and impulsive temper of Peter, and by numerous incidental details and picturesque touches betrays the observation of an eye-witness.

---

* See his testimony in Schaff's *Church History*, I. 315.

† Renan, also, admits as genuine nine Epistles of Paul, besides the Acts, and the narrative portions of John. He otherwise goes the full length of the negative critics of Germany both in the Old and New Testament.

The Johannean authorship of the fourth Gospel is still in dispute; but the latest discoveries—as the Diatessaron of Tatian (which begins with the Prologue of John), the last book of the pseudo-Clementine Homilies (referring to John 9:25), the knowledge of the Prologue by Basilides, one of the earliest Gnostics, made known by the *Philosophumena* of Hippolytus, the traces of Johannean phraseology in the *Didache*—have forced the critics to push the composition back from 170, or 150 (the date assigned to it by Baur), almost to the beginning of the second century, when many friends and pupils of John were still living; while the internal evidence in favor of its genuineness far outweighs the objections and justifies the conclusion that such a Gospel could only have been written by an eye-witness, by one of the twelve, by one of the favorite three, by the son of Zebedee and Salome, by the Apostle John under divine inspiration.*

II. THE OLD TESTAMENT. The higher criticism of the Hebrew literature has been carried on chiefly in the school of Heinrich Ewald (1803–1875), a younger contemporary of Baur, for ten years (1838–1848) his antagonistic colleague, and equal to him in genius and learning, honesty and earnestness.

This school has revolutionized the traditional opinions on the origin and composition of the Pentateuch (or Hexateuch, including Joshua), the authorship of the greater part of Isaiah (especially the exilic Deutero-Isaiah from chapters 40–66), of Daniel, of the Davidic Psalms, and the Solomonic writings. The doubts and objections of older scholars have been fortified, systematized, and an attempt made to reconstruct the entire history and literature of the Old Testament. The venerable Professor Delitzsch shortly before his death made large concessions to this advanced School. At present there is scarcely a scholar among the academic professors of Old Testament exegesis in Protestant Europe who defends the orthodox theory.†

---

* Professor Schürer, one of the ablest and most judicious scholars, meets the conservative critics half-way and concedes that A.D. 130 is the latest possible date to which the composition of the fourth Gospel can be assigned. See his article in *The Contemporary Review* for September, 1891, and two articles of Professor Sanday of Oxford on the Johannean question, in *The Expositor* for March and April, 1892. Dr. Ritschl, who was formerly a pupil of Dr. Baur, and then became the head of a new theological school, admitted the Johannean origin of the fourth Gospel.

† All the articles on Old Testament subjects in *The Encyclopædia Britan-*

But a reaction similar to that in the Tübingen School will no doubt take place on those difficult and complicated problems, and has already begun in the line of the search after the older sources from which the various documents of the Pentateuch are derived. It has been suggested that these documents furnish a parallel to the four canonical Gospels, which are themselves derived, in part at least, from older Gospel fragments, such as the Hebrew Matthew and the writings referred to in the Prologue of Luke.

The process of action and reaction will go on, and it would be unprotestant and unwise, as well as impossible, to stop it. Truth will slowly but surely make its way through the wilderness of conflicting hypotheses.

A theological teacher may shake the confidence of students in the Bible and thus unfit them for the ministry, either by obstinately shutting his eyes against new light and progress, or by presenting negative results without furnishing the antidote. In either case, he incurs a fearful responsibility. The cause of biblical criticism has been much injured in the eyes of devout Christians by the hasty and oracular assertions of unproved hypotheses.

To theological students I would give the advice, as the best safeguard against the danger of scepticism, to master first and last the contents of the Bible, and never to lose sight of its spiritual truths, which are immeasurably more important than all the questions of lower and higher criticism.

CHAPTER CXV.

THE FINAL RESULT.

The immense labor of Christian scholarship cannot be lost, and must accrue at last to the advantage of the Church. The result will be a clear and comprehensive restatement of the Bible literature as an organic whole on the basis of all the new facts brought to light by modern research.

We should remember that the Bible has a human as well as a divine side, and we must know both in order to enjoy its full

nica, under the editorship of W. Robertson Smith, are from negative critics. This is hardly consistent with impartiality, which should be one of the chief traits of an encyclopædia.

benefit. The person of our Lord and Saviour comes near to us by his humanity as our sympathizing friend and brother; and his humanity has never before been so fully brought to light as in the nineteenth century. So also the Bible is made more intelligible, interesting and useful to the devout student by a full knowledge of its humanity, its human birth and growth, its various fortunes, its variety and beauty, its historic setting and environments, its fitness for its own time and for all subsequent times.

Healthy criticism, animated by the love of truth, is a blessing to the Church, and keeps theology from stagnation. Every real progress in biblical learning must ultimately have a beneficial effect upon Christian life. Faith in the Bible must be grounded upon the rock of its divine truth, not upon the shifting sand of human theories. The Bible need not fear the closest scrutiny. The critics will die, but the Bible will remain—the Book of books for all ages. Human opinions and systems fade away; in the New Testament blooms the eternal spring.

FOURTH SECTION: BIBLICAL HERMENEUTIC AND EXEGESIS.

CHAPTER CXVI.

NATURE OF HERMENEUTIC.

Hermeneutic is the science of the laws and principles of interpretation, by which the meaning of an author is ascertained from his language.

It is closely related to Logic or the science of the laws of thought, and to Grammar and Rhetoric or the science of the laws of language and speech.

Biblical Hermeneutic is general Hermeneutic applied to the books of the Old and New Testaments. It precedes exegesis or the actual work of interpretation, but on the other hand it presupposes exegetical skill and experience. It embraces some account of the languages of the Bible, discussions on the qualifications of an interpreter, on different methods of interpretation, on metaphors, symbols, types, parables, and also a history of interpretation.

Hermeneutic is derived from ἑρμηνεύω, *to interpret, to explain*, and this from Ἑρμῆς, the son of Zeus and Maia, the messenger of the gods and interpreter of their will. The Greek Hermes corresponds to the Roman Mercurius (from *merx, mercari*), who was originally the god of commerce and gain; and hence especially worshiped by merchants. Ἑρμηνεία and ἐξήγησις mean the same thing; but *hermeneutic* now denotes the theory, *exegesis*, the practice of interpretation.

LITERATURE: Works on Hermeneutic by ERNESTI (Leipzig, 5th ed., 1809); LÜCKE (Göttingen, 1817); SCHLEIERMACHER (edited by Lücke, 1838); KLAUSEN (Leipzig, 1841); WILKE (Leipzig, 1843); CELLERIER (Paris, 1852); KUENEN (Leiden, 1858); PATRICK FAIRBAIRN (Glasgow and Philadelphia, 1859); IMMER (Wittenberg, 1873, translated by ALBERT H. NEWMAN, Andover, 1877); LANGE (Bonn, 1878); J. CHR. VON HOFMANN (posthumous, ed. by VOLCK, 1880); VOLCK (in Zöckler's *Encykl.*, 3d ed. 1889); * M. S. TERRY (New York, 1883, revised ed. 1892).

A full list of hermeneutical books down to 1883, in Terry, pp. 738–752.

On the *History of Interpretation*: * L. DIESTEL: *History of the Old Testament in the Christian Church* (Jena, 1869). F. W. FARRAR: *History of Interpretation* (London, 1886).

CHAPTER CXVII.

AIM OF INTERPRETATION.

Every literary composition, sacred or secular, consists of ideas expressed in words connected into sentences. The ideas are the soul, the words are the body. The aim of interpretation is to draw out the idea from the words or to ascertain and unfold, according to the recognized laws of speech and thought (grammar and logic), the true sense of the writer from his own vocabulary and range of thought, without addition, abstraction or any other change, so that the reader may be put as far as possible into the very situation and experience of the author.

This work becomes more difficult and complicated in proportion to the distance of time and place of composition, and the doctrinal difference between the writer and his interpreter.

The Bible is the clearest and yet the most obscure of all books. It has been compared to a river with depths for an elephant to swim in, and with shallows that a lamb can wade. "Oftentimes the same Scripture is at once a depth for one and a shallow for another." It is sufficiently intelligible for practical purposes to every reader who seeks in it spiritual edification and comfort and uses it as a guide in the battle of life. Hence it is the daily food of the people of God. But it is also the most difficult to understand and interpret, because it is the most profound and most universal book in the world. Hence it has occupied the minds of theologians and scholars for these eighteen centuries, and is now more extensively studied than ever. "*Habet Scriptura haustus primos, haustus secundos, haustus infinitos.*" (Augustin).

An absolute understanding of the Bible is impossible in this world. The prophetic portions will only be fully understood in the light of their fulfilment. But there is a progressive understanding through the course of the Christian centuries among scholars, and a growing demand for a popular diffusion of the best results of exegetical research among the laity. Each generation digs new treasures from this inexhaustible mine; each commentary creates a taste for another and a better one; and the occupation of the exegete will never cease till "we shall see face to face and know even as we are known."

CHAPTER CXVIII.

QUALIFICATIONS OF AN INTERPRETER.

The qualifications for the office of an exegete are natural and acquired, intellectual and moral.

I. The INTELLECTUAL and EDUCATIONAL qualifications are:

(1) Common sense and sound judgment, which enable one to follow the author's train of thoughts and to understand them in their connection and bearing.

A lively imagination controlled by sober judgment is likewise a desirable (though rare) gift of a commentator, by which he can realize the situation of the writer and penetrate into his state of mind and feeling during the composition.

(2) Knowledge of the author's language, which is the key to his thought, the bearer of his meaning. In the case of the Old Testament the Hebrew and Aramaic, in the case of the New the Greek. (See *Biblical Philology*, pp. 101 sqq.)

(3) Knowledge of the historical relations and conditions in which the book was written. In the interpretation of the Bible, which was composed in the distant East many hundreds of years ago, much antiquarian learning is required. (See chapters on *Archæology*, pp 140 sqq.)

II. MORAL and SPIRITUAL qualifications.

(1) Honesty or a conscientious regard for truth, to which all preconceived notions and dogmatic prejudices must be sacrificed. The aim of the interpreter is not, to make the author say what he *might* have said, or *ought* to have said, but to find out what he actually *did* say and mean. A great deal of pretended *ex*egesis is *eis*egesis, or *im*position rather than *ex*position. This is especially true of the allegorizing method which turns the Bible into a nose of wax.

(2) Sympathy with the spirit and subject of the writer. Only a poet or at least a mind endowed with love and taste for poetry can understand and expound a Homer or Dante or Shakespeare.* Only a philosopher can understand and appreciate Plato or Aristotle or Spinoza or Leibnitz or Kant or Hegel.

For the same reason the proper exposition of the Bible re-

---

* "*Wer den Dichter will verstehen,*
  Muss in Dichter's Lande gehen."
      Goethe (*Westöstlicher Divan*).

quires a religious mind, enlightened by the Holy Spirit who spoke through the prophets and apostles. Without this we may understand the letter or the body, but can never penetrate to the living soul of the Bible. No amount of grammatical and historical learning can compensate for the want of spiritual affinity and insight. "The natural man receiveth not the things of the Spirit of God: for they are foolishness unto him: and he cannot know them, because they are spiritually judged. But he that is spiritual judgeth all things." (1 Cor. 2 : 14, 15.)

CHAPTER CXIX.

TRANSLATIONS, PARAPHRASE, COMMENTARY.

We now enter upon the field of exegesis proper, or the actual interpretation of the Scriptures.

There are three degrees of interpretation: translation, paraphrase, commentary.

I. A TRANSLATION is a simple transfer of the original into a vernacular tongue. There are two kinds of translation:

1. A translation for scholarly and private use, as a basis of a critical commentary, should be as close and faithful as possible, with exclusive regard to accuracy.*

2. A translation for popular and public use should be an idiomatic reproduction; free as well as true, and adapted to the genius of the language into which it is made, so as to come home to the reader with all the power and beauty of an original work. Model translations of this class are: the Syriac Peshitta, the Latin Vulgate, Luther's German Bible, the Authorized English Version, and other Protestant versions of the Reformation period.

The Roman Catholic Church requires all authorized translations into modern languages to be conformed to the Latin Vulgate. Hence they are translations of a translation, and latinizing to a degree that makes them in some places almost unintelligible, as compared with the popular Protestant versions which are made directly from the original.†

---

* Ewald's translations in his commentaries are models of accuracy. He goes so far as to defy the German idiom, in rendering ὁ λόγος "*der* Wort," instead of "*das* Wort," to indicate the personality of the Logos, John 1 : 1.

† The Rheims version of the New Testament (1582), in its first editions, had a large number of Latinisms, such as "supersubstantial" (*supersub-*

II. A PARAPHRASE is an explanatory and extended translation. Clearer and simpler terms and phrases are substituted for obscure ones and made part of the text.

Examples: the Aramaic Targums (*i.e.*, translations) of the Old Testament which became necessary after the Babylonian Exile when the Hebrew as a spoken language gave way to the Aramaic. Erasmus's *Paraphrase of the New Testament*. Doddridge's *Family Expositor*.

III. A COMMENTARY is an explanation of the text distinct from the text itself. It may be brief in the form of glosses and hints, or may be full and exhaustive.

There are three kinds of commentaries: philological, theological, and practical or homiletical; and there are commentaries which combine all three. There are critical commentaries for scholars, and popular commentaries for general use.

CHAPTER CXX.

THE ENGLISH VERSION AND REVISION.

Every student and minister (in his pulpit preparations) ought to use the Revised Version of 1885 in connection with the Authorized Version of 1611 and the original text.

The English Version, which bears the name of James I. (though he had nothing to do with it except to appoint the forty-seven translators), is the result of several revisions from the time of Tyndale (1525). It is the best version that could be made at the beginning of the seventeenth century, and surpasses all other authorized versions in accuracy. It is the first of English classics, and so deeply interwoven with English and American literature that it can never be ignored, even if the Revised Version should supersede it in public use. F. William Faber, after his conversion from Anglo-Catholicism to Romanism, could not forget its "uncommon beauty and marvellous English."

stantialis) for daily bread (in the Lord's Prayer), "impudicity" (*impudicitia*) for uncleanness (Gal. 5: 19), "contristate" (*contristare*) for grieve the Holy Spirit (Eph. 4: 30), "exinanite" (*exinanivit seipsum*) for emptied himself (Phil. 2: 7; in later editions, "debased himself"), "prepuce" for foreskin, "pasch" for passover, "breads of proposition" for shew breads, "holocaust" for burnt-offering, "agnition," "azims," "scenopegia." The Rheims-Douay Bible has, however, undergone improvements in later editions, and most of these Latinisms have given way to idiomatic terms; but some still remain, as "supersubstantial" for daily (in Matt. 6: 11).

But the received English Version has its imperfections, like everything human. The chief defects may be classified as follows:

1. It rests upon the unrevised textus receptus (the Masoretic text in the Old Testament, and the editions of Stephens and Beza in the New Testament). It was made before the science of textual criticism was born, before the oldest manuscripts were discovered, and before the ancient translations and patristic quotations were properly examined.

2. It has many obsolete and unintelligible words and phrases, such as "besom" (broom), "bewray" (betray), "bosses" (knobs), "botch" (boil), "cabins" (cellars), "cankerworm" (caterpillar), "chapiter" (capital), "chapman" (trader), "clouts" (patches), "daysman" (arbitrator), "earing" (ploughing), "knop" (bud), "minish" (diminish), "neesing" (sneezing), "ware" (aware), "to fetch a compass" (to make a circuit).

3. It uses familiar words in a different sense from what they now have, as "atonement" for reconciliation, "coast" for border, "prevent" for precede, "let" for hinder, "conversation" for conduct, "damn" and "damnation" for condemn and condemnation, "carriage" for baggage, "nephews" for grandchildren, "to wit" for to know, "by-and-by" for immediately, "by myself" for against myself (1 Cor. 4:4), "instantly" for urgently, "lively" for living, "sometimes" for once, "charger" for platter, "to hail" for to drag (Luke 12:58; Acts 8:3), "his" for its, "lunatic" (moonstruck) for epileptic, "occupy" for trade, "painful" for toilsome, "quick" for living, "turtle" for turtle-dove, "wench" for maid-servant (2 Sam. 17:17), "well" for spring, "witty" for clever.

4. It occasionally employs unseemly phrases in the Old Testament which can scarcely be read without offense in the family or pulpit (1 Sam. 25:22, 34; 1 Kings 14:10; 2 Kings 9:8; 18:27; Isa. 36:12).

5. It creates artificial distinctions which do not exist in the original, by translating the same word by different words, where it has the same meaning.

Examples: "Eternal" and "everlasting" ($αἰώνιος$, Matt. 25:46); "overseer" and "bishop" ($ἐπίσκοπος$, Acts 22:28; Phil. 1:1; 1 Tim. 3:1, etc.); "Passover" and "Easter" ($πάσχα$, Matt. 26:2, etc.; Acts 12:4); "atonement," "reconciling," and "reconciliation" ($καταλλαγή$, Rom. 5:11; 11:15; 2 Cor. 5:18,

19); "comforter." and "advocate" (παράκλητος, John 14:16, etc., used of the Holy Spirit; 1 John 2:1, used of Christ). Λόγος has no less than twenty-three renderings; τύπος, eight; ὄχλος, six; παιδίσκη, five; μένω, ten, etc. The Hebrew "Sheol" is translated by three words, "hell," "grave" and "pit."

Needless variations are also introduced in proper names, as Elijah and Elias; Elisha and Eliseus; Jeremiah, Jeremias and Jeremy; Timotheus and Timothy. "Jesus" is substituted for Joshua, Acts 7:45 and Heb. 4:8.

6. It obliterates or obscures real distinctions of the original in translating two or more Hebrew or Greek words by one and the same English word, such as "hell" for both Hades (Sheol, the spirit-world) and Gehenna (the place of torment); "devil" and "devils" for the one devil and for the many demons or evil spirits; "beasts" for wild beasts (θηρία), and the beast from the abyss (θηρίον, Rev. 13:1, 2, etc.), and the living creatures before the throne of God (ζῶα, Rev. 4:6, etc.); "crown" for crown (στέφανος) and diadem (διάδημα); "servant" for servant (διάκονος) and bondman (δοῦλος).

7. It contains a vast number of inaccurate or inadequate translations, especially through disregard of the Greek article, the Greek tenses and particles, which were imperfectly understood at the time.

Examples of the neglect of the article: "Christ" instead of *the* Christ (the official title); "*a* law" instead of *the* law (of Moses); "many" (opposed to few) instead of *the* many, that is, all (opposed to "the one," Adam or Christ, in Rom. 5:15–19; comp. 1 Cor. 15:22); "*the* root" instead of *a* root (1 Tim. 6:10); "*the* woman" instead of *a* woman (John 4:27).

Examples of the neglect of the tenses, that is the distinctions between the narrative aorist (or preterit for completed action), imperfect (incomplete or continuous action), perfect (an act or event continued in its effects), and the pluperfect: ἀπεθάνομεν τῇ ἁμαρτίᾳ, we who *died* to sin (at the time of our conversion), not "are dead" (which substitutes a state or condition for a past act or event), Rom. 6:2, 7, 8; Gal. 2:19; Col. 2:20; 3:1, 3; ἥμαρτον, they sinned, not "have sinned," Rom. 5:12; ἀποθανόντες, having died, not "being dead," Rom. 7:6; εἰσ ὑπὲρ πάντων ἀπέθανεν, ἄρα οἱ πάντες ἀπέθανον, one died for all, therefore all died, not "then were all dead," 2 Cor. 5:14; ἐκάλουν, they were calling, not "called," Luke

1:59; ἔτυπτε τὸ στῆθος αὐτοῦ, he kept smiting his breast, not "smote," Luke 18:13; ἤρχοντο, they were going, not "they went," John 6:17.

The prepositions, pronouns, conjunctions and adverbs are likewise very often confounded or mistranslated.

8. A considerable number of false and misleading translations.

Examples from the Old Testament: "apothecary" for perfumer (Ex. 30:25); "borrow" for ask (Ex. 11:2); "dragons" for monsters (Ps. 74:13); "foxes" for jackals (Judg. 15:4); "grove" and "groves" for pillar (or Asherah, Asherim and Asheroth, which denote the wooden symbols of a goddess, Judg. 2:17; Ex. 34:13, etc.); "galleries" for curls of hair (Cant. 7:5); "hell" or "pit" or "grave" for Sheol (the underworld or state of the departed, corresponding to the Greek Hades, the unseen world of the dead); "hypocrite" for ungodly (Job 8:13, etc.); "meat offering" for meal offering (Ex. 30:9, etc.); "owl" for ostrich (Lev. 11:16); "plain of Mamre" for oaks of Mamre (Gen. 18:1); "paper reeds" for meadows (Isa. 19:7); "river of Egypt" (the Nile) for brook of Egypt (Num. 34:5); "satyrs" for he-goats (Isa. 13:21); "spider" for lizard (Prov. 30:28); "unicorn" for wild ox (Num. 23:22).

Examples from the New Testament: "all the children" for all the male children (τοὺς παῖδας, Matt. 2:16); "ship" for boat (4:21, 22, and often); "before instructed" for urged or impelled (14:8); "strain at a gnat" (probably a printing error) for strain out a gnat (23:24); "testament" for covenant (26:28, etc.); "taxing" for enrolment (Luke 2:2) "search" for ye search (John 5:39; the Greek ἐρευνᾶτε admits of both translations, but the context and the known zeal of the scribes for a pedantic study of the letter of the Old Testament require the indicative rather than the imperative rendering); "one fold" for one flock (John 10:16, ποίμνη, not αὐλή, a mischievous error copied from the Vulgate *ovile*); "supper being ended" for during supper (13:2 comp. 26); "such as should be saved" for were being saved (in the process of salvation, Acts 2:47); "Easter" for Passover (12:4); "too superstitious" for somewhat superstitious or overreligious (17:22); "hold" for hold down or hinder (κατέχειν, Rom. 1:18); "remission of sins" for prætermission or passing over (διὰ τὴν πάρεσιν, Rom. 3:25); "made himself of no reputation" for emptied himself (ἑαυτὸν ἐκένωσε, Phil. 2:7); "conversation" for citizenship (πολίτευμα, 3:20); "vile body" for body of humiliation (3:21); "gain is godliness" for godliness is a way of gain (1 Tim. 6:5); "took on him," a double error for takes hold of, helps (ἐπιλαμβάνεται, Heb. 2:16); "answer" for interrogation, inquiry or seeking after God (ἐπερώτημα, 1 Pet. 3:21).

These defects and many more are nearly all corrected in the Anglo-American Revision which was begun in 1870 and completed in 1885. It is now very generally used as a commentary on the received version, and will ultimately supersede it. It is far more thorough than the official Revision of Luther's Version, which was undertaken by the Eisenach Church Conference in 1855, provisionally printed as "Probebibel" in 1883, and published in its final shape at Halle, 1892.

For further information on the Anglo-American Revision of the received version, see PHILIP SCHAFF (President of the American Committee on Revision): *Companion to the Greek Testament and the English Version* (New York and London, 1883, 4th revised ed. 1892), chapters VII. and VIII. (pp. 299–496), and Dr. TALBOT W. CHAMBERS (a member of the Old Testament Company of Revisers): *A Companion to the Revised Old Testament*, New York, 1885.

CHAPTER CXXI.

PHILOLOGICAL AND HISTORICAL EXEGESIS.

Philological or grammatical, and historical (grammatico-historical) exegesis is chiefly concerned with verbal and critical questions. It ascertains the true reading; brings out the meaning of words and phrases, according to the general rules of grammar and the *usus loquendi* of the writer, his age and country; explains the psychological situation of the writer, the historical surroundings of the book, and the state of society and religion in which it was written. It must stick closely to the text in its direct aspect and bearing, and be free from dogmatic and sectarian prejudice. It is the basis of all sound interpretation. It requires a thorough knowledge of Semitic languages for the Old Testament, and of classical and Hellenistic Greek for the New.

Grammatical exegesis was scarcely known in the first three centuries, or made subordinate to allegorical and practical exposition. It began properly in the Antiochian School (Chrysostom, Theodore of Mopsuestia, and Theodoret). It was not unknown to Jerome, who had a rare genius for languages and knew the Bible lands from personal observation, but was inconsistent, timid, anxiously concerned for his orthodoxy, and often wandered into allegorizing. It was well-nigh forgotten in the middle ages, together with the knowledge of Greek and Hebrew, till the time of the Revival of Letters. The Reformers felt the primary importance of sound grammatical exposition; Calvin practiced it with full faith in the divine truths of the Bible; the Arminians (Grotius, etc.) cultivated it with the aid of classical learning, but on a lower theory of inspiration; the Rationalists used and abused it in opposition to orthodoxy. A new epoch of grammatical exegesis was introduced by Winer's Grammar of the New Testament idiom, which made an end to the arbitrary handling of the Hellenistic dialect by the earlier Rationalists.

CHAPTER CXXII.

THEOLOGICAL EXEGESIS.

Theological exegesis draws out and unfolds the religious and moral ideas or doctrines of the text, considered in themselves and in connection with the general teaching of the Scriptures, according to the analogy of faith; yet not in any sectarian interest. This requires congeniality of mind or intelligent sympathy with the spirit and aim of the sacred authors.

Theology transcends, but does not contradict, grammar and logic. It is the logic of God. The spiritual sense of the Bible must be fairly deducible from, and be in harmony with, the literal. The Bible undoubtedly has a soul as well as a body; but the soul lives *in* the body, not out of it. The allegorical interpretation is wrong, not in maintaining a sense deeper than the letter, but in arbitrarily putting a subjective idea or fancy into the word, instead of taking the objective meaning of the Spirit out of the word.

The Bible is a unit, not a dead, mechanical unit, but a living organism with many members, each having its special office and use. There is in the Old Testament a Patriarchal, a Mosaic, a Prophetic, an Exilic and post-Exilic theology; and there is in the New Testament a theology of Jesus (Synoptic and Johannean), a theology of James, of Peter, of Paul and of John. Theological exegesis has to unfold the variety as well as the unity and harmony of Scripture teaching.

CHAPTER CXXIII.

PRACTICAL AND HOMILETICAL EXEGESIS.

This is the application of the Word of God to the religious wants of the people, on the basis of a sound philological and theological interpretation, and belongs properly to the pulpit.

It is the oldest form of exegesis both among Jews and Christians; for the Bible was written and read for edification and comfort (comp. 2 Tim. 3:15, 16; Rom. 15:4; 2 Pet. 1:19). It is also the last form, to which the other two look forward. Exegetical science must benefit the Church. The professor's chair should never lose sight of the preacher's pulpit.

The three kinds of exegesis should agree. A vast amount of practical exegesis, as found even in some of the greatest sermons, is based upon allegorical fancies. These must be avoided. The homiletical use of a passage must either be consistent with the plain grammatical sense, or it must not pretend to be an interpretation, but simply an extension and application. The word of God needs no fanciful and arbitrary helps; it has of itself an endless *applicability* to all classes and conditions of men. Like a diamond, it casts its lustre whichever way you turn it.

CHAPTER CXXIV.

EXHAUSTIVE COMMENTARIES.

The ideal of a commentary would be a combination of the philological, theological, and practical exegesis, under three distinct divisions, with a critically revised text as the basis. The practical division should be confined to brief hints and suggestions, not a substitute for, but a stimulus to, preparation for the pulpit and the Bible class.

CHAPTER CXXV.

POPULAR COMMENTARIES.

The rapid growth of the theological lay public in Protestant countries, and the large number of Sunday-schools and Bible classes, call for popular commentaries on the whole Scriptures, especially on the historical books.

The object of a popular commentary should be to present in brief the clean results of the latest biblical researches, without the critical apparatus, for the instruction and edification of the general reader. The value depends on accuracy, clearness, point, and a devout spirit, which should prevade the whole. It is better to edify indirectly by sound instruction, than to have a separate department of practical remarks or improvements, although these have their uses and are preferred by many.

CHAPTER CXXVI.

EXEGESIS OF THE OLD AND NEW TESTAMENTS.

The key to the true exposition of the Old Testament we find in the New Testament. It is contained in the declaration of Christ, Matt. 5:17: "I came not to destroy the law or the prophets, but to fulfill." Christ is the fulfiller of the Scriptures: he is the light which illuminates every page; without it, they remain a sealed book. The Old Covenant is a preparation for the New, the New Covenant is the fulfillment of the Old. They are one in the idea of Covenant, different as Old and New. "*Vetus Testamentum in Novo patet, Novum Testamentum in Vetere latet*" (Augustin).

Paul represents the law as a schoolmaster to lead men to Christ (Gal. 3:24). Christ and the Apostles see in the Old Scriptures the Word of God spoken through his servants Moses and the Prophets (Acts 1:16; 3:7; 4:7; 9:8). "Moses wrote of me," says Christ (John 5:46). "Holy men spake from God, being moved by the Holy Spirit" (2 Pet. 1:21).

But the Old Testament is not the final revelation of God; it is full of pregnant hints to the future; it is Messianic in its predictions; its institutions and ceremonies; even the law points beyond itself to the gospel. So the Apostles find everywhere Christ in the Old Testament, but Christ in his preparatory stages, Christ foreshadowed, Christ coming, not Christ come.

The exegesis of our Saviour is wonderful. He reveals depth in the Scriptures undreamed of before, yet without any unnatural allegorizing or putting anything into the Word, but by taking out its deepest sense and making it so plain as to excite our astonishment that we never saw it before. Examples: In Matt. 22:32, he proves before the Sadducees the resurrection from the Pentateuch, from the designation of God as "the God of Abraham, Isaac and Jacob," for "God is not the God of the dead, but of the living." In the same chapter, ver. 42–45, he argues before the Pharisees his own divinity from Ps. 110, where David calls the Messiah his Lord.

Matt. 5:17 implies the unity as well as the difference of the two covenants.

False interpretations of the Old Testament as a whole, ignore either the unity or the difference.

1. The harmony of the Old and New Testaments may be denied by the Gnostic heresy and those pseudo-Pauline Rationalists, who make Christianity something abrupt and sudden. The Gnostics rejected the Old Testament altogether as the work of the demiurge.

2. The difference may be obliterated in two ways:

(a) By lowering the New Testament to the level of the Old and making Christianity a mere completion or improvement of Judaism. So Ebionism and all Judaizing schools of theology.

(b) By raising the Old Testament to the position of the New and making it already teach the specific doctrines of Christianity and the experience of Christian believers. This has been done mainly through means of the allegorizing method. The old orthodoxy, Catholic and Protestant, used the Old Testament and the New for doctrinal proof-texts without the least discrimination, and found the doctrine of the Trinity in the plural name of God (Elohim), the three guests of Abraham, and the trisagion of Isaiah. In this way the originality of the New Testament is destroyed.

Scripture is the record of a *progressive* revelation of God, who, as a wise educator, adapted himself to the capacity of his people. "God, having of old time spoken unto the fathers in the prophets by divers portions and in divers manners, hath at the end of these days spoken unto us in his Son" (Heb. 1 : 1, 2). Even Christ did not reveal the whole truth to the disciples while on earth. He left many things unsaid, because they could not bear them (John 16 : 12), but he promised them the Holy Spirit, who would teach them all things and bring to their remembrance all he said unto them (John 14 : 26; 15 : 26; 16 : 7–14). And even the pentecostal illumination did not supersede the need of special revelations, such as the one given to Peter at Joppa concerning the admission of Gentiles, or those given to Paul at critical epochs in his life, or that of the seer of the Apocalypse concerning the struggles and final triumph of the Church.

It is the office of the interpreter to follow these progressive periods of divine revelation and to show their difference as well as their connection. "*Distingue tempora, et concordabit Scriptura*" (Augustin).

CHAPTER CXXVII.

HISTORY OF EXEGESIS.

The history of biblical interpretation is a history of misinterpretation as well. No book has been so much misunderstood and abused as the Bible. There are commentaries which shed light upon the Bible, and other commentaries which obscure the light of the Bible or pervert its true meaning. Christ charged the scribes of his day, that they "have made void the word of God, because of their tradition" (Matt. 15 : 6). They searched the Scriptures, and yet would not come to Christ (John 5 : 39, 40). They built a stone wall around the law so that nobody could get at it and see it face to face. The same story has been repeated in the history of the Christian Church. The mediæval papacy erected hierarchical, patristic, scholastic, and ritualistic forts around the Bible. It required all the courage and energy of Luther, Zwingli and Calvin to storm these forts and to open the treasures of the divine book to the people. There is no heresy that has not been read into the Bible and defended by the Bible. All churches and sects of Christendom appeal to it alike for support.

It is one of the strongest arguments for the divine origin and imperishable value of the Bible that it has outlived so many attacks from without and so many misapprehensions from within.

The Bible is no more responsible for its misinterpretations than Nature for the errors and contradictions of scientists. Man cannot fly on wings to the mountain-top of knowledge, but must slowly ascend it step by step.

The Roman Church maintains "a unanimous consensus of the Fathers" in the interpretation of the Bible, and uses the confusion among interpreters as an argument against the Protestant principle of the supremacy and sufficiency of the Bible, as a rule of faith. But the unanimous consensus of the Fathers is a fiction of the Council of Trent, which was not especially distinguished for exegetical and historical learning. The ancient Fathers are worthy of all respect, but they differed as widely and erred as frequently in their comments on the Scripture as the Reformers. The further up we go, the greater is the freedom and variety; as the oldest manuscripts of the Greek Testament present the largest number of textual variations. The ablest exegetes among the Fathers are the most independent. The growing principle of church authority and the narrowing orthodoxy imprisoned exegesis and kept it confined till the Reformation burst the chains and opened the prison door. The variety of interpretation is the inevitable result of freedom or the right of private judgment, and of the inexhaustible depth of the Bible.

There is, however, a steady progress and approach to agreement among competent scholars. The Bible languages, archæology, history, and the principles of interpretation are now better understood than ever before. Exegesis has become almost an exact science in ascertaining the precise meaning of the biblical writers.

CHAPTER CXXVIII.

JEWISH EXEGESIS.

Exegesis began among the Jews, to whom were given the Scriptures of the Old Covenant. The humble and believing souls who waited for the hope of Israel, derived from them spiritual nourishment and comfort; but the proud hierarchs and pedantic scribes searched only the letter of the Scriptures without seeking and finding the Christ to whom they bear witness (John 5 : 39). They obscured the true meaning by their traditions and made void the word of God. "Their minds are hardened: for until this very day the same veil remaineth unlifted; which veil is done away in Christ" (2 Cor. 3:14).

Nevertheless rabbinical scholarship has been of much use and is entitled to a respectful hearing in all matters which relate to Hebrew grammar and archæology. In the middle ages Jewish rabbis had the monopoly of Hebrew learning. They furnished the first grammars and dictionaries for the use of Christians. To the scrupulous care of the Masoretic scholars we owe the Hebrew text of the Old Testament.

Jewish exegesis may be divided into a pre-Christian and a post-Christian period.

CHAPTER CXXIX.

JEWISH EXEGESIS BEFORE CHRIST.

It began soon after the close of the canon. Ezra (B.C. 457), the priestly scribe, may be called the first biblical scholar. He collected and edited the books of the canon as far as they existed at his time. He was regarded as a second Moses and a restorer of the law. "He transformed the theocracy into a nomocracy," and raised "the scribe" above "the priest." He organized the synagogue-worship and the reading of Moses every Sabbath-day. He inaugurated the *Midrash* and the *Targum*, that is, the body of interpretation, which embraced the entire theological and literary wisdom of the Jews. (Ezra 7:6, 25; Neh. 8:7, 8; 13:24.)

The Jewish exegesis referred chiefly to the law (Thorah) and determined the individual and social duties and relations by deduction from the Pentateuch. It was divided into HALAKHA, *i.e.*, "decision," rule, legalized precept, and HAGGADA, *i.e.*, "discourse," narration, legend. The former was binding, the latter was not. The Halakha is compared to bread, the Haggada to water; the one to an iron fortress, the other to a flowery promenade within the fortress.

The interpretations were first propagated by oral tradition; after the time of Christ they were collected in the *Mishna, i.e.*, Learning, Repetition (about A.D. 200 or 220), and the *Gemara, i.e.*, Completion (A.D. 490). They together constitute the Jewish *Talmud*, or Doctrine (from למד, to teach).

There were two kinds of exegesis among the Jews.

1. The RABBINICAL or LITERAL exegesis was carried on in Palestine by the Pharisees. It excluded all foreign ideas, and was subservient to strict legalism and to carnal Messianic expectations, which formed the bridge between the past glory and the future hope of the Jews over the abyss of their present degradation. The spirit was sacrificed to the letter. Distinction of two senses, the proper or innate sense (*sensus innatus*, which is again either literal or figurative or mystical), and the derived sense (*sensus illatus*), obtained by logical inference or linked to the words by arbitrary combination.

2. The HELLENISTIC or ALLEGORIZING method of Alexandria was borrowed from the Stoic and Platonic philosophers, who applied it to Homer and the heathen mythology to get rid of its incongruities, absurdities, and impossibilities. It began in the period of the Apocrypha (comp. Wisdom 18 : 24), and was completed by Philo, who died A.D. 40. He held the most rigid view of verbal inspiration, but depended on the Septuagint with its countless errors, and endeavored to harmonize the Mosaic religion with Greek (Platonic) philosophy by means of allegorical interpretation. He thought that Plato had borrowed from Moses. He sacrificed the letter to a foreign spirit. He distinguished between an exoteric and esoteric understanding, in other words, between the *literal* or *historical* sense * and the *spiritual* or *mystic* sense.† The latter outruled the former. The Old Testament was turned into a storehouse of philosophical ideas, which more or less obscured or perverted the religious truths of revelation.

The allegorizing method exerted great influence on Christian exegesis, especially upon the Alexandrian school of Clement and Origen, and ruled for fifteen hundred years.

Examples of the allegorical interpretation of Philo : Adam in Genesis is the lower, sensuous man, the ἄνθρωπος χοικός; Cain, selfishness; Abel, devotion to God; Noah, righteousness; Abraham, contemplation and knowledge; Sarah, virtue; Hagar, wisdom; Moses, the prophetic spirit; Egypt, body; Canaan, piety; the sheep is the image of the pure soul; the ringdove, the emblem of divine wisdom; the house-pigeon, of human wisdom.

Generally Philo admits the literal sense in the Mosaic history, but sometimes, especially in the details, he denies it, where it seemed to imply

* ἡ ῥητὴ ἑρμηνεία, ἡ ῥητὴ ἀπόδοσις.
† ἡ ἀλληγορία, ἡ τροπική, ἡ συμβολικὴ διήγησις, ἡ διὰ τύπων, διὰ συμβόλων ἀπόδειξις.

materialistic, anthropomorphic, anthropopathic, or otherwise unworthy ideas of God. Thus, in the account of the creation, only the creative act is historic, not the details of the hexahemeron. The trees in paradise, the serpent, the expulsion from Eden, are only symbolic representations of the truths of a higher life. In such cases the allegorizing method approaches the mythical interpretation of Strauss, who denies the supernatural facts and admits only the ideas. Comp. C. Siegfried, *Philo als Ausleger des Alten Test.*, Jena, 1875.

CHAPTER CXXX.

JEWISH EXEGESIS AFTER CHRIST.

1. The TALMUDIC interpretation is a continuation of the Pharisaic, orthodox, traditional exegesis, partly slavishly literal, partly allegorizing. Overestimate of rabbinical learning. "Scripture is like water, the Mishna like wine, the Gemara like spiced wine." "The Scripture is as salt, the Mishna as pepper, the Gemara as spice." Among the chief Rabbis are Hillel (d. A.D. 8); Shammai (his rival); Johanan ben Zakkai (a pupil of Hillel); Aqiba (d. 135); Juda the holy (or simply the "Rabbi," d. 200), who made Tiberias the metropolis of rabbinism and compiled the Mishna; Ashî (d. 427), who chiefly systematized and completed the Gemara. The Babylonian Talmud fills 2947 folio pages, and contains the theology, the law and the ceremonial of the Jews. It is a continent of rabbinical wisdom and folly.

2. The sect of the KARAITES (the Protestants of Judaism) rejected talmudic traditions and aimed at a more simple and spiritual view of the Old Testament.

3. The GRAMMATICAL school of the middle ages produced valuable commentaries, grammars, and dictionaries. It flourished in Spain, where oriental learning had taken refuge. It began to influence Christian exegesis in the fourteenth century.

Rabbi Saadias Gaon (d. 942), Ibn Ezra (b. at Toledo, 1092, d. at Rome, 1167), R. Salomo Isaaki (or Rashi, erroneously called Jarchi, d. 1105), David Kimchi (or Qimchi, d. 1190), Maimonides (R. Mose ben Maimon, b. at Cordova, 1135, d. in Palestine, 1204), Abrabanel (1436–1507). Their commentaries are printed separately, and collected in the so-called rabbinical Bibles, *e.g.*, Buxtorf, Bas. 1618, 3 tom. f.

CHAPTER CXXXI.

EPOCHS OF CHRISTIAN EXEGESIS.

Christian exegesis has, like every other branch of theological science, its creative epochs, followed by periods of preservation and assimilation or transition.

The three prominent epochs are the PATRISTIC, the REFORMATORY, and the MODERN.

The first is essentially Catholic (Græco-Latin); the second, Protestant and anti-papal; the third, critical and evangelical Catholic. The exegesis of the Fathers was matured in the victorious conflict with the heresies of Ebionism, Gnosticism, Arianism, Pelagianism, etc.; the exegesis of the Reformers in the conflict with the unscriptural traditions of Rome; the modern evangelical in the conflict with rationalism in all its phases.

The patristic and reformatory exegetes agree in being predominantly doctrinal and practical, and devoted to the *divine* character of the Bible on a common theory of inspiration; the modern Protestant exegesis is grammatico-historical as well as theological, and explains the *human* as well as the divine side of the Bible. The older commentators move within opposite ecclesiastical and denominational channels; the best modern commentators rise above sectarian and polemical considerations to the comprehension of revealed truth in its comprehensive catholicity.

The mediæval exegesis is a continuation of the patristic; the exegesis of the seventeenth and eighteenth centuries is a development of the reformatory, with two branches, Lutheran and Reformed. The rationalistic exegesis lies between the second and third epochs, and prepared the way for the modern evangelical Catholic exegesis.

CHAPTER CXXXII.

PATRISTIC EXEGESIS. A.D. 100–600.

The first use made of the Bible in the Christian Church was practical and homiletical. Then followed the doctrinal use for the refutation of heresies. The Old Testament was regarded as a preparation for the New, full of prophecies and types of Christ, in opposition to the Jews. The New Testament was vindicated against Ebionism, and the harmony of the two Testaments against Gnosticism. The fundamental truths were elaborated and supported by proof-texts. The grammatical sense was neglected. The Greek Fathers had the advantage of a knowledge of the original language of the New Testament; the Latin Fathers depended mostly on the faulty Itala and the improved Vulgata of Jerome; the Hebrew was understood by very few. Allegorical fancies were freely substituted for sound expositions.

The most valuable exegetes among the Fathers are CHRYSOSTOM for his homiletical wealth, JEROME for his philological and archæological knowledge, and AUGUSTIN for his theological depth and spiritual insight.*

I. THE GREEK EXEGETES. The founder of exegesis proper is ORIGEN (180–254), the teacher of the catechetical school of Alexandria, a genius, a scholar, and an indefatigable worker. He wrote three kinds of commentaries: Annotations (σημειώσεις, *scholia*), Commentaries proper (τόμοι), and familiar Sermons (ὁμιλίαι, *sermones, tractatus*). He founded a theory of interpretation, based upon that of Philo and the Platonic trichotomy of σῶμα, ψυχή and πνεῦμα. He was a Christian Philo and a Christian Plato, or Platonic Christian. Viewing the Bible as a living organism of body, soul and spirit, he distinguished three senses: (1) the somatic, or the literal, historical; (2) the psychic, or moral (1 Cor. 9:9), and (3) the pneumatic, or spiritual, mystic, usually called allegorical sense (Gal. 4:24). He abandons the historical sense where it seemed to him inapt (anthropomorphic, anthropopathic), or morally offensive (ἄλογος, ἀδύνατος, containing σκάνδαλα and προςκόμματα). He mainly dwells on the spiritual or allegorical sense.

Two schools of patristic exegesis in the Oriental Church. (Comp. Schaff's *Church History*, II. 793, 813 sqq.; III. 705 sqq.)

1. The ALEXANDRIAN School followed the allegorical method of Origen. To this belong Eusebius (d. 340), Athanasius (d. 373), Basil (d. 379), Gregory of Nazianzus (d. 390), Gregory of Nyssa (d. 394), Ephraem Syrus (d. 373), Cyril of Alexandria (d. 444).

2. The ANTIOCHIAN, or Syrian, School was more sober, grammatico-historical, rationalizing, yet practical. *Chrysostom, the prince of Greek pulpit orators and commentators, who explained in his *Homilies* most of the books of the New Testament, Diodorus of Tarsus (d. 394), Theodorus

* The exegetical and other works of Augustin (8 vols.), Chrysostom (6 vols.), and Jerome (1 vol.), are now accessible to the English reader in "the Nicene and Post-Nicene Library," first series ed. by Schaff, second series ed. by Schaff & Wace, and published at New York (Christian Literature Co.) and Oxford (Parker & Company), 1886 sqq. See also *St. Chrysostom and St. Augustin* by Philip Schaff, New York (Thomas Whittaker), 1891.

of Mopsuestia (called ὁ ἐξηγητής, d. 429), Theodoret of Kyros in Syria (d. 457).

II. LATIN EXEGETES. Dependent on the Greeks, ignorant of Hebrew (except Jerome) and mostly even of Greek; hence worthless in matters of grammar and criticism, but rich in doctrinal and practical exposition.

Tertullian (d. 220), Cyprian (d. 254), Hilary (d. 368), Ambrose (d. 397), Pelagius (d. 420), *Jerome (d. 419), the translator of the Latin Vulgate, *Augustin (d. 430), Leo I. (d. 461), Gregory I. (d. 604), the last of the Fathers and the first of the popes.

The best patristic commentators admit the correct principle that we should first ascertain the historical truth and determine the spiritual sense in accordance with it, but they often mistake or pervert the natural sense and resort to arbitrary allegorizing. Origen, Chrysostom and Jerome resolve the collision between Paul and Peter at Antioch (Gal. 2:11–14) into a theatrical farce, and by trying to save the credit of Peter involve both Apostles in the charge of hypocrisy. The superior moral sense of Augustin protested against this monstrous misinterpretation, but his defective knowledge of the original led him into other errors; he even opposed from timid conservatism Jerome's revision of the old Latin version, which teemed with inaccuracies. Pope Gregory—one of the best popes, but excessively credulous and superstitious—was the last of the Fathers who produced an independent exegetical work. His exposition of the book of Job (translated in 3 vols. for the Oxford "Library of the Fathers," 1844) is useless as a commentary, as he knew neither Hebrew nor Greek, but valuable as a system of Christian morals (hence called *Magna Moralia*). He pursues the text in three separate threads, the literal, the allegorical, and the moral, for the edification of the Church. In the allegorical part he sets forth the life of Christ in the history of Job. The names of persons and things embody a spiritual meaning: Job represents Christ; Job's wife, the carnal nature; his seven sons, the apostles or the clergy; his three daughters, the three classes of the faithful laity worshiping the Trinity; his friends, the heretics; the seven thousand sheep, the perfect Christians; the three thousand camels, the heathen and Samaritans, etc. He deemed the question of authorship to be of no more consequence than the enquiry about the pen of a great writer; for the biblical authors were only pens of the Holy Spirit. This is a fair specimen of patristic and mediæval exegesis.

We should guard alike against a Roman Catholic overestimate and a Protestant underestimate of the Fathers. Their exegetical writings contain a vast amount of "gold, silver, and precious stones," but also of "wood, hay, and stubble" (1 Cor. 3:15). Even in the best of them we find profound views mixed with childish fancies. Luther spoke most disparagingly of the Fathers, except Augustin; Calvin knew them better and prized them higher; Anglican divines, especially of the high-church school, claim them for their *via media* between Rome and Geneva. Of all Protestant divines Bishop Christopher Wordsworth is the greatest admirer of the Fathers, and fills his commentary on the Old and New Testament with extracts from their writings, with a polemical aim both against Romanism and German Rationalism.

CHAPTER CXXXIII.

MEDIÆVAL EXEGESIS. A.D. 600–1500.

Mediæval exegesis is a repetition and continuation of patristic exegesis. The Schoolmen took the place of the Fathers, and analyzed and systematized their labors. Reproduction followed production. Exegesis became compilation. Commentaries were called "Chains," binding the Fathers together as so many links.*

Chrysostom, Augustin, and Pope Gregory furnished the chief material. The favorite books were the Gospels and the Psalms.

In the Eastern Church the Greek language continued to be spoken; hence the superior value of the exegetical labors of Œcumenius, Theophylactus, and Euthymius Zigabenus.

The Western Church Christianized and civilized the barbarians of Europe, built convents, churches, the papal hierarchy and the scholastic systems of theology, engaged in the heroic crusades, organized monastic orders, and produced self-denying missionaries, holy monks, commanding popes and emperors, but neglected exegetical and historical studies. There was no taste for critical investigation. The eternal truths of the Bible, however, could not be forgotten, and inspired all the great enterprises of that period. They shone through the stained glass of Gothic windows; they were expounded in profound theological treatises, and expressed in heart-stirring hymns, like the *Dies Irae*, the *Stabat Mater*, and *Jesu dulcis memoria*. Biblical learning was the monopoly of the clergy. The laity could not read and were even forbidden to read the Bible by the popes, who yet constantly quoted, in support of their theocracy, the Old Testament and the words of Christ to Peter: "Thou art Rock;" "Feed my sheep."

Exegesis was the slave of dogma, and was utilized for the support of the Catholic faith of the Church, handed down from the Fathers. It was based upon the distinction of a fourfold sense of the Bible, as expressed in the mnemonic couplet (attributed to Nicolas of Lyra):

"*Litera* gesta docet; quid credas, *Allegoria*;
Moralis, quid agas; quo tendas, *Anagogia*."

* *Catenæ Patrum* ; σεῖραι τῶν πατέρων, or συλλογαὶ, ἐπιτομαὶ ἐξηγήσεων.

The first sense is the literal or historical (*gesta docet*); the other three are ramifications of the spiritual or mystic sense, and correspond to the cardinal Christian virtues of faith, hope, and love. The allegorical sense strictly so-called refers to faith (*credenda*); the moral sense, to charity or good works (*agenda*), the anagogical (uplifting, exalting) sense to hope (*speranda* and *desideranda*). Thus Jerusalem means, literally, the city in Palestine; allegorically, the Church; morally, the believing soul; anagogically, the heavenly Jerusalem. Babylon: the city on the Euphrates; heathen Rome; the enemies of the Church; eternal perdition. The exodus from Egypt: the historical fact in the history of Israel; the redemption by Christ; the conversion of the soul; the departure from this life to the heavenly world.

The fourfold sense was an expansion of the threefold sense of Origen. It was suggested by Augustin, and more clearly set forth as a hermeneutical canon by Eucherius (d. 450), Cassianus (d. 450), and Rabanus Maurus (d. 856). Dante (in the *Convito* and in a letter to Can Grande della Scala) defends it as applicable to his *Divina Commedia*. Savonarola's sermons are full of the fourfold sense. Luther followed it in his first commentary on the Psalms (1513) before he became a reformer; he distinguished at times even six senses, and only gradually emancipated himself from the allegorizing method.

The mystic sense was the most important in the ages of faith and superstition. The commentators feasted upon the boundless wealth of revelation and derived from it lessons of holy living and dying. Even errors are overruled for good. Nevertheless this kind of exegesis turns the Bible into a *nasus cereus*, and makes it a slave of human caprices. By trying to evade difficulties, it creates new and greater difficulties. Starting from a profound reverence for the spiritual depths of the Bible, it destroys trust in its plain meaning. It substitutes arbitrary imposition for honest exposition. The Song of Songs and the Apocalypse even down to our day have suffered most from allegorizing commentaries, which fairly teem with pious sense and nonsense.

I. GREEK commentators: ŒCUMENIUS, bishop of Tricca in Thessalia (d. about 990), on the Acts and Epistles.—THEOPHYLACTUS, archbishop of Bulgaria (d. 1107), on nearly the whole New Testament.—EUTHYMIUS ZIGABENUS, a monk near Constantinople (d. 1118), on the Gospels and the

Psalms.—NICEPHORUS compiled an exegetical work from fifty-one writers. Chrysostom was the chief source. A series of Greek "Chains" on the whole New Testament was edited by J. A. Cramer, Oxford, 1838, sqq. in 8 vols.

II. LATIN commentators: WALAFRIED STRABO or STRABUS (abbot of Reichenau, d. 849), author of the *Glossa ordinaria*, compiled from Augustin, Ambrose, Gregory, Isidor, Beda, Alcuin, and Rabanus Maurus, with anonymous glosses,—the chief authority for the following centuries.— ANSELM OF LAON (d. 1117, not to be confounded with the more famous Anselm of Canterbury): *Glossa interlinearis*, next to the former in popularity, but defective and uncritical.—Cardinal HUGO DE S. CARO (d. 1263): *Postillæ in universa Biblia secundum quadruplicem sensum* (Venice, 1487, 6 vols.). He wrote also a Latin Concordance and introduced the chapter division, which, like the versicular division of the sixteenth century, is unfortunately very faulty.—THOMAS AQUINAS, "the angelic doctor" and standard divine of the Roman Church (d. 1274), compiled a devotional and exceedingly popular commentary on the Gospels, called *Catena aurea in Evangelia* (English translation by Pusey, Keble, and Newman, Oxford, 1841–45, 4 vols.), and explained also several epistles of Paul. He was a great admirer of Chrysostom, especially of his commentary on Matthew. The monkish legend says that St. Paul appeared to him in a dream and told him that no one understood him so well; but he did not correct his errors. Thomas says that the name of Paul cannot be of Hebrew origin, because the Hebrew lacks the letter P, but it may be from a similar word and mean "wonderful" or "elect"; if it be from the Greek, it means "quiet"; if Latin, it means "small." He proceeds to show from the Scripture that all these meanings suit St. Paul.

Other biblical scholars of less importance: Cassiodorus (d. 562), the Venerable Bede (d. 735), Alcuin (d. 804), St. Bernard (d. 1153; Sermons on the Canticles), Ruprecht of Deuz (d. 1135), John of Salisbury (d. 1182; on Paul), Albert the Great (d. 1280; on the Prophets, Gospels and Apocalypse), Bonaventura ("*doctor seraphicus*," d. 1274; on Ecclesiastes, the Gospels of Luke and John, etc.).

John Wiclif (d. 1384), one of the Reformers before the Reformation, deserves mention as the first translator of the whole Bible (from the Latin Vulgate) into English.

CHAPTER CXXXIV.

THE PERIOD OF THE RENAISSANCE.

The Revival of Letters and Arts, which began in Italy and spread over Europe during the fourteenth and fifteenth centuries, roused the spirit of free inquiry, and promoted the cause of biblical learning by the cultivation of the original languages. The first-fruits were shown in the exegetical works of Nicolas Lyra and Laurentius Valla, the last in Reuchlin and Erasmus. The German Reuchlin and the Dutch Erasmus, called "the two eyes of Europe," are the connecting links between the Renaissance and the Reformation, the one by his Hebrew, the other by his Greek learning.

The invention of the printing-press, the art-preserving art, gave wings to thought and prepared the way for the general circulation and use of the Bible among the laity as well as the clergy. The Latin Bible was the first large book that was printed (1455); but during the first half century of that art not a single new and important exegetical work appeared. The Church was silently gathering strength for a new productive epoch in biblical learning.

NICOLAS OF LYRA or LYRANUS ("*doctor planus et utilis,*" born at Lyre in the diocese of Evreux in Normandy, about 1270, d. at Paris, 1340): *Postillæ perpetuæ sive commentaria brevia in universa Biblia* (first printed ed. Rom. 1471, 5 vols., and very often, last ed. Antwerp, 1634, 6 vols.). He was a Franciscan monk, and doctor of theology, and taught with success in Paris. He is "the Jerome of the fourteenth century," and marks an epoch in the history of exegesis. His knowledge of Hebrew gave rise to the unsupported conjecture that he was the son of a Hebrew mother. He based his commentary on the original text, and first made use of Jewish scholars (especially Rashi); yea, he dared sometimes to prefer their explanations to those of the Fathers. He adopted the seven useless rules of Tichonius, and the traditional fourfold sense (in the preface), but maintained that the literal sense is the foundation, and should alone be used in proving doctrines. Practically he admitted only two senses, the literal (or historical) and the mystical (or typical and prophetical), the latter of which must be based upon the former. He complains that the mystical sense has been allowed almost to choke (*suffocare*) the literal. He followed the rule: "*Scriptura loquitur secundum modum nostrum loquendi.*" He wrote with great modesty, and submitted his works to the decisions of the Church; yet he quietly undermined the exegetical tyranny, and had considerable influence upon the Reformers. Hence the well-known lines:

"*Si Lyra non lyrasset, Lutherus non saltasset.*" *

LAURENTIUS VALLA (LORENZO DELLA VALLE, canon of St. John in the Lateran, 1406–57), the best Latinist and most independent scholar of his age, and the pioneer of historical criticism, who first disproved the fiction of the Donation of Constantine, prepared *Annotations to the New Testament*, which were published by Erasmus in 1505. He dared to criticise Jerome's Vulgate and St. Augustin, and to doubt the traditional text. Bellarmin calls him a forerunner of Luther, but he was simply a skeptical humanist, destitute of religious sincerity and moral earnestness. He

* To which somebody added: "*Et totus mundus delirasset.*" Luther greatly admired Lyranus, and closely followed him in his commentary on Genesis, almost verse for verse, but he blames him for his dependence on Jewish rabbis.

escaped punishment by a cynical submission to the authority of Mother Church and became a secretary of Nicolas V., the liberal patron of the Renaissance.

JACQUES LE FÈVRE (LE-FÈVRE D'ETAPLES, usually called FABER STAPULENSIS, 1450–1536) made a new Latin translation of the Epistles of Paul with a commentary (1512), and the first French version of the entire Scriptures (the New Testament in 1523, the Old in 1528), which formed the basis of the translation of Olivetan (1535). He was a humanist and pioneer of French Protestantism, though he died in the Roman Catholic Church. His exegesis is uncertain and wavering between the old and new methods. He proclaimed five years before the Reformation the Protestant principles of the supremacy of the Bible and of justification by faith, and uttered, in his work on Paul, the prophetic word: "The signs of the times announce that a Reformation of the Church is near at hand, and while God opens new ways for the preaching of the Gospel by the discoveries of the Portuguese and Spaniards, we must hope that he will also visit his Church and raise her from the abasement into which she has fallen." About the same time, he told his pupil, William Farel, the pioneer of the Reformation in French Switzerland: "My son, God will renovate the world and you will see it."* He fled from persecution to Strassburg, but spent his last years in peace under the protection of Queen Marguerite of Navarre in her little capital at Nérac. There Calvin, on his flight from Paris in 1533, saw the octogenarian scholar, who, in prophetic vision, saluted the youth as the future restorer of the Catholic Church in France, and suggested to him to take Melanchthon for his model.

JOHN REUCHLIN (1455–1522), called "the Phœnix of Germany," is the father of Hebrew learning in the modern Christian Church, though he must share this honor with Pellican. He learned the rudiments of Hebrew from John Wessel and from some rabbis. He paid ten gold pieces to a Jew for the explanation of a single phrase. On the basis of David Qimchi, he wrote a Hebrew grammar and dictionary (1506), from which the Reformers acquired their knowledge of that language. He was unduly addicted to the mysterious superstitions of the Kabala. He had to suffer much persecution from the intolerant champions of monastic obscurantism, but was supported by all progressive scholars.

DESIDERIUS ERASMUS of Rotterdam (1466–1536), the prince of the humanists and undisputed sovereign in the realm of letters, published, from a few manuscripts at Basel, where he spent the best years of his life, the first edition of the Greek Testament (1516), which became the basis of the *textus receptus* and of the Protestant versions. He accompanied this work with a new and elegant Latin translation and brief *Annotations*, which had a large circulation and exerted an immense influence.† He also began to publish, in 1517, *Paraphrases* on the New Testament (except the Apocalypse), in which

---

* "*Mon fils, Dieu renouvellera le monde et tu en seras le temoin.*" See Herminjard, *Correspondance des Réformateurs dans les pays de langue française*, vol. I. (1866), p. 5.

† *Annotationes*, with a manifesto of liberal exegesis *contra morosos ac indoctos*.

he repeated the text in different words.* His object was practical as well as literary. He wished that the theologians might study Christianity from its fountain-head, and that the Scriptures might be translated into every tongue and put into the hands of every reader, to give strength and comfort to the husbandman at his plough, to the weaver at his shuttle, to the traveler on his journey. Tyndale echoed this noble desire when he said: "If God spare my life, ere many years I will cause the boy that driveth the plough to know more of Scripture than you do," speaking to one of those ignorant priests who "prefer the laws of the pope to the laws of God."

Erasmus lived and died on the threshold of the middle ages and modern times. Stunica said by way of reproach: "*Erasmus lutherissat*"; Erasmus replied: "*Lutherus erasmissat.*" He displeased both parties. The Romanists charged him with laying the egg which Luther hatched; the Protestants called him a traitor to the Reformation; but Zwingli and Melanchthon never lost respect for him and his eminent services. His work was a necessary literary preparation for the greater work of the Reformers. He raised Greece from the dead "with the New Testament in her hand."

CHAPTER CXXXV.

EXEGESIS OF THE REFORMERS.

Humanism was an important intellectual factor in the Reformation, but could never have produced it. The deeper roots of this movement were moral and religious. The Renaissance was a revival of classical heathen learning, the Reformation was a revival of primitive Christianity. As the literature of ancient Greece and Rome preceded the advent of Christianity, so a revival of that literature preceded and prepared the way for a revival of Christianity. The Greek language furnished the key to both.

The Reformation of the sixteenth century, by raising the standard of the Bible, as the sovereign rule of Christian faith and life, in opposition to the yoke of papal and scholastic tyranny, kindled an intense enthusiasm for biblical studies. It cleared away the obstructions of traditional dogmatism and brought the believer into direct contact with the Word of God

---

* In his own definition: "*ita temperare παράφρασιν, ne fiat παραφρόνησις, h.e. sic aliter dicere ut non dicas alia.*" Luther, in his wrath, called the *Paraphrases* of Erasmus *Paraphroneses* (derangements, *deliria*); but Herder deemed them worth their weight in gold, and Reuss calls them "an inestimable benefit" to that age. Leo Judæ translated them into German. By a royal injunction of 1547, a copy of the Paraphrase on the Gospels was set up in every church of England for the use of the parishioners. Hardwick, *Hist. of the Reform.*, p. 195, note 1 (Stubbs' ed.). On the value of these Paraphrases see also R. Stähelin in Herzog, 2d ed., IV. 283 sq.

in the original Hebrew and Greek, and in idiomatic vernacular versions. It enabled him to drink from the fresh fountain instead of the muddy river, and to walk in the daylight of the sun instead of the night-light of the moon and the stars.

The Reformers were all in full sympathy with the spirit of the Bible, as witnessing, in unbroken harmony, that Jesus of Nazareth is the Son of the living God and the Saviour of mankind. To them Christ was the beginning, the middle, and the end of the written revelation, yet not in the way of forced allegorical interpretation. They had a sound instinct for the natural grammatical sense and laid aside arbitrary allegorizing, though not entirely.

The Bible was made the chief object of theological study, and a book of the people as well as the clergy. Exegesis, heretofore confined to the Greek and Latin languages and to scholars, was carried on for the benefit of laymen as well as ministers. But it was also often abused for polemical purposes and made to promote disunion rather than union among Christians.

Luther is the prince of translators, Calvin the prince of commentators, among the Reformers. Melanchthon, Zwingli, Œcolampadius and Beza occupy, next to them, the highest rank as expounders of the Scripture.

I. Exegesis in the LUTHERAN Church. MARTIN LUTHER (1483-1546) gave to the German people an idiomatic version of the Old and New Testaments (begun at the Wartburg, 1522, and finished at Wittenberg, 1534, last revision, 1545). It is his best and most useful work and an immortal monument of his genius, industry and piety. His commentaries on Galatians (which he called his "wife,"), Psalms and Genesis are original, deep, fresh and suggestive, but unequal and irregular. He often hits the nail on the head, but as often wanders away from the text, using or abusing it as a mere starting-point for polemical excursions against Papists and radical Protestants (*Schwarm—*und *Rottengeister*). He condemned allegorizing as a monkey-game (*Affenspiel*), but often resorted to it in Job, the Psalms and Canticles. He was at times slavishly traditional and literal, at times boldly independent and spiritual. He objected to some parts of the Bible (Esther, James, Hebrews, Apocalypse), and anticipated modern criticism, but had the profoundest reverence for the word of God in the Bible.

PHILIP MELANCHTHON (1497-1560) was a superior philologist and the best Greek scholar of his age. He thought in Greek, and could hardly write a letter to a learned friend without inserting a rare Greek word or phrase. He maintained the correct principles, that "the Scripture cannot be understood theologically unless it be first understood grammatically," and that "the Scripture had one certain and simple sense" (*una certa et simplex sententia*), which must be ascertained by the laws of grammar and rhetoric. But he required piety as well as knowledge of the grammar. Diestel gives him credit for having clearly pointed out the unity of the sense of the Scripture under the influence of his classical studies. Yet his brief comments are meager and dogmatical rather than grammatical. His *Loci theologici* grew out of his lectures on the Epistle to the Romans.

Secondary Lutheran commentators: Bugenhagen (d. 1558), Brenz (d. 1570), Flacius, the author of the *Clavis Scripturæ Sacræ* (d. 1575), Chemnitz (d. 1586), Chytræus (d. 1600), Osiander (d. 1604).

II. REFORMED Church. The Reformed exegesis was less dogmatical and more grammatico-historical than the Lutheran.

JOHN CALVIN (1509-64) is the first commentator of the sixteenth century, and both for quantity and quality has no superior in ancient or modern times. This is the unanimous judgment of competent scholars of different schools (like Scaliger, Tholuck, Winer, Diestel, Meyer, Reuss, Merx, Farrar) and expository preachers (like Spurgeon, who calls him "the most candid" commentator and of "priceless value"). His knowledge of the Bible as a whole and in all its parts is amazing and unsurpassed. He combined all the hermeneutical qualifications: classical culture, knowledge of Greek and Hebrew, mastery of Latin and French, familiarity with the best of the Fathers, fairness, freedom from prejudice, exegetical tact, acute perception, sound judgment, lucid method, spiritual insight, and profound sympathy with the biblical authors, especially Paul. He commented on the most important books of the Old Testament, and the whole New Testament, except the Apocalypse. Diestel calls him "the creator of modern exegesis." (See his *Geschichte des A. T.'s in der christl. Kirche*, pp. 267 sqq., and Schaff's *Church Hist.* VII. 524-538.) A complete English translation of Calvin's commentaries in 45 vols. was published by the Calvin Translation Society at Edinburgh, 1844 sqq.

ZWINGLI (1484-1531), the Reformer of Zurich and German Switzerland, had superior classical culture, was a great admirer of Erasmus, copied the Greek text of the Epistles of Paul at Einsiedeln (1516, before he had heard of Luther), and studied the Scriptures with a reverent and independent spirit for the practical purpose that he might "preach Christ from the fountain." He began with a continuous exposition of the Gospel of Matthew, while Luther and Melanchthon started from the Epistles to the Romans and Galatians. His commentaries on Genesis, the Psalms, Isaiah, Jeremiah, and several epistles, show sound common sense, sober judgment, and a preference for the simple, obvious sense, but are brief, fragmentary and immature. He died in the prime of manhood on the battlefield of Cappel.

JOHN ŒCOLAMPADIUS (1482-1531), the Reformer of Basel, was the best Hebrew scholar of his age, and well acquainted with the Fathers. He wrote useful commentaries on Genesis and the Larger and Minor Prophets, and ably defended the figurative interpretation of the words of institution in the eucharistic controversy.

THEODORE BEZA (DE BÈZE, 1519-1605), the friend and successor of Calvin, combined rare classical culture with a rigorous theology. He edited several standard editions of the Greek Testament, a new Latin version, and a brief commentary (1565 sqq.), which were very popular in the Reformed Churches of the Continent, and especially in England during the reign of Elizabeth. He exerted considerable influence upon the Geneva English Version (1557), and the Authorized Version of 1611, not always for the best.

Minor exegetes: MARTIN BUCER (d. 1551), the Strassburg Reformer and mediator between Luther and Zwingli, at last professor in Cambridge; PELLICAN (d. 1556), a self-taught Hebraist, professor at Zurich, who commented on the whole Bible (1532–39, 7 vols.); BIBLIANDER (d. 1564), likewise professor at Zurich, an Erasmian rather than a Calvinist; and HENRY BULLINGER (d. 1575), the friend and successor of Zwingli, and best known as the author of the Second Helvetic Confession (1566).

WILLIAM TYNDALE (d. 1536) deserves an honorable place among the primary translators and secondary Reformers. By his New Testament (1525) he shaped the idiom of the Authorized Version of 1611.

In his *Obedience of a Christian Man*, written in 1528 (ed. by the "Parker Society," 1848, p. 303 sq.), he lays down his hermeneutical principles in the following remarkable passage: " The Papists divide the Scriptures into four senses, the literal, tropological, allegorical, and anagogical. The literal sense is become nothing at all, for the pope hath taken it clean away, and has made it his possession. He hath partly locked it up with the false and counterfeited keys of his traditions, ceremonies, and feigned lies; and partly driveth men from it with violence of sword: for no man dare abide by the literal sense of the text, but under a protestation, 'If it shall please the Pope.' The tropological sense pertaineth to good manners (say they), and teacheth what we ought to do. The allegory is appropriate to faith; and the anagogical to hope, and things above. Tropological and anagogical are terms of their own feigning, and altogether unnecessary. For they are but allegories, both two of them; and this word allegory comprehendeth them both, and is enough. For tropological is but an allegory of manners; and anagogical, an allegory of hope. And allegory is as much to say as strange speaking, or borrowed speech. . . .

" *Thou shalt understand, therefore, that the Scripture hath but one sense, which is the literal sense. And that literal sense is the root and ground of all, and the anchor that never faileth, whereunto if thou cleave, thou canst never err or go out of the way.* Nevertheler, the Scripture uses proverbs, similitudes, riddles, or allegories, as all other speeches do; but that which the proverb, similitude, riddle or allegory signifieth, is ever the literal sense, which thou must seek out diligently: as in the English we borrow words and sentences of one thing, and apply them unto another, and give them new significations."

CHAPTER CXXXVI.

PROTESTANT EXEGESIS OF THE SEVENTEENTH TO THE MIDDLE OF THE EIGHTEENTH CENTURY.

The seventeenth century is the period of Protestant scholasticism. It furnishes a parallel to the Catholic scholasticism of the Middle Ages, but is much richer in biblical learning. Its exegesis bears the same relation to the exegesis of the Reformers (henceforward revered as protestant Fathers) as the mediæval exegesis to the patristic. It has the prevailing character of reproduction, compilation, and confessional contraction. It was based on a mechanical theory of verbal inspiration or dictation, which was most minutely formulated, and acted as a check upon independent research. An infallible Book was set over against an infallible Church. The Protestant Confessions of Faith acquired the authority of Catholic tradition. Exegesis was controlled by dogmatic systems and made subservient to polemic confessionalism. The Bible was used as a repository of doctrinal proof-texts, without discrimination between the Old and New Testaments, and between the different books. A vast amount of patient, pedantic, antiquarian learning was accumulated. The exegetical compilations of Calovius and the *Critici Sacri* correspond to the *Catenæ Patrum* of the Middle Ages.

1. The Lutheran Church took the lead in Protestant scholasticism. She claimed the monopoly of orthodoxy or doctrinal purity, in opposition to Romanism and Calvinism, and assumed that all orthodox Christians are Lutherans, either consciously, or unconsciously under other names. Luther's version of the Bible, which he himself had improved in every successive edition, became as unchangeably fixed as the textus receptus of the Greek Testament and as the Latin Vulgate. Adam, Noah, Abraham, Moses and the prophets were pressed into the service of pure unmixed Lutheranism. Calixtus advocated a more liberal tendency on the broad basis of the œcumenical creeds, but was silenced as a dangerous syncretist and latitudinarian.

The Pietistic school of Spener and Francke broke down the dominion of scholasticism and symbololatry, laid stress on experimental piety as the key to the understanding of the Scriptures, and developed practical and devotional exegesis.

The best Lutheran commentator of the eighteenth century was Bengel, a pietest of the Swabian type. His hermeneutic principle was: to exhibit the force and significance of the words of the text, so as to express everything which the author intended, and to introduce nothing which he did not intend.

After Bengel the old Tübingen school of Storr and Flatt maintained a moderate orthodoxy against the rising tide of Rationalism which broke in with Semler and gradually flooded Germany.

2. The Reformed Church elaborated the same theory of a literal inspiration, as a bulwark against popery, and gave it even symbolical authority in the Helvetic Consensus Formula (1675), but only for Switzerland and for a short period. In other respects, she presents in the seventeenth century more life, progress and variety than the Lutheran Church.

Holland stood first in critical learning, archæological and chronological investigations, and produced, on the one hand, the rigid orthodoxy of the Synod of Dort (1620), and on the other, the liberal school of Arminianism, which emancipated exegesis from dogmatic domination and reintroduced through Hugo Grotius the Erasmian spirit of philological and historical interpretation. Arminianism assumed great practical importance in the revival movement of Wesleyan Methodism.

England was agitated by the conflicts between prelacy or semi-popery and puritanism, which stimulated theological activity and furnished the most interesting chapter in the contemporaneous history of Protestantism. The Episcopal commentators made large use of the Fathers of the undivided Church of antiquity. The Puritan (Presbyterian and Independent) commentators followed the principle that the Holy Spirit is the proper interpreter of the Scripture, and that the Scripture explains itself. The seventeenth century was the palmy period of Puritanism and the most fruitful of biblical study.

I. LUTHERAN exegetes.

(1) The *Orthodox* School.

ABRAHAM CALOV, professor at Wittenberg (d. 1686): *Biblia illustrata*, 1672, 4 vols. fol., a dogmatico-polemical catena of Lutheran Bible learning, chiefly against Grotius.

W. GEIER, professor at Leipzig (d. 1680): *Psalms, Proverbs, Daniel*.

SEB. SCHMIDT, professor at Strassburg (d. 1696): several books of the Old and New Testaments, and *Collegium biblicum*.

SAL. GLASS, professor at Jena (d. 1656): *Philologia Sacra*, 1623, etc. *Sensus duplex, literalis et mysticus;* the former holding the priority of order, the latter of dignity.

SCHÖTTGEN (d. at Dresden, 1751): *Horæ Hebraicæ et Talmudicæ*, Dresden, 1733 and 1742.

J. C. WOLF, professor of Oriental languages in Hamburg (d. 1739): *Curæ philologicæ et criticæ in Novum Testamentum*, etc. Basil., 1741, 5 vols.

CHRISTOPH STARKE, orthodox but not polemical, aiming at edification, like the Pietists (d. 1744): *Synopsis bibliothecæ exeget.*, on the Old and New Testaments (German), Leipzig, 1733 sqq., 9 vols.; new ed. Berlin 1865 sqq. Replaced by Lange's *Bibelwerk*.

(2) The *Pietistic* School, aiming chiefly at edification. *Collegia philo-*

biblica. Methodism did for the Church of England, on a larger, more practical and methodical scale, what Pietism had done for Germany. Pietists and Methodists, originally terms of reproach for experimental Christians.

"*Was ist ein Pietist? der Gottes Wort studirt
Und nach demselben auch ein heilig Leben führt.*"

SPENER (d. 1705), on several Epistles. FRANCKE (d. 1727): *Manuductio ad lectionem S. Script.*—PAUL ANTON (d. 1730), a voluminous writer on the New Testament.—J. HEINRICH MICHAELIS (d. 1738): Notes on the Old Testament.—RAMBACH (d. 1735).

JOACHIM LANGE (d. 1744): *Licht und Recht*, 1729 sqq., 7 vols.

The *Berleburger Bibel*, 1726–42, 8 vols.

Many works, mostly worthless, on the Apocalypse with a millennarian tendency.

(3) JOH. ALBRECHT BENGEL (d. 1752): *Gnomon Novi Testamenti*, Tübing. 1742 and often (also in English). He occupies a *via media* between orthodox Lutheranism and Pietism; sound in doctrine, reverential in spirit, acute in judgment, sparing in words, pregnant in meaning, a sober chiliast, upon the whole the best exegete of the eighteenth century. His *Gnomon* is truly a pointer or indicator, like a sun-dial. Farrar (p. 393) calls it a "mine of priceless gems." It is one of the very few commentaries which, like Chrysostom's and Calvin's, have outlasted their generation, notwithstanding his faulty exposition of the Apocalypse, which was exploded June 18, 1836 (the supposed date of the destruction of the beast). A warning of humility and caution to lesser lights.

II. REFORMED exegetes, partly (and mostly) orthodox Calvinists, partly Arminians. The former developed the dogmatic and practical, the latter the scientific and historical element, in Calvin's exegesis.

(1) *Dutch Reformed.* (*a*) *Orthodox.*

J. COCCEJUS (KOCH), professor at Leyden (d. 1669), wrote commentaries on most of the biblical books (*Opera*, Amst. 1675, 10 vols. fol.) and founded a biblical rather than scholastic theology and exegesis, on the basis of the idea of the Covenant of God with man in a gradual historical evolution: (1) the Covenant of nature and works, made with Adam in Paradise (imaginary); (2) the Covenant of grace and faith, after the fall, under three administrations, viz. before the law, under the law, under the gospel. Immense learning. Excessive typology substituted for the manifold mystic sense. The Old Testament theocracy made a picture frame of the Christian Church. "*Verba S. S. significant id omne quod possunt.*" Coccejus found "Christ everywhere in the Old Testament, Grotius nowhere." Grotius, however, recognized messianic prophecies. On Ps. 15:10, he says: "*Latet sensus mysticus . . . ut in plerisque Psalmis.*" The covenant theology maintained itself in Holland till the eighteenth century.

CAMPEGIUS VITRINGA (d. 1722, at Franeker), a pupil of Coccejus, but more moderate, very learned and profound. His commentaries on Isaiah, Zach., Epp., Apoc., etc., are still valuable.

JOS. SCALIGER, professor at Leyden (d. 1609), the greatest scholar of his age, master of thirteen languages, an admirer of Calvin, founder of the first system of biblical chronology, *Thesaurus Temporum.*—J. DRUSIUS (d.

1616).—BOCHART (d. 1667), on biblical zoology and geography.—SAL. VAN TIL (d. 1713).—RELAND (d. 1718) made an epoch in Palestine geography and biblical antiquities.—J. MARCK (d. 1731).—SCHUTTENS (d. 1750) was the best Arabic scholar of the eighteenth century.—VENEMA (d. 1787).

(*b*) The *Arminian* commentators were free from the dogmatic prepossessions and intolerance of orthodoxy, and prepared the way for grammatico-historical exegesis, but also for rationalism by their lower view on inspiration and indifference to doctrine.

HUGO GROTIUS (DE GROOT, d. 1645), a great scholar, jurist, statesman and divine: *Annotationes* on the whole Bible, 1641–44. Himself a layman, he wrote for laymen, from the standpoint of a statesman and historian. Illustrations of the Bible by parallel passages from the Greek and Latin authors and secular historians. Afterwards superseded by Wetstein. Grotius was called a papist because he would not denounce the pope as the antichrist of prophecy, and the Romish priests as ministers of antichrist.

J. CLERICUS (LE CLERC, d. 1736): Commentaries on most of the Old Testament books, and Latin translation of Hammond on the New Testament, with many additions.

SIM. EPISCOPIUS (d. 1643).—PHIL. VON LIMBORCH (d. 1712).

(2) *German* and *Swiss Reformed.*

DAVID PAREUS, at Heidelberg (d. 1622): Commentaries on Gen., Min. Prophets and several books of the New Testament.

JOH. PISCATOR (FISCHER), at Herborn (d. 1625), on the whole Bible, in 24 vols. 8vo, afterwards in 4 vols.

D. TOSSANUS (TOUSSAINT), at Hanau (d. 1629), on the New Testament.

J. H. HEIDEGGER, professor at Zürich (d. 1697): *Exercitia biblica.*

F. A. LAMPE (b. at Bremen, 1683, professor at Utrecht, d. at Bremen, 1729) wrote a most learned commentary on John, 3 vols. 4to. He was a rigid Calvinist and yet a sweet hymnist (author of "*Mein Leben ist ein Pilgrimstand;*" "*O Liebesglut, die Erd und Himmel paaret,*" etc.).

JOHN JACOB WETSTEIN (1693–1754, professor at Basel, deposed and exiled from his native city for heresy, 1730, then professor at the Arminian College in Amsterdam) *Novum Testamentum Græcum,* Amsterdam, 1751–52, 2 vols. fol. A herculean work of forty years' labor, a thesaurus of classical, patristic and rabbinical learning in illustration of the text, and a quarry for commentators. As a textual critic he was inferior in judgment to the contemporary Bengel, but much richer in resources and collations. He introduced the system of citations of uncial manuscripts by Latin capitals (A, C, D, etc.) and of cursive manuscripts by Arabic numerals. His text (Elzevir) is superseded, but his notes of parallel passages are invaluable.

(3) *French Reformed.*

LUD. DE DIEU (d. 1642).—JAQ. CAPPELLE, at Sedan (d. 1624).—His brother, LOUIS CAPPELLE, at Saumur (d. 1658).—IS. DE BEAUSOBRE (d. 1738, at Berlin).

(4) *English* divines, of the Episcopal and of Dissenting Churches, rivaled each other in biblical learning and its application to the practical life of the Church, and produced more works of permanent homiletical value than those of the continent. The Puritan commentators excel in practical application and are rich mines for preachers. Spurgeon prized them

above all others, and characterizes them pithily in his *Lectures on Commenting and Commentaries* (London, 1876). Farrar ignores them.

HENRY HAMMOND (Canon of Christ Church, Oxford, d. 1660): *Paraphrase and Annotations upon the New Testament*, London, 1653 (best ed. 1702); also on the Psalms and Proverbs. Churchly and Arminian. (Spurgeon calls him "churchy.")

CRITICI SACRI, compiled as an appendix to Walton's Polyglot, under the direction of Bishop PEARSON, and others, first edition, London, 1660, 9 tom., followed by two suppl. vols. and four more, called Thesaurus Theologico-Philologicus; best ed. Amsterd. 1698–1732, 13 vols. Contains extracts from Reformed and Roman Catholic commentators, viz. Erasmus, Seb. Münster, Fagius, Vatablus, Castellio, Clarius, Drusius, Grotius, Scaliger, Casaubonus, Capellus, and a few others. A huge cyclopedia of the wisdom and folly of commentators. (See a full table of contents of the several volumes in Darling's *Cyclopedia Bibliographica*, pp. 815–820.)

MATTHEW POOLE (POLUS, Presbyterian divine, ejected for non-conformity in 1662, d. 1679): *Synopsis Criticorum aliorumque S. Scripturæ interpretum*, London, 1669–76, 4 vols. in 5 fol. (which is better than the incorrect Francf. reprints of 1688 and 1712). A useful abridgment from the *Critici Sacri*, and many other commentators (including Lutherans), the names being marked on the margin.

MATTHEW POOLE wrote also *Annotations upon the whole Bible*, 4th ed. London, 1700, 2 vols. fol.; London, 1840, 3 vols. imp. 8vo; London, 1853. This is an English synopsis from Poole's Latin synopsis and intended for popular use. The books from Isaiah to the end were done after his death by different authors. Spurgeon puts Poole next to Matthew Henry in value for practical use.

JOSEPH HALL (bishop of Norwich, d. 1656): *Contemplations on the Historical Passages of the Old and New Testaments*, in numerous editions, one at Edinburgh, 1844.

JOHN TRAPP (vicar of Weston-upon-Avon, 1611–69): *A Commentary on the Old and New Testaments*, London, 1654, 5 vols. fol.; new ed. 1867. Original with much quaint wit and illustrative anecdotes. Spurgeon says (p. 7): "Trapp is my especial companion and treasure; I can read him when I am too weary for anything else. Trapp is salt, pepper, mustard, vinegar, and all the other condiments."

PATRICK, WM. LOWTH, WHITBY and LOWMAN: *A Critical Commentary and Paraphrase on the Old and New Testaments and the Apocrypha*, London, 1679–94; ed. Pitman, London, 1822, 6 vols.; Philadelphia, 1844, in 4 vols. The New Testament with the exception of Revelation, by Whitby. Episcopalians and Arminians classed among the "Latitudinarians." *

---

* The meaning of the term Latitudinarianism as employed in England is well explained by Dr. John Stoughton, in his *Ecclesiastical History of England. The Church of the Restoration*, vol. II. p. 359 (London, 1870): "The term Latitudinarian, both as a term of praise and a term of reproach, intended by friends to signify that a man was liberal, intended by enemies to denote that he was heterodox, came to be applied to thinkers holding very different opinions. Amongst the divines, often placed under the generic denomination, very considerable diversities of sentiment existed. Indeed, the name is so loosely used as to be given to some persons

MATTHEW HENRY (Dissenting minister at Chester, 1662–1714, the son of Philip Henry, who was deposed for non-conformity in 1662): *An Exposition of the Old and New Testaments,* London, 1705–15, 5 vols. fol., often republished in England and America (also condensed in Jenk's *Comprehensive Commentary*). It is fresh, pithy, quaint, suggestive and full of spiritual wisdom and experience. It holds its ground to this day as the best practical and devotional commentary for English readers. Spurgeon advises ministers to read Henry "entirely and carefully through once at least" (p. 3). But we must not go to him for the solution of any critical difficulty.

JOHN GILL (Baptist minister, d. 1771): *An Exposition of the Old and New Testaments,* London, 1728–67; again London, 1810, in 9 vols. 4to. A supralapsarian Calvinist, great rabbinical scholar, but very dry and diffuse. "The Corypheus of hyper-Calvinism." (Spurgeon.)

JOHN LIGHTFOOT (professor in Cambridge, a member of the Westminster Assembly, d. 1675) must be mentioned here on account of his unsurpassed rabbinical learning made subservient to the illustration of the Scriptures: *Horæ Hebraicæ et Talmudicæ in quatuor Evangelistas, in Acta Apostol., partem aliquam Epistolæ ad Rom. et priorem ad Corinthios,* 1684, in 2 vols.; ed. Lips., by Carpzov, 1675, 1679; best ed. London, 1825. Lightfoot also largely assisted Walton in his Polyglot, and Poole in his Synopsis.

JOSEPH CARYL (one of the Westminster Puritans, 1602–73) wrote an *Exposition of Job, with Practical Observations,* in 12 volumes, 4to, which it required the patience of a Job to write, and requires as much patience to read. It is a Puritan parallel to Pope Gregory's Job. An abridgment appeared in Edinburgh, 1836. Another colossal Puritan commentary on a single book is JOHN OWEN'S *Exposition of the Hebrews,* in 4 fol. vols., London, 1668–74, also in 7 vols. 8vo., ed. by Goold, abridged by Williams, 1790. The richest modern commentary on the Psalms, of the Puritan type is CHARLES HADDON SPURGEON (d. 1892): *The Treasury of David,* London and New York, 1870 sqq., in 7 vols. It is a storehouse for preachers by the greatest of modern preachers. We mention it in this natural connection by anticipation.

PHILIP DODDRIDGE (an eminently pious Independent divine, d. 1751): *Family Expositor of the New Testament,* London 1736, 6 vols., and many other editions. Sound judgment and taste, devout spirit, excellent practical observations.

THOMAS SCOTT (Calvinistic Episcopalian, 1747–1821): *The Holy Bible,*

whose orthodoxy is above all just suspicion—to others not only verging upon, but deeply involved in considerable error. When we examine the essence of Latitudinarianism, and find that it consisted in the elevation of morals above dogmas, in the assertion of charity against bigotry, in abstinence from a curious prying into mysteries, yet in the culture of a spirit of free investigation, we see that there might be lying concealed under much which is truly excellent elements of a different description. Scepticism might nestle under all this virtue, and all this tolerance—under this love of what is reasonable, and this habit of liberal inquiry. Faith in that which is most precious might live in amicable alliance with the distinctive Latitudinarian temper, or scepticism might secretly nestle beneath its wings."

with Explanatory Notes, Practical Observations, and Copious Marginal References, London, 1792, and often since; best ed. London, 1841, in 6 vols. The favorite commentary of low-church Episcopalians of a former generation. Much esteemed and used chiefly for its practical value.

ADAM CLARKE (a Wesleyan minister and scholar, 1760–1832): *The Holy Bible, with a Commentary and Critical Notes*, London, 1810–23, 8 vols.; best ed. London, 1844, 6 vols. imp. 8vo. Replete with antiquarian but not always accurate and apposite learning, practical piety, defective in taste and judgment. A curiosity shop. The model commentary of the Methodists, and more used by preachers than any English commentary, except, perhaps, Matthew Henry.

Bishop LOWTH, of Oxford (d. 1787), opened the understanding for Hebrew poetry and may be called in this respect the English forerunner of Herder: *De Sacra Poesi Hebræorum* (1753); Commentary on Isaiah (1779).

CHAPTER CXXXVII.

THE COMMENTATORS OF THE ROMAN CATHOLIC CHURCH IN THE SIXTEENTH AND SEVENTEENTH CENTURIES.

The Roman Church cares more for the teaching priesthood and the sacraments than for the Bible; while Protestantism makes the Bible the chief means of grace and nourishment of piety.

The Council of Trent laid chains on progress in Biblical learning by raising the Latin Vulgate (even without a critical text) to equal dignity with the Greek and Hebrew Bible, and forbidding all departure from an imaginary *unanimus consensus patrum*, as the *ne plus ultra* of exegetical wisdom.

Nevertheless there were several learned commentators, especially among the Jesuits, who were ambitious to defeat the Protestants with their own weapons of learning and energy.

FRANÇOIS VATABLE (VATABLUS, professor of Hebrew in Paris, d. 1547), the author of learned annotations to the Old Testament, the first edition of which was condemned by the doctors of the Sorbonne. (Paris, 1545, 2d ed. 1584; also in the *Critici Sacri*).

J. MALDONADO (or. MALDONATUS, a learned Spanish Jesuit, professor at Paris, d. 1583), on the Gospels, Psalms, larger prophets. His commentary *in quatuor evangelistas* was reprinted, Mogunt., 1841–45, in 5 vols. 8vo.

EM. DE SA (a Portuguese Jesuit, 1530–96): *Notationes in totam S. Scripturam*, Antw. 1598.

Cardinal ROBERT BELLARMIN (1542–1621), the greatest champion of Romanism versus Protestantism, wrote a Latin *Commentary on the Psalms*, which was translated by the Ven. John O'Sullivan into English, London, 1866. Spurgeon (p. 81) characterizes it as "popish, but marvelously good for a Cardinal. He is frequently as evangelical as a Reformer. He follows the Vulgate text in his comment."

WILLIAM ESTIUS (b. in Holland 1542, studied at Utrecht and Louvain, professor in Douay, d. 1613): *Commentarius in Epistolas Apostolicas*, 3 vols., 1631. One of the best works of the kind, endeavoring to find out the literal meaning; Augustinian in spirit.

CORNELIUS À LAPIDE (VON STEIN, a learned Jesuit, professor of Hebrew at Louvain, d. 1637): *Commentaria in Vetus et Novum Testamentum* (exclusive of Job and Psalms). Antw. 1616–27, 12 vols. fol. and in many other editions. Gives the literal, allegorical, moral, and anagogical sense; full of patristic quotations, allegories and legends.

RICHARD SIMON (1638–1712), is the founder of biblical Isagogic by his critical histories of the text and versions of the Bible.

AUGUSTIN CALMET (a pious and learned Benedictine, abbot of Senones in the Vosges, 1672–1757): *Commentaire littéral sur tous les livres de l'Ancien et du Nouveau Testaments*, Paris 1724, 8 vols. in 9; several editions. A work of great learning and value. Translated into Latin by Mansi, Lucca, 1730–38, 9 vols. The same author wrote a *Dictionary of the Bible* (English ed. by Charles Taylor and Dr. Robinson), and *Biblical Antiquities*.

Minor commentators: J. MARIANA (d. 1624); ESCOBAR MENDOZA (d. 1609); JAC. TARINUS (d. 1636); MENOCHIUS (d. 1655); J. HARDOUIN (d. 1729).

To these orthodox writings must be added two exegetical works which were condemned by the Roman Church as Jansenistic or Quietistic.

PASQUIER QUESNELL (a half-evangelical Jansenist, b. at Paris, 1634, exiled 1681, d. 1719): *Le Nouveau Testament avec réflexions morales sur chaque verse*, etc., 1687; Amst. 1736, 8 vols. 12mo; English translation, London, 1719–25, 4 vols. The Gospels also separately edited by Bishop Wilson. Much admired for spiritual unction and rich piety.

Mme. JEANNE MARIE BOUVIER DE LA MOTHE-GUYON (1648–1717): *La Ste. Bible avec des explications et réflexions qui regardent la vie intérieure*, Col. 1713, 20 vols. The work represents her fervid, but eccentric, mystic piety of disinterested love. Quietism was condemned. She recanted thirty articles which were drawn from her writings. She led an exemplary Christian life, like Bishop Fénelon, her friend.

CHAPTER CXXXVIII.

RATIONALISTIC EXEGESIS, FROM THE MIDDLE OF THE EIGHTEENTH CENTURY TO THE PRESENT TIME.

A radical revolution in theology, similar to the political and social revolution in France, threatened to undermine the very foundations of Christianity since the middle of the eighteenth century. Its phases are Deism in England; Deism and Atheism in France; Rationalism and Pantheism in Germany.

Reason was raised above faith and made the judge of revelation; the Bible treated as a merely human production; its inspiration denied; its genuineness questioned; its doctrines assailed; its merits reduced and measured by the standard of a utilitarian morality. The supernatural and miraculous is the chief obstacle. The older, deistic Rationalism of Paulus (called *rationalismus vulgaris*) explains the miracles of the gospel history away as natural events, which the disciples misunderstood; the modern, pantheistic Rationalism of Strauss and Renan resolves them into myths and legends which arose in the religious imagination of a later generation.

Rationalistic exegesis, like Pharisaism of old, but from an opposite point of view, diligently searches the letter of the Bible, but has no sympathy with its life-giving spirit. It investigates the historical and human aspects of Christianity and ignores or denies its divine character.

The mission of Rationalism is chiefly negative and destructive. It was justifiable and necessary just as far as the human authorship and literary form of the Bible were neglected by the orthodox exegesis in its zeal for the eternal truths. It was a reaction against bibliolatry and symbololatry. It emancipated the mind from the tyranny of dogmatic systems. It aimed at a true historical understanding of the literature of the Bible in its origin and gradual growth. It achieved great and lasting merits in grammatical, critical, historical and antiquarian research. It forms a transition to a new age of faith in harmony with enlightened reason and fortified by critical learning.

1. The latest form of the supernaturalistic school of Germany, in its attempt to defend the faith against rising opposition, made concessions to the enemy and gradually approached Rationalism. J. DAVID MICHAELIS (Prof. in Göttingen, d. 1791): *Introduction to the Bible*, and *Translation with Com. on the Old and New Testaments*, etc.—J. A. ERNESTI (Prof. in Leipzig, d. 1781): *Institutio interpretis N. T.* (5th ed. 1809).—MORUS (d. 1792).—J. G. ROSENMÜLLER (d. 1815): *Scholia in N. T.* (1777, 6th ed. 1831).—E. F. C. ROSENMÜLLER (son of the former, d. 1835): *Scholia in V. T.*, 1788–1835, 24 tom.—Also KÜHNÖL, see below.

2. JOHANN SALOMO SEMLER (Prof. in Halle, d. 1791), the father of German neology, educated in the school of Pietism, to which he adhered in what he called his "private piety," but, carried away by the revolutionary spirit of the age, yet at last afraid of its consequences, unsettled the traditionary notions of the canon, distinguished the Bible from the word of God contained in it, and introduced the accommodation theory, which tries

to explain the Bible from the notions and prejudices of the times and peoples in which it originated. He left no school or permanent work, but scattered the seeds of doubt in every direction. And yet he opposed Lessing and the Wolfenbüttel Fragmentist. His style is prosy, inelegant and intolerably prolix.

3. The most distinguished Rationalists in the field of biblical learning.

J. G. EICHHORN (in Göttingen, d. 1827) : *Hist. Critical Introduction to the Old and New Testaments* (4th ed. 1823, 5 vols.) ; *Com. on Revelation*. He is sometimes called the founder of higher criticism, but was preceded by Semler, as Semler was preceded by Richard Simon.

H. E. G. PAULUS (Heidelberg, d. 1851) : *Com. on the Gospels*, and *Life of Jesus*. The natural explanation of the Gospel miracles, ably refuted by Strauss.

F. H. W. GESENIUS (Prof. in Halle, d. 1842) : *Hebrew Grammar* (25th ed. by Kautzsch, 1889) ; *Dictionary* (11th ed. 1890) ; *Thesaurus* (completed by Rödiger, 1829–58, 3 vols.) ; *Com. on Isaiah* (1829), etc.

C. F. A. FRITZSCHE (Prof. in Rostock and Giessen, d. 1846, a thorough classical philologist and investigator) : *Latin Com. on Matthew and Mark* (1826–30), and *Romans* (3 tom. 1836–43).

CHRIS. KÜHNÖL (or in Latin KUINOEL, Prof. in Giessen, d. 1841) : *Latin Com. on the New Testament* (Lips. 1825–43). A rational supernaturalist.

AUG. KNOBEL (Prof. in Giessen) : *Com. on Pentateuch, Isaiah*, etc.

HITZIG (Prof. in Zürich and Heidelberg, a most learned and acute critic), and nearly all the other contributors to the *Exeg. Handbook on the Old Testament* (later edd. by Dillmann and others).

DE WETTE (Prof. in Basel, d. 1849, whose religious heart and fine taste were in advance of his skeptical understanding) * : *Introduction to the Old and New Testaments* (1817 ; 8th ed. by Schrader, 1869) ; *Com. on the Psalms* (5 edd.) ; *Exeg. Handbook on the New Testament* (1835 sqq. and posthumous edd. by various writers, a model of comprehensive brevity and sound judgment) ; *Biblical Dogmatics* (3d ed. 1831) ; *German Translation of the Scriptures* (3d ed. 1839). He belongs to the school of Schleiermacher in a wider sense.

4. The *older* Tübingen school, represented by STORR (d. 1805), FLATT (d. 1821), the younger BENGEL (d. 1826), and STEUDEL (d. 1837), as also the isolated KNAPP in Halle (d. 1825), HESS in Zürich (d. 1828), manfully and faithfully defended the sinking ship of biblical (not churchly) supernaturalism in the midst of the raging storms of Rationalism. (Not to be confounded with the *modern* Tübingen school headed by BAUR.)

5. J. G. HERDER (d. 1803 at Weimar), one of the German classics, a man of almost universal genius and taste, more poet than divine, neither orthodox nor scriptural, yet deeply religious, a harbinger of a brighter era in theology, kindled enthusiasm for the sublime beauties of the Bible (es-

* He gave expression to his honest and sad skepticism shortly before his death in these touching lines :

"*Ich fiel in eine wirre Zeit :
Des Glaubens Einfalt war vernichtet.
Ich mischte mich mit in den Streit,
Doch, ach ! ich hab' ihn nicht geschlichtet.*"

pecially by his *Geist der Hebräischen Poesie*, 1782), and led a rising generation to the portal of the temple of inspiration. His influence is felt on many Rationalists, as Eichhorn, De Wette. In Ewald has arisen a new Herder with less poetry but more learning.

CHAPTER CXXXIX.

THE SWEDENBORGIAN EXEGESIS.

EMANUEL SWEDENBORG, the Swedish seer or visionary (1688–1772), in extreme contrast with the skepticism and infidelity of his age, came out with a new revelation and theory of Scripture interpretation, but exerted no influence on the regular course of historical development. He stood outside of the main current of history.

He distinguishes between the literal or natural, and the spiritual or celestial sense. "All and every part of the Scripture, even to the most minute, not excepting the smallest jot and tittle, signify and involve spiritual and celestial things." (*Arcana Cœlestia*, I. No. 2.) This deeper sense is in the literal as the thought is in the eye, or the soul in the body, but was lost until it was revealed to Swedenborg. His allegorizing is arbitrary and fanciful, often ingenious, often absurd. Examples: The first chapter of Genesis, in its spiritual sense, represents the regeneration of man; the six days, the successive stages of regeneration; Adam in paradise, the oldest church; the four rivers in Eden, goodness, knowledge, reason and science. All the geographical and personal names of the Old Testament are filled with mysteries. In this respect he goes further than Philo and Origen in their allegorical method, but differs entirely in the application, and especially also in his views of the canon.

With an ultra-supernaturalistic inspiration theory Swedenborg unites a rationalistic view on the extent of the canon. He rejects from the Old Testament the Solomonic writings and Job; from the New Testament he excludes the Acts and Epistles, especially those of St. Paul, from whose doctrine of the atonement and justification he entirely dissents. Even in the remaining books, the Gospels and the Apocalypse, he admits only the words of the Lord or of an angel, as strictly divine, while the words of an apostle or evangelist reflect the limited knowledge of enlightened men and have only one sense, the literal.

The exegesis of Swedenborg is original, but critically and theologically worthless, and hence ignored in commentaries. *Arcana Cœlestia* (Com. on Genesis and Exodus), London, 1749 sqq. (ed. Tafel, Tüb. 1833–42. English translation in 10 vols., New York, 1870). *Apocalypsis explicata secundum sensum spiritualem,* 3 vols. (English translation in 6 vols., published in London and New York by the Swedenborg Publication Society).

CHAPTER CXL.

MODERN EVANGELICAL EXEGESIS.

In conflict with the rationalistic movement, there arose in Germany a new evangelical theology, based upon a revival of faith in the Bible and in the principles of the Reformation, the tercentennial of which was celebrated in 1817. The leaders of this new theology were Schleiermacher, Neander, Tholuck, Nitzsch, Twesten, Julius Müller, Bleek, Lücke, Rothe, Dorner, Lange and others, who form a generation of thinkers and scholars such as had not been seen in the Church since the sixteenth century. England, Scotland and North America were much less affected by Rationalism than the Continent of Europe, but are passing now through a similar crisis, aided by the experience of the past.

The modern exegesis is not a simple restoration of the old Protestant exegesis, but a reconstruction and adaptation of it to the present state, and with a full appreciation of the grammatico-historical exegesis, as cultivated by the better class of Rationalists. Winer's Grammar of the New Testament marks an epoch in the strict grammatical exegesis of the New Testament, Gesenius' and Ewald's Hebrew Grammars in that of the Old Testament.

The exegetical apparatus and facilities have accumulated beyond all previous experience. The Bible languages and Bible lands are better known than ever before. Egypt, the Sinaitic Peninsula, Palestine, Syria, ancient Babylonia and Assyria, are made as familiar by recent discovery and research as our native lands. New branches of exegetical theology have been developed. There is an international co-operation and rivalry in biblical studies. Germany is the chief workshop, but Protestant Switzerland, Holland, France, Great Britain, and North America are taking an active part in every movement, and even the Roman Church keeps up with the progress. By the indefatigable labors of Lachmann, Tischendorf, Tregelles, Westcott and Hort we have now a pure and trustworthy text of the Greek Testament. The emendation of the Hebrew text has begun. The revision of the German, English and other Protestant versions is the practical result of critical study, and stimulates it in turn to new achievements. Altogether, the Bible is now more extensively circulated and studied than in any previous age.

The learned commentaries on single books and on the whole Bible which the nineteenth century has produced are so numerous and so varied that it is difficult to classify them. They represent all shades of theological opinions between the right wing of conservatism and the left wing of progressivism. Some German commentaries are like a symposium in which all parties are heard and criticised by the author as the presiding judge.

1. The conservative orthodoxy of modern times (mostly of the new Lutheran type) is represented in exegesis and biblical criticism by Hengstenberg, Hävernick, Caspari, Stier, Keil, Delitzsch, Von Hofmann, Philippi, Luthardt, Zahn, Zöckler, Strack. The last four lean toward the next class. None of them holds the mechanical inspiration theory of the seventeenth century, not even Hengstenberg.

2. The liberal and progressive evangelical orthodoxy: Neander (Life of Christ, Apostolic Age, popular commentaries), Tholuck (Romans, Sermon on the Mount, Hebrews), Olshausen, Bleek (Biblical Introduction, Hebrews, etc.), Lücke (the Johannean writings), Meyer, Lange, Ebrard, Hupfeld, Schlottmann, Riehm, Reuss, Lechler, Heinrici, B. Weiss, etc. With these Germans may also be numbered Van Oosterzee of Utrecht, and Godet of Neuchâtel (the best French commentator of recent times).

Among English commentators, Alford, Ellicott, Lightfoot, Westcott and Farrar represent the evangelical broad-church tendency, which comes very near the liberal evangelical school of Germany. Most of the Americans of the younger generation sympathize with it.

3. Ewald (d. 1875) founded a school of his own in the Old Testament by his epoch-making commentaries on the poetical and prophetical books and his history of Israel. In his wake followed, with more or less independence, Hitzig, Lagarde, Dillmann, Diestel, Wellhausen, Merx, Stade, Siegfried, Cornill, Kautzsch. In England, W. Robertson Smith, Cheyne, Driver.

4. Baur (d. 1860) and the new Tübingen school (Zeller, Schwegler, Hilgenfeld, Volkmar, etc.) have done little for exegesis proper, but a great deal for a critical reconstruction of the origin and growth of the literature

of the New Testament. In this department Baur has exerted more influence than any exegete. Strauss, his pupil, revolutionized the gospel history and stimulated the rich modern literature on the life of Christ, to be refuted as he has refuted Paulus. Ritschl (d. 1889) has created a fatal split in the Tübingen school (on the question of Paulinism and Petrinism), and has given rise to a new school in early Church history, of which Harnack is the leader, and Schürer's "Theologische Literatur Zeitung" the chief organ.

5. A liberal, but less radical school than that of Tübingen is represented by the school of Ritschl, and by Holtzmann, Lipsius, and other contributors to the *Handcommentar* on the New Testament.

6. Biblical scholars and commentators in England and Scotland: Pusey (Minor Prophets), Wordsworth (on the whole Bible), Stanley (Corinthians), Jowett (Pauline Epistles), Tregelles (textual criticism of the New Testament), Alford (New Testament), Ellicott (Pauline Epistles), Lightfoot (Galatians, Philippians, Colossians, etc.), Westcott (on John's Gospel and Epistle to the Hebrews, Introduction to the Gospels, Canon of the New Testament), Hort (textual criticism of the New Testament), Perowne (Psalms, etc.), Plummer (several Epistles), Farrar (Luke, Hebrews, Life of Christ, and St. Paul, etc.), A. B. Davidson (Job), W. Robertson Smith (Old Testament Criticism), Cheyne (Isaiah, Jeremiah, Psalms), Driver (Old Testament Introduction), Gloag (Acts, Johannean writings, Cath. and Pauline Epp., etc.), Kirkpatrick, Wright, Dods, and others.

7. American biblical scholars: Moses Stuart (Commentaries on several books of the Old and New Testaments), E. Robinson (Biblical Researches, Hebrew and Greek lexicography, Harmony of the Gospels), Barnes (the pioneer of popular commentators for Sunday-school teachers), Jos. A. Alexander (on Isaiah, the Psalms, Mark and Acts), Charles Hodge (Romans, Ephesians, Corinthians), Shedd (Romans), Tayler Lewis (additions to Lange on Genesis, Job, Ecclesiastes, etc.), Cowles (Commentaries on the whole Bible), Conant (Hebrew grammar, Proverbs, Matthew), Broadus (on Matthew, etc.), Hackett (on Acts), Hovey (the Gospel of John), Lyman Abbott (popular commentaries on the Gospels. Acts, Romans), Ezra Abbot (on textual criticism of the Greek Testament, on the authorship of the fourth Gospel, etc.), Thayer (Lexicon of the Greek Testament), Dwight, Briggs, Brown, Harper (in Hebrew learning), Marvin R. Vincent (Word Studies on the New Testament). As to the higher criticism of the Old Testament, Dr. Green of Princeton (like Hengstenberg in Berlin and Pusey in Oxford) represents the conservative orthodox, Dr. Briggs of New York (like Dillmann in Berlin and Driver in Oxford), the progressive and liberal school; but both stand on evangelical ground against Rationalism.

8. COMMENTARIES ON THE WHOLE BIBLE. England is most productive in general commentaries for the lay-reader. America comes next. But the German works are the most scholarly and critical.

J. PETER LANGE (ed., d. 1884): *Bibelwerk*, Bielefeld, 1857 sqq.; 4th ed. 1878 sqq., 16 vols.; Anglo-American ed. (enlarged and adapted) under the title *Lange's Commentary*, by PHILIP SCHAFF, New York and Edinb., 1864 sqq., 25 vols., several editions. Textual, exegetical, theological, and practical (homiletical). A composite work of twenty German and over forty American writers, differing in merit. Professor Terry (*Hermeneutics*, p.

727): "Lange is by far the most learned and comprehensive commentary on the whole Bible which has appeared in modern times." Spurgeon: "The American translators have added considerably to the German stock, and in some cases these additions are more valuable than the original matter. For homiletical purposes these volumes are so many hills of gold."

CH. K. JOSIAS BUNSEN (projector and general ed., d. 1860): *Vollständiges Bibelwerk für die Gemeinde*, Leipzig, 1858-70, 9 vols. Aided by Ad. Kamphausen, Joh. Bleek, and others, completed by H. Holtzmann.

E. REUSS (Professor in Strassburg, d. 1891): *La Bible*. New French translation with introductions and commentaries, Paris, 1874-79, 13 vols. The work of one scholar!

STRACK and ZÖCKLER: *Kurzgefasster Commentar zu den Schriften des A. u. N. T., sowie zu den Apokryphen*, Nördlingen, 1887 sqq., 10 vols. By moderately orthodox Lutherans and two Reformed Swiss divines (C. v. Orelli and Oettli).

Bible Annotée par une Société de théologiens et de pasteurs. Ed. by F. GODET, and others. Neuchâtel et Genève, 1878 sqq. Popular.

French Bible works by Roman Catholics: BACUEZ *et* VIGOUROUX: *Manuel Biblique*, etc., 1881 sqq.; Paris,1880 sqq.—Abbé ARNAUD, Paris, 1881 sqq.—TROCHON, LESÊTRE, and others, the Vulgate, with French translation and commentaries.

Bishop CHR. WORDSWORTH (d. 1885): *The Holy Bible*, etc., London, 1864 sqq., several editions, 6 vols. (the New Testament with the Greek text). Scholarly, reverential, patristic, high Anglican, uncritical, full of "apostolic succession" and "sacramental grace."

Canon F. C. COOK (editor, d. 1889): *The Holy Bible*, etc., usually called "The Speaker's Commentary" (because suggested by the Speaker of the House of Commons in 1863 for apologetic purposes), London and New York, 1871-81, 10 vols. By a number of Episcopal divines. Represents the average conservative scholarship of the Church of England prior to the Revised Version.

Canon SPENCE and Rev. JOS. S. EXELL (editors): *The Pulpit Commentary*, London, 1880 sqq. (40 vols. so far). By about one hundred contributors, mostly from the Church of England. On the plan of Lange, but more extended; a rich mine for preachers.

JAMESON, FAUSSET and BROWN: *The Library Commentary*, Edinb. 1871 sqq., 6 vols. Popular.

Bishop ELLICOTT: *Com. for English Readers by Various Writers*, London, 1877 sqq., the New Testament in 3, the Old Testament in 5 vols. Popular and useful. The Old Testament behind the latest scholarship. The New Testament is better.

J. C. GRAY (ed.): *Biblical Museum*. Old Testament 10 vols., New Testament 5 vols. London and New York, 1871 sqq., several edd. Popular and devotional.

Bishop PEROWNE (ed.): *Cambridge Bible for Schools*, by various scholars of the Church of England, Cambridge, 1877 sqq. Scholarly and popular.

DAN. D. WHEDON (ed., Methodist, d. 1885): *Commentary on the Old and New Testament*, New York, 1880 sqq., 12 vols.

JAMES GLENTWORTH BUTLER; *Biblework*, New York, 1883 sqq. Compilation from other commentaries.

W. ROBERTSON NICOLL (ed. of "The London Expositor," Presbyt.): *Expositor's Bible*, London and New York, 1888 sqq., to be completed in about 40 vols. Explanatory lectures, by writers of different denominations, English, Scotch and American.

9. COMMENTARIES ON THE OLD TESTAMENT.

KEIL und DELITZSCH: *Biblischer Commentar zum A. T.*, Leipzig, 3d ed. 1878 sqq. Conservative. The parts by Franz Delitzsch are the best. English translation published by Clark, Edinb. In 27 volumes, 1864–78.

Kurzgefasstes exeg. Handbuch zum A. T., Leipzig, 1841 sqq., 5th ed. 1886 sqq., by DILLMANN, DIESTEL, THENIUS, BERTHEAU, and others. Critical and somewhat rationalistic. See § 138.

M. S. TERRY and F. H. NEWHALL (Methodists): *Commentary on the Old Testament*, New York, 1889 sqq. Evangelical.

10. COMMENTARIES ON THE NEW TESTAMENT.

CALVIN and BENGEL are still invaluable.

HERMANN OLSHAUSEN (1796–1839): *Biblischer Commentar*, etc., continued by EBRARD and WIESINGER, Königsberg, 1830 sqq., 7 vols., several editions (transl. Edinb. 1847 sqq., and New York, 1856, in 6 vols.).

DE WETTE (d. 1849), in several posthumous editions already mentioned in § 138.

H. A. W. MEYER (d. 1874): *Kritisch exegetischer Kommentar über das Neue Testament*. Aided by a number of scholars. Göttingen, 1832 sqq., 16 vols.; 8th ed. by B. WEISS, and others, 1890 sqq.; in English (from older editions), published in Edinburgh, 1873–82, in 20 vols., and with sundry additions in New York. The best students' book for strict philological exegesis. Olshausen was superseded by De Wette, De Wette by Meyer, Meyer by Weiss. Every new edition of Meyer keeps up with the progress of science and makes the older editions useless for critical purposes. Meyer was one of the most honest and conscientious exegetes, and it is a pity that his work should almost disappear in the latest editions.

HOLTZMANN, LIPSIUS, SCHMIEDEL, VON SODEN: *Handkommentar zum Neuen Testament*, Freiburg, 1889 sqq., 4 vols. Popular, yet critical and somewhat rationalistic.

Dean H. ALFORD (d 1871): *The Greek Testament*, London, 6th ed., 1868 sqq., 4 vols. The Greek text, critical and exegetical commentary for the use of students and ministers. Makes use of Olshausen, De Wette and Meyer, but is better adapted for English students.

PHILIP SCHAFF (ed.): *The International Illustrated Commentary*, New York and Edinburgh, 1879–82. Contributors: Drs. Riddle, Howson, Milligan, Moulton, Plumpre, Dykes, Dods, Gloag, Lumby, Salmond, Spence, Brown. Maps by A. Guyot, illustrations by Drs. W. M. and W. H. Thomson. The editor wrote the general introduction and the Commentary on Galatians.

J. J. G. PEROWNE (ed.): *Cambridge Greek Testament for Schools*. Text, notes and maps. Cambridge, 1881 sqq. Contributors: Carr, Maclear, Farrar, Plummer, Lumby, Lias. Excellent for its purpose.

The commentaries on the several books, especially Genesis, Psalms, Gospels, Romans, are so numerous that we have no room for them here. See the Bibliographical Appendix.

CHAPTER CXLI.

BIBLICAL HISTORY AND BIBLICAL THEOLOGY.

The results of exegesis are summed up in Biblical History and Biblical Theology.

Biblical History exhibits the origin and growth of the kingdom of God from the creation to the close of the apostolic age, and properly belongs to Historical Theology. Biblical Theology presents a systematic account of the teaching of the Bible on faith and duty, and is the basis of Systematic Theology. History and theology are organically united in the Bible. History is teaching by example, and teaching is itself part of history.

These two branches of biblical learning lie on the border line of Exegesis, Church History and Systematic Theology. They are the end of the first, and the beginning of the second and third. Exegetical Theology is not complete without them, and Historical and Systematic Theology can still less omit them. A Church History without the life of Christ and the apostolic age would be like a river without a fountain, or like a building without foundation. And so also Systematic Theology, both dogmatic and moral, strikes its roots in the teaching of the Bible and must be guided by it throughout.

For these reasons as well as for considerations of just proportion, I prefer to treat Biblical History under Historical Divinity, and Biblical Theology under Systematic Divinity.

The History of Biblical Times likewise belongs to Historical Theology rather than to Exegesis.

CHAPTER CXLII.

HINTS FOR EXEGETICAL STUDY.

1. Read first the Scripture in the original text, with nothing but grammar, dictionary and concordance, and a good version (the Anglo-American revision).

2. Ascertain the meaning for yourself as nearly as you can.

3. Then, use the best grammatico-historical commentary within reach, to aid you in the solution of difficulties. Too

many commentaries are embarrassing and misleading to the beginner.

4. Consult other commentaries, doctrinal and homiletical, as you have need, but do not make yourself the slave of any.

5. Apply your whole self to the text, and the whole text to yourself. (*"Te totum applica ad textum : rem totam applica ad te."* Bengel.)

6. Never lose sight of the practical and spiritual aim of the Bible.

7. "He rightly reads Scripture who turns words into deeds." (St. Bernard.)

BOOK III.
HISTORICAL THEOLOGY.

CHAPTER CXLIII.
GENERAL CONCEPTION OF HISTORICAL THEOLOGY.

For a fuller introduction to Church History see SCHAFF: *History of the Apostolic Church* (1853), pp. 1–134, and *Church History* (1889), 3d revision, vol. I. pp. 1–55. C. DE SMEDT (Rom. Cath.): *Introductio generalis ad historiam ecclesiasticam critice tractandam.* Gandavi (Ghent), 1876 (pp. 533). JOS. NIRSCHL (Rom. Cath.): *Propædeutik der Kirchengeschichte,* Mainz, 1888 (pp. 352). For a list of works on introduction to history and church history see ED. BRATKE: *Wegweiser zur Quellen—und Litteraturkunde der Kirchengeschichte,* Gotha, 1890, pp. 86–89.

HISTORICAL THEOLOGY, or CHURCH HISTORY, in the widest sense of the term, exhibits the rise and progress of the kingdom of God from the beginning to the present time.*

We must distinguish between *objective* and *subjective* history. They differ as a man differs from his portrait. Objective history is history itself as it occurs. Subjective history is the representation or reproduction of it by the historian. The value of subjective history depends on the degree of its faithfulness to objective history. Subjective history is not the light itself, but a witness to the light. "*Historia est testis veritatis.*"

Church History is the connecting link between Exegetical

---

* *History* from ἱστορία (ἱστορέω, *to inquire into, to examine, to know by inquiry, to narrate*), means *research, knowledge* (ἡ περὶ φύσεως ἱστ., ἡ περὶ τὰ ζῷα ἱστ.), also *account, narrative*; ἱστορικός, *historical*; ἱστοριογραφέω, *to write history*; ἱστοριογραφία, *historiography*; ἱστοριογράφος, *historian, writer of history.* The Greek terms convey the *subjective* idea of history. The German word *Geschichte,* from *geschehen, to happen, to occur,* suggests the *objective* idea, the sum of what has happened. The writing of history is essential to the preservation of history itself in the memory of man. Mere oral tradition could not secure its integrity and identity. I prefer the term *church history (Kirchengeschichte)* to the longer and Latinized term *ecclesiastical history.*

and Systematic theology. It embraces all that is of permanent interest in the past fortunes of Christendom. But in a wider sense it covers also the whole extent of exegesis and runs parallel with it. The revelation of God in the Bible, which is the subject of exegesis, has its own history, and admits of a historical as well as an exegetical treatment. The exegete is the miner who brings to light the Scripture facts and Scripture truths; the historian is the manufacturer or artist who works the gold and gives it shape and form for actual use. Moreover, exegesis itself and all other departments of theology have their history and are constantly furnishing contributions to its material.

Historical Theology is by far the most extensive and copious part of sacred learning, and supplies material to all other departments. If exegesis is the root, church history is the main trunk. We are connected with the Bible through the intervening links of the past and all its educational influences, and cannot safely disregard the wisdom and experience of ages. Christ has never forsaken his Church, nor left himself without witnesses. If our fathers and forefathers have labored in vain, we who are of the same flesh and blood, have a poor prospect of better success.

Church history is a running commentary on Christ's twin parables of the mustard seed and the leaven (Matt. 13 : 31–33), and of his parting promise to his disciples, "Behold, I am with you all the days even unto the end of the world" (Matt. 28 : 20).

CHAPTER CXLIV.

BIBLICAL AND ECCLESIASTICAL HISTORY.

Church History in the widest sense embraces both biblical and ecclesiastical history: it begins with the creation and will end with the final judgment.

Biblical History runs parallel with the Bible. It follows the divine revelation and the growth of the kingdom of God in the Jewish dispensation, the life of Christ and the founding of the Christian Church by the Apostles to the close of the first century.

Ecclesiastical History or Church History in the narrower sense is a history of Christianity from the advent of Christ to the present time. Some date it from the day of Pentecost, when the Christian Church first appeared as a distinct and separate organization. But the miracle of Pentecost has no meaning without the preceding miracle of the resurrection and ascension, which is the consummation of the life of the Founder of Christianity.

The relative goal of history is the time of the historian, the absolute goal is the end of time and the beginning of eternity. The historian is a retrospective prophet, but the future is only known to God.

CHAPTER CXLV.

AGENTS OF HISTORY.

History in general is the product of divine, human, and satanic agencies.

1. On the part of *God*, history is his revelation in time, as nature is his revelation in space. It is his epos. It gradually unfolds an eternal plan of wisdom and goodness for the redemption of the human race and the triumph of his kingdom. Man ought to do all for the glory of God; God does all for the good of man. As nature reveals God's power and wisdom, so history reveals his justice and mercy.

The recognition of God in history is the first principle of all sound philosophy of history. God is no God unless he is almighty, omniscient and omnipresent. "In him we live, and move, and have our being" (Acts 17: 28). He is immanent as well as transcendent in his relation to the world. He made it and he upholds it continually by the all-pervading presence of his power. He rules and overrules even the sins and follies of man for his own glory and the good of his people. "Are not two sparrows sold for a farthing? and not one of them shall fall on the ground without your Father: but the very hairs of your head are all numbered" (Matt. 10: 29, 30). "We know that to them that love God, all things work together for good" (Rom. 8: 29).

This is the cheering and encouraging view of history. It is illustrated on every page. He who denies the hand of Providence in the affairs of the world and the church is intellectually or spiritually blind. The historian has good reason to be an optimist, notwithstanding all the dark and dismal chapters in history.

Atheism denies, Deism ignores, the presence of God in history. Both resolve it into an aimless and hopeless play of human passions. But the atheist is simply a fool (Ps. 14: 1), and the deist belittles God by making him a mere watchmaker or an idle spectator of the world he has made, and the events which come to pass

> "What were a God who only from without
> Upon his finger whirled the universe about?
> 'Tis his, within himself to move the creature,
> Nature in him to warm, himself in nature;
> So that what in him lives, and moves and is,
> Shall ever feel the living breath of his."

2. On the part of *man*, history is the biography of the human race. It is the development of all his physical, intellectual and moral faculties, the actualization of his dominion over nature, and the progress and triumph of civilization. Man is a free and responsible agent who must render an account for the part he acts in his public and private life.

God limits the exercise of his own sovereignty to give fair play to human freedom, and yet overrules it for his own holy purposes. "Man proposes, God disposes." All sins and errors in the world must be traced to man's agency, but God in his wisdom brings good out of evil; he makes the fall of Adam the occasion for the plan of redemption, the treason of Judas a means to the crucifixion and the consequent salvation. "He hath shut up all unto disobedience, that he might have mercy upon all. . . . For of him, and through him, and unto him are all things" (Rom. 11: 32, 36; Gal. 3: 22).

The pantheistic and fatalistic view of history is the direct opposite of the atheistic and deistic view. It is destructive of the freedom and responsibility of man, and substitutes a dark fate or iron necessity for Providence and paternal government. It turns history into a Moloch who devours his own children. It begins and ends in darkness.

3. *Satan* represents the preternatural or subnatural agency of history, in direct opposition, yet in final subserviency, to the supernatural and providential agency of God. The kingdom of darkness, as well as the kingdom of light, is organized under one head. Otherwise it would fall to pieces; for "a house

divided against itself cannot stand." Satan is the personification of all evil influences in the world. He is the everlasting denier, a part of that "power which ever wills the bad and ever works the good." He is the tempter and seducer of the human race and the director-in-chief of all the movements which counteract the plan of redemption and tend to the ruin of man. He brought about the original fall; he controlled Cain, and corrupted the generation before the Flood; he figured in the trial of Job; he attempted to seduce Christ into an abuse of his Messianic powers; he controlled the demoniacal possessions; he nursed the opposition of the Jewish hierarchy to Christ and inspired their bloody counsel as well as the treason of Judas; he is the fiend that scatters tares among the wheat; he has much to do with heresies and schisms, with false doctrines and bad practices, with uncharitable orthodoxy, hypocrisy and spiritual tyranny; he stirs up religious intolerance and persecution; he erects his temples and schools in all Christian lands.

> "Wherever God erects a house of prayer,
> The devil always builds a chapel there."

Satan is most dangerous in the garb of an angel of light. He finds his way into pews and pulpits, prayer-meetings, synods, general assemblies, and œcumenical councils. More than once he has occupied the chair of St. Peter in Rome and changed the vicar of Christ into an Antichrist. He can speak the language of orthodoxy and piety as well as of heresy and blasphemy. He quotes the Scriptures when it suits his purpose. He is utterly unscrupulous in the use of means, and succeeds best where he is least suspected, and where even his existence is denied.

There are Satanic depths in many a bold, bad man, and in many dark chapters in history, both secular and religious. We may deny the one devil, but we cannot deny the many devils in human shape.*

The incessant activity of Satan and his host imparts a fearful, tragic interest to history, covers it with crime and blood, and turns it into a scene of fierce conflict of light with the powers of darkness.

---

* As Goethe says of infidels:

> "*Den* Bösen sind sie los,
> *Die* Bösen sind geblieben."

4. *Relation* of these agencies to each other. God rules supreme; he sets all the powers of history in motion; he preserves and directs them, and he will stand at last on the dust as the Judge of all men and angels, giving to every one his due.

Man is the battle-ground of God and Satan. He is under the power of the devil as far as he sins and disbelieves; he is under the power of God as far as he acts rightly and obeys his will. He is to be delivered from the power of the prince of darkness and to become a free child of God and follower of Christ; but his life is a constant conflict, and he daily prays: "Lead us not into temptation, but deliver us from the evil one." *

Satan has more influence in the world than any man or combination of men, and will keep and exercise it till the judgment-day, but he is again and again defeated by God, and will at last be completely and finally overthrown, that God may be all in all.

In the prologue to the wonderful book of Job, God and Satan appear as the supernatural movers of the history of man on earth, and in the end Satan is defeated, and Job comes out of his trial purified and perfected. Goethe reproduces the same idea in the prologue to the tragedy of *Faust*.

CHAPTER CXLVI.

HISTORICAL DEVELOPMENT.

PHILIP SCHAFF: *What is Church History? A Vindication of the Idea of Historical Development*, Philadelphia, 1846.—JOHN HENRY (afterwards Cardinal) NEWMAN: *Development of Christian Doctrine*, London and New York, 1845.—LYMAN ABBOTT: *The Evolution of Christianity*, Boston, 1892.

History is a constant motion and progress, but with many obstructions, retrogressions and diseases caused by sin and error. It progresses, like a sailing-vessel, not in a straight but in a zigzag line on its course to the harbor. Whatever is living is also moving and growing. The dead only is done. Secular history is the progressive development of the idea of humanity, with its "struggle for existence and survival of the fittest"; ecclesiastical history is the progressive development of the idea of Christian-

---

* "Something in us near to hell; something strangely near to God. . . . In our best estate and in our purest moments there is a something of the Devil in us which, if it could be known, would make men shrink from us." F. W. ROBERTSON on 51st Psalm.

ity or the history of the origin, growth and triumph of the kingdom of God.

Revelation is gradual and progressive, adapted to the capacity of man. It culminates in Christ.

Humanity and the Church as a whole are subject to the same laws of growth with its attendant obstructions and diseases, as the individual man and the individual Christian. Every member of the body and every faculty of the soul exist at first in a potential state and attain their full proportions only by degrees. The believer, too, like Christ himself (Luke 2 : 52; Heb. 5 : 8), has to pass through the different stages of life to perfect manhood in Christ (Eph. 2 : 20; 3 : 18, 19; 4 : 12, 13; 1 Pet. 2 : 5). Regeneration by the Spirit is the beginning, the resurrection of the body is the end, of this spiritual growth. So the Church at large goes through a process of outward expansion and inward consolidation till it shall cover the earth and be perfected in unity and holiness.

The law of progress for his kingdom is laid down by our Saviour in the twin parables of the mustard seed and the leaven (Matt. 13 : 31, 32): the one illustrates chiefly the external growth; the other, the internal mission of the Church in pervading, transforming and sanctifying humanity.

The true theory of development is that of a constant growth of the Church *in* Christ the head, or a progressive understanding and application of Christianity, until Christ shall be all in all. The end will only be the complete unfolding of the beginning. All other theories of development which teach a progress of humanity *beyond* Christ and *beyond* Christianity are false and pernicious. Christ is the beginning, the middle, and the end of church history.

False theories of development:

1. The Roman Catholic theory: an accumulation of dogmas and institutions without and beyond the Scriptures, under the guidance of an infallible pope. This leaves no room for reformation and revolution, and would exclude the Greek and the Protestant Churches.

Cardinal Newman's essay on Development shows the logical process of transition from Anglo-Catholicism to Romanism by overleaping the Reformation and the development of Protestantism, which fills two-thirds of modern history.

2. The Rationalistic theory: a diminution and destruction of dogmas and institutions which interfere with the supremacy of reason. This negative theory would make the immense labor of centuries as useless as a child's play.

AUXILIARY SCIENCES. 241

The true theory of development must be both conservative and progressive, and provide for what is good and valuable in all ages and divisions of Christendom,—Greek, Latin and Protestant, ancient, mediæval and modern. No labor in the Lord can ever be lost.

The modern scientific theory of evolution in nature corresponds to the theory of development in history, which was previously discovered by historians and philosophers (like Hegel). But evolution in nature presupposes a creative beginning and God's continued omnipresence and immanence. In the same way, development in history implies a supreme intelligence which endowed man with reason and will, set history in motion and directs it by an omnipotent will. Christ founded the Church, is ever present with it, and his teaching and example are the inspiring force in all true moral and spiritual progress.

CHAPTER CXLVII.

CENTRAL POSITION OF CHRIST IN HISTORY.

Jesus Christ, the God-Man and Saviour of the world, is the center and turning-point of history, and the key which unlocks its mysteries. All history before him was a preparation for his coming, all history after him is the execution of his work.

He appeared in the fullness of the time (Mark 1:15; Gal. 4:4), when everything was ripe for him, and from his birth we justly date our chronology. He is "the desire of all nations." He came "to fulfill the law and the prophets," and all the nobler aspirations and unconscious prophecies of the ancient world.

"All things were created by him, and for him" (Col. 1:16). He is the prophet, priest and king of redeemed humanity. All events must directly or indirectly, positively or negatively, nearly or remotely, advance his kingdom, until he shall reign king of nations as he now rules king of saints in his Church. The great empires of the world are rising and passing away one by one, but his kingdom is constantly advancing and will last forever.

CHAPTER CXLVIII.

AUXILIARY SCIENCES: ECCLESIASTICAL PHILOLOGY, GEOGRAPHY, CHRONOLOGY, DIPLOMATICS, SECULAR HISTORY.

Historical Theology presupposes several preparatory and auxiliary sciences.

I. Ecclesiastical PHILOLOGY. This embraces the knowledge of the languages in which the sources of Church history are written, namely, the Greek and Latin for ancient, the Latin for mediæval, the German, French, English and other European languages for modern times.

The Greek is the official language of the Greek Church, and was used by the apostles and the Eastern Fathers.

The Latin became an ecclesiastical language with Tertullian at the end of the second century, and continues to be the official language of the Roman Church to this day. It was also used largely by the Reformers (Melanchthon, Zwingli, Calvin, etc.) and the older Protestant divines down to the end of the seventeenth century. Luther, Cranmer and Knox preferred their vernacular. The Latin is still employed in academic dissertations and festivities.

Modern Church history is mostly written in the popular languages which were developed in the Middle Ages under the influence of Christianity and rose to independence with the Renaissance and the Reformation. Dante exerted a creative influence upon the Italian, Wiclif and Chaucer upon the English, Luther upon the German, Calvin upon the French, language and literature. The German, French, and English languages are now the chief organs of the intellectual and practical activity of Christendom. They are emphatically the languages of religion and civilization. They occupy the position of the Hebrew, Greek and Latin in the ancient Roman empire. No student should neglect to master them sufficiently to use the ever-growing treasures of their literature.

II. Ecclesiastical GEOGRAPHY. It is the basis of history. The use of maps is indispensable for orientation. There is a close correspondence between nations and countries. The East has shaped the Greek; the South, the Latin; the North and West, the Protestant Churches. The organization of the Church—the division into dioceses, bishoprics, parishes, presbyteries, synods, etc.—is usually adapted to the existing political divisions. The territory of ancient Church history is that of the Roman empire, around the Mediterranean Sea. The geography of the middle ages extends farther north and west. The geography of modern history takes in the Western Continent and Australia, and the missionary fields in Asia and Africa.

A comparative historical geography would show the extent of Christianity and the different religions with which it came in contact,—Judaism, Mohammedanism and heathenism.

III. Ecclesiastical CHRONOLOGY. This includes the various systems of determining the dates of events, from the creation, from the year of Rome, from the birth of Christ, from the flight of Mohammed, etc.

IV. Ecclesiastical DIPLOMATICS is the science of diplomas or official documents, such as bulls, briefs, statutes, patents, etc., and teaches their value and right use. Special departments are: *Palæography,* the science of ancient writings and manuscripts of the Bible, etc.; *Sphragistics,* the science of seals; *Numismatics,* of coins; *Heraldics,* of weapons.

V. Secular History or the GENERAL HISTORY of the world. It is so intimately interwoven with Church History that the one cannot be understood without the other. In the widest sense the former includes the latter as its most important department. The Church is in the world and meets it at every point in friendly or hostile contact. During the middle ages, church and state were united. The history of the papacy is also a history of the German empire, and *vice versâ.* This union has prevailed under a different form in the history of Europe down to this day, and in America during the colonial period. But even where church and state are separated, as in the United States, they act and react upon each other, and religion enters into all the ramifications of national and social life.

LITERATURE.

I. Helps for Ecclesiastical Greek and Latin: SUICER and DU FRÈSNE, see Chapter LXXX.—KOFFMANE: *Geschichte des Kirchenlateins,* Breslau, 1879 sqq.—DIEZ: *Etymologisches Wörterbuch der roman. Sprachen,* Bonn, 4th ed. 1878.

II. The historical atlases of WILTSCH, W. SMITH, SPRUNER, DROYSEN, FREEMAN, LABBERTON, DORT (Groningen, 1884), WERNER (Freiburg i. B., 1888), GRUNDEMANN: *Missionsatlas* (Gotha, 1867-70).

III. IDELER: *Lehrbuch der Chronologie,* Berlin, 1831.—PIPER: *Kirchenrechnung,* Berlin, 1841.—BRINKMEIER: *Handbuch der histor. Chronologie,* Leipzig, 2d. ed. 1382.—BROCKMANN: *System der Chronologie,* Stuttgart, 1883.

IV. MABILLON: *De re diplomatica,* Paris, 1681, and later edd.—GARDTHAUSEN: *Griech. Paläographie,* Leipzig, 2d ed. 1877.—WATTENBACH: *Das Schriftwesen im Mittelalter,* Leipzig, 2d. ed. 1877.—FICKER: *Beiträge zur Urkundenlehre,* Innsbruck, 1877, 2 vols.

V. Works on general history are too numerous to be mentioned. Among brief compends, KARL PLOETZ (Berlin, 8th ed. 1884) and GEO. P. FISHER (*Outlines of Universal History,* New York, 1885, etc., with good maps) are very useful.

CHAPTER CXLIX.

BRANCHES OF CHURCH HISTORY.

The kingdom of God is as comprehensive as humanity. It embodies the redemption, regeneration and sanctification of the race. It aims to consecrate the individual, the family, the state and all the ramifications of society. It penetrates science, art, literature, and makes them subservient to the glory of God till he be all in all. It is the divine leaven which gradually pervades the whole lump of humanity. This is a slow but sure process, passing through many obstructions and apparent defeats, but approaching ever nearer its final goal. A thousand years for God are as one day.

Church history has as many departments as human life and society. The principal topics are: Missions and Persecutions (expansion and contraction); Toleration and Freedom; Organization (Church Polity and Discipline); Worship (including Rites and Ceremonies); Christian Life and Activity; Theology and Dogma.

These departments have an organic relation to each other, and form one living whole. Each period is entitled to a peculiar arrangement, according to its character. The number, order and extent of the different divisions must be determined by their relative prominence and importance at a given time.

CHAPTER CL.

HISTORY OF MISSIONS.

The history of MISSIONS is a history of the extension of Christianity throughout the world. It will go on till the whole race is Christianized.

There are three great missionary ages: the planting of the Church among the Jews, Greeks and Romans by the apostles; the conversion of the barbarians of Europe in the middle ages; the modern missions in all parts of the globe looking to the conquest of all nations to Christ.

1. *Foreign* Missions, or the spread of the Christian religion among non-Christian nations, civilized, semi-civilized, and bar-

HISTORY OF PERSECUTION. 245

barian. Heathen Missions, Jewish Missions, Mohammedan Missions (the last still in the future).

2. *Domestic* Missions follow the tide of emigration to new countries and settlements under the government of Christian nations (as the British Provinces, the United States and Territories, the Asiatic possessions of Russia, the European possessions in Africa).

3. *Inner* Missions and *City* Missions, or the revival of vital Christianity in dead or indifferent sections of the Church, especially among the neglected and worse than heathenish populations of large cities, as London, Paris, Berlin, New York.

The Literature on missions is immense, especially in the English language. The most complete list is by Rev. SAMUEL M. JACKSON in *The Encyclopædia of Missions*, ed. by E. M. Bliss, New York, 1891, vol. I. pp. 575–661.

CHAPTER CLI.

HISTORY OF PERSECUTIONS.

The history of PERSECUTIONS in the widest sense embraces all forms of persecution, from without and from within, of Christians by non-Christians, of Christians by Christians, of heretical Christians by orthodox Christians, and *vice versâ*, of churches against sects, of state-churches against dissenters and non-conformists, of the Church by the State, of Jews by Christians. There is bloody and unbloody persecution. The former has nearly ceased, the latter still continues and will continue to the end of time.

1. *Foreign* persecution of the Church by antagonistic religions. Jewish persecution culminated in the crucifixion of the Messiah, expelled the apostles from the synagogue and lasted till the destruction of Jerusalem. Then followed the persecution of the Jews by the Christians down to the present time. Heathen persecution continued for three hundred years and ended in the conversion of the Roman empire. Mohammedan persecution began with the conquest of the Holy Land and reached its climax in the conquest of Constantinople (1453).

2. *Domestic* persecution of Christians against Christians. Romanists persecuted Protestants, Protestants persecuted Romanists, both persecuted heretics and dissenters. The difference is only one of degree and extent. All Christian sects have

persecuted except those which never had a chance. For persecution comes from human nature, its selfishness, narrowness and love of power, and from the alliance of priest-craft and state-craft, or religion with politics. But the Quakers and the Baptists, to their great credit, have made liberty of conscience an article of their creed.

LITERATURE: Closely connected with the Literature on missions. RUINART: *Acta Martyrum. The Acta Sanctorum.*—JOHN FOXE: *Book of Martyrs.*—UHLHORN: *Kampf des Christenthums mit dem Heidenthum* (translated by Smyth and Ropes, New York, 1879).

CHAPTER CLII.

HISTORY OF RELIGIOUS LIBERTY.

The history of persecution is at the same time a history of RELIGIOUS LIBERTY. The blood of patriots is the seed of civil liberty; the blood of martyrs is the seed of religious liberty. The end of persecution is toleration, and the end of toleration is freedom. Religious freedom is the highest form of freedom; it is a gift of God and an inalienable right of man who is made in the image of God.

This principle is now recognized, in theory at least, by the most enlightened nations, and is becoming more and more a fundamental element of modern civilization and Christianity. "For freedom did Christ set us free" (Gal. 5:1).

PHILIP SCHAFF: *The Progress of Religious Freedom, as shown in the History of Toleration Acts,* New York (Scribners), 1889.

CHAPTER CLIII.

HISTORY OF ORGANIZATION.

The history of ORGANIZATION implies the government and discipline of the Church. Christ founded a visible Church (Matt. 16:18), appointed officers, and instituted the sacraments of baptism and the Lord's Supper, to be perpetually observed by his followers.

On this foundation have been built, in the course of time, various forms of church polity: the Apostolic, the Primitive Episcopal, the Metropolitan and Patriarchal, the Papal, the Anglican, the Presbyterian, the Independent, the Methodist Episcopal, etc.

The relation of church and state has passed through several distinct phases: (1) hostile separation (in the ante-Nicene age); (2) union, (*a*) the church ruling the state: hierarchy or theocracy (as in the mediæval papacy), (*b*) the state ruling the church: cæsaropapacy or Erastianism (as in the Byzantine empire, the Protestant state-churches, and in Russia); (3) friendly separation and independence (as in the United States of America).

LITERATURE: PLANCK: *Geschichte der christlich-kirchlichen Gesellschaftsverfassung* (1803–5), 5 vols.—ROTHE: *Anfänge der christlichen Kirche und ihrer Verfassung* (1837).—RITSCHL: *Die Entstehung der altkatholischen Kirche* (1887).—HATCH: *The Growth of Church Institutions* (1887).

The history of the papacy, which is in fact a history of Latin Christianity, has been especially treated in whole or in part by PLATINA, PAGI, BOWER, PLANCK, SPITTLER, BAXMANN, WATTENBACH, GREENWOOD, RANKE, CREIGHTON, PASTOR, and others. Monographs on single popes: LAU, and BARMBY on Gregory I.; VOIGT on Gregory VII.; REUTER on Alexander III.; HURTER on Innocent III.; DRUMANN on Boniface VIII.; ROSCOE on Leo X., etc.

CHAPTER CLIV.

HISTORY OF COUNCILS.

The history of COUNCILS, or deliberative church assemblies, from the apostolic conference at Jerusalem (A.D. 50) to modern times, is to a large extent a history of Christian doctrine and discipline.

The most prominent and influential councils are the œcumenical councils, from that of Nicæa (325) to that of the Vatican (1870). They formulated the dogmas and canons of the Greek and Latin Churches.

The most important synods of the Reformed Church are the Synod of Dort (1620), and the Westminster Assembly (1647), which framed Confessions of Faith, and Directories of Worship and Discipline.

The Presbyterian Churches have regular Synods and General Assemblies; the American Episcopal Church holds triennial Conventions; the Methodist Episcopal Church, quadrennial General Conferences; the Congregationalists and Baptists have occasional conventions of a voluntary character without legislative power.

Besides official conventions, there are in modern times Roman Catholic Congresses, General Conferences of the Evangelical Alliance, Pan-Anglican, Pan-Presbyterian, and Pan-Methodist Councils, etc., which have no legislative but great moral power.

LITERATURE: *The Acts of Councils*, by LABBEUS and COSSART, HARDUIN, and MANSI. The best history of Councils from a liberal Roman Catholic standpoint is the *Conciliengeschichte* of Professor (afterwards Bishop) HEFELE, continued by Cardinal HERGENRÖTHER (2d ed. revised, 1873–87, 8 vols.). It is a history of Latin Christianity. For the history of Protestant Synods and free Conferences, the official minutes and proceedings must be consulted.

CHAPTER CLV.

HISTORY OF WORSHIP.

The history of WORSHIP includes an account of sacred seasons and places, a history of preaching and catechetical instruction, liturgies, the administration of the sacraments, religious rites and ceremonies, ecclesiastical art (architecture, sculpture and painting), church poetry and church music.

Organization and worship of the ancient Church are often combined under the name of *Ecclesiastical Antiquities*, which corresponds to Biblical Antiquities or Archæology in Exegetical Theology. An important part of Church Archæology, of recent origin, relates to the catacombs of Rome, which present an interesting view of the manners and customs, of the life and death of the early Christians.

LITERATURE: BINGHAM, AUGUSTI, BINTERIM, SIEGEL, KRAUS.—On Christian Antiquities: SMITH and CHEETHAM: *Dictionary of Christian Antiquities* (London, 1780, 2 vols.).—DE ROSSI: *Roma sotterranea cristiana* (Rom. 1864–78, 4 vols. fol.).—On Liturgies: RENAUDOT, PAMELIUS, NEALE, PALMER, HAMMOND.—Numerous works on Church architecture, by BUNSEN, KUGLER, LÜBKE, etc.—The best work on hymnology is JULIAN'S *Dictionary of Hymnology*, London and New York, 1892, pp. 1616.

CHAPTER CLVI.

HISTORY OF CHRISTIAN LIFE.

The history of CHRISTIAN LIFE or Christian morality and piety embraces the biographies of martyrs and saints (Martyrology and Hagiology), the history of asceticism and monasticism, the progress of Christian philanthropy and benevolence, and the purifying and ennobling influences of Christianity upon individual, domestic, social and national life.

LITERATURE: *Acta Sanctorum*, by the Bollandists (a colossal work begun at Antwerp, 1643–1875, 61 vols. fol., with a supplement).—ALBAN BUTLER: *Lives of the Saints* (1756–59, 4 vols., a popular and abridged reproduction of the *Acta Sanctorum*).—S. BARING-GOULD: *Lives of the Saints* (1872–77, 15 vols.).—Numerous histories of Monasticism, and the various Monastic Orders. Biographies of St. Benedict, St. Bernard, St. Francis of Assisi, etc.—The histories of Asceticism, Mysticism, Pietism, Methodism.—MAX GOEBEL: *Geschichte des christlichen Lebens in der rheinisch-westphälischen evangel. Kirche* (1860, 3 vols.).—PIPER: *Evangelischer Kalender* (1873).—UHLHORN: *Die christliche Liebesthätigkeit in der alten Kirche* (1881), im Mittelalter (1884).—C. L. BRACE: *Gesta Christi;* or, *A History of Humane Progress under Christianity* (New York, 1883, 5th ed. 1890).—Histories of hospitals, reformatories, prison discipline, temperance, etc.

CHAPTER CLVII.

HISTORY OF DOCTRINES AND DOGMAS.

1. A history of THEOLOGY in the widest sense embraces the whole intellectual and literary activity of the Church. Every department of theology, exegetical, historical, systematic and practical, has its own history. Christian literature in all civilized languages surpasses in extent and variety all other kinds of literature.

2. History of Christian DOCTRINES or history of dogmatic theology traces the origin and progress of every article of the Christian faith. The doctrines are developed in a certain order: first those of the Trinity and incarnation (in the Nicene age and Post-Nicene age); then those of sin and grace (in the Pelagian and semi-Pelagian controversies); next those of the rule of faith, justification, faith and good works (in the Reformation period).

3. A special and the most important department in Doctrine History is the History of DOGMAS (*Dogmengeschichte*). Truth comes from God and is revealed in the Bible; doctrine is the conception and comprehension of truth by individuals; dogma is doctrine formulated by the Church and made a law for its members. Dogma involves the element of authority.*

* *Dogma* is derived from δοκέω, ἔδοξε, *placuit*, it seemed good, and means a public decree or ordinance; comp. Luke 2:1; Acts 17:7 (imperial

The Greek Church recognizes the dogmatic decisions of the seven œcumenical councils; the Roman Church holds in addition the decisions of Trent (1563) and of the Vatican Council (1870). The dogmatic system of the Lutheran Church was completed with the Formula of Concord (1577), that of the Calvinistic Churches with the standards of the Westminster Assembly (1647).

4. The history of HERESIES or perversions of Christian truths is an important part of the history of doctrines and dogmas. It is usually through conflict with heresies that the knowledge of Christian truth is evolved in the militant Church. Thus Arianism led to the Nicene Creed; Apollinarianism, Nestorianism and Eutychianism prepared the way for the Chalcedonian Christology; Pelagius stimulated the development of the Augustinian anthropology; the Reformation theology was brought out in conflict with the papacy; the Council of Trent formulated the modern Roman Creed in opposition to the Protestant doctrines; the Vatican Council settled the controversy between papal infallibilists and anti-infallibilists, or Ultramontanists and Gallicans, within the Roman Church.

LITERATURE: Histories of Dogmas in German by MÜNSCHER, BAUMGARTEN — CRUSIUS, NEANDER, GIESELER, BAUR, HAGENBACH (6th ed. by Benrath, 1888), THOMASIUS, FR. NITZSCH, HARNACK (1886–90, 3 vols., and *Grundriss*, 1889, 2d ed. 1892), LOOFS (3d ed. 1893).—Roman Catholics: PETAVIUS (Latin, the father of this science), KLEE, SCHWANE, BACH.

In English: HAGENBACH (translated from an older ed. by Buch, revised and enlarged by H. B. Smith, 1861, 2 vols., new ed., Edinburgh, 1880, 3 vols.), SHEDD (1863, 2 vols.), SHELDON (1886, 2 vols.), SCHAFF (the first vol. of his *Creeds of Christendom*, 5th ed. 1890), HARNACK (the *Grundriss*), *Outlines of the History of Dogma*, transl. by E. K. Mitchell, 1893, G. P. FISHER (in course of preparation for the series of theological textbooks, edited by Briggs and Salmond).

decree); Eph. 2 : 15; Col. 2 : 14 (the ordinances of Moses); Acts 16 : 4 (the decision of the Council of Jerusalem). The Old Testament puts monotheism in the form of a dogmatic statement, Deut. 6 : 4. The New Testament mentions no dogma, strictly so called; for the "decrees" ordained by the Apostles and Elders, Acts 16 : 4, were not doctrinal, but disciplinary, and not intended to be permanent. From the beginning of the fourth century a closer distinction was made between *dogma* and *canon*, and the former confined to doctrinal, the latter to disciplinary, decisions of councils.

CHAPTER CLVIII.

SOURCES OF CHURCH HISTORY.

The sources of Church History furnish authentic information of the facts and dates. They are partly written, partly unwritten. Before the invention of the printing-press the written sources existed in manuscripts, which are still preserved in the old libraries of Europe, especially that of the Vatican, and must be referred to, in doubtful cases, for the verification of the original texts. But since that time nearly all the written sources are printed and published in book form.

CHAPTER CLIX.

THE WRITTEN SOURCES.

For biblical history, we have the books of the Old and New Testaments, with supplementary and illustrative records of contemporary nations.

Ecclesiastical history is embodied in the immense and evergrowing literature of the Christian Church.

The post-biblical sources may be divided into three classes of works:

1. Official documents of ecclesiastical and civil authorities: Acts of councils, creeds, canons, liturgies, laws, monastic rules, briefs and bulls of popes, pastoral letters of patriarchs and bishops, proceedings of synods and other ecclesiastical bodies.

COLLECTIONS: Councils by HARDUIN (12 vols.) and MANSI (31 vols.). Papal Bulls by CHERUBINI (1586), CHEVALIER (1730), COCQUELINES (1740), BARBERI (1856), GAUDE (1857 sqq.). Liturgies by GOAR (1647), RENAUDOT (1716), MURATORI (1748), ASSEMANI (1766), DANIEL (1847), NEALE (1849). Creeds and Confessions of Faith by HAHN, RECHENBERG, NIEMEYER, SCHAFF. Monastic Rules by HOLSTEN and BROCKIE. Imperial Laws, the Theodosian and Justinian codes. The *Monumenta Germaniæ* for the mediæval history of the papacy and the holy Roman empire. The documentary sources of modern history are increasing with the growth of the Church and the multiplication of denominations and sects.

2. Private writings of prominent actors in history: The church fathers, heretics and heathen, for the first six centuries; the missionaries, monks, schoolmen and mystics, for the middle

ages; the Reformers and their Roman Catholic opponents, for the sixteenth century; and the leading writers of all denominations in more recent times. These works are the richest mines for the historian. They give history in its birth and actual movement. But they must be carefully sifted and weighed, especially the controversial writings, in which fact is generally more or less colored by party spirit, heretical and orthodox.

COLLECTIONS: The works of the Apostolic Fathers by GEBHARDT, HARNACK and ZAHN (1878), HEFELE-FUNK (1887), LIGHTFOOT (1869-90; Greek text ed., 1890). The Apologists by OTTO (3d ed. 1876 sqq.). All the Fathers by MIGNE (1844-66, the Latin Fathers in 222, the Greek in 167 vols.). Select works of the Fathers in English in the Ante-Nicene, Nicene, and Post-Nicene Libraries, ed. by COXE, SCHAFF and WACE.—The *Corpus Reformatorum* contains so far the works of Melanchthon, ed. by BRETSCHNEIDER and BINDSEIL (1834-60, 28 vols.), and the works of Calvin, ed. by BAUM, CUNITZ, REUSS, and ERICHSON (1863 sqq., so far 47 vols.). Separate editions of the works of Luther, Zwingli, Beza, Cranmer, Knox, etc.—The writings of Spener and Francke, for Pietism; Zinzendorf and Spangenberg, for the Moravian community; Wesley (John and Charles) and Whitefield, for Methodism; Pusey, Newman, and Keble, for Anglo-Catholicism; Döllinger, Reinkens, and Von Schulte, for Old Catholicism, etc., etc.

3. Accounts of contemporary historians, whether friends or foes, who were eye-witnesses of the events. Also autobiographies of the actors in history. The value of such works depends on the opportunities, capacity and credibility of the authors, which must be determined by careful criticism.

EXAMPLES: Eusebius on the life of Constantine, and the Palestinian Martyrs. Augustin's Confessions. Eginhard's Life of Charlemagne. Eadmer's Life of Anselm. The correspondence of the Reformers, especially the letters of Luther and Calvin. Melanchthon's Life of Luther. Beza's Life of Calvin. Knox's History of the Scotch Reformation. Cromwell's Letters. Clarendon's History of the Rebellion (anti-puritan). Newman's Apologia (for the inner history of Anglo-Catholicism).

4. Historians who lived after the events may be counted among the direct and immediate sources so far only as they have drawn from trustworthy and contemporary records which have either been wholly or partially lost, like many of the authorities of Eusebius for the ante-Nicene period, or are inaccessible to historians generally, as were formerly the papal *Regesta* and other documents of the Vatican library and papal Archives. Thus Baronius, in his *Annales*, largely drew from these treas-

ures, to which no Protestant would have been admitted before the liberal policy of Leo XIII. (1885).

Other historians who used documents already published are only secondary and indirect sources, and their value depends upon the degree of accuracy and faithfulness with which they made use of the primary sources.

CHAPTER CLX.

THE UNWRITTEN SOURCES.

1. To the unwritten sources belong churches, convents, works of sculpture, paintings, ruins, relics and other monuments; also the countries in which the history was transacted.

These sources have been largely increased by recent discoveries and excavations in Bible lands. The Egyptian and Assyrian literature is a supplement to the Old Testament. The Sinaitic Peninsula and Mt. Sinai are a commentary on Exodus and the Decalogue. Palestine is "a fifth Gospel." The Roman catacombs with their symbols illustrate the sufferings and trials, the simplicity and humility, the faith and hope of the Christians under heathen persecution. This source of ancient Church History, ignored by Mosheim and Gibbon, by Neander and Gieseler, was not properly opened up till after the middle of the nineteenth century. The basilicas and baptisteries embody the spirit of the Nicene age. The Byzantine churches are characteristic of Byzantine Christianity. The Gothic cathedrals symbolize the genius of mediæval Catholicism. The churches, sculptures and paintings of the Renaissance characterize the transition from the middle ages to modern times and the revival of classical taste.

2. The habits and customs of the Christian nations and their surroundings supplement and illustrate the written and unwritten sources. The historian should be a traveler, and put himself in contact with living and moving history. The present is the outcome of the past, and the tree is known fully by the fruit.

The Greek Church can be studied best in Turkey, Greece and Russia; the Roman Church, in Italy, Spain, France, Austria, Ireland and South America; the Lutheran Church, in Germany and Scandinavia; the Reformed Churches, in Switzerland,

France, Holland, Great Britain and North America; the Episcopal Church, in England, the British Provinces and the United States; Congregationalism, in England and New England. In the mother countries of the Churches, we find not only the largest collections of written and printed sources, churches, museums, picture-galleries and monumental remains, but also the oral traditions and living representatives of the past, who exhibit the national genius and social condition of their forefathers in a far more instructive manner than ponderous volumes.

CHAPTER CLXI.

DUTY OF THE HISTORIAN.

There are different historical talents: For production and reproduction, for original research and artistic composition, for philosophic comprehension and special investigation. There are historical miners who bring raw material to light; historical manufacturers who work up the material into readable shape; and historical retailers who epitomize and popularize scholarly labors for general use. Few are gifted with a deep insight into the secret laws, forces, currents and connections of events. We have several philosophies of general history; but a philosophy of Church history is still a desideratum. Every man must follow his inclination and taste, and not despise another for doing what he cannot do and does not pretend to do.

The first and last duty of the historian—whether he be a producer or reproducer, a generalist or specialist—is truthfulness. As the exegete has to explain the Scriptures according to their natural sense, without dogmatic bias, and to draw out all that is in them, but to put nothing foreign into them, so it is the business of the historian to reproduce history as God and men made it, without omission or addition, and not to pervert and utilize it for selfish or sectarian purposes. But alas! many commentaries are impositions rather than expositions, and many histories are caricatures rather than portraits.

The historian is a witness who must tell the truth, the whole truth, and nothing but the truth; and he is also a judge who must do strict and full justice to every person and event which comes before his tribunal.

To be thus faithful and just, he needs a threefold qualification: scientific, artistic, and moral; in other words, knowledge of the sources, power of composition, and a Christian spirit.

So far as the historian combines these qualifications, he fulfills his office. We can, at best, only approach perfection in this or in any other branch of study, but we must strive after it. Absolute success would require infallibility; and this is denied to mortal man. The Pope of Rome claims to be officially infallible, but he is mistaken sometimes, and his claim does not extend to matters of history. Even St. Paul knew only in part and saw "in a mirror, darkly." It is the exclusive privilege of the divine mind to see the end from the beginning with the eye of omniscience.

The final solution of the mysteries of history is reserved for that heavenly state when we shall see "face to face," and shall survey the developments of time from the heights of eternity. What St. Augustin so aptly says of the mutual relation of the Old and New Testament, "The New Testament is concealed in the Old, the Old Testament is revealed in the New" (*Novum Testamentum in Vetere latet, Vetus in Novo patet*), may be applied also to the relation of this world and the world to come. The history of the Church militant is, throughout, but a type, and a prophecy which can be perfectly understood only in the light of its fulfillment.

There is a concealed and a revealed God in history as well as in nature: sufficiently concealed to try our faith, sufficiently revealed to strengthen our faith.

CHAPTER CLXII.

THE MASTERY OF THE SOURCES.

The historian must first make himself master of the sources. This is a well-nigh endless task, but no one should attempt to write history without some knowledge of the primary sources of information; as no one should attempt to write a commentary without a knowledge of the original languages of the Bible. He must look the actors in the face, and feel the pulse of events.

The first thing for the historian is to select the sources for the particular period or topic which he wishes to investigate. Then he has to examine the genuineness and integrity of the sources, according to the laws of textual and literary criticism, and to measure the capacity and credibility of the witnesses. Thus only can he separate facts from fiction, truth from error.

As history progresses, the sources multiply beyond the power of any individual to read and digest them. We may do exhaustive work in a special department of limited extent; but for many fields of history even the greatest scholars have to depend upon the labors of others, and avail themselves—with grateful acknowledgment—of collections, digests, indexes, and monographs of specialists. The general historian and the specialist are indispensable to each other. The one looks out for the whole, the other for the parts.

CHAPTER CLXIII.

ARTISTIC COMPOSITION.

The historian is an artist as well as a scholar. He ought to be endowed with historical imagination as well as with critical acumen. Familiarity with poetry and general literature will be of much benefit to him. He is more than an annalist and reporter. History is not a heap of dry bones, but a living organism, filled and ruled by a rational soul. The historian must reproduce the movements of the past, clothe the actors with flesh and blood, and make them live their lives over again. He is not permitted, indeed, to color history or to turn it into a romance, for the purpose of making it more interesting than it really is, but he must set the events in their true light and relation to their age, their antecedents and results, and give them a freshness and interest as if they were occurring before the eyes of the reader.

In this respect the Church historians (especially the Germans) are far behind the secular historians. They have been so much absorbed by the contents as to neglect the graces of style, method and arrangement. Hence Church history is confined to a professional class, and has not yet taken a place in general literature. You may find Gibbon and Macaulay in every gentleman's library, but very rarely Neander and Gieseler. And yet the history of Christianity is the most interesting, as well as the most profound and most important, part in the annals of the human race.

The first requisite of a readable history is a lucid arrangement and grouping of the material. The best method is to combine judiciously the chronological and topical principles of division, so as to present at once the succession of events and the several parallel departments of history in due proportion. Accordingly, we would first divide the whole history into periods, not arbitrarily, but as determined by the actual course of events; and then present each of these periods in as many sections or chapters as the material itself suggests.

Another requisite, in these days of rapid motion and multiplied studies, is to combine brevity and condensation with completeness. In general Church history condensation becomes more and more a necessity and a virtue as the material increases. Brevity is the soul of wit not only, but also of a good speech and a good book. Life is too short and time too precious to read (except for reference) the thirteen folios (covering so many centuries) of the Magdeburg Centuries, the thirty-eight folios of the Annals of Baronius, the sixteen quartos of Tillemont, the forty volumes of Fleury, the forty-five volumes of Schroeckh, and the twenty-nine volumes of Rohrbacher.

"*Wie die Welt läuft immer weiter,*
Wird stets die Geschichte breiter;
Und uns wird je mehr, je länger
Nöthig ein Zusammendränger."

CHAPTER CLXIV.

THE CHRISTIAN SPIRIT.

The moral qualification of the historian may be comprehended in the Christian spirit, which is the spirit of truth and love. "Malice to none, charity for all." The secular historian must have a general sympathy with humanity, according to the motto:

"*Homo sum: humani nihil a me alienum puto.*"

The Church historian must have a general sympathy with Christianity in all its forms and phases, and follow the motto:

"*Christianus sum: Christiani nihil a me alienum puto.*"

No one can interpret poetry without poetic feeling and taste, or philosophy without speculative talent; so no one can rightly comprehend and exhibit the history of Christianity without the spirit that animates and controls it. An unbeliever could produce only a repulsive caricature, or at best a lifeless statue.

The higher the historian stands on Christian ground, the wider is his horizon, and the clearer and fuller his view of the regions below. Even error can be fairly seen only from the position of truth. "*Verum est index sui et falsi.*"

Christianity is the absolute truth, which, like the sun, both reveals itself and enlightens all that is dark.

CHAPTER CLXV.

USES OF CHURCH HISTORY.

(From SCHAFF's *Church History*, I. 20 and 21.)

Church history is the most extensive, and, including the history of the Old and New Testaments, the most important branch of theology. It is the storehouse from which theology derives its supplies. It is the best commentary on Christianity itself. The fullness of the stream is the glory of the fountain from which it flows.

1. Church history has a general interest for every cultivated mind, as showing the moral and religious development of our race, and the gradual execution of the divine plan of redemption. A knowledge of it should be an essential part of general culture.

2. It has special value for the theologian and minister of the Gospel, as the key to the present condition of Christendom and the guide to successful labor for the future. The present is the fruit of the past, and the germ of the future. No work can stand unless it grows out of the real wants of the age and strikes firm root in the soil of the past. Those who despise their fathers have no claim upon the respect of their children. Church history is no mere curiosity shop; its facts are not dead men's bones. It embodies living realities, the general principles and laws for our own guidance and action. Who studies Church history studies human nature under the influence of Christianity as it was, as it now is, and as it will be to the end of time.

3. The history of the Church has practical value for every Christian as a storehouse of wisdom and experience, warning

and encouragement. It is the philosophy of facts, Christianity in living examples. History in general is described by Cicero as "*testis temporum, lux veritatis, et magistra vitæ*," and by Diodorus as "a handmaid of Providence, a priestess of truth, and a mother of wisdom." This is true in the highest degree of Church history. Next to the holy Scriptures, which are themselves a history and depository of divine revelation, there is no stronger proof of the continual presence of Christ with his people, no more thorough vindication of Christianity, no richer source of useful learning, no stronger incentive to virtue and piety, than the history of Christ's kingdom. Every age has a message from God to man, which it is of the greatest importance to understand.

The Epistle to the Hebrews describes in stirring eloquence "the cloud of witnesses" from the old dispensation for the encouragement of the early Christians. But we are "compassed about" with a far greater and brighter cloud of apostles, evangelists, martyrs, confessors, fathers, reformers and saints of all ages and tongues, and this cloud is constantly increasing. In reading the thoughts and prayers, the lives and deaths of those heroes of faith and love, who were living epistles of Christ, the salt of the earth, the benefactors and glory of our race, we are elevated, edified, comforted and encouraged to follow their example that we may at last, by the grace of God, be received into their fellowship to spend with them a blessed eternity in the praise of the same God and Saviour of the world.

CHAPTER CLXVI.

PERIODS AND EPOCHS.

Church history is divided into several *ages* or *periods* which represent the various stages of its progress. The dividing line between two periods is called an *epoch:* it marks the close of one and the beginning of another period, and introduces a new principle or a new phase of development. Thus the birth of Christ, the Day of Pentecost, the conversion of Paul, the council of Nicæa, the fall of Constantinople, the invention of the printing-press, the discovery of America, the outbreak of the Reformation, the Edict of Nantes, the Toleration Act of 1688, the American Declaration of Independence, the French Revolution, the Vatican Council of 1870, are epoch-making facts or events, followed by new periods. The term *age* is often used also in the limited sense of a generation, as when we speak of the age of Constantine, of Charlemagne, of Hildebrand, of Queen Elizabeth.

The periods of history should not be artificially made after a certain mechanical scheme of equal time-divisions of years or centuries. They must faithfully represent the successive ages of history itself, which in different times and countries moves with very unequal degrees of rapidity, corresponding to the means of communication from the slow pace of the caravan to the speed of the railroad and magnetic telegraph.

CHAPTER CLXVII.

PERIODS OF BIBLICAL HISTORY.

Biblical or sacred history is the development of the divine Revelation and the kingdom of God from the Creation to the close of the Apostolic age. It runs parallel with the Scriptures from Genesis to Revelation.

Here we must distinguish the dispensation of the law and the dispensation of the gospel, or the history of the Old Testament religion and that of the New Testament religion.

I. Under the OLD DISPENSATION: from the Creation down to John the Baptist, or the advent of Christ.

II. Under the NEW DISPENSATION: Christ and the Apostles, or primitive and normative Christianity in its divine-human founder and inspired organs, from the birth of Christ to the death of John at the close of the first century (A.D. 1–100).

CHAPTER CLXVIII.

PERIODS OF CHRISTIAN CHURCH HISTORY.

Church History in the narrow sense, or the History of Christianity, begins with the birth of Christ, and includes the second division of Biblical history, already mentioned.

Main divisions: Ancient, Mediæval, and Modern Christianity.

I. ANCIENT CHRISTIANITY embraces the first six centuries to Gregory I. (590): The Græco-Latin, patristic, old catholic

PERIODS OF CHRISTIAN CHURCH HISTORY. 261

Church, the common stock from which the Greek, the Roman, and the Protestant Churches have sprung.

Ancient Christianity corresponds to the patriarchal period in Jewish history. Its theatre is the Old Roman empire around the Mediterranean, *i.e.*, western Asia, northern Africa, southern Europe; its nationalities, the Jews, the Greeks, and the Romans; the language of its literature is chiefly the Greek, and, after the close of the second century, also the Latin.

Subdivisions:

(*a*) The Life of Christ, and the Apostolic age, stand by themselves as the culmination of Biblical history and the beginning of Church history.

(*b*) The Ante-Nicene Age, 100–325. The period of persecution under the Roman empire to the conversion of Constantine the Great and the first œcumenical council of Nicæa.

(*c*) The Nicene and Post-Nicene Age, 325–600. The period of Græco-Roman State-Christianity, ruled by Christian emperors, patriarchs, and œcumenical councils, from Constantine the Great to Pope Gregory the Great.

II. MEDIÆVAL CHRISTIANITY from the close of the sixth to the beginning of the sixteenth century, or from Gregory I. to the Reformation, A.D. 590–1517. Character: The partial conversion and civilization of the barbarians in Europe, and preparation for modern Christianity and civilization. The Greek and Roman Churches, divided, pursue their independent course; the Latin Church extends west, among the Celtic and Germanic races; the Greek, northeast among the Slavonians (in Russia). The rise and progress of the papacy, monasticism, scholasticism, and mysticism; the crusades; the papal schism and the reformatory councils. The anti-catholic sects. The revival of letters and arts. The invention of printing. The discovery of America. The rise of independent nationalities. The abuses and corruptions of the Church. The forerunners of Protestantism (Wiclif in England, Hus in Bohemia, Savonarola in Italy, Wessel in Holland, Reuchlin and Erasmus in Germany and Switzerland).

Mediæval Christianity corresponds to the Mosaic theocracy in the old dispensation. It moves chiefly on European soil, northward and westward, among the Latin and barbarian (Celtic, Germanic and Slavonic) races, and its literature is chiefly Latin, the official language of the Roman Church.

Subdivisions:

(a) The missionary period of the middle ages from Gregory I. to Gregory VII. (590–1073).

(b) The palmy period of the papacy from Gregory VII. to Boniface VIII. (1073–1294).

(c) The decay of the mediæval papacy and scholasticism, the revival of letters, and preparation for a Reformation, from Boniface VIII. to Leo X. and Martin Luther (1294–1517). The last period has a striking resemblance to the nineteenth century: Old things passing away, all things becoming new.

III. MODERN CHRISTIANITY, from the Reformation of the sixteenth century to the present time. Latin Christianity is divided between conservative Romanism and progressive Protestantism. The founding of the evangelical churches, Lutheran, Reformed, and Anglican, by the labors of Luther, Zwingli and Calvin on the continent, Cranmer in England, and Knox in Scotland. Reaction of Romanism; the Council of Trent; the order of the Jesuits, henceforth the chief support of the revived papacy, and the indefatigable enemy of Protestantism. The disastrous Thirty Years' War in Germany, ending with the legal recognition of the Lutheran Church by the treaty of Westphalia (1648). The heroic war of emancipation of the Hollanders against the tyranny of Spain. The Synod of Dort (1620). The Edict of Nantes by Henry IV. (1598), its revocation by Louis XIV. (1685); the expulsion of the Huguenots from France, who became a blessing to other nations, while a remnant remained at home as a church of the desert, hoping for better times. The Puritan rebellion, or rather the second reformation in England; the Westminster Assembly and Westminster standards of the Presbyterian Churches (1647); the Cromwellian commonwealth; the restoration of episcopacy; the revolution of 1688, the Act of Toleration, and consequent division of English Church history into separate denominational channels. The Pietistic and Moravian movements in Germany. The Methodist revival in England and the American colonies. The rise and progress of Deism and Rationalism all over Europe. The American secession from England, and the peaceful separation of Church and State, with full religious liberty guaranteed by the national Constitution. The French Revolution and the temporary abolition of Christianity, followed by the restoration of the Roman Catholic Church under

Napoleon with toleration and government support of other churches (Reformed and Lutheran), and the Jewish synagogue. Then began the revival of Protestantism and Romanism all over Europe. The centennial celebration of the Reformation and the union of the Lutheran and Reformed Churches in Prussia (1817). The old Lutheran reaction in Germany. Oxford Tractarianism or Anglo-Catholicism in England resulting in a large secession to Rome (1845), headed by Newman and Manning (both subsequently made cardinals), and a ritualistic revival of Christian life within the Church of England. Triumph of Ultramontanism over Gallicanism in the Vatican Council of 1870, which declared the dogma of papal infallibility, thus completing the hierarchical pyramid; but this was followed by the Old Catholic secession under the lead of Döllinger. The Franco-German war, and the establishment of a Protestant empire under the headship of Prussia. The *Culturkampf* with Rome; the May-laws, and their abrogation. Prince Bismarck and Pope Leo XIII. on the way to Canossa but at a respectful distance, and asking and granting a *quid pro quo*. The papacy and the French republic. The school question in connection with religious instruction. Conflict between religion and the various forms of skepticism and infidelity. Growing activity in all departments of theological learning and popular literature, in foreign and domestic missions, in practical works of philanthropy and benevolence. Tendencies towards union among different Churches. Bible Societies; Sunday Schools; Young Men's Christian Associations; Christian Endeavor Societies. Evangelical Alliance; pan-Anglican, pan-Presbyterian, pan-Methodist Councils. Opening up of the heart of Africa. An age of discoveries and inventions, which stimulate and facilitate the conversion and civilization of the whole world.

At the end of the nineteenth century, Christianity stands on the threshold of a glorious past and a more glorious future which no man can forecast.

Subdivisions:

(*a*) The age of the Protestant Reformation, and the papal counter-Reformation (1517–1648).

(*b*) The age of scholastic and polemic confessionalism in conflict with nonconformity and subjective piety (from the middle of the seventeenth to the middle of the eighteenth century).

(c) The age of revolution, revival and progress in all Churches and upon all continents (down to the close of the nineteenth century).

CHAPTER CLXIX.

HISTORY OF ISRAEL.

We now proceed to a brief survey of the most important branches of Historical Theology.

The Jewish Church History begins with Abraham and closes with John the Baptist.

It is a history of the positive preparation for Christianity by a divinely organized theocracy. "Salvation is from the Jews" (John 4: 22). This wonderfully gifted and indestructible people, whose fit symbol is the burning bush, was chosen by God to know and to worship him amidst surrounding idolatry, and to prepare the way for the coming of the Messiah. Theirs are "the adoption, and the glory, and the covenants, and the giving of the law, and the service of God, and the promises"; theirs are "the fathers"; and of them is "Christ as concerning the flesh, who is over all, God blessed forever" (Rom. 9: 4, 5). Herein lies the universal and permanent interest and value of the Jewish history and the Old Testament literature. It represents two concurrent movements: a descending revelation of God to man, and an ascending moral and spiritual aspiration of man to God, both culminating in the divine-human Messiah and Saviour.

In a wider sense, the History of the Old Covenant includes also the antediluvian history of religion from the creation of man, and the connections of the Jewish nation with the surrounding heathen empires of Egypt, Assyria, Babylonia, Persia, Greece and Rome.

The principal divisions are the following:

1. The primitive or antediluvian period, from the creation of Adam to Noah and the call of Abraham. The creation of man; the state of innocence; the fall; the antediluvians; the flood; Noah and his sons; the dispersion of nations.

2. The patriarchal period, from Abraham to Moses. Abraham; Isaac; Jacob; Joseph; the sojourn in Egypt; the growth into a nation; the oppression by Pharaoh (Rameses II. or Sesostris); the preparation and call of Moses.

3. The Mosaic period, from Moses to Samuel. The Exodus from Egypt; the miraculous passage through the Red Sea; the establishment of the theocracy from Mount Sinai; the Decalogue; the Mosaic legislation and worship; the wanderings through "the great and terrible wilderness" of the Sinaitic Peninsula; the conquest of Canaan under Joshua; the anarchical period of the Judges; the peaceful episode of Ruth.

4. The period of the Jewish monarchy and prophecy. The undivided monarchy (B.C. 1095–975): The reigns of Saul (forty years), David (forty), and Solomon (forty). The divided monarchy: The kingdom of Judah from Rehoboam to the destruction of Jerusalem and the Babylonian Captivity (B.C. 588). The kingdom of Israel from Jeroboam to the end of the kingdom (B.C. 722). The older prophets: Elijah and Elisha, Isaiah, Jonah, Amos, Hosea, Micah, Nahum, Zephaniah, Habakkuk, Jeremiah (till B.C. 588).

5. The Babylonian Captivity, B.C. 588 to 536. Contact with foreign nations and ideas. The prophets Daniel and Ezekiel.

6. The period of reconstruction under Ezra, the model priest and scribe, and Nehemiah, the model statesman and patriot, and the post-exilian prophets, Haggai, Zechariah, and Malachi. Gradual formation of the Hebrew canon. Dispersion of the Jews.

7. The Maccabæan period, or the whole period intervening between Nehemiah and John the Baptist. The invasion of Alexander the Great; Palestine subjected to Macedonian rule. The heroic Maccabæan war of independence against Antiochus Epiphanes (175–164 B.C.). The Jewish Apocrypha. The Greek Version (Septuagint) of the Hebrew Scriptures. The Hebrews and the Hellenists. The sects of the Pharisees, Sadducees and Essenes. The Messianic expectations. John the Baptist, the last of the prophets. Palestine subject to Roman rule since Pompey and Cæsar.

8. The history of the Jewish theocracy closes with the destruction of Jerusalem and the Temple (A.D. 70), which was foretold by Christ, and graphically and minutely described by Josephus as an eye-witness.

This part of its history may be embraced in what is called the History of New Testament Times. (See next chapter.)

The history of the Jews after the destruction of the theocracy lies outside of biblical or ecclesiastical history, but the treatment of the Jews by the Christian Church belongs to the history of religious persecution.

LITERATURE: The chief sources for the history of Israel are the books of the Old Covenant, and the Archæology of Josephus. The works of Philo on Moses, etc., are of little historical value, on account of their allegorical interpretation. The Greek and Latin historians depend upon Josephus. The Egyptological and Babylonio-Assyrian discoveries throw side-lights on the Jewish history.

HEINRICH EWALD (d. 1875): *History of the People of Israel*, Göttingen, 1843, 3d ed. 1864–68, 7 vols.; English translation, London, 1868–76, 5 vols. Marks an epoch as the first critical and yet profoundly religious construction of the history of Israel, as the unique people of divine revelation. Comp. also his *Prophets*, and *Poetical Books of the Old Testament*.

DEAN STANLEY (d. 1881): *Lectures on the History of the Jewish Church*, London and New York, 1863–76, 3 vols. A picturesque popular condensation of Ewald, who once told him, when a student of Oxford, that the little New Testament contained the whole wisdom of the world.

The conservative orthodox school is represented by HENGSTENBERG, in his posthumous *History of the Kingdom of God in the Old Covenant* (Berlin, 1870); KURTZ, in his unfinished *History of the Old Covenant* (Berlin, 1848 and 1855); KÖHLER, in his *Lehrbuch der biblischen Geschichte* (Erlangen, 1875–88); also by VON HOFMANN, in an independent way; and by EDERSHEIM (in several works).

Since Ewald, a new critical reconstruction has gradually been elaborated, which reverses the traditional order of the relation of the law and prophecy. This theory puts the prophetic development before the priestly, and regards the levitical priest-code (based in part on Ez. 40–48), with its stiff, narrow legalism and elaborate ritual, as an exilian and post-exilian contraction and petrifaction of the grand prophetic ideas, which at last were revived and fulfilled by Christ. It was first suggested by Reuss in lectures (1833), and independently by Vatke (1835) and George (1835), and carried out by Graf (1869) and Kayser (1874)—two pupils of Reuss,—and especially by Wellhausen (1878), who gave to it unity and consistency. Wellhausen starts from the facts that the oldest sources know nothing of a concentration of worship in Jerusalem, nor of a minute sacrificial ritual, nor of a levitical and priestly hierarchy. Kuenen in Holland (1869 and 1875) and Renan in France (1887) have arrived, by independent research, at similar conclusions, and the advanced Hebrew scholars of England (as W. R. Smith, Cheyne, Driver) and of America (as Briggs, Brown, Toy, H. P. Smith, Moore) have substantially adopted the chief results, but with higher views of inspiration. This theory is closely connected with the complicated critical investigations of the sources of the Pentateuch or Hexateuch (including the book of Joshua), which are not yet concluded, and will probably undergo considerable modifications. It can only be superseded by another historical construction which is equally consistent and does justice to all the facts in the case.

WELLHAUSEN (formerly of Marburg, now of Göttingen, originally a disciple of Ewald): *History of Israel*, Berlin, 1878; 2d ed. under the title *Prolegomena to the History of Israel*, 1883; 3d ed. 1886; English translation with introduction by W. R. Smith, London, 1885. Comp. the abridgment in the art. "Israel" in the *Encycl. Brit.*, vol. xiii.

STADE (Giessen): *Geschichte des Volkes Israel*, Berlin, 1881 sqq.

KUENEN (Leiden, d. 1881): *The Worship of Israel*, Haarlem, 1875; *The Prophets and Prophecy in Israel*, Leiden, 1875; *Historico-Critical Introduction to the Old Testament*, Leiden, 1885 sqq. Translated, in part, from the Dutch.

RENAN: *History of the People of Israel*, Paris, 1887 sqq., 4 vols. Translated. Brilliant, but radical and secular.

ED. KÖNIG: *The Chief Problems of the Old Israelitic History*, Leipzig, 1884. He adopts the Wellhausen hypothesis, but without surrendering the inspiration and authority of the Old Testament.

KITTEL: *History of the Hebrews*, Gotha, 1888 sqq. Occupies a middle position and writes from the standpoint of universal history.

JAMES ROBERTSON (University of Glasgow): *The Early Religion of Israel*, Edinburgh and New York, 1892 (324 pp.). Conservative.

CHAPTER CLXX.

HISTORY OF BIBLICAL TIMES.

The History of Biblical Times is auxiliary to Biblical History, and supplies the frame-work to it. We may treat it as a whole, or divide it into History of Old Testament Times, and History of New Testament Times. The former deals with the heathen nations with whom the Jews came in contact from the time of Moses to the exile, and derives much material from the recent researches in Egyptology and Assyriology. The latter gives an account of the environments of Christ and the Apostles, and facilitates the understanding of the Gospels, Epistles and the Apocalypse. It has been recently raised to the dignity of a separate branch of Church history.

The History of New Testament Times proves that Christ appeared when "the time was fulfilled" (Mark 1:15; Gal. 4:4), that is, when the preparations for the coming of Christ among the Jews, Greeks, and Romans were completed, and when the world had reached the point of the greatest need of a Saviour. It shows that Christianity was fully adapted to the wants of the times in which it appeared, and yet cannot be derived from any of the then existing forces and circumstances. It was a new revelation, towards which all previous revelations of God and aspirations of men were tending. The religion of the Jews, the literature of Greece, and the polity and law of Rome contributed their share, but could not of themselves produce it.

The History of New Testament Times includes three parts:
1. The state of Judaism at the time of Christ and the Apostles.
2. The state of Heathenism in the Roman Empire at the same period.
3. The contact between Judaism and Græco-Roman Heathenism.

The chief sources on the political and moral condition of the Jews from the time of Malachi to the destruction of Jerusalem are the Jewish Apocrypha and the works of Josephus, especially his Archæology. The sources on the condition of the Roman Empire are the Greek and Roman classics, especially Tacitus.

LITERATURE: The History of Biblical Times (*Biblische Zeitgeschichte*), as a separate department, was founded by SCHNECKENBURGER (Professor in Bern, d. 1848), in his *Vorlesungen über die Neutestamentliche Zeitgeschichte* (posthumously edited by Löhlein, Frankf. 1862). HAUSRATH of Heidelberg followed with a larger work in four parts, under the same title (1868; 3d ed. 1879). SCHÜRER'S admirable *Lehrbuch der Neutestamentlichen Zeitgeschichte* (Leipzig, 1874) has been greatly enlarged in a second edition under the new title: *History of the Jewish People at the Time of Christ* (Leipzig, 1885 and 1890, 2 vols.; English translation, Edinburgh, 1885 sqq.). It is a masterpiece of exact critical learning, but confined to Jewish history. GEORGE P. FISHER (of Yale University, New Haven), in *The Beginnings of Christianity* (New York, 1877), covers in part the same ground, and enters also into the field of Gospel criticism.
Contributions to this department: WELLHAUSEN: *Pharisees and Sadducees* (1874). REYNOLDS: *John the Baptist* (1874). DELITZSCH on *Jesus and Hillel* (3d ed. 1879); and *A Day in Capernaum* (1871). WEBER: *System of the Palestinian Jewish Theology* (1880). PICK: *The Life of the Jews at the Time of Christ* (1881). LÜCIUS: *Essenism in its Relation to Judaism* (1881). MERRILL: *Galilee in the Time of Christ* (1885). STAPFER: *Palestine at the Time of Christ* (3d ed. Paris, 1885, also in English). DRUMMOND: *The Jewish Messiah* (1877). STANTON: *The Jewish and Christian Messiah* 1888).

CHAPTER CLXXI.

THE LIFE OF CHRIST.

Jesus Christ is the founder of Christianity. His life on earth is the fountain-head of its history. His advent marks the turning-point of ages, the end of the past, and the beginning of an endless future. He is the fulfiller of the law and the prophets, and of all the noble aspirations of heathendom, the Redeemer and Saviour of men. His person is the great moral miracle of history, and rises in solitary grandeur above the surrounding plane of a fallen and sinful race—the one only sinless and perfect man, in whom 'all the fullness of the Godhead dwelleth bodily" (Col. 2:9).

A biography of Christ is the most difficult task of the church historian. It was written by the Evangelists, only in fragments, but with unsurpassed simplicity, frankness, modesty and reverence; and it can never be done any better for the general reader and for practical purposes. All attempts to versify or beautify the gospel story are failures. It is above all poetry. But it must be written and rewritten for scholars as well as for the common people. Every age must renew for itself the picture of Christ, who is the inspiration of all ages and the model for all classes and conditions of men. He is, in the language of a distinguished man of letters, "our divinest symbol, a symbol of quite perennial, infinite character, whose significance will ever demand to be anew inquired into, and anew made manifest."*

The dogmatic theologian may construct his Christology in a descending line, beginning, like John, with the eternal Logos in the bosom of the Godhead, and coming down to the incarnation. But the historian must follow rather the Synoptical Gospels, which begin with the human genealogy of Jesus, as the son of Abraham and of Adam, thus connecting him with the Jewish race and the whole human family. He must endeavor to construct a truly human history of Jesus of Nazareth, from infancy to manhood, and mark the stages of his Messianic consciousness and his ethical development. Jesus lived, spoke, suffered and died like a man, and became in all things like unto us. "The child grew, and waxed strong, filled with wisdom: and the grace of God was upon him" (Luke 1:40). "He was tempted in all points, like as we are, yet without sin" (Heb. 4:15). "He was made perfect through sufferings. . . . In that he himself hath suffered, being tempted, he is able to succor them that are tempted" (Heb. 2:10, 18).

* Thomas Carlyle: *Sartor Resartus*, Book III., chapter 3. Neander (in the preface to his *Leben Jesu*) says: *"Das Christusbild ist das, was nicht von gestern und heute, doch immer mit der Menschheit sich verjüngt und mit neuer himmelanstrebender Jugendkraft die alternde Welt durchdringt."*

But we search in vain for any moral defect in his private or public character. All his biographers (even Strauss and Renan) admit that history presents no parallel to him, and that religion has never risen so high, nor is likely ever to rise higher than in the person of the Son of Mary. The perfection of Christ's humanity compels the recognition of his divinity, according to his own claim and the testimony of his disciples. The sinless Son of Man is truly the Son of God, and all his amazing claims become intelligible and consistent only on the basis of his divine origin and character. With this admission, his miraculous works appear to be the natural and necessary manifestations of his miraculous person.

> "Deep strike thy roots, O heavenly vine,
>   Within our earthly sod!
> Most human and yet most divine,
>   The flower of man and God!"

CHAPTER CLXXII.

LITERATURE ON THE LIFE OF CHRIST.

The life of Christ has always been the shining light of the Church, and the richest source of edification, comfort and worship. It has been reproduced, and will continue to be reproduced to the end of time, in countless sermons, books of devotion and works of art.

The "Harmonies" of the Gospels began in 170 with Tatian's Syrian *Diatessaron,* which has been recently recovered in an Arabic translation (1888). The first biographies of Christ were ascetic or poetic, and largely legendary, for edification.

The critical period was opened by the attacks of infidels in the last century (Reimarus and others), who revived the Jewish lie of the resurrection fraud (Matt. 28: 11–15). They occasioned the noble apologetic works of Hess (1774, 8th ed. 1823), Herder (1796), and Reinhard (*Der Plan Jesu,* 1781, 5th ed. 1830).

A most powerful impulse to the modern literature on the subject was given by the rationalistic theory of Paulus of Heidelberg (1828), which explains away the miracles of Christ as real but natural events and skillful medical cures; next by the mythical theory of D. F. Strauss (1835), which dissolves them into innocent poems of the religious imagination; and thirty years later by the legendary theory of E. Renan (1863), which lowers them to the level of incredible legends of mediæval hagiology, or an interesting romance, and, in the case of the resurrection of Lazarus, even resorts to the exploded hypothesis of imposture. Paulus, Strauss, and Renan agree only in their opposition to the supernatural, but otherwise refute each other. Indeed, it is a merit of Strauss that he has annihilated the theory of Paulus. Strauss wrote for German scholars, Renan for French novel-readers. Both combined genius and learning, and were masters of style.*

Their works created a great sensation and called forth a vast number of apologetic replies; these again were followed by independent books of more or less permanent value.

The chief biographies of Christ: *HASE (*Leben Jesu*, 1829, 5th ed. 1865, very valuable for its literature; and his *Geschichte Jesu*, 1875); SCHLEIERMACHER (1832, posthumously published, 1864, very unsatisfactory); STRAUSS (1835, 4th ed. 1840, 2 vols.; popular ed. 1864, 5th ed. 1889); *NEANDER (1837, 7th ed. 1873); *LANGE (1844–47, 3 vols.); VAN OOSTERZEE (Dutch, 1855–71, 3 vols.); EBRARD (1868); EWALD (1867); RENAN (1863, in many editions and translations); *PRESSENSÉ (1865, 7th ed. 1884); *KEIM (1867–72, 3 vols.); *ANDREWS (1863, revised 1891, unpretending, but very valuable in chronology and topology); *FARRAR (1874, in many edd.); GEIKIE (1878, several edd.); *WEISS (1882, 3d ed. 1888, Engl. trsl. in 3 vols.); *EDERSHEIM (1884, 2 vols.); STALKER (1884); *BEYSCHLAG (1885, 2d ed. 1888, 2 vols.); UHLHORN (*Das Leben Jesu in seinen neueren Darstellungen*, 4th ed. 1892; a review of the works of Renan, Strauss, Keim, Delff, Weiss, Beyschlag).

On the moral character of Christ, as an evidence of his divinity, ULLMANN: *The Sinlessness of Jesus* (1828, 7th ed. 1864, Engl. trsl. 1870); BUSHNELL: *The Character of Jesus Forbidding His Classification with Men* (1861); SEELEY: *Ecce Homo* (1864, several editions and translations); SCHAFF: *The Person of Christ* (1865, 12th ed. 1882, in several languages).

---

* It is noteworthy that these writers outlived the false theories which they represent. Strauss sank from an ideal Hegelian pantheism to a Darwinian materialism. Both he and Renan were pessimists, and lost, with their faith in Christ, all faith in immortality. They substituted a gospel of death for the gospel of resurrection. Strauss declared that the hereafter (*das Jenseits*) is the last enemy to be conquered by scientific criticism, and called the resurrection of our Saviour "the great world-humbug"; he died

CHAPTER CLXXIII.

THE APOSTOLIC AGE.

The period of the founding of Christianity by the inspired Apostles begins with the Day of Pentecost, A. D. 30, the birthday of the Christian Church, and ends with the death of St. John, about A. D. 100. It may be subdivided into three sections:

1. The founding of Christianity among the Jews, or the Jewish Christian Church, under the lead of St. Peter and with Jerusalem as its centre.

2. The founding of Christianity among the Greeks and Romans, or the Gentile Christian Church, under the lead of St. Paul, with Antioch as the starting-point and Rome as the termination and the place of the martyrdom of Peter and Paul.

3. The amalgamation and consolidation of Jewish and Gentile Christianity into one community, under the presiding genius of St. John, the apostle of love, who survived all the other apostles and continued at the head of the churches of Asia Minor till the reign of Trajan.

The Apostolic Age differs from all subsequent periods of the Church by the supernatural outfit of the Apostles, and the authoritative character of their writings, by which the Church must always be guided and, if necessary, reformed and reconstructed. The Apostolic Church has a prophetical and typical import; it anticipates, in its three stages of progress and types of doctrine, the whole subsequent development of Christianity. As the Jewish Church is a type of the Christian Church, so the Apostolic Church prefigures and foreshadows the history of Catholicism, Protestantism, and the Church of the future till the second Advent of Christ, who will reconcile all antagonisms and harmonize all discordant creeds.

like a Stoic, and was buried without any religious ceremony (1874). Renan, who was brought up for the priesthood, but ended in agnosticism, said to his wife a few hours before his death (October 2, 1892): "Be calm and resigned. We undergo the laws of that nature whereof we are a manifestation. We perish; we disappear; but heaven and earth remain, and the march of time goes on forever." He was buried in the Pantheon with Voltaire and Rousseau.

PATROLOGY AND PATRISTIC.   273

LITERATURE: Histories of the Apostolic Age by * NEANDER (1832, 5th ed. 1862; trsl.); THIERSCH (1852, 3d ed. 1879); EWALD (1858, 3d ed. 1868); RENAN (*Les Apôtres*, 1866; *St. Paul*, 1869; *L'Antechrist*, 1873); LANGE (1854); * LECHLER (3d ed. revised, 1857); G. P. FISHER (*The Beginnings of Christianity*, 1877); * WEIZSÄCKER (1886, 2d ed. 1892); PFLEIDERER (*Das Urchristenthum*, 1887); SCHAFF (separate *History of the Apostolic Church*, in German, 1851 and 1854; in English, 1853, etc.; also, as a new work, the first vol. of his general *Church History*, third revis. 1889); MCGIFFERT (in preparation).

Special works on Paul: PIERSON (*Annales Paul.*, 1688); PALEY (*Horæ Paulinæ*, 1790); * BAUR (1845, 2d ed. 1867, 2 vols.); * CONYBEARE and HOWSON (1853 and later edd.); * LEWIN (1875); * FARRAR (1879, 2 vols.); PFLEIDERER (1885); SABATIER (1887); * G. R. STEVENS (1892).

The recent critical reconstruction of the history of the Apostolic Age is represented by two schools, the one headed by Neander in Germany and Lightfoot in England, the other by Baur of Tübingen and Renan of France. See a *résumé* in Schaff's *Church History*, Vol. I., pp. 207-217 and 853-863 (third revision, 1889); and Lightfoot's *Dissertations on the Apostolic Age*, 1892.

CHAPTER CLXXIV.

PATROLOGY AND PATRISTIC.

(Altchristliche Literatur-Geschichte.)

I. Definition. Patrology, or Patristic, is a biographical and literary account of the Christian Fathers and ecclesiastical writers during the Græco-Roman age of Christianity, *i. e.*, during the first six or seven centuries, before the separation of the Eastern and Western Churches. It is a history of ancient Christian literature. It includes also an exposition of the doctrinal and ethical opinions of the Fathers. It begins with the Apostolic Fathers, so called, at the close of the first century, and ends with Gregory I. (d. 604) in the West, and with John of Damascus (d. about 750) in the East.

Sometimes a distinction is made between Patristic and Patrology; in this case the former (*patristica doctrina* or *theologia*) is confined to the theological and doctrinal, the latter to the biographical and literary part. But they cannot be separated.

II. Division. Patristic embraces:

1. The APOSTOLIC FATHERS, *i. e.*, the immediate disciples of the Apostles, who flourished at the end of the first and the beginning of the second century and present a faint echo of the age of inspiration. Clement of Rome, Polycarp, Ignatius

(and pseudo-Ignatius), Barnabas, Papias, Hermas, the anonymous author of the beautiful Epistle to Diognetus, and the unknown writer of *The Teaching of the Twelve Apostles.*

2. The ANTE-NICENE FATHERS, or the apologists and theologians of the second and third centuries, who were chiefly engaged in the defense of Christianity against Jews and Gentiles, and the refutation of the Ebionite and Gnostic heresies.

(*a*) Greek Church: Aristides (under Hadrian), Justin Martyr (d. 166), Irenæus (d. 202), Hippolytus (d. 236), Clement of Alexandria (d. 220), Origen (d. 254), Methodius (d. 311), and others of less importance. Of these, Irenæus is the soundest divine, Origen the greatest thinker and scholar.

(*b*) Latin Church: Tertullian (d. about 220), Cyprian (d. 258), Minutius Felix, Arnobius. Tertullian is the most vigorous and independent thinker, Cyprian the most churchly character.

3. The NICENE FATHERS of the fourth century, who chiefly developed and defended the doctrines of the Trinity and the Incarnation in the Arian conflict from 325 to 381.

(*a*) Greek Church: Eusebius (the historian, d. 340), Athanasius ("the father of orthodoxy," d. 373), Gregory Nazianzen ("the theologian," d. 391), Gregory of Nyssa (d. 395), Basil the Great (d. 379), Cyril of Jerusalem (d. 386), Chrysostom (the prince of pulpit orators, d. 407), Epiphanius (the zealot for orthodoxy, d. 403).

(*b*) Latin Church: Hilary of Poictiers (the "Athanasius of the West," d. 368), Ambrose of Milan (d. 397).

4. The POST-NICENE FATHERS, who developed the orthodox christology and the fundamental doctrines of Christian anthropology and soteriology.

(*a*) Greek Church: Cyril of Alexandria (d. 444), Theodoret (d. 458), John of Damascus (d. 754).

(*b*) Latin Church: Jerome (d. 419), Augustin (d. 430), Leo the Great (d. 604), Gregory the Great (d. 604).

III. Value. The Fathers laid the foundations for theological literature. They were the first commentators, the first apologists, the first controversialists, the first homilists. Their position near the source of Christianity gives them a special importance as early witnesses. But they are far inferior to the apostolic grandfathers, and must be judged by the Scriptures, like all other divines. The New Testament alone is worth more than all the patristic and scholastic works put together.

To read all the Fathers is a task which can only be expected from the professional historian, and would be an idle waste of time for the ordinary student. But some knowledge of them is indispensable. Every student ought to read select works, such as the *Didache*, the Epistle of Clement to the Corinthians, the Epistle of Polycarp, the Epistles of Ignatius, the Epistle to Diognetus, the *Apologies* of Justin Martyr; the *Apologeticus* of Tertullian, Cyprian's *Unity of the Church*, Origen *Against Celsus*, Eusebius's *Church History*, Augustin's *Confessions* and his *City of God*, and some *Homilies* of Chrysostom.

NOTES.

1. The title CHURCH FATHER is given to those divines of the early ages who excelled in learning, judgment, piety, and orthodoxy; but in a wider sense it is also extended to other ecclesiastical writers of merit and distinction. The line of the Greek Fathers is closed with John of Damascus (d. 754), the line of the Latin usually with Gregory I. (d. 604); but the latter is sometimes extended so as to embrace the most distinguished schoolmen and mystics, as St. Anselm, St. Thomas Aquinas, St. Bernard, and St. Bonaventura.

2. The Roman Church makes a distinction between PATER ECCLESIÆ, DOCTOR ECCLESIÆ, and AUCTOR ECCLESIASTICUS. This distinction is more or less arbitrary, and made without regard to literary merit, in the interest of Roman orthodoxy.

(*a*) PATRES ECCLESIÆ are all ancient teachers who combine *antiquitas, doctrina orthodoxa, sanctitas vitæ,* and *approbatio ecclesiæ* (which may be expressed, or silent). These requisites, however, are only imperfectly combined even in the most eminent of the Fathers. Some excel in learning (Origen, Jerome); some in piety (Polycarp); some in orthodoxy (Irenæus, Athanasius, Leo I.); some in genius, vigor, and depth (Tertullian, Augustin); some in eloquence (Chrysostom); but none could stand the test of Roman orthodoxy of the Tridentine, still less of the Vatican or Ultramontane stamp, and many of them would have to be condemned as heretics. This is especially the case with the Fathers of the ante-Nicene age. See Schaff's *Church History*, Vol. I., pp. 625 sqq.

(*b*) DOCTORES ECCLESIÆ are the most authoritative of the Church Fathers, who in addition to the above requisites excel in learning (*eminens eruditio*) and have the express approbation of the Church (*expressa ecclesiæ declaratio*). See the bull of Benedict XIV., 1754: "*Militantis ecclesiæ*."

Greek Church doctors: Athanasius, Basil the Great, Gregory Nazianzen, Chrysostom, Cyril of Alexandria, John of Damascus. Latin Church doctors: Ambrose, Augustin, Jerome, Leo the Great, Gregory the Great, also Hilary of Poictiers, Anselm, Bernard of Clairvaux, Thomas Aquinas, Bonaventura, to whom have been added more recently Alfonso da Liguori (1871), and Francis of Sales (1877).

(*c*) AUCTORES ECCLESIASTICI: those who are less important for didactic theology, or who held questionable or heterodox opinions, as Tertullian,

Clement of Alexandria, Origen, Eusebius, Arnobius, Lactantius, Theodoret. Among these are some of the most learned and useful of the Fathers, especially Tertullian, Origen, and Eusebius.

CHAPTER CLXXV.

PATRISTIC LITERATURE.

The patristic literature is exceedingly rich. It began with ST. JEROME'S *Catalogue of Illustrious Men* (*De Viris Illustribus*), which comprises, in 135 numbers, brief notices of the biblical and ecclesiastical authors from St. Peter down to Jerome, and was completed in 393. It was continued by GENNADIUS about 490.*

Patristic learning has been cultivated mostly by Roman Catholic and Anglican scholars during the seventeenth century, in the apologetic or polemic interest of using the Fathers as witnesses for or against disputed doctrines and institutions.

The principal older writers on Patristic are:

1. Roman Catholics: BELLARMIN (1613), *TILLEMONT (1693), DUPIN (1715), CEILLIER (1763), LUMPER (1799), MÖHLER (1840), FESSLER (1852).

2. Protestants: SUICER (1682), CAVE (1698), OUDIN (1722), *FABRICIUS (the most learned and most useful of bibliographers, d. 1736), J. G. WALCH (1770), SCHÖNEMANN (1792).

RECENT DISCOVERIES.

Important discoveries have been made since about 1850 in biblical and ecclesiastical literature and antiquities, which supersede in large part older works and require a reconstruction and completion of the Patristic history of ante-Nicene Christianity.

The *Codex Sinaiticus* of the Greek Bible, with the Greek Barnabas and the Greek Hermas, found by Prof. Tischendorf on Mt. Sinai, 1859, and published 1863. In connection with this discovery may be mentioned the photographic facsimile edition of the *Codex Vaticanus* at Rome, 1889 (which was imperfectly known before). These two oldest known uncial manuscripts are the chief sources of the latest critical editions of the Greek Testament by Tischendorf, Tregelles, Westcott and Hort, and of the Anglo-American Revision of 1881.

The *Philosophumena* of HIPPOLYTUS of Rome, edited by Duncker and Schneidewin, 1859. They shed much light on ancient heresies and the commotions in the Roman Church at the beginning of the third century.

The Commentary of HIPPOLYTUS on *Daniel* has been made better known to us by the fourth book, which was discovered and first published by Prof. Georgiades at Athens, in 1885, and again by J. H. Kennedy in 1888, and last by Prof. Ed. Bratke, in Bonn, in 1891, with introduction and notes. Hippolytus was a millennarian, like most of the Ante-Nicene Fathers, but at the close he warns against fanatical expectations and

---

* Both are translated by E. C. Richardson in Schaff and Wace's *Library of Nicene and Post-Nicene Fathers*, Vol. III., pp. 353–402 (1892).

chronological calculations of a *near* approach of the millennium, since Christ would not come before the close of the sixth millennium of the world. In this connection he notices incidentally the date of the nativity and crucifixion. He says (in Bratke's edition, p. 19): "The first advent of the Lord in the flesh by his birth in Bethlehem took place on the 25th of December, on a Wednesday, in the 42d year of Augustus, or 5500, dating from Adam. He suffered in his 33d year, on the 25th of March, on a Friday, in the 18th year of Tiberius, under the consuls Rufus and Rubellius." Consequently he put off the second advent to the year 500 after Christ's birth, i.e., to A. M. 6000, when the seventh millennium, or the great world's Sabbath (Rev. 20:1-6) will begin.

The Tenth Book of the *Pseudo-Clementine Homilies*, first published by Dressel, 1853. It supplements our knowledge of a curious type of distorted Christianity in the post-apostolic age, and furnishes, by an undoubted quotation, a valuable contribution to the solution of the Johannean problem.

The Greek HERMAS from Mt. Athos (the *Codex Lipsiensis*), published by Anger and Tischendorf, 1856.

A new and complete Greek manuscript of the *First Epistle* of the Roman CLEMENT, with several important new chapters, and the oldest written Christian prayer (about one-tenth of the whole). It was found in the Constantinopolitan or Hierosolymitan Codex belonging to the library of the Greek patriarch of Jerusalem (whose chief residence is at Constantinople) by Bryennios, 1873, and first published by him in 1875. The *Second* (falsely so called) *Epistle* of CLEMENT in its complete form (twenty chapters instead of twelve), found by the same scholar, in the same Codex. It is a post-Clementine homily, and gives us the first post-apostolic sermon.

A new Greek text of the *Epistle* of BARNABAS in the same Codex, which has since been transferred to Jerusalem.

A Syriac Version of CLEMENT in the library of Jules Mohl, now at Cambridge (1876).

The *Didache*, or *Teaching of the Twelve Apostles*, the most interesting and valuable of the post-apostolic writings, by an unknown author, probably of Syria, at the end of the first or the beginning of the second century, discovered by Bryennios in 1873, and first published in 1884. It created an unusual sensation, and called forth a small library of books (see the literature in Schaff's edition, pp. 140 sqq.).

TATIAN's *Diatessaron* (the first Harmony of the Gospels), in an Arabic Version, discovered and published by Ciasca, 1888. Fragments of it, in an Armenian Version, with EPHRAEM's *Commentary* on it, had been previously discovered and published in Latin by Mösinger, 1878

A Syriac translation of the *Apology* of ARISTIDES, found at Mt. Sinai, by J. R. Harris, 1889. This Apology has been identified with the Greek text in *The Lives of Barlaam and Josaphat* (edited by J. A. Robinson, 1891).

Fragments of the apocryphal *Gospel* and *Apocalypse* of PETER, discovered in Upper Egypt, 1887, published by Bouriant, Paris, 1392, and by Harnack, with notes, Leipzig, 1893. Facsimile ed. by O. v. Gebhardt, 1893.

A palimpsest of a *Syriac translation of the Gospels*, discovered by Mrs. A. S. Lewis in the Convent of St. Catherine on Mt. Sinai, February, 1892.

The modern researches in the Roman Catacombs by CAVALIER DE ROSSI, GARRUCCI, PARKER, ROLLER, and LANCIANI are important for a knowledge of the humble life and pious death of the ancient Christians in the times of persecution, and for the beginnings of Christian art.

For new discoveries or critical discussions of old Christian literature, see OSCAR VON GEBHARDT and ADOLF HARNACK: *Texte und Untersuchungen zur Geschichte der Altchristlichen Literatur.* Leipzig, 1882 sqq.

SOURCES—THE WORKS OF THE FATHERS.

The Benedictine editions of the Fathers, repeatedly published in Paris and Venice, are the best so far as they go, but need supplementing and correcting from more recent researches and discoveries.

Abbé MIGNE (1800–75): *Patrologiæ Cursus Completus,* etc. Petit Montrouge (near Paris), 1844–66, new ed. since 1878. The cheapest and most complete, but not the most critical, patristic library, reaching down to the thirteenth century, the Latin in 222 vols., the Greek in 167 vols., reprinted from the Benedictine and other good editions, with Prolegomena, Vitæ, Dissertations, Supplements, etc. Some of the plates were consumed by fire in 1868, but have been replaced. To be used with caution. The work is continued by Abbé HOROY and is to be brought down to the Council of Trent, in the *Medii Ævi Bibliotheca Patristica, ab anno* 1216 *ad Conc. Trid.,* Paris, 1879 sqq. But this continuation belongs to mediæval Church history.

Corpus Scriptorum Ecclesiasticorum Latinorum, published by the Imperial Academy of Vienna and edited by a number of scholars, Vienna, 1866 sqq. More critical than Migne but not complete.

Separate Editions of the Apostolic Fathers.

J. B. LIGHTFOOT (late Lord Bishop of Durham, and the best patristic scholar in the Church of England): *The Apostolic Fathers.* Edited and completed by J. R. Harmer, London and New York (Macmillan & Co.), 1891. The Greek text with English translations and brief introductions, in 568 pp. It includes the *Didache,* without which no edition of the Apostolic Fathers, hereafter, can be complete. The most convenient edition for students.—Also the *Editio minor* of O. von Gebhardt, Harnack and Zahn.

Larger editions, with notes, by BP. HEFELE (R. Cath.), continued by FUNK (5th ed. 1878–81, 2 vols.); O. VON GEBHARDT, HARNACK and ZAHN (2d ed. 1878, 3 vols.); JACOBSON (2 vols.); and especially the monumental editions of the three chief Apostolic Fathers, by BP. LIGHTFOOT, namely: *St. Clement of Rome* (1869, 2d ed. 1890, 2 vols.); *St. Ignatius* and *St. Polycarp* (1885, 2d ed. 1891, 3 vols., a complete *Corpus Ignatianum*).

Separate editions of *The Teaching of the Twelve Apostles* (briefly called *The Didache*), by BRYENNIOS (Greek, Constantinople, 1884); HARNACK (German, Leipzig, 1884); SCHAFF (English, New York, 1885; 3d ed. revised, 1889); and JACQUIER (French, Lyons, 1892). A facsimile of the text was published by J. RENDEL HARRIS at Baltimore (Johns Hopkins University), 1887.

The works of the *Apologists* have been edited by OTTO (3d ed. 1876, 9 vols.); a new edition by O. VON GEBHARDT and E. SCHWARTZ is in course of preparation (Leipzig. 1888 sqq.).

English Translations of the Fathers.

The Oxford *Library of the Fathers of the Holy Catholic Church, anterior to the Division of the East and West.* Translated by Members of the English Church, Oxford (1837 sqq., 48 vols.). Edited by DRS. PUSEY, NEWMAN, KEBLE, and CHARLES MARRIOTT (chiefly by PUSEY and MARRIOTT) in the interest of the Tractarian or Anglo-Catholic School. Unfinished.

The *Ante-Nicene Christian Library,* edited by ROBERTS and DONALDSON (Edinburgh, 1866–72, 24 vols.); republished, with additions, by the Christian Literature Co., under the editorship of BISHOP A. CLEVELAND COXE (New York, 1886, 8 vols.).

A Select Library of the Nicene and Post-Nicene Fathers. In two series, published by the Christian Literature Co., New York and Oxford, 1886 sqq. The first series, edited by PHILIP SCHAFF, embraces the works of Augustin in 8 vols., and of Chrysostom in 6 vols. The second series, edited by PHILIP SCHAFF and HENRY WACE, now in course of publication, will embrace in 13 or 14 vols. the works of the other Fathers from Eusebius to John of Damascus (4 vols. were published till 1892, embracing, I., Eusebius; II., Socrates and Sozomenus; III., Theodoret, Jerome, and Rufinus; and IV., Athanasius).

PATRISTIC MANUALS.

ALZOG (R. Cath., d. 1878): *Grundriss der Patrologie oder der älteren christl. Literärgeschichte* (Freiburg, 1866; 4th ed. 1888).

NIRSCHL (R. Cath.): *Lehrbuch der Patrologie und Patristik* (Mainz, 1881–85, 3 vols.).

*ADOLF HARNACK (aided by PREUSCHEN): *Geschichte der Altchristlichen Litteratur bis Eusebius* (1st Part, Leipzig, 1893, pp. 1020).

PATRISTIC BIOGRAPHIES.

WM. SMITH and HENRY WACE (Anglicans): *A Dictionary of Christian Biography, Literature, Sects and Doctrines during the first eight centuries* (London, 1877–87, 4 vols.). By far the best patristic biographical dictionary in the English or any other language. A noble monument of the learning of the Church of England. Indispensable to scholars.

FREDERIC W. FARRAR (Archdeacon, Evangelical Broad-Church): *Lives of the Fathers. Sketches of Church History in Biographies* (London and New York, 1889, 2 vols.).

The Fathers for English Readers. A series of popular biographies in small volumes, published by the "Society for Promoting Christian Knowledge," London and New York, 1879.

PHILIP SCHAFF: *St. Chrysostom and St. Augustin* (New York, 1891).

CHAPTER CLXXVI.

CHRISTIAN ARCHÆOLOGY.

(Comp. pp. 140 sqq.)

Christian Archæology, or Ecclesiastical Antiquities, embraces an account (fuller than Church History can give) of the institutions, creeds, liturgies, laws, canons, rites, and ceremonies of the ancient undivided Church of the East and the West. It is usually confined to the first six centuries, but sometimes carried down to the age of Charlemagne or even later.

Christian or Ecclesiastical Archæology occupies the same position and answers the same purpose in Church History as Biblical or Jewish Archæology does in exegetical literature. Works of this sort may also be arranged in alphabetical order for more convenient reference.

LITERATURE.

* JOSEPH BINGHAM (Anglican, 1668–1723): *Origines Ecclesiasticæ*, or *The Antiquities of the Christian Church* (new ed. by Pitman, London, 1840, 7 vols.). Still very valuable.

BINTERIM (R. Cath.): *Denkwürdigkeiten der christl.-kathol. Kirche aus der ersten, mittleren und letzten Zeit* (Mainz, 1825 sqq., 7 vols; 2d ed. 1830–40).

K. CH. F. SIEGEL: *Handbuch der christlich-kirchlichen Alterthümer in alphabetischer Ordnung* (Leipzig, 1835–38, 4 Bände).

J. A. MARTIGNY (R. Cath.): *Dictionnaire des antiquités chrétiennes*, etc. (Paris, 1848; new ed. 1877). With illustrations.

* WM. SMITH and S. CHEETHAM: *Dictionary of Christian Antiquities, being a continuation of the Dictionary of the Bible* (London, 1875–80, 2 vols.).

F. X. KRAUS (R. Cath.): *Real-Encyklopädie der christlichen Alterthümer. Unter Mitwirkung mehrerer Fachgenossen.* With illustrations, mostly taken from Martigny (Freiburg, 1882–86, 2 vols.).

* CHARLES W. BENNETT (Methodist): *Christian Archæology.* With an introductory notice by Dr. Piper (New York, 1888).

CHAPTER CLXXVII.

THE REFORMATION.

The Reformation of the sixteenth century is, next to the Apostolic Age, by far the most important and interesting part of Church History. It was a revival of primitive Christianity, and an assertion of the freedom and purity of the gospel against the tyranny of ecclesiastical tradition and corruption. It is the turning-point from the Middle Ages to modern times. It is the formative period of the Evangelical denominations, when the principles and institutions of Protestantism were elaborated in opposition to the papacy.

The Reformation extends, on the Continent, from A.D. 1517 to the Peace of Westphalia in 1648, which secured the legal existence of the Lutheran and Reformed Churches in the German Empire. In England, it extends to the Westminster Assembly of 1648, or rather to the Toleration Act in 1689, which gave legal existence to orthodox Dissenters.

The sixteenth century is also the time of the papal counter-Reformation under the lead of Jesuitism and the Council of Trent. It was then that mediæval Catholicism was consolidated and contracted into Romanism in opposition to the evangelical doctrines of the Reformers. In the further course of its development, it eliminated also Jansenism, Gallicanism, and other liberal tendencies, and culminated in the Vatican decree of an absolute and infallible papacy. Hence modern ultramontane Romanism, while far better than at the time of the Reformation, at least in Protestant countries and under the stimulus of Protestant energy, is in principle more opposed to Protestantism than ever before.

Since the Reformation the Christianity of Europe runs in two distinct channels: the Protestant, which represents liberty and progress, and the Roman Catholic, which represents authority and conservatism. This separation is broader and deeper than the separation of the Latin from the Greek Church in the ninth century.

The schism of the sixteenth century became the fruitful mother of other divisions. At first the Reformation resulted in three orthodox evangelical Churches: the Lutheran, the Reformed (Calvinistic), and the Anglican; while the more radical sects of the Anabaptists, Socinians, etc., were persecuted by Protestants and Romanists alike. After the long struggle between Puritanism and Prelacy in England, which was a second Reformation, and after the expulsion of the semi-popish dynasty of the Stuarts through the peaceful Revolution of 1683, the Toleration Act of May 24, 1689, gave partial relief to the Dissenters or Nonconformists and allowed them to form independent and self-governing church organizations.

From that time English Church History is divided into several denominational channels: Episcopalians, Presbyterians, Congregationalists, Baptists, Quakers; to whom were afterwards added Methodists, Unitarians, Universalists, and others. The principle of toleration was at first very limited, and denied altogether to Romanists and Socinians; but it gradually developed into the principle of religious freedom and legal equality, which is making steady progress in Europe, and was fully carried out in the United States. Toleration is a grant of the government, and implies disapproval or censure; liberty is a gift of God, and an inalienable right of every man. Turkey and Russia are tolerant towards religions which they despise, but cannot exterminate and must tolerate as a nuisance. England and America respect and protect the freedom of every man to worship God according to the dictates of his conscience. This is the legitimate result of the Reformation, though it took three centuries to bring it about.*

The great counter-movements of Romanism and Protestantism, and the rival movements of Protestant denominations are still in progress, with no apparent approach to a reconciliation, but with a multiplication of agencies for the conversion of the whole world to Christ. Providence has great surprises in store for the future. We may hope for a higher, deeper, and broader reformation, and a new pentecostal effusion of the holy spirit of wisdom and love, which will unite what the sin and folly of man have divided. Christ's prophecy of one flock under one shepherd must and will be fulfilled in God's own good time.

LITERATURE.

I. *Protestant Works on the Reformation.*

The chief sources are the works of the Reformers: LUTHER, MELANCHTHON, BUCER, ZWINGLI, BULLINGER, CALVIN, BEZA, CRANMER, KNOX.

GIESELER, in his *Church History* (Vols. IV. and V. of the English translation) gives a good sketch of the Reformation, with extracts from the sources.

K. R. HAGENBACH (d. 1874): *Geschichte der Reformation, vorzüglich in Deutschland und der Schweiz* (5th ed. edited by Nippold, 1887). Part of his *General Church History*. English translation by Miss Eveline Moore (Edinburgh, 1878, 2 vols.).

---

* Tolerance is a virtue and an element of Christian charity, but toleration is an intolerable insult to the divine right of religious freedom. Lord Stanhope (in a speech in the House of Lords in 1827, on the bill for the repeal of the Test and Corporation Acts) said: "The time was when toleration was craved by Dissenters as a boon; it is now demanded as a right; but a time will come when it will be spurned as an insult."

MERLE D'AUBIGNÉ (d. 1872) : *Histoire de la réformation du 16me siècle* (Paris, 1835–53, 5 vols. ; 4th ed. 1861 sqq.). Extends to 1531. By the same : *Histoire de la réformation en Europe au temps du Calvin* (Paris, 1863–78, 8 vols., including a posthumous volume). Extends to 1542. Translated into German by Runkel (Stuttgart, 1848 sqq.). Several English editions (some of them mutilated), the best published by Longmans, Green & Co. (London, 1865 sqq.) and republished by Robert Carter & Bros. (New York, 1870–79), the first work in 5, the second in 8 vols. The first division of Merle's *History of the Reformation*, owing to its evangelical fervor, intense Protestantism, and dramatic eloquence, has had an enormous circulation in England and America by means of the Tract Societies and private publishers.

LEOPOLD VON RANKE (d. 1886) : *Deutsche Geschichte im Zeitalter der Reformation* (6th ed. Leipzig, 1881, 6 vols.). A standard work from the standpoint of secular history. English translation in part.

L. HÄUSSER (d. 1867) *Geschichte des Zeitalters der Reformation*, 1517–1648. Edited by Oncken (Berlin, 1868, 867 pp.). Abridged English translation by Mrs. Sturge (New York, 1874).

GEO. P. FISHER (Prof. of Church History in Yale College): *The Reformation* (New York, 1873; also in 1891). A comprehensive work, clear, calm, judicial, with a useful bibliographical Appendix (pp. 567–591).

GEORG WEBER: *Das Zeitalter der Reformation* (new ed., Leipzig, 1886; the 10th vol. of his *Weltgeschichte*).

CHARLES BEARD (Unitarian, d. 1888): *The Reformation in its Relation to Modern Thought and Knowledge*, Hibbert Lectures (London, 1883; 2d ed. 1885). Liberal and able. German translation by F. Halverscheid (Berlin, 1884).

G. EGELHAAF: *Deutsche Geschichte im Zeitalter der Reformation* (Halle, 1885). In the spirit of Ranke, with polemical reference to Janssen; it extends from 1517 to the Peace of Augsburg, 1555 (450 pp.).

FR. VON BEZOLD: *Geschichte der deutschen Reformation* (Berlin, 1886).

L. KELLER: *Die Reformation und die älteren Reformparteien* (Leipzig, 1885). In sympathy with the Waldenses and Anabaptists.

PHILIP SCHAFF: *History of the Christian Church*; Vol. VI., the German Reformation (New York and Edinb., 1889); Vol. VII., the Swiss Reformation (1892). Full lists of the Reformation literature in Vol. VI., pp. 89–97 and 99–105; Vol. VII., 12–20 and 223–232.

Biographies of the Reformers:

Leben und ausgewählte Schriften der Väter und Begründer der luther. Kirche, herausgeg. von J. HARTMANN *u. A., eingeleitet von* K. J. NITZSCH (Elberfeld, 1861–83, 10 vols., including KÖSTLIN'S *Luther*, which was published last).

Leben und ausgewählte Schriften der Väter und Begründer der reformirten Kirche, herausgeg. von J. W. BAUM, R. CHRISTOFFEL, K. R. HAGENBACH, *und A., eingeleitet von K. R. Hagenbach* (Elberfeld, 1857–63, 10 vols.).

The best biographies of Luther by JULIUS KÖSTLIN (large ed. in 2 vols., 1883, small ed. in 1 vol., with illustrations; English translation, 1883); of Zwingli by MÖRIKOFER (1869, 2 vols.); of Calvin by P. HENRY (1835–44, 3 vols.); STÄHELIN (1863, 2 vols.) and KAMPSCHULTE (1872, unfinished); of

Cranmer by STRYPE (*Memorials by Cranmer*, new ed. 1840); of Knox by THOS. MCCRIE (1841) and WM. TAYLOR (1885).

II. *Roman Catholic Works on the Protestant Reformation.*

IGNATIUS DÖLLINGER (Prof. of Church History in Munich, since 1870 Old Catholic, d. 1891): *Die Reformation, ihre innere Entwicklung und ihre Wirkung im Umfange des Luther. Bekenntnisses* (Regensburg, 1846-48, 3 vols.; 2d ed. 1853). A learned collection of testimonies against the Reformation and its effects from contemporary apostates, humanists, and the Reformers themselves (Luther and Melanchthon), and those of their followers who complain bitterly of the decay of morals and the dissensions in the Lutheran Church. The author has, nevertheless, after he seceded from the Roman communion, passed a striking judgment in favor of Luther's greatness (quoted in Schaff's *Church History*, VI. 742).

JOH. JANSSEN (d. 1892): *Geschichte des deutschen Volkes seit dem Ausgang des Mittelalters* (Freiburg i. B. 1876-88, 6 vols.), down to the beginning of the Thirty Years' War, 1618. This masterpiece of ultramontane historiography is a counterpart of Ranke's work, and is written with great learning and ability from a variety of sources (especially the archives of Frankfurt, Mainz, Trier, Zürich, and the Vatican). It soon passed through twelve editions, and called out able defences of the Reformation by Kawerau, Köstlin, Lenz, Schweizer, Ebrard, Baumgarten, and others, to whom Janssen calmly replied in *An meine Kritiker* (Freiburg i. B., tenth thousand, 1883, 227 pp.), and *Ein zweites Wort an meine Kritiker* (Freiburg i. B., twelfth thousand, 1883, 144 pp.). He disclaims all "tendency," and professes to aim only at the historical truth. Admitted, but his *standpoint* is false, because he views the main current of modern history as an apostasy and failure; while it is an onward and progressive movement of Christianity under the guidance of Divine Providence and the ever-present spirit of its Founder. He reads history through the mirror of Vatican Romanism. Pope Leo XIII. has praised Janssen as "a light of historic science and a man of profound learning."

III. *The Papal Counter-Reformation.*

The chief sources are the polemical writings of ECK, COCHLÆUS, EMSER, PIGHIUS; the *Regesta* of Leo X., ed. by Hergenröther; the *Monumenta Reform. Lutheranæ* (1821-25), ed. from the papal archives by Balan, 1884; and the *Acts of the Council of Trent*, collected by Le Plat (*Monumenta ad Hist. Conc. Trid.*, 1781-87, 7 vols.).

L. V. RANKE (Prot.): *Die römischen Päpste in den letzten vier Jahrhunderten* (1834; 8th ed. Leipzig, 1885, 3 vols.). A standard work on the revival of the papacy among the Romanic nations from the Protestant standpoint.

MANDELL CREIGHTON (Anglican): *History of the Papacy during the Period of the Reformation* (London, 1882-87, 4 vols.). Includes the earlier period of the Renaissance.

LUDWIG PASTOR (R. Cath.): *Geschichte der Päpste seit dem Ausgang des Mittelalters* (Freiburg i. B., 1886 sqq.; to be completed in 6 vols.). A counterpart of Ranke's *Popes*, as Janssen is of his *Germany* in the period of the Reformation; a standard work of modern ultramontane historiography, equal to Janssen's *History of Germany*. Pastor includes, like Creighton, the popes of the Renaissance.

WILHELM MAURENBRECHER (Prot., d. 1892): *Geschichte der katholischen Reformation* (Nördlingen, Vol. I., 1880).

The histories of the Council of Trent (Sarpi and Pallavicino) and the literature on the order of the Jesuits.

CHAPTER CLXXVIII.

AMERICAN CHURCH HISTORY.—ROMAN CATHOLIC AMERICA.

"Westward the course of empire takes its way;
  The four first acts already past,
A fifth shall close the drama with the day;
  Time's noblest offspring is the last."
                    BISHOP BERKELEY.

America is the middle continent, looking eastward to Europe and Africa, and westward to Asia and Australia.

Providence has divided the Western Hemisphere between the Latin and the Teutonic races, and assigned to the former the southern, to the latter the northern half of the continent. The South is almost entirely Roman Catholic, the North predominantly Protestant, as in Europe.

The history of the Roman Church in America may be divided into three periods: Spanish, French, and modern Anglo-American (in the United States).

Spanish America.

American Church History, in the widest sense, begins with the discovery of America at the end of the Middle Ages, a quarter of a century before the Reformation. Christopher Columbus[*] was an ambitious adventurer, an avaricious gold-hunter, and a cruel despot, but also a great explorer, a devout Catholic, and a religious enthusiast. He believed in the existence of a new world, and he found it in spite of the combined opposition of ignorance, prejudice, and bigotry. All things are possible to faith, and nothing great and good is possible without faith. True to his name, "Christbearer," he planted the cross on the first island he discovered (October 12, 1492), and called it *San Salvador* in honor of the Saviour. He hoped to apply the profits of his discovery to a new crusade for the res-

[*] An Italian by birth (*Cristoforo Colombo*), a Spaniard by adoption (*Christóbal Colón*), a cosmopolitan by mission and merit. America ought to have been called *Columbia*.

cue of Jerusalem from the tyranny of the Turks. He concludes his first letter, after his return from the first voyage, addressed to Gabriel Sanchez, Treasurer of the King of Spain, with this eloquent appeal:

"Therefore let the king and queen, the princes and their most fortunate kingdoms, and all other countries of Christendom give thanks to our Lord and Saviour Jesus Christ, who has bestowed upon us so great a victory and gift. Let religious processions be solemnized; let sacred festivals be given; let the churches be covered with festive garments. Let Christ rejoice on earth as he rejoices in heaven, when he foresees coming to salvation so many souls of people hitherto lost. Let us be glad also, as well on account of the exaltation of our faith, as on account of the increase of our temporal affairs, of which not only Spain, but universal Christendom, will be partaker. These things that have been done are thus briefly related. Farewell.

"Lisbon, the day before the Ides of March [March 14, 1493]." *

His royal patron, Isabella the Catholic, whom Shakespeare calls "the queen of earthly queens," pledged her jewels for his enterprise, in the prospect of extending the kingdom of Christ as well as that of Spain, and ordered that the Indians should be treated with the utmost kindness and carefully instructed in religion.

The West India Islands, Mexico and Peru, and all the countries of Central and South America, were discovered and peopled by Spaniards and Portuguese, and were nominally converted to the Roman Catholic faith. Unfortunately, the conversion was darkened by the curse of filthy lucre and by atrocious cruelties to the innocent natives. An Indian chief of Cuba declared before he was burned alive, that gold was the real god of the Christians, and he refused the offer of a place in heaven if Spaniards should be found there. But we must not forget the noble Christian philanthropy of Bartholomeo de las Casas, "the apostle of the Indies," and the unselfish devotion of the Dominican and Franciscan missionaries who have earned a place among the heroes and martyrs of the Christian Church.

The Spanish missions, radiating from Mexico, extended across the continent from Florida to California. The oldest city in the present (not in the original) territory of the United States is St. Augustine, in Florida, which was founded in 1565,

* See the translation of *The Letter of Columbus on the Discovery of America, a facsimile of the Pictorial Edition; printed by order of the Trustees of the Lenox Library* (New York, 1892, p. 12).

forty-two years before the settlement of Jamestown, in Virginia (1607); but Florida is spotted with the first Protestant blood shed on American soil. An ominous beginning of sectarian strife.*

The Roman Church thus gained a vastly larger territory in America than she lost in Europe through the Protestant Reformation.

But the conquests of Spain north of Mexico were of short duration. Spain ceded Florida to the United States in 1819; Mexico lost Texas in 1845, and California and New Mexico in 1848.

Alexander VI. (a Spaniard, and the most wicked of popes) made a great mistake when, in the fullness of his apostolic power as the Vicar of Christ, he divided the New World between the crowns of Spain and Portugal (ignoring the French), as a perpetual inheritance. So Columbus was mistaken to the hour of his death in the belief that he had simply discovered a western passage to India. The mistake was perpetuated in the name of the natives.

New France.

In the seventeenth century, Catholic France entered the lists for the possession of the new hemisphere, and extended her magnificent empire from the mouth of the St. Lawrence over the Northwest, and down the Mississippi Valley to the Gulf of Mexico. That empire was not founded by the voluntary immigration of individuals and companies, like the English and Dutch settlements, but by the despotic will of a king for the extension of his power and of the Roman Church, and was kept under his control. It was not based upon political and religious liberty, but upon the feudalism and sacerdotalism of mediæval Europe. It transplanted the principles of the papal counter-Reformation under the lead of the order of the Jesuits.

Quebec, founded by Champlain in 1608, and Montreal, founded

* The Spaniards, in 1564, attacked the Huguenot settlers and hanged them on the trees, "Not as Frenchmen, but as heretics." The Frenchmen soon afterwards avenged this barbarity by hanging the Spanish garrison on the same trees, "Not as Spaniards, but as cut-throats and murderers." The Spaniards held the Fort of St. Augustine till 1586, when it was captured by Sir Francis Drake. In 1763 the whole province of Florida was ceded to Great Britain in exchange for Cuba. By the treaty of 1783 it was retroceded to Spain, and the greater part of the inhabitants moved to the United States. Finally in 1819 Spain ceded the whole province to the United States. Florida was admitted as a State into the Union in 1845.

in 1642, became the strategic centers of New France, and of the Roman Catholic propaganda. All honor to the missionaries of the type of Xavier! The apostolic labors of Isaac Jogues, Brébeuf, Charles Garnier, Gabriel Lalemant, and other Jesuits, in the well-nigh fruitless attempt to convert and civilize the Indian savages, form one of the brightest chapters in the missionary history of Christianity. They combined the bold enterprise of the crusaders with the patience of the early martyrs. They encountered incredible dangers and hardships in the unbroken wilderness and among untamed savages, and met the most cruel death with cheerful composure. The long sufferings of Jogues (1607–46) among the Mohawks, who killed him at last, are almost without a parallel in the annals of martyrdom.

The unrighteous revocation of the Edict of Nantes (1685) was applied also to New France, and Louis XIV. directed the governor of Canada to quarter his troops in the houses of any Huguenots, or to imprison them. The governor informed the king that there was not a heretic in Canada. To this day the French Canadians are stricter Romanists than the French themselves.

But France lost her magnificent empire in Canada and on the Mississippi in the long conflict with England, which culminated in the victory of Wolfe over Montcalm on the Plains of Abraham at Quebec, 1759, and was concluded by the peace of 1763. France took revenge by aiding the American Colonies in the War of Independence. Napoleon sold the territory of Louisiana to the United States in 1803.

The loss of the Latin race was the gain of the Anglo-Saxon race, and led to the supremacy of the United States and of Protestantism on the northern continent.

The present strength and future importance of the Roman Church in America must be sought not in French Canada, nor in Spanish America, but in the United States, where she is enriched by Teutonic and Celtic blood, and stimulated by the progressive spirit of Protestantism. There is good ground for the expectation that in becoming Americanized she will be also liberalized.

LITERATURE.

I. Spanish America:—The principal authorities on the Columbian discovery and the conversion of the Indians are the letters and journals of COLUMBUS; the writings of BART. DE LAS CASAS, BERNALDEZ, OVIEDO, PETER MARTYR, HERRERA; and the invaluable collection of documents by

NAVARRETE (d. 1844, *Coleccion de viages*, etc., Madrid, 1825-37, 5 vols.; French translation, Paris, 1828, 3 vols.; also an Italian version).

Of modern writers we mention ROBERTSON (*History of America*); WASHINGTON IRVING (*Life and Voyages of Columbus*, a rose-colored view); PRESCOTT (*History of the Reign of Ferdinand and Isabella*); HEFELE (*Der Cardinal Ximenes*, 2d ed. 1851); WINSOR (*Columbus*, 1891, very unfavorable to Columbus); JOHN FISKE (*The Discovery of America*, 1892, 2 vols.); CASTELAR (*Life of Columbus*, 1892); EDWARD JOHN PAYNE (*History of the New World called America*, London and New York, 1892 sqq.); and the extensive Columbus literature of 1892.

II. French America:—JOHN GILMARY SHEA (R. Cath., d. 1892): *History of the Catholic Missions among the Indians of the United States* (New York, 1855).—FRANÇIS PARKMAN: *France and England in North America* (Boston, 1865-92, 6 parts in 7 vols.). Especially Part II., under the separate title: *The Jesuits in North America in the Seventeenth Century* (Boston, 1867, and several later editions). This is the standard work on the conflict between France and England in North America, based upon original documents. Parkman does full justice to the heroic Jesuit missionaries, but distinguishes two periods in their missions, the earlier of which was strictly religious, the later more political and unsuccessful.

CHAPTER CLXXIX.

CHURCH HISTORY OF THE UNITED STATES.

North America was first discovered under the flag of England (by John Cabot, 1497, and his son Sebastian C., 1498). It was settled chiefly by Englishmen, and predestinated for the Teutonic races of northern Europe. It was built up by Protestant genius and enterprise. It has far outstripped Latin America in progress, prosperity, and influence upon the Church and the world, and will soon rival with Europe as a theater of history.

American Church History, in the narrower sense, is therefore chiefly a church history of the United States and of Canada. It begins in the seventeenth century, with the settlements of Virginia (1607), of New York (1609), and of New England (1620). The Puritan colonies of Plymouth Salem, Boston, Hartford, and New Haven were of a strictly religious character, and have determined and controlled American theology and church life in the colonial period.

No nation, except the Jewish, has such a religious origin. The fathers and founders of this Republic fled from persecution, and made sacrifices for their faith; they were not gold-hunters, like the Spaniards and Portuguese, but sought first of all a home for the free worship of God according to the dictates of their conscience. The blessing of their piety and virtue, their reverence for the Word of God, the Lord's Day, and the Church of God, remain to this day as a safeguard against the influx of modern worldliness, indifference, and infidelity.

The roots of the American Churches are in Europe. New England Congregationalism is directly descended from English Puritanism; the Presbyterian Churches are chiefly derived from Scotland and the north of Ireland; the Protestant Episcopal Church from the Church of England; the Dutch Church from Holland; the Lutheran Church from Germany and Scandinavia; the German Reformed Church from the Palatinate and Switzerland; the Roman Catholic Church is recruited from all countries of Europe, but chiefly from Ireland and Germany. The two largest denominations, however, the Baptist and the Methodist, were from the start Anglo-American, and grew up simultaneously in England and in the American colonies, the one through the labors of Roger Williams in Rhode Island, the other through the evangelistic visits of John Wesley and George Whitefield. Unitarianism, Universalism, and Mormonism are of native American origin; the first, however, was preceded by a similar movement in England.

It is remarkable that the older denominations are more conservative and orthodox in America than in Europe. While Rationalism has revolutionized the Protestant Churches of Germany, Switzerland, France, and Holland, the Churches of the United States hold fast to their traditional creeds. One reason is that the universities of Europe, including the theological faculties, are institutions of the State, which is indifferent to creeds; while American schools of theology are founded, supported, and ruled by the Churches.* But a change is coming on with the immense progress of biblical and historical research in recent times. An increasing number of American scholars complete their studies in European universities and in Bible lands, and on their return take an active share in solving the problems of modern theology.†

* There are exceptions, as the Union Theological Seminary of New York, and some Congregational and Baptist institutions, which were founded by individuals.

† The pioneer of independent theological learning in America is Dr. Edward Robinson, the author of the *Biblical Researches*, and of a Hebrew

American Christianity starts with the invaluable inheritance of the Christian civilization of Europe. It covers an immense field of virgin territory with inexhaustible natural resources. It is rapidly increasing by peaceful emigration from the different nationalities of the Old World, with many of its best as well as its worst elements. It embraces all the Churches and sects, which import their traditions and peculiar gifts as moulding forces of the future, and enjoy full liberty of action on a basis of equality before the law. It furnishes all the material for a final settlement of the controversies of Christendom.

To a superficial observer blinded by papal or infidel preconceptions, the ecclesiastical map of the United States presents a wilderness of warring sects, a *bellum omnium contra omnes*. But they are nearly all imported from Europe, and only brought into closer proximity. There are as many sects in England, and as many monastic orders in the Roman Church; while there is in America a growing tendency towards practical co-operation in common Christian and philanthropic work and moral reform movements.

American Church History is divided into a colonial and a national period. The colonies were from the beginning refuges for people of different denominations—Puritans, Presbyterians, Huguenots, Baptists, Quakers, Roman Catholics, etc.—and were thus predestined to protect religious freedom on a larger scale than any other country. But this manifest destiny was not fully understood till after the War of Independence, which united the separate colonies with their different sects into one nation under one Constitution, with equal protection to all.

The distinctive character of American Christianity since the adoption of the Federal Constitution is the voluntary principle of self-support and self-government in friendly relation to the State. The Apostolic and ante-Nicene Church was likewise self-supporting and self-governing, but persecuted by the heathen State; while the American government is based upon Christian civilization. There is here no State Church domineering over dissenting sects. No apology is needed for being a Dissenter. The law makes no difference between churches and sects, or churchmen and dissenters, but recog-

and a Greek Lexicon (d 1863). He was in his day almost the only American divine known in Europe. Sidney Smith used to ask: "Who reads an American book?" Now he might ask: "Who does *not* read American books?"

nizes all Christian denominations alike and treats them with even justice. We have a free Church in a free State. The relation of Church and State is based upon Christ's declaration to "render unto Cæsar the things that are Cæsar's, and unto God the things that are God's" (Matt. 22 : 21). Each of the two powers is entirely independent in its own sphere, and not allowed to intermeddle with the rights and duties of the other; but the State protects the Church in her property and liberty of action, and the Church strengthens the moral foundations of the State.

The separation of Church and State, therefore, is not owing to religious indifference or disrespect, and must not be understood to be a separation of the nation from the Church; on the contrary, the American people are as Christian as any people in Europe, and do much more for the support of Church and school than any government.* But they have learned from the past that the union of Church and State is a source of religious persecution and civil war, and that religion flourishes best in the atmosphere of freedom. Hence the first Amendment of the Federal Constitution forbids Congress to establish a State Church, or to interfere with the liberty of religion. Similar guarantees are given in the constitutions of the several States.

The voluntary principle has so far worked very successfully, and shown its superiority over State-churchism. It has not diminished the respect for the Church and the clergy, but increased it, and has improved the quality and efficiency of ministers. It has stimulated and developed individual energy and liberality in building churches, supporting pastors, establishing colleges, theological seminaries, and other literary and benevolent institutions, and in promoting the cause of Christianity at home and abroad. There is no good cause which appeals in vain to American generosity.

This freedom of a self-supporting and self-governing Christianity is a new chapter in history, and the strength and glory of America. The spread of the gospel and the future of the

* In this judgment the most intelligent foreign writers on America who have visited the country, are fully agreed. Alexis de Tocqueville says that "there is no country in the whole world in which the Christian religion retains a greater influence over the souls of men than in America" (*Democracy in America*, I. 285). The incidental judgment of Prof. James Bryce of Oxford on religion in America is equally favorable (*The American Commonwealth*, II., 246, 567).

human race will largely depend upon the combined energies of the people of Great Britain and the United States.

The Church History of the United States has yet to be written, and this is a task worthy of the time and strength of rising scholars; for this is the land of freedom and of the future. Denominational and local histories we have in abundance, and the number is fast increasing, but there is no worthy history of American Christianity which represents it as an organic whole, in its genesis and growth, its connections with the mother Churches in Europe, its characteristic peculiarities, and its great mission for the future.

Special chairs ought to be established in our seminaries for American Church History.

LITERATURE.

ROBERT BAIRD (Presbyt., d. 1863): *Religion in America* (New York, 1856). Not a history, but a collection of material for history down to that year.

DANIEL DORCHESTER (Methodist): *Christianity in the United States from the First Settlement down to the Present Time* (New York, 1888, pp. 795). A considerable improvement upon the former, as an industrious collection of facts, statistical tables and maps, but marred by numerous inaccuracies. The author is a sanguine optimist with Methodist sympathies.

PHILIP SCHAFF: *Church and State in the United States, or the American Idea of Religious Liberty and its Practical Effects. With Official Documents* (New York, 1888).—*America; a Sketch of its Political, Social, and Religious Character* (New York, 1855. Lectures delivered in Berlin and first published in German).—*Der Bürgerkrieg und das christliche Leben in Nord Amerika* (Berlin, 1866).—*Christianity in the United States* (New York, 1879. An address before the Seventh General Conference of the Evangelical Alliance at Basel).—Art. "Nord Amerika" in Herzog[2], X. (1882), 631-642.

JOHN F. HURST: *Short History of the Christian Church* (New York, 1893), pp. 431-643.

FRIEDRICH NIPPOLD (Prof. of Church History in Jena): *Amerikanische Kirchengeschichte seit der Unabhängigkeitserklärung der Vereinigten Staaten* (Berlin, 1892, pp. 270). This is the first part of the 4th vol. of his *Handbuch der neuesten Kirchengeschichte seit der Restauration von 1814* (Elberfeld, 1867 sqq.; 4th ed. revised 1889 sqq.). The American history, as may be expected, is inferior in size and importance to any of the first three vols., which are devoted to the modern Church History of Europe, but fuller and more accurate than other German works on the American Churches. Nippold is an admirer of Bunsen and Döllinger, and finds his Church ideal in Anglo-American episcopacy (with lay representation and two houses), and in Old Catholicism. He gives lists of the leading divines of the different denominations, and has used some of the latest sources of information (as the "Papers of the American Society of Church History"). He marks a great advance over the views of Gieseler on America (quoted p. 11), who thought that love of money, cold selfishness, hypocritical piety, overweening conceit, and contempt for everything European are the leading traits (*Hauptzüge*) of the American character, especially of the Yankees, New Yorkers and Pennsylvanians! (See the posthumous volume of his *Kirchengeschichte*, V. 372). Such an opinion, which makes the very truth lie, was very common among scholars on the Continent some thirty or fifty years ago. The philosopher Schelling told me that Mormonism seemed to him the only important fact in the Church history of America. Hegel ignores America altogether in his *Philosophie der Geschichte*, although he teaches (p. 546) that the history of the world is the development of the idea of *liberty*.

The best foreign works on the *political* institutions of the United States are ALEXIS DE TOCQUEVILLE'S *Democracy in America* (1835, translated by Henry Reeve, 1845), and JAMES BRYCE'S *American Commonwealth* (2 vols., 1889, 3d ed. rev. 1892).

The chief secular historians of America, who must be consulted by the Church historian, especially in the colonial period, are GEORGE BANCROFT (Colonial History down to Adoption of the Federal Constitution, last revision, 1882-85); RICHARD HILDRETH (Colonial History to the End of Sixteenth Congress, 1849-52); JUSTIN WINSOR (*Narrative and Critical History;* a collection of independent essays by a number of scholars, with a full bibliography; 8 vols., 1889-92); H. VON HOLST (*Constitutional and Political History of the United States*, from 1750 to 1859, translated by J. J. Lalor and A. B. Mason; 6 vols., 1876-89); J. B. MCMASTER (*History of the People of the United States*, vols. 1-3, 1884-91, to be completed in 5 vols.); JAMES SCHOULER (*History of the United States under the Constitution*, 1783-1861; 5 vols., 1880-91); HENRY ADAMS (Histories of the Administrations, beginning with Jefferson's; 9 vols. covering period from 1801 to 1817, thus far published, 1889-91); and EDWARD JOHN PAYNE, already noticed in Chapter CLXXVIII.).

"The American Society of Church History," founded in 1888, at its third meeting, held in Washington, December 31, 1890, resolved to undertake the preparation of a critical American Church History, in a series of denominational histories on a uniform plan by a number of competent and unsectarian scholars. It will be published in New York, under the supervision of an editorial committee, consisting of Dr. Schaff, Bishop Potter, Prof. Geo. P. Fisher, Bishop Hurst, Prof. E. J. Wolf, Rev. H. C. Vedder, and Rev. S. M. Jackson, LL.D., in ten or more volumes, to be concluded by a compendious history of American Christianity as a whole.

CHAPTER CLXXX.

ECCLESIASTICAL MONOGRAPHY.

Monography is a most useful department, and indispensable to the general historian. It furnishes him with characteristic details and fills the gaps. In the ever-widening extent of history the monographic treatment is the best way of effectually promoting an accurate general history. Few are called to write a universal history of Christianity, but many may successfully cultivate portions of it.

A monographer views his subject under all its aspects and environments, in its antecedents and consequents, and weaves into it a picture of the whole age to which it belongs. He may select a person, or a doctrine, or any specific topic of history.

1. BIOGRAPHICAL monographs are thorough and exhaustive histories of distinguished persons of more or less representative character. They follow them from the cradle to the grave, into the secrets of their private life as well as into their public labors, and show how they are children of their age, and in turn have influenced and shaped their age.

2. DOCTRINAL monographs follow a particular doctrine from its germ in the New Testament through the successive ages of its development to its ultimate matured shape as it appears in the formulated statements of creeds and confessions of faith.

3. Any other topic of church history may be treated monographically, *i. e.*, with minute reference to all the details and subordinate relations which must necessarily be omitted in a general Church History.

LITERATURE.

I. Biographical monography begins, we may say, with Eusebius' *Life of Constantine* (d. 337), which, however, is more of a eulogy than impartial and independent history. The most extensive collection of biographies of Saints is the *Acta Sanctorum* of the BOLLANDISTS, begun in 1643 and not yet completed. TILLEMONT treated the history of the first five centuries monographically (*Mémoires*, 1693 sqq.).

Among Protestants, NEANDER has given the greatest impulse to this method of historiography, by his *Julian the Apostate, Tertullian, St. Chrysostom, St. Bernard*. We have now monographs on most of the great church fathers, popes, schoolmen, mystics, monks, reformers and missionaries, too numerous to mention. One of the latest and best is Dr. R. S. STORRS' *Bernard of Clairvaux* (New York, 1892). FR. BÖHRINGER (assisted by his son, PAUL B.) has written the history of the whole Church, from the second century to the Reformation, in biographies (*Die Kirche Christi und ihre Zeugen*, new ed. 1873-78, in 12 vols.).

II. Doctrinal and dogmatic-historical monographs are of more recent origin. The ablest specimens are BAUR'S *History of the Doctrine of the Trinity and Incarnation* (1843, 3 vols.), and his *History of the Doctrine of the Atonement* (1838); DORNER'S *History of Christology* (1839, enlarged ed. 1856, 2 vols.); MÜLLER'S *Doctrine of Sin* (6th ed. 1878, 2 vols.; more dogmatic than historical); RITSCHL'S *The Christian Doctrine of Justification and Atonement* (3d ed. 1889, 3 vols.; the first vol. is historical); EBRARD'S *History of the Doctrine of the Lord's Supper* (1846, 2 vols.); AL-

GER'S History of the Doctrine of a Future Life (1863; 12th ed. 1885; with bibliography by Prof. Ezra Abbot, which is a model of accuracy and completeness).

CHAPTER CLXXXI.

LITERATURE OF GENERAL CHURCH HISTORY.

A fuller account in SCHAFF'S Introduction to his *History of the Apostolic Church* (1853), pp. 51–135, and in his *History of the Christian Church*, vol. i., 27–53 (third revision, 1889).—BAUR: *Die Epochen der kirchlichen Geschichtsschreibung* (1852).—HASE: *Kirchengeschichte auf der Grundlage akademischer Vorlesungen* (1885), vol. i., 35–60.

The literature of Church History is the most extensive, next to that of the Bible. The time is coming when a general knowledge of the history of Christianity will be considered an essential part of liberal culture. For the Church of Christ is the central institution in the world, as the Bible is the Book of books. The profoundest theme of history is the problem of religion and the conflict between faith and unbelief.*

But as the Bible, owing to its very importance, has been more frequently misunderstood and misinterpreted than any book, so has Church History been more misrepresented and perverted than secular history, for partisan and sectarian interests. Facts may be obscured, exaggerated, or underestimated under the bias of preconceived notions; and thus the truth itself may be " made void because of tradition " (comp. Matt. 15 : 6).

The ancient historians, in their zeal for orthodoxy, rarely do justice to heretics. The historians of the Greek Church are polemical against the Latin, and the historians of the Latin Church against the Greek. Heretical historians are equally unjust to orthodoxy.

The war between Romanists and Protestants is reflected in their historians, and carried on even to our days.

---

* This was acknowledged even by such a worldly poet as Goethe, who says: "*Das eigentliche, einzige und tiefste Thema der Welt—und Menschengeschichte, dem alle übrigen untergeordnet sind, bleibt der Konflikt des Glaubens und des Unglaubens. Alle Epochen, in welchen der Glaube herrscht,—sind glänzend, herzerhebend und fruchtbar für Mit- und Nachwelt. Alle Epochen dagegen, in welchen der Unglaube, in welcher Form es sei, einen kümmerlichen Sieg behauptet, und wenn sie auch einen Augenblick mit einem Scheinglanz prahlen sollten, verschwinden vor der Nachwelt, weil sich niemand gern mit Erkenntniss des Unfruchtbaren abquälen mag.*"—(*Israel in der Wüste*, 1797, *Westöstl. Divan*, p. 313.)

At the end of the last century, rationalism took hold of Church History in the spirit of hostile neutrality and indifference, and turned the most important doctrinal controversies into worthless logomachies, and the whole history into a bedlam.*

But the true historic spirit which aims at the truth, the whole truth and nothing but the truth, is making steady progress and dominates in the great historians of the nineteenth century.

CHAPTER CLXXXII.

CHURCH HISTORIANS BEFORE THE REFORMATION

EUSEBIUS, "the father of Church History," or the Christian Herodotus, who saw the last persecution and the triumph of the Church (d. 340): 'Εκκλησιαστικὴ 'Ιστορία, from the birth of Christ to Constantine the Great (324). A work of permanent value as a source.

His successors in the Greek Church: SOCRATES till 439, SOZOMEN till 423, THEODORET till 423.

Best English translation of the Greek historians, with commentary, in the Second Series of the *Nicene and Post-Nicene Library of the Fathers* (N. Y. and Oxf., 1890–92, vols. i.–iii.).

The Latin Church contented itself with extracts from Eusebius and his continuators.

CASSIODORUS (d. 562): *Historia tripartita.*—RUFINUS (d. 410) supplemented Eusebius.—SULPICIUS SEVERUS (d. 410): *Historia Sacra* or *Chronica*.

The Middle Ages produced valuable material for history, especially in the form of annals and biographies of popes, bishops, monks, missionaries, and saints, but no great general Church History.

In the period of the Renaissance, the spirit of historical criticism was awakened by LAURENTIUS VALLA (d. 1457), who may be called a forerunner of Erasmus. He ventured to criticise and correct Jerome's *Vulgate*, rejected Christ's letter to King Abgar of Edessa as a forgery, threw doubts on the apostolic origin of the Apostles' Creed, and destroyed the hierarchical fiction of the *Donation of Constantine* as "contradictory, impossible, stupid, barbarous and ridiculous." For these views, which are now universally accepted even by Roman Catholic scholars, he excited the suspicion of the Roman Inquisition, but escaped its punishment by the hypocritical confession that he believed as Mother Church believed.

---

* Of this kind of Church historiography Goethe said in the *Zahme Xenien*:
"*Mit Kirchengeschichte was hab ich zu schaffen?
Ich sehe weiter nichts als Pfaffen!
Wie's um die Christen steht, die Gemeinen,
Davon will mir gar nichts erscheinen.*"

CHAPTER CLXXXIII.

HISTORIANS OF THE SIXTEENTH AND SEVENTEENTH CENTURIES.

Church History, as a critical science, began with the Reformation, which emancipated the mind from the tyranny of an infallible traditionalism. It roused the spirit of inquiry which separates facts from fiction and truth from error by proving all things and holding fast to what is good (I. Thess. 5:21). But for a long time history was subordinated to dogmas and carried on in a polemic and sectarian spirit. The Protestant historians saw in the pope the Antichrist, in the mediæval Roman Church the great apostasy predicted in prophecy, and in the Reformation the restoration of the Apostolic Church; while the Roman Catholic historians represented the Reformation as an apostasy from the true historic Church of Christ, and blackened the character of the Reformers as rebels and archheretics.

MATTHIAS FLACIUS, a learned and zealous Lutheran and unsparing foe of Papists, Calvinists, and Melanchthonians (d. 1575), aided by princes and cities and by several Protestant divines then at Magdeburg (the stronghold of the uncompromising enemies of the Imperial Interim), prepared the *Magdeburg Centuries* (*Ecclesiastica Historia N. Testamenti*, Basil., 1559-74), covering thirteen Christian centuries in as many large folio volumes, the first history from a Protestant point of view in opposition to the claims of Romanism. An epoch-making work of herculean labor, but overgrown with polemics.

In the Reformed Church, *J. H. Hottinger* (1651), *Frederic Spanheim* (1689), and *Sam. Basnage* (1699) wrote with equal learning and zeal, but more sober judgment, against the papal Church.

Their pessimistic view of the "dark" ages, illuminated by a few sporadic witnesses of the truth, controlled and obscured Protestant Church History down to the eighteenth century, and still prevails in popular antipopery literature, though abandoned by the best Protestant historians.

Cardinal CÆSAR BARONIUS (1538-1607), the father of papal historiography, wrote *Ecclesiastical Annals*, in 12 folio volumes, down to the year 1198 (published at Rome 1588-1607), in rhetorico-polemical style, and in defense of Romanism against the Greek Church and against Protestantism, with occasional reference to Flacius, whose *Centuries* he called "Centuries of Satan." It is a work of immense learning and unwearied industry, drawn largely from the treasures of the Vatican and still valuable for its material, but to be used with caution on account of the numerous chronological errors, spurious documents and legends. It was continued in the same spirit and style, but with inferior talent by Raynaldi till 1565, by Laderchi till 1571, by Theiner till 1585, and others. Two French Franciscans, Antoine and François Pagi, wrote correcting and supplementary criticisms (*Critica hist.-chronologica in Annales Baronii*, 1705-27, 4 vols.), which are incorporated in Mansi's ed. of Baronius and his successors, Lucca, 1738-59, 38 vols. fol.; new ed. by Aug. Theiner, Bar-le-Duc, 1864 sqq. (to be finished in about 50 vols.).*

The monumental works of Flacius and Baronius furnished abundant material for abridgments, with which the two Churches were contented for many years, till, in the middle of the seventeenth century, a new zeal for history was stimulated in the French Catholic Church by the controversy with Protestants and Jansenists. The best work was done by Gallicans and Jansenists. They were aided by the invaluable patristic and archæological labors of the Benedictines of the Congregation of St. Maur, as Mabillon, Massuet, Montfaucon, and others.

NATALIS (NOEL) ALEXANDER, a Dominican at Rouen, professor in Paris (d. 1724, eighty-six years old and blind), wrote an *Historia Ecclesiastica, V. et N. Testamenti* till 1600, in 26 vols. (Paris, 1676-83). Put on the Index by Innocent XI. (1684) on account of its Gallicanism; hence expurgated editions.

SEBASTIEN LE NAIN DE TILLEMONT (d. 1698), a pupil and friend of the Jansenists, in his still valuable *Memoires* (Paris, 1693-1712, 16 vols.), prepared in thirty years the history of the first six centuries (till 513) from the words of the original sources, translated into French after the bibliographical model of Plutarch, and in the spirit of liberal Gallican Catholicism.

CLAUDE FLEURY (educated under Bossuet and Fénelon, confessor of Louis XV., d. 1723) carried his *Histoire ecclesiastique* down to 1414, in 20 vols. (Paris, 1691-1720); continued by CLAUDE FABRE till 1595, in 16 vols. Popular, Gallican, in elegant French. Partly translated under the direction of John H. (Cardinal) Newman before his transition to Rome (Oxford, 1842).

---

* Hase (i., 36 sq.) thus characterizes the two representative Church historians of the sixteenth century: "*Flacius und Baronius im schroffsten Gegensatze stehn doch auf gleichem Standpunkte. Gemeinsam ist ihnen die Anerkennung der apostolischen Kirche als der vollkommenen Gestalt der Kirche, auch der ersten 5 Jahrhunderte, als massgebend für alle Zeit, doch so dass Flacius einzelne* NAEVI, *Muttermale, bei den grossen Kirchenlehrern findet. Gemeinsam die supernaturale Betrachtung: im alttestamentlicher Anschauung unmittelbar aus Gottes Hand Lohn und Strafe. Beide haben ihre Lust am Wunderbaren, die Centurien haben ein eignes Kapitel für* MIRACULA *und* PRODIGIA, *doch weniger zur Verherrlichung der Heiligen, mehr als göttliche Strafgerichte. Gemeinsam endlich die dualistische Weltanschauung: die Welt- und Kirchengeschichte ein Kampf der beiden jenseitigen Mächte, des dreieinigen Gottes und des Satan, wenn auch kein unentschiedner. Ihr Grundunterschied ist: Flacius ist historischer Pessimist, Baronius Optimist.* Ihm [Baronius] *erscheint die katholische Kirche wesentlich immer als dieselbe siegreich über alle Gegensätze. Er leugnet nicht dunkle Zeiten, das 10te Jahrhundert eine vorübergehende Verdunkelung, um die rettende Wundermacht desto glänzender zu zeigen. Christus im Seesturm ist ihm ein Sinnbild für alle Zeiten: immer bleibe dem Frommen der Trost, auch wenn Christus schlafe, dass er im Schifflein des h. Petrus schläft. Nur die gottlosen Neuerer, die nichts wissen vom Glauben, auf den sie sich berufen, verfallen, wenn sie das Schifflein Petri einmahl von den Wogen überfluthet sehn, in die Lästerung, dass Christus nicht mehr darin sei. Flacius dagegen sah nach dem 5ten Jahrhundert eine immer dunklere Verfinsterung, nach dem gemeinsamen Glauben seiner Kirche: Rom Babylonien, das Papstthum das Mysterium Iniquitatis, der Papst der Endchrist, der sich im Tempel Gottes anbeten lässt. Eine revolutionäre Geschichtsanschauung, die nichts Vergangenes zu achten hat.*"

CHAPTER CLXXXIV.

HISTORIANS OF THE EIGHTEENTH CENTURY.

GOTFRIED ARNOLD (d. 1714), a learned mystic of the Pietistic school of Spener, took a new departure, in opposition to the intolerant orthodoxy of the Lutheran Church, in his *Impartial History of the Church and of Heretics,* to A.D. 1688 (*Unpartheiische Kirchen- und Ketzerhistorie*, Frankfort, 1699 sqq., 4 vols. fol.). He advocated the interests of practical piety, and the claims of heretics and schismatics, and all those who suffered persecution from an intolerant hierarchy and orthodoxy. His historical pessimism goes farther than that of Flacius, and hands the whole historic Churches—Greek, Roman and Protestant—over to the reign of Antichrist, leaving in each only a little flock that never bowed the knees to Baal. But he boldly broke down the walls of bigotry, and without intending it, prepared the way for a skeptical treatment of history. He first substituted the German for the customary Latin in learned works, but his style is rude and insipid.

The *History of the Church of Christ* by JOSEPH MILNER (Vicar of Hull, d. 1797; continued by Isaac Milner and Stebbing) is written in the Pietistic spirit of Arnold, but for popular edification, and is free from polemics.

J. LORENZ VON MOSHEIM (Chancellor of the University of Göttingen, d. 1755): *Institutes of Ecclesiastical History*, in Latin (Helmstädt, 1755). Mosheim marks an epoch. He was a moderate and impartial Lutheran, educated in the school of the classical and French historians, and the first German who raised Church History to the dignity and interest of an art. In this respect he may be compared to Bossuet. He surpassed all his predecessors in skillful construction, clear though mechanical and monotonous arrangement, critical sagacity, pragmatic combination, freedom from polemical passion, almost bordering on cool indifferentism, and in easy elegance of Latin style. He follows the centurial plan of Flacius, but in simpler form, and combines it with the division into four periods (from Christ to Constantine, from Constantine to Luther, from the Reformation to 1700), and with the mechanical division into external and internal history, into prosperous and calamitous events. His *Institutes* were translated and supplemented by Maclaine and Murdock (5th ed. New York, 1854, 3 vols.; best ed. by W. Stubbs, London, 1863), and continued in use as a text-book much longer in England and America than in Germany.

J. M. SCHRÖCKH, a pupil of Mosheim, but touched with the neological spirit of Semler, and professor of poetry, afterwards of history, at Wittenberg (d. 1808), is the author of the most extensive German work on *Christian Church History* (Leipzig, 1768–1810, in 45 vols.). It reaches with its continuation by TZSCHIRNER to the end of the eighteenth century, is compiled from the sources in a mild and candid spirit, and written in clear but diffuse style. It adopts the periodic plan instead of the centurial, which was still followed by Mosheim. Very unequal in different parts, but useful for occasional reference. Nobody ever read it through except the author and proof-reader.

The *Church History* of H. P. C. HENKE (Professor in Helmstädt, d. 1809), continued by VATER (Braunschweig, 1788–1820, 9 vols.), is rationalistic and ignores the divine side of the Church. He derives the chief events from hierarchical ambition, and represents "Athanasius as a stubborn crank, Augustin as an unmasked Manichæan and dialectical babbler, and Catherine of Siena as a silly old woman." (Hase, vol. i., p. 43.)

SPITTLER (d. 1810) of Göttingen wrote a compend (1782, 6th ed. 1827) in the same derogatory spirit, which destroys all real interest in Church History except that of mere literary and antiquarian curiosity.

CHAPTER CLXXXV.

HISTORIANS OF THE NINETEENTH CENTURY.

(1) The Protestant historians take the lead.

AUGUST NEANDER (originally DAVID MENDEL, a convert from Moses and Plato to Christ, a Christian Nathanael without guile, Professor of Church History in Berlin—where he lived like one of those learned Benedictines of Paris, absorbed in patristic studies and in teaching enthusiastic students; d. 1850) marks an epoch in this study, and is called the modern "father of Church History." He rescued it from the icy grasp of rationalism, infused into it the warm love of Christ, the ever-present Head of the Church, and made it a rich fountain of edification as well as instruction. His *General History of the Christian Religion and Church* (Hamburg, 1825–52, 11 parts; 3d ed. 1856 in 4 large vols., with an introduction by Dr. Ullmann; translated by Torrey, Boston, 1847–52; new ed. with complete index, 1881, 6 vols.) extends to the Council of Basel, 1430. It is characterized by profound learning, impartial judgment, spiritual insight into religious life and the development of Christian doctrines, and by evangelical catholicity and loving sympathy with all types of Christian piety. It is defective in the secular, political and artistic sections, and somewhat diffuse and monotonous in style. Neander's motto was, *"Pectus est quod theologum* [not *dissertum] facit."* He felt most at home in the invisible church of thought and spiritual life, and in those periods where religion has nothing to do with politics, nor the Church with the State—except to be persecuted, as in the first three centuries. He dictated the last pages, on "the Friends of God," the forerunners of the Reformation, a few hours before his death, and then said to his faithful sister: "I am weary; let us go home." *

Equally valuable, though of an altogether different plan and spirit, is the *Church History* of J. C. L. GIESELER (Professor in Bonn, afterwards in Göttingen, d. 1854). It was published in Bonn, 1824–56, in 5 vols. (nominally in 3 vols., but in 8 parts); 4th ed. 1844–57; the last two volumes, from 1648 to 1848, were posthumously edited from lectures by Dr. Redepenning (1855 and 1857), and are of inferior merit as they lack the critical notes. English translation by Davidson and Hull in England, revised and completed by

* Comp. Schaff: *August Neander. Erinnerungen* (Gotha, 1886); and Harnack, *Rede auf Neander zur Feier seines* 100 *jähr.-Geburtstags,* 17 Jan. 1889 (Berlin, 1889).

H. B. Smith, and after the death of the latter, 1877, by Lewis French Stearns and Miss Mary Robinson of New York (with preface by Philip Schaff, 1857-80, in 5 vols.).*

Gieseler was an honest, sober, level-headed rationalist of the school of Wegscheider, but with more learning and appreciation of history than his rationalistic predecessors. The first three volumes, edited by himself, extend to the Treaty of Westphalia, 1648 (in the English translation, the first four and a part of the fifth volume). The text (except in the last two volumes) is a dry, meager and unsympathetic, but impartial skeleton of facts and dates; the body of the work consists of carefully selected extracts and proof texts from the sources which furnish the data for an independent judgment. He makes each age speak for itself. He follows the method of Tillemont, but reverses his order by throwing the sources into footnotes. His critical and literary notes are also very valuable. Neander and Gieseler have been the chief feeders of modern manuals. They supplement each other; the one furnishes a subjective reproduction, the other the raw material, of Church History. They are not yet superseded.

The *Church History* of FERDINAND CHRISTIAN VON BAUR, the founder of the Tübingen School (d. 1860), was partly published after his death (Tübingen, 1863, in 5 vols.). The first two volumes comprising the first five centuries are the best, and contain his original investigations. He was an indefatigable scholar, distinguished for philosophic grasp, critical combination, and bold conjectures in the treatment of the apostolic and post-apostolic ages, and the ancient heresies and systems of doctrine. He revolutionized the history of apostolic and post-apostolic Christianity, and resolved its rich spiritual life of faith and love into an intellectual process of conflicting tendencies, which started from an antagonism of Petrinism and Paulinism, and were ultimately reconciled in the compromise of ancient Catholicism. He applied the Hegelian conception of a dialectical process of thesis, antithesis, and synthesis to primitive Christianity; but he overstated the conflict of Peter and Paul, who were agreed in principle, and he put all but four of Paul's epistles into the post-apostolic age of reconciliation. He fully brought to light, by a keen critical analysis, the profound intellectual fermentation of the primitive Church, but eliminated from it the supernatural and miraculous element; yet as an honest and earnest skeptic he admitted at last a psychological miracle in the conversion of St. Paul, and bowed before the greater miracle of the resurrection of Christ, without which the former is an inexplicable enigma. A most important concession. His critical researches and speculations gave a powerful stimulus to a reconsideration and modification of the traditional views on early Christianity; but the Tübingen school had to abandon some of his positions, and is now superseded by the more positive school of Ritschl and Harnack.

The *Church History* of CARL RUDOLPH HAGENBACH (Professor in Basel, d. 1874; published at Leipzig, 1873, 7 vols.; revised ed. by Nippold, 1885

---

* The section on American Church History (vol. v., pp. 370 sqq.) is omitted in the translation, as it betrays so much ignorance and prejudice that it would diminish the just respect for his great learning and good judgment in the body of the work. See above, pp. 293 sq.

sqq.) is a well-written, popular, yet scholarly digest for the educated lay reader in the irenic, evangelical, catholic spirit of Neander, and gives also due attention to ecclesiastical poetry and art. His history of the Reformation has been translated into English by Miss Eveline Moore (Edinburgh, 1878, 2 vols.), and his history of the eighteenth and nineteenth centuries by Bishop Hurst (New York, 1869, 2 vols.).

KARL HASE (Professor at Jena) began to publish his *Lectures on Church History* in 1885, when death interrupted him at the age of ninety (Jan. 3, 1890), but the second and third vols. were edited by Dr. Krüger (Leipzig, 1892). They are an expansion of his *Manual*. Hase was an amiable and most accomplished scholar, a master of elegant, clear, pithy historiography, with kindly sympathy for all that is great, good, and beautiful, and with cultivated taste for the poetry of religion.

To Hase and to Hagenbach belongs the merit of having introduced Church History into general literature and made it interesting to the cultivated laity. Their works should be translated or reproduced in English.

GEORGE WADDINGTON (Dean of Durham, d. 1869) prepared three volumes on the history of the Church before the Reformation (London, 1835), and three volumes on the Continental Reformation (1841), in the spirit of evangelical and liberal Anglicanism.

JAMES CRAIGIE ROBERTSON (Canon of Canterbury and Professor of Church History in King's College, d. 1882) brings his *History of the Christian Church* from the apostolic age down to the beginning of the Reformation (64–1517). The work was first published in four octavo vols. (1854 sqq.), and then in eight duodecimo vols. (London, 1874), and is the best, as it is the latest, general Church History written by an Episcopalian. It deserves praise for its candor, moderation, and careful indication of authorities.

ETIENNE L. CHASTEL (a descendant of the Huguenots, Professor of Church History in the National Church at Geneva, d. 1886): *Histoire du Christianisme depuis son origine jusqu' à nos jours* (Paris, 1881–85, 5 vols.). An able work, influenced by Neander.

PHILIP SCHAFF (Professor of Church History in New York): *History of the Christian Church* (New York and Edinburgh, 1859 sqq., 5th ed. revised and enlarged, 1889–92, 7 vols. Vol. v. is not yet completed. The first three vols. appeared also in German, Leipzig, 1868, but are superseded by the later English revisions. The work so far comes down to the close of the sixteenth century, and will be continued. It is written from the Anglo-German and Anglo-American standpoint, and brings the past in living contact with the present.

(2) Roman Catholic historians.

COUNT STOLBERG (a convert, d. 1819): *Geschichte der Religion Jesu Christi*, to A.D. 430 (1806–18, 15 vols.); continued by KERZ and BRISCHAR to 1245 (1825–64, 38 vols.). This work is nearly as extensive as the Annals of Baronius, and marks the beginning of the Roman Catholic revival in Germany, but has no critical value.*

---

* Hase (i., 56) thus happily characterizes Stolberg: "*Dem Göttinger Dichterbund angehörig mit Hölty und Voss unter Klopstock's Patronat, dann mit Goethe hat er ein Stück Jugend in übersprudelnder Kraft durchlebt, bis die aristokratische Natur durchbrach, welche im Mittelalter ihre Ideale fand, bei weiblicher Sehnsucht nach Fesseln. Er hat der katholischen Kirche sein*

J. ADAM MOEHLER (d. 1838): *Kirchengeschichte*, published after his death by Gams, Regensburg (1868, 3 vols.). It is very unequal, and lacks the author's own finish.

J. J. DÖLLINGER (since 1870 an Old Catholic, and excommunicated, d. 1891): *Manual of Church History till* 1517 (2d ed. 1843, 2 vols.). English translation by Dr. Edward Cox, London (1840-42, 4 vols.). Döllinger was regarded in the Roman Church before he opposed the Vatican Council and the dogma of papal infallibility as the most learned Church historian.

ABBÉ ROHRBACHER (Professor of Church History at Nancy, d. 1856) wrote an extensive *Histoire universelle de l'Église catholique*, including that of the Old Testament, down to 1848 (Nancy and Paris, 1842-49, 29 vols.; 4th ed. by Chantral, 1864 sqq.). A free German translation by Hülskamp, Rump, and others appeared at Münster, 1860 sqq. He is less liberal than the great Gallican writers of the seventeenth century.

DARRAS BAREILLE and FÈVRE: *Histoire de l'Église* (Paris, 1861-88, 44 vols.). According to Dr. Funk, who is himself a Roman Catholic historian, this extensive work is still more behind the age than Rohrbacher's.

CHAPTER CLXXXVI.

MANUALS, TEXT-BOOKS, AND TABLES OF GENERAL CHURCH HISTORY.

Most of the recent Manuals of Church History have been written by German Protestants, because Church History is more thoroughly studied in the universities of Germany than elsewhere.

(1) Protestant Manuals:

* HASE (Prof. in Jena, d. 1891), 11th ed. 1886 (a masterly miniature picture).—NIEDNER (Prof. in Berlin, d. 1865), 1866 (very learned and very heavy).—GUERICKE (Prof. in Halle, d. 1878), 9th ed. 1866 (high Lutheran, contracted in spirit and involved in style); freely translated, in part, by Dr. Shedd.—EBRARD (Prof. in Erlangen, d. 1888), 1865-67, 4 vols. (Reformed and polemical).—* KURTZ (Prof. in Dorpat, d. at Marburg, 1889), 13th ed. 1892, 2 vols.; translated from the 9th and partly from the 10th ed. by J. Macpherson, 1888-90, 3 vols. (evangelical Lutheran, more liberal in the later edd.).—HASSE (Prof. in Bonn, d. 1862), 1864 (posthumous).—HERZOG (Prof. in Erlangen, d. 1884), 1880-82, 3 vols., 2d ed. by Koffmane (evangelical Reformed).—H. SCHMID (Prof. in Erlangen, d. 1885), 1881, 2 vols. (Lutheran).—* WILHELM MOELLER (Prof. in Kiel, d. 1891), 1891, 2 vols.

warmes Herz und seine protestantische Bildung gebracht. Als er zu den Füszen des Papstes den Frieden gefunden, hat er mehr mit dem Enthusiasmus des frommen Dichters als mit dem Ernste des besonnenen Geschichtschreibers die alttestamentliche Geschichte, die er nicht verstand, und die Geschichte des kirchlichen Alterthums, die er so eben lernte, geschrieben. Es war doch von grosser Wirkung; ähnlich wie Baronius stand Stolberg einer neuen Weltbildung gegenüber, man erfuhr, dass auch die moderne Bildung zur Verherrlichung der katholischen Kirche zu brauchen sei, und der Katholicismus fasste wieder Vertrauen zu seiner Vorzeit."

(the first vol. translated by A. Rutherford, 1892).—*K. MÜLLER (Prof. in Breslau, School of Ritschl), 1892 sq., 2 vols.

HARDWICK (Anglican, d. 1859), 1853; 3d ed. by Stubbs, 1873, 2 vols.; one on the Middle Ages and one on the Reformation.—PHILIP SMITH, London and New York, 1881 and 1885, 2 vols. to the Reformation, with illustrations (vol. i. largely extracted from Schaff).—* G. P. FISHER (Prof. in Yale University), New York, 1887.—JOHN F. HURST, New York, 1893.

(2) Roman Catholic Manuals:

RITTER, 6th ed. 1862 —*ALZOG (Prof. in Freiburg, d. 1878), 10th ed. by Kraus, 1882, 2 vols.; English translation, Cincinnati, 1874, in 3 vols. —*JOSEPH HERGENRÖTHER (Cardinal, d. in Rome, 1890): *Handbuch der allgemeinen Kirchengeschichte*, 3d ed. Freiburg, 1884, 3 vols.—BRÜCK, 4th ed., 1888.—* KRAUS (successor of Alzog in Freiburg), 3d ed. 1887.—* FUNK (successor of Hefele in Tübingen), 2d ed. 1890, 1 vol. (liberal but too brief).

(3) Greek Orthodox Manuals:

PHILARET BAPHEIDES (Prof. of Church History in Chalce): Ἐκκλησιαστικὴ Ἱστορία. Constantinople, vols. i. and ii., 1884 and 1886. Extends to the fall of Constantinople, 1453. Bapheides is the successor of Bryennios (the discoverer of the *Didache*), and, like him, is well acquainted with German Protestant literature.

Another compend of Church History in Greek by DIOMEDES KYRIAKOS appeared at Athens, 1881, in 2 vols.

(4) Chronological Tables:

WEINGARTEN: *Zeittafeln*, Berlin, 3d ed. 1874.—H. B. SMITH: *History of the Church of Christ in Sixteen Chronological Tables*, New York, 1860 (the best, but too large in size for convenient use).—F. X. KRAUS (Roman Catholic Professor, first in Strassburg, then at Freiburg, i. B.): *Synchronistische Tabellen zur Kirchengeschichte*, Trier, 1876; and *Synchronistische Tabellen zur christlichen Kunstgeschichte*, Freiburg, 1880.

(5) Historical Atlases have been mentioned in Chapter CXLVIII., p. 243.

CHAPTER CLXXXVII.

HINTS FOR THE STUDY OF CHURCH HISTORY.

1. The study of Church History, like that of the Bible, should run through the whole course, instead of being made an appendix, as is the case in many theological seminaries.

2. Church History and the Bible are the training-school for forming theological opinions. Facts should control dogmas, and not *vice versâ*.

3. God made history, and not man, and man could not make it any better. Our business is humbly to learn, and to adore Providence even in its darkest chapters. What we cannot understand now we shall understand hereafter.

4. Impress on the memory and imagination a general chrono-

logical map of the leading epochs, dates, events, and personalities of history, with the help of the latest and best manuals, tables, and atlases.

5. Study first and last Biblical history, especially the Life of Christ and the Apostolic Age, which are of perennial interest, ever fresh and ever new, and must regulate the Church in all ages.

6. Study next the Reformation history, which is the fountain of modern history.

7. Then the history of your own country and denomination in which you expect to labor.

8. Select one particular period or department for exhaustive study, and cultivate it as your favorite field.

9. Aim always, first and last, at an accurate knowledge of the facts and truth.

10. Study Church History not only for instruction, but also for warning and encouragement to work for the kingdom of God in the sphere to which God has assigned you.

11. The most useful manuals are those of HASE, KURTZ, MÜLLER, and FISHER. The first three give the literature in the respective sections; Fisher is the best guide for recent English and American Church History, which is very imperfectly treated in German works, although there is a steady improvement in the more recent editions. For an advanced study, Gieseler and Neander are recommended, but need supplementing, especially in the Ante-Nicene age.

12. Church History may be profitably introduced into the pulpit and lecture-room by a series of sketches of great and good men, as Abraham and faith; Moses and the law; Isaiah and the promise; Peter the Confessor; Paul the Missionary; John the Seer; Polycarp the Martyr; Justin Martyr the Apologist; Tertullian the Polemic; Origen and Christian scholarship; Athanasius and the divinity of Christ; Augustin and Christian experience; Chrysostom and the pulpit; Hildebrand and the papacy; St. Bernard and monasticism; Columbus and the Discovery of America; Erasmus and the Greek Testament; Luther and justification by faith; Calvin and election by grace; Wesley and revival; Zinzendorf and heathen missions; Livingstone and darkest Africa; the Salvation Army and darkest England.

BOOK IV.

SYSTEMATIC THEOLOGY.

CHAPTER CLXXXVIII.

GENERAL CONCEPTION.

Systematic Theology represents the Christian religion as a scientific system. It derives its material from three sources: the Bible, the Church, and Christian experience. It arranges the material so as to form an organic whole, and adjusts it to the prevailing spirit of the Church and the existing state of philosophic and scientific culture. In its method it is often more or less influenced by the current philosophy, but it may and ought to be independent in spirit and aim.

Christianity is not systematic as to outward form, any more than nature is a system of natural science and natural philosophy. It is a divine revelation, a series of supernatural truths and facts; it is spirit and life, and has the freshness and directness of life. But its truths and facts are all consistent with each other and constitute together a beautiful organism. It is the business of the systematic theologian to bring out the unity, harmony and completeness of the revealed religion.

Systematic Theology may also be called *Philosophical*, or better, *Speculative* Theology, because it aims to show the reasonableness of the Christian religion and brings it into contact with the scientific thinking of the age.

CHAPTER CLXXXIX.

DEPARTMENTS OF SYSTEMATIC THEOLOGY.

Systematic Theology embraces:
1. Christian Apologetic. 2. Biblical Theology. 3. Christian Dogmatic. 4. Christian Symbolic. 5. Christian Polemic and

Irenic. 6. Christian Ethic. 7. Ecclesiastical Geography and Statistic. 8. Formal Encyclopædia.

Apologetic is a vindication of Christianity against its opponents. Biblical Theology is a systematic view of the teaching of the Scriptures. Dogmatic is an exposition of the doctrines of Christianity. Symbolic is comparative Dogmatic. Polemic is directed against false conceptions of Christianity and internal controversies. Irenic seeks a higher unity above the dogmatic differences, or the concord in the discord of creeds. Polemic and Irenic may as well be combined with Symbolic. Ethic is the theory of Christian life. Ecclesiastical Geography and Statistic is a description of the social status of the Christian world. Encyclopædia is an outline of all the theological sciences in their unity and mutual relations. This is substantially the same with Propædeutic, but gives also an outline of the contents.

Schleiermacher and Rothe comprise Systematic Theology under Historical Theology, except Apologetic and Polemic, which Schleiermacher assigns to Philosophic Theology, while Rothe assigns Ethic and Apologetic to what he calls Speculative Theology, and Polemic to Practical Theology.

FIRST SECTION: APOLOGETIC, OR EVIDENCES OF CHRISTIANITY.

CHAPTER CXC.

IDEA AND AIM OF APOLOGETIC.

Apologetic or Apologetic Theology is the proper scientific term for what is popularly called "Evidences of Christianity."

It means a self-vindication of the Christian religion against the attacks of its enemies. It aims to prove the divine origin and character of Christianity, as the perfect religion for the whole human race.

Hence Apologetic must take the first place (in order, though not in importance) among the branches of Systematic Theology. It lays the foundation for all the rest.

It is closely connected with Philosophy of Religion, and forms, together with Dogmatic and Ethic, the connecting link between Philosophy and Theology.

NOTES.

Apologetic is from ἀπολογία, *apologia*, a defense or a discourse in defense of some person or doctrine or cause which has been assailed or misrepresented. It has the claim of priority over other terms. The earliest defenses of the Christian faith by Justin Martyr, Tertullian, etc., were called *Apologia*, *Apologeticus*, and the writers are called *Apologists*. The theological use of *apology* must be carefully distinguished from the popular English use of the term, which makes it equivalent to an *excuse*, and implies weakness and censurableness of the person or thing excused. The existence of apologies of Christianity presupposes simply the fact of its being assailed, and its readiness and ability to defend itself. Some German writers distinguish between *Apology*, a *popular* defense, and *Apologetic*, a *scientific* or *learned* defense. So Stirm, who calls his valuable popular work: *Apologie des Christenthums für gebildete Leser* (Stuttg., 2d. ed. 1856).

Schleiermacher makes Apologetic the first in the order of the theological sciences. But Christianity cannot be defended before it is made known from the Bible and Church History.

CHAPTER CXCI.

NECESSITY OF APOLOGETIC.

Apologetic is chronologically the oldest branch of Christian theology. It was called forth by the attacks of Jews and Gentiles to which Christianity was exposed at its first appearance (comp. Luke 2 : 34). In more recent times it is required by the assaults of skepticism, and infidelity within the Church. Christians should be "ready always to give answer* to every man that asketh them a reason concerning the hope that is in them, yet with meekness and fear, having a good conscience" (I. Peter 3 : 15).

Apologetic has also an inward necessity. It arises from the impulse of the Christian faith to justify itself before the tribunal of our own reason and to arrive at a clear insight into the grounds on which its convictions are based. Even if idolatry and infidelity should entirely disappear, there would still be room for Apologetic to satisfy the mind of believers. It is an integral part of theology as a science.

The attacks upon Christianity may proceed either from rival religions, as Judaism, heathenism, Mohammedanism; or from the various forms of infidelity within the Church, as Deism, Rationalism, Pantheism, Atheism, Materialism, Agnosticism. The former attacks have long since been overcome, or have ceased to be formidable; the latter are still going on and will continue to the end of time. In this world the Church will always be a militant body. Error assumes ever new shapes and forms, and must be met in all its varieties. Every age must produce its own apologies adapted to prevailing tendencies and wants.

The principal objections to Christianity are in substance always the same, and have been often refuted. Celsus, Porphyry and Julian have anticipated the most plausible arguments of modern Deists and Rationalists.

On the other hand, the chief arguments for Christianity are also the same now as they were in the first and second centuries. Justin Martyr, Origen and Tertullian already urged with

---

* Literally: for apology, ἕτοιμοι ἀεὶ πρὸς ἀπολογίαν.

great freshness and force the arguments from prophecy and types, from miracles, from the rapid spread of Christianity amidst persecution, from its moral fruits, its reasonableness, and its general adaptation to all classes and conditions of man; in short, all the more important external and internal evidences, which reappear in every modern Apology, and will retain their convincing force to the end of the world.

But the evidences change in force and importance according to the wants of the times and modes of attack. At present the internal and moral evidences are of far greater weight than the external evidences of prophecies and miracles. It is now better understood than ever before that the best argument for Christianity is Christ himself.

While error grows weaker with every defeat, truth grows stronger with every victory. If it were not for the obstinacy of the human heart, and the fact that infidelity borrows its best weapons from Christian civilization, it would have disappeared long ago.

CHAPTER CXCII.

LIMITS OF APOLOGETIC.

Apologetic is confined to a discussion of the fundamental claim of Christianity—that is, to the proof that it is the final and perfect religion of God for all men. It does not enter into the several doctrines of Christianity, nor into denominational differences.

In the general defense of Christianity we ask not for the church relations of the apologist, but stand on common ground against the common enemy. Unitarians, like Priestly, Channing and Martineau, as well as Roman Catholics, have written excellent works in defense of Christianity. Apologetic is polemical only against outsiders and unbelievers, and stops at the outer court of the temple. To extend it to internal controversies is to confound it with other branches of Systematic Theology, and to anticipate discussions which properly belong to Dogmatic, Symbolic and Polemic, or to the historical criticism and defense of the Bible.

At the same time there is room for popular apologetic works of a more extended range, as well as for special discussions of particular objections to Christianity. Every doctrine of the gospel may be assailed or misrepresented and is capable of an apologetic or polemical treatment. We only wish to guard the boundary lines of the theological sciences and to prevent interference and repetition.

CHAPTER CXCIII.

VALUE AND USE OF APOLOGETIC.

The value of Apologetic is not so much the conversion of infidels, who seldom read theological books. The Roman emperors and provincial governors to whom the Apologies of Justin Martyr and other fathers were addressed probably never saw a copy of them. Infidelity strikes its roots in the heart and the will rather than in the intellect.*

The Christian system is far more rational than any other religion or system of philosophy, and needs not fear the closest scrutiny. It is the most satisfactory solution of the problems of life. If many difficulties still remain, they are such as can as little be solved by philosophy. Christianity numbers among its adherents the greatest intellects and profoundest thinkers from St. Paul, Origen and Augustin down to Luther, Calvin, Pascal, Bossuet, Dante, Shakespeare, Milton, Bacon, Newton, Kepler, Leibnitz, Schleiermacher, Schelling, Tennyson, Gladstone, and many others, before whom the stars of infidelity dwindle into obscurity.

Conversion begins with a sense of sin and the need of redemption. With the humility and trust of little children must we enter the kingdom of heaven. All honest doubters, like Thomas, who sincerely seek after truth and long for salvation, may be materially aided by apologetic discussions; but proud and self-righteous Pharisees and frivolous Sadducees cannot be converted by any amount of argument.

The chief use of Apologetic is for the Church itself. It strengthens the faith of the believer, it gives him a clearer insight into the immovable foundations of his faith, and shows that Christianity has been equal to any emergency, has outlived

---

* This is popularly expressed in the well-known lines:
"A man convinced against his will
Is of the same opinion still."

all attacks, and grows stronger and stronger with every generation. Every assault ends in a defeat of the assailing force and a new triumph of the assailed. Every new form of error leads to a clearer and stronger statement of the correspondent truth; and so it will be to the end of time. The past of Christianity is sure, and insures the future. The gates of hell shall never prevail against the Church. It is the only possible religion for the civilized world, and religion is as necessary to society as the air we breathe.

CHAPTER CXCIV.

EPOCHS OF APOLOGETIC.

The history of Apologetic may be divided into two main periods:

I. Defense of Christianity against rival religions.
1. Against Judaism. 2. Against Paganism (polytheism, idolatry, Græco-Roman mythology). 3. Against Mohammedanism.

These enemies have been defeated by argument long ago, although Judaism and Mohammedanism remain unchanged. Of modern forms of heathenism the only formidable rivals are Brahmanism, Buddhism, and the state religion of Confucius in China. These must be met by learned missionaries.

II. Defense of Christianity against modern infidelity, which is nominally Christian and fights Christianity with the weapons of Christian culture.
1. Against Deism in England. 2. Against Deism and Atheism in France. 3. Against Rationalism and Pantheism in Germany and other countries. 4. Against Materialism and Positivism. 5. Against the objections of the natural sciences (geology, astronomy, biology, etc.). 6. Against Agnosticism.

The former enemies opposed to Christianity another religion and form of worship; the latter would substitute for it the supremacy of reason and science or literary culture and humanitarianism—in one word, modern civilization, which, in its best elements, is itself a product of Christianity.

CHAPTER CXCV.

APOLOGETIC LITERATURE.

I. ENGLISH WORKS.

JOSEPH BUTLER (Bishop of Durham, d. 1752): *The Analogy of Religion Natural and Revealed to the Constitution and Course of Nature* (1736, and very many edd., English and American). The chief philosophical work against English Deism. It exerted and still exerts a great influence among English-speaking people, but is little known on the Continent. Butler vindicates the Christian religion by analogical evidence from the beautiful harmony of the system of nature and the system of revelation. His argument is negative and probable rather than positive and demonstrative, and hence better calculated to silence objections than to establish truth; yet in its total effect it carries strong conviction to the mind.

NATH. LARDNER (a Presbyterian, leaning to Arianism, d. 1768): *Credibility of the Gospel History* (1727-57) and *Collection of Ancient Jewish and Heathen Testimonies* (1764-67). The most learned historical work against Deism, and a storehouse of external evidences of the Gospels.

WILLIAM PALEY (Archdeacon of Carlisle, d. 1805): *Evidences of Christianity* (1794, many edd.); *Natural Theology* (1802). Against Deism. His *Horæ Paulinæ* (1790) show the credibility of the Acts from undesigned coincidences in the Acts and the Epistles of Paul.

ADAM STOREY FARRAR (Canon and Professor in the University of Durham): *Critical History of Free Thought*, Bampton Lectures for 1862.

HORACE BUSHNELL (Congregational minister at Hartford, Conn., d. 1876): *Nature and the Supernatural as together Constituting the One System of God* (New York, 1858). The work of an original genius.

JAMES MCCOSH (late President of Princeton College): *The Supernatural in Relation to the Natural* (New York, 1862).

* GEORGE P. FISHER (Professor of Church History in Yale University): *The Grounds of Theistic and Christian Belief* (New York, 1883).

RICHARD S. STORRS (Congregational minister in Brooklyn): *The Divine Origin of Christianity indicated by its Historical Effects*, Ely Lectures in Union Theological Seminary (New York, 1884).

LEWIS FRENCH STEARNS (Professor of Theology at Bangor, Me., d. 1892): *The Evidences of Christian Experience*, Ely Lectures for 1890 (New York, 1890).

* ALEXANDER B. BRUCE (Professor of Apologetics in Glasgow): *Apologetics; or, Christianity defensively stated* (Edinb. and New York, 1892). He concludes his work (p. 514) as follows: "In the foregoing pages the authority of Christ has been exalted above that of all other claimants. But it has not been set in antagonism to any legitimate authority. Christ's attitude is not one of zealous antagonism, but of grand comprehension. His teaching sums up and crowns the best thought of the wise in all ages and lands. It is throughout in affinity with reason. The just, wholesome authority of the Church depends on the measure in which Christ's spirit dwells in her. 'The testimony of Jesus is the spirit of prophecy.' Therefore Christianity is the absolute religion. It is indeed, God's final word to men. On the simple principle of the survival of the fittest, it is destined to perpetuity and to ultimate universality."

G. M. MEAD (Professor in Hartford, Conn.): *Supernatural Revelation: An Essay concerning the Basis of the Christian Faith* (New York, 1889).

Small but useful *Manuals of Christian Evidences*, by C. A. ROWE (London, 1887), and G. P. FISHER (New York, 1892).

The BAMPTON LECTURES, a series of eight lectures or sermons, annually delivered at the University of Oxford since 1780, instituted by John Bampton, Canon of Salisbury.

The ELY LECTURES, and MORSE LECTURES of the Union Theological Seminary, New York, since 1866.

II. GERMAN WORKS.

CHR. E. LUTHARDT: *Apologetische Vorträge über die Grundwahrheiten des Christenthums* (Leipzig, 1864; 10th ed. 1883; Engl. transl., *The Fundamental Truths of Christianity*, Edinb., 1865; 6th ed. 1885). *Die modernen Weltanschauungen und ihre praktischen Konsequenzen* (Leipzig, 1880; 3d ed. 1892). Against Rationalism, Pantheism, Materialism and Pessimism.

J. H. A. EBRARD (d. at Erlangen, 1888): *Apologetik* (Gütersloh, 1874 sq., 2 vols.; 2d ed. 1878-81; English translation by W. Stuart and J. Macpherson, Edinburgh, 1887, 2 vols.).

THEODOR CHRISTLIEB (Professor in Bonn, d. 1889): *Moderne Zweifel am christlichen Glauben* (2d ed. Bonn, 1870; English translation, Edinburgh and New York, 5th ed. 1885). Compare his *The Best Methods of Counteracting Modern Infidelity*, a paper read before the Sixth General Conference of the Evangelical Alliance, held in New York, 1873 (New York, 1874). This was the most popular paper read in that Conference, and was translated into several languages.

CH. ERNST BAUMSTARK: *Christliche Apologetik auf anthropologischer Grundlage* (Frankf., 1872-89, 3 vols.).

J. KAFTAN: *Die Wahrheit der christlichen Religion* (Basel, 1888).

FRANZ HETTINGER (Roman Catholic Professor at Würzburg, d. 1890): *Apologie des Christenthums* (Freiburg, i. B., 1863-67; 6th ed., in 5 parts, 1886). *Lehrbuch der Fundamental-Theologie oder Apologetik* (Freiburg, 1879, 2 vols.; 2d. ed. 1888). An able and learned defense both of Christianity and of the Roman Church.

P. SCHANZ (Roman Catholic Professor at Tübingen): *Apologie des Christenthums* (Freiburg, i. B., 1887-88, 3 vols.).

Der Beweis des Glaubens (Gütersloh, 1864 sqq.). An Apologetic Monthly, edited by Zöckler and Grau.

SECOND SECTION: BIBLICAL THEOLOGY.

CHAPTER CXCVI.

NATURE AND OBJECT OF BIBLICAL THEOLOGY.

Biblical Theology, in its modern technical sense, is a systematic representation of the revealed or biblical religion in its primitive form, as laid down in the canonical books of the Old and New Testaments, and as distinct from its subsequent development and comprehension in different ages and branches of the Church.

The Bible itself is no more a system of theology than nature is a system of natural philosophy or natural science, but it contains all the facts and truths which make up such a system.

Biblical Theology embraces both Dogmatic and Ethic, which form an organic unit in the Bible, but they may be separately treated.

It must have frequent reference to the history of revelation, especially in the Old Testament, which teaches doctrine mostly in the form of example; yet the history proper should be left to Historical Theology (History of Israel, Life of Christ, History of the Apostolic Church).

Biblical Theology sums up the scattered results of exegesis and arranges them so as to exhibit the organic unity and completeness of revealed religion. Notwithstanding the great variety of its authors, topics, styles of composition and modes of representation, the Bible contains a harmonious, self-consistent system of divine truth. It stands alone in this respect in the entire history of literature.

But we must distinguish different stages in the revelation of this truth, and different types of teaching. God revealed himself, like a wise educator, in condescending adaptation to man's expanding wants and capacities. The germ of salvation lies already in the first promise (Gen. 3 : 15), the rich fruit appeared in the death and resurrection of Christ. Moreover, the same revealed truth reflects itself differently in different minds and is expressed in different styles. Inspiration must not be confounded with dictation. The various talents which God has distributed among men are not abolished or suspended by inspiration, but purified, invigorated, ennobled and elevated to the highest degree of usefulness. Every prophet of the Old Testament has his peculiar style and temperament. In the New Testament every Gospel is aimed at a particular class of readers—Matthew to Jews, Mark to Romans, Luke to Greeks, John to mature Christians—and reflects the same Christ under a special aspect, as the Messiah, or the great Conqueror, or the healing Physician, or the incarnate Son of God. In the Epistles we may discern four distinct types of doctrine, of James, Peter, Paul and John.

CHAPTER CXCVII.

CONNECTION OF BIBLICAL THEOLOGY WITH OTHER BRANCHES.

Biblical Theology is the connecting link between Exegesis, Church History, and Systematic Theology. Inasmuch as it has to do only with the teaching of the Bible and derives all its matter from the Bible, it belongs to the exegetical department; but its comprehensive systematic form and method connect it more naturally with Systematic Divinity, especially with Dogmatic and Ethic. It is also the starting-point of the doctrinal section of Church History; for in the Bible are contained the vital truths which were subsequently discussed, opposed, perverted, defended, defined and reduced to dogmas by the doctors and councils of the Church.

Biblical Theology then is both exegetico-systematic and exegetico-historical. It is the first and fundamental form of Didactic Theology, on which ecclesiastical and philosophical Dogmatic and Ethic must rest throughout.

It is neither apologetic nor polemic, but objective and impartial; yet not on that account cold or indifferent. He who would fairly exhibit the teaching of the Bible, must sympathize with its spirit and aim.

CHAPTER CXCVIII.

IMPORTANCE OF BIBLICAL THEOLOGY.

Biblical Theology should be the guiding star in all departments of sacred learning, "a focus of light in theological study." It refreshes, fructifies, directs and rectifies dogmatic and moral theology by leading them back to the fountain-head of revealed truth. It brings us face to face with the divine oracles in all their original power and freshness. It contains the living roots of all sound tendencies and developments in the history of Christianity, and furnishes a standard for the proper estimate of theological schools and parties, as well as for a correction of errors.

In the periods of scholastic theology, during the Middle Ages and in the seventeenth century, the Bible was subjected to dogma, and furnished merely proof-texts for a preconceived system of doctrine, whether Roman Catholic, or Lutheran, or Calvinistic. The proofs were taken from any book without discrimination or regard to the connection and the progressive periods of revelation. A passage from Job or Chronicles was deemed as conclusive as a passage from John or Romans. The Westminster Assembly first sent the Westminster Confession of Faith to Parliament (in 1647) without any Scripture proofs, but added them afterwards, by express direction of Parliament, "that the texts of Scripture be printed with the Articles of Faith."

The normal way is to make the Bible the basis of dogma. It is of far more consequence to know the exact teaching of Christ and the Apostles than that of the Fathers, Reformers and Councils.

In the age of the Reformation the zeal for Biblical Theology asserted its supremacy over mediæval scholasticism, and produced such works as Melanchthon's *Loci Theologici* and Calvin's *Institutio Christianæ Religionis*. In our age Biblical Theology again claims the supremacy over Confessional and Speculative Theology, and will give rise to new systems of greater depth and wider breadth than those which have preceded them.

NOTE.—The growing sense of the importance of Biblical Theology has led to the establishment of special chairs in two or three of our theological seminaries. One of them has already become famous and, we may say, historic. Dr. Charles Butler, the only surviving founder of the Union Seminary in New York, endowed such a chair in 1890 by the munificent gift of one hundred thousand dollars, in honor of his friend, the late Dr. Edward Robinson, the pioneer of Palestine exploration and biblical scholarship in America, and one of the first professors of that institution. Dr. Charles A. Briggs, as the first incumbent of the "Edward Robinson Chair of Biblical Theology," delivered, on January 20, 1891, an inaugural address on *The Authority of Holy Scripture* (published by Charles Scribner's Sons), which created an exceptional sensation, and led to the most important heresy trial in America. His transfer to that chair from the chair of Hebrew was vetoed by the General Assembly of the Presbyterian Church at Detroit, May, 1891, and the Presbytery of New York, the largest in that denomination, tried him for unsound views on the fountains of divine authority (Bible, Church, and Reason), the inspiration and the (imaginary) "inerrancy of the original autographs," the Mosaic origin of the Pentateuch and higher criticism generally, and "progressive sanctification after death." The long trial ended in the full acquittal of Dr. Briggs, January 9, 1893. This was a substantial victory for freedom of investigation beyond the narrow bounds of the creeds of the seventeenth century. But the Committee on Prosecution intends to appeal to the General Assembly, which is to meet in May, 1893, and may reverse the decision of the Presbytery of New York. This would lead to serious consequences in the Presbyterian Church.

CHAPTER CXCIX.

DIVISION AND METHOD.

Biblical Theology may embrace the entire Bible, or treat each Testament separately. In the latter case we have Theology of the Old Testament and Theology of the New Testament. The connected treatment brings out more prominently the harmony of the two Covenants; the separate treatment gives a more complete view of each Covenant in its peculiar character as a whole.

The method of Biblical Theology is historico-genetic, and traces the truths of Revelation from the germ through the various stages of growth to the mature fruit. Revelation is an educational process by which God revealed himself gradually to man according to man's expanding wants and capacities.*

The method, moreover, may differ as to the order under

---

* "God having of old time spoken unto the fathers in the prophets by divers portions ($\pi o \lambda v \mu \varepsilon \rho \tilde{o}_{\varsigma}$) and in divers manners ($\pi o \lambda v \tau \rho \acute{o} \pi \omega \varsigma$)," etc. (Heb. 1:1; comp. 6:1). See Canon Bernard's *Progress of Doctrine in the N. T.*

which the subjects are discussed. We may either divide the Old and the New Testament Revelation into distinct periods and treat the doctrines of each in full; or we may run each doctrine continuously through all the periods; or finally, the two methods may be so combined as to present first a general sketch of the distinctive religious character of the several periods, and then a special history of the various doctrines systematically arranged in accordance with their prominence and mutual connection.

CHAPTER CC.

THE OLD AND NEW TESTAMENTS.

(Compare Chapter CXXVI., p. 197.)

The two Testaments or Covenants sustain to each other a relation of unity and a relation of difference. They are one in the idea of revelation and the idea of covenant. They emanate from the same God, they record the same plan of salvation, and aim at the same holiness and eternal happiness of men by communion with God. There is not a single doctrine or precept in the New Testament which has not its germ and root in the Old. There is not a doctrine or precept in the Old Testament which is not set in a much clearer light and brought to perfection in the New. But they differ as the Old and the New, as different degrees in the progressive development of Revelation and the history of redemption.

The Old Testament is the preparation for the New, the New is the fulfillment of the Old. Judaism is the cradle of Christianity, and points prophetically and typically to it as its proper meaning and end. The Old Testament is the dispensation of the law, the New Testament is the dispensation of the gospel. The one is the prophecy, the other the accomplishment, of salvation. Yet there is gospel or promise and comfort also in the Old Covenant, as there is law in the New. Even the law implies the promise of divine grace, without which it would be a cruel irony. The New is the key that unlocks all the mysteries of the Old. The one is unintelligible without the other. Both relations are comprehended in the declaration of our Lord that he came, not to destroy, but to fufill the law and the prophets.

This twofold relation is taught in the Bible itself. The Old Testament, on the one hand, regards the plan of salvation and the kingdom of God revealed therein as embracing all times and nations (Gen. 12:3; 18:18; 26:4; Num. 14:21; Isa. 45:23; 54:10; Ps. 22:27; 86:9; Mal. 1:11); on the other, it acknowledges its own transitory character and prophesies a new covenant of the heart and spirit, as distinct from the covenant of the flesh and letter (Jer. 31:31–33; Ezek. 37:26–28; Heb. 8:6–13; 10:9). The whole religion of the Old Testament culminates in the Messianic hopes and prophecies; and its genius is best represented by John the Baptist, who was willing to decrease that Christ might increase (John 3:30). The New Testament continually refers to the Old as an unbroken testimony to Christ and his salvation (John 5:46, and in many other passages); but just as clearly it asserts its own superiority and represents the law as a schoolmaster to lead men to Christ, as a shadow of the substance of the gospel, as a beggarly religion (Gal. 3:24 sq.; 4:9; Col. 2:17; Heb. 10:1 sq., etc.), so that even the least in the kingdom of Christ occupies a higher position than the greatest saint in the Old Testament (Matt. 11:11). "The law was given by Moses, grace and truth came by Jesus Christ." (John 1:17).

CHAPTER CCI.

THEOLOGY OF THE OLD TESTAMENT.

The Theology of the Old Covenant exhibits a comprehensive and connected view of the revealed religion in its growth, as contained in the Hebrew Scriptures; or the development of the Jewish theocracy in its doctrinal and ethical features.

The Apocryphal books of the Old Testament, being written after the extinction of genuine prophecy, form no part of the Hebrew or Palestinian canon, but are included in the Septuagint and the Egyptian canon, and must be either ignored, or treated in a separate chapter with a view to show the later development of Jewish theology in the period intervening between the age of Ezra and the coming of Christ. (Oehler excludes the Apocrypha, but Schultz, in the later editions, includes them.)

In the history of Revelation before Christ we may distinguish five periods: the PRIMITIVE, before the flood; the PATRIARCHAL; the MOSAIC; the PROPHETIC; and the POST-EXILIC.

I. The PRIMITIVE or ANTEDILUVIAN age, from Adam to Noah. (Genesis 1–12.) It includes:

(*a*) The pure, childlike religion of our first parents before the Fall: the belief in one God as the Maker and Preserver of all things, the doctrine of the divine image in which man was created, his original communion with God in a state of innocence and holiness.

(*b*) The disturbed religion after the Fall: the origin and nature of sin and death, the first promise of redemption (Gen. 3: 15).

We have then here already the fundamental elements of the Old Testament religion.

II. The PATRIARCHAL age, from Abraham to Moses. (Genesis 12 to Exodus 20.) The age of faith and promise. A religion of boundless trust in the only true and living God; the obedience of faith. The evangelic element prevails here over the legalistic. Abraham "the friend of God" and "the father of the faithful" (Isa. 41:8; James 2:23; Rom. 4:16, 17; Gal. 3:7). He stands at the head of the three monotheistic religions of the world. The covenant of circumcision. The promises given to the patriarchs constitute the prophetic and Messianic element. They include:

(*a*) The land of Canaan as a perpetual possession to the posterity of Abraham (Gen. 17:8); while he himself dwelt there as a stranger (Gen. 12:6) and had to buy even the place of his burial (Gen. 23; comp. Acts 7:5).

(*b*) An innumerable posterity, through the son of promise born according to God's counsel, and not according to the ordinary course of nature (comp. Rom. 4:16–22; 9:8). There is a distinction between Jews according to the flesh and Jews according to the spirit; as there is a distinction between circumcision of the flesh and circumcision of the heart (Rom. 2:25–29; Col. 2:11). Change of the name Abram into Abraham, that is, the father of nations (Gen. 17:5).

(*c*) A blessing to all the nations of the earth through the posterity of Abraham: "In thee shall all the families of the earth be blessed" (Gen. 12:3; comp. Gal. 3:8, 16). This is the Messianic part of the promise.

The typical character of the patriarchal age: circumcision—baptism; Canaan—the heavenly home; Isaac's offering—the sacrifice of Christ; Melchisedek, the mysterious outsider, the priest-king (Heb. 7).

III. The MOSAIC age, from Moses to Samuel, the last of the Judges and the first of the Prophets, properly so called. The theocratic legislation began with Moses on Mount Sinai, but was gradually developed, and perhaps not brought into its final shape till the time of Ezra, the second Moses, the restorer of the law (B.C. 458). Israel becomes a nation and a Church on the basis of an act of divine mercy, the deliverance from the bondage of Egypt, which again is a type of the redemption from sin. The Ten Commandments enjoin love to God (first table) and love to man (second table), as the sum and substance of true religion (Ex. 20; comp. Matt. 22 : 38–40). Pedagogic and typical import of the Mosaic law : it developed the sense of sin and guilt and the need of atonement, and thus served as a schoolmaster to lead men to Christ (Rom. 3 : 20 ; 5 : 20 ; 7 : 7, 13; Gal. 3 : 24). Clearer revelation of God as Jehovah, the covenant God of his people, his justice, holiness, long-suffering, patience and mercy. The training of this people by the long pilgrimage through the desert, where they were alone with their God, away from the contaminating influences of idolatrous nations, and where they had to depend solely on him for temporal and spiritual blessing, for care and protection under all trials and dangers.

Moses was the divinely appointed deliverer and law-giver of Israel and the organ of all the powers of the theocracy. In this view he occupies a unique position and had no successor. Joshua and the Judges merely carried out and defended what he had established. Like Abraham, he is equally revered by the followers of three religions. He controlled the whole history of Israel; he furnished the best elements to Mohammedanism; the Decalogue as explained and fulfilled by Christ is the rule of Christian life and underlies all good government; in the whole history of religion, he is only surpassed by Christ, of whom he wrote (Deut. 18 : 15 ; John 5 : 46) and for whom he prepared the way.*

* Heinrich Heine, an infidel Jew, but a great genius, gives in his *Confessions*, written 1854 (*Werke*, vol. iv., p. 45), the following striking description of Moses: "What a gigantic figure! I cannot imagine that Og, King of Bashan, was greater. How small appears Mount Sinai if Moses stands on the top! This mountain is only the base on which stand the feet of a man whose head reaches into heaven, where he speaks with God. . . . He took a tribe of poor shepherds and created them a people which was to defy the centuries, a great eternal, holy people which was to serve as a model to all other nations: he created Israel!"

IV. The PROPHETIC age, from Samuel to Malachi. The prophetic office was organized by Samuel. Before there were isolated prophets, Moses himself being one of the greatest of prophets, who stood in constant communication with Jehovah and was the organ of his revelation to his people. Prophetic utterances are scattered through all the historical books and reach back to the beginning of the race (Gen. 3:15). But Samuel gave prophecy an institutional character and established "Schools of Prophets," which flourished two or three hundred years.*

From his time on there was an almost unbroken succession of divinely inspired teachers called "prophets," who in connection with, and often in opposition to, the kings and priests controlled the history of the theocracy during the undivided and the divided monarchy, the exile and the restoration under Ezra and Nehemiah. Sixteen of them left writings.

The prophetic office represented the spiritual part of the theocracy, and the divine presence and power in the forms and ceremonies of religion; it acted upon the kingly and sacerdotal offices; it kept them from stagnation and degeneracy; it stimulated the consciences of rulers and people; it communicated to them the oracles of God; it expounded the law, warned them of sin and danger, urged them to repentance and faith; it announced the judgments, but also the mercies, of God, and unfolded the picture of the suffering and conquering Messiah as the hope of Israel.

The Messianic predictions are the flower of the prophecy. They culminate in Isaiah, the evangelist among the prophets, especially in the second part, called Deutero-Isaiah, written towards the close of the exile by "the Great Unknown."

The powerful influence of the prophets may be seen in Nathan at the court of David, and in Elijah and Elisha in the

* I. Sam. 8:7; 9:6, 19-27; 15:16-30; I. Chron. 9:22; 26:28; 29:29. Hence the phrase πάντες οἱ προφῆται ἀπὸ Σαμουήλ (Acts 3:24). There were prophetic schools and societies at Ramah, Bethel, Gibeah, Gilgal, Mizpah, and the region of Jericho (I. Sam. 7:16, 17; 8:1, 2, etc.; comp. II. Kings 2:3–5; 4:38). The members were called "sons of the prophets" (*bene hanephiim*). (I. Kings 20:35; II. Kings 2:3, 5, 7, 15; 6:1; 9:1.) They were at times very numerous; Obadiah concealed one hundred prophets; from Jericho fifty were sent to seek Elijah (I. Kings 18:4 sq.; 22:6; II. Kings 2:7). Of course not all pupils became really prophets, nor was the training by older prophets sufficient; it required first and last a divine call, and divine inspiration and enthusiasm to be a real messenger of God and an organ of his revelation.

kingdom of Israel. The prophets speak in the name of God, hence the phrase, "Thus saith the Lord," or "Oracle of God." They challenge obedience to their message as the word of God. Even King David submitted to the rebuke of Nathan (II. Sam. 12:13 sq.; comp. 24:11 sq.). The prophets were statesmen as well as teachers and preachers, but both from the theocratic standpoint; their activity referred exclusively to the kingdom of God, and to foreign nations only so far as they were connected with the fortunes of the people of God. They were watchmen on the walls of Zion, and from this their vision extended to the uttermost nations of the earth and the end of time. They were the Reformers and Puritans of the Jewish theocracy.

The writings of the prophets constitute a unique body of literature which has no parallel among other nations, and is as remarkable and grand as the epistles of the New Testament.

During the prophetic period was also developed the poetic literature of the Hebrews. Job is very important for the doctrine of God and of his providential government. The Psalms contain Hebrew theology in the form of devotion; the Proverbs and Ecclesiastes furnish a system of ethic in the shape of brief sentences or maxims of practical wisdom and experience.

V. The POST-EXILIAN period, from Ezra to John the Baptist, the last representative of the Old Covenant and immediate forerunner of Christ. The organization of the synagogue; the origin of the religious sects of the Pharisees, Sadducees and Essenes; the hedging of the law by the traditions of the elders; the Greek Version of the Scriptures; the whole literature of the Jewish Apocrypha and Pseudepigrapha; contact with Greek thought and Platonic philosophy (Philo of Alexandria).

CHAPTER CCII.

THEOLOGY OF THE NEW TESTAMENT: THE TEACHING OF JESUS.

In the Theology of the New Testament, we must first distinguish between the Theology of Christ as derived from his teaching in the Gospels, and the Theology of the Apostles as contained in the Acts and Epistles. The former is the living germ of the latter.

The teaching of Jesus is altogether unique. He was neither self-taught, nor school-taught, nor inspired like the prophets and apostles. He spoke directly out of the fullness of the indwelling God, as his only-begotten Son. He was not simply a witness of the truth, but the Truth itself, and the Light of the world. His teaching is a self-revelation of his divine-human person, as the Son of God and the Son of Man, as the Messiah and Saviour of the world, as the founder of the New Covenant and the Kingdom of Heaven upon the earth. His teaching is a reflection of his life, and is as free from error as his life was free from sin. It is the union of infallible teaching with a sinless life which raises him above the founders of other religions, and above all moral philosophers, ancient and modern.

As Jesus himself wrote nothing, we have to depend upon the reports of his disciples in the canonical Gospels.

The Synoptic teaching relates chiefly to the Kingdom of God and the duties of those who enter therein, and is brief, sententious, parabolic and pictorial. This style was best calculated to impress itself upon the heart and memory of the common people in Galilee.

The Johannean discourses, which were mostly delivered in Jerusalem before the learned Pharisees and Scribes and in the private circle of his disciples, discuss the deepest mysteries of faith and eternal life, of the relation of the Son to the Father, to the world and to believers. They differ also in style, which strikingly agrees with that of the Johannean Epistles. They were evidently reproduced by the congenial mind of the beloved disciple, as understood in the light of the promised illumination of the Holy Spirit, and presented in his own language for the second or third generation of Christians. But no human genius could have invented such heavenly discourses, any more than the miracles of Jesus; no honest writer could have practiced such a deception upon his readers as the hypothesis of invention involves.

On close investigation there is no material contradiction between the Synoptic and the Johannean teaching of Christ. They supplement each other. It is the duty of the biblical theologian to show the harmony as well as the difference.

NOTE.—Weiss acknowledges the Johannean Gospel discourses as genuine throughout, though subjectively colored. Wendt distinguishes in them original sayings (as the λόγια in Matthew) and later additions from the school of John. Beyschlag represents the Synoptic and Johannean teaching separately in the full conviction of the entire genuineness of the fourth Gospel (vol. i., pp. 212 sqq.), but he explains away the passages on the preëxistence of Christ (John 6 : 62; 8 : 58; 17 : 4, 5, 24, and in the prologue).

If the fourth Gospel in whole or in part were the product of an unknown and unknowable Christian Plato of the second century, it could not be a source for the teaching of Jesus, but only a record of post-apostolic tradition, or a theological romance. This would make the Johannean problem more difficult and absolutely insolvable.

CHAPTER CCIII.

THE TEACHING OF THE APOSTLES.

In the apostolic period three main types of doctrine may be distinguished, which are respectively represented by Peter, Paul and John, with subordinate differences in the Epistle of James, the Epistle to the Hebrews, and the Apocalypse.

The Petrine type, to which also James belongs, may be called the Jewish Christian; the Pauline type, the Gentile Christian; the Johannean type, the harmonious adjustment of the two. The first views Christianity predominantly in its harmony with the Old Testament; the second in its distinction, its newness and independence; the third rises above the antagonism of Jewish and Gentile Christians and represents a new generation. The first was the gospel for the Jews; the second the gospel for the Gentiles; the third harmonizes the national and religious differences in the higher union of Christ.

The Epistle of James, "the brother of the Lord," is probably the oldest of the New Testament writings and also nearest to the Old Testament, like the Gospel of Matthew. It represents the gospel itself as law, but as the "perfect law of liberty" (James 1 : 25), which implies that the Mosaic law was imperfect and a law of bondage.

Peter is the connecting link between James and Paul, as the Gospel of Mark mediates between Matthew and Luke. He first made the confession that Jesus is the Messiah, the Son of the living God (Matt. 16 : 16), which is the foundation article of the Christian faith. He agreed with Paul in the principle that Jews and Gentiles alike are saved without the unbearable yoke of the ceremonial law, simply and solely "through the grace of the Lord Jesus Christ" (Acts 15 : 11); and he rose to the liberal conviction that "in every nation he that fears God and works righteousness is acceptable to him" (Acts 10: 35).

Paul's fundamental idea is righteousness in Christ, apprehended by faith and operative in love, in opposition to the legal self-righteousness of the Jews. His doctrinal system turns on the great antithesis of sin and grace. Out of Christ, sin and death reign; in Christ, righteousness and life.

The anonymous Epistle to the Hebrews forms the transition from Paul to John, and gives us the fullest insight into the eternal priesthood and sacrifice of Christ.

John, the mystic seer among the Apostles, penetrates most deeply into the character of Christ, on whose bosom he leaned, and strikes the keynote of the highest type of Theology in the word: "God is love." God's love to all mankind manifested in Jesus Christ, is the central idea of John's Dogmatic; man's love to God and the brethren, is the sum and substance of his Ethic. John and Paul meet in the idea of love, as the highest of the Christian graces, which binds and makes fruitful all the other graces and shall abide forever, when faith shall have passed into sight, and hope into fruition.

The best representations of New Testament Theology enter into all the differences, and give us almost as many apostolic types of teaching as there are books in the New Testament. But there is unity as well as diversity in the teaching of Christ and his Apostles, and we need a work in which this unity is more fully brought out.

CHAPTER CCIV.

HISTORY OF BIBLICAL THEOLOGY.

Biblical Theology as to spirit and substance is as old as the Bible, but as to scientific form it dates only from the eighteenth century. It is, we may say, a child of German Rationalism and was born at the same time with higher or literary criticism, but it is perfectly consistent with faith, and is cultivated also by evangelical and orthodox theologians.

As long as the teaching of the Bible was identified with that of the Church or with orthodoxy, there was no motive for the special treatment of the former; but when the two were more or less clearly distinguished, Biblical Theology began to be cultivated, first in a spirit of hostility to Church orthodoxy; then in opposition to the Bible itself, as being a mixture of facts and myths, of truth and error; but at last, in a spirit of impartial historical inquiry. The third phase represents the true standpoint. Supreme regard is due to the teaching of the Bible, subordinate regard to the teaching of the Church derived from it.

Patristic Theology was both biblical and traditional; it derived all its material and arguments from the Bible as interpreted by the rule of faith. Scholastic Theology was traditional and ecclesiastical, and rested on the Fathers rather than the Bible. The theology of the Reformation was a revival of Biblical Theology (in spirit and aim, though not in form), but was soon succeeded by another phase of scholasticism intensely confessional and polemical. Then followed the radical reaction of Rationalism, which broke loose from all restraint of Church authority and viewed the Bible itself as a mere human production to be explained and judged like any other book.

Rationalists made the first attempts to treat the Bible doctrines historically in distinction from and in alleged opposition to all subsequent systems of Church orthodoxy. To this class belong the now antiquated biblical theologies of Ammon (1792), G. L. Bauer (1796–1800), Kayser (1813), De Wette (1st ed. 1813, 2d ed. 1830, the ablest among them), Baumgarten-Crusius (1828), Cramer (1830), Cölln (ed. by D. Schulz, 1836).

The revival of evangelical faith since Schleiermacher and Neander gave a new spirit and character to Biblical Theology. Neander's *Planting and Training of the Apostolic Church* (1832 and since) marks an epoch and enters into the discussion of the apostolic types of doctrine with deep spiritual sympathy and with an eye to their unity as well as diversity. Since that time Bible Theology of the New Testament has been chiefly cultivated by Schmid, Reuss, Messner, Van Oosterzee, Weiss and Beyschlag; that of the Old Testament, by Hengstenberg, Hävernick, Vatke, Steudel, Von Hofmann, Oehler, Ewald, Kuenen and Schultz.

CHAPTER CCV.

LITERATURE OF BIBLICAL THEOLOGY.

I. OLD TESTAMENT THEOLOGY.

G. F. OEHLER (Ephorus in Tübingen, d. 1872): *Prolegomena zur Theologie des Alten Test.* (Stuttgart, 1845).

H. A. C. HÄVERNICK (d. 1846): *Vorlesungen über die Theologie des A. T.; herausg. von Hahn mit Vorwort von Dorner* (Erlangen, 1848; 2d ed., with notes by Herm. Schultz, Frankf.-a-M., 1863). Orthodox and learned, in the spirit of Hengstenberg.

* HEINRICH EWALD (d. 1874): *Die Lehre der Bibel von Gott oder Theologie des Alten und Neuen Bundes* (Leipzig, 1871-75, 4 vols.). The last work of this great scholar. It comprehends the Old and New Testament theology. Translated in part, by Th. Goadby (Edinb. 1888).

* HERMANN SCHULTZ (Professor in Göttingen, School of Ewald): *Alttestamentliche Theologie. Die Offenbarungsreligion auf ihrer vorchristlichen Entwickelungstufe* (1869 ; 4th ed., entirely revised, Göttingen, 1889, 821 pp.). English translation by J. A. Paterson, Professor of Old Testament theology in the United Presbyterian College, Edinburgh (Edinburgh, 1892, 2 vols.).

* G. F. OEHLER (d. 1872): *Theologie des A. T.* (Tübingen, 1873, 2 vols.; 3d ed. Stuttgart, 1891, 1 vol.). English translation by E. D. Smith and S. Taylor (Edinburgh, 1874), revised by George E. Day, *Theology of the Old Testament* (New York, 1883, 1 vol.). Very useful for students.

ABR. KUENEN (d. 1891): *De Godsdienst van Israel tot den ondergang van den Joodschen Staat* (Haarlem, 1869-70, 2 vols.). Hypercritical. English translation by A. W. May: *The Religion of Israel to the Fall of the Jewish State* (London, 1874-75, 3 vols.).

* CHARLES A. BRIGGS (Professor in Union Seminary, N. Y.): *Biblical Study: its Principles, Methods and History* (New York and Edinburgh, 1883; 4th ed. 1891). Ch. XI., 367-405.

F. W. SCHULTZ (of Breslau) in Zöckler's *Handbuch der Theol. Wissenschaften* (1883), vol. i., pp. 289-338.

A. DUFF (United Presbyterian): *Old Testament Theology* (Edinburgh, 1891).

B. STADE (Professor in Giessen): *Alttestamentliche Theologie* (in course of preparation, 1893).

A. B. DAVIDSON (Professor of Hebrew, New College, Edinb.): *Theology of the Old Testament* (in course of preparation for the Briggs-Salmond "International Theological Library," 1893).

The CHRISTOLOGY of the Old Testament, or MESSIANIC PROPHECIES, are treated in special works by HENGSTENBERG (Berlin, 1829-32; 2d ed. 1854-57, 3 vols. transl. by Theod. Meyer, Edinb., 4 vols.); RIEHM (Gotha, 1875; 2d ed. 1885); JAMES DRUMMOND (*The Jewish Messiah*, London, 1877); P. J. GLOAG (Edinburgh, 1879); ED. BÖHL (Vienna, 1882); C. VON ORELLI (Vienna, 1882; English transl., Edinb. 1885); C. A. BRIGGS (*Messianic Prophecy*, New York and Edinb., 1886); FRANZ DELITZSCH (*Messianische*

Weissagungen in geschichtlicher Folge, 1890; transl. by Samuel Ives Curtiss of Chicago, Edinburgh, 1891).

II. NEW TESTAMENT THEOLOGY.

* NEANDER (d. 1850): *History of the Planting and Training of the Church under the Apostles* (second part, Hamburg, 1832; 5th ed. 1862; English translation by Ryland, Edinb. 1842, 2 vols.; revised by Ez. G. Robinson, New York, 1864).

CHR. FR. SCHMID (d. 1352 at Tübingen): *Biblical Theology of the N. T.* (edited by Weizsäcker, Stuttgart, 1853, 2 vols.; 4th ed. 1869). Eminently biblical and sound. The abridged English translation by G. H. Venables (Edinburgh, 1870) omits the general statements which are very important.

ED. REUSS (d. at Strassburg, 1891): *Histoire de la théologie chrétienne au siècle apostolique* (*History of the Christian Theology of the Apostolic Age*) (Strassburg, 1852, 2 vols.; 3d ed. 1864). Translated into English by Miss A. Harwood (London, 1872), also into Dutch and Swedish. Able and critical.

* THOMAS DEHANY BERNARD (Canon and Chancellor of Wells): *The Progress of Doctrine in the New Testament* (Bampton Lectures, London, 1864; 4th ed. 1878). Compare his more recent work quoted on p. 332.

F. C. BAUR (d. at Tübingen, 1861): *Lectures on New Testament Theology* (German). Published after his death by his son (1864). Independent, critical, and suggestive, but he makes Paul almost the founder of Christianity.

J. J. VAN OOSTERZEE (Professor at Utrecht, d. 1882): *The Theology of the New Testament* (Dutch; German transl., Barmen, 1869; English transl. by Maurice J. Evans, London, 1870, and by George E. Day, New York, 1871). A brief manual for students.

A. IMMER: *New Testament Theology* (Bern, 1878).

* BERNHARD WEISS (Professor in Berlin): *Handbook of the Biblical Theology of the New Test.* (Berlin, 1868; 5th ed. 1888; transl. from the 3d ed. by Dav. Eaton and J. E. Duguid, Edinb. 1882-83, 2 vols.). The most complete and accurate work, which rests on a thorough exegetical and critical study of all the details.

R. GRAU, in Zöckler's *Handbuch der Theol. Wissenschaften* (1833 sqq.), vol. i., pp. 549-633.

* WILLIBALD BEYSCHLAG (Professor in Halle): *Neutestamentliche Theologie oder geschichtliche Darstellung der Lehren Jesu und des Urchristenthums nach den neutestamentlichen Quellen* (Halle-a-S., 1891-92, 2 vols.). The most important work after that of Weiss, and more full on the teaching of Jesus.

Professor SCHÜRER and Professor GRAFE are preparing manuals on *New Testament Theology* (1893).

(a) The Teaching of Jesus:

JOS. P. THOMPSON (d. 1870): *The Theology of Christ* (New York, 1870).

W. F. GESS (d. 1891): *Christi Person und Werk, nach Christi Selbstzeugniss und der Apostel* (Basel, 1870-78).

E. WÖRNER: *Die Lehre Jesu* (Basel, 1882).

* H. H. WENDT (b. 1853, Professor in Heidelberg, School of Ritschl): *Die Lehre Jesu* (Göttingen, first part, on the sources, 1886; second part, 1890). The second part was translated by John Wilson: *The Teaching of Jesus* (New York, 1892, 2 vols.).

THOMAS DEHANY BERNARD: *The Central Teaching of Jesus Christ. A Study and Exposition of the Five Chapters of the Gospel according to St. John*, 13-17 inclusive (London and New York, 1892). Reverential and devout, but less important, scientifically, than his former work quoted on p. 331. Compare the literature on the Life of Christ, ch. clxxii., p. 271.

(b) The Teaching of the Apostles (*Apostolische Lehrbegriffe*):

Discussed by LUTTERBECK (Roman Catholic, 1852, 2 vols.), MESSNER (1856), and also in the respective sections of the works on the Apostolic Age by NEANDER, LECHLER, SCHAFF, WEIZSÄCKER, and PFLEIDERER.

(c) The Teaching of the Several Apostles:

Paul by USTERI (1824; 6th ed. 1851), DÄHNE (1835), STANLEY LEATHES (1869), W. J. IRONS (1876), A. SABATIER (1870; 2d ed. 1881; transl. from the French by J. G. Findlay, with preface by Sabatier, N. Y., 1891), HOLSTEN (1868 and 1880), O. PFLEIDERER (1873; in English, 1885), LORENZ (1884), R. T. KNOWLING (1892), G. B. STEVENS (1892).

The Teaching of *Peter* by B. WEISS (1855).

The Teaching of the Epistle to the *Hebrews* by RIEHM (1859; 2d ed. 1866).

The Teaching of *John* by FROMMANN (1839), K. R. KÖSTLIN (1843), HILGENFELD (1849), B. WEISS (1862).

The Teaching of *James* by W. SCHMIDT (1869) and KÜBEL (1880).

The Teaching of the *Apocalypse* by H. GEBHARDT (1873) and WILLIAM MILLIGAN (1886).

Compare the literature on the Apostolic Age, p. 273.

THIRD SECTION: DOGMATIC THEOLOGY.

CHAPTER CCVI.

DEFINITION AND CONTENTS OF DOGMATIC THEOLOGY.

Dogmatic or Didactic Theology, usually called Systematic Theology,* is a comprehensive scientific statement of Christian truth contained in the Scriptures and believed and taught in the Church. A dogma in the technical ecclesiastical sense (*statutum, decretum*) is a doctrine formulated by Church authority or a publicly recognized article of faith.†

Dogmatic Theology formerly embraced also Moral Theology or Christian Ethic; but now they are distinct and separately treated.

Each system of Dogmatic must embrace the following departments (*Loci Theologici* ‡):

1. BIBLIOLOGY: a discussion of the Bible, viewed as the supreme rule of faith and duty, and its relation to the subordinate rules of tradition and reason.

2. THEOLOGY, in the narrower sense, that is, the doctrine of God: the knowableness or cognoscibility of God (gnosticism and agnosticism); the arguments for his existence; his names and attributes; the unity and trinity of the Godhead (Father, Son and Spirit; the trinity of essence, and the trinity of revelation). Theism in opposition to Deism and Pantheism.

3. COSMOLOGY: God's relation to the world. The doctrine of creation, preservation and providence. The decrees, or the

---

* *Theologia dogmatica,* as distinct from *Theologia moralis;* also *Doctrina Christiana; Institutio* or *Institutiones Christianæ Religionis* The term Systematic Theology is customary among English and American writers, but is too wide, and would embrace also Apologetic, Symbolic, Polemic and Ethic.

† On the meaning of dogma and the difference between truth, doctrine and dogma, see above, pp. 249 sq.

‡ *Loci Communes* means, in philosophical usage, fundamental ideas and self-evident truths. Melanchthon gave this title, and also the title *Loci Theologici,* to his dogmatic work, and later Lutheran divines accepted it in the sense of chief articles of the dogmatic system.

eternal purpose of creating and saving mankind in Christ. The *Theodicy*. The best system of the moral universe.

4. ANGELOLOGY: the doctrine of good and bad angels. Satanology or Diabolology is a part of it and treats of Satan and the prehistoric fall.

5. ANTHROPOLOGY, or the doctrine of man in his relation to God: the image of God; the rational and moral constitution of man; the origin of souls; free-will; the state of original innocence; the fall and its consequences. The state of redemption (conversion, regeneration, sanctification) is embraced in Soteriology.

6. HAMARTOLOGY, or PONEROLOGY: the doctrine of sin, in all its aspects and consequences. Part of Anthropology and Ethic.

7. CHRISTOLOGY, or the doctrine of Christ's person: his humanity, his divinity, and the relation of the two.

8. SOTERIOLOGY, that is, the doctrine of salvation, or Christ's work and office as Prophet, Priest and King; the atonement, its nature and extent.

9. PNEUMATOLOGY: the doctrine of the Holy Spirit; his person and his relation to the Father and the Son; his office and work in the regeneration, sanctification and glorification of believers.

10. ECCLESIOLOGY: the doctrine of the Church and the kingdom of God; its constitution, attributes, authority and aim.

11. SACRAMENTOLOGY: the doctrine of the sacraments and the means of grace.

12. ESCHATOLOGY, or the doctrine of the last things: death and immortality; hades and the middle state; the second advent; the general resurrection and the judgment; heaven and hell; the beatific vision and life everlasting.

These are the deepest and highest themes which can engage human thought. Hence the great importance and interest of Dogmatic Theology.

CHAPTER CCVII.

THE SOURCES OF DOGMATIC THEOLOGY.

There are three sources of Dogmatic Theology: the Bible, the Church, and the Christian consciousness or experience.

The Bible contains the word of God written by holy men

as they were moved by the Holy Spirit (2 Pet. 1:21). It is, therefore, the infallible rule of faith and practice, and nothing can claim the authority of a dogma or an article of faith which is not founded on the teaching of Christ and the Apostles.

The Church is the keeper and expounder of the Bible, but any particular branch of the Church universal is liable to err, and may be corrected and reformed as it advances in the knowledge of truth.

The Christian consciousness and experience appropriates and digests the matter supplied by the Bible and the creeds of the Church.

Dogmatic Theology, therefore, comprises a biblical, a churchly or confessional, and a personal and experimental element. It is a rational and critical digest of the teaching of the Bible and the Church. These three elements may be combined in one work, or may be separately treated with more fullness.

CHAPTER CCVIII.

BIBLICAL DOGMATIC.

Biblical Dogmatic is a systematic exhibition of the Bible doctrine of faith and duty as an organic whole. It is essentially the same as Biblical Theology, but differs from its genetic historical method. It gives the results systematically arranged, while Biblical Theology traces the revealed religion in its gradual growth and its various stages and types.

Every dogmatic system should begin with a brief statement of the teaching of the Bible as containing the germs of the subsequent confessional developments.

LITERATURE.

K. IM. NITZSCH (d. 1868): *System der christlichen Lehre* (Bonn, 1829; 6th ed. 1851; Eng. transl. by Robert Montgomery and Hennen, Edinburgh, 1849). Embraces Biblical Dogmatic and Ethic, but with constant reference to modern opinions.

JOHANN TOBIAS BECK (1804–78; Professor in Tübingen since 1843), following in the line of Bengel and Oetinger, endeavored to build up in various writings a purely biblical theology without any regard to historical developments. His theology may be called pneumatic and realistic Biblicism. He was a colleague of Dr. Baur and his antipode, but in respectful personal relations with him, and exerted a great influence upon the students by his enthusiasm for the depth and sufficiency of the Bible. He wrote, *Einleitung in das System der christlichen Lehre* (*Propædeutik*) (Stuttgart, 1838; 2d ed. 1870). *Christliche Lehrwissenschaft nach den biblischen Urkunden* (Stuttgart, vol. i., 1841; 2d ed. 1875; unfinished). *Umriss d. biblischen Seelenlehre* (Stuttgart, 1843; 3d ed. 1877; translation, *Outlines of Biblical Psychology*, Edinburgh, 1877). *Christliche Liebeslehre* (1875). *Leitfaden d. christl. Glaubenslehre für Kirche, Schule, und Haus* (1862; 2d ed. 1869). *Christliche Ethik* (published after his death by Lindenmeyer, 1882–83, 3 vols.). See an article on Beck's theology by Kübel in Herzog[2], vol. xvii., pp. 693–706.

ROBERT B. KÜBEL (Beck's pupil and successor as Professor in Tübingen) : *Das christliche Lehrsystem nach der heiligen Schrift* (Gütersloh, 1874, 2 vols.). Embraces Ethic and Dogmatic.

CHAPTER CCIX.

CONFESSIONAL OR CHURCHLY DOGMATIC.

Confessional or Churchly (Ecclesiastical) Dogmatic exhibits the doctrinal system of a particular Church as laid down in the symbolical books or confessions of faith. It is chiefly historical, as Biblical Theology is chiefly exegetical. Its object may be either purely objective and historical, or also personal and denominational (but not necessarily sectarian).

Denominational differences are not always confessional or doctrinal. The Presbyterians, Methodists, and Baptists are divided into several denominations or independent organizations, which acknowledge the same creeds or confessions, and differ only in minor matters of worship and discipline.*

There are as many kinds of Ecclesiastical Dogmatic as there are creeds or confessions of faith. Each has its own standard of orthodoxy and heterodoxy.

The dogmatic systems of the Greek and Roman Churches are based on the Bible and tradition, as equally authoritative sources and binding rules of faith and public teaching; but with this difference, that the Greek Church confines tradition to the first seven Œcumenical Councils, while the Roman Church extends it to the twentieth Œcumenical Council of

---

* According to the census of the United States of 1890, there are in the United States over one hundred (145) denominations and sects, and according to Whitaker's Almanack for 1892, there are as many or even more (254) in Great Britain. But they may be reduced to less than a dozen creeds or confessions. See the statistical tables on p. 24, and the *Census Bulletins* published in numbers by Dr. Henry K. Carroll, Washington, 1892 and 1893.

1870, and lodges it permanently in the official infallibility of the Pope. The Protestant systems of Dogmatic are based upon the Scriptures, as the only infallible rule of faith, use tradition with critical discrimination, and allow larger liberty to reason and private judgment. Rationalism makes reason the judge of both Scripture and tradition.

We shall now give a brief outline of the principal dogmatic systems in their chronological order.

CHAPTER CCX.

DOGMATIC THEOLOGY OF THE GREEK CATHOLIC CHURCH.

Catholicism, in its technical, ecclesiastical sense, has two branches: the Oriental or Greek, and the Occidental or Roman. They show the influence, one of the Greek, the other of the Roman, spirit. The former is older, more metaphysical, and stationary; the latter is more practical and progressive, and was completed in the Vatican Council of 1870. They are very similar in theory, yet very antagonistic in fact. The Pope of Rome and the Czar-Pope of Russia are the greatest rivals.

The Dogmatic of the Eastern or Greek Church, which claims the monopoly of pure, primitive orthodoxy, is based upon the doctrinal decisions of the first seven Œcumenical Councils (325–787), especially the Nicæno-Constantinopolitan Creed of 381 (without the *Filioque*). Its chief authorities among the Fathers are Athanasius, Gregory of Nazianzen, Gregory of Nyssa, Cyril of Alexandria, and especially John of Damascus (d. after 750).

The Greek Dogmatic is metaphysical and lays chief stress on the œcumenical doctrines of the Trinity, the Incarnation, and the duo-physitic and dyo-thelitic personality of Christ. It adheres to the older anthropology and soteriology, and has never been affected by the Augustinian doctrine of total depravity and the loss of free-will.

LITERATURE.

St. John of Damascus (Chrysorrhoas): Ἔκδοσις ἀκριβὴς τῆς ὀρθοδόξου πίστεως (*De Fide orthodoxa*), in Migne's *Patrologia Græca*, tom. xciv., pp. 789–1228 (Paris, 1864). It is in process of translation by Professor Salmond of Aberdeen for the "Post-Nicene Library of the Fathers."

338   THEOLOGICAL PROPÆDEUTIC.

THE ORTHODOX CONFESSION OF THE EASTERN CHURCH (1643), and THE EIGHTEEN DECREES OF THE SYNOD OF JERUSALEM (1672). Both in Greek and Latin in Schaff's *Creeds of Christendom*, vol. ii., pp. 275–444.

PHILARET (b. 1782, d. 1867, Metropolitan of Moscow): *The Longer Catechism of the Orthodox Russian Church*, revised and published by the Holy Synod of St. Petersburg (Moscow, 1839, in several languages and many editions; English translation by Blackmore, Aberdeen, 1845). The doctrinal part of this catechism is printed in Schaff's *Creeds*, vol. ii., pp. 445–542.

LE QUIEN : *Oriens Christianus* (Paris, 1740, 3 vols.).

W. GASS : *Symbolik der Griechischen Kirche* (Berlin, 1872).

ARTHUR P. STANLEY: *Lectures on 'the History of the Eastern Church* (London and New York, 4th ed. 1869).

For other works on the Greek and Russian Church, see Schaff, *Creeds of Christendom*, vol. i., pp. 43, 46, 50, 54, 61, 68; also the "Schaff-Herzog Encycl.," vol. ii., p. 904.

CHAPTER CCXI.

DOGMATIC THEOLOGY OF THE ROMAN CATHOLIC CHURCH.

Roman Catholic Dogmatic is founded on the theology of the Fathers, the doctrinal Decrees of the Council of Trent (1563), and of the Council of the Vatican (1870). It is best expounded and defended by Bellarmin, Bossuet, Möhler, and Perrone.

It is essentially the same with Greek orthodoxy, but differs from it in the doctrines of the Papacy, the double Procession of the Holy Spirit, the Immaculate Conception of the Virgin Mary as defined by Pius IX. in 1854, and the Infallibility of the Pope as decreed in 1870. It is also more fully developed in anthropology, soteriology and eschatology.

The Roman Catholic Creed is the most complete and most logical of all dogmatic systems, as the papacy is the most complete and absolute form of government; but it requires the sacrifice of reason and freedom, which God himself has given us, and for the use of which we are individually responsible.

LITERATURE.

The chief builders of the Roman Catholic creed before the Reformation were St. Augustin, Gregory the Great, and Thomas Aquinas. The last is the favorite divine of Pope Leo XIII., who recommended him for study in an encyclical of August 4, 1879, and ordered a magnificent edition of all his works at his own expense.

HENRICUS DENZINGER (Professor at Würzburg, d. 1862): *Enchiridion Symbolorum et Definitionum, quæ de Rebus Fidei et Morum a Conciliis Œcu-*

menicis et summis Pontificibus emanarunt (Wirceburgi, 6th ed. by Stahl, 1888). A very convenient compend.

GIOVANNI PERRONE (b. 1794, Professor in the Jesuit college in Rome, d. 1876): *Prælectiones theologicæ* (Rome, 1835 sqq., 9 vcls., and often republished at Turin, Paris, Brussels and Ratisbon). The *Compend* by the same author has appeared in different languages and many editions.

German works on Roman Dogmatic by F. BRENNER (1830, 3 vols.), MÖHLER (*Symbolik*, several edd.), H. KLEE (4th ed. 1831), F. R. DIERINGER (5th ed. 1865), FR. FRIEDHOFF (1871), J. B. HEINRICH (1874–89, 7 vols.), HETTINGER (1888), and SCHEEBEN (1892, 3 vols.).

French works: BOSSUET: ("The Eagle of Meaux," "The Last of the Fathers," d. 1704): *Exposition de la doctrine de l'église catholique* (many edd.). TH. M. J. GOUSSET: *Théologie dogmatique ou exposition des preuves et des dogmes de la relig. cathol.* (Paris, 1850, 4 vols.).

English works: Cardinal WISEMAN: *Lectures on the Principal Doctrines and Practices of the Catholic Church* (London, 1836, several editions).

JOS. BERINGTON and JOHN KIRK: *The Faith of Catholics on Certain Points of Controversy, Confirmed by Scripture and Attested by the Fathers of the First Five Centuries of the Church.* Third edition, revised and greatly enlarged by JAMES WATERWORTH (London, 1846, 3 vols.).

JAMES GIBBONS (Cardinal, and Archbishop of Baltimore): *The Faith of our Fathers: Being a Plain Exposition and Vindication of the Church founded by our Lord Jesus Christ* (Baltimore, 1876, 36th revised ed. 1890). Not scientific, but popular and very plausible, like Cardinal Wiseman's *Lectures*.

CHAPTER CCXII.

DOGMATIC THEOLOGY OF THE LUTHERAN CHURCH.

The Dogmatic of the Lutheran Church is based upon the Augsburg Confession (1530) and the Formula of Concord (1577). It agrees with the Roman Church in the œcumenical doctrines, is Augustinian in anthropology and soteriology, and original in the doctrines of justification by faith alone (which expresses Luther's personal experience) and the eucharistic presence of Christ "in, with, and under" the elements of bread and wine.*

There are, however, two types of Lutheranism: the strict or high Lutheranism of the Formula of Concord, and the moder-

* Kahnis (vol. i. 1): "*Die Dogmatik der lutherischen Kirche hat die Glaubenslehren lutherischen Bekenntnisses aus dem Formalprincipe der Schrift zu beweisen und aus dem Materialprincipe der Rechtfertigung aus dem Glauben zu entwickeln.*" This definition omits the doctrine of the Lord's Supper by which Lutheranism differs from the Roman and the Reformed doctrines; but Kahnis surrendered the literal interpretation of the words of institution, on which Luther so strongly insisted at Marburg.

ate, Melanchthonian Lutheranism of the altered Augsburg Confession of 1540. The chief champions of the former theology are the Lutheran scholastics from the latter part of the sixteenth to the middle of the eighteenth century : Chemnitz (1591), John Gerhard, Hutter, Calov, Quenstedt, Hafenreffer, König, Baier, and Hollaz. In the nineteenth century, Lutheran orthodoxy was revived in opposition to Rationalism and Unionism, but in a milder form, and with some changes, by the leading theologians of Erlangen (Von Hofmann, Thomasius and Frank), Rostock (Philippi and Dieckhoff), and Leipzig (Kahnis and Luthardt).

Melanchthon, the pure and noble scholar, the "Præceptor Germaniæ," the inseparable companion of Luther who wrote to him his last letters, the admiring friend of Calvin, in whose bosom he wished to die, is the author of the Augsburg Confession and the proper founder of Lutheran Theology. He was far less original and productive than Luther, who cut out the stones from the quarry, but more scholarly and methodical. His *Loci Theologici* (1521), which grew out of his exegetical lectures on the Epistle to the Romans, and which Luther thought worthy of a place in the Canon, are the first attempt at an Evangelical Dogmatic, and, in their improved forms, continued to be the text-book in Lutheran universities till the beginning of the seventeenth century, when they were thrown into contempt by an uncharitable orthodoxy. It seems incredible that Leonhard Hutter, in a public disputation at Wittenberg, tore the likeness of Melanchthon from the wall and trod upon it. But the spirit of Melanchthon revived in Calixtus, Spener, Mosheim, Bengel, in the modern irenical Lutheranism, and in the evangelical Union Theology of Germany. His memory was celebrated throughout Protestant Christendom in 1860 at the third centennial of his death, and will ever be honored.

LITERATURE.

I. Historical representations of the scholastic Lutheran orthodoxy of the seventeenth century.

KARL HASE: *Hutterus Redivivus, Dogmatik der Evangelisch-Lutherischen Kirche* (Leipzig, 12th ed. 1883). The amiable author differed widely from the orthodoxy of the seventeenth century, but he knew how to appreciate it as a historian. He says in the preface : *" Das dogmatische System des 16 und 17 Jahrhunderts kam mir vor wie einer unsrer alten deutschen Münster mit seinen himmelstrebenden Spitzbogen und wunderlichen sinnvollen Zierrathen. Nicht allezeit ist der Herr in solch einem steinernen Hochwalde ver-*

ehrt worden. Als Er selbst noch auf Erden wandelte, war der Himmel und die Erde seine Kirche, ein Berg seine Kanzel; darnach hielt man das Liebesmahl in Werkstätten und in Katakomben; zu andrer Zeit erschallte das Te Deum laudamus unter den heitern Säulenhallen und Kuppelgewölben des Südens; und überall wo Zwei oder Tausende sich in seinem Namen versammelt hatten, war der Herr mitten unter ihnen. Einen Dom wie unsre Vorfahren kann unsre Zeit nicht wieder bauen, vor einigen Jahrzehnten hielt man's sogar für ein altgothisch barbarisch Bauwerk; es wird einem aber doch ganz besonders wie in einem Gotteshause darin zu Muthe." Hase presents his own dogmatic views in his *Evangelische Dogmatik* (Leipzig, 1826; 6th ed. 1870); and in his *Gnosis, oder protestantisch-evangelische Glaubenslehre, für die Gebildeten in der Gemeinde, wissenschaftlich dargestellt* (1827–29, 3 vols.; 2d ed. 1869–70, 2 vols.). This judgment applies to Calvinistic scholasticism as well.

HEINRICH SCHMID (of Erlangen, d. 1885): *The Doctrinal Theology of the Evangelical Lutheran Church*. Translated from the 5th German ed. by Charles A. Hay and Henry E. Jacobs (Philadelphia, 1876).

II. Modern reproductions and modifications.

A. D. C. TWESTEN (successor of Schleiermacher in Berlin, d. 1876): *Vorlesungen über die Dogmatik der Evangelisch-Lutherischen Kirche* (Hamburg, 1837; 4th ed. 1838, 2 vols.). Represents the movement from Schleiermacher to Lutheranism but within the United Church of Prussia. Very able and clear, but unfortunately never finished.

H. MARTENSEN: *Die christliche Dogmatik* (Kiel, 1850; 3d ed. 1855; English translation in Clark's Foreign Theological Library). Very fresh and genial.

F. A. PHILIPPI: *Kirchliche Glaubenslehre* (Stuttgart, 1854–72; 3d ed. 1864–88, 6 vols.). Strictly Lutheran.

GOTTFRIED THOMASIUS (Professor in Erlangen, d. 1875): *Christi Person und Werk. Darstellung der evangelisch-lutherischen Dogmatik vom Mittelpunkte der Christologie aus* (Erlangen, 1852–61; 3d ed. 1888, 2 vols.). Christocentric. Departs from Lutheran orthodoxy by the theory of kenosis. Compare also his *Dogmengeschichte* (new ed. by Seeberg, 1888).

CHR. ERNST LUTHARDT (Professor in Leipzig): *Kompendium der Dogmatik* (Leipzig, 1865; 6th ed. 1882). A very useful manual.

K. FR. A. KAHNIS: *Die Lutherische Dogmatik historisch-genetisch dargestellt* (Leipzig, 2 vols., 1861 and 1864; new ed. in 2 vols., 1875). Progressive Lutheran orthodoxy in touch with modern thought. Compare his *Zeugniss von den Grundwahrheiten des Protestantismus gegen Dr. Hengstenberg* (Leipzig, 1862).

F. H. R. FRANK (Professor of Theology in Erlangen): *System der christlichen Gewissheit* (Erlangen, 1870–73, 2 vols.; 2d ed. 1881–84). *System der christlichen Wahrheit* (Erlangen, 1878–80, 2 vols.; 2d ed. 1885–86). *Dogmatische Studien* (Leipzig, 1892).

American works:

CHARLES B. KRAUTH (of Philadelphia, d. 1883): *The Conservative Reformation and its Theology* (Philadelphia, 1872). Not a system, but a series of essays in defense of the distinctive doctrines of orthodox Lutheranism, of which the author was the chief representative in America.

SAM. SPRECHER (President of Wittenberg College, Springfield, O.): *Groundwork of a System of Evangelical Lutheran Theology* (Phila., 1879).

CHAPTER CCXIII.

DOGMATIC THEOLOGY OF THE REFORMED AND CALVINISTIC CHURCHES.

The Dogmatic Theology of the Evangelical Reformed Churches agrees with the evangelical Lutheran system, except in the doctrines of predestination, the sacraments and the ubiquity of Christ's body. It is based on the same pessimistic anthropology of St. Augustin, but is more logical and severe, and has gone through similar phases of development, but has been less influenced by Rationalism. It is embodied in the Reformed Confessions of the sixteenth and seventeenth centuries, and is held by the Reformed Churches in Switzerland, Germany, France, Holland, by the Presbyterian Churches of England, Scotland and America, by the Congregational or Independent Churches, and, with the exception of the doctrine of baptism, by the Regular or Calvinistic Baptists. It was developed by Calvin, Bullinger, Danæus, Ursinus, Zanchi, Francis Turretin, Coccejus, Witsius, Heidegger, and all the Puritan divines of England and New England (Jonathan Edwards and his school). In the modern age it has been reproduced, with various modifications, by Alex. Schweizer, Heinrich Heppe, Ed. Böhl, Aug. Ebrard and Van Oosterzee in Europe, and by Dwight, Taylor, Park, Hodge, Shedd, H. B. Smith, and E. V. Gerhart in America.

There are two types of Calvinism, as there are of Lutheranism: the strict, scholastic Calvinism of the Canons of Dort and the Westminster Confession; and the moderate Calvinism of the Heidelberg Catechism, the Second Helvetic Confession, and the Thirty-nine Articles of the Church of England. Moderate and progressive Calvinism omits or softens the five knotty points of Dort and seeks to reconcile divine sovereignty and human liberty, divine justice and divine love. It is in sympathy with the Melanchthonian type of Lutheranism; it enters as an important factor into the evangelical Union Theology of Germany, and is gaining ground in all the Reformed Churches of Europe and America.

LITERATURE.

JOHN CALVIN: *Institutio Christianæ Religionis* (1st ed. 1536; last revised ed. 1559). A classical masterpiece of permanent value. Many edd. in

DOGMATIC THEOLOGY OF THE REFORMED CHURCH. 343

different languages; see the literary notices in SCHAFF'S *Church History*, vol. vii., pp. 327 sq.

HEINRICH HEPPE (Professor in Marburg, d. 1879): *Die Dogmatik der evang. reform. Kirche* (Elberfeld, 1861).—*Dogmatik des deutschen Protestantismus im 16ten Jahrh.* (Gotha, 1857, 3 vols.). Compare also his *Bekenntnissschriften der altprotestantischen Kirche Deutschlands* (Cassel, 1855).

ALEXANDER SCHWEIZER (Professor in Zürich, d. 1888): *Die Glaubenslehre der Evang. Reform. Kirche, dargestellt und aus den Quellen belegt* (Zürich, 1844–47, 2 vols.). Compare his *Centraldogmen der Reform. Kirche* (Zürich, 1854–56, 2 vols.). Two very important historical works. A. Baur (in his *Zwingli's Theologie*, ii. Preface) calls Schweizer "the genuine successor of Zwingli in his chair and pulpit." He was the ablest Reformed pupil of Schleiermacher, as Twesten was his ablest Lutheran pupil. He gives his own dogmatic system in his *Christliche Glaubenslehre nach protestantischen Grundsätzen dargestellt* (Leipzig, 1863–72, 3 parts; 2d ed. 1877).

J. H. A. EBRARD : *Christliche Dogmatik* (Königsb., 2d ed. 1863, 2 vols.). Moderately Calvinistic (Melanchthonian), and polemic against Schweizer.

JOHN PETER LANGE (Professor first at Zürich, then at Bonn, d. 1884): *Christliche Dogmatik* (Heidelberg, 1849–52 ; new ed. 1870, 3 vols.). Divided into three parts: 1. Philosophical Dogmatic ; 2. Positive Dogmatic ; 3. Polemic and Irenic. Full of original thoughts and fancies.

J. J. VAN OOSTERZEE (Professor in Utrecht, d. 1382): *Christian Dogmatics: A Textbook for Academic Instruction and Private Study*. Translated from the Dutch (London and New York, 1874, 2 vols.).

Scotch Presbyterian works by G. HILL, J. DICK, and THOMAS CHALMERS.

CHARLES HODGE (Professor in Princeton, d. 1878) : *Systematic Theology* (New York and Edinburgh, 1872, 3 vols., with an index vol.). The standard work of the Old School type of American Presbyterianism.

ARCHIBALD A. HODGE (son and successor of the former, d. at Princeton, 1886) : *Outlines of Theology* (New York, 1860 ; rev. and enlarged, 1879). A popular epitome of his father's work.

HENRY B. SMITH (Professor in Union Theological Seminary, d. 1877) : *System of Christian Theology* (New York, 1st ed. 1884 ; 4th ed. 1890). A posthumous work, published from lectures by William S. Karr, and therefore incomplete, but very able, acute and philosophical. Progressive Calvinism in transition to Christocentric theology, and in living touch with modern German systems of thought.

WILLIAM G. T. SHEDD (Professor in Union Theological Seminary, resigned 1890) : *Dogmatic Theology* (New York, 2d ed. 1889, 2 vols.). A clear, strong, logical reproduction of the high Calvinism of the Westminster Confession.

AUGUSTUS H. STRONG (Professor in Rochester Theological Seminary, Baptist) : *Systematic Theology* (New York, 1886 ; 2d ed. 1889). High Calvinistic, except on the baptismal question.

EMANUEL V. GERHART (Professor in the German Reformed Seminary at Lancaster, Pa.) : *Institutes of the Christian Religion* (New York, 1891, to be completed in two more vols.). Christocentric. The fruit of the Mercersburg movement.

LEWIS FRENCH STEARNS (a pupil of Henry B. Smith, Professor in the

Theological Seminary at Bangor, Me.; d. 1892): *Present Day Theology: A Popular Discussion of Leading Doctrines of the Christian Faith* (New York, 1893). With a biographical Introduction by Professor George L. Prentiss. A. M. FAIRBAIRN: *The Place of Christ in Modern Theology* (New York, 1893).

CHAPTER CCXIV.

DOGMATIC THEOLOGY OF THE ANGLICAN CHURCH.

The Church of England and her independent daughter, the Protestant Episcopal Church of the United States, is the most conservative of the evangelical Churches and nearest the Roman Catholic in organization and worship. She was once intolerant and exclusive, and she still insists upon conformity to episcopacy and the rubrics of her liturgy; but in theology, she is very liberal and allows almost as much latitude, at least in England, as the Protestant State Churches on the Continent. She nursed at her breast Calvinistic Puritans, Arminian Methodists, liberal Latitudinarians, and Romanizing Tractarians and Ritualists. She has room for divines as Calvinistic as Toplady and as Arminian as Wesley, as high-church and Romanizing as Dr. Pusey and as broad-church and latitudinarian as Dean Stanley. Recent judicial decisions in the cases of Hampden (1836), Gorham (1850), Bennett (1871), and others, have all been decided in favor of the liberty of holding different opinions, even to the denial of baptismal regeneration and the real presence.

This comprehensiveness of the Church as a whole is quite consistent with the narrowness and exclusiveness of parties within her bosom. It repels and attracts; it caused the large secessions which have occurred at critical junctures, but it explains also the individual accessions which she continually and quietly receives from the clergy and laity of other churches. The English mind is not theorizing and speculative, but eminently practical and conservative; it follows more the power of habit than the logic of thought; it takes things as they are, makes haste slowly, mends abuses cautiously, and aims at what is attainable rather than at what is ideal.

The Anglican theology is composite and eclectic, like the English language. It was first moulded by the influence of Melanchthonian Lutheranism, afterwards more strongly by Calvinism. The Thirty-nine Articles drawn up by Cranmer in 1553 with the aid of Bucer and Peter Martyr, revised under

Queen Elizabeth in 1563 in Latin, and 1571 in English, and again revised by the American Episcopal Church in 1801, must be classed upon the whole with the Reformed or moderately Calvinistic confessions. They accept the three œcumenical creeds (the Athanasian Creed, however, is wisely omitted in the American revision). They are moderately Augustinian in the doctrines of free-will, sin and grace; Lutheran in the articles of justification and the Church; and Reformed or moderately Calvinistic in the doctrines of predestination and the Lord's Supper. They were supplemented by the Nine Lambeth Articles (1595), which go to the full extent of Calvin's doctrine of absolute predestination (with reprobation and preterition). The same rigorous Calvinism was taught in the Irish Articles of Archbishop Ussher (1615), some of which were literally incorporated into the Westminster Confession. In the Elizabethan age, Calvin was the greatest theological authority in England. Even the moderate and judicious Richard Hooker prized him most highly, and says that "the perfectest divines were judged they which were skillfullest in Calvin's writings; his books almost the very canon to judge both doctrine and discipline by." The Church of England was represented by five delegates at the Calvinistic Synod of Dort (1619), among them, John Davenant and Joseph Hall.

In the reign of Charles I., chiefly through the influence of Archbishop Laud, Calvinism gave way to Arminianism, but it revived again in the low-church or evangelical party. This was followed by the Oxford or Anglo-Catholic and Ritualistic revival, and later by the broad-church liberalism. The Thirty-nine Articles have lost much of their authority. The Nicene Creed has risen in estimation, and is offered by the Lambeth Conference of Bishops as a sufficient doctrinal basis for the reunion of Christendom.

LITERATURE.

The chief dogmatic works of Anglican divines are expositions of the Apostles' Creed, and of the Thirty-nine Articles.

RICHARD HOOKER (d. 1600): *Eight Books of the Laws of Ecclesiastical Polity* (London, 1594 sqq., not completed; best edition by John Keble, Oxford, 1841, 3 vols.).

JAMES USSHER (Archbishop of Armagh and Primate of Ireland, d. 1656): *Body of Divinity* (1638) and *Principles of the Christian Religion* (1654). Calvinistic. Complete ed. of his *Works* (Dublin, 1847 sqq., 16 vols.).

JOHN PEARSON (Bishop of Chester, b. 1612, d. 1686): *An Exposition of the Creed.* Third ed. by the author, 1669, fol., and very often since. Ed. with notes by Dobson (London, 1840), by Burton (Oxford, 1847), Chevallier (Cambridge, 1849). One of the most valuable works on theology in the English language.

GEORGE BULL (d. 1710): *Defensio Fidei Nicænæ* (London, 1685; a new translation, Oxford, 1851, 2 vols.).

WILLIAM BEVERIDGE (Bishop of St. Asaph, d. 1708): *Thesaurus Theologicus; or, A Complete System of Divinity* (London, 1710–11, 4 vols.; new ed. 1828, 2 vols.).

E. HAROLD BROWNE (Bishop of Winchester since 1873, resigned 1890): *An Exposition of the Thirty-nine Articles* (London, 1850–53, in 2 vols., and often since; American ed. by Bishop Williams, New York, 1865, etc.).

Other commentaries on the Articles by THOMAS ROGERS, GILBERT BURNET, RICHARD LAURENCE, THOMAS R. JONES, A. P. FORBES, R. W. JELF, J. MILLER. See the literature and a full discussion of the Anglican standards in Schaff's *Creeds*, vol. i., pp. 592–665.

SAM. BUEL (Professor in the General Theological Episcopal Seminary, New York, d. 1892): *Treatise of Systematic Theology* (New York, 1889,2 vols.).

NOTE.—The most recent authoritative deliverance of the Episcopal Church of England and America is the four articles of the Pan-Anglican Conference, held at Lambeth Palace, London, 1888, as a basis of union for English-speaking Churches.

"1. The Holy Scriptures of the Old and New Testaments, as 'containing all things necessary to salvation,' and as being the rule and ultimate standard of Faith.

"2. The Apostles' Creed, as the Baptismal Symbol; and the Nicene Creed, as the sufficient statement of the Christian Faith. (Nothing is said about the *Filioque*.)

"3. The two Sacraments ordained by Christ himself,—Baptism and the Supper of the Lord,—ministered with unfailing use of Christ's words of institution, and of the elements ordained by him.

"4. The Historic Episcopate, locally adapted in the methods of its administration to the varying needs of the nations and peoples called of God into the unity of his Church."

. This is the shortest and most liberal creed ever set forth by any orthodox Church. But the fourth article, which refers to government rather than doctrine, has met with serious objection in the non-episcopal Churches.

CHAPTER CCXV.

ARMINIAN AND METHODIST THEOLOGY.

The Arminian Theology arose in the Reformed Church of Holland in reaction against strict scholastic Calvinism, and is expressed in the Five Articles of the Remonstrants of 1610, which relate to predestination, the extent of the atonement, the nature of faith, the irresistibility of grace, and the perseverance of saints. It teaches that foreordination is conditioned by foreknowledge; that the atonement is universal and sufficient for all men, although efficient only for the elect; that divine grace may be resisted, since man has still a remnant of freedom to accept or reject the offer of salvation; and that regenerate believers may totally and finally fall from grace and be lost.

Arminianism was rejected and banished by the National Synod of Dort (1619); but after the death of Prince Maurice of Nassau (1625), the expelled Arminians were allowed to return with full liberty to establish churches and schools in every town of Holland. Their doctrines were defended with much learning and ability by Hugo Grotius, Episcopius, Limborch, Curcellæus, Clericus (Le Clerc), and Wetstein.

The Arminian system assumed a much wider field and practical power in England and America than in Holland. It has largely influenced the Church of England since the time of Archbishop Laud, and was adopted by John Wesley and his followers.

The Methodist Theology is a modified evangelical Arminianism. It differs from the Dutch Arminianism by a stronger Augustinian view on natural corruption; it lays greater stress on the subjective experience of conversion and regeneration; and adds a few additional doctrines, namely:

1. The doctrine of the universality of divine grace not only in its intention, but in its actual offer. (This was derived from the Quaker doctrine of universal light.)

2. The doctrine of the witness of the Spirit or the assurance of salvation (Rom. 8: 15, 16).

3. The doctrine of perfectionism (also borrowed from the Quakers, and based on such passages as Matt. 5: 48; Phil. 3: 15; Heb. 6: 1; 10: 4; 1 John 3: 6; 5: 18).

LITERATURE.

JAMES ARMINIUS (Professor in Leyden, d. 1609): *Works*, translated from the Latin by James and William Nichols (London, 1825-75, 3 vols.; *Opera Theol.*, 1631).

PHILIP VAN LIMBORCH (Professor in the Arminian College at Amsterdam, and chief defender of religious toleration in his age; d. 1712): *Institutiones Theol. Christianæ* (Amsterdam, 1686, 5 edd. till 1735; English translation by William Jones, London, 1702, 2 vols.).

JOHN WESLEY (founder of Methodism, and the most apostolic man that England has produced; d. 1791): *Sermons on Several Occasions* (London,

1771, 4 vols.; many edd.). Compare his *Explanatory Notes upon the New Testament* (based upon Bengel's *Gnomon*).

Methodist *Articles of Religion*, a liberal and judicious abridgment of the Thirty-nine Articles of the Church of England, drawn up by Wesley for the American Methodists, and adopted at a Conference in 1784, and again in 1804. They are printed in the official Manual of the Methodist Episcopal Church, and in Schaff's *Creeds of Christendom*, vol. iii., pp. 807-813.

RICHARD WATSON (Wesleyan, b. 1781, d. in London, 1833): *Theological Institutes; or, A View of the Evidences, Doctrines, Morals, and Institutions of Christianity* (London, 1823-24, 3 vols.; many edd.). With a copious Index and Analysis by Dr. John McClintock (New York, 1850, 2 vols.). "The moral and scientific standard of Methodism."

WILLIAM BURT POPE (Professor in Didsbury College, Manchester): *A Compendium of Christian Theology* (London and New York, 1875-76; revised ed. 1879-81, 3 vols.).

MINER RAYMOND (Professor in Garrett Biblical Institute since 1864, Evanston, Ill.): *Systematic Theology* (Cincinnati, O., 1877-79, 3 vols.).

JOHN MILEY (Professor of Systematic Theology in Drew Theological Seminary, Madison, N. J.): *Systematic Theology* (New York and Cincinnati, 1892, pp. xvi., 533, to be continued).

CHAPTER CCXVI.

SOCINIAN AND UNITARIAN THEOLOGY.

Socinianism of the sixteenth century, and Anglo-American Unitarianism of the nineteenth century may be classed together as radical departures from the general orthodoxy of the historic Churches, Greek, Roman, and Evangelical. They are alike opposed to the Nicene Theology and the Augustinian anthropology. They reject the doctrines of the Trinity and the Incarnation, the vicarious atonement of Christ, original sin and total depravity, and materially modify other essential articles of the Catholic creeds.

But, while they are indifferent or hostile to dogmas, they firmly maintain the ethical teaching of Christianity and emphasize the moral perfection of Christ as the highest model for imitation. This accounts for the noble and refined type of Christian character which is often found among Socinians and Unitarians.

Socinianism has produced a meager, but definite system of theology. It is laid down in the Rakow (Racovian) Catechism and the writings of Faustus Socinus and his followers which are collected in the *Bibliotheca Fratrum Polonorum* (1656, 6 vols. fol.). The Socinian sect flourished awhile in Poland, but was expelled by the Diet of Warsaw under the influence of the Jesuits in 1658, and found a refuge in Transylvania and in Holland. It became the mother of English Unitarianism, and exerted much influence upon the theology of the Lutheran and Reformed Churches.

Servetus, who was burned for heresy at Geneva in 1554, is sometimes called the author and martyr of Unitarianism, but his system is Christopantheistic rather than Unitarian, and was not properly understood in his day, not even fully by Calvin his great antagonist.* The real founder is the younger Socinus (d. 1604) and other Italian refugees who settled in Switzerland, but were repelled by the rigor of the Calvinistic system, and offended by the execution of Servetus. They were among the first advocates of religious toleration.

The Socinian Theology is not a system of pure rationalism, but of rational supernaturalism. It rejects the tri-personality of God and the essential divinity of Christ, and reduces the Holy Spirit to a divine power or influence; but it teaches the absolute necessity of a divine revelation as laid down in the Bible, accepts the New Testament as an infallible guide in matters of faith and duty, and makes Christ an object of divine worship. Christ was conceived without sin, divinely illuminated by a rapture to heaven (*raptus in cœlum*) and deified after his resurrection in reward for his perfect obedience in life and death by being elevated to a participation in the divine majesty and government. Faustus Socinus refused to recognize as Christians those who would not pay divine honors to Christ.

Unitarianism in England and America has no formulated creed or dogmatic system, and allows greater latitude of development, both in the direction of heresy and orthodoxy, between a purely humanitarian and a high Arian Christology, with corresponding freedom in other doctrines. The only article of Unitarian belief is the acceptance of Christ as Lord and Saviour, and as the model of moral conduct. Beyond this it is liberal and elastic. It professes to be "not a fixed dogmatic state-

---

* See a full account of the theological system of Servetus from his *Restitutio Christianismi*, and of the toleration controversies connected with it, in Schaff's *Church History*, vol. vii., pp. 736-757. Servetus was a theological genius of great originality and speculative power.

ment, but a movement of ever-enlarging faith, welcoming inquiry, progress, and diversity of individual thought in the unity of spiritual thought."

The chief Unitarian divines are James Martineau, William E. Channing, Andrews Norton, George E. Ellis, James F. Clarke, Andrew P. Peabody, Joseph H. Allen. The radical or left wing is represented by Theodore Parker, who sympathized with Strauss, but had a higher view of Christ and an enthusiasm for humanity and moral reform.

CHAPTER CCXVII.

RATIONALISTIC THEOLOGY.

Rationalism goes further than Socinianism and the conservative wing of Unitarianism. It makes reason the chief fountain of authority and an arbiter of the Church and the Bible. It rejects or minimizes revelation and inspiration, and treats the Bible like any other book, though assigning it the highest place among works of religious genius. It is not organized as a religious society, but is simply a school or tendency within the Protestant State Churches of Europe. It resembles in this respect the schools of Gnosticism in the ante-Nicene age.

Rationalism arose at the end of the last century in Germany in opposition to Lutheran orthodoxy, and as a reaction against symbololatry, and has there developed great scientific and literary activity. At one time it had the controlling influence in the universities and Church judicatories. It has spread its influence over the Protestant Churches of the Continent, and is exerting itself of late also in England and America. It is chiefly negative and destructive, but has a critical value in exposing the weak points of traditional orthodoxy and stimulating progress. Thus it serves a similar purpose to modern Protestantism as Gnosticism did to the ancient Church.

In Rationalistic Theology, we must distinguish chiefly two phases, the theistic or Kantian, and the pantheistic or Hegelian.

The older Rationalism, represented by Wegscheider and Bretschneider, retained the fundamental articles of the personality of God, the freedom and moral responsibility of man, and the immortality of the soul.

The later Rationalism, represented by Strauss and Biedermann, begins by denying the personality of God, and ends in the annihilation or absorption of the personality of man.

The Hegelian philosophy originally produced a quasi-orthodox theology, which was represented by Marheineke and Daub, or the right wing. It treated vulgar Rationalism with contempt, and defended the fundamental doctrines of Christianity, especially the Trinity and Incarnation, but gave them a different and speculative meaning. The left or radical wing denies the historicity of the gospel facts, and thus undermines the firm foundation of the eternal truths which those facts are supposed to embody.

The latest phase is more positive and constructive, partly in connection with the revival of Kant's philosophy (Lipsius), partly on the basis of the Hegelian philosophy (Pfleiderer).

LITERATURE.

I. Theistic Rationalism.

J. A. L. WEGSCHEIDER (Professor in Halle, d. 1849): *Institutiones Theologicæ Christianæ Dogmaticæ* (Halle, 1815; 8th ed. 1844).

K. G. BRETSCHNEIDER (Professor at Wittenberg, 1804, General Superintendent at Gotha, 1816; d. 1848): *Handbuch der Dogmatik der evang.-luther. Kirche* (Leipzig, 1814 sqq.; 4th ed. 1838, 2 vols.); also, *Systemat. Entwickelung aller in der Dogmatik vorkommenden Begriffe* (Leipzig, 1805; 4th ed. 1841).

II. Pantheistic Rationalism.

PHIL. MARHEINEKE (Professor in Berlin, d. 1846): *Die Grundlehren der christlichen Dogmatik* (Berlin, 1819; 2d ed. 1827).—*System der christlichen Dogmatik* (1847). Orthodox Hegelianism.

D. F. STRAUSS (d. 1874): *Die christliche Glaubenslehre in ihrer geschichtlichen Entwickelung und im Kampfe mit der modernen Wissenschaft* (Tübingen, 1840–41, 2 vols.). Purely destructive, like his *Leben Jesu*. His last sad work was *Der alte und der neue Glaube* (11th ed. 1881), in which he retracts all his former concessions to Christianity and avows the gospel of materialism and pessimism.

A. E. BIEDERMANN (Professor in Zürich, d. 1885): *Christliche Dogmatik* 1869; 2d ed. Berlin, 1885. 2 vols.). He was an earnest Christian man, and tried to combine practical Christianity with pantheistic theology.

III. R. A. LIPSIUS (Professor in Jena, d. 1892): *Lehrbuch der evangelisch-protestantischen Dogmatik* (Braunschweig, 1876; 2d ed. 1879). On the basis of Kant and Schleiermacher. He opposes the modern Lutheran orthodoxy, but also the school of Ritschl. He has great respect for Biedermann, but differs from him, as Schleiermacher differed from Hegel.

OTTO PFLEIDERER (Professor in Berlin since 1875): *Grundriss der Glaubens- und Sittenlehre* (Berlin, 1880; 4th ed. 1888). Comp. his *Philosophy of Religion* (2d ed. 1884). He belongs to the philosophical school of Hegel.

and the critical historical school of Baur, and closely approaches Biedermann, but allows more influence to the convictions of the heart (*Gemüth*). He defines religion to be essentially a matter of the heart (*wesentlich Herzenssache*, p. 12), and faith as a dedication of the heart to the revelation of divine mercy in the gospel (*centraler Herzensakt der Hingabe an die Gnadenoffenbarung Gottes im Evangelium*, p. 7).

CHAPTER CCXVIII.

EVANGELICAL UNION THEOLOGY.

The Evangelical Union Theology arose with the revival of evangelical religion after the dreary winter of Rationalism. In Germany, it is connected with the ecclesiastical Union of the Lutheran and Reformed Confessions, which was introduced at the third jubilee of the Reformation in 1817 in Prussia and other German States. But it is quite independent of this governmental Union and has sympathizers in all Protestant countries and churches. It has exerted more influence upon modern English and American thought than any other German school.

This type of Evangelical Theology rests on the consensus of the two leading Protestant Confessions, which is not formulated in a creed, but has practically superseded the exclusive confessionalism, and is allowed to shape itself freely with the progressive march of knowledge.* The doctrinal differences of the Lutheran and Reformed Churches are theological rather than religious, and do not prevent Christian and ecclesiastical communion, but admit of reconciliation in a higher type, and demand a further development. For this reason this theology is sometimes called the Theology of Mediation or Reconciliation.†

It rises also above the antagonism of Rationalism and Supernaturalism, and finds the essence of Christianity not in a body of doctrines, but in a divine fact and a new life, namely, the revelation of God in Christ for the salvation of the world.

The Union Theology was foreshadowed by the genial Herder and men of kindred spirit. It was first advocated and constructed into a scientific system by Schleiermacher, who eman-

---

* Dr. Julius Müller made an important contribution towards a formulated consensus from the Lutheran and Reformed Confessions in his work, *Die evangelische Union, ihr Wesen und göttliches Recht* (Berlin, 1854), pp. 170-205, but it has no official character.

† *Vermittlungstheologie*, also used in the sense of mediating between faith and philosophy, orthodoxy and liberty.

cipated German Theology from the dominion of Rationalism, and, together with Neander, his colleague, introduced a new era. It was modified and developed by Twesten, Schweizer, Nitzsch, Julius Müller, Rothe, Ullmann, Lange, Dorner, and others. Schleiermacher was the son of a Reformed minister and educated among the Moravians, and shows the influence of these connections in his system (the Calvinistic element in his conception of religion as a sense of absolute dependence, and the Moravian influence in his Christocentric principle); but the majority of evangelical Union divines are of Lutheran descent and mode of thinking. They have the conciliatory and liberal spirit of Melanchthon. They reject the double predestinarianism (not election by free grace, which is acknowledged by all, but what Calvin called the *decretum horribile* of eternal reprobation), and emphasize the fatherhood and love of God rather than his sovereignty and justice. But they mostly accept Calvin's doctrine of the spiritual real presence in the Lord's Supper, which was a point of agreement between him and Melanchthon in his later phase of development.

The Union Theology of Germany is confined to the Lutheran and German Reformed type. A corresponding theology in Great Britain and America must enlarge its scope and include as far as possible the post-Reformation forms of English-speaking evangelical Protestantism, which in our generation are gradually coming into closer sympathy and fellowship; but an evangelical catholic consensus creed and theology is as yet a matter of the future.

LITERATURE.

FRIEDRICH SCHLEIERMACHER (Professor in Berlin, d. 1834): *Der christliche Glaube nach den Grundsätzen der evangelischen Kirche* (Berlin, 1830; 3d ed. 1835, 2 vols.). Ritschl ranks this work with the *Summa* of Thomas Aquinas and the *Institutio* of Calvin, as one of the three great dogmatic systems. But we would rather compare Schleiermacher with Origen, and his theology with the work *De Principiis*. It is epoch-making and suggestive even in its errors, but unsatisfactory as a system. It is built upon the Christian consciousness or experience of sin and grace as expressed in the evangelical confessions, and prepares the way for Christocentric Theology. His best pupils have gone beyond him in the direction of positive faith. He himself protested earnestly "against the honor of being the head of a new theological school" (Preface to the second ed., 1830, p. 5).

To the Evangelical Union school of theology as to spirit and aim, but with various modifications, belong the dogmatic works (already mentioned in preceding chapters) of Nitzsch, Twesten, Liebner, Martensen, Hase, J. P. Lange, Schweizer, Ebrard, Heppe, and Van Oosterzee.

JULIUS MÜLLER (Professor in Halle, d. 1878): *Die christliche Lehre von der Sünde* (Breslau, 1838; 7th ed., Bremen, 1889; English translation by William Urwick, *The Christian Doctrine of Sin*, from the 5th ed., Edinb. 1868; new ed. 1877, 2 vols.). The best book on hamartology. (In connection with this work may be mentioned Tholuck's popular and very effective book on *Sin and Redemption*, 1825, in a series of letters between Julius, *i.e.*, Julius Müller, and Guido, *i.e.*, his friend Tholuck. Both were colleagues in Halle.)—*Dogmatische Abhandlungen* (Bremen, 1870).—*Die evang. Union* (Berlin, 1854).

Julius Müller was one of the purest, ablest and soundest divines of Germany, and his lectures on Theology (of which I have a good manuscript) would have been welcomed in print, but in his extreme modesty he ordered all his manuscripts to be destroyed. Dr. Henry B. Smith has published Müller's scheme and the collection of his proof-texts.

KARL ULLMANN (Professor of Church History at Heidelberg, d. 1865) was a Church historian, but his *Das Wesen des Christenthums* (*The Essence of Christianity*, 1845; 5th Germ. ed. 1865; English translation by John W. Nevin, 1846) and *Die Sündlosigkeit Jesu* (*The Sinlessness of Jesus*, 7th ed. 1863; English translation, by Sophia Taylor, 1870) must be mentioned here for their dogmatic contents.

RICHARD ROTHE (Professor in Heidelberg, d. 1867): *Dogmatik* (published from manuscript, by D. Schenkel, Heidelberg, 1870, 2 vols.).—*Zur Dogmatik* (Gotha, 1863). Compare also his *Theologische Ethik* (2d ed. 1867-71, 5 vols.), which contains a great deal of dogmatic theology. Rothe was one of the profoundest speculative divines of the nineteenth century, and worked up some of the best elements of Hegel's philosophy and Schleiermacher's theology into an independent system. He combines strong faith in supernatural revelation with a liberal view on inspiration. He says (in the Preface to his *Zur Dogmatik*): "*Mein strenger Supranaturalismus und Offenbarungsglaube stösst den theologischen Liberalismus vor den Kopf, meine Weise, die heil. Schrift anzusehen, die orthodoxe Richtung.*" To him may be applied the words of Cardinal Cajetan to Luther: "He has profound eyes and marvelous speculations in his head."

ISAAC A. DORNER (Professor in Berlin, d. 1884): *System der christlichen Glaubenslehre* (Berlin, 1879-81, 2 vols.; 2d ed. 1886; English translation by Cave and Banks, *A System of Christian Doctrine*, Edinburgh, 1880-82, 4 vols.). A profound work of permanent value, influenced by Schleiermacher and Hegel, but biblical and positive. Compare also his classical history of Christology (2d., 2 vols.), his collection of Theological Essays (1883), his *History of Protestant Theology* (1867) and his theological correspondence with Martensen from 1839 to 1881 (posthumously published, Berlin, 1888, 2 vols.).

FR. REIFF: *Die christliche Glaubenslehre als Grundlage der christl. Weltanschauung* (Basel, 1872, 2 vols.; 2d ed. 1876). Popular and biblical.

A. GRETILLAT (Professor of theology in La Faculté Indépendante de Neuchâtel): *Exposé de Théologie Systématique* (Neuchâtel, 1892).

The "Studien und Kritiken," a theological quarterly, started by Ullmann and Umbreit, 1828, and still published (at present by Köstlin and Kautzsch), and Herzog's "Theol. Real-Encyclopædie" (especially the first ed., 22 vols.) are chiefly, though by no means exclusively, controlled in their doctrinal articles by evangelical Unionists.

CHAPTER CCXIX.

THE THEOLOGY OF RITSCHL.

The latest school of German Theology was founded by Dr. Ritschl (1822–89), and spread rapidly in the last quarter of the nineteenth century. He belonged originally to the critical Tübingen school of Baur, who was a Hegelian in philosophy; but he took a new departure in 1857, first on questions of apostolic and post-apostolic Church history, and then also in philosophy and theology.*

This school is largely influenced by Schleiermacher, but it takes its stand on the objective records of primitive Christianity rather than the subjective experience of the religious consciousness.† It rises, like the Evangelical Union Theology, above the confessional antagonism of Lutheranism and Calvinism, but sympathizes with the spirit of the former; while Schleiermacher's system has an affinity with the latter. His orthodox opponents denounce his theology as a new form of Rationalism, but it differs from the Rationalism of Kant and Hegel by its evangelical spirit and by recognizing the supernatural revelation of God in Christ as its basis.

Ritschl agrees with Schleiermacher in keeping theology free from philosophy. He expels all metaphysical dogmas and arguments from the domain of Christian doctrines. He leaves no room for Natural Theology.‡ He claims to deliver theology from all collision with philosophy, science and biblical criticism, and to simplify the problem of faith by relieving it of foreign matter which has no necessary connection with faith and religious life. He hopes to commend Christianity to educated and thinking people who have lost all confidence in dogmas, which can at best be made only plausible, but cannot compel conviction.

---

* Ritschl maintained against Baur the originality and priority of the Gospel of Mark, and took a different view on the origin of the old Catholic Church, in the second edition of his work, *Die Entstehung der altkatholischen Kirche* (1857).

† See Kattenbusch, *Von Schleiermacher zu Ritschl, zur Orientirung über den gegenwärtigen Stand der Dogmatik* (Giessen, 1892).

‡ He once startled an American student, who in broken German magnified the importance of Natural Theology, by the cool reply: "*So ein Ding giebt's ja gar nicht*" (There is no such thing)! But it lives and will survive.

But his theology is not unphilosophical, any more than Schleiermacher's. He has a philosophy of his own, which controls his thinking. He admits that every scientific theologian must proceed according to a definite theory of cognition. He adopts Kant's theory of cognition, as modified by Lotze. He distinguishes, with Kant, between the thing-in-itself, which we cannot know, and the thing-for-us, or the phenomenon, which we can know. Religious judgments are judgments of value (*Werthurtheile*), that is, affirmations as to what persons and things are *worth*, not in themselves, but to *us*.* Ritschlianism is connected with the rise of New Kantianism; it is a wholesome reaction of agnosticism, which recognizes the boundaries of human knowledge, against the Hegelian gnosticism, which claims absolute knowledge.†

Here is the philosophical ground of Ritschl's hostility to metaphysical dogmas, and to the modern Lutheran orthodoxy. He assigns to Luther the highest place among theologians, and professes to follow him in his earliest stage, that is, Luther as an evangelical Christian and Reformer, but not Luther as a Catholic dogmatist and reactionist. Luther ought consistently to have made an end of dogma instead of originating new dogmas (like the ubiquity of Christ's body, and the *communi-*

---

* "*Alle Erkenntnisse religiöser Art sind directe Werthurtheile.*" *Die christl. Lehre von der Rechtfertigung und Versöhnung* (vol. iii., pp. 195, 376; third ed.).

† The agnosticism of Kant, Sir William Hamilton and Mansel, who believed in the Christian revelation, must not be confounded with the skeptical agnosticism of Darwin, Spencer and Huxley. I quote an interesting passage from Sir William Hamilton's *Dissertations*, which states his theory in an extreme form:

"There are two sorts of ignorance: we philosophize to escape ignorance, and the consummation of our philosophy is ignorance. We start from the one, we repose in the other; they are the goals from which and to which we tend; and the pursuit of knowledge is but a course between two ignorances, as human life is itself only a traveling from grave to grave. The highest reach of human science is the scientific recognition of human ignorance: *Qui nescit ignorare, ignorat scire.* This learned ignorance is the rational conviction by the human mind of its inability to transcend certain limits: it is the knowledge of ourselves—the science of man. This is accomplished by a demonstration of the disproportion between what is to be known and our faculties of knowing the disproportion, to wit, between the infinite and the finite. In fact, the recognition of human ignorance is not only the one highest but the one true knowledge, and its first-fruit is humility. Simple nescience is not proud: consummated science is positively humble. The grand result of human wisdom is thus only a consciousness that what we know is as nothing to what we know not—an articulate confession, in fact, by our natural reason, of the truth declared in Revelation, that "*now* we see through a glass darkly."

catio idiomatum), which were afterwards imposed on the Church as articles of faith in the Formula of Concord and developed and vindicated by the scholastics of the seventeenth century. In the controversy with Zwingli he fell back more and more into the subtleties of the schoolmen whom he formerly had despised as sophists and followers of the "accursed heathen Aristotle." *

The historians of Ritschl's school, under the lead of Harnack, regard the Nicene Creed as the product of the Hellenic philosophy working upon Christian material, rather than the product of Christian faith aided by the forms of Hellenic philosophy. The orthodox terminology of "person," "nature," "essence," "coequality," "incarnation," etc.,† as applied to the Trinity (three persons in one nature) and to the person of Christ (one person in two natures), served its purpose in the Greek Church, but has lost its meaning and significance for our age. ‡ Even the two clauses of the Apostles' Creed, ' Conceived by the Holy Ghost, born of the Virgin Mary," are ruled out of the essential articles of apostolic teaching. §

This theology is therefore anti-dogmatic and anti-scholastic; it is still more anti-mystic. Herein lies both its strength and its weakness.

Ritschl emphasizes the moral element in the religious life and exalts practice and experience above theory and speculation. He bases theology on the historical person of Christ and

---

* Comp. here Harnack's *Dogmengeschichte*, vol. iii., pp. 755 sqq. He confines *Dogmengeschichte* to the history of dogmas properly so called, and strangely excludes Calvinism and Arminianism, the two leading dogmatic systems of the Reformed Church; while he devotes 73 pages to Lutheranism (691–764) and 38 pages to Socinianism (653–691). German divines have no proper conception of the extent and power of the Reformed Church beyond Germany and Switzerland, and are apt to regard Zwingli and Calvin as mere epigoni of the Reformation.

† These and other terms belong to ecclesiastical Greek, and are not found in the New Testament. See p. 138.

‡ See the Christological section in Ritschl's *Die christl. Lehre von der Rechtfertigung und Versöhnung* (vol. iii., p. 364 sqq.), and the second volume of Harnack's *Dogmengeschichte*. The same view is carried out more fully in the posthumous work of Edwin Hatch (a friend of Harnack), *The Influence of Greek Ideas and Usages upon the Christian World* (The Hibbert Lectures for 1888), ed. by Fairbairn, London, 1890. Hatch regards the elevation of dogma over conduct as the *damnosa hereditas* bequeathed by Greek thought to Christendom.

§ Schleiermacher, also, denied the supernatural conception, but held strictly to the sinlessness of Christ and assumed that the Holy Spirit kept him free from all contact with sin from the beginning (vol. ii., p. 64 sqq.).

the facts of primitive Christianity as ascertained by critical and historical research, with the fullest liberty of dissent from traditional opinions on the authorship and canonicity of the books of the Bible (as exercised by Luther in his early stage).

Dogmatic Theology is essentially Christological and Christocentric.* Christ is the first and only sinless man, and the supreme revelation of the love of God. He founded the kingdom of heaven, which is the aim of divine revelation. The divinity of the risen and exalted Lord is admitted, but his *personal* preëxistence is declared to be unessential and of little practical consequence.† It is left an open question, like the apostolicity of the fourth Gospel, on which the Ritschlians are divided. Justification, or the pardon of sin, is the foundation of personal piety. The Church is the medium of the experience of justification. We must exercise individual faith, but the object of faith is presented to us through the religious community with which we are connected. Mysticism, which rests on the pretense of a direct personal revelation in communication with Christ, is discarded as a fanatical delusion. ‡

In a private letter to me, Dr. Ritschl, shortly before his death, condensed his theological system into the following summary: "Strictest recognition of the revelation of God through Christ; most accurate use of the Holy Scripture as the fountain of knowledge of the Christian religion; view of Jesus Christ as the ground of knowledge for all parts of the theological system; in accord with the original documents of the Lutheran Reformation respecting those peculiarities which differentiate its type of doctrine from that of the middle ages." §

Among the chief dogmatic followers of Ritschl are Kaftan in Berlin, Herrmann in Marburg, Hæring and Schultz in Göt-

* With this I fully agree. See chapter ccxxi., p. 362.

† But preëxistence is closely connected with the fact of the incarnation, and is clearly taught by John and Paul and by Christ himself (John 6: 62; 8: 58; 17: 4, 24). On this point, also, Ritschl followed Schleiermacher.

‡ Ritschl shows his inability to appreciate mysticism and pietism in his very able *Geschichte des Pietismus* (Bonn, 1880–86, 3 vols.). Mysticism as represented by Bernard of Clairvaux, Tauler, Thomas à Kempis, and some of the Pietists and Moravians, introduces us into the holy of holies of religious life.

§ "*Strengste Anerkennung der Offenbarung Gottes durch Christus; genauste Benützung der heiligen Schrift als Erkenntnissgrund der christlichen Religion; Verwendung Jesu Christi als des Erkenntnissgrundes für alle Glieder des Systems; im Einklang mit den Urkunden der lutherischen Reformation in Hinsicht des eigenthümlichen von der Theologie des Mittelalters abweichenden Lehrtypus.*"

tingen, Gottschick in Tübingen, Kattenbusch and Reischle in
Giessen, Lobstein in Strassburg, and G. von Schulthess-Rechberg in Zürich. His views have affected the recent researches
in ancient Church history, and especially the conception and
treatment of the history of dogmas by Harnack and Loofs.
His school is opposed on the one hand by orthodox Lutherans
(Frank of Erlangen, Luthardt of Leipzig, and Dieckhoff of
Rostock), as a new phase of Rationalism; and on the other, by
speculative rationalists (Lipsius and Pfleiderer) on account of
its hostility to philosophy.

LITERATURE.

ALBRECHT RITSCHL (Professor in Göttingen, d. 1889): *Die christliche
Lehre von der Rechtfertigung und Versöhnung* (Bonn, 1870–74, 3 vols.; 3d
ed. 1888–89). The first vol. is historical, the second exegetical, the third
dogmatic, and gives the author's views on two of the important doctrines,—
justification and atonement. It is his chief work. He has not left a
full system, but only a brief popular outline in his *Unterricht in der christlichen Religion* (Bonn, 1875; 3d ed. 1886, 84 pp.). Compare also his *Theologie und Metaphysik* (Bonn, 1881). Ritschl is an original and vigorous
thinker, but not a clear writer. His biography was written by his son, Otto
Ritschl (1891).

J. W. M. KAFTAN (Professor in Berlin since 1883): *Das Wesen der christl.
Religion* (Basel, 1881; 2d ed. 1888).—*Die Wahrheit der christl. Religion*
(Basel, 1889).—*Glaube und Dogma* (Bielefeld, 1889).

J. G. HERRMANN (Professor in Marburg since 1879): *Die Religion im
Verhältniss zum Welterkennen und zur Sittlichkeit* (Halle, 1879).—*Die Gewissheit des Glaubens und die Freiheit der Theologie* (Freiburg, 1887; 2d ed. 1889).

FRIEDRICH NITZSCH (Professor in Kiel since 1872, son of K. I. Nitzsch):
Lehrbuch der evangelischen Dogmatik (Freiburg, 1892). Mediates between
Schleiermacher and Ritschl.

MAX REISCHLE: *Das Wesen der Religion* (Freiburg, 1891).

To the school of Ritschl belong, as regards their historico-dogmatic
standpoint, the *Dogmengeschichte* of HARNACK (1886–90, 3 vols.), the *Dogmengeschichte* of Loofs (2d ed. 1890, 1 vol.), and the *Symbolic* of KATTENBUSCH (*Lehrbuch der vergleichenden Religionskunde*, Freiburg i.B., 1891 sqq.;
dedicated to the memory of Tholuck and Ritschl; to be completed in
3 vols.).

The periodical organ of the school is the *Zeitschrift für Theologie und
Kirche*, ed. by J. Gottschick (Freiburg i.B., 1891 sqq.).

The series of text-books now in course of publication by Mohr in Freiburg is largely under the influence of the same school.

Against Ritschl: F. H. R. FRANK: *Die kirchliche Bedeutung der Theologie A. Ritschl's* (Erlangen, 1888).—R. A. LIPSIUS: *Die Ritschl'sche Theologie*
(Leipzig, 1888).—W. SCHMIDT: *Die Gefahren der Ritschl'schen Theologie für
die Kirche* (Berlin, 1888).—O. PFLEIDERER: *Die Ritschl'sche Theologie* (1893).

NOTE.—An important incident in the history of the Ritschl school is the recent agitation about the Apostles' Creed, which brought it into serious conflict with Lutheran orthodoxy and the Church authorities. Mr. Schrempf, a clergyman in Würtemberg, was deposed for refusing the customary recital of that creed in the services of baptism and confirmation. This case induced some students of theology to ask Professor Harnack's opinion on the expediency of petitioning the *Oberkirchenrath* (the highest Protestant Church tribunal in Prussia) to abolish or to relax the obligatory use of the Creed in public worship. Harnack, who sits in Neander's chair and is the chief representative of the Ritschl school among Church historians, counseled against the petition, but wrote a pamphlet, *Das Apostolische Glaubensbekenntniss* (Berlin, 1892, pp. 44), in which he showed the comparatively late origin of the Creed (as a Gallican enlargement of the older and simpler Roman form dating from the third century), and objected to the clause on the supernatural conception by the Holy Ghost, as not belonging to the original preaching of the Gospel, since it is not contained in the Gospels of Mark and John or any of the Epistles (but it is taught in the first chapters of Matthew and Luke). He also objects to the articles on the communion of saints and the resurrection of the flesh (*carnis*) in their original sense. The Creed, he holds, is venerable and permanently valuable as a confession of God, the almighty Father, and Jesus Christ, his Son our Lord, through whom we have the remission of sin and eternal life; but it fails to point to the teaching of Christ and his saving personality (?). "The symbol," says Harnack (p. 34), "contains only titles. In this sense it is imperfect; for no confession is perfect which does not paint the *Saviour* before the eyes and impress him upon the heart."

This pamphlet passed in a few weeks through more than a dozen editions, and provoked a widespread orthodox opposition all over Germany. The Ritschlians, in a conference at Eisenach, beneath the Wartburg, protested against the legally binding force of the Apostles' Creed, but not against its practical use. The *Oberkirchenrath* in Berlin tried to satisfy both parties and counseled tolerance and moderation. The chief pamphlets called forth by this controversy on the Apostles' Creed are by Kattenbusch in Giessen, Cremer in Greifswald, and Zahn in Erlangen (the last two against Harnack, who answered Cremer in the "Hefte zur Christlichen Welt," No. III.).

CHAPTER CCXX.

SPECULATIVE AND CRITICAL DOGMATIC.

Speculative Dogmatic is a scientific exposition and rational vindication of the Christian faith. It rests on the conviction that revelation and reason, faith and knowledge, are not opposed in principle and aim, but that they proceed from the same God of truth and must harmonize. Speculative theology reproduces, criticises and advances the exegetical and historical material, and adjusts it to the religious thought of the times. No Confession of Faith, however elaborate, can legislate for all future generations and supersede independent thinking. If it does, it becomes a yoke of bondage and a symbol of stagnation. Every age must produce its own theology adapted to its specific wants.

Speculative theology is akin to the philosophy of religion, and has often been more or less influenced by philosophy;. in the patristic age by Plato, in the scholastic period by Aristotle, in modern times by Descartes, Locke, Leibnitz, Wolff, Kant, Schelling, Hegel, Lotze. But theology derives its material from the Bible and the Church, and ought to be independent of any particular system of philosophy. For this reason we call it speculative, rather than philosophical. Schleiermacher and Ritschl disconnect theology from philosophy; but their theology is nevertheless the product of speculative thought. Speculation and criticism are necessary to progress. Without them we would not have any dogmatic systems.

From time to time there arises a great genius who by deeper views, bold combinations, or original methods marks an epoch and opens new avenues in the history of Dogmatic Theology. This was done by Origen, Athanasius, John of Damascus, among the Greek Fathers; Augustin among the Latin fathers; Anselm and Thomas Aquinas among the schoolmen; Luther and Calvin among the Reformers; Jonathan Edwards in New England; Schleiermacher, Rothe and Ritschl among the modern divines of Germany. Such men usually dissent from the prevailing traditions and are heterodox, if judged by an earlier or later standard of orthodoxy. But they cannot be counted heretics; they are rooted in the Christian faith, and have the mission to present it under new aspects, to rouse investigation, to keep theology in motion and to adapt it to the wants of the age.

Systems pass away, but their influence continues. In the New Testament blooms the eternal spring.

> "Our little systems have their day;
> They have their day and cease to be;
> They are but broken lights of Thee,
> And Thou, O Lord, art more than they."—TENNYSON.

CHAPTER CCXXI.

CHRISTOCENTRIC THEOLOGY.

A dogmatic system, whether biblical, confessional or speculative, ought to have a central idea which dominates the several parts and sheds light upon them. We may distinguish three fundamental principles and methods of arrangement.

1. THEOCENTRIC Theology. The absolute sovereignty and glory of God. The history of the world is suspended on eternal decrees of election and reprobation. Scholastic Calvinism. The Westminster Confession, chapter iii. 1: "God from all eternity did by the most wise and holy counsel of his own will freely and unchangeably ordain whatsoever comes to pass." Calvin, however, in his *Institutes*, follows the trinitarian and historical scheme of the Apostles' Creed, and discusses election in the third Book (iii. 21).

2. ANTHROPOCENTRIC Theology. The doctrine of sin and redemption. Paul in the Epistle to the Romans. St. Augustin, Luther, Melanchthon (law and gospel). The Heidelberg Catechism, Quest. 2, lays down as the essential articles of knowledge, "first, the greatness of my sin and misery, second, how I am redeemed from all my sins and misery, third, how I am to be thankful to God for such redemption." The later Epistles of Paul (Colossians and Philippians) and the anonymous Epistle to the Hebrews are Christological, and mark the transition to John.

3. CHRISTOCENTRIC Theology. John's Gospel and Epistles. The divine-human person of Christ, the highest manifestation of the love of God for the salvation of man, the sum and substance of Christianity, the article of the standing or falling Church. This system affords a common ground of agreement for all evangelical catholic divines. God is known to us only in Christ. "No man cometh to the Father but by the Son" (John 14: 6–10; Matt. 11: 27). Christ is the first and fundamental article of faith. It is the burden of Peter's confession (Matt. 16: 16). Paul's preaching was summed up in "Jesus Christ, and him crucified" (1 Cor. 2: 2), "delivered for our trespasses, and raised for our justification" (Rom. 4: 25). In Christ are "hid all the treasures of wisdom and knowledge"

(Col. 2: 3). When Paul was asked by the jailer of Philippi, "What must I do to be saved?" he did not say, "Believe in the Bible," or "in the Church," or "in divine sovereignty," or "in justification and election," or in any other particular dogma, but simply, "Believe in the Lord Jesus, and thou shalt be saved" (Acts 16: 31). The test of orthodoxy and heresy is the assertion or denial of Jesus Christ come in the flesh for our salvation (John 1: 14; 1 John 4: 2). All other doctrines derive their significance from their connection with it. Christian life starts with living faith in Christ, and its progress is growth in Christ. What is the foundation of Christian experience should also be the ground of Christian theology.

The Christocentric method does not require that Dogmatic should begin with Christology. The center is not the beginning, but it throws light on the beginning and the end. Christology furnishes the key for theology and anthropology. It illuminates the doctrine of eternal election "in Christ" (Eph. 1: 4-6), and the doctrine of the future life when "we shall be like him" and "see him as he is" (1 John 3: 2). It determines the doctrine of inspiration and the authority of the Bible, which reflects the mystery of his personality all human and yet all divine. We believe in the Bible because we believe in Christ who is the light and life of the Bible.

The Christocentric method may be combined with the trinitarian method (adopted by Calvin and Martensen), which is based upon the Apostles' Creed, as the Apostles' Creed is only an expansion of Peter's confession with Christ in the center. The Creed follows the historical order of God's revelation as Father in creation, as Son in redemption, and as Holy Spirit in sanctification. The holy Trinity is the most comprehensive dogma, and is revealed to us fully in Christ, who explained the Father and sent the Spirit. The best theology is the theology of God's saving love in Christ to the world; as the best Christian ethic is that which enjoins, as the sum and substance of duty, supreme love to God and love to our neighbor.

The best modern systems of evangelical theology in Europe and America are tending more and more toward the Christocentric theology.

NOTE.—Henry B. Smith struck the keynote of Christocentric theology in America, but did not live to carry it out. "The central idea," he says, "to which all the parts of theology are to be referred, and by which the system is to be made a system, or to be constructed, is what we have termed the Christological or Mediatorial idea, viz., that God was in Christ reconciling the world unto himself. This idea is central not in the sense that all the other parts of theology are logically deduced from it, but rather that they center in it. The idea is that of an Incarnation in order to Redemption. This is the central idea of Christianity, as distinguished, or distinguishable, from all other religions, and from all sorts of philosophy; and by this, and this alone, are we able to construct the whole system of the Christian faith on its proper grounds. This idea is the proper center of unity to the whole Christian system, as the soul is the center of unity to the body, as the North Pole is to all the magnetic needles. It is so really the center of unity that when we analyze and grasp and apply it, we find that the whole of Christian theology is in it" (*System of Christian Theology*, p. 341). Among Smith's papers was found this remarkable passage, which shows that he had virtually surmounted Calvinistic Predestinarianism: "What Reformed theology has got to do is to *christologize* predestination and decrees, regeneration and sanctification, the doctrine of the Church, and the whole of eschatology."

Schleiermacher, Liebner, Lange, Thomasius, Gess, Ritschl, Godet, Nevin, Smith, Stearns, and Gerhart may be called, as to their spirit and tendency, Christocentric theologians. Comp. Schaff's Introduction to Gerhart's *Institutes of the Christian Religion* (1891).

CHAPTER CCXXII.

HISTORY OF DOGMATIC THEOLOGY.—THE PATRISTIC PERIOD.

In the history of Dogmatic Theology we may distinguish six principal periods: the Patristic, the Mediæval-Scholastic, the Reformatory, the Protestant-Scholastic, the Rationalistic, and the modern Evangelical. Each period makes some contribution to the knowledge of revealed truth. The Christian doctrines are first produced or evolved by the aid of reason out of the Scriptures, the faith of the Church, and the religious experience; then analyzed and systematized; then criticised and dissolved, but only to be revived and reconstructed in new and better forms. Thus the process of Christian thought will go on to the end of time and present the Christian truth in all its aspects, without being able to exhaust its depth in this imperfect world of limited knowledge. For we shall always have to confess, with the inspired Apostle, that we here see in a mirror darkly and know only in part till we shall see face to face (1 Cor. 13:12).

The Patristic period, embracing the first eight centuries, developed, in a natural order, the several doctrines of the Bible: first, theology proper (the Divine unity and tripersonality), and Christology (the divine-human personality of Christ); then anthropology and soteriology (sin and redemption). The former was the work of the Greek, the latter the work of the Latin Church.

1. The first attempt at a systematic representation of the whole body of Christian truth was made by Origen (185–254), the greatest genius and scholar of his age. He was a Christian Platonist, the father of speculative theology, and also the father of exegesis and of the allegorical interpretation and misinterpretation of the Scriptures. He exerted a commanding influence on all the Greek divines, but his Platonic ideas provoked opposition during his life-time and were at last condemned by a local council of Constantinople in 543 (not, as is often falsely stated, by the fifth œcumenical council of 553). The Roman Church never admitted him to the rank of the saints and the orthodox Fathers.

His dogmatic work *De Principiis* (Περὶ 'Ἀρχῶν) * is built upon the freedom of the will and the prehistoric fall of each individual soul, and ends in the final restoration of all rational creatures, men and angels (ἀποκατάστασις τῶν πάντων). He assumed a succession of worlds before and after the present one, since God reveals himself from eternity to eternity.

His ablest and most faithful follower was Gregory of Nyssa, a profound thinker of the Nicene age (331–394).†

The great Athanasius is "the father of orthodoxy." ‡

The last dogmatic work of the Greek Fathers is the *Exposition of the Orthodox Faith*, by St. John of Damascus, the champion of image worship (d. after 750). He summed up the results of the doctrinal controversies of the Nicene and post-Nicene ages from the works of Athanasius, Basil, Gregory Nazianzen, Gregory of Nyssa, Cyril of Alexandria, and Maximus; he constructed them into a scholastic system with the help of Aristotle and the mystic Pseudo-Dionysius, and furnished a clas-

---

* Preserved in the paraphrastic and inaccurate Latin translation of Rufinus (and some Greek fragments); English translation by Dr. Crombie in the "Ante-Nicene Library" (New York ed., vol. iv.).

† Translated for the first time by W. Moore and H. A. Wilson in the second series of the ' Nicene and Post-Nicene Library," vol. v. (1893).

‡ English translation of his chief works in the 4th vol. of the "Library" just quoted (1892). He is the defender of the Nicene dogma of the Trinity.

sical standard work which enjoys the same authority in the orthodox Greek and Russian Church as the "Summa" of Thomas Aquinas in the Latin. (See chapter ccx.)

2. By far the greatest and most influential divine among the Latin Fathers is St. Augustin, bishop of Hippo in North Africa (353–430). He meditated and speculated profoundly and devoutly on almost every topic of faith and philosophy, especially on the dark problem of sin, the eternal purpose of God, and the final outcome of history. He ascended the highest heights and sounded the deepest depths of divine and human knowledge and of Christian experience.

His chief dogmatic works are the *Enchiridion*, a handbook on faith, hope and love; Four Books *De Doctrina Christiana*, a compendium of instruction in the development of Christian doctrine from the Holy Scripture; Fifteen Books on the *Holy Trinity*, against the Arians; and the comprehensive apologetic work on the *City of God*, which is the first attempt at a philosophy of history viewed under the aspect of two antagonistic kingdoms. His doctrines of sin and grace are developed in his anti-Pelagian writings and constitute what is usually called "the Augustinian system," which was substantially adopted by the Reformers. In Christology he was less productive.*

Augustin's system is the very reverse of that of Origen. Both battle with the problems of sin and redemption; but Origen starts from the freedom of the will and the prehistoric fall of every soul, Augustin, from the single sin of a single man and the slavery of the will. Origen ends with the final salvation of all men; Augustin with the eternal salvation of an elect minority and the eternal damnation of the vast majority of the human race, including all unbaptized infants. Sin was permissively decreed from eternity and overruled for the redemption of the elect, in whom God reveals the glory of his grace, and for the damnation of the reprobate, in whom he shows the glory of his terrible justice. The freedom of will was lost after its first exercise, and gave way to the slavery of sin or the necessity of sinning, from which we can only be delivered by the regenerative grace of Christ. Augustin suspends the temporal and eternal destiny of mankind upon the fall of Adam, viewed as the fall of the whole race. He assumes an

---

* English translation of his works by several writers in Schaff's "Nicene and Post-Nicene Library," first series (New York, 1886–88, in 8 vols.).

unconscious yet responsible preëxistence of all men in their first parent, and derives from it their consequent participation in his sin and guilt. This hypothesis of a generic preëxistence at the beginning of history transcends our experience as much as Origen's Platonic hypothesis of a prehistoric individual preëxistence, and is less reconcilable with personal responsibility. It is based on a false interpretation of Rom. 5 : 12.*

The unity and solidarity of the race in sin and redemption is indeed taught in Rom. 5 : 12–21 ; 1 Cor. 15 : 21, 22, and is sustained by philosophy and history. But so is also the equally important doctrine of individual responsibility. Moreover, the consequences of the sin of the first Adam are more than counterbalanced by the righteousness of the second Adam. Paul teaches that "where sin abounded, grace did *much more* abound." We are born into a dispensation of saving grace as well as of sin and death. Christ welcomes children as belonging to the kingdom of heaven. To send them to hell in consequence of a sin they never heard of, is a doctrine which shocks the reason and all the moral sensibilities of man, and is inconsistent with divine justice. God is a loving Father as well as a Sovereign, and has made superabundant provision for the salvation of all his rational creatures on the sole condition of repentance and faith.

Augustin's anthropology is pessimistic and only partially relieved by a limited plan of salvation, however glorious. He ignores the general love of God to all mankind (John 3 : 16), his sincere will to save all men (1 Tim. 2 : 4 ; 2 Pet. 3 : 9), and the universality of the atonement (1 John 2 : 2). His doctrine of an absolute double predestination which immutably fixes all human events and actions, and his total denial of human freedom, seem, logically, destructive of moral responsibility ; and yet, by a happy inconsistency, Augustinians and

---

* Following the wrong translation of the Vulgate, Augustin misunderstands the neutral phrase, ἐφ' ᾧ (*for that*), in the masculine sense, *in quo* (*in whom*), and refers it to Adam. *De Pecc. Mer. et Rem.*, iii. 7 : "*In Adamo omnes tunc peccaverunt, quando in ejus natura, illa insita vi qua eos gignere poterat, adhuc omnes ille unus fuerunt.*" *Contra Jul.*, v. 12 : "*Fuerunt omnes ratione seminis in lumbis Adami quando damnatus est . . . quemadmodum fuerunt Israelitæ in lumbis Abrahæ, quando decimatus est*" (Heb. 7 : 9, 10). *Opus imperf.* i. 47 : "*Fuit Adam, et in illo fuimus omnes ; periit Adam, et in illo omnes perierunt.*" Comp. on this exegetical question and the doctrinal inferences, my annotations to Lange's *Comm. on Romans*, pp. 178 sqq. and 191 sqq.

Jansenists, Calvinists and Puritans have always been the strictest moralists; and Calvinists have also been the chief promoters of civil and religious liberty in Holland, England and America; their fear of God made them fearless of man.

Augustin controlled the Christian thinking of the Latin Church during the Middle Ages; but he was entirely ignored by the Greek Church, which adheres to the doctrine of the freedom of the will. He is still justly revered by the Roman Church as the greatest among the Fathers, but she has never sanctioned his doctrines of absolute predestination and the slavery of the human will, and has, indirectly, condemned them by condemning Jansenism. The Evangelical Churches, on the contrary, have adopted his anti-Pelagian anthropology, but ignored his opinions which gave aid and comfort to the Roman theology.

Augustin may be quoted on both sides of the Protestant controversy with Rome. He is the author of the theory which sanctions the right and duty of religious persecution, and based it upon a false interpretation of the words, "Compel them to come in" (Luke 14: 23, which would lead to a compulsory salvation rather than persecution). He suggested some of the most objectionable doctrines of the Roman Church, as purgatory (on the ground of Matt. 12: 31, 32; 1 Cor. 3: 15), the sinlessness of the Virgin Mary,* and even papal infallibility.† He furnishes the most remarkable example, in history, of a man of the greatest genius and deepest piety, who blessed the Church with his truths and hindered its progress by his errors.

CHAPTER CCXXIII.

THE SCHOLASTIC PERIOD.

The second period of Dogmatic Theology extends from the twelfth to the close of the fifteenth century.

Scholastic theology is the theology of the Schoolmen as dis-

---

* Speaking of universal depravity (*De Nat. et Gratia*, chapter lxii.), he excepts the Virgin Mary, "concerning whom" (he says) "I wish to raise no question concerning sin, out of honor to the Lord."

† The sentence often quoted by Romanists, "*Roma locuta est, causa finita est*," though not literally found in Augustin's works, is substantially his. *Sermo*, cxxxi., cap. 10, § 10: "*Jam enim de hac causa duo concilia missa sunt ad sedem apostolicam : inde etiam scripta venerunt. Causa finita est, utinam aliquando error finiatur.*" But he had reference to the single case of the condemnation of Pelagius, not to a general principle. He himself pro-

tinct from the Fathers, and reduces their doctrines to a scientific system. It is an attempt or series of attempts to reconcile revelation and reason, faith and philosophy. It is built upon the Bible and the Fathers. Its principle is that faith precedes knowledge (*fides præcedit intellectum*), but that it also leads to knowledge and is confirmed by knowledge (*credo ut intelligam*). Some trace Scholasticism back to Scotus Erigena, the first distinguished Irish divine, who lived in France in the middle of the ninth century. He was a transcendental, pantheistic philosopher, and was not understood by his age; else he would have been burnt as a heretic. He taught, in his *Division of Nature*, the identity of philosophy and theology, and introduced into the Latin Church a translation of the mystic writings of Pseudo-Dionysius, which exerted great influence on the Schoolmen and Mystics of the Middle Ages.*

Anselm of Canterbury (d. 1109), "the second Augustin," gave the first splendid specimens of the scholastic method by proving the existence of God (*Monologion* and *Proslogion*) and the necessity of the incarnation and the vicarious atonement (in answer to the question *Cur Deus homo ?*). He was a Realist and refuted the Nominalism of Roscellin.

Peter Abelard (1079–1142), who is as well known by his erotic tragedy in the history of romance as of philosophy and theology, represents the skeptical and rationalistic type of scholasticism. He applied his dialectic skill and audacity to the doctrine of the Trinity, and was condemned for heresy by the Council of Sens (1141) under the influence of St. Bernard, the champion of orthodox mysticism and the greatest saint of his age. But after this conflict, Scholasticism became a pillar of orthodoxy.

Peter the Lombard, "*Magister Sententiarum*" (d. 1164), and his commentators, called *Sententiarii*, covered the whole ground of doctrinal theology and constructed from the sentences of the Fathers coherent systems, illuminating every nook and corner and answering every question. The dialectal method was further developed with the aid of the Aristotelian philosophy

tested against the decision of Pope Zosimus. Comp. the learned discussion of Reuter, in *Augustinische Studien*, pp. 322 sqq.

* He was not only a profound thinker, but also a bright wit. When asked by King Charles the Bald of France at the dinner-table, "What is the difference between a Scot and a sot?" (*Quid distat inter Scotum et sottum ?*) the Scotch-Irishman quickly replied: "The table (*tabula*), your Majesty."

which became known, during the crusades, in translations from the Arabic, and afterwards in the original Greek. Aristotle was first suspected and opposed, but soon took the place of Plato, as a forerunner of Christ, or as a philosophical John the Baptist. He kept his authority as the master-thinker till he was dethroned by Luther, who denounced him as an "accursed heathen," but he was soon reinstated by Melanchthon and the Protestant Scholastics.

Scholasticism reached its height in Thomas Aquinas, "*Doctor Angelicus*" (d. 1274), of the Dominican order, who is to this day the standard divine of the Roman Church (specially commended by Leo XIII.), and in his contemporary, Bonaventura, "*Doctor Seraphicus*" (d. 1274), of the Franciscan order, who combined mysticism with scholasticism. The later Schoolmen were divided into two rival schools: the followers of Thomas Aquinas, who were Dominicans, and were called "Thomists" or "Summists" (*Summistæ*, from *Summa Theologiæ*), and the followers of Duns Scotus, "*Doctor Subtilis*" (d. 1308), who were Franciscans, and were called "Scotists."

The decline of Scholasticism began with the skeptical William Occam (d. 1347), who dared to renew the philosophical heresy of Nominalism, hence called "*venerabilis inceptor*," also "*Doctor singularis et invincibilis*." The last eminent Schoolmen were Gabriel Biel of Tübingen, a Nominalist (d. 1495), and Cardinal Cajetan, a standard commentator of the *Summa* of Thomas Aquinas, who confronted Luther at Augsburg in 1518 and judged of this arch-heretic that he had "*profundos oculos et mirabiles speculationes in capite suo.*" *

The scholastic systems are majestic cathedrals of thought, and furnish a parallel to the contemporary papal hierarchy and to the structures of Gothic architecture. The Schoolmen mirrored all the learning and wisdom of the times. They solved the highest problems of speculation to the satisfaction of the mediæval Church, but they attempted too much and lost themselves at last in the labyrinth of empty speculations and hair-splitting distinctions. They turned theology into a logical skeleton. They squeezed the soul out of it and left it a mere corpse (*corpus divinitatis*). They neglected the study of the Scriptures,.

---

* Cajetan's commentaries on Thomas Aquinas are reprinted in the magnificent edition of the *Opera S. Thomæ Aquinatis*, published under the patronage of Leo XIII. (1882 sqq.).

but discussed with great seriousness such silly questions as how many angels could dance on the eye of a needle, and what effect the sacrament would have upon a mouse. Some answered that the sacred wafer would sanctify the mouse; others, that it would kill it; still others answered more wisely, because less foolishly, that it would have no effect at all, because the wafer could be eaten by an animal only *accidentaliter*, not *sacramentaliter*.

Thus Scholasticism by the abuse and excess of speculation dug its own grave, and provoked the double opposition of mysticism, which cultivated spiritual piety, and the skepticism of the Renaissance, which undermined traditional beliefs and superstitions.

The best scholars of the fifteenth century called for a biblical theology and a return to the living waters of the original Scriptures. Reuchlin and Erasmus promoted the study of the original languages. Melanchthon and Zwingli carried the best elements of the humanistic culture into the service of the Reformation.

But the Roman Church, after recovering from the shock of the Reformation, revived the patristic and scholastic theology, sanctioned it in the Council of Trent (1563), defended and further developed it in opposition to Protestantism, Jansenism, and Gallicanism, until it was completed in 1870 by the Vatican dogma of papal infallibility. (See chapter ccxi.)

CHAPTER CCXXIV.

THE THEOLOGY OF THE REFORMATION.

The evangelical theology of the Reformers of the sixteenth century is a revival of biblical theology in opposition to Roman Scholasticism. It is built upon an infallible Bible, as Scholasticism was built upon an infallible Church.

Luther, the first and greatest among the Reformers, was a prophet rather than a systematic thinker and theologian. He passed in the convent at Erfurt through a severe personal experience of sin and justification, which shaped his theological views, and he developed them gradually, in constant conflict with papists and "sacramentarians," under the inspiration of the moment, without regard to their coherence; leaving the systematic and scholarly statement to his more learned and moderate friend and colleague, Melanchthon, whose *Loci Theologici* (1521; last revised ed. 1559) was used for nearly a century as a textbook in Lutheran universities.

Zwingli laid down his dogmatic system in the *Commentarius de Vera et Falsa Religione* (1525), in *Fidei Ratio ad Carolum V.* (1530), and in *Christianæ Fidei brevis et clara Expositio ad Franciscum I.* (1531), and his view on predestination in the tract *De Providentia* (1530). They were far surpassed in depth, completeness and literary finish by the *Institutio* of Calvin (Basel, 1536; 5th revised edition, Geneva, 1559).

Calvin is beyond question the greatest commentator and dogmatic theologian among the Reformers. He has been called the Aristotle and Thomas Aquinas of the Reformed Church.* He fortified and intensified the Augustinian system by his severe logic and unrivaled knowledge of the Scripture, but he liberalized it also by making the electing and saving grace of God independent of the visible means, and extending it beyond the limits of baptized members of the Church. The Spirit of God is not bound, and "worketh when, and where, and how he pleaseth," as the Westminster Confession (ch. x. 3) expresses the Calvinistic view. A most important advance beyond the Augustinian and Roman Catholic exclusiveness. It is not inconsistent with John 3:5, which seems to make water-baptism a necessary condition of salvation; for this applies only to the *ordinary* method for those who are brought to a knowledge of the gospel, and must be supplemented by our Lord's blessing of unbaptized children as members of the kingdom of heaven, and by the fact that the penitent thief and all the Old Testament saints were saved without baptism.

Zwingli, the most liberal among the Reformers, had ventured a step further, and positively asserted the salvation of all children dying before the age of responsibility, and of the virtuous heathen who live up to the light of nature. This view was a natural result of his enthusiasm for the classics, in which Erasmus had preceded him. He was also the only Reformer who departed from the Augustinian hamartology and taught that natural depravity, inherited from Adam, was a disease and misfortune, rather than a sin and guilt. His view on the Lord's Supper was a still greater departure from the tradi-

---

* See the judgments in Schaff's *Church History*, vol. vii., pp. 270–295.

tional belief in the real presence, but fails to appreciate the deep mystical element of the sacrament. He was a rational supernaturalist, and anticipated modern opinions.

On two fundamental doctrines all the Reformers agreed: first, that the word of God contained in the Bible is the only infallible rule of faith and duty; second, that we are saved by the free grace of God in Christ without any merit of our own. These are the two vital and fundamental principles of evangelical Protestantism in opposition both to Romanism and Rationalism.

The fresh productive theology of the Reformation was folowed by the scholastic Lutheranism and Calvinism of the seventeenth century, which corresponds to the Catholic Scholasticism of the Middle Ages, and shares its virtues and defects, but adheres more closely to the Bible under a rigid theory of inspiration by mechanical dictation of every letter. It degenerated into bibliolatry and symbololatry, and a dead orthodoxy. This provoked various reactions—Arminianism in Holland, Pietism in Germany, Methodism in England, and at last the destructive critique of Rationalism which swept over the whole Continent. But as the mediæval Renaissance prepared the way for the Reformation, so Rationalism was succeeded by the revival of evangelical theology.

These modern schools have been sufficiently characterized in the preceding chapters. There remains only the American development of Protestant theology, which is little known, and yet deserves our special attention.

LITERATURE.

G. J. PLANCK: *Geschichte der Entstehung, der Veränderungen und der Bildung unsers Protestantischen Lehrbegriffs* (Leipzig, 1791–1800, 6 vols.). The most learned work on the doctrinal controversies in the Lutheran Church till the Formula of Concord.

W. GASS: *Geschichte der Protestantischen Dogmatik in ihrem Zusammenhang mit der Theologie überhaupt* (Berlin, 1854–67, 4 vols.).

K. F. A. KAHNIS: *Der innere Gang des deutschen Protestantismus* (Leipzig, 3d. rev. ed. 1874).

G. W. FRANK: *Geschichte der Protestantischen Theologie* (Leipzig, 1862–75, 3 parts).

Is. A. DORNER: *Geschichte der Protestantischen Theologie* (München, 1867; English translation, Edinburgh, 1871, 2 vols.).

OTTO PFLEIDERER: *Die Entwicklung der Protestantischen Theologie in Deutschland seit Kant und in Grossbritannien seit 1825* (Freiburg i.B., 1891; also in English).

CHAPTER CCXXV.

AMERICAN THEOLOGY.

[American Theology is ignored by German historians except Dorner, who devotes to it a few remarks at the end of his work. Even Dr. Shedd, in his *History of Christian Doctrine* (1863, 2 vols.), barely alludes to it. Contributions: HENRY B. SMITH, additions to Hagenbach's *History of Doctrines*, vol. ii., pp. 435–452 (New York, 1862); and *Chronological Tables* (New York, 1860). EDWARDS A. PARK: *New England Theology*, in "Schaff-Herzog," vol. iii., 1634–38; and separate articles on New England divines in the same Encyclopædia. GEO. P. FISHER: *Discussions in History and Theology* (New York, 1880, pp. 227 sqq.). Other works are quoted below.]

America welcomes all nationalities and creeds of Europe and gives them equal freedom before the law. It knows no distinction between Church and Sects, between Churchmen and Dissenters.

Nevertheless it adheres very closely to the inherited and imported creeds. It may be strange, but it is true, that "the westward course of empire" is a course of orthodoxy rather than heresy. England is more orthodox than the Continent, New England is more orthodox than Old England, the Western and Southern States are more orthodox than the Eastern States. The Roman Catholic, the Protestant Episcopal, the Presbyterian, the Congregational, the Lutheran, the Dutch and German Reformed, and other Churches are more conservative in theology, while they are more progressive in every other department of Christian life and activity than their mother Churches in Europe. Professors of rationalistic tendency and champions of radical biblical criticism, who enjoy the full freedom of academic teaching in German, Swiss and Dutch universities, could not be elected to a chair in any of our theological seminaries, not even in the Divinity School of Harvard University. Church and theology are much more closely identified in a free Church which supports and governs itself, than in a State Church which is supported and governed by the civil power. Heresy trials have ceased in Protestant Europe, but not in America.

Calvinism and Arminianism have been so far the ruling theological systems in American Theology. Unitarianism or modern Socinianism is a native growth of New England, but is confined to a limited circle among the cultured classes of

Boston and other large cities. Universalism, as an organized denomination, is also an American product. More recently German Theology, as developed since Schleiermacher, is exerting a growing influence, especially in exegesis and Church history.

Out of these different forces will grow new systems of theology adapted to the cosmopolitan and pan-Christian composition and destiny of the United States.

NOTES.

"Christian Theology in America," says Henry B. Smith, "has received some peculiar modifications adapting it to the new position and relations of the Church. Its most marked and original growth has been in the line of the Reformed or Calvinistic system. The separation of the Church from the State, the unexampled immigration, and the rapid growth of the country, made the pressure to come upon the practical rather than the theoretical aspects of Christian truth. Hence, the most thorough discussions and controversies have been chiefly upon questions of anthropology and soteriology. Systems of theology have all been preached. Controversy, too, has been sharpened by the fact that in the New World are representatives of all the ecclesiastical divisions of the Old World, with many sectarian subdivisions. The minor sects in Europe have had the sway in America."—Hagenbach's *History of Doctrines* (Am. edition, vol. ii., p. 435).

Dr. Dorner concludes his *History of Protestant Theology* (p. 918) with the following judicious remarks: *"Amerika steht noch in seinen theologischen Anfängen, aber die Zukunft des Protestantismus hängt grossentheils von der weiteren Entwicklung dieses kräftigen, nunmehr auch von dem Banne der Sclaverei befreiten Volkes ab; daher die Erhaltung und Mehrung des Verkehres mit dem deutschen Protestantismus und seinen Gütern von unberechenbarer Bedeutung ist. Jetzt ist die Zersplitterung noch gross und der Gegensatz der Parteien oft mehr ein Spiel der Willkür und äusserer Interessen, als dass er zu ernstem wissenschaftlichem Kampf gediehe. Aber je mehr der Sinn für Wissenschaft zunimmt und mit ihr die Kraft des Gedankens, dem eine einigende Macht beiwohnt, weil er auf das Allgemeine und an sich Wahre gerichtet ist, desto mehr müssen von den dortigen Denominationen viele von selbst verschwinden, andere aber in einen Process der Verständigung eintreten, der ihnen eine gemeinsame Geschichte auch des geistigen und religiösen Lebens sichert, welche wie Grossbritannien ebenbürtig und fruchtbar mit deutscher Wissenschaft wetteifern wird."*

CHAPTER CCXXVI.

THE CALVINISTIC THEOLOGY IN AMERICA.

The Reformed or Calvinistic Theology is the most potent and prolific in North America. It is not confined to a single denomination; it rules, with various modifications, the Congregationalist, the Baptist, the Presbyterian, the Dutch and German Reformed Churches. Nearly all the advances have been made on this line. Calvinism was imported into this country by the early settlers of English-Puritan, Dutch, Huguenot, Scotch and Scotch-Irish descent. It regulated the religious life and shaped the character of the people of New England during the Colonial period (1620–1776), when the church and schoolhouse were the center of the town, the Bible the statute-book of the community, the pastor the watchman of public morals, the sermon the intellectual food and topic of conversation, and church membership the condition of citizenship. The theology and theocracy of Geneva were transplanted into the unbroken wilderness of Massachusetts and Connecticut, and became the training-school of the Fathers of the Anglo-Saxon Republic.

The history of American Calvinism from the middle of the seventeenth to the close of the nineteenth century, first in provincial isolation, then in national expansion, with its changes and "improvements" from extreme supralapsarianism to the verge of semi-Pelagianism, forms an interesting and as yet unwritten chapter in the history of scholastic theology. Compared with older forms of scholasticism, it shows the same power of logical distinction and minute analysis, but also the same danger of running into barren abstractions. Its first advocates were not secluded monks or learned professors, as in Europe, but pastors and preachers. Their sermons were theological lectures. Hence the close connection of theology with practical religion. Theology and the Church, the clergy and the people, are inseparable in America.

We must distinguish between PURITAN CALVINISM, or NEW ENGLAND THEOLOGY properly so called, and PRESBYTERIAN CALVINISM which prevails in the middle, southern and western States. The former is of English-Puritan, the latter chiefly of Scotch and Scotch-Irish origin. Both are based upon the Westminster standards of 1647, which present the Scotch-English development of the Calvinism of Geneva and Dort. Both are divided into a conservative Old School and a progressive New School.

CHAPTER CCXXVII.

NEW ENGLAND THEOLOGY.

The New England divines paid chief attention to anthropology and soteriology, but neglected Christology and eschatology. They discussed with great acuteness the freedom and slavery of the will, the difference between the will and the sensibilities, between native and natural depravity, between natural and moral ability and inability, the doctrine of mediate and immediate imputation, the nature of sin and holiness, the problem of sin in a moral universe and its necessity in the best system (Optimism), the character and extent of the atonement and its relation to divine justice. The eternal decrees, efficient and permissive, election and reprobation, foreordination and foreknowledge, supralapsarianism and sublapsarianism, also occupied the devout attention of the Puritan Calvinists. Like Milton's fallen angels,

> "Sitting apart on a hill retired, they reasoned high
> Of providence, foreknowledge, will, and fate,
> Fixed fate, free will, foreknowledge absolute;
> And found no end, in wandering mazes lost." *

But the leading New England divines were by no means slavish followers of Dort and Westminster. They soften the Calvinistic system and endeavor to reconcile it with the principle of freedom and moral responsibility by a metaphysical distinction between natural and moral ability, and by affirming the former and denying the latter. They maintain that man has the natural ability to repent, to believe, and to keep the law, but that he will never use this power without the grace of God; that he does not choose the wrong inevitably, but certainly; that he may fall away totally and finally, but that he will not fall away because the grace of God will infallibly keep him. By asserting the natural ability or faculty, they approach the Pelagian system.† By asserting with equal emphasis the moral inability (a mild term for total depravity) they

---
* *Paradise Lost*, Bk. II., 555.
† Pelagius distinguished between *posse* (natural ability), *velle*, and *esse* (*bonum*), the power, the will, and the act: the first comes from God, the other two depend upon man's free choice (*liberum arbitrium*).

agree with the Augustinian system. But a natural ability which is never exercised seems to be a mere abstraction.*

The first and ablest theologian of New England, and the greatest metaphysician of America, was JONATHAN EDWARDS (1703–58), first pastor at Northampton, then missionary at Stockbridge, and at last for a few weeks president of the Presbyterian College at Princeton. He may be called the American Calvin.† He was equally distinguished for metaphysical subtlety and devout piety. He had a vein of ardent mysticism (like other profound thinkers, as Augustin, Anselm, Thomas Aquinas, Bonaventura). Though far removed from the rich libraries of Europe, and often threatened by wild beasts and savage Indians, he meditated and wrote on some of the deepest problems of thought, and left 1400 manuscripts neatly written and arranged by his own hand. While engaged in metaphysical speculations he preached powerful sermons and led, with Whitefield, "the Great Awakening" of 1740.

He out-calvined Calvin in his awful descriptions of the sinfulness and guilt of sin, and the endless torments of the impenitent. His imprecatory sermons (bearing such titles as "Wicked Men Useful in their Destruction Only," "The Sinners in the Hands of an Angry God") have scarcely a parallel in homiletical literature and would not now be tolerated by any Christian congregation even in New England, but in his day they produced tears and outcries and sincere conversions. He believed in the corporeal roasting-theory of hell, and made it as hot as Dante's "Inferno." He describes God as holding the damned "over the pit of hell much as one holds a spider or some loathsome insect over the fire."‡ He repeatedly avows his belief that the great majority of mankind, including the whole heathen world, and large masses of Christendom with many members of his own congregation, were or will be lost

---

* This distinction was first made by John Cameron of Glasgow, Professor at Saumur (d. 1625), the teacher of Amyrault, whose hypothetical universalism was disapproved in the Helvetic Consensus Formula (1675). Shedd rejects the distinction and charges Edwards with self-contradiction (*Dogm. Theol.*, vol. ii., p. 219). But he substitutes for it another distinction which amounts to the same thing, namely, between capability and ability, and asserts that the natural man "is capable of loving God supremely, but not able to love him supremely."

† He died, like Calvin, in the prime of manhood, in his fifty-fifth year.

‡ When at college he made original and minute observations on the habits of spiders.

forever.* The saints in glory are callous to the sufferings of the damned, though they be their fathers, mothers and children. They are absorbed in adoring wonder at the terrible justice of God toward the reprobate as well as at his mercy toward the elect. Divine justice in the destruction of the wicked will appear as light without darkness and will shine as the sun without the clouds." But the prevailing severity of his preaching is broken somewhat by sweet tenderness and affecting appeals to emotion. "He had," says his best biographer, who is not in sympathy with his theology, "the power of inspired appeal and exhortation. Refinement, dignity and strength, and always and everywhere a fresh and intense interest in his theme, make his sermons not only readable, but still forcible and impressive, as if the preacher were even yet standing in our midst. . . . Above the preacher, above the thinker, there towered also the majestic purity of the man entirely sincere and devoted—a character that seems well-nigh flawless; so that in his own age he was, if possible, more deeply revered as a Christian man than as the dauntless, unwearied champion of the Puritan theology." †

Edwards defended Calvinism against Arminianism, which had crept into the New England churches during the time of the "Half-Way Covenant," through the writings of Daniel Whitby and John Taylor. His chief works in this line are on the *Free-*

* "The bigger part of men," he says, "who have died heretofore have gone to hell" (see Allen, p. 124). This was the prevailing belief in Christendom till recent times, and is still the doctrine of the Roman Church, which makes water-baptism and Catholic Church membership a necessary condition of salvation. (*Extra ecclesiam nulla salus* is understood to mean *extra ecclesiam Romanam*.) The horrible doctrine of infant damnation was held in New England and incorporated in a popular poem, *The Poem of the Day of Doom*, by the Rev. Michael Wigglesworth, of Malden, Mass., a graduate and tutor of Harvard College (d. 1705). It was published in 1662, passed through six editions till 1715, and was reprinted as a curiosity by the American News Company, New York, 1867. God is represented there on the judgment day as reasoning with reprobate infants, who "from the womb unto the tomb were straightway carried," about the justice of their eternal damnation; and in consideration of their lesser guilt, he assigns to them (like St. Augustin) "the easiest room in hell." A change began with the younger Edwards (*Against Chauncy*, xiv.), who denied that it is an article of his faith that "only a small part of the human race will finally be saved." Hopkins (*Future State*, v.) asserts that "there is reason to believe that many more of mankind will be saved than lost; yea, it may be many thousands to one " Drs. Hodge and Shedd go still farther (see next chapter). On the subject of infant salvation there is probably now absolute unanimity among Protestant divines of America.

† Allen (Episcopalian), pp. 104, 105.

dom of the Will (1754) and on *Original Sin* (1758). He starts from the absolute sovereignty of God, and finds the last end of creation in the revelation of his glory, not, as the Arminians, in the happiness of his creatures, which he makes only a subordinate aim. He vindicates with subtle logic Locke's determinism and the prior certainty of all choices by antecedent causes or motives. Herein he differs from Augustin and Calvin, who gave to Adam the liberty of choice, which was lost by the fall. He makes every man responsible for Adam's sin, not by the federal theory of representation, but by the theory of identity. We are identical with Adam in his nature and constitution, and therefore identified with him in sin and guilt. Adam is not the federal head, but the generic type and root of humanity. Every man comes into this world with the nature of Adam and falls like him by a permissive decree of God. And this is called original sin. Adam's sin is not imputed to us until we consent to it by voluntary sinning. All sin is voluntary and so far a free act, and yet inevitable. It is difficult to evade the logical conclusion that God is the author of sin, and that sin is necessary.

Edwards makes the metaphysical distinction between natural ability and moral inability, by which he tried to maintain a certain kind of freedom of the will with the denial of it. Hence his constant pathetic appeals to the will to repent and to escape the impending danger by accepting Christ. He urged his hearers to take the kingdom of heaven by violence. But this freedom is "a *deus ex machina* ready to relieve the theological situation when the stress became unendurable."

The central idea of his Ethic (*On the Nature of Virtue*) is holy love, as the gift of irresistible divine grace. He defines the nature of virtue as "love to Being in general," or disinterested benevolence. What he calls "Being" is God, as the most sacred and awful of realities, like "the Substance" of Spinoza. God should be loved first of all for his infinite existence and intrinsic excellence, without regard to what he has done for us. Spinoza says, "He who loves God must not demand that God should love him in turn." But love is the very essence of God (1 John 4 : 16). "In making the motive of true virtue consist in devotion to an Infinite Being, Edwards marks the beginning of a transition in the Calvinistic churches to a theology in which love is the central principle of the creation, and the law of all created existence." *

Another great work of Edwards is the *History of Redemption* (posthumously published, 1774). It was intended to be an introduction to a comprehensive system of theology which he did not finish.

His intention was to strengthen Calvinism by his metaphysical and ethical speculations, but in effect he weakened it as a theological system.†

The Followers of Edwards.

The writings of Edwards created a school of divines called "Edwardeans," or "New Theology Men" or "New Lights." They emphatically asserted the Calvinistic doctrine of divine sovereignty and election, but generally discarded the imputation of Adam's sin and guilt to his posterity, and advocated a universal, instead of a limited atonement.

---

* Allen, p. 314.

† Editions of his Works, published at Worcester, Mass., 1809, 8 vols. (republished in New York, 1847, in 4 vols.), and by Dwight, New York, 1830, 10 vols. (also a London ed., 1817, and an Edinburgh ed., 1847). See his biography in Dwight's ed.; Alex. V. G. Allen, *Jonathan Edwards*, Boston, 1889 (in the series of "American Religious Leaders"); and Dr. Park, in the Schaff-Herzog Encycl. (vol. ii., pp. 697 sqq.). Park says: "Edwards did more, perhaps, than any other American divine in promoting the doctrinal purity, and at the same time quickening the zeal, of the churches; in restraining them from fanaticism, and at the same time stimulating them to a healthy enthusiasm. His writings were in his own day, and are in our day, a kind of classic authority for discriminating between the warmth of sound health and the heat of a fever. He did not remain stationary, like the center of a circle; he moved in an orbit not eccentric, but well-rounded and complete." Robert Hall considered Edwards "the greatest of the sons of men." Dr. Chalmers recommended his treatise on the Will as the best defense of Calvinism. Allen, a liberal Episcopalian, discriminates between Edwards, who "asserted God at the expense of humanity," and Edwards the seer, who beheld by direct vision what others knew only by report. "Among the great names," he says, "in America of the last century, the only other which competes in celebrity with his own is that of Benjamin Franklin, who labored for this world as assiduously as Edwards for another world." (p. 385).

Edwards was well known through his writings in his age by British divines who called American theology "Edwardean Theology," but was almost unknown on the Continent till quite recently. I learned his name first from Dr. Park when he studied at Berlin in 1843, and I suggested to Dr. Herzog, who had never heard of him, to secure a contribution from Dr. Park or Dr. Stowe in Andover for his "Real-Enclyklopædie." This is the origin of the article "Edwards," by Stowe, which appeared in the first edition of that great work (1854), and passed unaltered into the second edition (vol. iv., pp. 44–50), retaining a reference to Leonard Woods and Lyman Beecher as the *living* representatives of the two wings of the Edwardean School, although they had died years before.

The principal phases through which Edwardeanism passed may be designated as Hopkinsianism, Emmonsism, Taylorism and Parkism.

The younger JONATHAN EDWARDS * (1745–1801), president of Union College, Schenectady, N. Y.) edited his father's works and credits him with "ten improvements" on the older Calvinism. He modified the Anselmic view of the atonement, and elaborated what is called after him "the Edwardean theory," which substantially agrees with the governmental theory of Grotius, that the atonement is a satisfaction to the public justice of God as a moral governor.†

SAMUEL HOPKINS (1721–1803), a student of Jonathan Edwards, pastor at Newport, R. I., and one of the earliest advocates of the abolition of slavery and the slave-trade, matured a complete system of theology called "Hopkinsianism."‡ It does not materially differ from that of Edwards. He equally enforced the divine sovereignty and the obligation of immediate repentance. He held that sin is the necessary means to the greatest good and is overruled for the advantage of the universe.§ He resolved all sin into selfishness, and taught that all actions, even the prayers, of impenitent men are sinful, repentance being a prior duty. Hence it is wrong to exhort men to pray for their own conversion.

He is best known by his theory of virtue. He carried Edwards's view of love, as disinterested benevolence, to the extent

---

* Called Doctor Edwards, in distinction from his father, President Edwards. The College of New Jersey, at Princeton, where he was graduated in 1765, conferred on him the degree of D.D. See Park, in the Schaff-Herzog Encycl., vol. ii., pp. 699–701. Emmons said of the two Edwardses: "The father had more reason than his son, but the son was a greater reasoner than his father."

† See E. A. Park, *The Atonement: Discourses and Treatises, by Edwards, Smalley, Emmons, etc., with an Introductory Essay* (of 80 pp.), Boston, 1860; also the introduction of Frank H. Foster (a pupil of Park) to his edition of the famous essay of Grotius, *On the Satisfaction of Christ* (Andover, 1889, pp. xlv. sqq.).

‡ *System of Doctrines contained in Divine Revelation* (1793, 3 vols.; 2d ed., Boston, 1811, 2 vols.). Best edition of his Works, with a Biographical Memoir by Dr. Park (Boston, 1852, 3 vols.). See also Park's article, "Hopkinsianism," in Schaff-Herzog, vol. ii., p. 102. Hopkins is the hero of *The Minister's Wooing*, a theological novel by Mrs. Harriet Beecher Stowe, who, herself a daughter of the Puritans, describes the lights and shades of Puritan theology and piety, and contrasts them with the infidelity and immorality of Aaron Burr, the unworthy grandson of Jonathan Edwards.

§ The title of his first work is *Sin through the Divine Interposition an Advantage to the Universe.*

of unconditional submission and willingness to be damned forever for the glory of God. A similar view was held by Fénelon and Madame Guyon. It is a noble error, which rests on a literal misinterpretation of the wish of Paul (Rom. 9:3), and ignores the inseparable connection of love and happiness.

NATHANIEL EMMONS (1745–1840), for fifty-four years pastor of a Congregational Church at Franklin, Mass. (which he made a parish of theologians), and teacher of a hundred candidates for the ministry, was one of the chief advocates of Hopkinsianism, and one of the most original divines of Puritan New England. He held to verbal inspiration and literal interpretation. He strongly believed in the Trinity and the divinity of Christ, but irreverently called the Nicene doctrine of the eternal generation of the Son "eternal nonsense." He said: "Strict Calvinism brings God near to us; all opposing systems put him far away." He made the "five points" of this system, with the exception of *limited* atonement, the staple of his sermons, and even declared belief in the decree of reprobation to be necessary to salvation. He pressed the doctrine of divine sovereignty to the revolting extent of making God the efficient cause of all sinful, as well as holy, acts ("exercises") of the will; yet with happy inconsistency he maintained the responsibility of the sinner on the ground of his natural power to thwart the divine decrees, and earnestly enforced the claims of disinterested benevolence. Under his advice the severe creed of Andover Seminary was adopted.*

* His Works were edited by Dr. Jacob Ide, and published by the Congregational Board (Boston, 1861, in 6 vols.). Dr. Park has written an admirable sympathetic *Memoir of Nathaniel Emmons, with Sketches of his Friends and Pupils* (Boston, 1861, 468 pp., with a portrait). With this should be compared an elaborate essay on *The Theological System of Emmons*, by Henry B. Smith, written in 1862, and republished in his *Faith and Philosophy* (New York, 1877, pp. 215–263). Smith sums up the scheme of Emmons in the formula: "God, by direct efficiency, produces all events and exercises for his own glory." It is reported that an eminent preacher said to him, "You and I agree that all sin and holiness consist in exercises;" and that Emmons replied, "Yes, but we differ as to where the exercises come from." Presbyterians generally opposed Emmons for opposite reasons: as a hyper-Calvinist on account of his supralapsarianism, and as an Arminian on account of his views on sin, ability, and the atonement. Emmons was a typical Puritan of the old style, known for sharp and quick repartees, and attracted attention by his three-cornered hat, small-clothes, and knee-breeches. In church polity he was an extreme Independent, and is credited with the saying: "Association leads to consociation, consociation to presbytery, presbytery to prelacy, prelacy to popery, popery to the devil."

The New Haven theologians, TIMOTHY DWIGHT (1752–1817) and NATHANIEL W. TAYLOR (1786–1858), represent a semi-Arminian form of Calvinism which is called the "New School."

President Dwight of Yale College, a grandson of Jonathan Edwards and a preacher and instructor of great influence, humanized the Edwardean system and relieved it of its extreme severity. He preached a system of theology and published it in a series of sermons.* He rejected the doctrines of the imputation of Adam's sin, of natural inability (total depravity), and of limited atonement, also the Hopkinsian view of the sinfulness of the prayers of impenitent men, and other Hopkinsian extravagances. He is best known in the churches by his classical hymn, "I love thy kingdom, Lord."

Dr. Taylor, his pupil, introduced further variations of the New England theology in the direction of semi-Pelagianism. He was, next to Jonathan Edwards, the most metaphysical of the New England divines, but apparently not familiar with the development of German philosophy from Kant to Hegel. He made theology subservient to the practical work of persuading men to turn to God by rousing their sense of personal responsibility. He taught, in opposition to the Old School, that election is founded in benevolence, guided by wisdom, and so dispenses grace as to insure the best results; that sin is not "the necessary means of the greatest good," but may not be preventable in the best system of the universe; that "natural ability" involves a continued "power of contrary choice," but is checked by moral inability; that self-love is the spring of all moral action; that the atonement is to be vindicated not as a vicarious scheme, but (with Grotius) as an essential part of the moral government of God.†

---

* *Theology Explained and Defended* (1818, 5 vols.; several editions, American and English).

† His most elaborate work is *The Moral Government of God* (New York, 1859, 2 vols.). See G. P. FISHER, *The System of Dr. N. W. Taylor in its Connection with Prior New England Theology*, in his *Discussions in History and Theology* (New York, 1888, pp. 285–354). He vindicates Taylor against the charge of Pelagianism raised by Hodge and other Old School divines. "It is a curious fact," he says (pp. 351 sq.), "that men who are loud in their denunciation of Dr. Taylor's system profess themselves willing to tolerate the extreme Hopkinsians. They are shocked at the assertion of a power of contrary choice, but they can put up with the doctrine that God is the creator of sin! They can freely tolerate propositions which are not only denounced by all the creeds of Christendom, but, if logically carried out, would banish all religion from the earth."

Against this New Haven School, Dr. BENNET TYLER (1783–1858) reasserted strict Calvinism,* and founded a theological seminary at East Windsor, Conn. (1834), which was afterwards removed to Hartford. It has lately received liberal endowments and taken a much broader position in the direction of progress.

The last Old School divine in New England was Dr. LEONARD WOODS (1774–1854), professor in the theological seminary at Andover, which was founded in 1808 by the coöperation of the strict Calvinists (Hopkinsians) and the moderate Calvinists. It is the oldest theological school in America next to that of the Dutch Reformed Church in New Brunswick, which dates from the year 1784.† Dr. Woods took a leading part in the Unitarian controversy, and published his *Theological Lectures* and other essays at Andover (1849–50, 5 vols.). His son, LEONARD WOODS, Jr. (1807–78), translated Knapp's *Christian Theology* (1831–33, 2 vols.), which has been widely used as a text-book.

Dr. EDWARDS A. PARK (b. 1808, resigned 1881), a descendant of Edwards, succeeded and opposed Dr. Woods in the theological chair at Andover. He was a brilliant and magnetic lecturer and preacher, and had the singular faculty of making abstruse, logical definitions and distinctions interesting by illustrative anecdotes. His system essentially agrees with the modern New Haven divinity. ‡

Since about 1880 Andover theology, under the lead of Dr. Egbert C. Smyth (professor of Church History), has taken a new departure, which differs as widely from Dr. Park as Dr. Park differed from Dr. Woods. It has become an advocate of "progressive orthodoxy" beyond the strict sense of the "Andover Creed." The best known tenet of this newer New School is the modern German hypothesis of future (not second) probation for all who have not heard the gospel in this life. This hypothesis, though not professionally taught in the Seminary, created a great commotion in connection with the policy of the American Board of Foreign Missions, and led to a lawsuit for

---

* In several controversial pamphlets, and in his *Lectures on Theology*, published after his death (Boston, 1859), with a memoir by Nahum Gale.

† Dr. Livingston was chosen professor by the Dutch Reformed Church in 1784, and inaugurated at New York, May 19, 1785.

‡ See his *Discourses on some Theological Doctrines as related to the Religious Character* (Andover, 1885). His lectures on Systematic Theology have not yet been published.

alleged violation of the creed of the seminary. The court has decided in favor of a liberal construction (1892).

The Congregational Creed of 1883.

New England Puritanism has gradually drifted away from the Westminster Confession without falling out of the line of Reformed theology in its legitimate development. At the fourth session of the National Council of the Congregational Churches of the United States, convened at St. Louis, Mo., November, 1880, it was resolved to prepare a summary of the doctrines held by them. Accordingly, a committee of twenty-five able divines matured a new "statement of doctrine" in 1883, without imposing it upon the churches. It consists of twelve articles, and presents all the essential truths of evangelical Protestantism, but omits the offensive points of the Calvinism of Dort and Westminster. The first article states the orthodox doctrine of the Trinity with a skillful avoidance of the vexed difference about the double procession of the Holy Ghost by substituting "is sent" for "proceeds" (from the Father and Son). The second article treats of the difficult subject of divine sovereignty and human responsibility as follows:

"We believe that the Providence of God, by which he executes his eternal purposes in the government of the world, is in and over all events; yet so that the freedom and responsibility of man are not impaired, and sin is the act of the creature alone."*

CHAPTER CCXXVIII.

CHANNING AND BUSHNELL.

An account of New England theology would not be complete without a reference to two most eminent divines, who were of genuine Puritan stock, but departed considerably from Puritan orthodoxy.

Unitarianism is an important factor in the history of Puritan New England. It rose from the early Arminianism, which never died out, in spite of Edwards and his School, but increased in the later part of the eighteenth century. It is a radical re-

---

* The creed is printed, with a historical introduction, in the 5th edition of Schaff's *Creeds of Christendom*, vol. iii., pp. 910 sqq.

action against dogmatic Calvinism, and substitutes an optimistic for a pessimistic view of human nature. It denies original sin, and believes in the native dignity and nobility of man. It lacks that sense of sin and guilt which terrified the conscience of Paul, Augustin, Luther, Calvin, and Edwards, and which made them feel all the more the power of forgiving and saving grace. It forms an American parallel to German Rationalism in its milder types.

The ablest and noblest representative of American Unitarianism is WILLIAM ELLERY CHANNING (1780–1842), a man of high literary culture, moral purity, devout and fervent piety. He was not so much a scholar and theologian as a preacher, philanthropist and practical reformer.*

Unitarianism took possession of the cultivated society of Boston and Cambridge, the classical headquarters of Puritanism, and was connected with a literary and æsthetic renaissance. It turned theology from a metaphysical and dogmatic into an ethic and philanthropic channel, and produced a rich literature in poetry (Bryant, Longfellow, Lowell) and in history (Prescott, Bancroft, Motley).†

HORACE BUSHNELL of Hartford (1802–76), an original genius and great preacher, stands between Calvinism and Unitarianism, but nearer the former. He occupies an isolated position, yet has left a permanent impression on New England theology.

He renewed the Unitarian controversy in a milder form by his advocacy of the Sabellian view of the Trinity (*God in Christ*, 1849), and of the moral theory of the atonement (*The Vicarious Sacrifice, Grounded in Principles of Universal Obligation*, 1866). In his *Nature and the Supernatural* (1858), he showed the harmony of the two "as together constituting the one system of

---

* In Europe he is better known, perhaps, than most of American authors. A French Catholic writer calls him the American Fénelon. Coleridge said that he "had the love of wisdom and the wisdom of love." Dr. Döllinger regarded Channing and Nevin (very different in their tendency) as the two greatest American divines. His *Works* were published in Boston, 1848 (6 vols.), and in 1880; in London, 1865; German translation, Berlin, 1850; French translation, 1857 and 1861. See his *Memoir*, by his nephew (London and Boston, 1848; 10th ed. 1874, 3 vols.); George P. Fisher: *Channing as a Philosopher and Theologian*, in his *Discussions in History and Theology*, pp. 253–284; and Schaff, art. "Channing" in the Schaff-Herzog Encycl., vol. i., pp. 430 sqq.

† See ch. ccxvi., p. 349. It is characteristic that a number of distinguished Unitarian ministers, as Sparks, Everett, Bancroft, Emerson, Ripley, Palfrey, and Upham, left the pulpit to devote themselves to literature.

God," and inserted a chapter on "the Moral Character of Jesus forbidding his possible classification with men," which is one of the noblest tributes of genius to the superhuman perfection of our Saviour, and superior to Channing's admirable essay on the same subject.*

CHAPTER CCXXIX.

PRESBYTERIAN THEOLOGY.†

The history of Presbyterian theology in America is synchronous with the history of New England theology and passed through a similar conflict between a conservative and a progressive tendency, respectively called "Old Lights" and "New Lights," or "Old School" and "New School." Owing to the closer ecclesiastical organization of Presbyterianism this conflict resulted more than once in a split, but also in a reunion. The Old and New School are two rival sisters which cannot live without each other. The one preserves the good in the past and moderates the rate of speed; the other pushes hopefully forward into new fields of discovery and research. A ship requires heavy ballast to keep it steady, and steam and wind to drive it ahead.

JONATHAN DICKINSON (1688-1747) is the first notable theologian of the American Presbyterian Church. He was of Puritan stock, the grandson of one of the first settlers of Connecticut, and educated at Yale College. In 1706 he became pastor at Elizabethtown. In connection with his ministry he practiced medicine. He joined the Philadelphia Presbytery in 1717 and helped to frame the Adopting Act of 1729, which made the Westminster Confession of Faith the standard of Presbyterian orthodoxy, but with an important limitation to its "essential and necessary articles." He took a leading part in the controversy between the "Old Side," or "Old Lights," and the "New Side," or "New Lights," which led to a division into the Synod of Philadelphia and the Synod of New York in 1741, lasting till 1758, when the schism was healed. He sided with the

---

* *Life and Letters of Horace Bushnell*, edited by his daughter (New York, 1880).

† The chief dogmatic works of Presbyterian divines have been mentioned in ch. ccxiii., p. 343.

"New Lights." He was one of the founders and the first president of Nassau Hall, or the College of New Jersey, which was opened at Elizabethtown in 1747, and removed to Princeton in 1757.

Dickinson was a contemporary of Jonathan Edwards, his second successor in the presidency of the College of New Jersey, and, like him, took a leading part in the great revival conducted by Whitefield and Gilbert Tennent. He was less metaphysical but equally earnest and practical, and made Calvinistic theology a converting agency.

His chief theological work is a defense of the five knotty points of Calvinism, in five discourses, on Election, Original Sin, Irresistible Grace, Justification by Faith, and Perseverance of Saints.* He regarded the five points indorsed by the Synod of Dort against Arminianism as a "golden chain, which extends from everlasting to everlasting and connects a past and future eternity, which takes its rise in God's foreknowledge and eternal purpose of grace to the elect and reaches through their vocation and justification on earth into their eternal glorification in heaven."

At a joint meeting of the Synods of New York and Philadelphia, held in Philadelphia, May, 1788—the year after the framing of the Federal Constitution of the United States—the ecclesiastico-political articles of the Westminster Confession were changed and conformed to the separation of Church and State. This was a most important departure from original Calvinism, and the Synods of Dort and Westminster, which held to a union of ecclesiastical and civil government and the implied principle of religious persecution.†

I. *The Old School Theology.*

The founding of the theological seminary at Princeton by the General Assembly in 1812 (four years after the founding of the seminary at Andover) marks a new epoch in the history of

---

* *The Scripture Doctrine Concerning Some Important Points of Christian Faith*, first published in Boston, 1741, and often reprinted since (also by the Presbyterian Board of Publication, Philadelphia, 1841, pp. 292).

† See the changes in chapters xx., xxiii., and xxxi., with original statements placed in parallel columns in Schaff's *Creeds of Christendom*, vol. i., pp. 806 sqq. The American Episcopal Church, at the general Convention in Trenton, 1801, made a similar alteration in the Thirty-nine Articles, and omitted the Athanasian Creed (*Creeds*, vol. i., p. 653).

Presbyterian Calvinism. This seminary was singularly favored for two generations by two illustrious divines who, with their sons and successors, determined its character for a long period, and by their writings, as well as their pure and noble lives, made a lasting impression upon the Presbyterian Churches, and, we may say, upon American Christianity at large.

Dr. ARCHIBALD ALEXANDER (1772–1851), a Virginian by birth, was the first professor of systematic theology and the father of what, since about 1832, has been called "Princeton Theology," which was developed into a system by his colleague and successor, Dr. CHARLES HODGE (1797–1878), and popularized by the latter's son and successor, ARCHIBALD ALEXANDER HODGE (1823–86).

The elder Hodge studied in Germany at the time when Rationalism was still prevailing in the universities, but was not affected by it. He notices modern German opinions mostly to oppose them.*

The Princeton Theology is a scholarly, logical, luminous and warm-hearted reproduction of the Calvinism of the seventeenth century as laid down in the Westminster standards of 1647, and revised in America, 1788.† On the questions of inspiration

---

* Dr. Hodge, after his election to a professorship in Princeton (1826), spent two years in Halle to study oriental philology with Gesenius, and became intimately acquainted with Tholuck, who was just then beginning to turn the tide in favor of the evangelical revival. Hodge often spoke with great affection of Tholuck, and told me that he found as pious and godly men in Halle and Berlin as anywhere in America. Tholuck said to me once: "Charles Hodge, Henry B. Smith and George L. Prentiss are my American pets." Dr. Hodge's place during his absence was filled "with eminent ability" by John W. Nevin, who never visited Germany, but was much more influenced by its theology and afterwards, at Mercersburg, developed a very different theology. See *The Life of Charles Hodge*, p. 103, and Nevin's controversy with Hodge on the doctrine of the Lord's Supper, in the "Mercersburg Review" for 1850, pp. 421–549.

† The Princeton professors are sworn to the Westminster standards by a rigid subscription formula, which is as follows: "In the presence of God and of the directors of this seminary, I do solemnly and *ex animo* adopt, receive and subscribe the Confession of Faith and Catechisms of the Presbyterian Church in the United States of America as the confession of my faith, or as a summary and just exhibition of that system of doctrine and religious belief which is contained in Holy Scripture, and therein revealed by God to man for his salvation; and I do solemnly *ex animo* profess to receive the Form of Government of said Church as agreeable to the inspired oracles. And I do solemnly promise and engage not to inculcate, teach or insinuate anything which shall appear to me to contradict or contravene, either directly or impliedly, anything taught in the said Confession of Faith or Catechisms, nor to oppose any of the fundamental principles of Presbyterian Church government, while I shall continue a professor

PRESBYTERIAN THEOLOGY. 391

and imputation, which were not finally decided by the Westminster Assembly, Princeton follows the teaching of the elder Turretin of Geneva (1623–1687),* and of the Helvetic Consensus Formula (1675).†

The Helvetic Formula is the latest and most orthodox of the Calvinistic confessions, but its authority was confined to Switzerland, and of short duration. It was prepared in 1675 by Johann Heinrich Heidegger of Zürich (1633–98) in connection with François Turretin of Geneva (1623–87) and Lucas Gernler of Basel (1625–75), and signed by the clergy of Zürich, Bern, Basel and Schaffhausen, but not printed till 1714, and soon afterwards subscription to it was abolished in Switzerland, chiefly through the influence of the younger Turretin. ‡

This document deals with theological questions which were raised after the death of Calvin and Beza. It is directed against the liberal Reformed School of the Academy of Saumur in France, which flourished from 1598 till the revocation of the Edict of Nantes in 1685. It teaches verbal inspiration against Louis Cappel (Capellus, d. 1658), particular election, in opposition to the hypothetical universalism of Amyraut (Amyraldus, d. 1664), and immediate imputation of Adam's sin, against mediate imputation, taught by Joshua de la Place (Flacæus, d. 1655). §

in this seminary." This formula was adopted by the General Assembly in 1811, and is still in force (see Baird's *Digest*, p 436; Moore's *Digest*, p. 377). Under such restriction it is difficult to teach Church History, and almost impossible to make any doctrinal progress " directly or impliedly."

* François Turretin was the third descendant of the distinguished Turrettini (Turretin) family which emigrated from Lucca and settled at Geneva in 1593. His *Institutio Theologiæ Elenchticæ*, etc. (1679, ed. nova, Genev., 1688, 3 vols.; neatly republished in Edinburgh, and reprinted by Robert Carter in New York, 1847–48, in 4 vols. 8vo.), was made the theological text-book at Princeton by Dr. Alexander. He was one of the ablest of the numerous dogmatists of the seventeenth century, and a veritable *malleus hæreticorum*, who approved the burning of Servetus as most just ("*justissimas impietatis execrandæ pœnas tulit*," vol. i., ch. xvii.).

† "*Formula Consensus Ecclesiarum Helveticarum Reformatarum circa doctrinam de gratia universali et connexa alia nonnulla capita*," in Niemeyer's *Collectio Conf.*, pp. 729–739. An English translation in A. A. Hodge's *Outlines of Theology*, pp. 651–663.

‡ Jean Alphonse Turretin (1674–1733), a son of François, but a much more liberal divine and a hearty promoter of Christian union, exerted all his influence for the abolition of the subscription to the Consensus Formula in Geneva in 1725. There the venerable document lay decently buried, till it rose to new life in the American town of Princeton. See E. de Budé, *Vie de François et J. Alphonse Turrettini* (Lausanne, 1871 and 1880, 2 vols.).

§ Schweizer, *Centraldogmen*, vol. ii., pp. 439 sqq., 784 sqq.; and Schaff, *Creeds of Christendom*, vol. i., p. 477 sqq.

The Swiss Formula extends verbal inspiration even to the Hebrew vowel-points, or at least their force and significance (*potestas*), and meant to assert also the divine preservation of the Bible text so as to supersede the necessity of biblical criticism, which was feared as a dangerous science, undermining the authority of an infallible Bible against an infallible pope.*

Dr. HODGE does not go quite so far; he knows well enough that the Hebrew vowels cannot be traced beyond the sixth century after Christ; he allows more room for the human agency in the composition of Scripture; he even admits a few minor defects, as (to use his illustration) "here and there a speck of sandstone may be found in the marble of the Parthenon." But he asserts, nevertheless, the plenary inspiration of words as well as thoughts, and says that "inspiration is not confined to moral and religious truths, but extends to the statements of facts, whether scientific, historical or geographical." †

The theory of a literal inspiration and inerrancy was not held by the Reformers, is not taught by any other symbolical book, has no foundation in the Bible itself, is disproved by the free quotations from the Old Testament (*ad sensum* rather than *ad literam*), and is exposed to unanswerable objections. It is inconsistent with known facts which are truths. It cannot be

---

* "II. *In specie autem Hebraicus Veteris Testamenti Codex, quem ex traditione Ecclesiæ Judaicæ, cui olim Oracula Dei commissa sunt, accepimus hodieque retinemus, tum quoad consonas, tum quoad vocalia, sive puncta ipsa, sive punctorum saltem potestatem, et tum quoad res, tum quoad verba θεόπνευστος, ut fidei et vitæ nostræ, una cum Codice Novi Testamenti sit Canon unicus et illibatus, ad cuius normam, ceu Lydium lapidem, universæ, quæ extant, Versiones, sive orientales, sive occidentales exigendæ, et sicubi deflectunt, revocandæ sunt.*"—(Niemeyer's *Collectio*, p. 731.) In the translation of Dr. A. A. Hodge: "But, in particular, the Hebrew Original of the Old Testament, which we have received and to this day do retain as handed down by the Jewish Church, unto whom formerly 'were committed the oracles of God' (Rom. 3:2), is, not only in its consonants, but in its vowels—either the vowel points themselves, or at least the power of the points—not only in its matter, but in its words, inspired of God, thus forming, together with the Original of the New Testament, the sole and complete rule of our faith and life; and to its standard, as to a Lydian stone, all extant versions, oriental and occidental, ought to be applied, and wherever they differ, be conformed." Compare Turretin, *Locus Secundus, Questio* 10 (vol. i., pp. 96 sq.). He vindicates verbal inspiration for the existing original text as a faithful copy of the autographs. "*Textuum Originalium nomine, non intelligimus ipsa* AUTOGRAPHA *manu Mosis, Prophetarum et Apostolorum exarata, quæ desiderari hodie constat, sed eorum* APOGRAPHA, *quæ eo nomine veniunt, quia exprimunt nobis Verbum illud Dei illis ipsis verbis quibus Scriptores sacri id consignarunt sub immediata inspiratione Spiritus S.*"

† *Syst. Theology*, vol. i., p. 163.

claimed for any of the numerous translations of the Bible, which are confessedly imperfect and yet convey to the reader the word of God for all practical purposes; nor for the Hebrew text, which in its present form is of late rabbinical origin and presents many variations; nor for the Septuagint, which often differs from the Hebrew text, and yet is usually quoted by our Lord and the Apostles; nor for the Greek Testament with its many thousands of discordant readings, which have come to light since the seventeenth century by the discovery and examination of MSS., versions, and patristic quotations. It could therefore only apply to "the original autographs" (which nobody has seen since the days of the Apostles).*

Since God has made no provision for infallible transcribers and infallible translators of the Bible, we must infer that verbal inspiration was not necessary. Inspiration must not be confounded with dictation; the former is a free spiritual, the latter a mechanical, process. God acts upon men as free and responsible agents, and so inspired the organs of revelation that they became his faithful witnesses in preaching and acting as well as in writing, but always in accordance with their education, their mode of thought and speech, and without superseding the use of the ordinary means of information (as is very evident in the case even of the Gospels; comp. Luke 1:1-4). The fact of inspiration is manifest, the mode of inspiration is as mysterious as the influence of the mind upon the body.

Our faith in the Bible, as containing the very word of the living God and as the infallible guide in all matters of faith and practice, rests on its intrinsic value, and is independent of

---

* Drs. A. A. Hodge and B. B. Warfield, the successors of Charles Hodge in the theological chair at Princeton, confine inerrancy to these non-existing original autographs. See "Princeton Review" for 1881, p. 238. "The historical faith of the Church has always [?] been that all the affirmations of Scripture of all kinds, whether of spiritual doctrine or duty, or of physical or historical fact, or of psychological or philosophical principle, are without any error, when the *ipsissima verba* of the original autographs are ascertained, and interpreted in a natural and intended sense." Comp. Dr. Warfield's article on inspiration in "The Presbyterian and Reformed Review" for April, 1893, pp. 177-221.

The distinction between "inerrant autographs" and errant copies seems to have been first made by Richard Simon (1638-1712), the father of biblical isagogic, to prove the necessity of textual criticism and to silence the attacks of Protestant and Roman Catholic champions for the inerrancy of the *existing* text of the Bible. He also intended to show "*que les protestants n'avait aucun principe assuré de leur religion, en rejetant la tradition de l'Église*" (Preface to his *L'histoire critique du V. T.*).

any human theory of inspiration. As Dr. Hodge well says, "theories are of men, truth is of God."

In some important respects, the Princeton theology marks an advance and improvement upon the polemic orthodoxy of the seventeenth century. Dr. Hodge is free from narrow and uncharitable bigotry. He claims that his theology is "distinctly Christological," and quotes with approbation the words which Neander wrote in his album in Greek: "Nothing in ourself, all things in the Lord, whom alone to serve is a glory and a joy;"—adding, "These words our old professors would have inscribed in letters of gold over the portals of this seminary, there to remain in undiminished brightness as long as the name of Princeton lingers in the memory of man." *

He dissented from the traditional prejudice against Romanism, and had the courage to oppose by convincing arguments the decision of the Old School General Assembly held at Cincinnati in 1845, which out-poped the pope by unchurching the oldest and largest Church of Christendom, and declaring, by a vote of 169 to 8, Roman Catholic baptism invalid.†

The most important change refers to the number of the saved. Hodge holds the liberal views first advocated by Zwingli, and adopted by Arminians, Quakers, Baptists and Methodists, that all infants dying in infancy are saved, and closes his dogmatic work with the sentence that the number of those who are ultimately lost "is very inconsiderable as compared with the whole number of the saved." ‡

The Southern theologians, JAMES H. THORNWELL (1812–62), ROBERT J. BRECKINRIDGE (1800–71) and ROBERT L. DABNEY (b. 1820), represent, independently, the same system of Calvinism, but dissent from the federal scheme and the doctrine of imputation, and are more opposed to popery.

---

* See his Semi-centennial Address in *The Life of Charles Hodge*, by his son, A. A. Hodge (New York, 1880, p. 521).

† See his article in "The Princeton Review" for April, 1846, and his *Life*, pp. 340 sq. A similar action was attempted in the New School Assembly, 1853, but defeated by Dr. Henry B. Smith. In the united General Assembly, held at Cincinnati in 1885, a resolution was offered to confirm the action of 1845, but was fortunately rejected. Among the proposed changes in the Westminster Confession are those in ch. xxv., p. 6, which declares the pope of Rome to be the Antichrist predicted by Paul (2 Thess. 2: 3, 4), and in ch. xxiv. 3, which by implication classes papists with "idolaters."

‡ *Syst. Theology*, vol. i., p. 26; vol. iii., p. 879. A. A. Hodge was even more liberal than his father. Comp. Schaff, *Creeds*, vol. i., p. 795.

Dr. WILLIAM G. T. SHEDD, professor at Andover, and afterwards at Union Seminary, New York (b. 1820, resigned 1890), elaborated, in classical English, a different type of Old School Calvinism, with great ability and logical severity. He adheres strictly to the Augustinian anthropology, and the Westminster Confession. He is a Calvinist pure and simple, and makes no concessions to Arminianism or modern theology.* He advocates the infralapsarian scheme; the decree of reprobation, as the necessary corollary of the decree of election; the distinction between the secret and the revealed will of God in his offering salvation to all men, while he really means to make it effectual only for the elect. He teaches (herein differing from Augustin, but in harmony with the Westminster Standards) the perfect sanctification of believers at their death and their immediate passage into glory, and thus obliterates or at least minimizes the distinction between the middle state before, and the final state after, the resurrection.†

So far there is no difference between Shedd and Hodge. They also agree in mitigating the older Protestant eschatology by "the larger hope" for the salvation of the vast majority of men, including all infants dying in infancy. This is a triumph of the Christian heart over the cold logic of the intellect. ‡

But there is a material difference in the philosophy and anthropology of these two distinguished divines. Dr. Hodge is a nominalist and a creationist. Dr. Shedd is a realist and a traducianist. Dr. Shedd makes, with Augustin, a real distinction between the generic human nature and the individual man, and assumes that the whole race pre-existed and fell in Adam, and actually participated in his sin and guilt; while Dr. Hodge defends the federal view of Coccejus, that Adam by divine appointment acted as the representative head in behalf of his posterity, which did not yet exist except in the divine purpose. Dr. Shedd accounts for the propagation of sin by Tertullian's

---

* See his *Dogmatic Theology* (1888, 2 vols.), and his *Calvinism, Pure and Mixed: A Defence of the Westminster Standards* (New York, 1893).

† He denies the distinction between Hades and Gehenna, in opposition to the unanimous opinion of the ancient Fathers, modern commentators and the Anglo-American Bible Revisers. He always quotes King James's version, which renders both words by "hell."

‡ Dr. Shedd emphasizes the countless "multitude" of the saved, and reduces hell to "a narrow pit" (*Dogmatic Theology*, vol. ii., p. 747, and *Calvinism, Pure and Mixed*, pp. 121 sqq.). Yet he devotes only 3 pages to Heaven (vol. ii., pp. 664–666) and 87 pages to Hell (pp. 667–754)!

theory of traducianism, or the transmission of body and soul by natural generation, instead of ascribing the origin of each human soul to a creative act of God. His view furnishes a more rational ground for personal responsibility and for what he calls "the sinfulness of original sin," but it involves all the insuperable difficulties of the Augustinian theory.

II. *The New School Theology.*

The New School is nearer the Congregational Calvinism than the Old School, and keeps progress with modern thought.* The chief differences referred originally to the extent of the atonement—whether general or limited—and the nature of imputation—whether mediate or immediate. With these were connected conflicting views on the authority of the General Assembly, the "Plan of Union" with the Congregationalists (1801), the slavery question and moral reforms. In more recent times, other and more important differences in bibliology and eschatology have come to the front.

The earlier representatives of the New School before the separation were JAMES RICHARDS (1767–1843), BAXTER DICKINSON (1794–1876), ALBERT BARNES (1798–1870), LYMAN BEECHER (1775–1863), and THOMAS H. SKINNER (1791–1871). Richards wrote a system of theology, and presided over the Auburn Convention of the exscinded synods which adopted, in August, 1837, "the Auburn Declaration," setting forth, in sixteen articles, the true doctrines of the New School.† Barnes was the most popular commentator of his day; Beecher was one of the most powerful preachers, though surpassed afterwards by his son, Henry Ward Beecher; Skinner was chiefly distinguished as a preacher and saintly character. Barnes and Beecher were tried for heresy, but were acquitted. Nevertheless the friction between the two parties increased, until in 1837 the Old School obtained the majority in the General Assembly, abrogated the "Plan of Union," and cut off four entire synods (Western Reserve, Utica, Geneva and Genesee) without a trial. The split

---

* A number of distinguished New School Presbyterian divines (as Lyman Beecher, Wm. Adams, H. B. Smith, R. D. Hitchcock, G. L. Prentiss) were of New England origin.

† The Auburn Declaration was written by Dr. Baxter Dickinson (then professor in Lane Seminary, Cincinnati, afterwards in Auburn) as a protest against the sixteen articles condemned by the General Assembly of 1837. It was declared sound and orthodox by the Old School Assembly of 1869. It is printed in Schaff's *Creeds of Christendom*, vol. iii., pp. 777–780.

was completed by the General Assembly of 1338, which refused to recognize the commissioners of the four exscinded synods.

For more than thirty years the two Schools kept up their separate organizations at a respectful distance and in honorable rivalry, until in 1869 they were reunited into one Church on the basis of the Westminster Standards, without a surrender either of orthodoxy or of liberty, and pursued the common work of propagating Christianity at home and abroad with great energy and success.*

The reunion was a general and spontaneous movement, and was strongly promoted by the faculty of the Union Theological Seminary of New York, consistently with its name. This institution was founded in 1836, shortly before the separation, on liberal principles, and as a protest against extreme views on either side, and against "practical radicalism and ecclesiastical domination." It afforded ample room for different tendencies of Presbyterian theology (having among its professors Smith of the New School and Shedd of the Old School), on the basis of the fullest and freest investigation of the Scriptures and the history of the Church.†

The first exegetical professor in this seminary was EDWARD ROBINSON (1794–1863), the pioneer of Palestine exploration and of biblical philology in America.

Its first distinguished dogmatist was Dr. HENRY B. SMITH (1815–77), who passed from the historical to the dogmatic chair. He mediated between Old and New School and was the chief leader in the reunion. He was a keen metaphysician as well as a historically trained theologian, a favorite pupil of Tholuck, and in living sympathy with the best ideas of the modern evangelical theology of Germany. He marks the transition from Theocentric to Christocentric theology. His leading idea was "incarnation in order to redemption." Unfortunately, he did

* See *Presbyterian Reunion: A Memorial Volume*, 1837–1871 (New York, 1870).

† See George L. Prentiss: *The Union Theological Seminary in the City of New York* (New York, 1889, 294 pp.). An authentic history of the institution during its first fifty years, with biographical sketches of its founders and first professors. Dr. Prentiss wrote also an Appendix: *The Agreement between Union Seminary and the General Assembly* (New York, 1891). The Union Seminary was originally free from ecclesiastical control, but voluntarily sacrificed a part of its independence at the reunion in 1870 by giving the General Assembly the veto power over appointments of new professors (but not over transfers of professors from one chair to another). As this agreement led to unpleasant collisions instead of promoting peace, it was terminated on legal and constitutional grounds by the Board of Directors in 1892.

not live to elaborate his system for publication, but left behind him a strong influence over numerous pupils.*

Among these was LEWIS FRENCH STEARNS, his biographer, who was called to Smith's chair in 1890, but preferred to remain professor in the Congregational Seminary at Bangor, where he died in his forty-fifth year (1892). He carried out more consistently the Christocentric principle in his *Present Day Theology*.† This is not a complete scientific work, but a fresh popular discussion of the leading doctrines of the Christian faith by a devout and thoughtful American, who had studied with Hodge in Princeton, with Smith in New York, with Dorner in Berlin, and with Kahnis and Luthardt in Leipzig, and mediated between Presbyterian and Congregational Calvinism. He presents the most recent movements of evangelical thought on inspiration, creation, the providence of God, the Christological problem (the theories of kenosis and of progressive incarnation), election and predestination, and the future life. He reveres Augustin and Calvin as the greatest divines, "whose names should never be mentioned without reverence, and who have been most reviled by those who have known them the least" (p. 223); but he finds two defects in

* His *System of Christian Theology* was posthumously published from imperfect lectures by Karr (1884, 4th ed. 1890). Comp. the collection of his essays edited by Dr. George L. Prentiss, with an Introduction, under the title *Faith and Philosophy* (New York, 1877). The oration which he delivered on this subject before the "Porter Rhetorical Society" of the seminary at Andover in 1849, struck the keynote of his theology. Dorner called Smith "one of the first, if not the very first American divine of his time, deeply rooted in the Christian faith, large-hearted, far-sighted, of philosophical spirit, and unusually gifted for systematic theology." Godet, his friend and fellow-student under Neander, said: "*Il dominait chaque sujet, et me dominait en en parlant.*" Conversing with me once, Godet remarked: "Dr. Smith speaks from the heights." See *Henry Boynton Smith: His Life and Work,* ed. by his wife (New York, 1881), and *Henry Boynton Smith,* by Lewis F. Stearns (Boston and New York, 1892). Smith anticipated the central thought of his theology even in his twenty-first year, before he went to Germany, when he wrote to his Episcopal friend, Dr. Goodwin, from Bowdoin College at Brunswick, Me., Nov. 21, 1836: "My object is to make and harmonize a system which shall make Christ the central point of all important religious truth and doctrine. Such, I am convinced, is the biblical scheme. Such a system, too, would be a practical system; it would, at any rate, require that all preaching should be made in reference to Christ, of course in reference to redemption and sanctification, and Christ as the cause of both."

† Published by Charles Scribner's Sons (New York, 1893, pp. 508). Comp. his lectures before the Union Theological Seminary on *Evidences of Christian Experience* (New York, 1890), and his paper read before the International Congregational Council in London, July 15, 1891, which made a very marked impression.

their system—the limitation of the love of God, and the denial of freedom. Instead of vindicating Calvinism in antagonism to Arminianism, he aims at a reconciliation of the two, and subordinates both to Christology.*

The deep problem of divine sovereignty and human freedom, of particular election and the universal love of God, is still unsolved, and may never be satisfactorily solved in this world of imperfect knowledge. But far better to acknowledge the defect, than to deny the one or the other of these equally important truths. Practically, however, the problem is solved in our Christian experience. Augustinians and Calvinists preach and work as if all depended on man; Semi-Pelagians and Arminians pray and worship as if everything depended on God. Both can unite with equal fervor in Wesley's hymn, "A charge to keep I have," and in Toplady's "Rock of Ages, cleft for me." Paul himself, who first opened this controversy among Christian divines and is confidently quoted by both parties, calls upon Christians: "Work out your own salvation with fear and trembling"—that is, with the utmost diligence, as if you could not do enough; and adds, as the strongest encouragement, the Calvinistic reason: "For it is God who worketh in you both to will [by prevenient grace] and to work [by cooperative grace] for his good pleasure" [in fulfillment of his gracious purpose].

* "Calvinism," he says (p. 431), "has had one great and most praiseworthy object, to exalt God. It has aimed to bring men to the realization of their utter dependence upon God for all things here and hereafter. Believers owe their faith not to themselves or anything in them, but to God alone, working through Christ and the Holy Spirit. The practical effect of this doctrine has been to make strong Christians. The men who had come to believe that they were nothing and God everything, and yet that God was working in them and through them, could do their work in the world, since God gave it to them to do, without fear of men or the devil. The Protestants of Geneva, the Huguenots of France, the Covenanters of Scotland, the Puritans of the English Civil War, and our own Pilgrim Fathers, got the iron in their blood from their Calvinism.

"But there is another side to this doctrine. It reduces human freedom to a mere name, so far as spiritual things are concerned. Faith, instead of being the free personal surrender of man's will to God, is a divine act, wrought in the soul by overmastering power. Moreover, the doctrine throws a baleful light upon the divine righteousness. The non-elect never have the opportunity for salvation. It is to no purpose to say that they are justly condemned for their sins; for the sin is not really theirs but Adam's, and they are condemned for that which they have absolutely no power to help. If the arrangement by which Adam stood probation for the race was of God's appointment, then the sin and guilt and misery which resulted to the race were also of his appointment. Undoubtedly

The Revision Movement and the Briggs Controversy.

In 1890, the General Assembly held at Saratoga inaugurated a doctrinal revision of the Westminster Confession with a view to relieve it of its hard metaphysical and polemical features, and to adapt it to the present belief of the Presbyterian Church. The same Assembly appointed also a committee for the preparation of a brief, popular creed, which should express the consensus of the English-speaking Reformed Churches embraced in the Pan-Presbyterian Alliance.

This movement marks a new epoch of development. It reopened the old conflict between the conservative and progressive tendencies under a new form. It was followed and complicated since 1891 by the Briggs controversy about "the higher criticism," which involves the broader question of the academic liberty of teaching within the Presbyterian Church. This conflict has already led to two heresy trials in the presbyteries of New York and Cincinnati, with opposite results (1892). The Presbytery of New York (the largest in the country) acquitted Dr. Briggs on all the charges of heresy, but the General Assembly at Washington, June 1, 1893, by a large majority,

many who profess to hold the genuine Calvinistic doctrine find some way to evade its ethical difficulties at the expense of their logic. But the doctrine itself is open to insuperable objection. It stands the test neither of Scripture nor of reason.

"The most important rival theory bears the name of the Dutch theologian Arminius, but it was known long before his day, and is now held by multitudes who do not call themselves Arminians. The doctrine has been presented in two forms, which are at bottom the same. According to the first form, God's decree of predestination or election concerns the class of believers. God from eternity determined to save all who believe on the Lord Jesus Christ, and to condemn all who reject his grace. But when the Arminians are pressed to explain the relation in which individuals stand to the divine plan, they state the doctrine in a second form: God from eternity determined to save those individuals whom he foreknew would exercise faith and obedience; or the divine decree, so far as it relates to the destiny of individuals, is conditioned upon the foreknowledge.

"One cannot but feel respect for the moral earnestness of Arminianism. If human responsibility is to be maintained and the divine righteousness vindicated, the reality of human freedom must be admitted. Only upon this condition can the Gospel be offered freely to men, and the call be given to all who will to drink the water of life. Between a theory of election which shuts a large fraction of mankind helplessly and irremediably out from salvation, and the Arminianism which opens wide the gates of Christ's redemption to all who will enter, whether Christian or Jew or heathen, it seems as if there could be no question what our choice should be.

"Still, when all is said, Arminianism also has its difficulties. Its weak-

reversed the verdict and suspended him from the Presbyterian ministry. The minority entered a vigorous protest. What will be the consequences God only knows. The existence of two or more schools in one Church is a sign of strength rather than weakness: it shows vitality, encourages a noble rivalry, and insures progress. Controversy is preferable to stagnation, if it is conducted for the victory of truth.

The Revision Committee after two years of labor reported a large number of emendations, omissions and additions, but as, these proved unsatisfactory to both parties, they failed to receive the sanction of the necessary two-thirds majority of the two hundred and twenty presbyteries. This failure will stimulate the preparation of a new creed. The Westminster Assembly at first attempted only a revision of the Thirty-nine Articles of the Church of England, with a view to make them more explicitly Calvinistic, but after having revised the first fifteen Articles, it was directed by Parliament (Oct. 12, 1643) to frame a new confession of faith "for the three kingdoms according to the Solemn League and Covenant." The present condition of the Church demands a short popular creed which is less Calvinistic, but more evangelical and catholic than the Westminster Standards, and which, instead of perpetuating sectarian division, will serve as a bond of union with other branches of Christ's kingdom.

ness lies in the direction of the strength of Calvinism. It lays the emphasis too strongly upon the human factor in conversion and the Christian life. It does not bring into sufficient prominence the believer's dependence upon God. It is commonly connected with a doctrine of possible sinless perfection, which does harm by lowering the standard of the divine law to the level of human infirmity. Arminianism, likewise, fails to justify itself philosophically. To say that the divine decree of predestination is based upon the divine foreknowledge is to state the matter altogether superficially. How could God have any foreknowledge until he had formed his plan? If he foreknew that certain men would accept his grace if it was offered to them, and that certain others would reject it, and then decreed to create them and to put them in the circumstances in which he foresaw they would make these choices, then there must have been some real sense in which he foreordained these acts and their consequences. So strongly have some of the more thoughtful advocates of this theory felt the embarrassment of their position that they have withdrawn to the position that God predestinates only the class of believers, and have denied his foreknowledge with respect to the choices of individuals, thus maintaining their doctrine at the expense of the divine absoluteness.

"The question therefore arises, Is it possible to formulate a consistent doctrine of predestination, which shall combine the elements of truth to be found in both the great theories and avoid the mistakes of both—a doctrine which shall be Calvinistic in its assertion of the divine sovereignty and yet do justice to real truth to which Arminianism bears witness? I think it is possible."

CHAPTER CCXXX.

GERMAN THEOLOGY IN AMERICA.

Germans, Englishmen, Scotchmen, and Anglo-Americans are branches of the same Teutonic stock, and acted and reacted upon each other in different epochs of their history. Germany gave to England in the fifth century her Anglo-Saxon population and language, upon which was grafted in the eleventh century the Norman French. England gave to Germany the Christian religion through St. Boniface, an Anglo-Saxon, who organized the feeble churches planted by himself and by Irish missionaries, and subjected them to the jurisdiction of the bishop of Rome. Germany repaid the debt by the Reformation and consequent emancipation from the tyranny of popery. The movement of Protestant skepticism and unbelief started with English Deism and found its scientific development in German Rationalism. The Pietistic movement of Spener, and the Moravian revival of Zinzendorf had a marked effect upon the greater Anglo-American revival of the Wesleys and Whitefield, who did more for the evangelization of the masses and the promotion of practical Christianity than any evangelists since the days of the apostles.

The revival of evangelical theology in Germany, which may be dated from the third centennial of the Reformation, could not be fruitless in England and America. It is becoming more and more an important factor in American theology, but cannot replace our systems of thought. German ideas cannot take root in English, Scotch or American soil unless they are freely reproduced in the English language and adapted to the practical wants of a free Church in a free State.

The Christian religion has a stronger hold on the English-speaking race than on any nation of the continent of Europe, and as far as practical theology and practical Christianity are concerned, Germany may learn much from England and America. State churches have the tendency to make the people slavishly dependent upon the civil government for support; while free churches develop individual liberality and the capacity for self-government.

But in the development of theology as a science in all its branches, Germany unquestionably occupies the first rank in the nineteenth century. Her universities are the busy workshops of progressive exegesis, Church history, biblical and speculative theology, and will retain the leadership for some time to come. A theological education can hardly be complete without a knowledge of these achievements.

The recent developments of German theology, since the days of Schleiermacher and Neander, have been made known to us first through translations, more or less imperfect, of the most important works by Scotch, English, and American scholars. Not content with indirect acquaintance, American students, following the example of Edward Robinson, Charles Hodge, Henry B. Smith, George L. Prentiss, Edwards A. Park, and George P. Fisher, attend, in increasing numbers, German universities, to drink at the fountain new ideas and fresh inspiration for independent work. They find a hospitable reception in the lecture-rooms and homes of German professors, and learn to admire their plain living and high thinking, while they return the benefit by giving them a higher idea of American institutions and churches.*

The influence of Germany is both negative and positive; it tends to undermine old foundations, and aids in building up new constructions. It has been felt so far mainly in biblical and historical theology, but these are the foundation of systematic theology. The proper way is to proceed from the Bible to dogma, and not from dogma to the Bible.

On the other hand, English and American divines are beginning to influence German theology by their published works, which attract the favorable notice of the leading periodicals. "In reality," says Harnack, "there no longer exists any distinction between German and English theological science. The exchange is now so brisk that scientific theologians of all evangelical lands form already one concilium."

The future progress of evangelical theology is intrusted by

---

* Tholuck, Neander, Delitzsch, Dorner, Weiss, Harnack, and others will long be gratefully remembered for their kind attentions to American students. And these will appreciate the generous tribute given to them by the theological faculty of the University of Berlin: "The number of your pupils who cross the ocean to continue their studies with us is growing from year to year. We desire here to give expression to the special pleasure with which we welcome American fellow-students; for they form among our hearers a special group, which in lively interest and devoted zeal is not surpassed by any other." (From the semi-centennial *Epistola congratulatoria* to Dr. Schaff, Nov. 16, 1892.)

Providence chiefly to the combined efforts of German and Anglo-American scholars.

LITERATURE.

Clark's "Foreign Theological Library," published at Edinburgh since 1864 and republished in New York, embraces : (1) commentaries of Tholuck, Hengstenberg, Stier, Keil and Delitzsch, Olshausen, Meyer, Lange, Ebrard; Cremer's *Theological Dictionary of the Greek Testament;* Lange's *Life of Jesus;* Weiss's *Life of Christ,* his *Theology of the New Testament,* and *Introduction to the New Testament;* Godet's commentaries on John, Luke, Romans, and Corinthians, and his *Introduction to the New Testament;* Schürer's *History of the Jewish People at the Time of Christ;* (2) the Church histories of Neander, Gieseler, Kurtz, Hagenbach (in part) ; (3) Ullmann's *Reformers before the Reformation,* and his *Sinlessness of Jesus;* Dorner's *History of Christology,* his *History of German Theology,* and his *Dogmatic,* and *Ethic;* Müller's *Doctrine of Sin;* Martensen's *Dogmatic* and *Ethic;* Luthardt's, and Ebrard's *Apologetic,* etc. These translations were prepared mostly by Scotch Presbyterians, some by English Episcopalians and Independents, and belong to the evangelical school.

In 1873, a company of liberal scholars, including Principal John Tulloch, Professor Jowett, Dean Stanley, Prof. Samuel Davidson, Dr. James Martineau, John Caird, Henry Sidgwick, Prof. T. K. Cheyne, and others, formed a "Theological Translation Fund" for the publication of a theological literature of an independent character which should present the "best results of recent theological investigations . . . conducted without reference to doctrinal considerations, and with the sole purpose of arriving at truth." This company furnished and published through Williams & Norgate, London, translations of Keim's *History of Jesus of Nazara;* Baur's *Paul, the Apostle of Jesus Christ,* and his *Church History of the First Three Centuries;* Kuenen's *Religion of Israel to the Fall of the Jewish State;* Bleek's *Lectures on the Apocalypse;* Zeller's *Acts of the Apostles;* Ewald's *Prophets of the Old Testament,* and his *Psalms* and *Job;* Hausrath's *History of the New Testament Times;* Schrader's *Old Testament and the Cuneiform Inscriptions;* Pfleiderer's *Paulinism,* and his *Philosophy of Religion*; Reville's *Prolegomena of the History of Religions; A Protestant Commentary on the New Testament,* by Lipsius, Holtzmann and others.

American scholars have done their share in translations, and have added the results of original work. Prof. Edward Robinson, of the Union Theological Seminary in New York, laid the foundation for American biblical learning by his translation of Gesenius' Hebrew Lexicon (1836 ; 5th ed. 1854) and Wahl's *Clavis Philologica Novi Testamenti* (1825), which he superseded by his own superior *Greek and English Lexicon of the New Testament* (1836 ; thoroughly revised, 1850). Prof. Joseph H. Thayer, of Andover Theological Seminary (since 1884 professor in the theological department of Harvard University), followed in the same line with a translation of Winer's *Grammar of the New Testament Greek* (1869), A. Buttmann's *Grammar of the New Testament Greek* (1873), and Grimm's *Clavis Novi Testamenti* (1886, with valuable additions and references to the Anglo-American Revision). Neander was translated by an American Congregationalist

(Prof. Joseph Torrey). Gieseler was completed by an American Presbyterian (Prof. Henry B. Smith), and Hagenbach's *Dogmengeschichte* was enlarged by the same. Meyer's commentary on the New Testament, and Godet's commentaries were republished from the Edinburgh edition with considerable improvements. Mitchell translated Harnack's *Outlines of the History of Dogma* (1893). Lange s voluminous Bible-Work was (by authorization) reproduced and enlarged by forty American divines of different denominations, published in New York, and republished in Edinburgh, in 25 vols. The Schaff-Herzog "Encyclopædia" (3d revised ed. in 4 vols., 4to, 1891) is a condensed translation of the best articles of the second edition of Herzog (18 vols.), by arrangement with the German editors and publishers, with numerous bibliographical additions; while more than one-third of the work, embracing the articles on English and American and other topics, and the whole Supplement on Living Divines are original. The translated articles were submitted in proof to the German authors for revision.

In this connection we may remark that some of the best private libraries of Germany have been bought by liberal friends of American institutions. The invaluable library of Leander van Ess, which originally belonged to a Benedictine monastery in the diocese of Paderborn, and numbers 13,000 volumes, including 430 *incunabula* and the controversial literature of the Reformation period, is now in possession of the Union Theological Seminary at New York (Presbyterian). Neander's library belongs to the Theological Seminary of Rochester, N. Y. (Baptist). The library of Leopold von Ranke is the property of the University of Syracuse, N. Y. (Methodist). The Beck collection of the Luther literature, embracing over 1200 works, was bought by the Theological Seminary at Hartford (Congregationalist). The library of Paul de Lagarde, which is very rich in *Orientalia*, was recently acquired by the University of the City of New York (1893).

FOURTH SECTION: SYMBOLIC, POLEMIC AND IRENIC.

CHAPTER CCXXXI.

SYMBOLS OF FAITH, OR CREEDS AND CONFESSIONS.

Christendom is divided into a number of Churches and Confessions. All acknowledge the Holy Scriptures of the Old and New Testaments as divinely inspired and as an infallible rule of faith and practice, but they derive from them different systems of doctrine, government, and worship.

The various doctrinal systems are expressed in the symbolical books or confessions of faith. A symbol in the theological sense is a creed which holds the members of a church together and distinguishes them from other religious bodies. The earliest creeds were brief baptismal confessions. The later creeds are much fuller, and some embody a whole system of divinity (as the Lutheran Formula of Concord, and the Calvinistic Confession of Westminster). They profess to be a summary of the teaching of the Bible as understood by those who adhere to them. But they differ from the Bible in form. A string of Bible passages, systematically arranged according to topics, would have no distinctive character, and could not be called a symbolical book. A creed is the human answer to God's word, and the Church's interpretation of his revelation. The same may be said of a hymn, which is a devotional creed, as the Apostles' and the Nicene creeds are doctrinal hymns.

All creeds are more or less imperfect and fallible. The Bible alone is the rule of *faith* (*regula credendi*), the *norma normans*, and claims divine and therefore absolute authority; the creed is a rule of public *teaching* (*regula docendi*), the *norma normata*, and has only ecclesiastical and therefore relative authority, which depends on the measure of its agreement with the Bible. Confessions may be improved (as the Apostles' Creed is a gradual growth from the baptismal formula), or may be superseded by better ones with the increasing knowledge of the truth.

NOTES.

1. CONFESSIONS is the name used on the continent of Europe for the three leading Churches which differ in their creed, namely, the Roman and Greek Catholic, the Lutheran, and the Reformed. Other religious societies are usually termed *sects*, and were, until recently, excluded from civil rights. The Roman Church identifies herself with the Church Catholic, and regards all others as mere sects. In England the distinction is made between the *Church* (i.e., the Episcopal Church of England) and the *Dissenting* or *Nonconformist* bodies, and the members of the former call themselves *Churchmen*. In the United States, where all churches and sects are on a basis of equality before the law, the inoffensive term *Denomination* has come into use. There are, however, many more denominations than confessions, inasmuch as the leading Protestant denominations agree in their doctrinal standards, and differ only on minor matters of church polity and ceremonies.

2. SYMBOL, from the Greek σύμβολον (συμβάλλειν, to throw together, to compare) and the Latin *symbolum*, means a sign or emblem ; in theological language, a doctrinal sign, token, creed, confession of faith. It was first so applied in the third century to the "Apostles' Creed," which the Christians professed at baptism to distinguish them from Jews, heathen and heretics. It was also used in the sense of a watchword, military parole (*tessera militis Christiani*), with which the baptized entered upon their spiritual warfare against the flesh, the world and the devil, under the banner of Christ. The term "symbolical books" (*libri symbolici*) originated in the Lutheran Church, as also the term *theologia symbolica*. On the different meanings of *symbolum*, see Suicer, *Thesaurus*, sub σύμβολον; Bingham, *Antiq.*, bk. x., ch. 3 ; ° Schaff, *Bibl. Symbol.* vol. i., p. 3.

3. The AUTHORITY of creeds is absolute in the Roman Church, which co-ordinates the Bible and tradition, and claims infallibility. It is relative and limited in the Protestant churches, which subordinate tradition to the Bible, and deny infallibility and perfection to any particular or visible church. Symbololatry is a species of idolatry. Article 19 of the Thirty-nine Articles of the Church of England says : "As the Church of Jerusalem, Alexandria, and Antioch have erred, so also the Church of Rome hath erred, not only in their living and manner of ceremonies, but also in matters of faith." Papal infallibility was declared a dogma by the Vatican Council in 1870, contrary to the clear case of Pope Honorius I., who officially indorsed the Monothelebic heresy, and at the expense of the infallibility of the sixth and seventh œcumenical councils, and Pope Leo II., who officially condemned him as a heretic (see Schaff's *Church History*, vol. iv., pp. 500 sqq., and the literature there quoted).

CHAPTER CCXXXII.

CLASSIFICATION OF CREEDS.

The creeds may be divided into the following classes:

I. The three ŒCUMENICAL Creeds of the ancient Church, acknowledged, at least in substance, by all branches of orthodox Christendom: (1) The Apostles' Creed, so called, begun in the second century, and completed in the fifth; (2) the Nicene Creed, begun at the first œcumenical council in Nicæa, 325, completed at the second in Constantinople, 381 (or at Chalcedon, 451); (3) the Athanasian Creed, which is not from Athanasius, but of much later Gallican origin, in the sixth or seventh century. To these should be added the Chalcedonian symbol on the person of Christ, adopted by the fourth œcumenical council (451).

Strictly speaking, the Nicene Creed without the *Filioque* is the only one which is adopted by the Greek Church, and she protests against the later and unauthorized insertion of the clause *Filioque* by the Latin Church. She ignores the Apostles' and the Athanasian Creeds. The Apostles' Creed is used by Protestants and Roman Catholics more than the Nicene, and the Athanasian much less than either.

All these creeds, however, agree in the doctrine of the Trinity and Incarnation. They profess faith in one God the Father Almighty, maker of all things; and in one Lord Jesus Christ, the Son of God and Son of man in one person, who assumed human nature, suffered, died, and rose again for our salvation; and in the Holy Ghost, the regenerator and sanctifier; and in the holy Catholic Church, the forgiveness of sins, the resurrection of the body, and the life everlasting.

II. The distinctive Creeds of the ORTHODOX ORIENTAL or GREEK Church: (1) The Orthodox Confession (1643), drawn up by Peter Mogila and indorsed by the Eastern patriarchs and the Synod of Jerusalem; (2) the Decrees of the Synod of Jerusalem or the Confession Dositheus (1672); (3) the Russian Catechisms of Philaret sanctioned by the Holy Synod of Russia (1829).

III. The distinctive creeds of the ROMAN CATHOLIC Church: (1) The Canons and Decrees of the Council of Trent (1564); (2) the Confession of the Tridentine Faith, also called the Creed of Pius IV. (1564); (3) the Roman Catechism (1566); (4) the Decree of the Immaculate Conception of the Virgin Mary (1854); (5) the Decrees of the Vatican Council of 1870 (the dogma of papal absolutism and papal infallibility).

IV. The LUTHERAN Confessions: the Augsburg Confession and the Apology of the Augsburg Confession, both by Melanchthon (1530); Luther's Catechisms, the large and small (1529); the Smalcald Articles (1537); and the Formula of Concord (1577).

V. The REFORMED (mostly Calvinistic) Confessions: the Second Helvetic Confession (1566); the Heidelberg Catechism (1563); the Gallican Confession (1559); the Belgic Confession (1560); the Thirty-nine Articles of the Church of England (1562); the First and Second Scotch Confessions (1560 and 1581); the Canons of the Synod of Dort (1619); the Westminster Confession, and Larger and Shorter Catechisms (1647). The term Reformed is wider than the term Calvinistic and embraces several modifications. Calvinism is not the name of a Church, like Lutheranism, but of a theological school.

VI. Creeds of EVANGELICAL Churches organized since the Reformation, as the Arminians, Congregationalists, Quakers, Baptists, Methodists, Moravians, etc. They differ from older Protestant Confessions in some minor points of doctrine, which are embodied in separate standards, or held traditionally. The Congregationalists or Independents originally adopted the Westminster Confession and Catechisms with trifling variations (1658), but have recently prepared a briefer and more popular statement of doctrine (1883). The Arminians differ from the Calvinists in five articles, chiefly on predestination and the extent of the atonement. The Moravians accept the consensus of the Lutheran and Reformed Confessions The Twenty-five Articles of Wesley are an abridgment of the Thirty-nine Articles of the Church of England. But the Wesleyan Methodists hold in addition the five Arminian Articles. The Regular Baptists are Calvinists with the exception of the doctrine of infant baptism and immersion. The Free-Will or Arminian Baptists are a small minority. The Quakers depart farthest from the Augustinian anthropology, and from the catholic views on the ministry and the sacraments, but are otherwise evangelical.

VII. Those denominations which radically dissent from the evangelical doctrines of the Reformation as well as from Romanism, either substitute a new revelation for the old, like the Swedenborgians, or are opposed to all creeds. Their creed is no-creed or unlimited liberty of private judgment.

COLLECTIONS OF CREEDS.

PHILIP SCHAFF: *Bibliotheca Symbolica Ecclesiæ Universalis. The Creeds of Christendom with a History and Critical Notes* (New York, 1877; 4th ed. revised, 1884; 5th ed. 1890, 3 vols.). The only collection which contains all creeds and confessions. The fifth edition is enlarged in vol. ii. by Encyclical letters of Leo XIII. of 1885 and 1888 on Church and State; in vol. iii., by the Congregational Creed of 1883. The first volume contains a history of the creeds; the second, the Greek and Roman Catholic creeds in Greek, Latin and English; the third, the Protestant creeds down to 1883, in the original, with translations.

The PRIMITIVE CATHOLIC symbols by H. A. HAHN: *Bibliothek der Symbole und Glaubensregeln der apostolisch-katholischen Kirche* (Breslau, 1842; 2d ed. by G. L. Hahn, 1877).

The Confessions of the GREEK Church are collected by KIMMEL and WEISSENBORN: *Monumenta Fidei Ecclesiæ Orientalis* (Jen. 1843-50, 2 vols.).

The ROMAN CATHOLIC Confessions by DENZIGER: *Enchiridion symbolorum et definitionum*, etc. (Würzburg, 1856; 6th ed. by Ign. Stahl, 1888).

The LUTHERAN Confessions, which as a collection are called *Liber Concordiæ, Book of Concord*, have been edited in Latin by RECHBERG, HASE, *MÜLLER (Latin and German, 6th ed. 1886), and in English by HENRY E. JACOBS (Philadelphia, 1882 and 1883, 2 vols.).

The Confessions of the REFORMED Church in Latin by AUGUSTI (1828), NIEMEYER (1840), and in German by MESS (1828-46), BÖCKEL (1847), HEPPE (1860), and BODEMANN (1867).

CHAPTER CCXXXIII.

SYMBOLIC.

Symbolic, from σύμβολον (see notes in chapter ccxxxi.) is a new name for an old thing, called *Controversial* or *Polemic* Theology, but is an enlargement and improvement on it. In German it might be called *Confessionskunde*. Robertson and Shedd use for it the term *Symbolism;* but this has no analogy in theological nomenclature, and would, etymologically, designate the system of symbols rather than the science of symbols.

The number and variety of creeds and confessions necessitates a special branch of theology called Symbolic or Comparative Dogmatic. It deals with the doctrinal differences of the Christian Churches as far as they are publicly expressed and acknowledged in their doctrinal standards.

Symbolic lies on the boundary line between the History of Dogma and Dogmatic Theology. It agrees with both in the contents, but it differs from the former as the result differs from the process, and from the latter as comparative philology differs from philology. It represents the creeds not in their gradual historic growth, but as living and completed systems of faith. It covers not the whole field of Dogmatic, but only the controverted articles, and discusses them more fully.

Symbolic in its fullest extent implies a historical, polemical and irenical element. Some writers, however, exclude the second and third elements, and make it purely historical.*

CHAPTER CCXXXIV.

HISTORICAL SYMBOLIC.

Historical Symbolic is an objective exposition of the various Christian creeds, either in chronological order, or according to their importance. It may cover the whole ground of dogmatic teaching, or omit the parts in which the Churches are agreed. In either case the method may be purely historical, or comparative.†

The information must always be drawn from the symbolical books; but standard writers may be used for explanation and illustration.

CHAPTER CCXXXV.

POLEMICAL SYMBOLIC.

Theologia Polemica, from πόλεμος, war, πολεμικός, warlike. *Theologia Elenchtica*, from ἔλεγχος, proof, ἐλέγχω, to convict, to refute (Tit. 1: 9, 13; 2: 15). *Synopsis Controversiarum* (Calov). *Streittheologie* (Mosheim). *Polemik* (Schleiermacher and others).

Polemic, or controversial theology, in the wider sense, discusses the conflict of orthodoxy with the various forms of heresy as well as the differences between the orthodox creeds. In the narrower sense, it is confined to denominational controversies and is identical with Symbolic.

The polemical element consists in the argument for or against the doctrines in dispute. They must be subjected to the three-

* So Winer, Köllner, Baier, Kattenbusch.
† Winer follows the comparative method and exhibits the controverted doctrines in parallel columns representing as many churches and sects, for convenient use.

fold test of Scripture, tradition or church teaching, and reason; in other words, to an exegetical, historical, and dogmatic or philosophical examination.

The standpoint and the result vary according to the confessional conviction and aim of the writer. But justice and truth should be the supreme consideration.

CHAPTER CCXXXVI.

IRENIC.

From εἰρήνη, peace; εἰρηνικός, pacific. *Theologica irenica, pacifica,* or *henotica* (from ἕνωσις, ἑνωτικός). *Irenicon* or *Henoticon* is a formula of union, a device for securing peace. *Irenic* is the science of the harmony of confessions or the reunion of Christendom.

Controversy is or ought to be carried on for the triumph of truth. The end of war is peace. Paul, the most polemic of the apostles, always ready to fight for "sound doctrine," and "to convict the gainsayers" (Tit. 1:9), exhorts the Christians to "keep the unity of the Spirit in the bond of peace"; adding, "There is one body, and one Spirit, even as also ye were called in one hope of your calling; one Lord, one faith, one baptism, one God and Father of all, who is over all, and through all, and in all" (Eph. 4:3-6).

Symbolic fulfills its highest mission in Irenic. We can hardly call Irenic a distinct and separate discipline, but an irenic spirit should pervade and direct Symbolic and Polemic. This is the spirit of Christian liberality and comprehension, in opposition to narrowness, bigotry, and exclusiveness. The irenic temper is free from malice and full of charity even to an enemy. It does not minimize or compromise the doctrinal differences, but it never loses sight of the points of contact and the underlying unity, and endeavors to promote a better understanding and ultimate reconciliation of the doctrinal antagonisms of the Church. This irenic spirit is of comparatively recent growth, but there have always been advocates of peace, even in the most polemic ages of the Church, as Melanchthon, Baxter, Spener.

True catholicity and liberality are as far removed from indifferentism and latitudinarianism as from sectarian bigotry and exclusiveness. They are born of a larger Christian charity and a deeper insight into the vastness of the truth and the incapacity of any single mind or sect to comprehend it in all its various aspects. Those who are firmly rooted and grounded in the faith can best afford to be liberal toward those who honestly and earnestly differ. The higher the position, the broader the horizon of vision. Our theology should be as broad and comprehensive as God's truth and God's love, and as narrow and strict as God's justice. Denominational Christianity should be subservient to catholic Christianity. Loyalty toward a particular church is perfectly compatible with a catholic spirit of respect and love for all other branches of the same kingdom of our common Lord and Saviour. The one eternal truth of God reflects itself in each human mind in a peculiar form. The Holy Spirit speaks in ten thousand tongues.

Between truth and error, indeed, there can be no compromise, as little as between holiness and sin, God and Belial, Christ and Antichrist. As far as two parties teach contradictory doctrines, either one or both must be wrong; both cannot be right. But there are doctrinal differences which are simply opposite, not contradictory, and which on closer inspection appear to be only different aspects of one and the same truth. In such cases both parties may be right so far as they go in their positive statement, and wrong only so far as they exclude and deny the other side of the truth.

Of such character are the historical discrepancies among the Evangelists, and even the doctrinal differences among the apostles, *e.g.*, Paul and James in the article on justification by faith or works. There are undoubtedly various types of apostolic theology represented by James, Peter, Paul and John, and we behold in them the manifold wisdom of God, the depth and height and breadth of Christian truth, its variety, fullness, universality and adaptability to all classes of mind and spheres of labor.

So we must to a large extent admit the historical necessity and usefulness of doctrinal as well as disciplinary and ritual distinctions in Christendom. We should cheerfully recognize all that is good, beautiful and useful in them. We should bless all whom God blesses and wish them success, no matter to what branch of his kingdom they belong. Protestants should thank God for the progress of Catholicism, and Catholics for the progress of Protestantism, as a progress of Christianity. If only Christ is proclaimed and souls are converted, "I rejoice," says

Paul, "yea, and I will rejoice" (Phil. 1 : 18). Such a spirit must be educated and disciplined; for human nature is selfish and contracted, and inclined to bigotry and exclusiveness rather than to catholicity and charity.

It is the noblest mission of Symbolic to promote Christian union and harmony, not by ignoring or underrating the doctrinal differences, but by tracing them to their roots, showing their connections, pointing out the errors and defects, and opening new avenues for broader and higher conceptions. We can, of course, not attain to perfect knowledge in this world. Now we know the truth in fragments; in the other world we shall know it in its fullness and harmony.

In this way Symbolic and Polemic become Irenic. Honest and earnest controversy is the road to an honorable and lasting peace between the contending Churches of Christendom. All the discords of human creeds will be solved at last in the concord of divine truth.

NOTES.

I. The famous motto of Irenic: *"In necessariis unitas, in dubiis libertas, in omnibus caritas."* Not from St. Augustin in the fifth century, but from irenic divines of the polemic seventeenth century, Rupertus Meldenius in Germany (1627), and Richard Baxter of England (1679). For the origin and meaning of this sentence, see Schaff, *Church History*, vol. vi., pp. 650–653.

"Christianus sum: Christiani nihil a me alienum puto." A Christian application of the sentence of Terence: *"Humo sum: humani nihil a me alienum puto."* Christianity is the perfection of humanity.

II. Christian union and Christian freedom are inseparable. Compulsory union can only end in greater separation.

III. Christian union exists and has always existed as a spirit and principle, but is struggling for fuller manifestation, especially since the middle of the nineteenth century, in English-speaking Christendom, where the divisions are most numerous. Christian believers are one in Christ, and members of his mystical body. The nearer they approach to Christ in acts of worship and charity, the nearer they come to each other and forget their differences.

IV. Various kinds of union: voluntary, federal, organic.

1. Voluntary union and co-operation of individual Christians of different denominations without representative character or legislative power:

The Evangelical Alliance, a voluntary society of evangelical Christians of different denominations and countries, founded in London, 1846, for the promotion of Christian union and the defense of religious liberty. General Conferences held in London, 1851; Paris, 1855; Berlin, 1857; Geneva, 1861; Amsterdam, 1867; New York, 1873 (the largest and most successful of all); Basel, 1879; Copenhagen, 1884; Florence, 1891; Chicago, 1893.

The German Church Diet (*Kirchentag*), founded in 1848; confined to German Christians of the Lutheran, Reformed, Evangelical United, and Moravian Churches.

Bible Societies; Tract Societies; Sunday-school Unions; Young Men's Christian Associations; Christian Endeavor Societies.

2. Confederation of Churches, resembling the United States and the German Empire, but without a central government and without legislative power:

The Greek and Latin Churches before the great schism in the ninth century.

The Pan-Reformed or Pan-Presbyterian Alliance, organized in London, July, 1875, embracing most of the Reformed Churches of both hemispheres, and meeting from time to time in common council for co-operation, especially in mission fields and for the support of weak churches. The first council was held in Edinburgh, 1877; the second in Philadelphia, 1880; the third in Belfast, 1884; the fourth in London, 1888; the fifth in Toronto, Canada, 1892; the sixth will be held in Glasgow, 1896.

The Pan-Anglican Council, composed of bishops of the Protestant Episcopal Churches of Great Britain, the British colonies, and the United States, convened at Lambeth Palace, London, 1866, 1868, and 1888.

The Pan-Methodist Conference, held first in London, 1881, and the second in Washington, 1892.

The Old Catholic Union Conferences, held at Bonn, 1874 and 1875, under the lead of Dr. Döllinger, aimed at a confederation and intercommunion of the Old Catholic, the orthodox Oriental, and the Anglican Churches, on the basis of the œcumenical consensus of the ancient Græco-Latin Churches and the episcopal succession. They agreed on a consensus creed, but it has not received official recognition. (See Schaff, *Creeds*, vol. ii., pp. 545 sqq.)

3. Organic or corporate union under one government:

The Evangelical Union of the Lutheran and German Reformed Churches in Prussia and other German States, founded after the tercentennial of the German Reformation in 1817. (See NITZSCH: *Urkundenbuch der Evangelischen Union*, Bonn, 1853.)

The Reunion of the Old and New School Presbyterian Churches in the United States under one General Assembly, completed at Pittsburg, November, 1869. (See *Presbyterian Reunion*, New York, 1870.)

The Pan-Anglican Council of the Church of England (at the suggestion of the House of Bishops of the Protestant Episcopal Church of the United States, convened, at Chicago, 1886) issued from Lambeth Palace, 1888, a liberal basis for an organic union of English-speaking, evangelical Churches, consisting of four articles : the Holy Scriptures, the Apostles' Creed and the Nicene Creed, the sacraments of baptism and the Lord's Supper, and the "historic episcopate." The proposal has not as yet led to practical results. (See RANDALL T. DAVIDSON : *The Lambeth Conferences of 1867, 1878, and 1888*: London, 1889, pp. 280 sq.)

Organic union must embrace ultimately all Christendom, Greek, Roman, and Evangelical, under one head, Jesus Christ. It will not destroy, but preserve, the distinctive individualities of denominations as far as they are rooted in God's peculiar gifts, in different mental constitutions, and special missions. Unity is not uniformity, but implies the beauty of variety, like all the works of God. The labors of history cannot be in vain. The wood, hay and stubble of man's invention will be burned, but the gold, silver and costly stones will be preserved, and each builder on the foundation of Christ will receive a reward. An act of humiliation in which all Churches will confess their sins against God and against each other, and give all glory to Christ, will precede the feast of reconciliation. That union may not be realized before the glorious advent of Christ at the end of the present order of things; but it will surely come in a form much better than we can dream of; and it is the duty and privilege of all Christians to pray and labor for it.

CHAPTER CCXXXVII.

METHOD AND ARRANGEMENT.

The topical order adjusts the material of Symbolic to the dogmatic system, beginning with God and the creation and ending with the resurrection and life everlasting, and states under each topic the views of all the Churches. This is the method of Winer, who arranges the whole under twenty-one heads.

The historical order presents the doctrinal controversies as they appear in successive ages.

Both methods have their advantages. I would propose the following arrangement:

I. The Creeds of Christendom, that is, a brief account of the symbolical books or doctrinal standards of the different Churches (*Confessionskunde*).

II. The controversies between the Greek and Roman Churches. The procession of the Spirit; the supremacy of the pope.

III. Romanism and Protestantism. The rule of faith; the primitive state; the fall and its effects; justification; the Church and the sacraments; the papacy; purgatory; the worship of Mary and the saints, etc.

IV. Protestant controversies.
1. Lutheranism and Reform.
2. Calvinism and Arminianism (Methodism).
3. The Baptist controversy.
4. The Socinian and Unitarian controversy.
5. The Quakers.
6. Swedenborgianism.
7. Universalism.

CHAPTER CCXXXVIII.

HISTORY OF SYMBOLIC.

Symbolic was first created in an exclusively controversial and sectarian spirit down to the middle of the eighteenth century. Then followed a period of confessional indifferentism, which ignored or underrated doctrinal distinctions. In the nineteenth century Symbolic was revived and raised to the dignity of a theological science, partly in a purely historical interest, partly in the interest of confessionalism.

I. The oldest dogmatic works of Irenæus, Hippolytus, Tertullian, and of the Nicene and post-Nicene Fathers are directed against heresies, and are purely polemical.

Augustin (d. 430) made an approach to Symbolic in his treatise *De Fide et Symbolo* (393); but it is simply an exposition of the Catholic faith for popular instruction.

II. The antagonism of the creeds of rival Churches began in the ninth century with the Greek schism, which is not healed to this day. The two main points of difference between the Greek and Latin Churches are the eternal procession of the Holy Spirit from the Father and the Son, and the supremacy of the pope. The chief champion of the Greek dogma was Photius, patriarch of Constantinople (d. 891); his great opponent was Pope Nicholas I. (d. 867).

The controversy was carried on with great bitterness for centuries, and was occasionally interrupted by unsuccessful efforts for union.

III. The Reformation of the sixteenth century introduced the more comprehensive controversy between Romanism and Protestantism, which lasts to this day. Cardinal Robert Bellarmin (1542–1621), a Jesuit professor of controversial theology in the Collegium Romanum, was by far the most learned opponent of Protestantism. His *Disputationes de controversiis Christianæ fidei adv. hujus temporis hæreticos* (Rome, 1587–90, 3 vols., and often reprinted, *e.g.* Rome, 1832–40, 4 vols. 4to) furnished a rich arsenal for Roman Catholic polemics. Against him wrote Martin Chemnitz: *Examen Concilii Tridentini* (1565–73, 3 vols. fol., several edd.; abridged German translation by Bendixen, Leipzig, 1385).

IV. The Reformation gave rise to a number of Protestant denominations with special creeds and confessions, which largely increased the material of Symbolic. The war between these rival Churches and sects—the Lutherans and Calvinists, the Calvinists and Arminians, the Baptists and Pedobaptists, etc. —was conducted almost with the same bigotry and bitterness as that between Romanists and Protestants. The *rabies theologicorum*, from which Melanchthon prayed to be delivered, reached its height in the seventeenth century before, during, and after the Thirty Years' War. A Lutheran wrote a book to prove that "the damned Calvinistic heretics" hold six hundred and sixty-six theses (the apocalyptic number) in common with the Turks! When Calixtus of Helmstädt (1586–1656), a learned Lutheran of the Melanchthonian spirit, raised his voice in favor of moderation and peace, he was fiercely attacked from all sides as a Crypto-papist, Crypto-Calvinist, and dangerous syncretist.

The reaction of Rationalism went to the opposite extreme of disregarding all creeds.

V. The modern works on Symbolic were written by Planck, Marheineke, Winer, Neander, Köllner, Oehler, Hase, Kattenbusch and other scholars in a scientific and moderate spirit, and with better historical knowledge and appreciation of the different creeds. The Roman controversy was revived by Möhler and stimulated by the aggressive movements of ultramontanism. The antagonism between Lutheranism and Calvinism has been superseded by the tendency toward union and co-operation among evangelical Churches.

VI. In England, and especially in North America, where all denominations of Christendom meet in daily intercourse, the study of Symbolic and Irenic is more needed and more important than in any other country, and requires a considerable extension of the field and a modification of terminology. Though strangely neglected heretofore, it will no doubt be duly cultivated and incorporated in the regular course of instruction in our theological seminaries. English and American literature abounds in popular books and pamphlets on the Roman, the Arminian, the Baptist, the Unitarian, and minor doctrinal controversies, but has as yet not produced a single original scientific work on Symbolic. Two German works, by Möhler and Winer, have been translated.

CHAPTER CCXXXIX.

SYMBOLICAL LITERATURE.

PHIL. K. MARHEINEKE (1780–1846) : *Christl. Symbolik oder histor.-kritische und dogmatisch-comparative Darstellung des kathol., luther., reform. und socinianischen Lehrbegriffs* (Heidelberg, 1810–13, 3 vols.; 1st Part, *Katholicismus*).—*Institutiones symbolicæ doctrinarum Catholicorum, Protestantium, Socinianorum, ecclesiæ Græcæ minorumque societt. christ. summam et discrimina exhibentes* (Berol. 1812; 3d ed. 1830).

* G. B. WINER (Lutheran, 1789–1858): *Comparative Darstellung des Lehrbegriffs der veschied. christl. Kirchenparteien, nebst vollständ. Belegen aus den symbol. Schriften derselben* (Leipzig, 1824, 4tc; 4th ed. by P. Ewald, Leipzig, 1882; English translation by W. B. Pope: *A Comparative View of the Doctrines and Confessions of the various Communities of Christendom*, Edinb., 1873). A very useful and impartial book.

* J. A. MÖHLER (R. Cath., 1796–1838) : *Symbolik oder Darstellung der dogm. Gegensätze der Katholiken und Protestanten, nach ihren öffentl. Bekenntnissschriften* (Mainz, 1832; 10th ed. 1889, with supplements by Kihn and Raich; English translation by J. R. Robertson, under the misleading title *Symbolism*, London, 1843, 2 vols.). This masterly defense of Romanism created a great sensation in Germany, and called forth several able replies, especially from his colleague, F. C. BAUR, *Gegensatz des Protestantismus und Katholicismus* (Tübingen, 1834 ; revised and enlarged, 1836), from C. IM. NITZSCH, *Protestantische Beantwortung der Symbolik Möhler's* (Hamburg, 1835), and MARHEINEKE (Berlin, 1833). Möhler replied to Baur (1834), and Baur replied to Möhler (1834) with equal learning and ability. It was a battle of giants. Möhler was a devout and orthodox Catholic, but not an ultramontanist and infallibilist; Baur, a liberal Protestant, and founder of the Tübingen school of critics.

* ED. KÖLLNER (Lutheran): *Symbolik aller christl. Confessionen* (Hamburg, 1837–44, 2 vols.). The Roman and the Lutheran systems. Purely historical, and full of accurate information, but unfinished.

H. C. F. GUERICKE : *Allgemeine christl. Symbolik, vom luth.-kirchl. Standpunkte* (Leipzig, 1839; 3d ed. 1860 sq.). High-church Lutheran.

B. J. HILGERS (Roman Catholic): *Symbolische Theologie* (Bonn, 1841).

H. W. I. THIERSCH (Irvingite): *Vorlesungen über Katholicismus und Protestantismus* (Erlangen, 1845, 2 Parts; 2d ed. 1848). Irenical.

A. H. BAIER: *Symbolik der christl. Confessionen und Religionspartheien.* First vol., *Symbolik der röm.-kath. Kirche* (Greifswald, 1853 sq., 2 Parts).

F. R. MATTHES: *Comparative Symbolik aller christl. Confessionen vom Standpunkt der evang.-luth. Confession* (Leipzig, 1854).

RUD. HOFMANN: *Symbolik oder systemat. Darstellung des symbol. Lehrbegriffs der verschied. christl. Kirchen und namhaften Secten* (Leipzig, 1857).

* A. NEANDER: *Katholicismus und Protestantismus, herausgeg. von H. Messner* (Berlin, 1863). Posthumous.

F. W. BODEMANN : *Vergleichende Darstellung der Unterscheidungslehren der vier christl. Hauptconfessionen* (Göttingen, 1842 2d ed. 1869).

KARL GRAUL (d. 1864): *Die Unterscheidungslehren der verschiedenen christl. Bekenntnisse im Lichte des göttlichen Wortes* (Leipzig, 1845; 9th ed. by Theod. Harnack, 1872).

* G. F. OEHLER (Evang.): *Lehrbuch der Symbolik, herausg. von J. Delitzsch* (Tübingen, 1876; 2d ed. by Theod. Hermann, Stuttgart, 1891).

G. PLITT: *Grundriss der Symbolik* (Erlangen, 1875; 2d ed. by Wiegand, 1888).

K. H. Gez. VON SCHÉELE (Lutheran Bishop of Gotland): *Teologisk Symbolik* (Upsala, 1877, 2 vols.; German translation, with introduction, by O. Zöckler, Leipzig, 1881, 3 Parts). Schéele wrote also the *Symbolik* for Zöckler's *Handbuch der theol. Wissenschaften* (1883). He visited America in 1893 as delegate from Sweden to celebrate the third centenary of the Swedish Reformation in Minneapolis.

F. A. PHILIPPI (Lutheran): *Symbolik. Akad. Vorlesungen, herausg. von F. Philippi* (Gütersloh, 1883). Posthumous.

* K. HASE: *Handbuch der protestantischen Polemik gegen die römisch-katholische Kirche* (Leipzig, 1862; 5th ed. 1890).

P. TSCHACKERT: *Evang. Polemik gegen die röm. Kirche* (Gotha, 1885).

HERM. SCHMIDT: *Handbuch der Symbolik* (Berlin, 1890).

* FERD. KATTENBUSCH: *Lehrbuch der vergleichenden Confessionskunde* (Freiburg i.B., 1892 sq.; vol. i., the Greek Church; vols. ii. and iii. will be devoted to the Roman Catholic and Protestant Churches). He extends the limits of Symbolic and includes worship, discipline and statistic.

M. SCHNECKENBURGER (Professor in Bern; d. 1848): *Vergleichende Darstellung des luther. und reformirten Lehrbegriffs* (ed. by Güder, Stuttgart, 1855). This is confined to the differences between the Lutheran and Reformed Churches, but is remarkably acute and discriminating. The lectures of the same author on the doctrinal systems of the smaller Protestant Church parties, edited by Hundeshagen (Frankfurt, 1863) are less important.

I. E. Μεσολώπας: Συμβολικὴ τῆς ὀρθοδόξου ἀνατολικῆς ἐκκλησίας. Τὰ συμβολικὰ βιβλία, τόμος Α'. ('Εν 'Αθήναις, 1883, 494 pp.).

IRENICAL LITERATURE.

JUL. MÜLLER: *Die Evangelische Union; ihr Wesen und ihr göttliches Recht* (Berlin, 1854).

H. G. HASSE: *Grundlinien christl. Irenik* (Leipzig, 1882).

J. DÖLLINGER (d. 1891): *Kirche und Kirchen* (München, 1861).—*Die Wiedervereinigung der christlichen Kirchen (The Reunion of the Christian Churches)*.—Seven lectures delivered in Munich, 1872, after his excommunication from Rome, published in German, 1888, and previously translated from MS. into English by Oxenham (1872), and into French by Mrs. Loyson.

P. SCHAFF: *The Discord and Concord of Christendom*, or *Denominational Variety and Christian Unity*. An address delivered before the eighth General Conference of the Evangelical Alliance at Copenhagen, 1884, reprinted in his *Christ and Christianity*, pp. 293 sqq.—*The Reunion of Christendom*. An address prepared for the Parliament of Religions in Chicago, September, 1893.

W. R. HUNTINGTON (Episcopalian): *The Peace of the Church* (New York, 1891).

FIFTH SECTION: ETHIC AND STATISTIC.

CHAPTER CCXL.

CHRISTIAN ETHIC.

Ethic, ἠθική (sc., τέχνη, ἐπιστήμη, or φιλοσοφία), and *Ethics*, τὰ ἠθικά, are from ἔθος or ἦθος, *custom, habit, usage, disposition, character*. Aristotle, the founder of moral science (in his ἠθικὰ Νικομάχεια), gives this derivation, for the reason that virtue or moral habit is formed by repeated acts. Habit becomes a second nature. But he subordinates Ethic to Politic, and finds the realization of the moral ideal in the state.
Morals is from *mos, mores*.
Theologia Moralis.—Ethica Christiana.—Moral Theology, or *Moraltheologie* (Kihn and other Roman Catholic moralists).—*Christliche Moral* (Marheineke and Daub).—*Christliche Sittenlehre* (De Wette, Schmid, and Dorner).—*Theologische Ethik* (Rothe).—*Christliche Ethik* (Neander, Harless, and Martensen).—*Christian Ethics* (Newman Smyth).

Christian Ethic or Moral Theology is the science of Christian life. It is related to Dogmatic as works (ἔργα, ἀγάπη, *agenda*) are related to faith (πίστις, *credenda*), or as practice is to theory, or as morality is to religion.

It is usually divided into a general and a special part. The first discusses the fundamental principles on which morality rests: the moral character of God; the moral government of the world; the natural and revealed law of God; the moral constitution of man; the conscience; the freedom of the will; sin and evil; ability and inability; regeneration; and Christian life. The special part is subdivided into three sections: the doctrine of the highest good—the kingdom of God; the doctrine of duty—to God, to our neighbor, and to ourselves; the doctrine of virtue, which culminates in Christlike holiness or complete conformity to the will of God.

Several of these topics are treated also in Dogmatic, but under different aspects. Christ is viewed in Dogmatic as the God-man and Redeemer from sin; in Ethic, as model and exemplar to follow. The kingdom of God appears in the former as an established institution, in the latter as an ideal to be actualized. Sanctification is, dogmatically, the fruit of the grace of God, who "works in us both to will and to work"; ethically, it is the duty of man, who must "work out his own salvation with fear and trembling" (Phil. 2:13).

Definitions of Ethic.—Schleiermacher: The representation of the communion of the redeemed man with God through Christ, or of that mode of life which arises from the dominion of the Christian self-consciousness. Neander: Christian Ethic is the science which deduces from Christianity the laws of human action. C. F. Schmid: The part of systematic theology which has for its object the Christian life. Wuttke: The science of Christian morals. Harless: The theory of the normal Christian life. Martensen: The science of moral life determined by Christianity. Rothe: The science of the moral (*die theologische Wissenschaft von dem Moralischen*). He regards it as a branch of *speculative* theology. Kihn (R. Cath.): The scientific representation of those revealed truths which are the rules of our will and action. Sidgwick: The study of what ought to be. Martineau: The doctrine of human character. Newman Smyth: The science of living according to Christianity.

CHAPTER CCXLI.

ETHIC AND DOGMATIC.

Ethic has its roots in Dogmatic. Piety is the mother of virtue; love to God begets love to man. The first table of the Decalogue treats of duties to God; the second of duties to our neighbor; and the tenth commandment, in forbidding evil desire, points back to the secret springs of the heart, out of which are the issues of life. James says, "Faith without works is dead;" Paul says, "Works without faith are dead;" both demand a living faith in living works. "Faith working through love" (Gal. 5:6) is the irenicon between the apostle of faith and the apostle of works. In catechetical instruction, Dogmatic is usually taught on the basis of the Apostles' Creed; Ethic, on the basis of the Decalogue.

Before the seventeenth century, Ethic was treated as an integral part of Dogmatic, either under a separate section on law and an exposition of the Decalogue,* or in connection with re-

* So Thomas Aquinas and the scholastics who overrated Dogmatic and underrated Ethic. Among Protestant divines Charles Hodge (*Syst. Theol.*, vol. iii., chap. xix., pp. 259 sqq.) follows this inadequate method.

generation and the new life in Christ.* But the dignity and importance of morality require a separate treatment, which is now almost generally adopted. It was first introduced in the Reformed Church by Lambert Daneau (Danæus, 1530–95), a learned professor at Geneva and afterwards at Leyden, and a voluminous writer.† It was followed by Moses Amyraut of the school of Saumur, ‡ and, in the Lutheran Church, by G. Calixtus (1586–1656). §

CHAPTER CCXLII.

PHILOSOPHICAL AND CHRISTIAN ETHIC.

Ethic may be treated philosophically or theologically. Philosophical Ethic, or Moral Philosophy, is based upon the conscience or the inborn moral sense; Theological or Christian Ethic, upon the revealed will of God and the example of Christ. The former follows the unwritten law of nature and the light of reason; the latter, the law of Moses and the gospel of Christ. The one sees the highest good in the state, the other in the kingdom of God.

The relation of the two is the same as the general relation of philosophy and theology, reason and faith, natural virtue and supernatural grace. It is a relation of friendly independence. They often come into collision, but this is due to the imperfection of human knowledge. Each has its own mission. Starting from different premises and pursuing different methods, they yet mutually illustrate and strengthen each other, and arrive at the same end. The God of nature and of grace, of reason and of revelation, is one and the same. "The moral law within us," which filled the philosopher Kant with ever-growing reverence and awe, even more than "the starry heavens above us," points prophetically to the gospel, and finds its own subjective ideal (moral perfection, that is, conformity to the will of God) fully realized in the moral perfection of Christ. And the ideal state

---

* So Calvin, *Inst.*, bk. ii., ch. 8. (*legis moralis explicatio*); bk. iii., chs. 6–8 (*de vita hominis Christiani*, etc.).

† In his *Ethices Christianæ libri tres* (Geneva, 1577, and often). He tried to reconcile the Calvinistic doctrine of absolute predestination with severe morality. See a list of his works in *La France Protestante*, vol. v., pp. 62–91 (2d ed.).

‡ In his *Morale chrétienne*, 6 vols. (1652–60).

§ In his *Epitome Theologiæ Moralis* (Helmstädt, 1634, 1662).

of the philosopher coincides with the ideal Church of the theologian, that is, in the kingdom of God.

CHAPTER CCXLIII.

PAGAN AND CHRISTIAN MORALITY.

ED. ZELLER (Hegelian, afterwards eclectic): *Grundriss der Geschichte der griechischen Philosophie* (3d ed. 1889; trsl. by S. F. Alleyne and E. Abbot, *Outlines of Greek Phil.*, London, 1886). His larger work: *Die Philosophie der Griechen* (4th ed. 1876–88, 5 vols.).—WUTTKE: *Handbuch der christlichen Sittenlehre*, vol. i., pp. 18–94 (Leipzig, 3d ed. 1874).— THEOBALD ZIEGLER: *Die Ethik der Griechen und Römer* (Bonn, 1881).— LUTHARDT: *Die antike Ethik* (Leipzig, 1887).—HENRY SIDGWICK: *History of Ethics* (3d ed. London, 1892).—Comp. SCHAFF'S *Church History*, vol. ii., pp. 311–421 (5th ed. 1889).

Moral science, like all sciences and arts, was born in Greece, as Christianity was born in Palestine. Plato, in his *Dialogues*, represents Socrates as an ideal sage and moral hero in contrast with the sophists of his time. He almost prophesied the suffering Christ when he described the righteous man as one who without doing any injustice, yet suffers the greatest injustice, and proves his own justice by perseverance against all calumny unto death; adding that, if such a righteous man should ever appear on earth, "he would be scourged, tortured, bound, deprived of his sight, and, after having suffered all possible injury, be nailed to a post." Aristotle, who was less poetical and idealistic, but more sober and realistic, than Plato, came very near the Christian standpoint when he said: "It is the divine principle in us (τὸ ἐν ἡμῖν Θεῖον) which in some way sets everything in motion. Reason has its origin in something better than itself. What is there, then, which you may call better than rational cognition except God (Θεός)?" His definition of virtue as a happy medium between extremes or avoidance of contrasted errors,* as also his fourfold division of virtue,† have been accepted by the Fathers, but supplemented by the Christian graces of faith, hope and charity.

No wonder that the two greatest thinkers of the ancient world have exercised such a commanding influence on Christian

* Μεσότης ἡ ἀρετή, ὑπερβολὴ κακία. Μηδὲν ἄγαν. *Ne quid nimis.*
† Σοφία, ἀνδρία, σωφροσύνη, δικαιοσύνη.

theology, and were regarded as the intellectual forerunners of Christ.

Nevertheless, there is a fundamental difference between heathen and Christian Ethic. Pagan morality is based upon selfishness and pride; Christian morality, upon love and humility. Love, the gift of gifts, the fulfilling of the law, the bond of perfectness, is not one of the four cardinal virtues of Greek philosophy—wisdom, manliness (or fortitude), temperance (or self-restraint), and justice. The last comes nearest to it, as the virtue which harmonizes the other three, gives to every one his due, even to an enemy, and includes piety to the gods (ὁσιότης), gratitude to benefactors, and mercy to the helpless. But how far is this from the incomparable description of love by Paul (1 Cor. 13)! Humility, the crown of saintly character, denotes in classical Greek a servile, mean, abject spirit. Chastity, which lies at the base of personal purity and of family life, was unknown among the heathen, and the commendation of sensual love in its unnatural forms is a dark spot in Greek poetry and philosophy. Greek philosophy sees the greatest evil in guilt; Christianity, in sin. The former has no conception of sin, and therefore no conception of grace, which is the basis of higher morality.

Stoicism is the best type of Roman virtue, as Platonism is the highest form of Greek philosophy. Seneca, in his moral maxims, almost echoes Paul, though, in practice, he contradicted them, anticipating Francis Bacon, "the wisest, brightest, meanest of mankind." Epictetus, the slave, and Marcus Aurelius, the philosopher on the throne, representing the extremes of society, are the saints of classical paganism, and resemble Christian saints as the shadow resembles the substance. They shine like lone stars in the midnight darkness of prevailing corruption. We must admire their purity and superiority over the animal passions, their self-control, their disregard of pain, and their passive resignation to inevitable fate. But the stoic virtue of apathy which consigns wife and children to the grave without a tear, and hopelessly resorts to suicide when the house begins to smoke, is unnatural, and contrasts most unfavorably with the cheerful and hopeful submission of the Christian to the will of his heavenly Father, who doeth all things well. We are not to kill, but only to moderate and to purify the feelings of joy and sorrow, of pleasure and pain. We may rejoice with those who rejoice, and weep with those who weep. Our Saviour was in sympathy with all the sufferings of humanity: he shed tears of friendship at the grave of Lazarus, tears of sorrow over unbelieving Jerusalem, tears of agony in Gethsemane, and under the weight of a world of sin and guilt he cried on the cross, " My God, my God, why hast thou forsaken me ? " Yet in all this he submitted his own will to the will of his heavenly Father; and having drunk the cup of suffering to its dregs, he commended his soul to him, with the shout of triumph, " It is finished ! " He was most human, and yet most divine.

Christ presents the first and highest example of the purest teaching and the holiest life in perfect harmony. His advent was a new moral creation. The extent and depth of his influence upon all future ages is beyond calculation. " The simple record of his three short years of active life," says a liberal historian, " has done more to regenerate and soften mankind than all the disquisitions of philosophers and all the exhortations of moralists." *

From this pure fountain, the Christian Church in all its branches is continually drawing its highest inspirations and recuperative energies. By the influence of the teaching and example of the ever-present Christ we see, in unbroken succession, from age to age, sinners converted into saints, and savages into civilized beings, women emancipated from degrading slavery, and children from the tyrannical authority of parents, happy homes created, society regenerated, cruel laws and customs abolished, legislation reformed by the spirit of justice and humanity, the lower and unfortunate classes elevated, institutions of charity and philanthropy founded, missionaries going to the ends of the earth to dispel heathen darkness with the light of the gospel, and steady progress making to transform this sinful world into a kingdom of righteousness and peace.

CHAPTER CCXLIV.

ASCETIC AND EVANGELICAL MORALITY.

The difference of creeds is reflected in the sphere of Ethic. We must distinguish two main types of Christian morality: ascetic and evangelical. The former is represented by the

* Lecke, *History of European Morals*, vol. ii., p. 10.

Catholic Church, both Greek and Roman; the latter by the Protestant Churches. The one predominated in the Middle Ages, the other in modern times.

The Græco-Roman theory makes a distinction between a common morality for all, which consists in keeping the Ten Commandments, and an uncommon morality for a spiritual aristocracy or nobility of monks and priests, which in addition obeys "the evangelical counsels," so called, of voluntary poverty, voluntary celibacy, and absolute obedience. The Protestant theory enjoins the same obligations upon all, and teaches the right use of property and marriage rather than poverty and celibacy, temperance rather than abstinence. The Catholic finds the moral ideal in the ascetic and monastic life, which tends to raise exceptional saints, but to lower the morals of the people. The Protestant seeks the moral ideal in the faithful performance of the social duties in the family, the state, and the church. Flight from the world is the perfection of Catholic piety and virtue; transformation of the world which God has made is the perfection of Protestant piety and virtue.

Asceticism is found in all religions, but reached its noblest form in the Christian Church. It appeared first within the congregation; then in the isolation of hermit life; and last in the convent as a pure church of the elect, outside of the mixed Church of the world.*

Monasticism was a wholesome reaction against the corruptions of heathenism and against the worldliness which crept into the Church after Constantine. It became a powerful missionary agency in christianizing and civilizing the barbarians of Europe.

The saints of the Greek and Roman Church are monks and nuns and priests who led a life of ascetic self-denial and consecration, and performed miracles in their lives, or by the touch of their dead bones. The *Acta Sanctorum* record their extraordinary deeds. Laymen, and fathers and mothers of children, are not found in the Roman calendar.

Protestantism has few exceptional ascetic saints, but it has created the pastoral family and raised the standard of general morality for laymen as well as clergymen.

The results of the two systems are apparent when we com-

* On the development of asceticism and monasticism, see Schaff's *Church History*, vol. iii., pp. 147 sqq.

pare the intellectual and moral condition of Roman Catholic with that of Protestant countries and nations: Italy with Scandinavia, Spain with England and Scotland, Austria with Prussia, Belgium with Holland, the Roman Catholic cantons with the Protestant cantons in Switzerland, southern with northern Ireland, French Canada with English Canada, Mexico or Brazil with the United States.

This fundamental difference affects also the standard of the common morality. Romanists emphasize meritorious works and measure their value by quantity rather than by quality. Protestants lay stress on the spirit and motive of works and measure their value by quality rather than by quantity. The former, following the Epistle of James, make works as well as faith a condition of justification; the latter, with Paul, demand works as fruits of faith and evidence of justification. The Catholic is legalistic, can never do enough, and seldom attains to a serene assurance of faith and peace of conscience; the Protestant relies on the full satisfaction of Christ, disclaims any merit of his own, moves in the sphere of Christian liberty and cheerful gratitude. The one is governed by absolute obedience to the Church, and by self-imposed mortifications; the other by conformity to the law and example of Christ as an all-sufficient, living and ever-present Saviour, with whom it is the privilege of every believer to commune directly without human mediators.

CHAPTER CCXLV.

HISTORY OF CHRISTIAN ETHIC.—THE PATRISTIC PERIOD.

NEANDER: *Geschichte der christlichen Ethik* (posthumous, 1864).—WUTTKE: *Christliche Sittenlehre*, vol. i., pp. 108–242 (3d ed.).—H. J. BESTMANN: *Geschichte der christlichen Sitte* (Theil I.: *Die sittl. Stadien*, Nördl. 1880; Theil II.: *Die kathol. Sitte*; 1 Lief.: *Die judenchristl. Sitte*, 1882).—W. GASS: *Geschichte der christlichen Ethik* (Berlin, 1881-87, 2 vols.).—TH. ZIEGLER: *Geschichte der Ethik* (1881; Part II., Strasburg, 1892; also under the title, *Geschichte der christlichen Ethik*).—F. JODL: *Geschichte der Ethik in der neueren Philosophie* (Stuttgart, 1882).—CH. E. LUTHARDT: *Geschichte der christlichen Ethik* (Leipzig, vol. i., 1888, vol. ii., 1893).—W. E. H. LECKY: *History of European Morals from Augustus to Charlemagne* (London and New York, 1869, 2 vols.).—SIDGWICK: *Outlines of the History of Ethics* (London, 3d ed., 1892).

The history of Christian Ethic runs parallel with the history of Christian life, but the practice preceded the theory, and the science of moral theology followed the science of dogmatic theology.

The Ante-Nicene Period.

Ancient Christianity in the Roman Empire presents a striking contrast to the moral corruption and putrefaction of the Roman Empire. The doctrines of a common creation, common redemption and common destination of man for immortality and glory gradually wrought a peaceful moral revolution in society. Christianity recognized the divine image in every man; raised the humble and lowly; enjoined love to God and man, even an enemy, as the supreme duty; made chastity a fundamental virtue; elevated woman to dignity and equality with man; upheld the sanctity and inviolability of the marriage tie, and thus laid the foundation for a well-regulated family life and a happy home, from which the state is built up. It moderated the evils and undermined the foundations of slavery; it emancipated children from the tyrannical control of parents; denounced the exposure of children as murder; made relentless war upon the bloody games of the arena and the shocking indecencies of the theater, upon cruelty and oppression; infused into a heartless and a loveless world the spirit of love and brotherhood, and into legislation the spirit of justice and humanity, and established the first institutions of benevolence and charity, which have since been multiplied from generation to generation.

The oldest Church manual, called *The Teaching of the Twelve Apostles*, from the close of the apostolic age, begins with a Jewish-Christian catechism which is built upon the Sermon on the Mount, and presents the Christian life as the way of life, contrasted with the life of sin as the way of death. It rises far above the heathen moralists, and shows the predominant ethical character of early Christianity. It condenses man's duty into the sentence: "The Way of Life is this: first, Thou shalt love God who made thee; secondly, thy neighbor as thyself; and all things whatsoever thou wouldst not have done to thee, neither do thou to another." This is the negative form of the golden rule. The Gospels (Matt. 7:12; Luke 6:31) give the positive form, which is much stronger, since there is a great difference between doing no harm and doing good. The *Didache* directs that the Lord's Prayer be repeated thrice a day, lays much stress upon fasting, and seems to contain the germ of the ascetic doctrine of perfection or a higher morality when it says (ch. vi. 2), "If thou art able to bear the whole yoke of the Lord, thou shalt be perfect (comp. Matt. 19 : 21); but if thou art not able (comp. Matt. 19 : 11; 1 Cor. 7 : 7), do what thou canst."

The anonymous Epistle to Diognetus, the Apologies of Justin Martyr, the practical treatises of Tertullian, the Epistles of Cyprian, give us a full view of the holy lives and heroic deaths of the Christians in times of persecution, but with a decided leaning to ascetic morality, which began to be organized in the beginning of the fourth century.

The Post-Nicene Period.

With the union of church and state in the fourth century, the world, by a wholesale water-baptism, rushed into the Church and swept into it all the vices of heathen Rome. In opposition to this mixed and worldly Christianity the monastic system was developed and spread with great rapidity. It was strongly favored by all the Greek and Latin Fathers, though not without protest. The patristic and mediæval Church is ascetic in theory and so far unprotestant.

Athanasius, "the father of orthodoxy," wrote the life of St. Anthony of Egypt, "the father of monks," and made monasticism known in the West. St. Chrysostom, the greatest preacher of the Greek Church, was himself a monk, and reluctantly left the solitude of his cell for the pulpit in Antioch and Constantinople.

Ambrose of Milan (d. 397), an ethical character, and, like Cyprian, a model bishop of the old Roman type, describes the moral duties of clergymen in his work *De Officiis Ministrorum*, which is a pendant to Cicero's well-known work of the same name. He makes piety the foundation of all virtues, and lays stress on the grace of humility, which was unknown to the ancients. He places the highest aim of man's life in likeness to God. He christianizes the principal or cardinal virtues, *sapientia*—in reference to God, *justitia*—towards our fellow-men, *fortitudo*—in the trials of life, *temperantia*—towards our own person. The Christian realizes the ancient ideal of a *vir justus et sapiens.* In special tracts on virgins and widows, and in his epistles, he glorifies virginity as the perfection of Christian virtue. He praises the virgins who committed suicide to save their chastity under persecution, as holy martyrs. He makes no allowance for a second marriage of widows. He opposes resistance to violence in self-defense, and is averse to war and the death penalty. He raised a righteous protest against the first bloody execution of heretics (the Priscillianists in Spain). He commends charity and almsgiving as the chief virtues and as a second baptism, which has the power of covering a multitude of sins, not only once, but as often as these virtues are exercised.

Jerome (d. 419), the mediator between the East and the West, the translator of the Latin Bible, the Catholic ideal of a learned monk, exerted an incalculable influence upon his and future generations, inferior only to that of his younger contemporary, Augustin. He far surpassed all the Fathers as an enthusiastic and eloquent advocate of ascetic piety. He commended it in his epistles and legendary biographies of the earliest monks, and defended it against the objections of Jovinian, Helvidius, and Vigilantius. He induced the descendants of the proud patrician families of Rome to turn their sumptuous villas into monastic retreats. He himself labored hard, though not quite successfully, to gain absolute control over the animal passions, and fought many a battle with the devil in the Syrian wilderness. He praises "the desert where the flowers of Christ are blooming, the solitude where the stones of the New Jerusalem are prepared, the retreat which rejoices in the friendship of God." He exalts celibacy far above marriage, whose chief use consists in giving birth to brides of Christ.* "Since I am about," he says in his work against Helvidius, "to draw a comparison between virginity and marriage. I beseech you, my readers, not to think that I have disparaged marriage in praising virginity or made any severance between the saints of the Old and New Testaments. . . . The former were under a dispensation suited to their days, but we under another upon whom the ends of the world are come. Whilst that law remained, 'Increase and multiply and replenish the earth' (Gen. 1 : 28), and 'Cursed is the barren who does not bear children in Israel,' all married and were given in marriage, and, leaving

* "*Laudo nuptias, laudo conjugium, sed quia mihi virgines generant.*"— Ep. xxii., 20.

father and mother, became one flesh. But when that voice sounded, 'The time is short,' it goes on, 'Let them that have wives be as though they had none' (1 Cor. 7 : 29)." He then draws a vivid contrast between the distracting cares and trials of a married wife with the single devotion of a virgin to God; without considering that trials are a wholesome discipline for the development of Christian manhood and womanhood, and that celibacy also has its dangers and temptations. St. Anthony reminded the anchorites: "Woe to him that stands alone, for if he falls he has no one to raise him up." Jerome himself informs us how in the midst of his self-imposed ascetic mortifications his fancy tormented him with obscene images of Roman banquets and dances.

On the supreme duty of truthfulness he shared the loose notions inherited from the Greek sophists. He explained away the collision between Paul and Peter at Antioch (Gal. 2 : 11) as a mere stroke of pastoral policy, or an accommodation of both apostles to the weakness of the Jewish Christians, at the expense of truth—an interpretation against which Augustin rightly protested. In his controversial writings Jerome shows such vanity, intolerance and bitterness of temper that we are alternately attracted and repelled, and vacillating between admiration for his greatness and pity for his weakness.*

Augustin (d. 430) passed through the deepest experience of sin and grace, and left us in his *Confessions* an abiding monument of a holy life. He wrote valuable treatises on several moral topics, and a book, *De Moribus Ecclesiæ Catholicæ*. In these and in his life-work, *De Civitate Dei*, which was written in view of the approaching collapse of the Roman Empire, he scattered moral ideas which exerted almost as much influence as his dogmatic views. His pessimistic anthropology depreciated the value of the natural virtues, which, however praise-

---

* While Erasmus admired Jerome as "*theologorum princeps,*" Luther hated him, and called his book against Jovinian "*ein schändlich Buch*" (a shameful book). Cardinal Newman, before his transition from Anglo-Catholicism to Romanism, exhibited the conflict of sound moral feeling with Church authority in his judgment on Jerome: "I do not scruple to say, that, were he not a saint, there are things in his writings and views from which I should shrink; but as the case stands, I shrink rather from putting myself in opposition to something like a judgment of the catholic (?) world in favor of his saintly perfection." The first English translation of the principal works of Jerome has just been published by Canon Fremantle, and forms vol. vi. of Schaff and Wace's "Nicene and Post-Nicene Library," Second Series, New York and Oxford, 1893.

worthy and useful in civil life, he regards rather as vices, because they are inflated with pride.* He appeals to Rom. 14: 23: "Whatsoever is not of faith is sin;" but "faith" has in this connection a wider sense of moral conviction of duty or "the informing and confirming conscience" (as Bengel explains); moreover, the apostle speaks only of Christians, and not of the heathen, who have a guide of action in their conscience, as he asserts elsewhere (Rom. 2: 14). According to Augustin, it is the grace of God alone which creates a new spiritual and moral life in man, and this grace works irresistibly in the elect according to an eternal and unchangeable purpose. His denial of human freedom and his doctrine of absolute predestination seem to leave no room, logically, for a vindication of divine justice, and for human guilt. If man is only free to sin or if he *must* sin, how can God justly condemn him? But Augustin and Calvin escape the ethical difficulty at the expense of logic, and enjoin the strictest morality; for their sense of God's holiness is stronger than their sense of man's sinfulness, and they connect election inseparably with sanctification and perseverance to the end.

Augustin defended, in his treatises on *Marriage*, *Virginity*, and *Widowhood*, the monastic ideal, though with more moderation than Jerome. Herein he agreed with his opponent Pelagius, who advocated the freedom of choice and moral ability in the interest of monastic morality. He was influenced in his conversion by reading the life of St. Anthony, the pattern saint of the desert; he dismissed after his baptism his faithful mistress, the mother of his only son, and devoted himself to single life. He praised marriage as a sacrament, but placed virginity above it as more holy, and appealed to the example of Paul, who permits but does not recommend marriage. He finds, after all, the earthly perfection of a Christian in retreating from public life and in ascetic imitation of the example of Christ. He introduced monasticism into North Africa, but confessed that

---

* "*Vitia sunt potius quam virtutes.*"—*De Civitate Dei*, xix., 25. Another saying of Augustin (which I cannot just verify) is, "*Omnis infidelium vita peccatum est.*" The Lutheran Formula of Concord expresses nearly the same view (p. 700), and declares all good works of the natural man, "*revera coram Deo peccata, hoc est, peccatis contaminata, et a Deo pro peccatis et immunditio reputantur propter naturæ humanæ corruptionem.*" How different is Christ's merciful sentence on those who knew him not, in the parable of the judgment (of the heathen world)! (Matt. 25: 35–40.)

he had found some of the worst, as well as some of the best men and women in convents. He wrote a special work against the idleness and spiritual pride of monks.*

God is to Augustin the only true and highest good, and union with God is the end of man. Love to God is the virtue of virtues, which gives true value to all other virtues. In the present world the Christians are only pilgrims towards the heavenly home, but by hope and love they anticipate the future life of the vision of God and rise above the misery of the present existence.

CHAPTER CCXLVI.

MEDIÆVAL MORALS.

The pope and the monk ruled the Latin Church in the Middle Ages. Hierarchical domination and ascetic self-renunciation co-operated with each other for the conversion of the barbarians and the supremacy of the spiritual over the secular power. Gregory VII., the greatest of popes, was a monk bearing the triple crown; St. Bernard, the greatest of monks, was the arbiter of rival popes. The monks were the standing army of the popes in fighting against disobedient kings and emperors and in enforcing celibacy upon the clergy.

The morality of the Middle Ages presents startling contrasts of a sublime faith and degrading superstition, of angelic purity and gross sensuality, of self-denying charity to suffering Christians, and barbarous cruelty to infidels, Jews and heretics. When the crusaders, under the lead of Godfrey de Bouillon, who refused to wear a crown of gold where his Saviour had worn a crown of thorns, came in sight of Jerusalem, they fell on their knees, kissed the earth, laid aside their armor, and advanced as pilgrims with prayers and penitential hymns; but after the capture of the holy city they massacred the Mohammedan population to the extent of more than 70,000, burned the Jews in their synagogues, and waded in blood to the Holy Sepulchre to offer up their prayers and thanks. The Acts of Councils and the Penitential Books reveal a low state of morals, even among the clergy, who were charged with vulgar vices, and were tempted by celibacy to unnat-

* *De Opere Monachorum,* written after 401.

ural sins. The discipline of the Church was often perverted for the extortion of money, and the Roman curia, with its insatiable greed of gold, reaped the chief benefit, but finally also met the punishment of the Reformation.

Pope Gregory the Great (d. 604), a moderate Augustinian in theology, and a Benedictine, united the monastic ideal with the hierarchical interest, and thus fairly introduced the spirit of mediæval morality. He wrote *Magna Moralia*, a sort of compend of Christian Ethic, in the form of a threefold exposition of the Book of Job, whom he represents as the type of Christ. His *Regula Pastoralis* was the favorite text-book for pastors during the Middle Ages.

Thomas Aquinas (d. 1274) represents the height of the mediæval Ethic as well as Dogmatic. He treats the ethical material in the second part of his *Summa Theologiæ*.* He combined the views of Augustin and Aristotle and worked them up into a system. He makes, with Aristotle, happiness the end of human life, but finds happiness, with Augustin, in the vision of God and assimilation to God, who is the source and goal of all existence, and the supreme good. He divides the virtues into three classes, moral, intellectual and theological. The first two were known to Aristotle. The moral virtues are the four cardinal virtues. The three theological and highest virtues are faith, hope and charity; they are infused by divine grace and have a supernatural aim. Charity is the crown of all. Sins are divided into carnal and spiritual, and into venial (pardonable) and mortal. The three monastic vows of voluntary poverty (Matt. 19 : 21), celibacy (Luke 14 : 26 ; 1 Cor. 7 : 32), and obedience are the way to perfection (Matt. 6 : 44).

St. Thomas defends the papal power over the state to the extent of deposing princes and absolving subjects from the oath of allegiance. He gives to the people the right to depose a tyrannical ruler. He justifies the punishment of heretics by death, because murderers of the immortal soul are more dangerous and guilty than murderers of the mortal body. He teaches the doctrine of a treasury of hyper-meritorious works from which the pope can dispense indulgences for the release from the temporal punishments of sin. The abuse of in-

---

* In the *Prima Secundæ*, and *Secunda Secundæ*. They occupy about one half of the *Summa*, which is divided into three parts.

dulgences occasioned the reformation of Luther, who hated Thomas Aquinas as the abettor of all the heresies of popery.

The teaching of the "angelic doctor," as Thomas is called, rules the Roman Church to this day.

The discipline of the Church and auricular confession produced a number of penitential books which regulate the order of penitence and prescribe specific punishments for certain sins, as drunkenness, fornication, avarice, perjury, homicide, heresy, adultery. They were the first books of casuistry (see below, ch. ccxlix.).*

The Mystics advocated a more inward and spiritual piety in connection with ascetic practices. Some lost themselves in the maze of pantheism; others, like Tauler, Thomas à Kempis and Staupitz, preached and practiced a simple, fervent and practical piety in imitation of the humble life of Christ. The ripest fruit of this devotional mysticism is the well-known work of Thomas à Kempis (d. 1471), which has been published in all European languages and is to this day the most popular book of devotion for Catholics and Protestants. But the moral ideal even of this book is monastic. Staupitz, the fatherly friend of Luther, connects the mediæval piety with the Reformation, but he could not accept Luther's doctrine of justification by faith alone, nor the separation from the Catholic Church.

The imitation of Christ is the moral ideal of the best writers in the Greek, Latin and Evangelical Churches and forms a connecting link between them; but it is differently understood and carried out, by the Catholics in a literal and external sense, by the Protestants in a spiritual and internal sense.

CHAPTER CCXLVII.

HISTORY OF PROTESTANT ETHIC.

The Reformation introduced the evangelical and social, as distinct from the ascetic and monastic, ideal of morality (see ch. ccxliv.). Luther renewed the battle of Paul for Christian liberty against Jewish legalism and self-righteousness. His strongest weapon was the Epistle to the Galatians, which he

---

* The penitential literature has recently been enriched by an American historian, Henry Charles Lea: *A Formulary of the Papal Penitentiary in the Thirteenth Century* (Philadelphia, 1892).

called "my wife." He broke the bondage of papal tyranny and achieved at Worms the first decisive victory for liberty of conscience. He magnified the importance of personal responsibility over passive obedience to absolute authority. He found in the doctrine of justification by faith peace of conscience, which he had failed to obtain by the self-imposed mortifications of the cloister. He emphasized solifidian justification at the expense of progressive sanctification, and faith at the expense of good works. But he meant by faith a living power which, far from being idle, must do and always will do good works, as a good tree will produce good fruit. He rejected the antinomianism of Agricola, and deplored with Melanchthon the abuse of evangelical liberty which was the temporary consequence of the overthrow of Catholic discipline. In political life the Lutheran Church has always been an obedient handmaid of the State.

Melanchthon, the humanist among the Reformers, began the science of Protestant Ethic in his *Epitome of Moral Philosophy* (1538; thoroughly revised, 1550) on the basis of Aristotle, whom Luther hated; but he distinguished sharply between natural morality and Christian morality.*

The Lutheran Church, after the conflict with popery, was involved in internal dogmatic feuds, which were unfavorable to the cultivation of the theory and practice of Christian Ethic, and excited the worst passions. Melanchthon prayed to be delivered from "the fury of theologians." The champions of an intolerant orthodoxy forgot that charity is the chief of virtues, and uncharitableness the worst of heresies.

In opposition to dead orthodoxy, John Arndt (d. 1621) defended the claims of practical piety in his *True Christianity*, one of the most popular books of devotion. Spener (d. 1705), the founder of Pietism, labored in the same spirit and introduced wholesome reforms. Pietism produced many benevolent institutions and societies; it was the salt in the Lutheran state-churches during the rationalistic period, and is so largely even to this day, especially in Würtemberg. It bears some resemblance to asceticism in the Roman Church, and still more to Methodism.

The ethical factor was much stronger in the Swiss than in the

* On his merits as a moral teacher, see Gass, *Geschichte der christlichen Ethik*, vol. ii., pp. 92–105; and Ziegler, vol. ii., pp. 454 sqq.

German Reformers. Zwingli and Calvin opposed the paganism of papal Rome, and aimed at a complete moral renovation of Church and State. Calvin was a legislator and disciplinarian as well as a theologian. Himself a Christian stoic, fearing God, but fearless of men, he succeeded, after a long conflict with pseudo-Protestant libertinism, in establishing a model church in Geneva, which John Knox, the Scotch reformer, from personal observation declared to be "the most perfect school of Christ that ever was in the earth since the days of the Apostles," and which Dr. Valentin Andreæ, a bright and shining light of the Lutheran Church of Germany, fifty years after Calvin's death, characterized as "the perfect institute of a perfect republic and moral discipline"; adding, "What a glorious ornament of the Christian religion is such a purity of morals! We must lament with tears that it is wanting with us, and almost totally neglected. If it were not for the difference of religion, I would forever have been chained to that place [Geneva] by the agreement in morals, and I have ever since tried to introduce something like it into our churches. No less distinguished than the public discipline was the domestic discipline of my landlord, Scarron, with its daily devotions, reading of the Scriptures, the fear of God in word and in deed, temperance in meat and drink and dress. I have not found greater purity of morals even in my father's home." His father was the chief author of the Formula of Concord, the last of the symbolical books of the Lutheran Church.

Calvinism produced the severest, the most energetic and most aggressive morality of Protestantism. It is muscular Christianity, which bows before no earthly despot. It educated God-fearing, manly, independent characters, like the Huguenots of France, the defenders of liberty and independence in Holland, the Puritans of England, the Covenanters of Scotland, and the Fathers of New England, who were willing to sacrifice life for their conscientious convictions. It fortified statesmen and soldiers, like Coligny, Knox, William of Orange, and Oliver Cromwell, in their struggle with despotic power. The Reformed Churches, including the Waldenses, have suffered more persecutions from the Roman Church, and produced more martyrs during the single reigns of Mary Tudor of England, Philip II. of Spain, and Louis XIV. of France, than the whole Christian Church during the first three centuries under heathen emperors. The blood of these martyrs was the seed of political and religious liberty in modern Europe.

The separation of Ethic from Dogmatic, which was first made in the Reformed Church, promoted its scientific treatment.

Independent of the Church, the science of philosophical Ethic was cultivated by Spinoza (*Ethica,* 1677), Leibnitz (*Theodicy,* 1710), Wolff (*Philosophia Moralis,* 1750), and Kant (*Metaphysik der Sitten,* 1785, and *Kritik der Praktischen Vernunft,* 1788). Kant was a rationalist, but by his doctrine of the "categorical imperative" of practical reason, and of the "radical evil," made a near approach to Christian Ethic. Fries influenced De Wette.

Socinianism of the sixteenth and Rationalism of the eighteenth century departed from the Augustinian basis of the Reformation and developed a Pelagian morality, but without its ascetic and monastic features. The Unitarianism of England and America follows in the same line, and exalts the ethical above the dogmatic features of Christianity.

The revival of evangelical theology in the nineteenth century had a wholesome effect upon Christian life. Schleiermacher (d. 1834) marks an epoch in ethical as well as dogmatic theology. He broke the power of Rationalism. He was a master both of philosophical and theological Ethic, and derived the latter, like Dogmatic, from the Christian consciousness or experience, which comes down in an unbroken stream from the person and work of the Redeemer.

Since Schleiermacher the science of Christian Ethic has been greatly advanced by Rothe, Schmid, Martensen, Dorner, Gass, Harless, Wuttke, Luthardt, Frank, and Hermann Weiss.

English and American literature is very rich in works on Moral Philosophy, but very poor in works on Christian Ethic. This is surprising, if we consider that the Anglo-Saxon race has produced the finest type of Christian civilization and Christian character, and develops the greatest activity for the improvement of society and the spread of Christianity at home and abroad.

440 THEOLOGICAL PROPÆDEUTIC.

CHAPTER CCXLVIII.

LITERATURE ON ETHIC.

I. Roman Catholic writers. See a large list in KIHN, *Encyklop. und Method.*, pp. 444–447.

ALFONSO MARIA DA LIGUORI (1696–1787 ; founder of the order of Liguorians, a canonized saint, and created a doctor of the Church by Pius IX., 1871) : *Theologia Moralis*, based upon Busenbaum's *Medulla;* first published at Naples, 1748, and since in a great many editions ; also, in his *Works*, ed. by Hugues, Regensb. 1842–47, 38 vols.

P. JOH. PETRUS GURY (S.J., 1821–66) : *Compendium Theologiæ Moralis;* first published 1850, and very often since ; for the use of priests at the confessional, highly commended by Roman authorities for brevity and precision, but condemned by Protestants and moderate Catholics as jesuitical and dangerously minute in the description of the mysteries of married life.

German Catholic works on Ethic (*Sittenlehre*) by SAILER (1818), HIRSCHER (5th ed. 1851), PROBST (1877), WERNER (1888).

DÖLLINGER and REUSCH (Old Catholics) : *Geschichte der Moralstreitigkeiten in der röm. katholischen Kirche seit dem 16ten Jahrhundert* (Nördlingen, 1889, 2 vols.).

II. Protestant works. English :

W. WHEWELL (1794–1866, Cambridge) : *Elements of Morality, including Polity* (London and New York, 1845), and *Lectures on Systematic Morality* (1846).

ALEXANDER BAIN (Aberdeen) : *Mental and Moral Science: A Compendium of Psychology and Ethics* (London, 1868 ; new ed. 1872). The second Part (pp. 460–751) treats of the Ethical Systems from Socrates to Cousin and Jouffrey.

PAUL JANET : *Elements of Morals* (*Eléments de Morale*, Paris, 1869 ; transl. by Mrs. Corson, New York, 1884) ; and his *Theory of Morals* (*La Morale*, Paris, 1874 ; transl. by Mary Chapman, Edinburgh and New York, 1884).

L. P. HICKOK : *A System of Moral Science* (Boston, 1880).

NOAH PORTER : *Elements of Moral Science* (New York, 1885).

* JAMES MARTINEAU : *Types of Ethical Theory* (Oxford, 1885 ; 3d ed. rev., 1889, 2 vols.).

HENRY SIDGWICK (Professor of Moral Philosophy, Cambridge) : *The Methods of Ethics* (London, 4th ed. rev., 1890).

H. HUGHES : *Principles of Natural and Supernatural Morals* (London, 1890–91, 2 vols.). On the empirical basis.

BORDEN P. BOWNE (Boston) : *The Principles of Ethics* (New York, 1892).

* NEWMAN SMYTH (New Haven) : *Christian Ethics* (New York, 1892).

Popular Manuals on Moral Science by A. ALEXANDER (New York, 1852), F. WAYLAND (77th ed., Boston, 1865), M. HOPKINS (*The Law of Love and*

Love as Law, 1869), A. P. PEABODY (New York, 1873), H. CALDERWOOD (London, 7th ed. 1881), J. BASCOM (New York, 1879).

III. German works by SCHLEIERMACHER (*Die Christliche Sitte*, ed. by Jonas, Berlin, 1843), * RICHARD ROTHE (*Theologische Ethik*, Wittenberg, 1845–48, 3 vols.; 2d ed. 1867–71, 5 vols.), HARLESS (Stuttgart, 1872; 7th ed. 1875; translated by Morrison and Findlay, Edinb. 1868), * CHR. FR. SCHMID (Stuttgart, 1861; Engl. trsl. of the first Part by W. J. Mann, Philadelphia, 1872), * WUTTKE (Berlin, 1861; 3d ed. Leipzig, 1874–75, 2 vols.; abridged trsl. by J. P. Lacroix, Edinburgh, 1873, 2 vols.), * MARTENSEN (first in Danish, then in German, 1871; 6th ed. Berlin 1893; Engl. transl. of vol. i. from the Danish by C. Spence, vol. ii. from the German by Sophia Taylor, 1873–82), LANGE (Heidelberg, 1878), * LUTHARDT (*The Moral Truths of Christianity*, Leipzig, 1872; 4th ed. 1389; transl. by Sophia Taylor, Edinb., 1873), BECK (1882, 3 vols.), FRANK (Erlangen, 1883 and 1887), * DORNER (Berlin, 1885; trsl. by Mead and Cunningham, New York, 1887), GASS (Berlin, 1881–87, historical), HERMANN WEISS (Freiburg i.B., 1889; so far only the general introduction, to be followed by a systematic treatise).

CHAPTER CCXLIX.

CASUISTRY (CASUISTIK).

Casuistry is a branch of moral theology, and is also closely connected with pastoral theology (*cura animarum*). It deals with the cases of conscience (*casus conscientiæ*) which arise from the conflict of duties. It is a directory and method rather than a science. Kant calls it "the dialectic of conscience."

Casuistry has been cultivated as a separate science with great fullness by Roman Catholic moralists, especially by Jesuits, for the use of priests at the confessional. It discusses the permissibility of acts which are sinful in themselves, but may be justified, or at least pardoned, under extenuating circumstances, such as suicide to escape disgrace, tyrannicide to free the people from oppression, dueling (which is forbidden by civil law, but upheld by the military code of honor) homicide in self-defense, pious fraud or lying for a good purpose, sacrifice of chastity as an alternative for denial of faith. Casuists give general rules of conduct in such doubtful and embarrassing cases, which must ultimately be decided by the individual conscience.

Casuistry grew up during the Middle Ages in connection with the doctrine of penance and absolution, and for the use of confessors, who must know the degrees of guilt. The numerous *Libri Pœnitentiales* determine the ecclesiastical punishments for the different sins and offenses. A summary of penitential regulations passed into the canon law.

The first systematic work of the kind was prepared by the Dominican Raymond of Pennaforte (d. 1275) under the title, *Summa de Casibus Pœnitentialibus*, which came into general use in the thirteenth century. After the Reformation, the Jesuits cultivated casuistry in opposition to the rigor of the Jansenists, and brought it into disrepute by the minute anatomy of vices and indelicate discussion of immodest topics, on the plea of the requirements of the confessional, and by their lax theory of "Probabilism."* Pascal, in his *Provincial Letters* (1656), has severely chastised this jesuitical casuistry, which was corrupting in its effect, though not in design. The Popes Alexander VII. and Innocent XI. condemned several propositions of the Probabilists.

The Reformation was unfavorable to casuistry and the whole penitential system. Protestantism leaves the regulation of each man's conduct to his own conscience, as enlightened and strengthened by a study of the law of God. But most persons require some guidance in doubtful cases; hence in the seventeenth century casuistry was cultivated also by Protestant divines. In the University of Cambridge, England, there is a special professorship of *Moral Theology* or *Casuistical Divinity*.

LITERATURE.

The chief Roman Catholic Works on Casuistry are by PUSENBAUM (S.J., d. 1668), *Medulla Theologiæ Moralis;* ALFONSO MARIA DA LIGUORI (d. 1787): *Praxis Confessarii;* and GURY (S.J., d. 1866): *Casus Conscientiæ in Præcipuas Questiones Theologiæ Moralis*. See chapter ccxlviii. and a list in Kihn's *Encyklop.*, pp. 453 sq.

The chief Protestant casuists are PERKINS (1602), BISHOP HALL (1649), BISHOP SANDERSON (1678), JEREMY TAYLOR (*Ductor Dubitantium*, 1660), RICHARD BAXTER (*Christian Directory*, 1673), and SPENER (*Consilia et Judicia Theologica*, 1709).

CHAPTER CCL.

SOCIOLOGY.

Sociology, or the science of human society, its constitution, phenomena and development, is closely related to Ethic and

---

* The principle of Probabilism is: "*Si est opinio probabilis, licitum est eam sequi, licet opposita sit probabilior.*"

Political Economy, but it is narrower in one respect and wider in another. It falls within the line of duties to our neighbor, and embraces the question of the highest good (which is the kingdom of God). It may be treated philoscphically and theologically. Sociology is the theory of society; socialism is a practical movement which aims at the reconstruction of society and an improvement of the condition of the laboring classes. There are different kinds of socialism, peaceful and anarchistic, Christian and atheistic, with modifications between the extremes.

Socialism is a symptom of the present age in Europe and America. The burning questions of the relations between the rich and the poor, the employer and the laborer, the master and the servant, the right use and distribution of wealth, and the best methods of elevating the lower classes are of such practical importance as to demand a Christian Sociology which should treat these questions from the standpoint of the gospel. The best and only effective remedy of the social evils so much complained of is the consistent application of the Christian spirit of justice and charity to legislation and to individual and social life.

SOCIOLOGICAL LITERATURE.

ALEX. VON OETTINGEN: *Die Moralstatistik und die christliche Sittenlehre. Versuch einer Socialethik auf empirischer Grundlage* (Erlangen, 1868–74, 2 Parts; Theil I. in 2d ed. 1874). By the same: *Die Moralstatistik in ihrer Bedeutung für eine Socialethik* (3d. ed. Erlangen, 1882).

HERBERT SPENCER: *The Study of Sociology* (London and New York, 1873; 11th ed. 1885); *Principles of Sociology* (London, 1876; 3d. ed. 1885); *The Data of Ethics* (1879, 5th ed. 1888); *Descriptive Sociology* (1872–81, in 8 Parts). The last is a compilation by different writers, in which facts illustrating Spencer's doctrines are culled from the works of travelers and ethnologists.

ELISHA MULFORD (1833–85): *The Nation: The Foundation of Civil Order and Political Life in the United States* (New York, 1870; 9th ed. 1884).

R. D. HITCHCOCK (d. 1887): *Socialism* (New York, 1879).

J. H. W. STUCKENBERG (Berlin): *Christian Sociology* (New York, 1880). Compare the chapter on "Church and Socialism" in his *The Age and the Church* (Hartford, Conn., 1893, pp. 273 sqq.).

ROBERT ELLIS THOMPSON (Philadelphia): *De Civitate Dei. The Divine Order of Human Society* (Philadelphia, 1891).

CHAPTER CCLI.

ECCLESIASTICAL GEOGRAPHY AND STATISTIC.

Ecclesiastical Geography and Statistic is a systematic view of the present condition of Christendom. It exhibits history at rest.* But the Statistic of to-day becomes history to-morrow. This is true especially of numerical Statistic in a new and rapidly growing country like the United States, while in the Orient things are more stationary.

This branch of theological science includes the following divisions:

I. GEOGRAPHICAL STATISTIC. A description of the territorial extent of Christendom and the boundary lines of the different Churches. The Greek or Oriental Church has its home in the Turkish Empire, Russia and Greece; the Latin Church, in southern Europe, and Central and South America, with a very large representation in nearly all Protestant countries; the Protestant Churches, in western and northern Europe, and in North America, with mission fields in all heathen lands. The Greek Church is the Christianity of the East, the Latin is the Christianity of the South, the Protestant is the Christianity of the North and West. The first embraces the Greek and Slavonic, the second chiefly the Latin, the third the Teutonic races. The missionary geography extends to all heathen countries.

II. NUMERICAL STATISTIC. An account of the numerical strength of Christendom as a unit *versus* heathenism, Mohammedanism and Judaism, and of the various churches and denominations. This is Statistic in the narrow sense of the term. Figures are facts, but they often deceive. Numerical strength is no index of moral strength and influence. The handful of apostles and primitive disciples was a match for the whole Roman Empire. The same applies to countries: little Palestine did more for religion and morals, and little Greece more for philosophy and art, than the huge Assyrian, Babylonian, Medo-Persian, Roman and Russian empires. In modern times, Switzerland, Holland, England and Scotland have a historical importance far beyond their size as compared with much larger countries.

* Schlözer, "*Eine stillstehende Geschichte.*"

III. SOCIAL STATISTIC. A description of the moral status of Christendom and its branches and ramifications, as the result of its past history and the basis of its future development. It includes the creed, polity, administration, cultus, rites and ceremonies of the different churches, their relation to the civil power, their institutions, and organized activities and charities.

CHAPTER CCLII.

MATERIAL FOR STATISTIC.

The material for this science is found in the official census reports of governments and churches, in ecclesiastical almanacs or year-books, in reports of travelers, and in religious periodicals. Travel in different countries and personal intercourse with representative men are necessary for lively and accurate accounts. The adage of Goethe applies here:

" *Wer den Dichter will verstehn,*
Muss in Dichter's Lande gehn "

In old countries and churches, little reliable information on numerical Statistic can be obtained, least of all in the Greek Church and the Oriental sects, more in the Roman Church, most in the Protestant Churches. In Great Britain and the United States almost every denomination publishes the proceedings of its synods or conferences or conventions, and year-books with lists more or less complete of its ministers, churches, membership, sabbath-schools, contributions, etc. Much information can be gathered from the proceedings of the General Conferences of the Evangelical Alliance (nine were held between 1851 and 1891), the Pan-Presbyterian, the Pan-Anglican Councils, the Pan-Methodist Conferences, the Catholic and Protestant Church Congresses, and similar collective assemblies which convene regularly or occasionally in the large capitals from all parts of the world.

CHAPTER CCLIII.

COMPARATIVE STATISTIC.—LESSONS OF STATISTIC.

This statistical material should be so worked up as to show the comparative strength of the various sections of Christendom, and its progress over false religions.

The results are upon the whole encouraging. What Christianity may lose in one direction is more than made up in another. It moves with steady march with the sun from East to West, from Asia to Europe, from Europe to America and Australia, and acts back again from West to East. It gradually conquered the paganism in the old Roman Empire; it converted and civilized the barbarian races of the Middle Ages; it colonized America and Australia, and spreads the nets of missions over all the countries of the globe. It increases more rapidly than the population of the world, while nearly all other religions are declining. Protestantism is gaining over Romanism; evangelical religion is gaining over infidelity; the moral and spiritual condition of Christianity is upon the whole in advance of former ages, though it may be behind in some specific virtues; the final triumph of Christianity is secured by its past history. No other religion is possible for the civilized world. The only alternative is between the Christianity of Christ as exhibited in the New Testament, and agnosticism and unbelief which can never satisfy the human heart.

Nevertheless the parables and eschatological discourses of Christ do not warrant the hope of a universal conversion in the present dispensation; on the contrary, they predict a great apostasy and terrible conflict before the second Advent and the final consummation when "the kingdom of the world shall become the kingdom of our Lord and of his Christ, and he shall reign forever and ever" (Rev. 11 : 15).

LITERATURE.

Statistic is as yet in its rudiments, and a comprehensive scientific work is a desideratum.

WILTSCH: *Handbuch der kirchlichen Geographie und Statistik* (Berlin, 1846, 2 vols.; with an Atlas; English trsl. by John Leitsch, London, 1859, 2 vols.).

JULIUS WIGGERS: *Kirchliche Statistik* (Hamburg and Gotha, 1842-43, 2 vols.).

EDWARD A. FREEMAN: *The Historical Geography of Europe* (London, 1881, 2 vols.).

A large number of periodicals and special works on different countries. See a list in Hagenbach (12th ed.), pp. 386-390, but it needs to be supplemented by American periodicals, whose number is legion.

For American Statistic:

DANIEL DORCHESTER: *The Problem of Religious Progress* (New York, 1881, 603 pp.); *Christianity in the United States* (New York, 1888; chapters vii. and viii., pp. 750 sqq.). The author tries to show that during the nineteenth century evangelical Protestantism in the United States has steadily progressed in a greater ratio than the population.

The Census Bulletin, giving the results of the census of 1890, published in numbers, under the direction of Dr. Carroll, 1893. The fullest statistical information of any country, preceded by brief sketches of the different denominations and sects into which American Christianity is divided.

BOOK V.

PRACTICAL THEOLOGY.

CHAPTER CCLIV.

GENERAL CONCEPTION OF PRACTICAL THEOLOGY.

The term *Theologia Practica* for a special department of theological study was first introduced by Gisbert Voëtius (1588–1676; Professor of Theology at Utrecht), in his *Selectæ Disputationes* (1667), and adopted by Witsius, Vitringa, and other Dutch divines. (See Achelis, *Praktische Theologie*, 1890, vol. i., p. 2.) Kihn and other Roman Catholic and some English scholars (*e.g.*, A. Cave) prefer the title *Pastoral Theology;* but this is only a branch (*Poimenic*). Räbiger calls it *Ecclesiastic*, but this also is only a branch (the theory of the Church).

Practical Theology is the science and art of the various functions of the Christian ministry for the preservation and propagation of the Christian religion at home and abroad. It is the crowning consummation of sacred learning to which all other departments look, and by which they become useful for the upbuilding of the kingdom of God in the world. It forms the connecting link between the theological seminary or university and the Church, between the professor's chair and the pastor's pulpit. It shows how to utilize and popularize the results of biblical, historical and systematic theology for the general benefit of the Christian community. It makes the experience and wisdom of the past available for the present and the future.

Theology in all its branches is not a barren study for the satisfaction of intellectual curiosity; it is eminently practical and fruitful in its spirit and aim. But some parts of it are more directly practical than others, and constitute what is technically called Practical Theology.

Heretofore this department has been exclusively confined to

clerical duties and functions. But the recent development of the lay energies in Protestant Churches, especially in England and America, requires an additional branch, or a corresponding enlargement of the other branches. The Protestant doctrine of the general priesthood of believers implies the co-operation of the members of the congregation with the pastor in all departments of Christian activity, especially in church government, in the Sunday-school, and in mission work.

NOTES.

I. Practical Theology is itself a theory (Homiletic=theory of preaching; Catechetic=theory of teaching); and on the other hand all other branches of theology are practical in their bearing. Practical theology is an art (τέχνη) as well as a science (ἐπιστήμη). Preaching especially is the art of eloquence applied to the pulpit.

II. Definition: Vinet (*Théol. past.*, p. 1) defines Practical Theology: "*C'est l'art après la science, ou la science se résolvant en art. C'est l'art d'appliquer utilement dans le ministère les connaissances acquises dans les trois autres domaines, purement scientifiques, de la théologie.*" Ebrard: "Practical Theology is not a science [?], but an art by which the acquired knowledge becomes practical." Schleiermacher calls it "the crown of the theological study." Hagenbach: "Practical Theology embraces the theory of the ecclesiastical activities and functions as they proceed either from the Church as a whole, or from its individual members and representatives in the name of the Church." Similarly Nitzsch, Schweizer, Gaupp. Nitzsch: "*Die Theorie der kirchlichen Ausübung des Christenthums.*" M'Clintock: "It is an art and science. As an art, it seeks to employ usefully in the Church the scientific knowledge acquired in the three other departments of Theology which naturally precede it." Van Oosterzee: "The science of labor for the kingdom of God as called into exercise by the pastor and teacher of the Christian Church." Achelis: "The doctrine of the self-actualization (*Selbstbethätigung*) of the Church for its edification." Zezschwitz: "The theory of the continuous self-realization (*Selbstverwicklichung*) of the Church in the world." Cave: "Pastoral Theology is the science of the functions of the Christian Church." HEINRICI: "*Theorie des kirchlichen Handelns.*"

CHAPTER CCLV.

BRANCHES OF PRACTICAL THEOLOGY.

We divide Practical Theology into the following branches:
1. Theory of the Christian Ministry: The Minister an Ambassador of Christ (prophet, priest, and king).
2. Ecclesiology or Ecclesiastic (Church Law and Church Polity): The Minister as Ruler.
3. Liturgic: The Minister in Worship (as priest).

4. Homiletic: The Minister as Preacher.
5. Catechetic: The Minister as Teacher.
6. Poimenic: The Minister as Pastor.
7. Evangelistic: The Minister as Evangelist and Missionary. The duties of the laity should be considered in each department. These branches necessarily interlap each other more or less at various points. Liturgic, in the wider sense, includes Homiletic and Catechetic; in the narrower sense, only the acts of worship proper and the administration of the sacraments.

OTHER DIVISIONS.

Schleiermacher, Schweizer, Hagenbach, and Rothe: 1. Ministerial functions relating to Church service (*Kirchendienst*). 2. Church government (*Kirchenregiment*). Schleiermacher puts Church service first, Schweizer and Rothe reverse the order. An unequal division, which overloads the first. Moreover, Church government is also Church service, and Church service is Church government; the minister rules chiefly from the pulpit, and serves as a ruler, as Christ came not to be ministered unto, but to minister (Matt. 20 : 26–28).

Schweizer subdivides the theory of Church service as follows:
1. Theory of Worship: (*a*) Liturgic; (*b*) Homiletic. 2. Pastoral Theology: (*a*) Official; (*b*) Free. 3. Halieutic: (*a*) Catechetic; (*b*) Theory of Missions.

Hagenbach: 1. The gathering of a Christian congregation: (*a*) Halieutic; (*b*) Catechetic. 2. The guiding and furthering of Christian life in the congregation: (*a*) Liturgic; (*b*) Homiletic; (*c*) Pastoral Theology. 3. Organization and administration of the Church at large: (*a*) Church Polity; (*b*) Church Law.

Nitzsch arranges the ministerial functions into edifying (*erbauende*) and organizing (*ordnende*) functions.

Claus Harms: 1. The Preacher; 2. The Priest; 3. The Pastor.

Rothe: 1. Church Government: (*a*) Church Law; (*b*) Polemic. 2. Church Service: (*a*) Liturgic; (*b*) Homiletic; (*c*) Catechetic; (*d*) Poimenic.

Rothe, who first followed Schleiermacher's twofold division, proposed in his last lectures on *Encycl.* (p. 136) this arrangement: 1. Church Polity; 2. Liturgic; 3. Homiletic; 4. Catechetic; 5. Pastoral Doctrine; 6. The Person of the evangelical clergyman.

Räbiger: 1. Theory of Church organization: (*a*) Church Polity; (*b*) Church Law. 2. Theory of Worship: (*a*) Liturgic; (*b*) Homiletic; (*c*) Catechetic; (*d*) Pastoral Care. 3. The Science of Christian Culture: (*a*) Theory of Missions; (*b*) Ecclesiastical Sociology. 4. Ecclesiastical Didactic: (*a*) Symbolic; (*b*) Theory of the Ministerial Office.

Van Oosterzee: 1. Homiletic; 2. Liturgic; 3. Catechetic; 4. Poimenic.

Gretillat (1885): 1. *Oicodomique*: the theory of the edification of the Church. 2. *Alieutique*: theory of the extension of the Church. 3. *Polemique*: theory of the defense of the Church.

M'Clintock: 1. Functions of the Church. (*a*) Conservative Functions: Catechetic, Homiletic, Pastoral Care, Duties of the Laity. (*b*) Aggressive

Functions: Home Missions, Foreign Missions, Civilization. 2. Organization and Government of the Church.
Cave: 1. The Theory of the Church. 2. The Theory of Worship (Liturgic). 3. The Theory of Preaching (Homiletic). 4. The Theory of the Training of the Young (Catechetic). 5. The Theory of the Training of Pastors and Church Workers (Pedagogic). 6. The Theory of the Care of Souls. 7. The Theory of Christian Charities. 8. The Theory of Missions.
HEINRICI: 1. Liturgic. 2. Homiletic. 3. Catechetic. 4. Pastoral Theology. 5. Church Law. 6. Church Polity. 7. Theory of Missions.

CHAPTER CCLVI.

HISTORY AND LITERATURE OF PRACTICAL THEOLOGY.

1. The roots of Practical Theology are in the Pastoral Epistles of Paul to Timothy and Titus, which contain directions for founding, training and governing churches, and for the proper treatment of individual members, old and young, widows and virgins, backsliders and factious persons, with parting counsels of the Apostle to his beloved disciples and fellow-workers. They exhibit the transition from the simplicity of the apostolic age to the more definite Church polity and discipline of the second century. They are rich in practical wisdom and full of encouragement to every pastor. The Epistles to the Corinthians, the Epistle to Philemon, and the Epistles to the Seven Churches in the Apocalypse contain also important hints for practical theology.

2. The post-apostolic literature on the duties of the ministry and Church polity is closely interwoven with the ethical and casuistic literature which has been previously noticed. The first works of the kind are Church Manuals or Directories of worship and discipline, and Collections of laws and customs which claim, directly or indirectly, apostolic origin and authority. Such are the *Teaching of the Twelve Apostles*, the *Apostolic Canons*, and *Apostolic Constitutions*.

3. Chrysostom (347–407), the first pulpit orator among the Fathers, described in his work *On the Priesthood*, written before 381 with youthful fervor and eloquence, the importance, duties and trials of the Christian ministry on the basis of the then prevailing conception of a real priesthood and sacrifice.* He holds up Paul as a model for imitation, and requires whole-

* Περὶ ἱερωσύνης, *De Sacerdotio*, often translated, best by W. R. W. Stephens, in Schaff's edition of Chrysostom's *Works* (1889).

souled consecration to Christ and unselfish devotion to the Church. The book is marred by the justification of pious fraud under the name of economy or good management, which was shielded by the examples of Abraham, Jacob, David, and Paul (Acts 16 : 3; 21 : 26). The maxim that the end sanctifies the means is much older than Jesuitism. Origen and St. Jerome perverted the contention of Peter and Paul at Antioch (Gal. 2 : 11) into a hypocritical farce, for the purpose of convincing the Jewish Christians that circumcision was not necessary, and thus involved both Apostles in hypocrisy.

The Greek Church furnished the first works on Catechetic. Cyril of Jerusalem and Gregory of Nyssa.

Among the Latin Fathers, Ambrose takes the lead with his *De Officiis Ministrorum*, which belongs also to the literature on Ethic.

Augustin gives useful hints on homiletic in the fourth book of his *De Doctrina Christiana* (426), and on Catechetic in his *De Catechizandis Rudibus* (400).

The *Regula Pastoralis* of Pope Gregory I. was the chief manual of the clergy during the Middle Ages.

Isidor of Seville, Walafrid Strabo, and Rabanus Maurus wrote similar works for the instruction of the clergy. St. Bernard addressed to Archbishop Henry of Sens his *De Moribus et Officiis Episcoporum*. Duranti (d. 1292) wrote *Rationale Divinorum Officiorum* (8 books).

The Penitential books (*Libri Pœnitentiales*) belong both to pastoral and ethical literature.

Among the forerunners of the Reformation, Wiclif wrote a tract, *De Officio Pastorali*, which has been published by Lechler (1863).

4. After the Reformation the education for the priesthood became an education for the duties of the preacher and pastor.

Zwingli described his ideal of an evangelical minister in his "Shepherd" (*Der Hirt*).

The divines of the seventeenth century discussed the pastoral duties in connection with Dogmatic (*locus de ministerio*) and Ethic (*casus conscientiæ*). Valuable contributions by Hyperius (1562), Porta (1585), Kortholdt (1698), Spener (*Pia Desideria*, 1675), Baxter (*The Reformed Pastor*, and *Christian Directory*, 1673), Pierre Roques (*Le pasteur évangelique*, 1723), Mosheim (1754).

Special chairs for Practical Theology were first established at Helmstädt and Tübingen.

HISTORY AND LITERATURE OF PRACTICAL THEOLOGY. 453

5. The scientific treatment of Practical Theology as an organism dates from Schleiermacher, who was pastor (of Trinity Church, Berlin) as well as professor. In his *Outlines of Theological Study* (1811) he connected Practical Theology closely with the Church and assigned it the last and most important place in the course of theological study, calling it "the crown." He made the first attempt to organize the various branches under the two chief divisions of Church service and Church government. His brief hints have been fruitful. He delivered also special lectures on Pastoral Theology, which were published long after his death.

The field of Practical Theology as a systematic whole has since been cultivated by L. Hüffell (Giessen, 1822; 4th ed. 1843, 2 vols.), Claus Harms (Kiel, 1830; 3d ed., with notes, 1878), Ph. Marheineke (Berlin, 1837), * C. J. Nitzsch (Bonn, 1847-67; 2d ed. 1859-68, 3 vols.), K. F. Gaupp (Berlin, 1848-52), Schleiermacher (posthumous ed. by Frerichs, Berlin 1850; *Works*, vol. xiii.), *A. Vinet (Paris, 1850; German translation from the French by Hasse, 1852), C. B. Moll (Halle, 1853), J. H. A. Ebrard (Königsberg, 1854), F. Ehrenfeuchter (Göttingen, 1859), W. Otto (Dillenburg, 1867; Gotha, 1869, 2 vols.), F. L. Steinmeyer (Berlin, 1874-79, 5 Parts), G. von Zezschwitz (Leipzig, 1876-78, 3 Parts), Theodosius Harnack (Erlangen, 1877, 2 Parts), * J. J. van Oosterzee (translated from the Dutch into German by Matthiä and Petry (Heilbr., 1878 sq., 2 vols.), * E. Chr. Achelis (Freiburg i.B., 1890-91, 2 vols.), Alfred Krauss (Freiburg i.B., 1890-93, 2 vols.), K. Knoke (1892).

Roman Catholic writers: J. M. Sailer (München, 1788 sq.; 5th ed. Sulzbach, 1853, 3 vols.), J. Widmer (Augsburg, 1840), A. Graf (Tübingen, 1841), F. Vogl (7th ed. of Gollowitz, Regensburg, 1855, 2 vols.), J. Amberger (Regensburg, 1851 sq., 2 vols.; 4th ed. 1883 sq.), J. Schüch (6th ed. Linz, 1882).

In the English language we have no original work which embraces all the branches of Practical Theology, but numerous special treatises on Preaching and Pastoral Care, by Fairbairn, Kidder, Phelps, Hopkins, Shedd, Broadus and others. The *Practical Theology* of J. J. van Oosterzee, who was professor and preacher at Utrecht, is of all foreign manuals best adapted for English students, and has been translated from the Dutch by Maurice J. Evans.*

* In H. B. Smith and Schaff, "Theological and Philosophical Library" (New York and London, 1878).

CHAPTER CCLVII.

THEORY OF THE CHRISTIAN MINISTRY.

The Theory of the Christian Ministry discusses the general questions which underlie the other departments of Practical Theology, such as the origin, nature and aim of the Christian ministry; the difference between clergy and laity; the internal and external call to the ministry; preparation; examination; licensure; ordination; installation; support; personal character and conduct.

Our Saviour appointed twelve Apostles and endowed them with the Holy Spirit for the founding of the Christian Church among Jews and Gentiles. They were the first of an unbroken succession of ministers who should make disciples of all nations by baptizing and teaching them to observe all things whatsoever Christ commanded them; and for this purpose he promised to abide with them "all the days, even to the consummation of the world" (Matt. 28:20).

The apostolic office contains the germ of the various ministerial offices which gradually were developed according to the needs of the Church. The primitive officers are:

1. For the Church at large: Apostles, Prophets, and Evangelists.
2. For local congregations: Presbyters or Bishops for ruling and teaching, and Deacons (and Deaconesses) for the care of the poor and the sick, and the temporalities of the congregation.

The topics of this branch are usually discussed in Homiletic and Poimenic. The most important modern writers on the apostolic and post-apostolic ministry are Rothe, Ritschl, Lightfoot, Hatch, Harnack, Weizsäcker, Loening, and Ch. de Smedt. See the literature in Schaff, *Church History*, vol i., pp. 481–484.

CHAPTER CCLVIII.

DIFFERENT CONCEPTIONS OF THE MINISTRY.

The Christian minister is a servant and ambassador of Christ, acting in his name and by his authority, and carrying forward his work in the world. As Christ is prophet, priest, and king, so the minister unites, in a restricted sense, these three offices. As prophet, he teaches the people from the pulpit and the lecture-room the way of salvation in Christ. As priest, he offers the spiritual sacrifices of prayer and praise, and administers the sacraments and religious rites. As king, he rules his flock and takes part in the general government of the Church.

In the Greek and Roman Churches, the minister is lost in the priest and separated from the people. He offers sacrifice at the altar, and dispenses absolution at the confessional. His personal character is overshadowed and shielded by his official character.

In the Protestant minister the preaching and teaching function is the most prominent; the pulpit is his throne. Hence a higher order of education is required, and his official authority must be sustained by personal purity and dignity. He stands not aloof from the people as a member of a distinct class, like the priest in the Jewish dispensation, but is associated and interwoven with the life of the congregation.

CHAPTER CCLIX.

ECCLESIOLOGY.

Ecclesiology treats of the Church as a visible organization, its constitution, offices, administration, and relation to civil society.

The word *church* is derived from κυριακόν, *what belongs to the Lord*, and is used in four senses: (1) a particular congregation; (2) the Church universal; (3) a denomination or confession (as the Greek Church, the Roman Church, the Episcopal Church, the Lutheran Church, the Presbyterian Church, etc.); (4) a church building.* (The last two senses are extra-biblical.)

In the New Testament the corresponding term is ἐκκλησία, which means a congregation or assembly.† It occurs only twice in the Gospels, once in the local sense of a particular congregation (Matt. 18:17), and once in the general sense of the Church of Christ or the whole body of believers (Matt. 16:18); but in

---

* Κυριακὸν δῶμα, or κυριακὴ οἰκία, as *Basilica* from βασιλεύς, *Regia* from *rex*.
† From ἐκκαλέω, to call out. The word is used of any gathering of the people for deliberation (Acts 19:32, 41). In the Septuagint it is often equivalent to *kahal*, the assembly of the Israelites.

the Acts, Epistles and Revelation it occurs 111 times, mostly in the particular or local sense.

On the other hand, our Lord uses the term "kingdom of heaven" or "kingdom of God" 123 times in the Gospels (counting the parallel passages); while in all other books from the Acts to Revelation it occurs only 33 times.

This suggests a difference as well as a resemblance. The Church of Christ and the kingdom of God are intimately related, but not identical. The Church dates from the day of Pentecost after the Ascension. Christ speaks of it as future: "Upon this rock I will build my Church."* The kingdom is older and will last forever. It is a wider, deeper and more spiritual conception: the kingdom embraces heaven and earth, eternity and time, the whole moral government of God, all the spiritual forces and energies of his people, the saints of the Old and New Dispensation, the Church militant and the Church triumphant. It is chiefly, but not exclusively, manifest and embodied in the Church and operative through the Church as its organ. The Church on earth is the training-school for the kingdom of heaven. Hence it is so often spoken of by the Apostles, the builders of the Church.

The difference between the two ideas is apparent in many passages where we could not with propriety substitute the Church for the kingdom; as, "Thy kingdom come" (Matt. 6: 10); "Seek ye first the kingdom of God" (6:33); "Theirs," or "of such" (the poor in spirit, and the children) "is the kingdom of heaven" (5:3; 19:4); "The kingdom of God cometh not with observation, . . . it is within you" (or "in the midst of you," Luke 17:20, 21).† These words were spoken before the Church was founded. In other passages the kingdom is spoken of as future, to be fully realized only at the second advent (Matt. 25:34; 26:29; Luke 1:33; Acts 14:22; 1 Cor. 15:24; 2 Pet. 1:11; Rev. 11:15).

The Roman Church identifies herself with *the* Church, and the Church with the kingdom of God. She confines the Church to the dominion of the papacy, and excludes the Greek Church as a schism, the Protestant Churches as heretical sects. Protestants distinguish between the invisible Church, which is one and universal and includes all who believe in Christ as their

* Οἰκοδομήσω μου τὴν ἐκκλησίαν.
† Comp. also such passages as Rom. 14:17; 1 Cor. 4:20; 15:50.

Lord and Saviour, and the visible Churches, Greek, Roman and Protestant, which embrace all nominal and baptized Christians, good and bad. Distinct from both conceptions, but more nearly identical with the invisible Church, is the kingdom of God.

Ecclesiology is divided into two parts: Church Law (*Kirchenrecht*) and Church Polity (*Kirchenverfassung*).

LITERATURE.

J. MCELHINNEY: *The Doctrine of the Church: An Historical Monograph, with a Full Bibliography of the Subject* (Philadelphia, 1871).

JULIUS MÜLLER: *On the Visible and Invisible Church* (in his *Dogmatische Abhandlungen*).

A. B. BRUCE: *The Kingdom of God; or, Christ's Teaching according to the Synoptical Gospels* (Edinburgh, 4th ed. 1893).

On the development of the idea of the Church since St. Augustin, see SCHAFF, *Church History*, vol. vi., pp. 520–536, and the literature there quoted.

CHAPTER CCLX.

CHURCH LAW.

The Church Law or Ecclesiastical Law (*Kirchenrecht*), as distinct from State Law or Civil Law, comprehends all the canons and regulations which the Church from time to time has adopted for its government, administration, worship and discipline. It embodies the governmental experience and wisdom of many ages, as the creeds of the Church embody its doctrinal belief. The disciplinary rules of the Church are called *canons* (κανόνες), in distinction from the doctrinal decrees (*decreta*) or *dogmas* of the Church, and from the *laws* (νόμοι, *leges*) of the State.

I. The oldest collections of ecclesiastical law pretend to be directly or indirectly of apostolic origin and sanction, but are clearly post-apostolic. They originated in the Orient, and make no reference to the Roman Church, though some claim a fictitious sanction from Bishop Clement of Rome. They exist in various forms, in Greek, Syriac, Arabic, and Ethiopic MSS. The chief are the following:

(1) The DIDACHE, or TEACHING OF THE TWELVE APOSTLES, probably of Syrian origin, from the end of the first or the beginning of the second century. It forms in language and spirit the bridge from the apostolic to the episcopal age, or between the Pastoral and the Ignatian Epistles. It contains a

summary of moral instruction based on the Decalogue and the Sermon on the Mount; directions for the celebration of baptism and the eucharist, and concerning discipline and church offices; and concludes with an exhortation to watchfulness in view of the coming of the Lord and the resurrection of the saints. This remarkable book was much used in the early Church, and then disappeared till it was rediscovered by Bryennios in 1873, in a convent of Constantinople, and first printed in 1884. The substance of it survived in the seventh book of the "Apostolical Constitutions."*

(2) The (pseudo-) APOSTOLICAL CONSTITUTIONS are the most important and complete clergyman's manual of the ancient Church. This work is in its literary form a pious fraud, and professes to be a bequest by all the Apostles dictated to the Roman Bishop Clement, but it is a gradual growth and was not completed till the middle of the fourth century in Syria. It is based upon the Bible, oral tradition, the *Didache*, just mentioned, and the *Didascalia*, or *The Catholic Doctrine of the Twelve Apostles and Holy Disciples of Our Redeemer* (which dates from the middle of the third century and is extant in a Syriac version in twenty-six chapters). It embodies also the decrees of early councils at Antioch, Neo-Cæsarea, Nicæa, Gangra, and Laodicea. The "Constitutions" contain, in eight books, moral exhortations, ecclesiastical laws and usages, and liturgical formularies. The compiler shows some sympathy with Semi-Arianism and Apollinarianism. Later interpolations were rejected as heretical by the second Trullan Council in 692. The Latin Church has only adopted the fifty canons appended to the eighth book.†

(3) The (pseudo-) APOSTOLICAL CANONS (fifty, afterwards eighty-five), drawn up, according to tradition, by Clement of Rome, are brief rules and prescriptions for the clergy, appended to the "Apostolic Constitutions," and are probably from the same author or compiler; for he refers to them in the 85th canon as among the sacred Scriptures. The Greek Church adopted the whole collection of eighty-five canons as authentic

* The MS. is now in the library of the Greek patriarch of Jerusalem. Editions and monographs by Schaff (*The Teaching of the Twelve Apostles; or, The Oldest Church Manual;* New York and Edinburgh, 3d revised ed. 1889), by Bryennios (in Greek), Harnack (in German), Jacquier (in French), and Savi (in Italian).

† Editions by Turrianus, Mansi, Harduin, Ueltzen (1853), Paul de Lagarde (1854 and 1862), Pitra (1864). Comp. Fr. Xav. Funk, *Die Apostolischen Konstitutionen* (Rottenburg, 1891).

and binding, but the Latin Church only the smaller collection of fifty canons.*

II. The CANON LAW, or CORPUS JURIS CANONICI, is the code of laws and usages of the Latin Church in the Middle Ages, and rules the Roman Church in great part to this day. It forms a parallel to the Justinian *Corpus Juris Civilis*. The material is derived from the Bible, the old Roman law, the writings of the Fathers, the decrees of the general councils, the decretal epistles and bulls of the popes. It is based on older collections, including the pseudo-Isidorian decretals. The foundation of this codification is the *Decretum Gratiani*, published at Bologna, 1150, which arranged, systematized and harmonized the discordant canons, and became a useful text-book of lectures in the universities.† This *Decretum*, or *Liber Decretorum*, is divided into three parts. The first part treats, in 101 *Distinctiones*, of the sources of the canon law, the clergy, ordination, consecration, the papal power. The second discusses, in 36 *Causæ*, different legal questions, church property and the marriage laws. The third, called *Liber de Sacramentis*, is devoted to the sacraments, feasts and fasts. The expounders of the canon law are called canonists or decretists, in distinction from the legalists or expounders of the Roman civil law.

* Editions by Mansi, Harduin, in most collections of church laws, and by Paul de Lagarde in Greek and Syriac (Lips., 1856). The following are specimens:

"CANON I.

"Let a Bishop be ordained by two or three Bishops.

"CANON II.

"Let a Presbyter, or Deacon, and the other clergy be ordained by one Bishop.

"CANON V.

"No Bishop, Presbyter, or Deacon shall put away his wife, under pretext of religion; but if he put her away, let him be suspended; and, if he persist, let him be deposed.

"CANON VI.

"No Bishop, Presbyter, or Deacon shall engage in worldly business; and, if he do, let him be deposed.

"CANON VII.

"If any Bishop, Presbyter, or Deacon shall celebrate the holy day of Easter before the vernal Equinox, as the Jews do, let him be deposed."

† Gratian called it, *Discordantium Canonum Concordia*. He was a Camaldolensian monk, and taught church law in a convent at Bologna about the same time with Irnerius, the restorer of Roman jurisprudence, and teacher of the civil law. These two may be called the founders of the University of Bologna, which became for several centuries the nurse of civil and ecclesiastical law, with the proud device: '*Bononia docet*.'

The *Decretum Gratiani* was enlarged by the collections of several popes, Gregory IX. (1230), Boniface VIII. (1298), Clement V. (1313), John XXII. (1317), to which were added, in 1500, the *Extravagantes communes* (*i.e.*, *extra Decretum vagantes*). These six collections make up the full *Corpus juris canonici*, and were officially edited under this title by a papal commission of Gregory XIII., in Rome, 1582, in 5 vols.

The Canon Law of Christian Rome and the Civil Law of heathen Rome have exerted an incalculable influence on the civilization of Europe. Rome, conquered by the barbarians, reconquered their children, and, by substituting the law for the sword, ruled the Christian world for many centuries. The Canon Law shares the virtues and faults of the papacy with which it rose and declined. It fortified the hierarchical theocracy of the Middle Ages. It attempted to regulate human life from the cradle to the grave by the sacramental acts of the priesthood. It protected the sanctity of marriage. It was a wholesome check upon the wild passions of the barbarians and the brutal force of despotic princes. It is animated by a spirit of justice and humanity; it acknowledges the brotherhood of men, and prepared the way for the modern science of international law. But it sanctions the persecution of heretics by fire and sword, and put a restraint upon the progress of thought. This overgrown code became at last a burden too heavy to be borne, like the traditions of the Jewish Elders which made void the Word of God (Matt. 15: 6), and like the yoke of the ceremonial law against which Peter protested at the Council of Jerusalem (Acts 15: 10).*

Luther burned the Canon Law together with the papal bull, Dec. 20, 1520. Calvin called it a barbarous code and a tyranny of conscience; he maintained that the laws of the Church must be subject to the law of Christ.† But the Canon Law survived

* "*Customs and laws in every place,*
  Like a disease, an heirloom dread,
  Still trail their curse from race to race,
  And furtively abroad they spread.
  To nonsense, reason's self they turn;
  Beneficence becomes a pest;
  Woe unto thee, that thou'rt a grandson born!
  As for the law born with us, unexpressed,—
  That law, alas! none careth to discern."
  (From Goethe's *Faust*.)

† *Instit.*, Book IV., ch. x., § 9: "*Constitutiones quas vocant ecclesiasticas quibus Papa cum suis onerat ecclesiam, dicimus perniciosas esse et impias;*

the Reformation. It has a permanent historical value, and many of its provisions on Church property, benefices, ordination, marriage, etc., were revised and re-enacted in Protestant State Churches, especially in Germany and England; while others were abrogated even in the Roman Church by the Council of Trent, and by later papal decretals, and papal concordats with modern States which have outgrown the hierarchical supremacy, demand independence in civil legislation, and protect freedom and progress.

III. The various Protestant Churches have their own constitutions and directories of Church polity and worship. The best organized Protestant Churches are the Episcopal Church of England and the United States, the Presbyterian Churches, and the Methodist Episcopal Church. While the Canon Law is the product of the Catholic Church independent of the State, the ecclesiastical legislation of Protestant State Churches is the joint product of Church and State and recognizes the equal or superior authority of the State. The constitutions of the Churches in the United States are purely ecclesiastical and denominational.

CHAPTER CCLXI.

COLLECTIONS AND MANUALS OF CHURCH LAW.

I. Collections:

Corpus Juris Canonici, first published in Rome, 1582, 5 vols. fol.; best critical edition by Æmilius (Emil) L. Richter, Leipzig, 1839; new ed. (*ed. Lipsiensis secunda*) by Æmilius Friedberg (Leipzig. B. Tauchnitz, 1879, 1881, 2 vols. fol.).

JOHN FULTON (Episcopalian): *Index Canonum. The Greek Text. An English Translation and a Complete Digest of the Entire Code of Canon Law of the Undivided Primitive Church* (New York, 1872; 3d ed. 1892, 393 pp.). A useful collection.

WILLIAM BRIGHT: *Notes on the Canons of the First Four General Councils* (Oxford, 1882). A good commentary on the œcumenical canons.

W. ANDREW HAMMOND: *Definitions of Faith, and Canons of Discipline of the Six Œcumenical Councils* (Oxford, 1843); an American reprint with

adversarii nostri sanctus esse et salutares defendunt." § 11: "*Sunt alia quoque duo non levia vitia, quæ in iisdem constitutionibus improbamus. Primum quod magna ex parte inutiles, interdum etiam ineptas observationes præscribunt: deinde quod immensa earum multitudine opprimuntur piæ conscientiæ, et in Judaismum quendam revolutæ umbris sic adhærescunt ut ad Christum nequeant pervenire.*"

the addition of the constitutions and canons of the Protestant Episcopal Church in the United States (New York, 1850).

JOHN HENRY BLUNT: *The Book of Church Law* (London, 1872; 4th ed. revised by Sir W. G. T. Phillimore, 1885).

SIR ROBERT PHILLIMORE: *Ecclesiastical Law of the Church of England* (London, 1873–76, 2 vols.).

A Summary of the Laws and Regulations of the Church of Scotland (Edinburgh 1840, and more recent editions). Contains the Acts of the Scotch Parliament relating to the Church, the First and Second Books of Discipline, the Form of Process, Pardowan's Collections, etc.

II. Books on the theory of Church Law. See full lists in Friedberg, pp. 4–6, and in Kihn, pp. 520–531.

(*a*) Roman Catholic authors:

FERD. WALTER: *Lehrbuch des Kirchenrechts aller christlichen Confessionen* (Bonn, 1822; 14th ed. 1871).

H. GERLACH: *Lehrbuch des katholischen Kirchenrechts* (1869; 5th ed. by Fr. Xav. Schulte, Paderborn, 1890). A brief but convenient manual.

G. PHILLIPS: *Kirchenrecht* (Regensburg, 1845; 3d ed. 1855 sqq., 7 vols.).

F. H. VERING: *Lehrbuch des katholischen, orientalischen, und protestantischen Kirchenrechts, mit besonderer Rücksicht auf Deutschland, Oesterreich und die Schweiz* (Freiburg i.B., 1876; 3d ed. 1893).

For the history of the Canon Law, see FR. VON SCHULTE (Old Cath. Prof. in Bonn): *Die Geschichte der Quellen und Literatur des kanonischen Rechts von Gratian bis auf die Gegenwart* (Stuttgart, 1875–80, 3 vols.).

(*b*) Protestant authors:

J. H. BÖHMER: *Jus Ecclesiasticum Protestantium* (Halle, 1714; 5th ed. 1756 sqq., 5 vols. 4to). The first great Protestant work on Church Law.

EMIL L. RICHTER: *Lehrbuch des kathol. und evangel. Kirchenrechts* (Leipzig, 1841; 8th ed. 1877–86, 2 vols.).

PAUL HINSCHIUS: *Das Kirchenrecht der Katholiken und Protestanten in Deutschland* (Berlin, 1869–88, 4 vols.).

EMIL FRIEDBERG: *Lehrbuch des katholischen und evangelischen Kirchenrechts* (Leipzig, 1879; 3d ed. 1889).—R. SOHM: *Kirchenrecht*, 1892.

(*c*) American works:

MURRAY HOFFMAN (Episcopalian): *Law of the Protestant Episcopal Church in the United States* (New York, 1850); *Ecclesiastical Law in the State of New York* (New York, 1868); *Ritual Law of the Church* (New York, 1872).

J. W. ANDREWS (Episcopalian): *Church Law of the Protestant Episcopal Church in the United States* (New York, 1883).

CHARLES HODGE (Presbyterian): *Discussions in Church Polity* (New York, 1878).

J. A. HODGE: *What is Presbyterian Church Law?* (Philadelphia.)

WILLIAM STRONG (Presbyterian): *Two Lectures upon the Relation of Civil Law to Ecclesiastical Polity, Property, and Discipline* (New York, 1875).

The Constitution of the Presbyterian Church in the United States of America (new ed. Philadelphia, 1893, with the amendments adopted in 1891).

SAMUEL J. BAIRD (Presbyterian): *A Collection of the Acts, Deliverances, and Testimonies of the Supreme Judicatory of the Presbyterian Church in America to 1858* (1856; 2d ed., Philadelphia, 1858; Old School from 1837–58).

WILLIAM E. MOORE (Presbyterian): *The Presbyterian Digest of* 1886 *; A Compend of the Acts and Deliverances of the General Assembly of the Presbyterian Church in the United States of America* (Philadelphia, 1886).
W. A. ALEXANDER (Southern Presbyterian Church): *A Digest of the Acts and Proceedings of the General Assembly,* etc. (Richmond, Va., 1888).

CHAPTER CCLXII.

CHURCH POLITY.

We may distinguish the following forms of church polity in the order of historical development:

I. The APOSTOLIC Church government from the day of Pentecost to the death of St. John (A.D. 30–100). Christ undoubtedly founded a visible Church on earth (Matt. 16:18), which appeared as a distinct society on the day of Pentecost, and appointed officers (Apostles) and two sacraments (Baptism and the Lord's Supper).

Out of the apostolate grew gradually the following officers: Apostles proper, Prophets, Evangelists, for the Church at large; Presbyters or Bishops, and Deacons (with female Deaconesses), for the local congregations. The former are extraordinary officers, necessary for the founding of the Church; the latter are ordinary officers, necessary for its preservation. The original identity of Presbyters or Elders, and Bishops or Superintendents, is very evident from a number of passages of the New Testament, the *Didache,* and the Epistle of Clement to the Corinthians, and is acknowledged by all scholars.

II. CONGREGATIONAL EPISCOPACY, with a bishop at the head of each local church, and a number of presbyters and deacons under him. The Episcopate was raised above the primitive Presbyterate as a permanent presidency. The Ignatian Epistles (Shorter Greek recension), between 107 and 118, first distinguish between the Presbyter and the Bishop. Christ is the one universal Bishop of all the churches; the human bishop is the vicar of Christ and center of unity for each congregation; while the college of presbyters and deacons around him are the successors of the Apostles. No distinction of order is made between the bishops, nor is there a trace of a primacy. Ignatius is the first to use the term "Catholic Church," as if episcopacy and catholicity sprung up simultaneously.

III. DIOCESAN EPISCOPACY makes the bishop the head of

several congregations. It appears towards the end of the second century in the writings of Irenæus and Tertullian, and more fully in Cyprian, who is the typical high-churchman of the ante-Nicene age, and represents the solidarity of the Episcopate, in connection with, and yet independent of, the Roman see, as the center of ecclesiastical unity. The dioceses, however, were very small as to the number of congregations; for Cyprian could assemble, in 258, a synod of 87 bishops in proconsular Africa, and the schismatical Donatists held, in 308, a council of 270 bishops at Carthage. Some were only congregational bishops over single churches. In larger cities there was even more than one bishop; for Epiphanius says that "Alexandria never had two bishops, as the other cities had." *

IV. The METROPOLITAN and PATRIARCHAL system was developed after Constantine, when Christianity became the religion of the Roman Empire. It was to a large extent conformed to the political divisions into pretorian prefectures, dioceses, provinces, cities and parishes. The apostolic mother churches (*sedes apostolicæ, matrices ecclesiæ*), such as those at Jerusalem, Antioch, Alexandria, Ephesus, Corinth and Rome, were always held in special reverence as the chief bearers of the pure Church tradition, but acquired now also a political importance (with the exception of Jerusalem). The bishops of the chief cities were called Metropolitans in the East, or Archbishops in the West, and presided over the bishops of a province as *primi inter pares*. Over the Metropolitans and Archbishops rose the Patriarchs of Alexandria, Antioch, Rome, Jerusalem, and Constantinople. The title "Patriarch" was originally an honorary title for all bishops, but after the Council of Constantinople (381) it was restricted to the five mentioned. They had the oversight of two or more provinces or eparchies; they ordained the metropolitans; conducted the œcumenical councils, and united in themselves the supreme legislative and executive power of the hierarchy. They were equal in rights and jurisdiction, but differed in the extent of their diocese and in influence. Rome was first, Alexandria second, and Antioch third in rank. After the founding of Constantinople (330), the Bishop of this city, as the second capital of the empire, competed with Rome for the primacy of honor. The fourth œcumenical council at Chal-

* *Hæres.* lxviii., c. 7. Compare Hatch, *The Growth of Church Institutions*, p. 17.

cedon (451) ordained in its 28th canon that the bishop of New Rome, where the emperor and the senate resided, should enjoy the same privileges as ancient imperial Rome, and be the second after her (in honor, not in jurisdiction, which was equal).

From this dates the conflict between the Patriarch and the Pope. The Bishop of Rome protested against that canon and refused to be put on a par with the eastern Patriarchs. Constantinople owed its ecclesiastical power to its political significance; while the Roman see goes back to the apostolic age and claimed to derive its authority from Peter.

The Greek Church adheres to the Patriarchal oligarchy of the œcumenical councils, and added to the four Patriarchs of the East the Patriarch of Moscow, who was succeeded by the holy synod of St. Petersburg under the presidency of the Czar of Russia.

V. The PAPAL MONARCHY, ruled by the Bishop of Rome, who claims to be the successor of Peter and the Vicar of Christ, and as such the head of the Church universal. The Papacy is the most complete and imposing organization which the world has ever seen. It rests on the double significance of the city of Rome as the political metropolis of the old Roman Empire, and as the mother-church of western Christendom consecrated by the martyrdom of Peter and Paul. It gradually grew with the conversion of the barbarians, and controlled the history of Europe during the Middle Ages. It lost by the Reformation the most vigorous and progressive nations, but it still commands from the Vatican with infallible authority the largest portion of Christendom. After a long conflict between the episcopal or the Gallican and the curial or ultramontane Schools—that is, between a constitutional and an absolute monarchy—the Roman hierarchy was completed by the Vatican Council of 1870, which declared the pope to be the Bishop of bishops and the infallible and final judge in all matters of faith and discipline

VI. ANGLICAN EPISCOPACY, with two archbishops (Canterbury and York), and the royal supremacy (which Henry VIII. substituted for the authority of the pope). It is modified and improved in the Protestant Episcopal Church of the United States, which has no political headship, is independent of the State, self-supporting and self-governing, and admits the laity to a share in the legislative functions of the lower house of representatives.

VII. The EPISCOPAL GOVERNMENT of the Swedish and Danish Lutheran Churches, of the Moravians, and of the Episcopal Methodists, is equivalent to a general superintendency, and claims no divine right or essential distinction of function from the presbyterate.

VIII. The PRESBYTERIAN POLITY dates from Calvin, and was more fully developed in the Reformed Churches of France, Holland and Scotland. It is based upon the equality of ministers or presbyter-bishops under the sole headship of Christ, and the co-operation of the laity. It distinguishes several judicatories, congregational, presbyterial, and synodical. The Church Session consists of the pastor and ruling elders of a particular congregation, and attends to the maintenance of the local government. The Presbytery consists of all the ministers and one ruling elder from each congregation within a certain district, and exercises jurisdiction over that district. The Synod consists of ministers and lay delegates from the Presbyteries. The General Assembly is the highest judicatory in all matters of doctrine, worship and discipline, but does not claim infallibility for any of its decisions, and must submit all constitutional changes to the Presbyteries for ratification.

IX. The Lutheran Church in the United States unites the Presbyterian and Synodical government with Congregational independency; but some divines are in favor of restoring the episcopal superintendency, after the model of Sweden.

X. CONGREGATIONAL or INDEPENDENT POLITY lodges the government of the Church in each congregation or society of believers, who voluntarily, by mutual agreement and by covenant with God, confederate or unite for purposes of worship and Christian activity. It maintains two offices, that of bishop or pastor, who guides the Church by instruction and counsel, and that of deacons or helpers, who have charge of the secularities of the congregation and the relief of the poor. The churches and ministers associate in councils, conferences, associations and consociations, which have moral but not legislative authority. This form of Church government dates from the reign of Elizabeth and is adopted by the Independents of England, the Congregationalists of America, the Baptists, the Quakers, a branch of the Methodists, the Disciples of Christ, the Unitarians, and the Universalists.

CHAPTER CCLXIII.

LITERATURE ON CHURCH POLITY.

1. On the apostolic Church government and the origin of episcopacy, see ROTHE (1837), ZAEN, LIGHTFOOT, RITSCHL, HATCH, RENAN, HARNACK, JACOB, and GORE.

2. Older works by RICHARD HOOKER (*Ecclesiastical Polity*, 1594); JOSEPH BINGHAM (*Antiquities of the Christian Church*, 1710 sqq.), etc. See lists in SCHAFF, *Church History*, vol. i., pp. 481–484.

3. ARTHUR P. STANLEY: *Christian Institutions* (London and New York, 1881).

EDWIN HATCH: *The Growth of Church Institutions* (London and New York, 1881; 2d ed. 1883).

4. Denominational Church Manuals: Episcopalian by FRANCIS VINTON (New York, 1870); Presbyterian by SAMUEL MILLER, JOEL PARKER, T. RALSTON SMITH, J. A. HODGE; Methodist by ROBERT EMORY (New York, 1864), W. PIERCE (London, 1873); Congregational by H. M. DEXTER (Boston, 1865, 5th ed. 1879), and J. E. ROY (Chicago, 1869, and often since); Baptist by FRANCIS WAYLAND (New York, 1857).

CHAPTER CCLXIV.

CHURCH AND STATE.

The relation of Church and State belongs to the outward condition of the Church in this world, and materially affects the interests of both. It is a part of the theory of Church Polity.

According to the Bible, the two powers, like the family from which they spring, are divinely appointed, the Church for the spiritual welfare, the State for the temporal welfare—that is, for the protection of life and property and all the natural rights of man. Hence the civil magistrate, as well as the clergyman, is a servant of God (Rom. 13: 1–4). The State belongs to the kingdom of nature; the Church, to the kingdom of grace; but nature prepares for grace, and both work together for the same end. The law is the weapon of the one; the gospel, the weapon of the other. Offenses against the State deserve temporal punishment; offenses against the Church deserve spiritual punishment (admonition, suspension, excommunication).

Christ draws a clear line of distinction between the two powers, and requires us to render to God and to Cæsar what is due to each. But in history, the two have often been confounded or brought into hostile collision. A faithful observance of Christ's wise words in answer to the Pharisees on the question of tribute (Matt. 22 : 21) would have prevented religious wars and saved rivers of blood.

There are four different relations which have been heretofore developed:

I. The State hostile to the Church. In the Roman Empire during the first three centuries. The age of persecution. But while the Church was oppressed from without by the heathen government, she was independent within in building up her creed and polity.

II. The State ruling over the Church. Cæsaropapism, Erastianism. The old Byzantine, and the modern Russian, Empire, where the Czar is pope; also the national Protestant Churches of Europe, where the secular ruler is the highest ecclesiastical authority ("summus episcopus" in Germany; "supreme governor" in England).

III. The Church ruling the State. The hierarchy, copied from the Old Testament theocracy. It was (and is still) the theory of the Roman Catholic Church, and led to the conflicts between the pope and the emperor and kings. It was most fully carried out in the States of the Church (*Kirchenstaat*), with Rome as the capital and the pope as the temporal and spiritual sovereign; but it came to an end in 1870, when Rome was made the capital of the united kingdom of Italy, and the pope was confined to the possession of the Vatican, though with undiminished spiritual power.

IV. Independence of Church and State on a footing of friendly recognition. This is the condition in the United States, where all Christian Churches and sects are on the same footing before the law, equally protected by the law, but equally independent of State control in the management of their affairs, and are thrown upon the voluntary principle and the duty and privilege of self-support and self-government. This separation secures entire religious freedom and is most favorable for the development of the energies of the Church. It is the best, though not the final, status.*

* Cardinal Gibbons, at a banquet of the Catholic Club in Philadelphia, Feb. 6, 1893, made the following sensible speech in response to the toast "Church and State":

"I am firmly persuaded, both by study and observation, that the Church

V. The ultimate relation of Church and State will be the perfect kingdom of God on the new earth, or a universal Christocracy of righteousness and peace.

LITERATURE.

EMIL FRIEDBERG : *Die Grenzen zwischen Staat und Kirche und die Garantien gegen deren Verletzung* (Tübingen, 1872).
MARCO MINGHETTI : *Stato e chiesa* (Milan, 2d ed. 1878; German translation by the Empress Frederick, *Staat und Kirche*, Gotha, 1881). Defends Cavour's principle of *l'église libre dans l'état libre*.
ATTILIO BRUNIALTI: *Biblioteca di Scienze Politiche* (Torino, 1892, vol. viii.). The eighth volume contains a number of essays by various authors in different countries on Church and State.
PHILIP SCHAFF: *Church and State in the United States; or, The American Idea of Religious Liberty and its Practical Effects. With Official Documents* (New York, 1888). Translated into Italian by Brunialti, 1892.
A. TAYLOR INNES : *Church and State : A Historical Handbook* (Edinburgh and New York, 1893).
On the relation of Protestantism to religious liberty, compare SCHAFF'S *Church History*, vol. vi , pp. 50–86; and vol. vii., pp. 693–712.

CHAPTER CCLXV.

TOLERATION AND LIBERTY.

The relation of Church and State is closely connected with religious liberty. The union of the spiritual and secular power is always more or less a restraint on liberty, and in its extreme form leads to persecution by fire and sword ; while the peaceful separation of the two allows the full exercise of liberty within the limits of public order and peace.

State-churchism may be, and has in modern times become,

is more sturdy in her growth, and is more prosperous in her career, when she is free to pursue her divine mission without any interference on the part of the State. Here, thank God, the Church is free and therefore she is prosperous. Here the Church and the State run in parallel lines, each assisting the other, and neither of them unwarrantably intruding on the domain of the other. Here the Constitution holds over the Church its protecting arm without interfering in ecclesiastical affairs.
"We have no State religion or official Church in the United States. But it would be a great mistake to draw as an inference from this fact that therefore our Government is anti-Christian or anti-religious. I venture to say, on the contrary, that there is no commonwealth under the sun more strongly permeated by Christian and religious principles than the Government of the United States.
"For my part, I believe the relations between the Church and State are as close and cordial as we should desire. All we ask is a fair field and no special favor. I do not wish to see the day when the State will be called on to build our churches and subsidize our clergy. For it were to

tolerant towards dissenting sects, but to the same extent has the bond of union been relaxed. Toleration may proceed from necessity, or from prudence, or from indifference, or from liberality and enlarged views of truth and right.*

But there is a wide difference between toleration and liberty. Toleration is the gift of man; liberty is the gift of God. The one is a concession and an expedient; the other a right and a principle. Toleration implies, more or less, censure and disapproval; it may be extended or withdrawn by the power which grants it. The most despotic governments tolerate or endure what they dislike but cannot prevent. Russia and Turkey are tolerant towards subjects too numerous or too useful to be killed off or to be exiled, but they strictly forbid propagandism and punish apostates from the State religion with exile and death. In a free country, no self-respecting man asks to be tolerated for his religious opinions or sacred convictions. "Toleration is first sought and granted as a favor, then demanded and conceded as a right, and at last spurned as an insult."

Liberty is the greatest gift of God to man.† It is a natural, fundamental and inalienable right of every man created in the image of God. The most precious of all liberties is religious liberty. It is rooted in the sacredness of conscience, which is the voice of God in man, and above the reach and control of human authority. It is a law above all human laws that "we ought to obey God rather than man." Liberty of conscience requires liberty of worship. Despots allow the one because they cannot help it, but deny the other. Religion in its nature is voluntary, and ceases to be religion in proportion as it is forced. God desires free worshipers and hates hypocrites.

The principle of religious liberty is proclaimed in the New

---

be feared that, as soon as the Government began to support the Church, it would dictate to us what doctrines we ought to preach. And in proportion as State patronage would increase, the devotion and patronage of the faithful would wax cold. If it is a great wrong to muzzle the press, it would be a great wrong to muzzle the pulpit."

But the same Cardinal defends the restoration of the temporal power of the pope. The Roman Catholics demand and enjoy all the liberty they can get in Protestant countries, on Protestant principles, but they deny liberty to Protestants in Roman Catholic countries, on Roman Catholic principles.

* In the last sense, toleration or tolerance, as freedom from bigotry and forbearance towards the dissenting opinions of others, may be a positive virtue.

† So says even Pope Leo XIII. in his Encyclical, *Libertas præstantissimum naturæ donum*, issued June 20, 1888.

Testament, and was defended by the ante-Nicene Fathers, such as Justin Martyr, Tertullian and Lactantius, against heathen persecution, and by the Nicene Fathers, as Athanasius and Hilary, during the Arian persecution. It was acknowledged in the Toleration Edict of Constantine (313), but soon forgotten by his successors, the Christian emperors, who persecuted the heathen religion and Christian heretics and schismatics, as their heathen predecessors had persecuted the Christian religion. The Catholic Church, although holding the principle, "*Ecclesia non sitit sanguinem*," admitted and defended the right and duty of the civil power to punish heresy, as a crime and murder of the soul, with fire and sword.

The greatest divines, under the lead of Augustin and Thom as Aquinas, sanctioned the principle of persecution which condemned thousands of heretics to a cruel death, and made the annals of the Spanish Inquisition the most infamous in the history of cruelty.

The Reformation was the first breach in the external unity and exclusiveness of the Roman Church. But the reign of intolerance continued for a long time even among Protestants. Romanism and Protestantism fought for supremacy and excluded each other from their respective territories; and both persecuted heretics and dissenters, like Anabaptists and Unitarians. The burning of Servetus under the eye of Calvin was approved as a righteous act of the Christian magistrate by all the surviving reformers, even the gentle Melanchthon. The Lutherans and Episcopalians practiced intolerance and exclusion against all dissenters, Protestant as well as Catholic, as far as they had the power.

The principle of parity for Catholics and Protestants in one country and under the same civil government was first recognized in Switzerland (1531), and, after the terrible Thirty Years' War, in Germany by the Westphalia Treaty (1648), but confined to three parties (Romanists, Lutherans, and German Reformed). In France Henry IV. secured a legal status to the Huguenots, his former associates, by the famous Edict of Nantes (1598); but it was revoked by his grandson, Louis XIV., in 1685, who aimed at the complete annihilation of the Reformed Church. The government of Holland condemned and expelled the Arminians, at the Synod of Dort (1619), but recalled them after the death of Prince Maurice of Nassau (1625), and has since that time been a protector of religious liberty. In England, the conflict between prelacy and puritanism for exclusive dominion lasted till the fall of the Stuarts and the peaceful revolution of 1688, when William of Orange was called to the throne, and issued the Act of Toleration, which secured to orthodox Protestant dissenters, under certain restrictions, a legal existence and the right of public worship and self-government. The same right, with full civil privileges, was in the nineteenth century extended to Unitarians and Roman Catholics. The United States of America went a step further in the federal constitution of 1787 by abolishing "religious tests as a qualification to any office or public trust," and in the first amendment to the constitution (1789), by forbidding Congress "to make any law respecting an establishment of religion or prohibiting the free exercise thereof."

This principle of religious freedom and separation of Church and State is slowly, but irresistibly, making progress in Europe, and is becoming more and more an essential part of modern civilization. It develops the power of self-government which is inherent in the Christian Church. It favors, indeed, the multiplication of sects; but honest division is preferable to an enforced uniformity which breeds hypocrisy and infidelity. The principle of liberty secures also the possibility of a reunion of Christendom on the solid basis of freedom and voluntary consent.

LITERATURE.

Compare the literature in the preceding chapter.

ALEX. RUD. VINET (Professor of Theology in Lausanne, the modern Calvin, and the pioneer of the doctrine of religious liberty and the separation of Church and State as a guarantee for it; b. 1797, d. 1847): *De la liberté des cultes* (1826); and *Sur la manifestation des convictions religieuses et sur la séparation de l'église et de l'état* (Paris, 1842).

PHILIP SCHAFF: *The Progress of Religious Freedom as shown in the History of Toleration Acts* (New York, 1889, pp. 126). With the texts of the principal toleration Acts.

CHAPTER CCLXVI.

HOMILETIC OR KERYCTIC.

Homiletic is derived from $\delta\mu\iota\lambda\iota a$, intercourse, communion; instruction, lecture (from $\delta\mu\delta\varsigma$, joint, common, or $\delta\mu o\tilde{v}$, together, and $\iota\lambda\eta$ or $\tilde{a}\lambda\eta$, a crowd, a band). A *homily* designates usually only one kind of sermon, viz., a familiar discourse on a Scripture text, as distinct from an elaborate artistic oration ($\lambda\delta\gamma o\varsigma$) on a theme.

HOMILETIC OR KERYCTIC. 473

Keryctic is from κήρυγμα, κηρύσσω, the Scripture terms for proclaiming the gospel as a herald of God or Christ (κήρυξ, *præco*), Matt. 11:1; 12:41; Mark 1:38; Luke 11:32; Rom. 10:15; 1 Cor. 1:21; Titus 1:3; 2 Tim. 4:17; 1 Pet. 3:19; etc.

Homiletic is the theory of pulpit eloquence, or of preaching. It is rhetoric applied to the pulpit, or sacred rhetoric as distinguished from general rhetoric. It deals with the composition and delivery of sermons. The general laws of speech and delivery are the same, and have their origin in the constitution of our intellectual and moral nature, but they are modified by the subject and purpose.

Eloquence is the art of persuasion and conviction by means of speech. It is practical in its aim. Science acts upon the intellect, art upon the imagination, eloquence upon the will. Eloquence uses argument, illustration and appeal, with a view to influence the mind and produce action. It is logic set on fire. Hence the secret of its power lies in the intense earnestness of conviction, in the magnetism and electricity, of the speaker. Action, action, action is the first and last virtue of eloquence. Only a heart full of fire can kindle fire.

Of all kinds of eloquence, religious eloquence is the highest, both for its matter and aim. Preaching is a divinely appointed means of persuading, instructing, converting and saving men. A good and effective sermon is a communication of spiritual life. It is the testimony of truth in the name and by the authority of God. It goes to the quick of the conscience and to the mysterious point where finite man is connected with the infinite God. A preacher is a prophet who reveals the secrets of God's will and of man's heart. There is no greater work in this world than that of the preacher. It was the work of the Son of God himself.

Homiletic must deal first with the matter, and then with the manner, of preaching. The matter is taken from the Bible and Christian experience; the manner must adjust itself to the general laws of literary composition and effective delivery.

The word of God is the chief instrumentality for saving men. "Sanctify them through thy truth: thy word is truth" (John 17:17). "Being born again, not of corruptible seed, but of incorruptible, by the word of God" (1 Peter 1:23). "Of his own will begat he us with the word of truth" (James 1:18). This Word must be preached and heard. "How shall they hear without a preacher? And how shall they preach except they be sent?" (Rom. 10:15.) Conversions by the mere reading of the Scriptures are very rare exceptions. It is *living* Christianity proclaimed by *living* preachers that always has been, and will be to the end of time, the great missionary agency.

Preaching has a powerful rival in the daily press, but it keeps pace with it, and will continue with increasing power as long as men are born in time and for eternity, as long as they marry and are given in marriage, as long as they require nourishment for their spiritual hunger and encouragement in the struggle with temptation and sin, as long as they suffer in body and mind, and need comfort and an assured hope of immortality and glory in the face of death and the lonely journey to the other world.

CHAPTER CCLXVII.

DIFFERENT KINDS OF PREACHING.

Different wants and circumstances necessitate different kinds of preaching.

1. A plain testimony of divine facts and saving truths, with a personal application to the hearers. Such was the missionary discourse in the apostolic age. Peter's pentecostal sermon, simple, devoid of dogma and ornamentation, but earnest, pointed, forcible and most effective.

2. A homily, or expository and hortatory discourse on some portion of Scripture.

3. A regularly constructed oration with introduction, theme, parts and peroration, for public worship on the Lord's Day, and for special occasions. This is subject to all the rules of rhetoric, but its efficacy depends not so much on the observance of these rules as upon the vital truth and the vital force in its exposition and application.

French rhetoricians make nice distinctions between homilies, conferences, discourses, and sermons.

CHAPTER CCLXVIII.

HOMILETICAL HINTS.

1. A good sermon grows out of the secret communion of the soul with God, the study of the Bible and other good books, knowledge of human nature, and living intercourse with the people.

2. Prepare your sermon on your knees as well as at your study-desk, and reproduce it in the pulpit under the fresh inspiration of the audience.

3. Write out your sermons in full, or at least the leading thoughts. The Lord always rewards industry and faithfulness, but idleness and neglect have no promise.

4. A natural, clear, logical arrangement is half the sermon.

5. Commit the thought, if not the words, to memory, so as to be master of the manuscript, whether you read it or not.

6. The Bible supplies suitable themes and texts for all occasions. Like a laden tree, the more it is shaken the more abundant the fall of fruit.

7. The pulpit style is popular, direct, forcible and practical; not vulgar or superficial, but noble, chaste, dignified, and modeled after the discourses and parables of Christ.

8. Avoid all display of learning, and make your reading directly subservient to the practical aim. Think not of the few scholars and critics, but of the common people hungry for spiritual nourishment.

9. Aim at the conversion of sinners and the edification of believers.

10. Preach first to yourself before you preach to others, and your sermons will have double weight with your hearers.

11. Avoid personalities in the pulpit, and attacks on infidels, who are seldom present.

12. Make no apologies for Christianity, but take for granted that it is the truth and the power unto salvation. Suggest no doubts which might disturb devotion.

13. Preach Christ and his gospel, not dogma and theology.

14. Preach from the heart to the heart.

"Nothing which does not burn itself can kindle a flame in anything else." (Gregory I.)

15. Address your hearers as if it were the last occasion for you and them.

> "I preached as never sure to preach again,
> And as a dying man to dying men."—RICHARD BAXTER.

16. Honesty and earnestness rather than genius and eloquence are the secret of success in the pulpit.

17. Learn from all good preachers, but do not imitate any; be yourself, and work out your own individuality.

18. Aim to please God, and not men.

19. Be brief, and stop when the interest is at its height. The Sermon on the Mount, the parables, and Peter's pentecostal sermon were short. Brevity is the soul of a good speech as well as of wit. Long sermons must be justified by special occasions.

20. " Get up freshly;
    Open your mouth widely;
    Be done quickly." *

21. " Begin low:
    Proceed slow:
    Aim higher,—
    Take fire;
    When most impressed
    Be self-possessed."

22. After the sermon ask no one for his opinion; shut your ears against praise, but be open to censure from friend or foe; keep the blame to yourself, and give the glory to God.

23. Preachers whose sermons are worth studying: Chrysostom, Augustin.—St. Bernard.—Baxter, Jeremy Taylor, South, John Wesley, Robert Hall, Chalmers, Guthrie, F. W. Robertson, J. H. Newman, Liddon, Spurgeon, Alex. McLaren.—E. D. Griffin, John M. Mason, H. Bushnell, H. W. Beecher, R. D. Hitchcock, Phillips Brooks.—F. W. Krummacher, Theremin, Tholuck, Ahlfeld, Kögel, Gerok.—Bossuet, Massillon, Saurin, Adolphe Monod, Bersier.

---

* " *Tritt frisch auf;*
Mach's Maul auf;
Hör bald auf."—LUTHER.

CHAPTER CCLXIX.

HISTORY OF THE PULPIT TO THE TIME OF THE REFORMATION.

PANIEL: *Geschichte der christlichen Beredtsamkeit* (1839, only till Chrysostom and Augustin).—HOPPIN: *Homiletics* (1881), pp 13-242.—BROADUS: *History of Preaching* (1876).—CHRISTLIEB: *Geschichte der Predigt* (1888), in Herzog,[2] vol. xviii., pp. 466-653 (disproportionately long for an encyclopædia, but very valuable).—For the French pulpit: VINET: *Histoire de la prédication parmi les Réformés de France au xvii. siècle* (1860); VINCENT: *Histoire de la prédication protestante de langue française au xix. siècle* (1871); A. HUREL: *Les orateurs sacré à la cour de Louis XIV.* (Paris, 1873, 2 vols.). —For the English pulpit: KEMPE: *The Classic Preachers of the English Church* (1878, 2 vols.).—For American preachers: SPRAGUE: *Annals of the American Pulpit* (New York, 1866-69, 9 vols.; a 10th vol. remains unpublished).

The history of preaching runs parallel with the history of Christian worship and Christian life. Every age and every Christian nation has its own style of preaching. Chief among them are the Greek, Roman, French, German, English, Scotch, and American styles. Italy and Spain have few great preachers.

I. Apostolic preaching. Its theme: Christ the Messiah and Saviour from sin and death, crucified, raised up, and everliving. The gift of teaching (διδασκαλία) and the gift of prophesying (προφητεία). The extraordinary gift of tongues (γλωσσολαλία) on the day of Pentecost and in the church of Corinth was an act of worship addressed to God rather than to the people.*

The birthday of the Church was also the birthday of the Christian sermon under the inspiration of the Holy Spirit.

The sermons of Peter and Paul, in the Acts, are models for simplicity, spiritual force and wise adaptation to circumstances. Peter, addressing Jews, showed the fulfillment of prophecy in which they believed, and his pentecostal sermon resulted in the conversion of three thousand souls. Stephen's apology before the Sanhedrin is a good specimen of an historical sermon with a practical application. Paul, addressing the Greeks on the Areopagus, appealed to the religious consciousness and took his text from a heathen poet. He required of every pres-

* See Schaff, *Church History*, vol. i., pp. 230-243 and 436-439.

byter or bishop that he should be apt to teach (διδακτικός).
But preaching was not confined to ordained ministers. Every
disciple who had the gift of speech was an evangelist and told
the story of Jesus as the mariner tells of his rescue from shipwreck, and the soldier of his escape from death on the battlefield.

II. The ante-Nicene age. The oldest extant homily after the apostolic age is the so-called Second Epistle of Clement of Rome, from the middle of the second century, which has been recently recovered in full (1875). It is far inferior to the apostolic sermons and has no literary value, but is inspired by moral earnestness and strong faith. The unknown author, probably a Roman Christian, addressed the hearers as "brothers and sisters," and closes with this doxology: "To the only God invisible, the Father of truth, who sent forth unto us the Saviour and Prince of immortality, through whom also He made manifest unto us the truth and the heavenly life, to Him be the glory forever and ever. Amen."

Origen, the father of exegesis, is also the father of the biblical homily, as a running exposition and application of a Scripture text. He shows an extraordinary familiarity with the Bible, and introduced the ingenious but arbitrary method of allegorizing. He was invited, even before his ordination, by friendly bishops in Jerusalem and Cæsarea "to expound the sacred Scriptures publicly in the church," but his enemy, Bishop Alexander of Alexandria, disapproved of it; and preaching was afterwards forbidden to the laity and regarded as an exclusive privilege of the clergy, especially of the bishop. Even the deacons lost the right of preaching in the course of the third century.

From Justin Martyr we learn that the leading officer of the congregation read every Sunday a portion of the apostolic and prophetic writings and added in a free speech an exhortation and practical conclusion. Tertullian's moral essays on Prayer, Penitence, Patience, etc., closely resemble sermons, and are original, fresh, forcible and sententious, but often obscure. Cyprian was an elegant and popular preacher, but his sermons are lost.

III. The Greek Pulpit. The regular sermon as a work of rhetorical art dates from the Nicene age, and was modeled after the heathen orators, from Demosthenes down to Libanius. Basil the Great, bishop of Cæsarea in Cappadocia (d. 379), Gregory

Nazianzen (d. 390), Gregory of Nyssa (d. 394), John Chrysostom (d. 407). Add Ephraem (d. 378), the most fertile theological author, poet and preacher of the Syrian Church. The sermons of this period are more eloquent, theological and polemical than those of the ante-Nicene age, and partake of the virtues and vices of the heathen rhetoric in its declining stage. They abound in extravagant eulogies of martyrs and saints and the ascetic life.

John of the Golden Mouth (Chrysostomos), as posterity called him, is by far the greatest orator of the Greek Church, and the model of a fearless court preacher. He was a pupil of Libanius, but took Paul for his model. The sermons which he preached as presbyter at Antioch and as bishop at Constantinople are expository homilies on Genesis, the Psalms, the Gospels of Matthew and John, the Acts, and the Epistles of Paul. He delivered also discourses on separate texts of Scripture, on Church festivals, eulogies of apostles and martyrs, and twenty-one orations on the statues of the Emperor Theodosius and Flacilla, his wife (which in a popular revolt against the excess of taxation were thrown down and dragged through the streets of Antioch so as to enrage the emperor and endanger the destruction of the city). Chrysostom was not free from the defects of the artificial rhetoric of Libanius, and indulges in fulsome glorification of dead martyrs and living men; but he was mighty in the Scriptures, intensely in earnest, fruitful in thought, illustration and application, and fearless in rebuking vice in high and low places. He held his hearers spellbound to the close. They manifested their admiration sometimes by noisy applause, as in a theater, and when he protested against it they applauded all the more his eloquent rebuke. He was a martyr of the pulpit. When Eudoxia, the ambitious, intriguing and vicious empress, ordered the erection of her own statue in silver for public adoration, Chrysostom publicly rebuked the act on the commemoration day of John the Baptist, and let the imprudent words escape his lips: "Again Herodias is raging! Again she is dancing! Again she demands the head of John on a platter!" He was sent into exile, and died, as he had lived, giving "glory to God for all things." Dante assigns to him a place in Paradise at the side of Nathan the prophet, who roused the conscience of David to a sense of his great sin, but he did it by indirect preaching through a parable.

IV. The Latin Pulpit. Hilary (d. 366), Ambrose (d. 397), Augustin (d. 430), Peter Chrysologus (d. 450), Maximus of Turin (d. 465), Pope Leo I. (d. 461), and Gregory I. (d. 604). Augustin, who was helped in his conversion by the sermons of Ambrose and the singing of hymns, preached often daily, especially during Lent, without much preparation but never without prayer, on the Psalms, on the Gospel of John, on sacred seasons, and on different texts of the Old and New Testaments, from a profound knowledge of the Bible, and an equally profound experience of sin and grace.

Pope Leo is the first Roman bishop whose Latin sermons (ninety-eight in number) have come down to us. They are inferior to Augustin's homilies in originality and depth, but surpass them in elegance of diction. He celebrated annually his elevation to the chair of Peter by a memorial sermon in the full consciousness of the dignity and importance of his office.

Gregory I. followed Augustin, but moderated his theology in a semi-Pelagianizing spirit. His homilies on the Gospels, twenty-two on Ezekiel, and his allegorical, practical commentary on Job, together with his *Pastoral Theology*, were much used in the Middle Ages.

V. The Pulpit of the Middle Ages. This is comparatively meager, as the Church was engaged chiefly in the conversion of the barbarians, who had to be treated like children. Hence the sermons or homilies were mostly brief missionary addresses, or expositions of the Apostles' Creed, the Lord's Prayer and the Ten Commandments. Alcuin and Paulus Diaconus and others, by direction of Charles the Great, made collections of sermons (*Homilaria*) from Ambrose, Augustin, Leo, Gregory and others for priests, very few of whom were capable of preparing original sermons.*

The rarer the preachers, even among bishops, the greater was their power. Pope Urban II. roused the chivalry of Europe to the first crusade at the Council of Clermont (1095) by a sermon, after which the crowd unanimously broke out in the cry: " God wills it! God wills it!"

St. Bernard of Clairvaux (d. 1153) was the most eloquent and effective preacher of the Middle Ages. He preached to monks in the convent, to bishops and cardinals in the cathedral,

---

* Such sermons on the *pericopes* or Scripture lessons were read *post illa verba sacræ scripturæ*, and hence called *Postilla*.

to miscellaneous assemblies in the open air. We have nearly three hundred and fifty imperfect reports of his extemporaneous Latin discourses. His eighty-six sermons on the Song of Solomon, which to his mystic mind had peculiar attraction, read into this poem of love, by allegorical interpretation, the mysteries of Christian experience. The secret of his power lay in his holy personality, his pathos and solemnity, and the intensity of his conviction of the truth of the gospel. This humble monk with delicate and emaciated but graceful frame, pale face, fiery eyes, melodious voice, vivacious gestures, glowing love to God and man, exerted an irresistible influence over his hearers. Even the Germans, who could not understand his Latin or Romance language, felt the heavenly impulses vibrating on his lips. He spared neither emperor nor pope. He stirred up the half of Europe to the second crusade, which, however, turned out a disastrous failure which hastened his death. He glorified monasticism as the perfection of Christian life, mysticism as the true theology, the Virgin Mary as the mother of grace (though he denied the immaculate conception). He found Christ everywhere in the Old Testament as well as the New, and expressed his love for him in his passion hymns, and in his *"Jesu, dulcis memoria,"* the sweetest hymn of Latin poetry, which has been reproduced again and again in different languages. Dante, in his description of the heavenly Paradise, represents Bernard as a fatherly old man, clothed in light, sent by Beatrice to explain to him the Rose of the Blessed and to lead him to the beatific vision—the vision of the Holy Trinity, with which the *Divina Commedia* closes. For that consummation of bliss, Bernard prepares the poet by a fervent prayer to the "Virgin Mother, the daughter of her Son." Luther found in Bernard his favorite doctrine of justification by faith, and declared him the best preacher among the Doctors of the Church.

The most eccentric and naïve preacher of the Middle Ages was St. Francis of Assisi (1182–1226), a seraphic stranger in this world who was intoxicated with the love of God and man, and died of the wounds of Christ. He preached to the poor and the rich, before kings and popes, before the Sultan of Egypt at the head of the Mohammedan army, and sent forth his companions, two by two, in rough clothing, barefoot, without money, as messengers of the gospel. He loved all the creatures of

God, and preached even to the sun and the moon, to birds and fishes, as his brothers and sisters. He was the first to use the common Italian speech, instead of the Latin, for sermons and religious poetry.

His pupil, St. Anthony of Padua (1195–1231), preached with equal success, converted thousands, and is said to have been listened to attentively by fishes, as a Christian Orpheus.

The mendicant orders of the Franciscans (*Fratres Minores*) and the Dominicans (*Fratres Prædicatores*), in the thirteenth century, as also the order of the Augustinians, were founded especially for preaching the gospel to the neglected people in their popular tongue, and to counteract the heresies which had spread in Italy and France. The greatest popular preacher of the Franciscans was Berthold of Ratisbon (d. 1272), who traveled on foot as an evangelist in southern Germany, Switzerland and Austria, and addressed at times as many as 60,000 to 100,000 hearers in the open air. The Spanish Dominican, Vincentius Ferrer (1357–1419), preached often twice a day to great crowds in Spain, Italy and France, with marvelous success.

VI. The reformers before the Reformation preached in the vernacular tongues: Wiclif in English, Hus in Bohemian (Czech), Tauler in German, Savonarola in Italian.

Wiclif (d. 1384), the translator of the Bible and founder of English prose, opposed the biblical to the scholastic style of preaching, attacked popery and monkery, and established a society of poor traveling preachers, called Lollards, to counteract the mendicant friars. He died in peace, but his bones were dug up and burnt to ashes by order of the orthodox reformatory Council of Constance.

Hus accepted the doctrines of Wiclif and preached against the corruptions of the Church and the clergy, for which he was condemned to the stake by the Council of Constance (1415). His pupil, Jerome of Prague, shared the same fate (1416).

John Tauler (d. 1361) was the most edifying and effective of the mystic preachers of the Middle Ages, and was highly esteemed by Luther. His theme was the imitation of the lowly and humble life of Jesus.

Savonarola, an ascetic monk of extraordinary eloquence, aimed at a moral reform, in opposition to the heathen Renaissance of the Medici, without attacking the doctrines of the

Roman Church. By his flaming sermons at San Marco he shook the whole republic of Florence, and converted it into a short-lived republic of Christ; but he fell a victim to the wicked Pope Alexander VI. and was burnt to death (1498).

CHAPTER CCLXX.

THE PROTESTANT PULPIT ON THE CONTINENT.

The Reformation placed the pulpit above the altar, and gave rise to an unbroken and ever swelling stream of sacred eloquence which it would require volumes to describe, from Luther and Zwingli, Calvin and Knox, down to Monod and Bersier, Spurgeon and Lidḍon, Beecher and Brooks. The Catholic pulpit also received a new impulse from the Reformation, especially in Germany and France. We can only sketch the most prominent names.

I. The Reformers were preachers as well as scholars and writers, and their sermons were reforming agencies.

Luther (1483–1546), the creator of the modern German book language and German translator of the Bible, is also the founder of modern German pulpit eloquence. Many of his sermons, like his tracts, were deeds and bugle sounds in the battle with the pope and the devil; others are simple expositions of the Gospels and Epistles for the common people, who heard him gladly. Their chief theme is Christ as the only and sufficient Saviour, to be apprehended by a living faith which justifies, gives peace to the conscience, and overcomes the world. He had the rare gift of expressing deep thought in popular language, and of striking the nail on the head. He departed more and more from the domination of the allegorizing method which had prevailed since the days of Origen. His *Kirchenpostille* (1522, 1525) is still much read in Germany.

Melanchthon was not an ordained minister, but preached to students in the lecture-room and in his house in Latin (*Postilla*, 1549), and wrote three works on rhetoric (1519, 1535, and 1561).

Zwingli had acquired, before he became a reformer, a great reputation as preacher in Glarus and Einsiedeln, and was appointed papal chaplain, 1518. His sermons at the great Minster in Zurich, from 1519 to his death, in 1531, were biblical, plain, solid, sober, practical, impressive, more ethical than doctrinal. His object was "to preach Christ from the fountain," and "to insert the pure Christ into the hearts of the people." His method was to explain entire books, beginning with the Gospel of Matthew, so as to give his congregation a connected and complete idea of the life of Christ and the way of salvation. The people said, "Such preaching was never heard before," and, "This is a genuine preacher of the truth, a Moses, who will deliver the people from bondage." At Marburg he preached before a learned audience of Lutherans who could not understand his Swiss dialect a Latin sermon on Providence which he elaborated into a theological essay. Zwingli was also the model of a Swiss pastor and patriot, frank, manly, cheerful, kind and hospitable, took great interest in the education of young men and in all the affairs of the Swiss republic, and aimed at a political and moral as well as a religious reformation of his fatherland. His freedom in the choice of texts was followed in the Reformed Churches, while Luther adhered to the traditional *pericopes*, or prescribed Scripture lessons.

His fellow-reformers in German Switzerland, Leo Judæ and Bullinger in Zurich, Œcolampadius in Basel, Haller in Bern, Blaurer in Constance, Commander in Coire, were likewise useful, popular preachers.

The Reformers of French Switzerland were the first distinguished preachers in the French language. Viret was the most persuasive, Farel the most fiery, Calvin the most instructive among them. Amidst the incredible labors of Calvin in Geneva were his almost daily lectures and sermons. "During the week," says Beza, "he preached every alternate and lectured every third day." His sermons cannot be called popular, but they were thoughtful and didactic, and reveal his unsurpassed familiarity with the Bible. His friend and successor, Beza, a scholar of classical culture and poetic talent, was likewise an indefatigable preacher, but few of his sermons have been published.

Latimer was the principal preacher among the three English Reformers and martyrs, and kindled at the stake in Oxford, 1555, "with God's help, a torch in England which shall never be extinguished." Cranmer prepared, with Ridley and Latimer, the first Book of Homilies, 1547, to which Parker and Jewell added a second in 1563, to be read in the churches as substitutes for original sermons; but Cranmer's chief merit in the history of worship is the Anglican liturgy, which next to the Bible is still the richest feeder of devotion in Episcopal churches.

John Knox, the Reformer of Scotland, "who never feared the face of man," preached with such vehemence and force that he seemed "likely to ding the pulpit in blads [to beat it in pieces], and to flie out of it." The English ambassador wrote to Lord Burleigh that "Knox put more life into his hearers in an hour than six hundred trumpets." He found a worthy successor in the more learned Andrew Melville (d. 1622).

II. The orthodox Lutheran Pulpit of the seventeenth century introduced a dry, scholastic, artificial and polemical style of preaching. But it was counteracted by the Pietists and Mystics, and afterwards succeeded by the insipid moralizing preaching of the Rationalists. Mosheim (d. 1755), called the "German Bourdaloue," studied French and English models, and marks a new epoch in preaching, as well as in Church History.

III. The French Pulpit reached its golden age in the seventeenth century, both in the Roman and Reformed Churches.

(1) The restoration of classical eloquence was a part of the papal Counter-Reformation, and is represented by Bossuet (1627–1704), "the brilliant eagle of Meaux," equally distinguished as historian, controversialist and orator. He followed Chrysostom and Augustin, and surpassed them, not in depth but in grandeur and splendor of diction, especially in his funeral orations, which belong to the immortal masterpieces of French style.

The other luminaries of French pulpit eloquence are Bourdaloue (d. 1704), Fléchier (d. 1710), and Massillon (d. 1742). The last is distinguished for profound knowledge of the human heart, moral earnestness and rare boldness, which made even Louis XIV. "dissatisfied with himself." Fénelon (d. 1715), the gentlest, humblest and most amiable among the bishops of the age of Louis XIV, published few sermons, but expressed sound principles on preaching in his *Dialogues sur l'éloquence.*

(2) The Huguenot Pulpit was not far behind the Catholic in eloquence, and superior to it in biblical simplicity and depth.

Its flourishing period extends from the Edict of Nantes (1598) to its Revocation (1685). The latter almost annihilated Protestantism in France, but sent hundreds of its professors to other countries to bless them by their industry and piety.

The principal Huguenot preachers were Pierre du Moulin (1568–1658), Michel Le Faucheur (1585–1657), Jean Mestrezat (1592–1657), Jean Daillé (1594–1670), Moïse Amyraut (1596–1664), Raymond Gaches (1615–68), Jean Claude (1619–87), Pierre du Bosc (1623–92), Daniel de Superville (1657–1728), and especially Jacques Saurin (1677–1730). The last was preacher to the refugees in The Hague, where he addressed crowded audiences and commanded the admiration even of Roman Catholics.

The French preachers have been admirably characterized by Vinet in the work above mentioned.

(3) Modern Protestant preachers in France and French Switzerland:

Vinet of Lausanne (1797–1847) marks a revival of the theory and practice of pulpit eloquence and its literature in the French language. Adolphe Monod (d. 1856), minister at the Oratoire in Paris, was the greatest French Protestant preacher of the nineteenth century, full of faith and the Holy Ghost, and of captivating beauty of style, equal to the pulpit lights of the seventeenth century. Next to him should be mentioned Malan, Merle d'Aubigné, Coulin, all of Geneva; Coquerel, Ed. de Pressensé, Eugene Bersier, and Theodore Monod (nephew of Adolphe), all of Paris.

IV. The modern German Pulpit begins with the genial Herder (1744–1803), poet, historian, theologian, and court preacher at Bückeburg, and last general superintendent at Weimar, the contemporary of Goethe and Schiller. He emancipated preaching from the jejune, moralizing monotony of rationalism and infused into it his enthusiasm for universal humanity.

Lavater (1741–1801), the physiognomist, poet and preacher at St. Peter's in Zurich, represents Christianity as a matter of feeling and experience and living communion with Christ, which he has well expressed in his hymn:

"O Jesus Christ, grow thou in me,
And all things else recede."

Reinhard (d. 1812), court-chaplain at Dresden, "the inexhaustible," surpassed all German preachers of his age. His sermons fill forty volumes (1819-37).

Schleiermacher (d. 1834), a master of dialectical analysis of religious feeling, a preacher to the educated, the Plato of Germany.

Menken (d. 1831), Reformed pastor in Bremen, a master of expository sermons.

Claus Harms of Kiel (d. 1855), Lutheran, original, quaint, witty and fresh.

Dräseke (d. 1849), preacher in Bremen, and, last, bishop in Magdeburg, highly polished, and admired by cultivated audiences.

Theremin (d. 1846), court-chaplain in Berlin, the most polished preacher of Germany, faultless in style and thoroughly evangelical in sentiment.

Ludwig Hofacker (d. 1828), the most popular revival preacher of Würtemburg, and his brother Wilhelm Hofacker of Stuttgart (d. 1848), less popular but more learned and accomplished.

Gottfried Daniel Krummacher (d. 1837), pastor of the Reformed Church in Elberfeld, Calvinistic, severe, strictly biblical, but at times given to arbitrary typical allegorizing. His nephew, Friederich Wilhelm Krummacher (d. 1868), pastor at Elberfeld, then in Berlin, at last court-chaplain at Potsdam, the most eloquent pulpit orator of Germany, a painter in words, highly imaginative, dramatic, fruitful and suggestive. His *Elijah the Tishbite* has been translated into nearly all the languages of Europe and found a larger circulation in England and America than in Germany.

Tholuck (d. 1877), a model preacher for theological students, noble, thoughtful, spirited, polished, combining deep earnestness with warm feeling.

We can only mention in addition, Mallet of Bremen (d. 1865), Kohlbrügge of Elberfeld (d. 1875), Löhe of Bavaria (d. 1872), Nitzsch of Berlin (d. 1868), Wilhelm Hoffmann, general superintendent and court preacher at Berlin (d. 1873), Beck of Tübingen (d. 1878), Julius Müller of Halle (d. 1878), Arndt of Berlin (d. 1881), Ahlfeld of Leipzig (d. 1884), Gerok of Stuttgart (d. 1890), and Christlieb of Bonn (d. 1889), the author of a brief but comprehensive history of pulpit eloquence. Kögel, Stoecker, Dryander, all of Berlin, and Beyschlag of Halle, are among the best living preachers of Germany.

CHAPTER CCLXXI.

THE BRITISH PULPIT.

The English and American Pulpit is the richest of all, commands the largest audiences, and exerts the greatest influence.

The Reformation lasted longer in England than on the Continent, and extends from the breach of Henry VIII. with the pope and the appointment of Cranmer as Archbishop of Canterbury in 1532 until the Toleration Act under William and Mary, 1688. It may be divided into two great acts: the first was a conflict with popery till its final overthrow under Queen Elizabeth; the second was a conflict of Puritanism with semi-popery and despotism, and ended with the expulsion of the Stuarts, the re-establishment of the Episcopal Church, and a limited toleration for orthodox Dissenters. The second Reformation is the most stirring and interesting period in English history, and the golden age of the British Pulpit.

The Puritan Pulpit.

Baxter, Bunyan, and Howe are the chief heroes and also martyrs of the Puritan Pulpit, who after the Restoration of the Stuarts were ejected, exposed to poverty, fines, insult and imprisonment for no other crime than obeying their conscience, but who are still living forces in English theology and ascetic literature.

Richard Baxter (1615–92), the model pastor of Kidderminster, a promoter of peace between Prelatists and Puritans, Presbyterians and Independents, in an age of intense controversy, was the most learned and fertile author and most saintly character among the Puritans. He wrote one hundred and sixty books and tracts; the best are: *Call to the Unconverted* (of which 20,000 copies were sold in one year, 1657), *The Reformed Pastor*, and *The Saints' Everlasting Rest.* His sermons are solemn, searching and impressive; his style is clear and simple, but negligent and prolix. In his old age he dwelt more on the love of God and Christian charity, and "his sermons became hymns of praise." "His practical writings," says Isaac Barrow, "were never mended, and his controversial seldom refuted." He was in advance of his times in the principles of toleration and Church union. The notorious Chief-Justice Jeffries sentenced him to prison in 1685; but he was released after eighteen months through the exertions of a Roman Catholic nobleman, and lived to enjoy the Toleration Act of 1688, universally respected for his learning, courage and piety. Churchmen and Dissenters united in raising his monument at Kidderminster in 1875, and Dean Stanley of Westminster pronounced the dedicatory oration.

John Bunyan (1628–88), the unschooled tinker, preached in a Baptist chapel at Bedford, was silenced and imprisoned in Bedford jail for twelve years, and after his release continued to preach till his death. He was taught by the Holy Ghost through the Scriptures, a prophet in the apostolic sense of the term, bent upon the one aim—to save the souls of men by the simple power of the gospel. His most powerful sermon, however, is a religious novel or an extended allegory, *The Pilgrim's Progress*, which he composed in his prison cell. It has been called by Longfellow "the English *Divina Commedia*," and is one of the most popular books, if not the most popular, next to the Bible.

John Howe (1630–1706), called the "Platonic Puritan," the favorite chaplain of Cromwell, was a theological preacher, scholastic in form, abounding in learned and Latin phrases, but thoughtful, spiritual and broad.

Stephen Marshall, lecturer at St. Margaret's, Westminster, was the best preacher among the members of the Westminster Assembly, "the trumpet by whom they sounded their solemn fasts" (Fuller). He preached often before the Long Parliament, the Lord Mayor, and the Assembly. At the solemn fast, May 17, 1644, he prayed a sermon of two hours' length before the Parliament and Assembly. The religious exercises of that day, which the Scotch commissioner Baillie called "the sweetest day" he saw in England, lasted eight hours. Marshall was buried in Westminster Abbey, 1655, but shamefully disinterred with Cromwell and other Puritans after the Restoration.

The devotional fervor and endurance of the Puritan divines is almost without a parallel in the history of devotion. And yet if we consider the length of their prayers and sermons, their moral austerity, their peculiar phraseology and cant, their aversion to art and the innocent amusements of life, we need not wonder at the popular rebound to the opposite extreme under the frivolous and licentious Charles II., "who never said a foolish thing and never did a wise one."

The Episcopal Pulpit.

The Anglican Pulpit, or the Pulpit of the Established Church, which is still called national, but now represents only half of the nation, reached its height after the fall of Puritanism, in the latter half of the seventeenth century. It was in full sympathy with episcopacy and royalty, but had the benefit of Puritan training, and rebuked the immorality and vice which characterized the reigns of the last two Stuarts and which occasioned their final overthrow.

Jeremy Taylor (1613–67), the son of a Cambridge barber, chaplain to Archbishop Laud and King Charles I., appointed bishop of Down and Connor in 1660, has been called the Shakespeare of the British pulpit, and the Homer of divines, and his sermons "a garden of spices." He was gifted with a gorgeous imagination, not always controlled by reason and judgment, and was the most learned and brilliant preacher of his age, and as pious as any Puritan. His sermons are studded with classical quotations and allusions. During his exile under the Long Parliament, he advocated religious toleration in *The Liberty of Prophesying*, but changed his views after the restoration of the Stuarts.

Isaac Barrow (1630–77) preached profound and lengthy treatises on Christian doctrines and virtues, which are better fitted for reading in the study than for delivery from the pulpit.

Robert South (1633–1716), chaplain to Charles II., was a staunch royalist and prelatist, but at the same time a rigorous Calvinist and severe moralist, full of genius, wit and sarcasm, an unmerciful polemic, a master of trenchant English style. He had more grit than grace.

John Tillotson (1630–94), Archbishop of Canterbury, represents the Latitudinarian Pulpit. He was the son of a zealous Puritan, but under the influence of the Cambridge Platonists he became the most liberal churchman of the reign of William of Orange, who made him primate, against his inclination, and head of a commission for the reconciliation of Dissenters and the reform of abuses. Bishop Burnet says of him: "He was not only the best preacher of the age, but seemed to have brought preaching to perfection." He preached a mild, tolerant, undogmatic, yet evangelical Christianity, in easy, clear, almost colloquial style, and with the tact of a man cf the world. His sermons are free from learned quotations, artificial arrangement, endless subdivisions, and the whole pedantry of scholastic sermonizing. They were collected by his chaplain, Dr. Barker, and published in 1694, in fourteen volumes (3d ed. 1704), often reprinted, and translated by Mosheim into German.

The Methodist Pulpit.

The Methodist revival of the eighteenth century was the greatest religious movement in England after Puritanism, and produced a new line of great preachers, of whom Wesley and Whitefield are the chief. Their aim was the conversion and regeneration of sinners, and God crowned their labors with marvelous success. They differed in theology, but were one in heart and equally consecrated to their common Master. Wesley made the truth of Arminianism, Whitefield the truth of Calvinism, a converting agency. It was largely due to their labors that England was saved from the destructive wave of infidelity which swept over the Continent in the eighteenth century.

John Wesley (1703-91), of Puritan ancestry, a student of Oxford, and a preacher, organizer and spiritual reformer, lived, labored, and died in the communion of the Church of England, of which he was a presbyter, but became the founder of a new denomination which mediates between the Episcopal and the Nonconformist bodies, and has grown more rapidly than any Church, not only in England, but still more in the United States, where it outnumbers every other Protestant denomination. His sermons are short, plain, well arranged, pointed, doctrinal and practical. They preach a free and full salvation, sincerely offered to all. They are the chief theological and homiletical text-book of Methodist ministers.

George Whitefield (1714-70), a fellow-student and coworker of Wesley till 1740, when they separated on doctrinal grounds, was the greatest Calvinistic, as Wesley was the greatest Arminian, revival preacher of the last century. He had all the spiritual and physical qualities of a popular orator and dramatic actor. He was a genuine apostolic evangelist, who led thousands of hearers in Old England and New England to repentance and faith in Christ. He crossed the Atlantic seven times, and turned even the ship into a pulpit. His power was not in wealth or profundity of thought or in logical reasoning, but in the intense earnestness, pathos and solemnity, graceful and impressive delivery, and the vivid presentation of spiritual truth. It is said that "persons were driven mad with fear under his impassioned oratory." Even the sober, philosophic Franklin could not resist Whitefield's appeal for charity.

The English Pulpit of the Nineteenth Century.*

England has produced a large number of distinguished preachers during this century. We mention, among Episcopalians (low-church, high-church, and broad-church): Melvill, Stowell, MacNeil; Pusey, Newman, Keble, Manning, Bishop Wilberforce, Canon Liddon; Whately, Arnold, Maurice, Hare, Trench, Kingsley, Stanley, Robertson, Farrar. Among Baptists: Robert Hall, Andrew Fuller, John Foster, Spurgeon, Alex. McLaren. Among Independents: John Angel James, Thomas Binney, Alex. Raleigh, W. L. Alexander, John Stoughton, Robert William Dale, Henry Allon, Newman Hall, Joseph Parker. Among Methodists: Joseph Beaumont, Jabez Bunting, William Morley Punshon. Among Presbyterians: J. Oswald Dykes, Donald Fraser, W. G. Elmslie, Adolf Saphir (a converted Israelite). Among Unitarians: James Martineau, Stopford Augustus Brooke (who was formerly chaplain to the Queen, but left the Established Church in 1880).

We can only describe a few representative preachers in their leading characteristics.

(1) Episcopalians:

Henry Melvill (1798–1871), canon of St. Paul's Cathedral and Golden Lecturer on Tuesdays at St. Margaret's, was called "the evangelical Chrysostom." He confirmed the faith and ravished the ears of his hearers coming from the mart and the exchange, by the rich melody of his voice, sentence following sentence harmoniously, like wave upon wave. He selected unusual texts and handled them with great ingenuity. Christ shone out as the diamond in all his sermons.

John Henry Newman (1801–90), the master of poetic prose, and intellectual leader of the Anglo-Catholic movement towards Rome, preached his parochial sermons at St. Mary's in Oxford,

---

* George J. Davies, *Successful Preachers* (mostly Episcopalian), London. 1884. Also Kempe mentioned above.

before his secession to Rome, but they are still studied by Protestants, and his hymn, "Lead, kindly Light," will retain a favorite place in all English hymn-books.

Frederick William Robertson (1816–53) represents the evangelical Broad-Church School by his sermons, which combine intellectual strength with æsthetic beauty, the highest culture with deep spirituality and love of humanity and are well calculated to gain over thoughtful and honest skeptics.

Canon Henry Parry Liddon (1829–90) was the favorite preacher of the Ritualistic and Sacramentarian School which has grown out of the Oxford Tractarian movement. His university sermons are models.

Archdeacon Farrar (b. 1831) is the most fertile and exuberant living preacher of the evangelical Broad-Church School.

(2) Dissenters:

Robert Hall (1764–1831), minister of a Baptist chapel in Cambridge, though an intense sufferer from an acute disease, was one of the most powerful preachers of his day, full of thought, wit, and fancy expressed in racy English. His discourse on "Modern Infidelity" is a brilliant apology for Christianity and a masterpiece of English style. In theology he was a moderate Calvinist. When one of his hearers rebuked him for not preaching the five points of Calvinism, emphatically adding, "I believe in predestination," Robert Hall replied: "So do I. I believe you are predestinated to be a fool, and you have made your calling and election sure." When asked how many discourses a minister could write in a week, he gave this answer: "If he is a deep thinker and condenser, one; if he is an ordinary average man, two; if he is an ass, he will produce half a dozen."

Charles H. Spurgeon (1834–92), a strict Calvinist and liberal Baptist, was the most popular and successful preacher of his age in England, who for many years addressed from Sunday to Sunday five thousand hearers at the Metropolitan Tabernacle in London, and millions of readers in all parts of the world, pouring forth an inexhaustible stream of biblical and evangelical instruction and edification in homely, pithy and forcible Anglo-Saxon. He also founded and successfully conducted an orphanage, a theological seminary, and a missionary society. His influence for good far exceeded the limits of his Calvinistic creed, and of the English language.

The Scotch Pulpit.*

The Presbyterian Church of Scotland in its three branches, the Established or National, the United Presbyterian, and the Free Church, abounds in solid, instructive and fervent preachers. In no country is preaching better appreciated, and religious intelligence more general among the people, than in Scotland. The Presbyterian churches in London also and in the British provinces are well provided with preachers. Beginning with the Reformation, we may mention Knox, Melville, Craig, Bruce, Henderson, Rutherford, Dickson, John Livingstone, Gray, Gillespie, Leighton, Robert Douglas, Renwick, Ebenezer Erskine, Ralph Erskine, Hugh Blair, John Erskine, Thomas MacCrie, John Brown, Ralph Wardlaw, Irving, Chalmers, MacCheyne, Guthrie, Candlish, Norman Macleod, Marshall Lang, Principals Tulloch, Caird, and Cairns, James Hamilton, Donald Fraser, J. Oswald Dykes, John Ker, MacNeil, Alex. Whyte, Stalker, etc.

Edward Irving (1792–1834) was a friend of Thomas Carlyle, an assistant of Dr. Chalmers in Glasgow, and wound up his brilliant but erratic career at the Caledonian Church in London, where, by his commanding form, prophetic mien, musical voice, and flaming eloquence, he attracted men of the highest standing in Church and State, who listened with wonder to his orations on the oracles of God, till he was condemned by the presbytery of London for his views on the humanity of Christ (1830). He fell in with the voices of prophecy and the speaking in an unknown tongue, which gave rise to "the Catholic Apostolic Church," usually called after his name. To hear him repeat the Lord's Prayer was like listening to an exquisite piece of music. Thomas Carlyle regarded him as the victim of hallucination, but called him "the best man I have found in this world, or hope to find."

Thomas Chalmers (1780–1847), the leader of the heroic band who in 1843 sacrificed their livings for the great principle of the sole headship of Christ, and founded by a liberality without example the Free Church of Scotland, one of the most flourishing in Christendom, was a man of large heart, full of the

---

* For fuller information see Wm. Garden Blaikie, *The Preachers of Scotland* (Edinburgh, 1888); and William M. Taylor, *The Scottish Pulpit* (New York, 1887).

perfervidum ingenium Scotorum. His sermons contained generally a single thought, which he richly unfolded from center to circumference. They remind one of Ezekiel's vision of wheels within wheels of living creatures. The tendency to amplification and verbosity is overshadowed by the merits which made his pulpit at Glasgow and Edinburgh an inspiration to all English-speaking Christendom. He was a truly great and good man sent from God to revive and to re-establish Christianity in Scotland. He widened the sphere of the pulpit and brought it into contact with the culture and humanities of the age. He used science and philosophy as allies of the Christian faith and duty, and made the stars in heaven and the flowers on earth preach the gospel. He covered the Calvinistic theology with flesh and blood, extended the love of God to all mankind, and blended Christianity and philanthropy in inseparable union.

Thomas Guthrie (1803–73), who next to Chalmers did most in laying the foundations of the Free Church, and collected in one year £116,370 for the manse fund, was not the most intellectual, but the most poetic and pictorial speaker of Scotland, both in the pulpit and on the platform. His power of illustration was inexhaustible. He was also full of genial mirth and humor, but suppressed it in the house of God. He could have extemporized a sermon at any time, but he always carefully prepared himself. He minded the three P's—Proving, Painting, Persuading—that is, he addressed the reason, the fancy, and the heart. A Scottish elder thus described him: "Maister Guthrie! He never had to rummage long for a word. Lots of illustrations, frae the sea and the earth and the air and onything that cam handy. Illustrations—thousands—extraordinar—a ready wittit mon—I will say that—tall of stature—wi' a voice like thunder." Guthrie brought sunshine and fresh air, the spirit of the poetry of Walter Scott and Burns, into the Scottish pulpit, and showed that the gospel, as he used to say, is unfriendly to nothing in human nature except its corruptions. Like Chalmers, he was an ardent philanthropist, and took the liveliest interest in the neglected classes and "ragged schools."

Norman Macleod (1812–72), minister of the Barony Church, Glasgow, and a favorite chaplain of the Queen, was in his day the most eloquent preacher of the Established Kirk, and the shrewdest man in Scotland. He was a friendly and congenial rival of Chalmers, warm-hearted, broad and catholic in his sympathies, liberal yet thoroughly evangelical in his theology, and an enthusiastic advocate of missions. On his return from India he delivered, as Moderator of the Church of Scotland (1869), one of the most eloquent addresses on Missions which I ever heard. Dr. Blaikie, one of the last survivors of the Fathers of the Free Church, thus characterizes him: "Norman Macleod furnished a great contrast to the old moderates, in the intense fervor, the boundless sympathy, and the missionary enthusiasm of his character. A man of genius, and of great literary and dramatic power, it was his heart that made him a preacher, and the heart would hardly submit to the guidance of the head. Not seeing a way of reconciling the doctrines of the standards with that conception of the full and ever-diffusive love of God in which he delighted, he made the standards go to the wall. Neither Chalmers nor Guthrie, whose hearts were as large as his, had had to make any such surrender. But nothing could have been more admirable than the effect he gave in his latter years to his conviction that the gospel was good news for every creature. His visit to India and his ceaseless endeavors to rouse the home Church to a sense of missionary obligation form one of the noblest chapters of Christian biography, and claim the warmest admiration of every evangelical soul." *

CHAPTER CCLXXII.

THE AMERICAN PULPIT.

Sprague's *Annals of the American Pulpit*, above quoted (p. 477), contain about 1500 sketches of Congregational (vols. i. and ii.), Presbyterian (vols. iii. and iv.), Episcopalian (vol. v.), Baptist (vol. vi.), Methodist (vol. vii.), Unitarian (vol. viii.), Lutheran, Reformed, and other preachers (vol. ix.), from the earliest settlements down to 1855.

As all Christian denominations are represented in America, so also are all styles of preaching, in different languages, though prevailingly in English. The American Pulpit is untrammeled, aggressive, popular and practical. The gift of speech is very common in this free republic, and is early cultivated and stimulated by public life. The divinity which hedges the Greek and

* *The Preachers of Scotland*, p. 292.

Roman priest does not protect the Protestant preacher, who stands or falls with his personal character. No minister is respected who does not believe and practice what he preaches. Yet the clergy occupy a higher social position, are more respected and beloved, and better supported by the people in the United States than in the State Churches of Europe. No public men, except a few statesmen like Lincoln, and generals like Grant, have received such popular ovations as Henry Ward Beecher and Phillips Brooks, whose deaths were lamented as a national loss.

The press is a rival but also an ally of the pulpit, by publishing in the Monday issues the most popular discourses of Sunday, and thus multiplying their influence a thousandfold. This is not done by newspapers in Europe.

Puritanism and Presbyterianism take the lead in preaching as well as in theology, and are essentially Calvinistic and doctrinal. The Methodist and Baptist pulpits come next: less learned and intellectual, but more simple, emotional and popular. The pulpit of the Protestant Episcopal Church dates from its first two bishops, White of Pennsylvania, and Seabury of Connecticut, and the organization of that Church on an independent basis. The German churches, since the days of Mühlenberg and Schlatter, follow German models, but are becoming more and more Americanized and Anglicized.

The first generation of ministers in New England were mostly bred in English universities and had a scholastic style. The distinctive American preaching, however, began a century after the settlement of New England, with Jonathan Edwards (1703–58), who, together with Whitefield, led the great awakening of 1740. He thus united Calvinistic theology with evangelistic, Methodistic revival preaching. His sermons were hard and rugged in style, but carefully elaborated, full of deep and solemn thought, sustained by the purity and dignity of his character. They startled the conscience like the judgment trump of God, and resulted in many lasting conversions.

He was followed by a race of theological preachers, as the younger Edwards, Hopkins, Bellamy, Emmons, Dwight, Griffin, Charles G. Finney, Lyman Beecher, and many others. Their sermons are highly intellectual, doctrinal and instructive, like theological lectures, addressed to the head and conscience rather than the heart and affections.

Lyman Beecher (1775–1863), who labored as a Congregational pastor in Boston and afterwards as Professor of the New-School Presbyterian Seminary in Cincinnati, was a born orator, full of fire, and his discourses against intemperance and other moral evils produced a powerful effect. He was tried for heretical views on the doctrine of the atonement, but was acquitted (1835).

His more celebrated son, Henry Ward Beecher (1813–87), preached for forty years as an apostle of humanity, to an independent congregation in Brooklyn, "the city of churches," and we may say, to the whole reading world—ever fresh and ever new.* He was the most original, fertile and popular orator that America has produced, and shared with Spurgeon of London a world-wide fame and influence. He swayed an audience from the pulpit and the platform like a king, by enthusiasm, passion, argument, illustration, wit and humor. A perpetual spring of flowers seemed to bloom in his mind. He was a true poet in prose, but never quoted poetry. His preaching, like that of his father, was devoted to moral reform, and, like his sister's *Uncle Tom's Cabin*, prepared the public conscience for the abolition of slavery. His oratory reaped during the Civil War its greatest triumph in England, where he converted hostile audiences against their will. All his instincts were for freedom and progress. In theology, as far as he had any, he was independent of all systems.† He preached humanity and Christian morality rather than doctrine, but he was a firm believer in the divinity of Christ, who was to him the only God he knew. He belonged to no sect, but loved all who love Christ.

Horace Bushnell of Hartford (1802–76) published *Sermons for the New Life*, which are among the most original, brilliant and polished in the English language.

The same may be said of the *Discourses* of Professor Edwards A. Park (published in 1885). When he preached at Andover or Boston, it was a sort of event.

These were all Congregationalists of New England origin.

Next to the Puritan Pulpit is the Presbyterian, the Methodist, the Baptist, the Unitarian, and the Episcopal.

---

* He humorously said on his seventieth birthday: "My father gave me a healthy stomach, my mother dedicated me to foreign missions; but God had mercy upon the heathen and sent me to the Christians in Brooklyn."

† I heard him say in the pulpit: "Theology is nothing but logic stiffened and sanctified."

The most distinguished Unitarian preachers of New England are Channing, Theodore Parker, and Andrew P. Peabody. Among the numerous Presbyterian preachers should be mentioned Samuel Davies, John M. Mason, Erskine Mason, Archibald Alexander and his two sons, James W. and Joseph Addison, Charles and A. A. Hodge, Albert Barnes of Philadelphia, William Adams, Thomas Skinner, Roswell D. Hitchcock, and W. G. T. Shedd. Professor Hitchcock (d. 1887) left but few sermons in print, but was a consummate orator, unsurpassed in rich thought, terse, epigrammatic expression, and impressive delivery.

Among Methodist preachers we mention John P. Durbin, John McClintock, Bishop Simpson; among Baptists, Francis Wayland and Richard Fuller.

Phillips Brooks (1835–93) was by far the greatest pulpit orator of the Protestant Episcopal Church, and commanded the respect and affection of all other Churches by his evangelical catholicity and enthusiasm for humanity.

Among the preachers still living, we may mention the scholarly and accomplished Dr. Richard S. Storrs, who adorns a Congregational pulpit in Brooklyn, and is called "the American Chrysostom"; Lyman Abbott, the liberal successor of Beecher, and editor of "The Outlook"; and Thomas De Witt Talmage (b. 1832), a Presbyterian minister in Brooklyn, whose original, pithy and entertaining sermons are more widely circulated than any since the deaths of Beecher and Spurgeon.

Dwight Lyman Moody (b. 1837), a layman ordained by the Holy Ghost, deserves to be called the greatest evangelist since the days of Whitefield. Originally a Congregationalist and Calvinist, he belongs to no sect and to all sects, and unselfishly labors only for Christ and his kingdom. His truly Christian influence extends as far as the English language, and the fruits of his plain, direct, earnest and rousing sermons, full of Bible knowledge, wisdom, common sense and mother-wit, benefit all Churches.

CHAPTER CCLXXIII.

HOMILETICAL LITERATURE.

1. English works on the theory of preaching, by JAMES M. HOPPIN (New York, 1869), SHEDD (New York, 1869), JOHN A. BROADUS (Philadelphia, 5th ed. 1876), KIDDER (1864), R. S. STORRS (1875), HENRY BURGESS (1881), AUSTIN PHELPS (New York, 1882).

The Yale Lectures on Preaching, delivered in the Divinity School in New Haven by HENRY WARD BEECHER, PHILLIPS BROOKS, JOHN HALL, R. W. DALE, MATTHEW SIMPSON, WM. M. TAYLOR, HOWARD CROSBY, JAMES STALKER, R. F. HORTON, and others.

2. French works: A. VINET: *Homilétique ou Théorie de la Prédication* (Paris, 1853; English translation, Edinburgh, 1853).—M. BAUTAIN: *The Art of Extempore Speaking* (4th ed. New York, 1867).

3. German works on Homiletic by SCHOTT (Leipzig, 2d ed. 1828–49, 3 vols.), THEREMIN (1837), PALMER (6th ed. 1887), SCHWEIZER (1848), KRAUSS (1883), BASSERMANN (1885), CHRISTLIEB (posthumous, 1893, to be translated into English).

NOTE.—It has been my privilege during the last fifty or sixty years to hear some of the most eminent preachers of the age, who have deeply impressed me with a sense of the sublime mission of the Christian pulpit, and the variety in the unity as well as the unity in the variety of spiritual gifts in the service of the same divine Lord and Saviour. I may mention: Dann, W. Hofacker, and Gerok at Stuttgart; Tholuck and Julius Müller at Halle; Theremin, Gossner, Arndt, and Kögel at Berlin; Ahlfeld at Leipzig; Claus Harms at Kiel; Mallet at Bremen; F. W. Krummacher and Sander at Elberfeld; Gaussen, Malan, Merle D'Aubigné, and Coulin at Geneva; Adolphe Monod, Bersier, and Père Hyacinthe at Paris; Van Oosterzee at Utrecht; Hugh Stowell, Hugh MacNeil, Professor Maurice, Archbishop Trench, Dean Stanley, Canon Liddon, Archdeacon Farrar, James Hamilton, J. Oswald Dykes, and Spurgeon at London; Guthrie, Candlish, and Norman Macleod at Edinburgh; William Adams, James W. Alexander, Roswell D. Hitchcock, W. G. T. Shedd, G. L. Prentiss, Thomas S. Hastings, William M. Taylor, John Hall, C. H. Parkhurst, R. S. McArthur, J. R. Paxton, and Bishop Potter at New York; H. W. Beecher, Richard S. Storrs, Theodore L. Cuyler, and Thomas DeWitt Talmage at Brooklyn; H. Bushnell at Hartford; Edwards A. Park at Andover; and Bishop Brooks at Boston.

CHAPTER CCLXXIV.

CATECHETIC.

Catechetic is from κατηχεῖν or κατηχίζειν (κατά and ἦχος), to resound, to instruct orally; κατηχητής, teacher, catechist; κατηχούμενος, novice, catechumen, an applicant for church-membership in process of instruction. Luke 1:4; Acts 18:25; 21:22–24; Rom. 2:18; 1 Cor. 14:19; Gal. 6:6.

Catechetic is the science and art of religious instruction, preparatory to church-membership. It is based upon Pædagogic (Pedagogy), or the science of education, and applies it to religion. It embraces the elementary knowledge necessary for an intelligent profession of faith and obedience. It is usually confined to an exposition of the Lord's Prayer, the Apostles' Creed, and the Ten Commandments, or to an instruction how to pray, what to believe, and what to practice, in order to be useful on earth and to be saved in heaven.

The subjects of Catechetic are baptized children or unbaptized adults, proselytes and converts from other religions.

The first converts of Christianity were Jews, who by their knowledge of the Old Testament were already sufficiently prepared (Rom. 2 : 18), and needed only to be convinced of the Messiahship of Jesus of Nazareth. Hence the penitent hearers of the pentecostal sermon of Peter were at once baptized. The heathen were usually very ignorant. Even the educated and learned among them required more or less instruction in the fundamentals of religion. In large cities, special schools were founded for this purpose. The catechetical school of Alexandria became the first theological seminary, in which Clement and Origen taught.

In the early Church, catechetical instruction preceded baptism, and the same is still the case in all missionary fields. Where infant baptism is introduced, catechetical instruction succeeds baptism and looks to confirmation or some solemn act by which children, having grown up to the age of responsibility, ratify their baptismal vow made in their behalf by parents or sponsors, and are introduced to the rights and privileges of full communion.

Christ commands his disciples to teach all nations (Matt. 28 : 19). This includes children as well as adults. The importance of catechetical instruction was always admitted in the Christian Church. Ignorance is death to religion. Archbishop Ussher says: "The neglect of catechizing is the frustrating of the whole work of the ministry."

But catechizing is not the exclusive duty of the ministry, nor sufficient of itself to qualify for confirmation and the communion. The catechumen must give satisfactory evidence of repentance and faith. The compulsory system which requires all children to be catechized and confirmed is an abuse of State churches, and has created an unreasonable prejudice against catechetical instruction in the United States.

CHAPTER CCLXXV.

TYPICAL CATECHISMS.

The necessity of catechetical instruction gave rise to catechisms, especially at the time of the Reformation. Nearly all the Reformers, — Luther, Brenz, Justus Jonas, Œcolampadius, Bullinger, Leo Judæ, Calvin, Zacharias Ursinus and Caspar Olevianus, prepared such works.

We shall mention the chief catechisms, which have acquired symbolical authority and are still in use.

I. Luther's Catechisms, a large one for teachers, and a small one for children, were prepared in 1529 to meet the lamentable ignorance which then prevailed in Saxony and throughout Germany. The small catechism appeals directly to the heart, and is a model of childlike simplicity. It begins with the Ten Commandments (retaining the Roman division and abridging it); then follows an explanation of the Apostles' Creed, and the Lord's Prayer; to these three divisions are added two sections on Baptism, the Lord's Supper, and in later editions (since 1654) a sixth section on Confession and Absolution, or the Power of the Keys.*

II. The Heidelberg Catechism, prepared by Ursinus (a pupil of Melanchthon), and Olevianus (a pupil of Calvin), in 1563, for the Reformed Church of the Palatinate, hence also called the Palatinate Catechism, acquired great popularity among the Reformed Churches of the Continent, and has symbolical authority in the Dutch and German Reformed Churches in America. It represents a moderate, evangelical and irenical Calvinism. It is divided into three parts, following the order of the Epistle to the Romans: first, of man's sin; second, of Christ's redemption; third, of man's gratitude for redemption. It puts the Ten Commandments, as a rule of Christian life, in the third part, after the Apostles' Creed; while Luther reverses this order, and treats the law as a schoolmaster unto Christ. The answers express the knowledge and experience of a mature Christian. The admirable answer to the first question, "What is thy only comfort in life and in death?" strikes the keynote of this cate-

---

* See Schaff, *Church History,* vol. vi., pp. 550–557.

chism. It is less childlike, but fuller and richer and intended for a more mature age than that of Luther.

III. The Anglican Catechism (1549, enlarged 1604, revised 1661) is the standard catechism of the Episcopal Church of England and her daughters in the British colonies and the United States. It is the shortest and the most churchly of the leading Protestant catechisms. It begins with the questions, "What is your name?" and "Who gave you this name?" to which the answer is returned, "My godfathers and godmothers (sponsors) in my baptism; wherein I was made a member of Christ, a child of God, and an inheritor of the kingdom of heaven." Then follows a simple exposition of the Creed, the Decalogue, the Lord's Prayer, and the sacraments of Baptism and the Lord's Supper.

IV. The Westminster Catechisms, Longer and Shorter, prepared by the Westminster Assembly, 1647, are used in English-speaking Presbyterian and Independent Churches. The Shorter Catechism is a model of clear, precise, logical definitions, but lacks the glow of feeling, is more addressed to the head than the heart, and departs from the traditional order which makes the Apostles' Creed the basis of doctrinal exposition.* It begins characteristically with the question, "What is the chief end of man?" and the answer, "To glorify God and to enjoy him forever." It is impersonal, and gives the answers in the form of a theological definition embodying the question; while the other catechisms are addressed to the catechumen as a baptized church-member, who answers the questions of the catechist from his present or prospective religious experience.

V. The Catechism of the Council of Trent (1564) is intended for teachers rather than pupils. It is a compendium of Roman Catholic theology. It contains a full exposition of the Apostles' Creed (Part I.), of the seven Sacraments (Part II.), of the Decalogue (Part III.), and of the Lord's Prayer (Part IV.). It was prepared by three learned Dominicans, Leonardo Marini, Francesco Foreiro, and Ægidius Foscarari, with the aid of other theologians, and published by authority of Pope Pius V. It is the mother of a large number of shorter, popular catechisms in all languages.

* The Creed is added as an appendix, with a comment on the clause "he descended into hell," which is made to mean "he continued in the state of the dead and under the power of death until the third day." But "hell" in the Creed means "Hades," the spirit-world, the realm of the dead.

VI. The standard catechisms of the Orthodox Greek and Russian Church, Longer and Shorter, were prepared by Philaret (1782-1867), Metropolitan of Moscow, revised and sanctioned by the Holy Synod of St. Petersburg, 1839, and published in all the languages of the Russian Empire. The Longer Catechism, called "A Full Catechism," is an able and clear summary of Eastern orthodoxy, and is divided into three parts: (1) on Faith—an exposition of the Nicene Creed arranged in twelve articles; (2) on Hope—an exposition of the Lord's Prayer in seven petitions, and of the nine Beatitudes of the Sermon on the Mount; (3) on Love or Charity—an exposition of the Decalogue, as teaching, in two tables, love to God and love to our neighbor.

If we compare these catechisms of the leading Churches of Christendom, it is remarkable how much more they agree than they differ in all the essential articles of the Christian faith and duty.

CHAPTER CCLXXVI.

CATECHETICAL LITERATURE.

I. CYRIL OF JERUSALEM: *Catechetical Lectures*, addressed to catechumens in Jerusalem in 347 and 348 (κατηχήσεις φωτιζομένων, translated by Church, with preface by J. H. Newman, in the Oxford "Library of the Fathers").

GREGORY OF NYSSA (d. 395): *The Great Catechism* (λόγος κατηχητικὸς ὁ μέγας, translated by William Moore in Schaff and Wace's "Post-Nicene Library," Series II., vol. v., 1893).

AUGUSTIN: *De Catechezandis Rudibus*, and *De Doctrina Christiana*.

II. BISHOP CHARLES WORDSWORTH: *Catechesis, or Christian Instruction Preparatory to Confirmation and First Communion* (London, 1868; 2d ed. 1880).

A. J. C. ALLEN: *The Church Catechism: Its History and Contents. A Manual for Teachers and Students* (London and New York, 1892).

ALEXANDER WHYTE: *The Shorter Catechism* (Edinburgh, 1883).

ROBERT STEEL: *The Shorter Catechism, with Proofs, Analysis, and Illustrative Anecdotes* (London, 1884).

III. German works on Catechetic by PALMER (Stuttgart, 1844; 6th ed. 1875), ZEZSCHWITZ (Leipzig, 1872-74), KÜBEL (Stuttgart, 1877), PESTALOZZI (Zurich, 1884), PROBST (R. Cath., *Geschichte der katholischen Katechese*, Breslau, 1886).

A rich popular literature on Luther's and the Heidelberg Catechism.

CHAPTER CCLXXVII.

THE AMERICAN SUNDAY-SCHOOL.

Catechetical instruction is the work of the pastor, and trains for church-membership. It ought to be supplemented but not superseded by lay instruction in the Sunday-school. The American Sunday-school is a necessary addition to every well-organized church. It is the church for children, who are little benefited by public worship and require such praying, singing, teaching and preaching as is adapted to their childlike capacity. It forms the connection between the family and the church. From home to school, from school to church, from church to heaven. The Sunday-school scholars are divided into groups and instructed in the Bible and the Catechism by members of the congregation. The exercises are opened and closed by singing, prayer, and short addresses. This system gives an excellent opportunity to young men and women of the church for the exercise of their gifts for the benefit of the rising generation.

Robert Raikes, a pious and benevolent layman of Gloucester, England (1735–1811), a printer by trade, was the founder of the modern Anglo-American Sunday-school. Impressed by the need of the children in a manufacturing quarter of his city, he engaged in July, 1780, "four decent, well-disposed women," at a shilling a day each, to collect and teach children on Sunday in the A B C and the church catechism. He was assisted by Rev. Thomas Stock, the parish clergyman. In 1783 he called public attention to this movement in his newspaper *The Gloucester Journal*. This charity school became the fruitful mother of similar schools in England, but volunteers took the place of paid teachers. John Wesley incorporated the plan of Raikes in his religious reform movement. A Sunday-school society was organized in London, and multiplied schools throughout Great Britain in spite of the opposition of the Archbishop of Canterbury. A Sunday-school was organized in America in 1786 by the Methodist Bishop Asbury, and a Sunday-school society was formed at Philadelphia in 1791, out of which grew the national American Sunday-School Union in 1824.

In this country the Sunday-school is a vital part of the church itself, and is also the forerunner of the church in new settlements and neglected districts of large cities. It is a necessary supplement to the public schools, which make no provision for religious instruction. It is the main instrumentality for the religious education of the children of the vast host of immigrants. From America and England the institution has extended to the continent of Europe and foreign mission fields, and given fresh impulse to every kind of Christian work. It is supposed that about twenty millions of scholars were under the instruction of some two millions of Sunday-school teachers in 1890. This most benevolent and useful institution has created an immense juvenile literature of books and periodicals. Every denomination has, or ought to have, a Sunday-School Society and periodical, and every congregation a library for the young. The kingdom of God is built up out of the family, the catechetical class and the Sunday-school.

LITERATURE.

L. G. PRAY: *The History of Sunday-schools and of Religious Education, from the Earliest Times* (Boston, 1847).

W. H. WATSON: *The History of the Sunday-school Union* (London, 1853); *The First Fifty Years of the Sunday-school* (1873).

ALFRED GREGORY: *Robert Raikes, Journalist and Philanthropist* (London and New York, 1877).

JOHN H. VINCENT: *The Modern Sunday-school* (New York, 1877); *The Church, School, and the Normal Guide* (1889).

H. CLAY TRUMBULL: *Teaching and Teachers; or, The Sunday-school Teacher's Teaching Work* (Philadelphia, 1884); *Yale Lectures on the Sunday-school* (Philadelphia, 1888).

JAMES A. WORDEN: *The Bible-teacher's Guide; or, Methods of Work in the Sabbath-school* (Philadelphia, 1892).

Among the periodicals which have the largest circulation among all denominations we mention the *Sunday-school World*, and the *Sunday-school Times*, both published in Philadelphia.

NOTE.—The spread of Sunday-schools in Germany is due chiefly to the untiring activity of an American layman, Albert Woodruff (died 1891), who, without knowing a word of German, but aided by Mr. Broeckelmann, a retired merchant, traveled from city to city, and tried to persuade ministers and church dignitaries of the importance of introducing Sunday-schools. In the following year I had occasion to follow up his labors in company with Mr. Broeckelmann in the chief cities of Germany and to establish a flourishing Sunday-school in Stuttgart. On his return he founded in Brooklyn "The Foreign Sunday-School Association," and devoted the rest of his useful life to the spread and support of Sunday-schools all over Europe and in mission fields. He furnishes a striking example how useful a plain layman may make himself in the Church by single and unselfish devotion to one idea. In Germany, where catechetical instruction by the pastor is universal, the Sunday-school has assumed predominantly the character of a children's service (*Kinder-Gottesdienst*).

CHAPTER CCLXXVIII.

POIMENIC (PASTORAL THEOLOGY).

Poimenic (adopted by Van Oosterzee, Von Zezschwitz and Achelis) is derived from ποιμήν, pastor, shepherd, ποιμαίνω, to tend a flock, to rule, to nourish. The term "shepherd" is applied to God, to Christ, and to his ministers (Ps. 23:1; Ez. 37:24; John 10:16; 21:15–17; 1 Peter 2:25; Eph. 4:11, etc.). *Pastoral Theology.—Théologie Pastorale.—Pastoraltheologie; Theorie der kirchlichen Seelsorge.*

Poimenic or Pastoral Theology embraced originally the whole field of Practical Theology, but in the narrower modern sense it means the theory of pastoral care. It deals with the duties of the minister in his personal relations to the members of his parish as their spiritual guide. Pastoral visitation is, next to preaching, the greatest means of the usefulness of a minister. As preacher he instructs, exhorts and comforts from the pulpit; as pastor he meets them at home and in their daily occupations, administers to them spiritual counsel and comfort in time of need, especially in seasons of affliction.

Poimenic gives directions to the minister in dealing with different classes, the young and the old, the rich and poor, the sick and the dying, and his duty to the masses outside of the church.

LITERATURE.

The Poimenic literature is closely connected with Homiletic, which has been mentioned in chapter cclxxiii.

Special works by Gregory I. (*Regula Pastoralis*), Burgon, Patrick Fairbairn, W. G. Blaikie, Vinet (*Théologie pastorale*, 1854, translated by Thos. H. Skinner), Kidder, Shedd (in connection with his *Homiletics*, 1864; 8th ed. 1884), Hoppin (1885).

German works by Palmer (1860), Kübel (1874), Schweizer (1875), Steinmeyer (1878), Walther (St. Louis, 1885).

One of the most useful treatises is Richard Baxter's *Gildas Sylvanus; or, The Reformed Pastor* (1656). John Wesley made the reading of it one of the duties of his lay preachers.

It is very helpful for ministers to study the biographies of model pastors, such as Baxter, Sperer, Francke, John Wesley, Oberlin, Claus Harms of Kiel, Louis Harms of Hermannsburg, Löhe, John H. Wichern, Chalmers, MacCheyne, Barnes, Lyman Beecher, Spurgeon.

For a list of Roman Catholic works on Pastoral Theology see Kihn, pp. 469 sq.

CHAPTER CCLXXIX.

LITURGIC.

Λειτουργία (from λέϊτος, λήϊτος, λαός, λεώς, and ἔργον) means public service (*munus publicum*); in the New Testament a sacred ministration, Luke 1:23; Phil. 2:19; Heb. 8:6; 9:21; λειτουργός, an administrant or servant, Rom. 13:6; λειτουργέω, to officiate as priest, Heb. 10:11; to minister in the Christian Church, Acts 13:2.

The derivation from λιτή, λιταί, *preces*, whence the word *litany*, is erroneous.

Liturgic is the theory of public worship (λατρεία, *cultus*).

Worship is the highest spiritual act of man and the nearest approach he can make to the Deity. It embraces prayer with its various forms of adoration, petition, intercession, thanksgiving and praise; singing; reading of the Scriptures; preaching of the gospel; confession of sin and of faith; benediction; and the administration of the sacraments. The holy communion is the culmination of worship.

A complete system of Liturgic comprehends all these acts of devotion, discusses their nature, aim and proper order, and includes an account of sacred places and sacred seasons, especially the Church year. It describes the different modes of worship: the Greek, Latin, Anglican, Lutheran, and Reformed.

Homiletic and Catechetic are usually omitted from Liturgic, and separately treated.

CHAPTER CCLXXX.

LITURGICAL LITERATURE.

I. Collections:

H. A. DANIEL (d. 1871; the most learned Lutheran liturgist): *Codex Liturgicus Ecclesiæ Universæ in Epitomen Redactus* (Leipzig, 1847–53, 4 vols.; vol. i. contains the Roman, vol. ii. the Lutheran, vol. iii. the Reformed, vol. iv. the Oriental Liturgies).

FR. J. MONE (Roman Catholic): *Lateinische und Griechische Messen aus dem 2ten bis 6ten Jahrhundert* (Frankfurt-a-M., 1850; with valuable treatises on the Gallican, African, and Roman Mass).

J. M. NEALE (d. 1866; the most learned Anglican ritualist and liturgist, who studied the Eastern liturgies daily for thirty years, and almost knew them by heart): *Tetralogia Liturgica; sive S. Chrysostomi, S. Jacobi, S. Marci Divinæ Missæ; quibus accedit ordo Mozarabicus* (London, 1849). The same : *The Liturgies of S. Mark, S. James, S. Clement, S. Chrysostom, S. Basil, or according to the use of the Churches of Alexandria, Jerusalem, Constantinople* (London, 1859 ; in the Greek with an English translation and an introduction and appendices).

C. E. HAMMOND : *Ancient Liturgies* (Oxford and London, 1878).
C. A. SWAINSON : *The Greek Liturgies* (Cambridge 1884).
The Greek *Menæa* in 12 vols.
The *Missale Romanum* in many Latin editions.—The *Pontificale Rom.* in 3 vols.—The *Breviarium Romanum*, Eng. translation by John Marquis of Bute (Edinburgh and London, 1879, 2 vols.).
Older liturgical collections by Goar, 1647, Assemani, 1749–66 (13 vols.), Muratori, 1748 (2 vols.).

II. Works on the theory of worship :

H. A. KÖSTLIN : *Geschichte des christlichen Gottesdienstes* (Freiburg i.B., 1887).

The *Christian Antiquities* of BINGHAM, BINTERIM, SIEGEL, SMITH and CHEETHAM, BENNETT, quoted on p. 280.

On the Anglican Liturgy, see the works of PROCTER, BLUNT, BUTLER, LUCKOCK, and W. R. HUNTINGTON (1893). For the American changes see Bishop White's *Memoirs*, and the Proceedings of the General Convention of the Protestant Episcopal Church, held at Baltimore, 1892.

CHAPTER CCLXXXI.

WORSHIP AND ART.

Worship is closely related to art and calls it into the service of religion. There is a sacred architecture, sacred sculpture, sacred painting, sacred poetry, and sacred music, and all have a history full of deep interest.

God is the author of beauty, as well as of truth and goodness. There can be no more essential antagonism between religion and art than between religion and science. All emanate alike from God and must return to God in harmony.

It is true that religion is independent of art. It can even dispense with church buildings and chapels. God may be worshiped anywhere and at all times. Christ prayed and preached on the mountain, under the canopy of heaven, as well as in the synagogue and in the temple. And for three hundred years, and often since, in times of persecution, the Christians held their services in the humblest places. But the regular public worship requires certain fixed seasons and buildings.

With the progress of the Church and civilization, all the fine arts were drawn into the service of devotion. Poetry and music were from the beginning intimately connected with worship, and form an important part of Liturgic.

CHAPTER CCLXXXII.

HYMNOLOGY.

Hymnology is the theory of sacred poetry as a part of public worship. In close connection with it is the theory of sacred music. Both are sanctioned in the Bible. "Sing unto the Lord a new song: sing unto the Lord, all the earth" (Ps. 96:1). "Admonish one another with psalms and hymns and spiritual songs" (Col. 3:16; Eph. 5:19).

Poetry and Music are twin sisters of heavenly descent, and the highest and most spiritual of the fine arts. They are handmaids of religion, and give wings to devotion. More than one third of the Old Testament is poetry: the Psalter, the Book of Job, the Proverbs, the Song of Songs, and the greater part of the prophetical literature, besides a number of lyric songs scattered through the historical books. The Psalter was the hymn- and tune-book of Israel; it passed into the worship of the Christian Church and assumed a new and deeper meaning in the light of the gospel salvation. The advent of Christ was preceded and accompanied by sacred poetry. The *Magnificat* of the Virgin Mary, the *Benedictus* of Zacharias, the *Gloria in Excelsis* of the angelic host, and the *Nunc Dimittis* of Simeon are the last of Hebrew psalms and the first of Christian hymns. They struck the keynote for the history of Christian hymnody.

A hymn is a popular lyric poem on a religious theme adapted for singing. It is prayer and praise in the Sunday language of poetry. It differs from other forms of lyric poetry, as the ode, the elegy, the ballad, and the sonnet, by its simple, pure and melodious language, and its adaptation to music. It is to the church what the folk-song (*Volkslied*) is to the nation. It is the highest flower of Christian life arrayed in a festal garb of beauty. It gives expression to the deepest feelings and highest aspirations of the human heart, and is one of the most powerful helps to private and public devotion. A genuine hymn never grows old. The *Gloria in Excelsis* and the *Te Deum* will be sung to the end of time with undiminished fervor and delight.

Hymns, like the Bible, are not sectarian, but truly Christian and catholic. They belong to the whole Church. They represent the unity of the faith and the communion of saints. This is especially true of the hymns on Christ, the common object of worship to all Christians, before whom the discords of rival theologies and rival Churches are hushed into silence.

A student for the ministry, and every Christian as well, should store the memory with the choicest hymns and Bible passages. They will be to them an unfailing source of comfort, especially in lonely hours, in the night watches, on journeys, and in seasons of affliction. Hymns drive away melancholy and evil spirits. They are angels or ministering spirits "sent forth to do service for the sake of them that shall inherit salvation" (Heb. 1:14).

CHAPTER CCLXXXIII.

HISTORY OF HYMNODY.

The history of hymnody is one of the most interesting branches of Church History, and equally important for the development of worship and Christian life, but has only of late begun to be cultivated. It is like a garden filled with fragrant flowers. It exhibits piety in its purest forms. Many hymns have a rich history of their own, which is written in the biographies of saints.

I. Greek hymnody. It began with an amplified *Gloria in Excelsis* (Luke 2:14) and reached its classical period during the Iconoclastic Controversy between 650 and 820. Pliny wrote to Trajan, at the beginning of the second century, that the Christians were in the habit on Sunday, early in the morning, of singing songs to Christ as their God. Clement of Alexandria wrote a poem of praise to Christ as the Shepherd of children. The hymns of the post-Nicene age celebrate the Holy Trinity, the Incarnation, and the great Church festivals, but also the worship of the Virgin Mary, the martyrs and saints, and the sacred icons, in a manner that offends Protestant taste. They are incorporated in the ritual books, especially the twelve volumes of *Menæa*, which contain the daily devotions and correspond to the Latin Breviary. The Greek hymns, like the Psalms, are written in rhythmical prose for chanting. The chief hymnists are Gregory Nazianzen (d. 390), Anatolius (d. 458), St. John of Damascus (d. after 750), his friend and fellow-monk St. Cosmas of Jerusalem, called "the Melodist" (d. 760), St. Theophanes (d. 820), Andrew of Crete (d. 732), Stephen of Marsaba (d. 794). The last is well known to English readers by Neale's free reproduction of his touching expansion of the Saviour's invitation, "Come unto me":

"Art thou weary, art thou languid."

Ephraem Syrus (d. 378) is the father of Syriac hymnody.

II. Latin hymnody may be divided into three periods:

(1) The patristic period extends from Hilary (d. 368) and Ambrose (d. 397) to Venantius Fortunatus (d. 609) and Pope Gregory I. (d. 604). Its most precious legacy to the Church universal is the *Te Deum Laudamus*, popularly ascribed to Ambrose of Milan, but of later date. Augustin informs us how deeply he was moved by the hymns and canticles in the church of Milan: "Those strains flowed into mine ears, and the truth distilled into my heart. My feelings of piety were enkindled, and tears fell from my eyes." Prudentius (d. 409) was the best hymn writer of Spain. Fortunatus of Poitiers in France is the author of the famous musical passion hymns: *Vexilla Regis prodeunt*, and *Pange, lingua, gloriosi prœlium certaminis*.

(2) From the second period, extending to the twelfth century, we have two famous pentecostal hymns, of uncertain authorship, addressed to the Holy Spirit: *Veni, Creator Spiritus*, and *Veni, Sancte Spiritus*. Notker Balbulus of St. Gall (840–912) is the father of the sequences in rhythmic prose (e.g., *Media in vita in morte sumus*, "In the midst of life we are in death").

(3) The third period embraces the greatest Latin hymnists, as Bernard of Morlaix (monk of Cluny, about 1150), Bernard of Clairvaux (d. 1153), Adam of St. Victor (d. 1192), Bonaventura (d. 1274), Thomas Aquinas (d. 1274), Thomas à Celano (about 1250), Jacopone (d. 1306). It produced the best Catholic hymns, some of which have been received into the Breviary and the daily devotions of the priests. The *Jesu, dulcis memoria* is the sweetest, the *Stabat Mater* the most pathetic, the *Dies Iræ* the most sublime, hymn in the Latin or any language. They have been often translated and imitated, but never

equaled. It must be added, however, that the mediæval hymnody of the Latin, as well as of the Greek Church, abounds in Mariolatry and hagiolatry. Some hymns virtually put the Virgin in the place of Christ as the fountain of all grace.

III. German hymnody is the richest of all, and numbers more than a hundred thousand hymns, of which more than one thousand have outlived their generation. The German hymns before the Reformation were translations from the Latin. Luther struck the keynote of evangelical hymnody with his triumphant pæan of the Reformation,

"Ein' feste Burg ist unser Gott."

For a sketch of German hymnody I must refer to my article in Julian's *Dictionary of Hymnology* (pp. 412–419).

IV. English hymnody. The Churches of England and Scotland, like the Reformed Churches on the Continent, for nearly two hundred years used metrical versions of the Psalms and Scripture Paraphrases in public worship. Sternhold and Hopkins (1551), Rouse (1646), Tate and Brady (1696).

The fathers of English hymnody are Bishop Ken (d. 1711), the author of a morning and evening hymn, with the classical doxology, "Praise God from whom all blessings flow"; Isaac Watts, an Independent minister (1674–1748), who furnished the richest supply for English hymnals; and Charles Wesley (1708–88), who wrote over five thousand lyric pieces, of which the most popular is "Jesus, Lover of my soul." His brother, John (1703–91), was also no mean poet, and a translator of German hymns. Methodism was sung into the hearts of the people. But the Calvinistic Toplady (1740–78) equaled any of the Methodist hymns by his immortal

"Rock of Ages, cleft for me."

The second period of English hymnody dates from the "Olney Hymns," the joint production of John Newton and William Cowper (a genuine poet), first published in 1779, and ends with Bishop Heber's missionary hymn, "From Greenland's icy mountains" (1827).

The third period dates from the Oxford revival of Anglo-Catholicism, and is marked by John Keble, the author of the "Christian Year" (1827); J. H. Newman, who wrote his exquisite "Lead, kindly Light" in an orange boat sailing from

Palermo to Marseilles (1833), twelve years before his secession to Rome; F. W. Faber ("O gift of gifts! O grace of faith!"); and by John Mason Neale, the most successful reproducer of Greek and Latin hymns. Miss Winkworth, Miss Cox, Arthur J. Russell, and Massie have added translations of many German hymns, from Luther down to Spitta.

Churchmen and Dissenters of all schools, from Calvinism and Anglo-Catholicism to Unitarianism, have contributed to this treasury of devotion.

The Scotch have longest adhered to the exclusive use of the Psalms in divine worship. Horatius Bonar (1808–89) is a most prolific and popular Scottish hymnist, although he would not permit any of his hymns to be sung in his church. He wrote, "I heard the voice of Jesus say," "I was a wandering sheep," and "Beyond the smiling and the weeping." Miss Jane Bothwick and her sister Sarah Findlater, of the Free Church, who published *Hymns from the Land of Luther*, have enriched English hymnody by choice reproductions of German hymns, among which Schmolke's "My Jesus, as Thou wilt" has become a universal favorite in America.

V. American hymnody follows closely that of England and Scotland, and has added hymns which will live, such as, "I love thy kingdom, Lord" by Dr. Timothy Dwight (d. 1817); "My faith looks up to thee," and "Jesus, thou joy of loving hearts" by Ray Palmer (d. 1887); "Softly now the light of day" by George W. Doane (d. 1859); "Trembling before thine awful throne" by Augustus L. Hillhouse (d. 1859); "Gently, Lord, O gently lead us," and "Saviour, I look to thee" by Thomas Hastings (d. 1872); "I would not live alway," and "Like Noah's weary dove" by William Augustus Muhlenberg (d. 1877); "One sweetly solemn thought" by Phœbe Cary (d. 1871); "O where are kings and empires now?" and "When o'er Judea's vales and hills" by Arthur C. Coxe (b. 1818); "Stand up, stand up for Jesus" by George Duffield (d. 1888); "More love to thee, O Christ" by Mrs. Elizabeth Prentiss (d. 1878); "Jesus, I live to thee" by Henry Harbaugh (d. 1867); "At the door of mercy sighing" by Thomas McKellar (b. 1812); "O deem not, they are blessed alone" by W. C. Bryant (d. 1878); "Jesus, Saviour, pilot me" by E. Hopper (d. 1890); "Immortal Love! forever full" by John G. Whittier, the Quaker poet (d. 1892); "O Love Divine that stooped to share" by Oliver Wendell Holmes; and the patriotic hymn of Samuel F. Smith, "My country, 'tis of thee," written in 1832. James W. Alexander (d. 1859) deserves a place among the best translators of German hymns, especially of Paul Gerhardt's "O sacred Head, now wounded." The same is true of Dr. Thomas C. Porter.

The English and American hymnody now numbers nearly 50,000 hymns, and is likely to increase faster in the future than the German hymnody.

VI. We have no space for the French, Dutch, Scandinavian, and Bohemian hymnody. The French Protestants still use Clément Marot's psalter, finished by Beza (1541, 1562, etc.), with Goudimel's sweet music. Modern French hymnody dates from César Malan of Geneva (1787–1864), who wrote about one thousand hymns and composed several popular tunes. He was followed by Alexander Vinet, Adolphe Monod, Ami Bost, H. Empaytaz, Merle d'Aubigné, Felix Neff, Henri Lutteroth.

CHAPTER CCLXXXIV.

HYMNOLOGICAL LITERATURE.

I. Collections:

WILHELM CHRIST and M. PARANIKAS: *Anthologia Græca Carminum Christianorum* (Lips. 1871). The Greek text with Latin Prolegomena.

H. A. DANIEL (d. 1871): *Thesaurus Hymnologicus* (Lips. 1841-56, 5 tom.; vols. i., ii., iv., and v. contain Latin, vol. iii. Greek and Syrian hymns).

F. J. MONE: *Lateinische Hymnen* (Freiburg i.B., 1353, 3 vols.).

J. M. NEALE: *Hymns of the Eastern Church* (London, 1862; new ed. 1876); *Mediæval Hymns and Sequences* (London, 1862; 3d ed. 1867). Several of these free versions have passed into all modern English hymn-books.

EDWARD CASWALL (Anglican; joined the Roman Church in 1847; d. 1878): *Lyra Catholica, containing all the Breviary and Missal Hymns, together with Some Other Hymns* (London, 1849; New York, 1851; admirable translations).

PHILIP WACKERNAGEL (d. 1877): *Das deutsche Kirchenlied von der ältesten Zeit bis zum Anfang des xvii. Jahrhunderts* (Leipzig, 1864-77, 5 vols.; the last vol. edited by his two sons). A monumental collection of older German hymns; the first volume contains Latin hymns and sequences from the fourth to the sixteenth century.

ALBERT KNAPP: *Evangelischer Liederschatz* (Stuttgart, 3d ed. 1885).

PHILIP SCHAFF: *Christ in Song; Hymns of Immanuel Selected from All Ages, with Notes* (New York, 1868; London, 1879). SCHAFF and GILMAN: *A Library of Religious Poetry* (New York and London, 1884).

Of the numerous German hymn-books in use may be mentioned that of PHILIP SCHAFF: *Deutsches Gesang- und Choralbuch*, with notes on the authors, value and history of the hymns (Philadelphia and Cleveland, 1859; revised and enlarged, 1874, etc.).

II. Historical works on hymnology:

JOHN JULIAN: *A Dictionary of Hymnology, setting forth the Origin and History of Christian Hymns of all Ages and Nations* (London and New York, 1892, 616 pp.). The best general work on hymnology in the English or any other language, with contributions from a large number of specialists.

1. The Poetry of the Bible by PHILIP SCHAFF in his *Literature and Poetry* (New York, 1890, pp. 63–133). The literature is given on pp. 131–133. The principal writers on Hebrew poetry are Lowth, Herder, and Ewald.

2. On Greek hymnology: PHILIP SCHAFF: *Church History*, vol. iii., pp. 575 sqq.; vol. iv., pp. 402 sqq., and the literature there quoted.

3. On Latin hymnology: TRENCH: *Sacred Latin Poetry* (London, 2d ed. 1864). SCHAFF, *Church Hist.*, vol. iii., pp. 585 sqq., and vol. iv., pp. 416 sqq. Special discussions of the *Dies Iræ, Stabat Mater*, and St. Bernard's Hymns, in his *Literature and Poetry* (New York, 1890), pp. 134–255.

S. W. DUFFIELD: *The Latin Hymn-Writers and Their Hymns* (New York, 1889).

4. On German hymnology: ED. EMIL KOCH: *Geschichte des Kirchenlieds und Kirchengesangs in der christlichen, insbesondere der deutschen evangelischen Kirche* (Stuttgart, 3d ed. revised and enlarged, 1866-76, 8 vols.; vol. viii. by R. Lauxmann).

C. A. BECK: *Geschichte des katholischen Kirchenliedes von seinen ersten Anfängen bis auf die Gegenwart* (Köln, 1878).

A. F. W. FISCHER: *Kirchenlieder-Lexicon* (Gotha, 1878–79, 2 vols.; supplement, 1886, contains an alphabetical list of 4500 hymns with literary notes).

5. On English hymnology:

JOSIAH MILLER: *Singers and Songs of the Church* (London, 1869).

E. F. HATFIELD (d. 1883): *The Poets of the Church* (New York, 1884).

S. W. DUFFIELD: *English Hymns; Their Authors and History* (New York, 1884).

Also JULIAN, above quoted, and H. S. BURRAGE: *Baptist Hymn-Writers;* HUTTER: *The Annotated Methodist Hymnal;* JAMES KING: *Anglican Hymnology.*

The Union Theological Seminary in New York has a rich hymnological library, especially of English and American hymn-books, including over three hundred volumes purchased from Daniel Sedwick in London, and the collections of Hatfield (presented) and Bird (bought).

CHAPTER CCLXXXV.

EVANGELISTIC.

Evangelistic is a new term for a new science, from εὐαγγελίζω, or εὐαγγε-λίζομαι, *evangelizo* (Vulg.), to *evangelize*, to bring glad tidings (of the Messianic blessings, of the Christian salvation), often used in the Septuagint and the Greek Testament. The term εὐαγγελιστής, *evangelista* (Vulg.), a *bringer of good tidings*, is given to the heralds of salvation through Christ, or itinerant preachers who were not apostles, but acted under their direction in different places, such as Philip, Timothy, Titus, Silas, Luke (Acts 21 : 8; Eph. 4 : 11; 2 Tim. 4 : 5). Every apostle is an evangelist, but not every evangelist is an apostle. The same term was used afterwards for the writers of the four canonical Gospels.

Evangelistic is the science of Missions (*Missionswissenschaft*), that is, of the propagation of Christianity at home and abroad. It is a new branch of theological learning, demanded by the growing zeal in missions.

Christianity is a missionary religion and looks to the conversion of the world. Christ commanded his disciples to preach the gospel to every creature and to make disciples of all nations.* In connection with this command he said: "All authority has been given unto me in heaven and on earth." He illustrates the progress of the kingdom of heaven by the twin parables of the mustard-seed and the leaven.†

The missionary activity of the Church embraces the following divisions:

I. Missions among the heathen or idolaters: barbarian, semi-civilized and civilized.

II. Missions among the Jews.

III. Missions among the Mohammedans.

IV. Home Missions in neglected parts of Christian countries and among immigrants. Especially important in America.

V. Inner Mission. In Germany (since Wichern) it includes the revival of dead Christianity, and philanthropic and benevolent institutions. Young Men's Christian Associations, Christian Endeavor Societies, etc. The labors of Moody, and other evangelists.

* Mark 16 : 15; Matt. 28 : 19, comp. Matt. 24 : 14; Luke 24 : 47; Rom. 11 : 25.

† Matt. 13 : 31–33.

VI. City Missions. A special branch of Home and Inner Missions among the modern heathen and barbarians of large cities, as London, New York and Berlin. Here belongs also the remarkable work of the Salvation Army, founded by William Booth and his noble wife in 1865, a sort of aggressive military Christianity, impelled by a truly apostolic spirit, and followed with rich results in the English-speaking world.

There is a reciprocal influence between these different mission fields. Zeal for one stirs up zeal for another. One of the greatest blessings of foreign Missions is their inspiring effect upon the Churches at home.

CHAPTER CCLXXXVI.

EPOCHS OF MISSIONS.

I. Apostolic Missions. The planting of Christianity from Jerusalem to Rome among Jews, Greeks and Romans. Peter, the apostle of the Jews; Paul, the apostle of the Gentiles.

II. Ante-Nicene period. Spread of Christianity amid persecution in the Roman Empire, especially in Syria, Egypt, Italy and southern Europe. Hindrances: hostility of the Jews and Gentiles; slanderous reports; novelty; poverty and obscurity; a crucified founder; apparent want of patriotism. Helps: the perfect teaching and example of Christ; moral and spiritual power; regenerating and sanctifying influence; rationality of doctrines; the universality and adaptability of Christianity; compact church organization; the testimony of miracles and prophecy; the order and unity of the Roman Empire, and the prevalence of the Greek language and culture; the destruction of Jerusalem; the moral corruption and hopeless decay of the heathen religion. "Christ appeared," says Augustin, "to the men of a decrepit, decaying world, that while all around them was withering away, they might through him receive new, youthful life."

The total number of Christians in the Roman Empire at the beginning of the fourth century was, perhaps, nearly ten millions—that is, about one tenth or one twelfth of the estimated population of the empire. According to Chrysostom, the Christian population of Antioch in the year 380 was about 100,000, or one half of the whole.

EPOCHS OF MISSIONS. 519

III. Post-Nicene period. After the conversion of Constantine, the emperors aided the Church in the overthrow of paganism, which was completed in the fifth and sixth centuries. This triumph, however, was not achieved without great sacrifice of the purity of the Church. The conversion was to a large extent merely nominal, while heathen corruptions and practices continued.

IV. Missions in the Middle Ages. Conversion and civilization of the barbarians of central and western Europe, Celtic, Germanic, and Slavonic, by monks and priests mostly under the direction of the Bishop of Rome and with the aid of the civil and military power. The Irish missionaries were distinguished for zeal and independence. Ireland was called "the island of saints."

St. Patrick, the apostle of Ireland, Columba, the apostle of Scotland, Augustin, the apostle of England, Columbanus and Boniface, the apostles of Germany, Ansgar, the apostle of Denmark, Cyril and Methodius, the apostles of the Bulgarians. The conversion of Catholic France was determined by King Clovis after the victory of Tolbiac (496). Charles Martel gave effectual aid to Boniface (750). Charles the Great converted the rebellious Saxons by force (785). His example was the beginning of a crusade for the overthrow of heathenism, contrary to the spirit of the gospel and against the protest of Alcuin, who with all his admiration for the great emperor maintained that instruction, persuasion and love were the only proper means for converting the heathen. The crusaders tried to convert or to subdue the Mohammedans by the sword, but failed. The Sultan still holds the key to the Holy Sepulchre, and rules and ruins the once flourishing lands of the Bible.

Russia received her Christianity from the Greek Church by military command of Grand-Duke Vladimir, called "Isapostolos" (980–1015), who sent his subjects into the river Dnieper, while the priests read prayers from the cliffs on the shore. The greatest wholesale water baptism in history, "wonderfully curious and beautiful to behold," says Nestor, the Russian monk and annalist.

V. Spain and Portugal, which had the supreme command at sea in the fifteenth century, discovered and settled Central and South America, and added them to the domain of the papacy. The conversion of the Indians was brought about by Dominican,

Franciscan, and Jesuit monks, with the aid of the civil power and in the same spirit which prevailed in the Middle Ages towards the barbarians. The sword was more powerful than the cross. The work was darkened by fearful cruelty against the natives; but the noble spirit of Las Casas, the friend and emancipator of the Indians, rises far above his gold-seeking contemporaries.

The French Canadians are likewise Roman Catholics, descended from the settlers in the seventeenth century. The labors of the French Jesuits among the Indians are distinguished for heroic self-denial, but had little success.

These American conquests made up, numerically, for the losses in Europe which the Roman Church sustained by the Reformation.

VI. Rome has carried on her missionary operations without interruption, and in the same spirit, to this day in all heathen lands. They are under the direction of the *Congregatio de Propaganda Fide*, which was founded by Gregory XV., a pupil of the Jesuits (1622), and has its seat in Rome. Its chief organ is the *Annales de la Propagation de la Foi*, published at Lyons, and elsewhere in different languages. The greatest missionary of the Roman Church is the Jesuit Francis Xavier, "the apostle of the Indians," and patron of Catholic missions (1506–52), who with the authority of the Pope and the King of Portugal carried on a most successful mission in East India and Japan, and was only prevented by his death from entering into China. Among the latest missionaries of the Roman faith is Cardinal Lavigerie (d. 1893), the benefactor of dark Africa, who figures most prominently in the suppression of the African slave-trade.

The Greek Church follows in the van of the military power of Russia in her conquering march eastward across the northern continent of Asia.

VII. Protestantism was for a long time culpably indifferent to the missionary duty of the Church. The Reformers were so absorbed in the conflict with popery that they hardly thought of the heathen. Luther preached war against the Turks, and thought that the end of the world was near at hand. Calvin gave his aid to unsuccessful settlements in Brazil and Florida, but they were intended more for a refuge for persecuted Huguenots than for the conversion of the natives.

The door for Protestant missions was opened by the rise of

Holland and Britain, which first disputed, then shared, and at last surpassed the exclusive dominion of Spain and Portugal over the seas, and acquired large possessions in Asia and America. The Dutch East India Company was chartered in 1602, with an avowed subordinate purpose of converting the heathen, and Protestantism was forced upon the natives of Ceylon in 1636.

The earliest missionary efforts of England were connected with the colonies of North America. John Eliot (1604–90) was the first great missionary to the Indians in New England. He translated the whole Bible into an Indian dialect. The Mayhews, Sargent, David Brainerd, and the Moravian Zeisberger labored in the same spirit. A corporation for "Promoting the Gospel of Jesus Christ in New England" was chartered in 1662, the "Society for Promoting Christian Knowledge" in 1698, and the "Society for the Propagation of the Gospel in Foreign Parts" in 1701.

The British East India Company was at first hostile to missions, but the steady progress of conquest in the eighteenth century resulted in the vast Indian empire under the control of English Christianity and civilization.

In Germany, the missionary spirit was first awakened by the pietistic movement of Spener and Francke, and by the *Unitas Fratrum*, or Moravians. The latter are the pioneer mission Church, and have sent since 1732 to all parts of the world over 2300 missionaries of a truly apostolic spirit, even to the most degraded among the heathen. The Lutheran Church followed very slowly in the course pointed out by Count Zinzendorf. Her earliest missionaries were Ziegenbalg and Schwartz (d. 1798), who studied in Halle and were sent by the Danish Missionary Society of Copenhagen to Tranquebar, in India, where they labored with great success.

VIII. A new missionary era may be dated from 1792, when, under the inspiration of William Carey, the Baptist Missionary Society was formed. It was followed by the London Missionary Society, 1795, the Church Missionary Society, 1799, the American Board of Commissioners for Foreign Missions, 1810, the American Baptist Missionary Union, 1814, the Basel Missionary Society, 1815, the Wesleyan Methodist Missionary Society, 1816; also the several Presbyterian, the Protestant Episcopal, the Baptist, the Dutch and German Reformed, the

Episcopal Methodist, the Protestant Methodist, the Lutheran, and many other missionary societies in the United States and Canada. The total number of these societies to-day exceeds one hundred, mostly English, Scotch, Irish, and American.

In the providence of God, India, China, Corea, Japan, and, since the explorations of Livingstone and Stanley, even the interior of Africa, in fact the whole heathen world, is now open to missions. The work in Japan, though scarcely begun, is most encouraging, and may at no distant day result in the conversion of that empire which has already adopted many of the results of Christian civilization.

The English, Scotch, and Anglo-Americans are the richest, the most energetic and most successful missionary nations of modern times; indeed they control the commerce of the world by sea and land. The extraordinary progress of missionary zeal and enterprise is phenomenal, and one of the greatest evidences for the vitality of Christianity, and an assurance of its ultimate triumph to the ends of the earth, in obedience to Christ's command and in fulfillment of his promise.

CHAPTER CCLXXXVII.

MISSIONARY LITERATURE.

The Encyclopædia of Missions: Descriptive, Historical, Biographical, Statistical. Edited by EDWIN MUNSELL BLISS (New York, 1891, 2 vols.). A full bibliography of Foreign Missions by Samuel Macauley Jackson is added, vol. i., pp. 557-661.

G. WARNECK: *Evangelische Missionslehre* (Gotha, 1892 sqq.).

R. GRUNDEMANN: *Missionsatlas* (Gotha, 1867-70).

I. General History of Foreign Missions:

THEODOR CHRISTLIEB: *Protestant Foreign Missions, Their Present State* (Eng. translation, London and Boston, 3d ed. 1881; also in German, French, Swedish and Norwegian).—GEO. SMITH: *Short History of Christian Missions* (Edinburgh, 1884; 2d ed. 1886).—W. FLEMING STEVENSON: *The Dawn of Modern Missions* (Edinburgh, 1887).—GUSTAV WARNECK: *Outline of the History of Protestant Missions* (English translation, Edinburgh, 1884).— EDWIN HODDER: *Conquests of the Cross: A Record of Missionary Work throughout the World* (London, 1890-91, 3 vols.).—J. LOWE: *Medical Missions* (London, 1886; 3d ed. 1891).—G. F. MACLEAR: *History of Christian Missions in the Middle Ages* (London, 1860).

In German: C. G. BLUMHARDT: *Versuch einer allgemeinen Missionsgeschichte der Kirche Christi* (Basel, 1828-37, 5 parts).—H. GUNDERT: *Die evangelische Mission, ihre Länder, Völker und Arbeiter* (Calw, 1881; 2d ed.

1886).—C. H. KALKAR: *Geschichte der christlichen Mission unter den Heiden* (Gütersloh, 1879).—G. E. BURCKHARDT: *Kleine Missionsbibliothek* (Bielefeld, 2d ed. by Grundemann, 1876 sqq.).

II. Special Histories of Foreign Missions:
American Board, by R. Anderson (Boston, 1870-74, 4 vols.); *Baptist* (Northern), S. F. Smith (Boston, 1879; 2d ed. 1883); (Southern), H. A. Tupper (Phila., 1880, continued to 1890; Richmond, Va., 1891); *Methodist*, J. M. Reid (New York, 1879, 2 vols.); *Moravian*, A. C. Thompson (New York, 1882); *Presbyterian*, J. C. Lowrie (New York, 1855; 2d ed. 1868); *Reformed Dutch*, Mrs. M. E. Sangster (New York, 1887); The New Hebrides Mission of John G. Paton (Presbyterian), or, *Thirty Years among South Sea Cannibals* (New York, 1892).

III. Biographies of Foreign Missionaries. Collections:
C. D. YONGE: *Pioneers and Founders* (London, 1872).—W. P. WALSH: *Modern Heroes of the Mission Field* (London and New York, 1882; 3d ed. 1892).—A. H. JAPP: *Master Missionaries* (London, 1880; 3d ed. 1883).—MRS. E. R. PITMAN: *Heroines of the Mission Field* (London and New York, 1881).—MRS. F. E. ARNOLD-FORSTER: *Heralds of the Cross* (London, 1882; 2d ed. 1885).

IV. Individual Biographies of Foreign Missionaries:
W. C. Burns (China), by Islay Burns (Edinburgh and New York, 1870; 6th ed. 1871).—*William Carey* (India), by Geo. Smith (London, 1885; 2d ed. 1887).—*Alexander Duff* (India), by Geo. Smith (1879; 2d ed. 1881).—*William Ellis* (Polynesia), by J. E. Ellis (London, 1873).—*William Goodell* (Turkey), by E. D. G. Prime (New York, 1876).—*James Hannington* (Uganda), by E. C. Dawson (London and New York, 1887).—*Adoniram Judson* (Burmah), by E. Judson (New York, 1883).—*Robert and Mary Moffat* (Africa), by J. S. Moffat (London and New York, 1885; 6th ed. 1887).—*David Livingstone* (Africa), by Samuel Smiles (London and New York, 1885).—*Henry Martyn* (Persia), by Geo. Smith (London, 1893).—*John Coleridge Patteson* (Polynesia), by Charlotte M. Yonge (London, 1874, 2 vols.).—*John Williams* (Polynesia), by John Campbell (London, 1842; 2d ed. 1843).—*Samuel Wells Williams* (China), by F. W. Williams (New York, 1889).—*John Wilson* (India), by Geo. Smith (London, 1878; 2d ed. 1879).—*David Zeisberger* (North American Indians), by Edmund de Schweinitz (Philadelphia, 1870).

V. Revivals and Inner Mission:
TRACY: *The Great Awakening* (of 1740).—MACFARLANE: *Revivals of the Eighteenth Century*.—FINNEY: *Lectures on Revivals*. Biographies of Whitefield, John Wesley, Jonathan Edwards, Lyman Beecher, Charles G. Finney, Wichern.

VI. The work of "the Salvation Army," and missions among the heathen in Christian lands:
General WILLIAM BOOTH (founder of the Army): *Aggressive Christianity* (London, 1882; 5th ed. 1890); *In Darkest England and the Way Out* (1890).—BALLINGTON BOOTH: *New York's Inferno* (New York, 1893).— Also Mrs. CATHERINE BOOTH (wife of General W. Booth, and one of the most remarkable and useful women of the nineteenth century, d. 1892): *Popular Christianity* (1890); and her biography, by BOOTH-TUCKER (1893, 2 vols.). The Salvation Army publishes the weekly "War Cry" and the

monthly "Conqueror," which have obtained in a short time an enormous circulation.

I recommend the study of biographies of great missionaries, as Columba, Boniface, Ansgar, Xavier; Eliot, Brainerd, Zeisberger, Carey, Henry Martyn, Judson, Moffat, Livingstone, Duff, Patteson, Hannington, Paton.

The greatest missionary is Paul, and the most inspiring history of missions is the Book of The Acts—the record of a spiritual conquest of souls and their redemption from the slavery of sin to freedom in Christ.

TOPICAL INDEX.

Abelard, as rationalist, 65, 369.
Æthiopic, 122.
Alexander, A., 390.
Allen, A. V. G., quoted, 381.
America, Spanish, 285.
 sects in early, 291.
American Church history, 285.
American Church History Society literature, 294.
Anselm, St., as to faith, 66; 369.
Anthony of Padua, 482.
Antiquities, 145.
 ecclesiastical, 248.
Apocrypha, Jewish, 142.
Apologetic, 309.
 necessity, 310.
 epochs, 313.
Apostles' teachings, literature on, 332.
Apostolic age, 272.
Apostolical Canons, 458.
 Constitutions, 458.
Aquinas, T., 370.
Arabic, 121.
Aramaic, 108, 115, 128.
 biblical, 116.
Arcana Cœlestia, 227.
Archæology, 280.
 biblical, 140.
 classified, 141, 145.
 sources, 142.
 history, 146.
 Christian, 280.
Aristides' "Apology," 277.
Aristotle, as to theology, 77.
Arminianism, 374, 399.
Arnold, E., quoted, 47, 48.
Arnold, G., 300.
Aryan religion, 34.
Asceticism of St. Jerome, 431.
Assyrian, 118.
Athanasius, 365.
"Auburn Declaration," 396.
Augustin, quoted, 197, 199, 255.
 influence, 366.
 as to morals, 432.

Bacon, quoted, 84, 91.
Balder, 54.
Bampton Lectures, 315.
Baptism, validity, 394.
Barnabas's Epistle, 277.
Barnes, A., 396.
Baur, F. C. von, 228, 302.
Baxter, quoted, 476, 488.
Beecher, H. W., 498.
Beecher, L., 396, 498.
Bellarmin, R., 222.
Bengel, quoted, 158, 233.
Berkeley, quoted, 285.
Bernard, St., quoted, 233, 480.
Berthold, 482.
Beyschlag, as to John, 327.
Beza, 214.
Bible, the, 94.
 inspiration, 95.
 tributes, 97, 158.
 natural history, 144.
 various readings, 156.
 transcriptions, 158.
 in original, and the Septuagint, 160, 161.
 authorship, 179.
 defects in Authorized Version, 191, 198.
Biblical criticism, 153.
Biblical history, periods, 260, 267.
Biblical theology, 316.
 bearings, 317.
 method, 319.
 history, 328.
Bibliography, i., 6, 10.
Biel, G., 370.
Books, Milton on, 91.
 American 291.
Brahminism, 43.
Breckinridge, R. J., 394.
Breviarium Romanum, 509.
Briggs, C. A., 400.
Broad-church, 344.
Brooks, Phillips, 499.
Buddhism, 45, 49.
Buddhists, number, 45.

525

Bunyan, 489.
Bushnell, H., 387.
Cajetan, Cardinal, 370.
Calixtus, 216.
Calvin, 484.
  as commentator, 214, 372.
  on canon law, 460.
Calvinism, 373.
  scholastic, 374.
  five points, 389.
Cameron, J., 378.
Canon, theory of the, 168.
  Hebrew, 171.
  Hellenistic, 171.
  New Testament, history, 172.
  and Protestantism, 175.
Canon law, the, 459.
Catechetic, 500.
Catechisms, typical, 502.
Chalmers, T., 494.
Channing, W. E., 387.
Carlyle, T., quoted, 269.
Casuistical divinity, 442.
Casuistry, 441.
Catenæ Patrum, 207.
Catholicity, 412.
Cave, A., as to knowledge and religion, 65.
Census, eleventh, 28.
Chaldee, 116.
Christ, life of, 268.
Christian life, history, 248.
Christian union, 414.
Christianity, 21, 129.
  fullness, 59.
  in U. S. A., origin and orthodoxy, 290.
  distinctive feature, 291.
  among the English, 522.
Christocentric, 241, 358, 364, 398.
Chronology, ecclesiastical, 243.
Chrysostom, 479.
Church, 130, 455.
  organization, 246.
  law, 457.
  polity, 463.
  Church and State as related, 467, 469.
Church ethic, history, 428, 439.
Church history, 244.
  written sources, 251.
  unwritten sources, 253.
  uses, 258.
  periods, 259.
  Christian, periods, 261.
Church's development, the, 240.
Cicero, on *relegere*, 18.
  quoted, 259.
Classics, study of, 123.

Clement's Epistles and Syriac version, 277.
Codex, Vatican, 162.
  Sinaiticus, 276.
  Lipsiensis, 277.
Codices of New Testament, 164, 172.
Coleridge, on Channing, 387.
Columbus, 285.
Commentaries, exhaustive, 196.
  popular, 197.
  Roman Catholic of 17th century, 222.
  by the English, 229.
  American, 229.
Confessions, 406.
Confucianism, 41.
Congregational Creed of 1883, 386.
Conversion, 312.
Co-operative societies of to-day, 415.
Corpus Juris Canonici, 459, 461.
Council of Trent, 175.
Councils, history, 247.
Cranmer, 485.
Creationism, 395.
Creeds, revision, politically, 389.
  nature of, 406.
  authority, 407.
  classified, 408.
  historically, 410.
Critici Sacri, 216, 220.
Criticism, literary, 153.
Culture, mental and moral, 3.
Cyprian and sacerdotalism, 86.
Dabney, R. L., 394.
De Civitate Dei, 432.
De Officiis Ministrorum, 430.
Denominations, number, 336.
Denominationalism, useful, 413.
Descartes, 81.
Diatessaron, Tatian's, 270, 277.
Dickinson, B., 396.
Dickinson, J., 388.
Didache, the, 278.
Diplomatic, ecclesiastical, 243.
Divine sovereignty, 399.
Dogma, history, 249.
Dogmatic, content, 333.
  sources, 334.
  biblical, 335.
  confessional, 336.
  Greek, 337.
  Roman Catholic, 338.
  Lutheran, 339.
  Reformed and Calvinistic, 342.
  Anglican, 344.
  Arminian, 346.
  Socinian, 348.
  rationalistic, 350.

TOPICAL INDEX. 527

Dogmatic, Evangelical Union, 352.
Ritschl, 355, 360.
speculative, 360.
Christocentric, 362.
Patristic, 364.
Augustinian, 368.
Scholastic, 368.
Reformation, 371.
Calvinistic, in America, 376.
New England, 377.
Presbyterian, 388.
Old School, 389.
New School, 396.
German, in America, 402.
Dorner, on American theology, 375.
Dualism, 31.
Dwight, T., 384.
"*Ecclesia non sitit sanguinem,*" 471.
Ecclesiæ, patres, doctores, auctores, 275.
Ecclesiology, 455.
Education, object, 3.
 kinds, 3.
 religious, 4.
 value, 4.
 means, 4.
 degrees, 5.
Edwardeans, 381.
Edwards, Jon., 378, 381.
Edwards, Dr., 382.
Egypt's religion, 50.
Eloquence, 473.
Emmons, N., 383.
Encyclical, 7.
Encyclopædia, formal, i., 8.
 meaning, 6.
 theological, 9.
 divisions, 11.
 history, 11.
"Encyclopædia," Schaff-Herzog, 338.
English, roots in, 106.
Episcopacy, congregational, 463.
 diocesan, 463.
 metropolitan, 464.
 Anglican, 465.
 papal, 465.
 Lutheran, 466.
Episcopal Prayer-Book, 509.
Erasmus, quoted, 134; 211.
Erigena, S., 369.
Ethic, definitions, 422.
 Christian, 421, 423
 contrasted with dogmatic, 422.
 philosophical, 423.
 pagan, 424.
 Protestant, history, 436.
Eusebius, on the canon, 174.
Evangelical Churches, confessions, 409.

Evangelistic, branches, 517.
Ewald, H., on Bible, 97; 141, 228.
on ὁ λόγος, 189.
Exegesis, divisions, 189, 202.
 of Old and New Testaments, 197.
 history, 199.
 Jewish, 200, 203.
 before Christ, 201.
 rabbinical, 202.
 allegorizing, 202.
 after Christ, 203.
 Christian, 204.
 patristic, 205.
 mediæval, 207.
 of the Reformers, 212.
 Protestant, of 17th century, 215.
 Rationalistic, of 19th century, 223.
 Swedenborgian, 226.
 evangelical, 227.
 as to history and theology, 232.
Exegete, qualifications, 188.
Exegetes, Greek, 205.
 Latin, 206.
Exegetic, departments, 94.
Exegetical sense, fourfold, 208.
 mystic, 208.
Ezra, 201.
 legend of, 170.
Faber, on English of the Bible, 190.
"Faith precedes understanding," 66.
Farel, W., 484.
Farrar, F. W., 493.
Fathers, the, estimated, 206.
Feeling and piety, 71.
Ferrer, 482.
Fetichism, 41.
Francis of Assisi, 481.
Franklin, Benj., on pride, 70.
Free-will, 380, 399.
Fundamental theology, 93.
Gautama, 46.
Geibel, quoted. 85.
Gemara, 201.
General Assembly of Presbyterian Church, 394.
Geschichte, 234.
Geography, biblical, 143.
 ecclesiastical, 241, 444.
Gibbons, Cardinal, on church and state, 468.
Goethe, as to the Bible, 97.
 quoted, 183, 238.
 as to the Christian struggle, 269.
 as to Church history, 297.
 as to rules 460.
Greek, 123.
 dialects, 125.
 Hellenistic, 126, 128, 135.

TOPICAL INDEX.

Greek, apostolic, 127.
  sub-apostolic, 137.
  ecclesiastical, 138.
Greek Church Creed, 408.
Gregory I., 480.
  as exegete, 206.
  quoted, 475.
Gregory of Nyssa, 365.
Guthrie, Thomas, 495.
Hades, 395, 503.
Haggada, 201.
Hagiographa, 171.
Halakha, 201.
Hall, Robert, 493.
Hamilton, Wm., as to knowledge, 356.
Harnack, on community in theology, 403.
Harper, A. P., quoted, 45.
Harper, W. R., 114.
Hase, on earlier historians, 299.
Heathen, Bible view, 38.
Heathenism, 36.
Hebrew, 105, 106, 107, 128.
  rabbinical, 116.
Hebrew learning, history, 111.
Heine, H., on Moses, 323.
Helvetic Formula, 391.
Hell, extent, 395.
Herder, J. G., 486.
Heresies, 250.
Hermeneutic, definition, 186.
  aim, 187.
  philological, 194.
  theological, 195.
  homiletical, 196.
Higher criticism, 153, 177, 184, 400.
  as to the New Testament, 181.
  as to the Old Testament, 183.
Hippolytus, on Daniel, 276.
Historian, duty, 254.
History, biblical, 235.
  ecclesiastical, 235.
  agents, 236.
  progress, 239.
  secular, 243.
  art in, 257.
  spirit for, 257.
Hodge, C., 390.
Hofacker, L., 487.
Homiletic, 472.
Homiletical hints, 475.
Hopkins, S., 382.
Hopkinsianism, 382.
Horus, 51.
Humility, 130.
Hymnody, Greek, 511.
  Latin, 512
  German, 513.

Hymnody, English, 513.
  American, 514.
  French, 515.
Hymnology, 510.
Idolatry, 36.
  origin, 37.
"Independent, The," 23.
Indo-Germanic, 103.
Inerrancy of the Bible, 392, 393.
Infant damnation, 379.
Inspiration, verbal, 392.
Irenic, 412.
Isagogic defined, 149.
  value, 150.
  classified, 151.
  history, 152.
  special, 177.
Islâm, 59.
Israel, history, 264.
'Ιστορία, 234.
Itala, 165.
Jerome, St., quoted, 97, 110.
Jesus' teaching, 325.
John of Damascus, St., 337, 365.
John's style, 134.
Jonah, 40.
Josephus, in Greek and Hebrew, 124.
  as to canon, 171.
Judaism, 55.
Kahnis, as to eucharist, 339.
Kant, as to religion, 69.
Karaites, the, 203.
Keryctic, 473.
Kingdom of God, 456.
Knowledge, and humility, 4.
  and piety, 65.
Knox, 485.
Krummacher, F. W., 487.
Lactantius, as to *religare*, 18.
Lambeth Palace articles, 346.
Languages, classification, 103.
Latimer, 484.
Latinisms, 190.
Latitudinarianism, 220, 412.
Le Fèvre, J. 211.
Leo I., 480.
Lightfoot, J. B., as to Muratori, 174.
Liturgic, 508.
Lombard, Peter, 369.
Luke's style, 132.
Luther, 371, 476, 483.
  as commentator, 213.
  as theologian, 356.
  quoted, 476.
Lutheran Church Confessions, 409.
Lutheranism, scholastic, 373.
Lyra, N., quoted, 207.
Macleod, N., 495.
Man, religious constitution, 63.

Manichæism, 35.
Mark's style, 132.
Marshall, S., 489.
Masora, 110, 159.
Massillon, 485.
Matthew's style, 131.
Melanchthon, 483.
  as exegete, 213, 340.
Melvill, H., 492.
Methodism, 347.
Methodology, i., 6, 10.
Midrash, 201.
Milton, quoted, 91, 377.
Ministerial call, 87.
Ministers, indispensable, 86.
Ministry, Christian, theory, 454.
  different offices, 454.
Mirandola, P. à, quoted, 82.
Mishna, 201.
Missale Romanum, 509.
Missions, 518.
  history of, 244.
  ante-Nicene, 518.
  Middle Ages, 519.
  Roman, 520.
  Protestant, 521.
  modern, 521.
  histories, 523.
  biographies, 523.
  revivals, 523.
Moabite stone, 109, 147.
Moody, D. L., 499.
Mohammed, 57, 58.
Mohammedanism, 33, 57.
Monod, A., 486.
Monography, ecclesiastical, 294.
Monotheism, 31, 37, 55.
Morality, and piety, 69.
  heathen and Christian, 424, 430.
  evangelical, 426.
  ascetic, 427.
Morals, 421.
  mediæval, 434.
Moses, 323.
Mosheim, J. L. von, 485.
Müller, M., quoted, 65.
Music, 510.
Mysticism, 358.
Mythology, Roman, 53.
  Teutonic, 54.
Natural ability, 378.
Neander, on Christ, 269.
  to Hodge, 394.
Nevin, J. W., 387, 390.
New France, 287.
"New Lights," 388.
New School, 388.
New Testament, writers' peculiarities, 130.

New Testament MSS., 156.
  text sources, 163.
  cursives, 165.
  ancient translations, 165.
  received, and true text, 167.
  higher criticism, 181.
  and the Old, 320.
  theology, 325.
Newman, J. H., on Jerome, 432.
  as preacher, 492.
Nirvâna, 47.
Occam, W., 370.
Œcolampadius, J., 214.
"Old Lights," 388.
Old School, 388.
Old Testament, sources of text, 159.
  origin of, 170.
  higher criticism, 183.
  and the New, 320.
  periods of theology, 321.
Origen, quoted, 95.
  as to "Hebrews," 180.
  as exegete, 205.
Orthodoxy among peoples, 374.
Pædagogic, 500.
Paganism, 36.
  classical, 52.
Pantheism, 31.
Paraphrase, 190.
Park, E. A., 385, 498.
Pascal, quoted, 66.
Patristic, 273.
  late discoveries in, 276.
  libraries of, 279.
Paul's style, 133, 134.
Pelagius, on freedom, 377
Persecutions, 265, 471.
Peshitta, 165, 174.
Peter's "Gospel" and "Apocalypse," 277.
Piety, and orthodoxy, 67.
  five forms of, 75.
Philo, quoted, 161.
  as allegorizer, 202.
Philology, biblical, 101.
  ecclesiastical, 241.
Philosophumena, 276.
Philosophy and theology, 82.
Physica Sacra, 144.
"Plan of Union." 396.
Poetry, 510.
Poimenic, 507.
Polity, apostolical, 463.
  papal, 465.
  presbyterian, 466.
  congregational, 466.
  denominational, literature for, 467.
Polytheism, 31.

TOPICAL INDEX.

Postilla, 480.
Preaching, 474, 477.
    where strongest, 497.
Presbyter, 86.
Presbyterian new creed, 401.
"Present Day Theology," 398.
Press, influence of the, 474.
Princeton, professors' declaration, 390.
    theology, 394.
Probabilism, 442.
Propædeutic, iv., 6.
Prophets, the, 324.
Pseudo-Clementine homilies, 277.
Pulpit, history of, 477.
    Greek, 478.
    Latin, 480.
    Middle Ages, 480.
    Reformation, 483.
    Lutheran, 485.
    French, 485.
    Huguenot, 486.
    modern German, 486.
    English, 488.
    American, 496.
Puritanism, 438.
Raikes, Robert, 505.
Rationalism, 350.
Reformation, the, 281.
Reformed Church confessions, 409.
Religion, defined, 17.
    science, 18.
    history, 18.
    philosophy, 20.
    its value, 20.
    psychologically, 33, 65.
    intellectually, 65.
    practically, 69.
    emotionally, 71.
    experimentally, 73.
    and theology, 81.
    among the English, 402.
Religions, classification, 29.
    natural, 29.
    revealed, 30.
    civilized, 32.
    barbarian, 32.
    sensual, 33.
    ascetic, 33.
    ethical, 33.
    by ideas and aims, 35.
    tribal, 35.
    national, 36.
    universal, 36.
Religious liberty, 246, 470.
Religious tests, 472.
Renaissance, 209, 297.
Reuchlin, J., 211.
Reunion of Presbyterians, 397.

Revision of English Version of 1870, sqq., 190.
Ritschl, A., as to John, 183.
    in theology, 229, 355.
Robertson, F. W., quoted, 97.
    on man, 239.
    as preacher, 493.
Roman Church Creed, 408.
Rosetta stone, 119.
Samaritan, 117.
Savonarola, 482.
Schaff, quoted, 99.
Schiller, quoted, 66.
Schleiermacher, F., 487.
    on dependence, 71.
Scholasticism, 370, 373.
Schoolmen, the, 369.
Scotch Church laws, 462.
Scott, W., quoted, 97.
"Self-love," 384.
Semitic, 103, 104, 115.
Semitic religion, 34.
Semler, J. L., 224.
Septuagint, the, 127.
    editions, 162.
    concordance, 163.
Servetus, 471.
Shedd, W. G. T., theology of, 395.
Siloam inscription, 109.
Simon, R., on "inerrancy," 393.
Smith, H. B., quoted, 98.
    as to Christocentric, 363.
    on American theology, 375.
    on Emmons, 383.
Smyth, E. C., 385.
Socinianism, 439.
Sociology, 442.
South, R., 490.
Spinoza, quoted, 380.
Spurgeon, C. H., 494.
Statistic, religious, 21.
    universal, 23.
    by nations, 24.
    English denominations, 25.
    United States, 25, 28.
    by sects in U. S. A., 26.
    of Roman Catholics in U. S., 27.
    geographical and numerical, 441.
    social, 445.
    how composed, 445.
    lessons of, 446.
Stoicism, 425.
Storrs, R. S., 499.
Stoughton, J., quoted, 220.
Straus, D. F., last words, 271.
Students' library, 91.
Study, of theology, hints for, 87.

TOPICAL INDEX.   531

Study, of the Bible, 93.
  exegetical, 232.
  of Church history, 305.
  in German universities, 403.
Summa de Casibus Pœnitentialibus, 442.
Summa Theologiæ, 435.
Sunday-school, American, 505.
Symbolic, historical, 410.
  polemical, 410.
  history, 417.
Symbols of faith, 406, 407.
Syriac, 117.
Syriac translations of the Gospels, 277.
Systematic theology, 307.
Talmud, 142, 171, 201, 203.
Targum, 201.
Tauler, 482.
Taylor, J., 490.
Taylor, N. W., 384.
"Teaching of the Twelve Apostles," 137, 277, 327, 429.
Tennyson, quoted, 361.
Textual criticism, 154.
  variations, 155.
  of Old Testament, 158.
Theodosius I., penal laws, 39.
Theological definitions, 308.
Theology, defined, 77, 449.
  natural and revealed, 79.
  and religion, 80.
  and philosophy, 82.
  and the clergy, 85.
  its divisions, 92.
  Exegetical, 93.
  Jewish, 146.
  Historical, 234.
  spirit for, 257.
  Systematic, 307.
  use of apologetic, 312.
  Biblical, 316.
  patristic, 329.
  Dogmatic, 333.
  evangelical union, 352.
  anthropocentric, 362.
  christocentric, 362.
  theocentric, 362.
  in Germany, 402.

Theology, Practical, 448.
  how divided, 449.
  history of, 451.
  writers on, 452.
  Pastoral, 507.
Tholuck, 487.
  and American scholars, 390.
Thornwell, J. H., 394.
Tillotson, J., 490.
Tocqueville, A., de, on America, 292.
Toleration, 59, 282.
  and liberty, 469.
Traducianism, 395.
Trimurtti, 44.
"True Christianity," 437.
Turanian, 104.
  religion, 34.
Turretin, J. E., 391.
Tyler, B., 385
Tyndale, Wm., 215.
Union Seminary, 319, 397, 516.
Unitarianism, 349, 374, 386, 387.
United States of America, 289.
  Church history, 289.
  separation of church and state, 292.
Urban II., 480.
Viret, P., 484.
Waddington, G., 303.
Weiss, B., on John, 326.
Wesley, J., 491, 505.
Westminster Confession on the Bible, 97.
  its revision, 394, 400.
Whitaker's "Almanack," 24.
Whitefield, G. 491.
Wiclif, J., 209, 482.
Williams, M., on Buddhists, 45.
Woodruff, A., 506.
Woods, L., 385.
Wordsworth, Chr., as to the Fathers, 206.
Worship, history of, 248.
  æsthetic, 509.
Young, B., as polygamist, 58.
Zoölatry, 50.
Zoroastrianism, 49.
Zwingli, 102, 214, 371, 483.

INDEX OF AUTHORS.

Abbot, Ez., 137.
Abbott, Lyman, 239.
Achelis, E. C., 453.
Alexander, W. A., 463.
Alford, H., 231.
Alger, W. R., 296.
Allen, A. J. C., 504.
Alzog, J., 279.
Ambrose, 12.
Andrews, J. W., 462.
———, S. J., 271.
Aquinas, T., 209.
Arminius, J., 347.
Arnold, G., 300.
Athanasius, 365.
Augustin, 12, 366.
Bacuez, *et* Vigouroux, 230.
Baier, A. H., 419.
Bain, Alex., 440.
Baird, R., 293.
———, S. J., 462.
Bapheides, Phil., 305.
Bareille, *et* Fèvre, 304.
Baring-Gould, S., 249.
Barnaby, J., 247.
Baronius, C., 298.
Baumstark, C. E., 315.
Baur, F. C. v., 295, 331, 404.
Bautain, 500.
Baxter, R., 442, 488, 507.
Beard, C., 283.
Beauvais, V. de, 12.
Beck, C. A., 516.
———, J. T., 335.
Bengel, J. A., 218.
Bennett, C. W., 280.
Berington, and Kirk, 339.
Bernard, T. D., 331, 332.
Bestmann, H. J., 428.
Beveridge, W., 346.
Beyschlag, W., 271, 331.
Bezold, Fr. v., 283.
Biedermann, A. E., 351.
Biel, G., 370.
Bingham, J., 280.
Binterim, 280.
Blaikie, W. G., 494.
Bleek, F., 404.

Bliss, E. M., 522.
Blunt, J. H., 462.
Bochart, 146.
Bodemann, F. W., 419.
Böhmer, J. H., 462.
Böhringer, Fr., 295.
Booth, B., 523.
Bopp, F., 103.
Bossuet, 339.
Bowne, B. P., 440.
Brace, C. L., 249.
Bratke, Ed., 234.
Bretschneider, K. G., **351.**
Briggs, C. A., 330.
Bright, Wm., 461.
Brinkmeier, 243.
Brockmann, 243.
Brown, Francis, 121.
Browne, E. H., 346.
Buel, S., 346.
Buhl, F., 169.
Bull, G., 346.
Bullinger, 13.
Bunsen, C. K. J., 230.
Burrage, H. S., 516.
Busenbaum, H., 442.
Bushnell, H., 271, 314, **498.**
Butler, Alban, 249.
———, J., 314.
———, J. G., 230.
Bruce, A. B., 314, **457.**
Brunialti, A., 469.
Bryce, J., 294.
Calixtus, 216.
Calmet, A., 223.
Calov, Abr., 217.
Calvin, J., 342.
Carpzov, J. G., 149.
Caryl, Jos., 221.
Cassiodorus, 12, 297.
Castelar, 289.
Caswall, E., 515.
Cave, A., 16.
Chalmers, T., 343.
Chambers, T. W., 194.
Charteris, A. H., 169.
Chastel, E. L., 303.
Christ, and Paranikas, **515.**

INDEX OF AUTHORS. 533

Christlieb, Theod., 315, 477, 522.
Chrysostom, 12.
Clarisse, Jo., 14.
Clarke, A., 222.
——, J. F., 29.
Coccejus, J., 218.
Cook, T. C., 230.
Cornill, 160.
Cramer, J. A., 209.
Creighton, M., 284.
Cremer, H., 136, 404.
Crooks, and Hurst, 15.
Cyril of Jerusalem, 504.
Daniel, H. A., 508, 515.
Davidson, A. B., 113, 330.
——, G., 169.
Davies, G. J., 492.
Delitzsch, Franz, 268, 330.
——, Fr., 120.
Denziger, H., 338.
De Rossi, 248.
De Wette, 225.
Dick, J., 343.
Diestel, L., 186.
Diez, 243.
Dillmann, Bertheau, and others, 231.
Doddridge, Philip, 221.
Dœdes, I. T., 14.
Döllinger, I., 284, 304
——, and Reusch, 440.
Dorchester, D., 293, 447.
Dorner, I. A., 295, 354, 373, 441.
Drey, J. Seb., 13.
Driver, S. R., 160.
Drumann, 247.
Drummond, J., 15, 268.
Duff, A., 330.
Duffield, S. W., 516.
Ebrard, J. H. A., 295, 315, 343.
Edersheim, A., 271.
Edwards, Jon., 380.
Egelhaaf, G., 283.
Eichhorn, J. G., 225.
Ellicott, C. J., 230.
Erasmus, 12.
Ernesti, J. A., 224.
Estius, W., 223.
Eusebius, 297.
Ewald, H., 112, 266, 330, 404.
Fairbairn, A. M., 344.
Farrar, A. S., 314.
——, F. W., 271, 279.
Fénelon, 485.
Fick, 103.
Ficker, 243.
Finney, C. G., 523.
Fischer, A. F. W., 516.
Fisher, G. P., 243, 268, 283, 314, 315, 374, 384.

Fiske, J., 289.
Flacius, M., 298.
Fleury, C., 299.
Foxe, J., 246.
Francke, A. H., 218.
Frank, F. H. R., 341, 359, 441.
——, G. W., 373.
Freeman, E. A., 447.
Frèsne, C. du, 139.
Friedberg, E., 462, 469.
Fritzsche, C. F. A., 225.
Fulton, J., 461.
Gardthausen, 243.
Gass, W., 338, 373, 428.
Gebhardt, v., Harnack, and Zahn, 278.
Geier, W., 217.
Gerhart, E. V, 343.
Gerlach, H., 462.
Gesenius, F. H. W., 225.
Gess, W. F., 331.
Gibbons, J., 339.
Gieseler, J. C. L., 301.
Gill, J., 221.
Ginsburg, C. D., 159.
Glass, Sal., 217.
Glassius, S., 112.
Godet, F., 230, 404.
Goebel, M., 249.
Gousset, T. M. J., 339.
Graul, K., 420.
Gray, J. C., 230.
Gregory I., 12
—— of Nyssa, 504.
——, A., 506.
——, C. R., 163.
Gretillat, J., 16, 354.
Groot, de, and Pareau, 14.
Grotius, H., 219.
Grundemann, P. R., 243, 522.
Guericke, H. C. F., 419.
Gundert, H., 522.
Gury, P. J. P., 440, 442.
Guyon, Mme. de, 223.
Haering, 358.
Hagenbach, C. R., 302.
——, K. R., 14, 282, 283.
Hahn, H. A., 410.
Hall, Jos., 220.
Hammond, H., 220.
——, C. E., 509.
——, W. A., 461.
Hardouin, J., 248.
Hardwick, C., 305.
Harless, G. C. A., 14, 441.
Harnack, Ad., 169, 250, 278, 301, 357, 360.
Harris, J. R., 277.
Hartmann, J., 283.

INDEX OF AUTHORS.

Hase, K., 271, 296, 303, 340, 420.
Hasse, H. G., 420.
Hatch, Ed., 136, 357, 467.
——, and Redpath, 163.
Hatfield, E. F., 516.
Hausrath, A., 404.
Häusser, L., 283.
Hävernik, H. A. C., 330.
Hefele, C. J. v., 248, 289.
Heidegger, J. H., 152, 219.
Heinrici, K. F. G., 16.
Hengstenberg, E. W., 266.
Henke, H. P. C., 301.
Henry, Matt., 221.
Heppe, H., 343.
Herder, J. G., 13, 225.
Hergenröther, Jos., 305.
Herrmann, J. G., 359.
Hettinger, F., 315.
Hickok, L. P., 440.
Hilgers, B. J., 419.
Hill, G., 343.
Hinschius, P., 462.
Hitchcock, R. D., 443.
Hitzig, F., 225.
Hodder, E., 522.
Hodge, A. A., 343, 392, 394.
——, C., 343, 462.
Hoffman, M., 462.
Hofmann, J. K. v., 15.
——, Rud., 419.
Holst, H. v., 294.
Holtzmann, Lipsius, Schmiedel, von Soden, 231.
Hooker, R., 345.
Hopkins, M., 440.
Horoy, Abbé, 278.
Hottinger, J. H., 152.
Hughes, H., 440.
Hugo de St. Caro, 209.
—— of St. Victor, 12.
Huntington, W. R., 420.
Hurel, A., 477.
Hurst, J. F., 305.
Hurter, F. E. v., 247.
Ideler, 243.
Immer, A., 331.
Irving, W., 289.
Isidor of Seville, 12.
Jackson, S. M., 121, 245.
Jameson, Fausset, and Brown, 230.
Janet, P., 440.
Janssen, Joh., 284.
Jerome, 276.
Jodl, F., 428.
John of Damascus, 337, 365.
Josephus, 142.
Julian, J., 516.
Kaftan, J. W. M., 356.

Kahnis, K. F. A., 341, 373.
Kalkar, C. H., 522.
Kattenbusch, F., 243, 355, **420**.
Keil, and Delitzsch, 231.
Keim, T., 404.
Kempe, 477.
Kienlen, H. G., 14.
Kihn, H., 16.
King, J., 516.
Kittel, 267.
Knapp, A., 515.
Koch, E. E., 516.
Labbeus, and Cossart, 248.
Lagarde, P. de, 146, 163.
Lampe, F. A., 219.
Lange, J., 218.
——, J. P., 14, 229, 343, 404.
Lapide, C. à, 223.
Lardner, N., 314.
Lau, 247.
Lecky, W. E. H., 427.
Le Clerc, 219.
Le Quien, 338.
Levita, Elias, 159.
Lightfoot, J. B., 221, 273, 278.
Liguori, A. M. da, 440, 442.
Limborch, P. v., 347.
Lipsius, R. A., 351, 359.
Lombard, Peter, 369.
Lowe, J., 522.
Lowth, R., 222.
Lucius, P. E., 268.
Luthardt, C. E., 315, 341, 404, **424**, 428, 441.
Luther, 213.
Lyra, N., 110, 210.
Mabillon, 243.
McClintock, J., 14.
McCosh, J., 314.
Maclear, G. F., 523.
McElhinney, J., 457.
McMaster, J. B., 294.
Maldonado, J., 222.
Mansi, G. D., 248.
Marheineke, P. K., 351, **419**.
Martensen, H., 341, 404, **441**.
Martigny, J. A., 280.
Martin, E., 16.
Martineau, J., 440.
Matthes, F. R., 419.
Maurenbrecher, W., 285.
Mead, G. M., 315.
Melanchthon, 12.
Merle D'Aubigne, 283.
$M\epsilon\sigma o\lambda\acute{\omega}\pi a\varsigma$, I. E., 420.
Meyer, H. A. W., 231.
Michælis, J. D., 224.
Migne, Abbé, 278.
Miley, J., 348.

INDEX OF AUTHORS.

Miller, J., 516.
Milner, J., 300.
Minghetti, M., 469.
Möhler, J. A., 304, 419.
Mone, F. J., 508, 515.
Moore, W. E., 463.
Mosheim, J. L. v., 300.
Mulford, E., 443.
Müller, J., 295, 354, 420, 457.
Natalis, A., 299.
Navarrete, 289.
Neale, J. M., 508, 515.
Neander, A., 295, 301, 331, 419, 428.
Nestle, E., 117, 163.
Newman, J. H., 239.
Nicoll, W. R., 231.
Nippold, F., 293.
Nirschl, Jos., 234, 279.
Nitzsch, C. J., 453.
———, F., 359.
———, K. Im., 335.
Oberthür, 13.
Œcolampadius, J., 214.
Oehler, G. F., 330, 420.
Oettingen, A. v., 443.
Olshausen, H., 231.
Oosterzee, J. J. v., 331, 343, 453.
Origen, 365.
Pagninus, S., 152.
Paley, W., 314.
Paniel, 477.
Park, E. A., 374, 382.
Parkman, F., 289.
Pastor, L., 284.
Paton, J. G., 523.
Patrick, Lowth, Whitby, and Lowman, 220.
Paulus, H. E. G., 225.
Payne, E. J., 289.
Pearson, J., 345.
Pelt, A. F. L., 14.
Perowne, J. J. S., 230, 231.
Perrone, G., 339.
Pestalozzi, J. H., 504.
Petermann, J. H., 104.
Pfleiderer, O., 273, 352, 359, 373, 404.
Philaret, 338.
Philippi, F. A., 341, 420.
Phillemore, 462.
Phillips, G., 462.
Pick, B., 268.
Pin, L. E. du, 13.
Piper, K. W. F., 249.
Planck, G. J., 247, 373.
Plitt, G., 420.
Poole, M., 220.
Pope, W. B., 348.
Porter, N., 440.
Possevinus, A., 13.

Prætorius, F., 122.
Pray, L. G., 506.
Prentiss, G. L., 397.
Prescott, 289.
Pressensé, E. de, 271.
Quesnell, P., 223.
Rabanus Maurus, 12.
Räbiger, J. F., 15.
Ranke, L. v., 283, 284.
Rawlinson, H. C., 121.
Raymond, M., 348.
Reiff, Fr., 354.
Reinhard, 270.
Reischle, M., 559.
Reland, 146.
Renan, E., 267, 273.
Reuchlin, J., 111.
Reuss, E., 169, 230, 331.
Reuter, H. F., 247.
Réville, A., 404.
Reynolds, H. E., 268.
Richter, E. L., 462.
Ritschl, A., 247, 295, 359.
Ritter, C., 147.
Rivetus, A., 152.
Robertson, J., 267.
———, J. C., 305.
Robinson, E., 113, 147.
Rohrbacher, Abbé, 304.
Roscoe, W., 247.
Rosenkrantz, K., 13.
Rosenmüller, 224.
Rothe, R., 15, 247, 354, 441.
Rowe, C. A., 318.
Ruinart, T., 246.
Ryle, H. E., 169.
Sa, Em. de, 222.
Sabunde, R. de, 79.
Salmon, G., 177.
Sanday, W., 183.
Scaliger, J., 218.
Schaff, P., 127, 137, 194, 205, 231, 239, 246, 250, 271, 279, 293, 301, 303, 364, 420, 515.
Schanz, P., 315.
Schéele, K. H. G. v., 420.
Schleiermacher, F., 13, 355, 441.
Schmid, C. F., 331, 441.
———, H., 341.
Schmidt, H., 420.
———, S., 217.
———, W., 359.
Schneckenburger, M., 268, 420.
Schöttgen, Chr., 217.
Schouler, J., 294.
Schrader, E., 404.
Schröckh, J. M., 300.
Schulte, Fr. v., 462.
Schultz, F. W., 330.

Schultz, H., 330.
Schürer, E., 148, 268, 404.
Schweizer, A., 343.
Scott, T., 221.
Scrivener, F. H. A.,-163.
Seeley, J. R., 271.
Shea, J. G., 289.
Shedd, W. G. T., 343.
Sidgwick, H., 424, 440.
Siegel, K. C. F., 280.
Siegfried, C., 203.
Simon, R., 152.
Smedt, C. de, 234.
Smith, H. B., 305, 343, 397.
——, G., 522.
——, W. R., 184.
——, and Cheetham, 248, 280.
——, and Wace, 279.
Smyth, N., 440.
Sophocles, E. A., 139.
Spence, and Exell, 230.
Spencer, H., 443.
Spener, P. J., 442.
Sprague, W. B., 496.
Sprecher, S., 341.
Spurgeon, C. H., 221.
Stade, B., 267, 330.
Stanley, A. P., 266, 338, 467.
Stanton, V. H., 268.
Stapfer, E., 268.
Starke, Chr., 217.
Staudenmeier, F. A., 13.
Stearns, L. F., 314, 343, 398.
Steel, R., 504.
Stevenson, W. F., 522.
Stolberg, F. L., 303.
Storrs, R. S., 295, 314.
Strack, H. L., 104, 160.
——, and Zöckler, 230.
Strauss, D. F., 351.
Strong, A. H., 343.
Strong, W., 462.
Stuckenberg, J. H. W., 443.
Suicer, C., 139.
Swainson, C. A., 509.
Swedenborg, E., 226.
Taylor, J., 442.
——, W. M., 494.
Terry, M. S., 186.
——, and Newhall, 231.
Thayer, J. H., 404.
Thiersch, H. W. I., 419.
Thomasius, G., 341.
Thompson, J. P., 331.
——, R. E., 443.
Tillemont, de, 299.
Tischendorf, 163.
Tobler, T., 148.
Tocqueville, A. de, 294.

Trapp, J., 220.
Trench, R. C., 516.
Trumbull, H. C., 506.
Tschackert, P., 420.
Turretin, F., 391.
Twesten, A. D. C., 341.
Uhlhorn, G., 246, 249, 271.
Ullmann, K., 354, 404.
Ussher, J., 345.
Valla, L., 210.
Vering, F. H., 462.
Vincent, 477.
——, J. H., 506.
Vinet, A., 453, 500.
——, A. R., 472.
Vitringa, C., 146.
Voigt, J., 247.
Wace, Henry, 279.
Wackernagel, P., 515.
Walter, F., 462.
Warfield, B. B., 393.
Warneck, G., 522.
Watson, R., 348.
——, W. H., 506.
Weber, F., 268.
——, Georg, 283.
Wegscheider, J. H. L., 351.
Weidner, R. F., 15.
Weingarten, H., 305.
Weiss, B., 157, 271, 331, 404.
——, H., 441.
Wellhausen, J., 160, 266, 268.
Wendt, H. H., 331.
Wesley, J., 347.
Westcott, B. F., 169.
Wetstein, J. J., 219.
Whedon, D. D., 230.
Whewell, W., 440.
Whyte, A., 504.
Wiggers, J., 447.
Wildeboer, G., 169.
Williams, Monier, 45.
Wiltsch, J. E. T., 446.
Winer, G. B., 136, 419.
Winsor, J. D., 289, 294.
Wirthmüller, J. B., 14.
Wiseman, Cardinal, 339.
Worden, J. A., 506.
Wordsworth, C., 504.
——, Christ., 230.
Wörner, E., 331.
Wright, Ch. H. H., 153.
——, Wm., 104.
Wuttke, A., 424.
Wyss, C., 136.
Zahn, T., 169.
Zeller, E., 404, 424.
Ziegler, Th., 424, 428.
Zöckler, O., 16.